HUMAN DEVELOPMENT REPORT 1993

undp

Published
for the United Nations
Development Programme
(UNDP)

New York   Oxford
Oxford University Press
1993

Oxford University Press
Oxford   New York   Toronto
Delhi   Bombay   Calcutta   Madras   Karachi
Kuala Lumpur   Singapore   Hong Kong   Tokyo
Nairobi   Dar es Salaam   Cape Town
Melbourne   Auckland   Madrid

and associated companies in
Berlin   Ibadan

ISBN 0-19-508457-8 (paper)
ISBN 0-19-508458-6 (cloth)
ISSN 0969-4501

9   8   7   6   5   4   3   2   1
Printed in the United States of America on acid-free, recycled paper.

Cover and design: Gerald Quinn, Quinn Information Design, Cabin John, Maryland

Editing, desktop composition and production management: Bruce Ross-Larson, Alison Strong, Kim Bieler,
Jennifer Peabody, Tristan de Coquereaumont, Paige Morse, Katrina van Duyn, William Freeman,
Terry Anderson, Antje Kharchi and Katie Scott, all with American Writing Corporation, Washington, D.C.

Foreword

The past decade has been a decade of the people. The forces of democracy are spreading across many lands. New markets are springing up in former command economies, unleashing the creativity and productivity of their people. With free enterprise winning out over central planning, and the courageous voices of democracy quieting the terrors of authoritarianism, people everywhere are asserting their right to determine their own destiny.

But democracy is more than drawing up constitutions, designing new election procedures or holding elections as one-time events. Democracy is a way of life. It is a long-term process of reorganizing the institutions of a civil society. For some countries, the process is painful—involving political unrest, civil strife, even war. And many of today's struggles are more than struggles for access to political power. They are for access to the ordinary opportunities of life—land, water, work, living space and basic social services.

What is impressive is the great determination of people to participate in the events and processes that shape their lives. No more impersonal commands from above. Instead, a search for participatory patterns of development. No more directives from a distant centre. Instead, a demand for decentralization of power. No more stifling regulations from an all-powerful state. Instead, an urge to liberate human enterprise.

What is even more impressive is that even the severest hardships are not turning people away from their newly won econom-

ic and political freedoms. Just look at the sheer determination of the people in the newly independent states of the former Soviet Union—in the face of high inflation, falling output, rising unemployment, and the removal of long-enjoyed subsidies. And look, too, at the determination of people throughout the developing world to go through their own democratic and economic transitions, to scale back their overextended public sectors, to meet their human development needs.

The challenge for the development community in all this is to identify practical and pragmatic options. The best route is to unleash people's entrepreneurial spirit—to take risks, to compete, to innovate, to determine the direction and pace of development.

It is fitting, therefore, that this year's *Human Development Report* has people's participation as its special focus. As the Report stresses, we have to redefine our concept of security as security for people, not security for land. We have to weave development around people, not people around development. And we have to ensure that development cooperation focuses directly on people, not just on nation-states.

The *Human Development Report* has, since its introduction in 1990, become a tradition in contributing to the international development debate. For this, I must thank the Report team and especially Mahbub ul Haq, my Special Adviser and the Report's chief architect.

The views set forth in this Report have emerged from the team's professional, frank and candid analysis of the issues. They do not necessarily reflect the views of UNDP, its Governing Council or other member governments of UNDP. The usefulness of a report such as this continues to depend on its professional independence and intellectual integrity.

I am confident that this year's Report will again make a major contribution to the development dialogue by offering a new vision for the future of human development.

William H. Draper III

New York
March 17, 1993

Team for the preparation of
Human Development Report 1993

Special Adviser
Mahbub ul Haq

UNDP Team
Director: Inge Kaul
Members: Bernard Hausner, Saraswathi Menon, Kees Kingma and Selim Jahan with Babafemi Badejo, Lily Ohiorhenuan, Peter Stalker (editing) and Leo Goldstone, World Statistics Ltd., for the statistics, with the assistance of Carl Haub and Machiko Yanagashita, Population Reference Bureau, and Laura Mourino

Panel of consultants
Sudhir Anand, Lourdes Arizpe, Meghnad Desai, Xavier Greffe, Simon Johnson, Atul Kohli, Bernard Lecomte, Roger Riddell, Gustav Ranis, Amartya Sen, Guy Standing, Frances Stewart, Paul Streeten and Herbert Wulf

Acknowledgements

The authors of the Report are deeply indebted to numerous organizations and individuals for their valuable contributions in the preparation of this Report.

Several international agencies have generously shared their experience and research with the authors. The statistical elements of the Report are drawn from the databases and material from the United Nations Statistical Division, United Nations Population Division, United Nations Centre for Social Development and Humanitarian Affairs, United Nations Office at Vienna, United Nations University, United Nations Economic Commission for Africa, United Nations Economic and Social Commission for Asia and the Pacific, United Nations Economic Commission for Europe, United Nations Economic Commission for Latin America and the Caribbean, United Nations Economic and Social Commission for Western Asia, Food and Agriculture Organization of the United Nations, International Labour Organisation, International Maritime Organization, International Trade Centre, United Nations Children's Fund, United Nations Educational, Scientific and Cultural Organization, United Nations Environment Programme, United Nations Population Fund, United Nations Industrial Development Organization, World Food Programme, World Health Organization, International Monetary Fund, World Bank, Organisation for Economic Co-operation and Development, Statistical Office of the European Communities, International Centre for Urban Studies, International Food Policy Research Institute, Inter-Parliamentary Union, MACRO International, Inc., Stockholm International Peace Research Institute, University of Pennsylvania, World Resources Institute and World Priorities Inc.

Several offices in UNDP provided data and information in areas where international data collection is not yet well developed. They include several UNDP field offices, UNDP's Regional Bureaux, the Bureau for Programme Policy and Evaluation and the United Nations Development Fund for Women. The Office for Project Services provided the team with critical administrative support.

Colleagues in UNDP provided extremely useful comments and suggestions during the drafting of the Report. In particular, the authors would like to express their gratitude to Wally Abbott, Solomon Akpata, Ali Attiga, Thelma Awori, Herbert Behrstock, Sharon Capeling-Alakija, Nikhil Chandavarkar, Judy Cheng-Hopkins, Erling Dessau, Søren Dyssegaard, Gustaf Adolf Edgren, Daan Everts, Fawaz Fokeladeh, Sakiko Fukuda-Parr, Gary Gabriel, Peter Gall, Luis Maria Gomez, Jean-Jacques Graisse, Reinhart Helmke, Nadia Hijab, Keith Hillyer, Arthur Holcombe, Caspar Jan Kamp, Bahman Kia, Uner Kirdar, Robert Leigh, Thierry Lemaresquier, Elena Martinez, Paul Matthews, Pedro Mercader, Roy Morey, Ramanathan Natarajan, Timothy Painter, Elizabeth Reid, Juliette Remy, Ingolf Schuetz-Mueller, Krishan G. Singh, Ellen Sirleaf-Johnson, Luis Thais, Sarah Timpson, J. David Whaley, Carl-Erik Wiberg and Fernando Zumbado.

Secretarial and administrative support for the Report's preparation were provided by Linda Pigon-Rebello, Renuka Corea, Flora Aller, Gabriella Charles, Ida Simons,

Lisa Daniell, Liza Perkins, Karin Svadlenak and Ponnuswami Thayaparan. The team was assisted in background research by Nele Boehme, Dina Bunshah, Daan Everts, Jr., Michelle Perrot and Sandra Reinecke.

The Report has benefited greatly from intellectual advice and professional criticisms received from Dragoslav Avramovic, James Grant, Keith Griffin, Michael Hopkins, Richard Jolly, Jeni Klugman, Juhani Lönnroth, Jacky Mathonnat, Terry R. McKinley, Joan Nelson, Nafis Sadik, Helen Shapiro and Barbara Boyle Torrey.

The authors also wish to acknowledge their great debt to William H. Draper III, UNDP Administrator. His deep commitment to independent professional analysis and to the goals of human development has been a source of great strength to the team.

ABBREVIATIONS

DAC	Development Assistance Committee
EC	European Community
FAO	Food and Agriculture Organization of the United Nations
HDI	Human development index
IDA	International Development Association
ILO	International Labour Organisation
IMF	International Monetary Fund
ODA	Official development assistance
OECD	Organisation for Economic Co-operation and Development
UNCTAD	United Nations Conference on Trade and Development
UNDP	United Nations Development Programme
UNEP	United Nations Environment Programme
UNESCO	United Nations Educational, Scientific and Cultural Organization
UNFPA	United Nations Fund for Population Activities
UNHCR	Office of the United Nations High Commissioner for Refugees
UNICEF	United Nations Children's Fund
UNIDO	United Nations Industrial Development Organization
WHO	World Health Organization
WIDER	World Institute for Development Economics Research

Contents

CHAPTER FIVE
People in community organizations 84

HUMAN DEVELOPMENT INDICATORS 125

BOXES

TABLES

FIGURES

# Overview

People's participation is becoming the central issue of our time. The democratic transition in many developing countries, the collapse of many socialist regimes, and the worldwide emergence of people's organizations—these are all part of a historic change, not just isolated events.

People today have an urge—an impatient urge—to participate in the events and processes that shape their lives. And that impatience brings many dangers and opportunities. It can dissolve into anarchy, ethnic violence or social disintegration. But if properly nurtured in a responsive national and global framework, it can also become a source of tremendous vitality and innovation for the creation of new and more just societies.

The dangers arise as the irresistible urge for participation clashes with inflexible systems. Although the achievements in human development have been significant during the past three decades, the reality is continuing exclusion. More than a billion of the world's people still languish in absolute poverty, and the poorest fifth find that the richest fifth enjoy more than 150 times their income. Women still earn only half as much as men—and despite constituting more than half the votes, have great difficulty securing even 10% representation in parliaments. Rural people in developing countries still receive less than half the income opportunities and social services available to their urban counterparts. Many ethnic minorities still live like a separate nation within their own countries. And political and economic democracy is still a reluctant process in several countries. Our world is still a world of difference.

But many new windows of opportunity are opening. Global military spending is beginning to decline for the first time since the Second World War. The cold war in East-West relations is over, and there is a good chance of phasing it out in the developing world. The ideological battles of the past are being replaced by a more pragmatic partnership between market efficiency and social compassion. The rising environmental threat is reminding humanity of both its vulnerability and its compulsion for common survival on a fragile planet. People are beginning to move to centre stage in national and global dialogues. There are times in history when the human voice has spoken out with surprising force. These past few years have marked just such a watershed.

Humanity must choose between these dangers and opportunities. But there really is no choice, for the future of our planet depends on grasping the opportunities.

Many old concepts must now be radically revised. Security should be reinterpreted as security for people, not security for land. Development must be woven around people, not people around development—and it should empower individuals and groups rather than disempower them. And development cooperation should focus directly on people, not just on nation-states.

Many of the old institutions of civil society need to be rebuilt—and many new ones created. And because future conflicts may well be between people rather than between states, national and international institutions will need to accommodate much more diversity and difference—and to open many more avenues for constructive participation.

All this will take time, for participation is a process, not an event. It will proceed at different speeds for different countries and

People today have an impatient urge to participate in the events and processes that shape their lives

regions, and its form and extent will vary from one stage of development to another. That is why it is necessary to address not only the levels of participation, but also whether participation is increasing. What is important is that the impulses for participation be understood and nurtured.

The implications of widespread participation are profound—embracing every aspect of development. Markets need to be reformed to offer everyone access to the benefits they can bring. Governance needs to be decentralized to allow greater access to decision-making. And community organizations need to be allowed to exert growing influence on national and international issues.

This Report explores these themes in some detail. But it is not the details that matter. It is the overall vision of societies built around people's genuine needs. This calls for at least *five new pillars of a people-centred world order:*
- New concepts of human security
- New models of sustainable human development
- New partnerships between state and markets
- New patterns of national and global governance
- New forms of international cooperation.

1. New concepts of human security must stress the security of people, not only of nations.

The concept of security must change—from an exclusive stress on national security to a much greater stress on people's security, from security through armaments to security through human development, from territorial security to food, employment and environmental security.

The world has already made a good start:
- Global military expenditures have declined cumulatively by around $240 billion since 1987.
- Nuclear warheads will be cut by two-thirds by the year 2003 as a result of the recent US-Russia agreement.
- More than two million people have been demobilized from the armed forces

since the beginning of the 1990s.
- Defence industries are expected to have cut nearly a fourth of their workforce by 1998.

This is a beginning, but a formidable agenda still awaits policy-makers.
- *Use defence cuts to finance human development*—Despite major reductions in arms expenditure, the expected peace dividend in industrial countries has yet to materialize. A close link must be created between defence cuts and the unfinished social agendas in these countries.
- *Ease the transition from defence to civilian production*—Industrial countries need to plan the transition to a peace economy by retraining defence workers and creating more jobs for them in the civilian sector. Unless this is done, there will be pressures to give further export subsidies to the arms industries—pressures that several industrial countries have already succumbed to. This way of easing the adjustment problems of today's defence industry is bound to lead to enhanced conflict and deferred human progress in the developing world. It is irresponsible to entice poor countries to buy expensive military toys at the same time they are advised to reduce military spending. For developing countries, even partial demobilization of their standing armies will require large-scale job creation.
- *Accelerate disarmament in the developing world*—Although the cold war has ended between the East and the West, it remains to be phased out in the developing world. If developing countries merely froze their military spending at the 1990 level during the next decade, this would release nearly $100 billion for their essential human development agendas—which, combined with the restructuring of aid allocations proposed later, will be enough for universal literacy, primary health care and safe drinking water by the year 2000. This will also require some major initiative from industrial countries. Needed especially are time-bound targets to phase out military bases and military assistance, internationally monitored restraints on military shipments, and an enlightened donor-recipient policy dialogue on reductions in military spending.
- *Forge new regional and international alliances for peace*—Preventive diplomacy is

New concepts of security must stress the security of people, not only of nations

needed to diffuse tensions around the globe *before* there are blowups. This demands a new role for the United Nations, not just in peacekeeping but in peacemaking and peacebuilding. After all, an ounce of prevention is better than a ton of punishment. During 1992, the UN had to intervene in several internal conflicts, from Bosnia to Somalia, and the number of UN soldiers quadrupled to more than 50,000. With conflicts in countries displacing those between them, the time has probably arrived for the UN to have a permanent military force, mainly for the new goal of peacemaking. But military force is only a short-term response. The long-term solution is faster economic development, greater social justice and more people's participation. The new concepts of human security demand people-centred development, not soldiers in uniform.

2. New models of sustainable human development are needed—to invest in human potential and to create an enabling environment for the full use of human capabilities.

The purpose of development is to widen the range of people's choices. Income is one of those choices—but it is not the sum-total of human life.

Human development is development *of* the people *for* the people *by* the people. Development *of* the people means investing in human capabilities, whether in education or health or skills, so that they can work productively and creatively. Development *for* the people means ensuring that the economic growth they generate is distributed widely and fairly. Earlier *Human Development Reports* (1990–92) concentrated on these first two components. This Report advances the argument by concentrating on development *by* the people—on giving everyone a chance to participate.

The most efficient form of participation through the market is access to productive and remunerative employment. So, the main objective of human development strategies must be to generate productive employment. It has long been assumed that pursuing economic growth through increasing output would necessarily increase employment. This clearly has not happened. Over the past three decades, the growth rate for employment in developing countries has been about half that for output. And as output rose in many OECD countries in the last decade, employment lagged behind. ILO projections for the next decade hold no comfort. On present trends, employment's growth will continue to lag far behind that of both output and the labour force.

We are witnessing a new and disturbing phenomenon: *jobless growth*. And policymakers the world over are searching for development strategies that combine economic growth with more job opportunities. No comprehensive programme has yet emerged, but governments can do several things to increase employment. Governments can:

- *Invest* generously in basic education, relevant skills and worker retraining.
- *Liberate* private enterprise and make markets more accessible to everyone.
- *Support* small-scale enterprises and informal employment, mainly through reform of the credit system and fiscal incentives.
- *Create* an efficient service economy for the future by investing in the new skills required.
- *Encourage* labour-intensive technologies, especially through tax incentives.
- *Extend* employment safety nets through labour-intensive public works programmes in periods of major economic distress.
- *Reconsider* the concept of work and the duration of the work week, with a view to sharing existing work opportunities.

Policy-makers are searching not only for development models that are people-centred. They also want development to be more sustainable—to protect the options of future generations. This means that the conventional definition of capital must be broadened beyond physical capital to include human and natural capital.

The supposed choice between economic growth and sustaining the environment is false and dangerous. Growth is imperative if poverty is to be reduced. But the distribution of growth must change, and it must become less wasteful of natural resources in

We are witnessing a new and disturbing phenomenon: jobless growth

both rich and poor nations. The new models of development must also recognize that poverty is one of the greatest threats to the environment. That is why it is as important to address the "silent emergencies" of poverty (water pollution, land degradation, environmental diseases) as it is to focus on the "loud emergencies" (global warming, ozone depletion) that usually dominate the headlines.

In short, the new models of sustainable development must be much more sensitive to people and to nature.

Markets should serve people— instead of people serving markets

3. New partnerships are needed between the state and the market to combine market efficiency with social compassion.

Heated ideological discussions have often marred an objective analysis of the relative roles of markets and the state. Some believe in the benevolence of the state and the need for constantly correcting the ill effects of the market. Others glorify the virtues of the market-place and argue that the economy should be liberated from the dead hand of state bureaucracy. Both groups assume, to a large extent, that the state and the market are necessarily separate and even antagonistic—that one is benevolent, the other not. In practice, both state and market are often dominated by the same power structures.

This suggests a more pragmatic third option: that people should guide both the state and the market, which need to work in tandem, with people sufficiently empowered to exert a more effective influence over both.

If people's interests are to guide both the market and the state, actions must be taken to allow people to participate fully in the operations of markets and to share equitably in their benefits. Markets should serve people—instead of people serving markets. After all, markets are only the means—people the end.

Changing markets to make them more people-friendly would start by maintaining the dynamism of markets but adding other measures that allow many more people to capitalize on the advantages that markets offer.

- *Preconditions*—People need the education and health standards to take advantage of market opportunities. Also needed is a reasonable distribution of productive assets (particularly land) so that people do not come to the market with totally unequal buying or selling power. Since poorer people often have very little access to credit, governments need to reform their credit systems to give access to the poor. In addition, governments have to ensure that markets are open to all—irrespective of race, religion, sex or ethnic origin. Other preconditions for effective people-friendly markets include adequate physical infrastructure (particularly in rural areas), a free and rapid flow of information, a liberal trade regime and a legal system that encourages open and transparent transactions.
- *Accompanying conditions*—are needed to ensure that markets work as freely and efficiently as possible. One of the most important is a stable macroeconomic environment—especially to ensure stability in domestic prices and external currency values. But markets would also benefit from a comprehensive incentive system, with correct price signals, a fair tax regime and an adequate system of rewards for work and enterprise. Markets should also be able to work untrammelled by arbitrary and unpredictable government controls.
- *Corrective actions*—When markets do not produce a desirable outcome, the state needs to regulate and correct. This would include protecting competition through antimonopoly laws, consumers through regulations on product standards, workers through adequate and well-enforced labour legislation, and such vulnerable groups as children and the elderly. It would also include protecting the environment, by banning certain types of pollution and ensuring that polluters pay.
- *Social safety nets*—must be in place to catch the victims of the competitive struggle. Sometimes, this support need only be temporary, for the short-term unemployed, for example. But there will always be those excluded wholly or partially by the market: the very young, the very old, the disabled

and those with heavy domestic commitments. In several developing countries, such social safety nets include employment schemes for the unemployed, pension schemes for the old, feeding programmes for malnourished children and mothers, and free basic health and education for all low-income groups.

The need to create people-friendly markets is all the greater now that so many countries have embarked on strategies of economic liberalization and privatization. Many developing countries have already undertaken bold programmes to liberalize trade and finance, reform their taxation systems, deregulate the labour market and reform or privatize public enterprises. The countries of Eastern and Central Europe and the former Soviet Union have been undergoing an even more dramatic transition—from command economies to market economies. The experiences of 11 developing countries and transition economies—Argentina, Brazil, China, Egypt, Ghana, India, Kenya, Malaysia, Poland, Russia and Viet Nam—are analysed in this Report.

One of the most significant aspects of economic liberalization has been privatization. Between 1980 and 1991, nearly 7,000 enterprises were privatized, around 1,400 of them in the developing world, chiefly in Latin America. As one element in a coherent private sector development strategy, privatization can greatly stimulate private enterprise. But mistakes are already being made in the process of privatization. The Report lists "seven sins of privatization": maximizing revenue without creating a competitive environment, replacing public monopolies with private ones, using nontransparent and arbitrary procedures, using the proceeds to finance budget deficits, simultaneously crowding the financial markets with public borrowings, making false promises to labour, and privatizing without building a political consensus.

For economic transitions to be guided by the interests of the people—and for markets to be made people-friendly—requires new patterns of governance centred around the rising aspirations of the people.

4. New patterns of national and global governance are needed to accommodate the rise of people's aspirations and the steady decline of the nation-state.

Pressures on the nation-state, from above and below, are beginning to change traditional concepts of governance. On the one hand, globalization on many fronts—from capital flows to information systems—has eroded the power of individual states. On the other, many states have become too inflexible to respond to the needs of specific groups within their own countries. The nation-state now is too small for the big things, and too big for the small.

National governments must find new ways of enabling their people to participate more in government and to allow them much greater influence on the decisions that affect their lives. Unless this is done, and done in time, the irresistible tide of people's rising aspirations will inevitably clash with inflexible systems, leading to anarchy and chaos. A rapid democratic transition and a strengthening of the institutions of civil society are the only appropriate responses. Among the many specific steps that must accompany such a transition, the two main ones are to decentralize more authority to local governments and to give much greater freedom to people's organizations and non-governmental organizations (NGOs) —instruments of people's participation discussed at length in this Report.

The decentralization of power—from capital cities to regions, towns and villages —can be one of the best ways of empowering people, promoting public participation and increasing efficiency. Many industrial countries delegate 25% or more of total government spending to the local level. But the governments of developing countries remain much more centralized, delegating only 10% or less of budgetary spending and giving local governments few opportunities to raise funds through taxation or borrowing.

Where decentralization has taken place, it has often been quite successful, encouraging local participation, reducing costs and increasing efficiency. This is evident from

The nation-state now is too small for the big things, and too big for the small

experiences all over the developing world—from the Rural Access Programme in Kenya to the *gram sabhas* in the Indian state of Karnataka and the local bridge construction in the Baglung district of Nepal.

Decentralization also increases the pressure on governments to concentrate on human priority concerns. Given a fair chance, local people are likely to choose ready access to basic education and health care rather than the construction of distant colleges or hospitals.

One danger of financial decentralization is that the richer regions can raise more through local taxation and so will get better services. But experience shows how to overcome this. Brazil allows states to collect taxes but then redistributes them so that the richer states in the South and South-East get back only a quarter of the taxes collected from them, while the poorer states in the North get back more than twice what is collected there.

Decentralization can, however, end up empowering local elites rather than local people. So, there can never be effective local participation in developing countries without a redistribution of power—if decentralization is to promote human development, it must be accompanied by genuine democracy at the local level.

Another major instrument for people's participation is their organization into community groups. Indeed, people's organizations and NGOs have grown dramatically in recent years, offering a powerful means of correcting the failures of both markets and governments. People's organizations tend to be formed in response to a felt need or a common interest. People might simply form self-help groups to pool their labour, obtain credit or buy goods in bulk. Or they might be responding to a failure by government to provide infrastructure or social services or to a failure of markets to protect vulnerable groups.

Although NGOs have increased in number and financial clout, there have been few systematic evaluations of their effectiveness. In broad terms, they have had a clear impact in four main areas:
- *Advocacy on behalf of the disadvantaged*—On such issues as human rights, the environment, women, poverty alleviation and indigenous peoples, NGOs have organized powerful advocacy groups that have changed the thinking of national and international policy-makers.
- *The empowerment of marginalized groups*—In most developing countries, poverty is often caused less by an absolute shortage of resources than by their skewed distribution. NGOs' emphasis on empowerment and their support of people's organizations have often enabled marginalized groups to resist local elites and claim their rights. In many countries, particularly in Asia and Latin America, they have been pressuring governments to provide land for the landless and embark on agrarian reform.
- *Reaching the poorest*—NGOs often manage to reach groups that governments find the most difficult to help, particularly the poorest 20% of the population and those in the rural areas, where government services may be thin or non-existent. It is doubtful, though, that they reach the very poorest—most NGOs probably miss the poorest 5–10%.
- *Providing emergency assistance*—One strength of NGOs is the ability to respond quickly and effectively to emergencies. Their network of contacts allows them to give advance warning of disasters and urge international action. And their independence means that they can operate in circumstances that are politically difficult for official organizations.

Although NGOs are effective in these and other respects, it is important to keep the scale of their operations in perspective. In the early 1980s, one estimate suggested that NGOs touched the lives of about 100 million people in developing countries—60 million in Asia, 25 million in Latin America and some 12 million in Africa. Today, the figure is probably nearer 250 million and rising—but that is still only a fifth of the 1.3 billion people living in absolute poverty in developing countries.

The small impact of NGOs is also evident at the national level. In Bangladesh, the Grameen Bank, one of the most internationally renowned NGOs providing credit for the poor, accounts for a mere 0.1% of total national credit.

Democracy is unlikely to be so obliging as to stop at national borders

This is not a criticism of NGOs—it is a reminder of a stark reality: NGOs can supplement government but never replace it.

The decentralization of government authority and the emergence of NGOs are powerful processes for greater participation by people. But they can be effective only if the overall framework of national governance changes—to become genuinely democratic and participatory.

Let us also recognize that the forces of democracy are not likely to be so obliging as to stop at national borders. This has major implications for global governance. States and people must have the opportunity to influence the global decisions that are going to affect them so profoundly. This means making the institutions of global governance much broader and more participatory. There should, in particular, be a searching re-examination of the Bretton Woods organizations. And the United Nations must acquire a much broader role in development issues. To contribute effectively to sustainable human development will probably require some form of Economic Security Council within the UN, where all nations can participate on the basis of geographical representation—with none holding a veto—to provide a new decision-making forum.

5. New forms of international cooperation must be evolved—to focus directly on the needs of the people rather than on the preferences of nation-states.

The new emphasis on human security coupled with sustainable development will have to be matched by a fresh approach to international development cooperation.

So far, the basic motivation for donors to give aid has been to win friends in the cold-war confrontation between socialism and capitalism. Some bilateral donors did place greater emphasis on developmental and humanitarian concerns, and so did the multilateral agencies. But in general, the dominant objectives have been political.

More than half of US bilateral assistance in 1991 was earmarked for five strategically important countries: Israel, Egypt, Turkey, the Philippines and El Salvador. With five million people and a per capita income of $1,000, El Salvador received more US assistance than Bangladesh, with 116 million people and a per capita income of only $210. And the strategic significance of Egypt has been such that it received aid of $370 per poor person in 1991. Compare that with just $4 per poor person for India—even though Egypt has nearly twice the income of India.

Bilateral official development assistance (ODA) is badly allocated, showing the considerable potential for beneficial restructuring:

• Twice as much ODA per capita goes to high military spenders as to more moderate spenders.

• Only a quarter of ODA goes to the ten countries containing three-quarters of the world's poor.

• Less than 7% of ODA is earmarked for human priority concerns.

• Most of the $15 billion in technical assistance is spent on equipment, technology and experts from industrial countries—rather than on national capacity building in developing countries.

Aid is allocated this way because it suffers from the scars of the cold war, from a focus on nation-states rather than on people, from a bias towards the public sector and from a reliance on western development models.

The changed circumstances of the 1990s demand an entirely new approach to ODA:

• *Focus aid on human priority issues*—Aid should be directed at human priority issues, such as health and basic education, and at environmental security and reducing population growth. Clear and specific goals in these areas—identified, implemented and monitored—would obtain greater public and legislative support in donor nations. At least 20% of total aid should be allocated to human priority concerns, three times the present 6.5%.

• *Base ODA allocations on levels of poverty*—ODA should be allocated to people rather than to countries, and it should go where the need is the greatest, to the poorest people wherever they happen to be. For example, the ten countries containing three-quarters of the world's poorest peo-

At least 20% of total aid should be allocated to human priority concerns

*Poverty anywhere
is a threat to
prosperity
everywhere*

ple should get around three-quarters of ODA, not the present one-quarter.

• *Link ODA with mutual concerns*—ODA must be in the mutual interest of recipients and donors. Recipients would be justified in insisting that ODA allocations be guided by their priorities in the fields of human development, poverty alleviation, employment creation and accelerated economic growth. Donors, by contrast, could legitimately link their ODA policy dialogue with their concerns on such matters as human rights, reducing international migration pressures, pollution, nuclear proliferation and drug trafficking—as well as the control of terrorism. Perhaps as much as 3% of aid funds could be earmarked for spending within donor nations to prepare public opinion for these post-cold-war realities and to increase public awareness of the interdependence of the North and the South.

• *Adopt a new people-centred policy dialogue*—ODA should be accompanied by a new form of policy dialogue based on the real interests of people, rather than those of the developing country governments that negotiate aid. This means putting much more pressure on governments to improve the distribution of income and assets, to direct spending away from military towards social concerns and to attend to the larger issues of better national governance.

• *Use technical assistance for national capacity building*—Technical assistance should be used increasingly to hire national experts, to invest in local institutions and to accelerate human development in the recipient countries. The ultimate criterion for judging the success of any technical assistance programme must be that it has built adequate national capacity and phased itself out over a predefined period.

• *Place ODA in a larger framework of sharing global market opportunities*—ODA can make a significant contribution to developing countries, but it must also be conceived in a larger framework. As the 1992 Report pointed out, developing countries are being denied market opportunities worth ten times the annual flows of ODA. The long-term solution to poverty is not charity. It is more equitable access for poor nations to global market opportunities.

• *Create a new motivation for aid*—The old motive of fighting the cold war is dead. The new motive must be the war against global poverty, based on the recognition that this is an investment not only in the development of poor nations but in the security of rich nations. The real threat in the next few decades is that global poverty will begin to travel, without a passport, in many unpleasant forms: drugs, diseases, terrorism, migration. Poverty anywhere is a threat to prosperity everywhere.

* * *

The implications of placing people at the centre of political and economic change are thus profound. They challenge traditional concepts of security, old models of development, ideological debates on the role of the market and outmoded forms of international cooperation. They call for nothing less than a revolution in our thinking. This Report touches on only a few aspects of a profound human revolution that makes people's participation the central objective in all parts of life. Every institution—and every policy action—should be judged by one critical test: how does it meet the genuine aspirations of the people? A simple test, vast in its reach.

This is the vision national and global decision-makers must consider if the 1990s are to emerge as a new watershed in peaceful development—and if the 21st century is to see the full flowering of human potential all over the world. The process of change ushered in by the events of the past few years must now be carried forward—with great courage and resolution. There are no engraved milestones on this road. There are no decorated heroes. It is a process of change led by people—and a promising journey we all must join.

An opportunity for this will arise fairly soon. All nations are committed to meet in 1995 at a World Summit on Social Development. It is a chance to focus on the building blocks for a new people-centred world order. It is a time to agree on a concrete agenda of national and global actions. That agenda will be the theme of the 1994 *Human Development Report*.

CHAPTER 1

Trends in human development

The 1980s were, in many ways, a decade of the people. All over the world, people had an impatient urge to guide their political, economic and social destinies. The democratic transition in developing countries, the collapse of socialist regimes and the worldwide emergence of people's organizations —all were part of a restless wave of human aspirations. Frustrated at times, in many places still in chains, the human spirit soared in the past decade.

At first sight, this may appear too sanguine an interpretation. This was, after all, a decade that shattered many lives and many hopes—with mounting external debt, faltering economic growth, increasing unemployment, growing civil strife, rising ethnic tensions, threats to the environment and the persistence of abject poverty.

But amid these disturbing and painful trends is an undoubtable resurgence of the human spirit. There are times in history when the human voice has spoken out with surprising force. These past few years have marked just such a watershed.

Now that the cold war is over, the challenge is to rebuild societies around people's genuine needs. The world has already made a positive start. For the first time since the Second World War, global military expenditures are beginning to decline—between 1987 and 1990, they fell cumulatively by some $240 billion. Most of this reduction has been by the United States and the former Soviet Union. But the developing countries also cut expenditure, with a cumulative reduction of $11 billion, chiefly in the Arab States and South Asia. This happened despite the fact that the poorest nations in Sub-Saharan Africa have yet to reduce military spending, and for many poor countries, the ratio of military spending to social spending remains far too high (figure 1.1). But in 1991, military spending in developing countries rose back to its previous level, mainly because of the Gulf War.

Detente and disarmament negotiations between East and West have considerably diminished the threat of nuclear war. As a result of the Strategic Arms Reduction Treaties (START I and II), the number of strategic nuclear warheads is likely to decline from 24,000 at the end of the 1980s to about 7,000 by 2003 (figure 1.2). And since the beginning of the 1990s, more than two million men and women have been demobilized, two-thirds of them in industrial countries and one-third in developing (figure 1.3). Further demobilizations on a similar scale are expected in the next few years.

This represents considerable progress, but the nuclear threat is far from gone, and conventional weapons continue to take many lives. So, greater emphasis must be

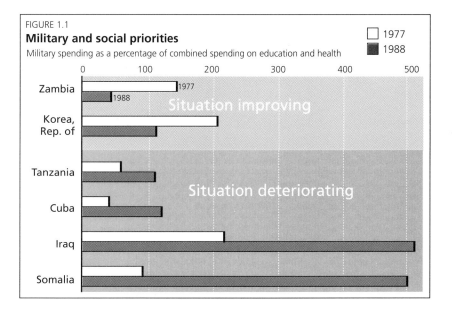

FIGURE 1.1
Military and social priorities
Military spending as a percentage of combined spending on education and health

1977
1988

placed not just on peacekeeping but on peacemaking and peacebuilding, demanding a new role for the United Nations (box 1.1).

Employment in the arms industry is beginning to fall. Having employed around 15 million workers at the end of the 1980s—90% of them in the former Soviet Union, China, the United States and the European Community (in descending size)—the industry will lose an estimated three to four million jobs (20–25%) by 1998.

As military threats have lessened, other dangers have surfaced—such as the ethnic and religious conflicts in Bosnia, India, Iraq, Liberia, Somalia and Sri Lanka. And many industrial countries have seen violent conflicts between different racial groups—from riots in Los Angeles to neo-Nazi attacks on immigrants and asylum-seekers in Germany. The world is entering a dangerous period: future conflicts may well be between groups of people rather than states.

All these changes highlight the urgent need to focus on human development, the concept defined in the first *Human Development Report* in 1990 as a process of widening the range of people's choices.

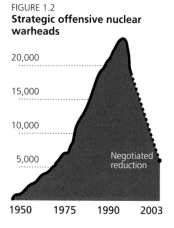

FIGURE 1.2
Strategic offensive nuclear warheads

20,000

15,000

10,000

5,000

Negotiated reduction

1950   1975   1990   2003

Assessing human development

The first *Human Development Report*, in introducing the concept of human development, argued that the real purpose of development should be to enlarge people's choices. Subsequent Reports have developed the basic concept, looking in particular at how human development could be financed and at its international dimensions—through trade, official development assistance and international migration flows. Each Report has also presented balance sheets for human development, for both industrial and developing countries (see boxes 1.2 and 1.3 for this year's balance sheets).

To quantify and clarify the process of human development, the 1990 Report also introduced a new yardstick of human progress: the human development index (HDI). By combining indicators of real purchasing power, education and health, the HDI offers a measure of development much more comprehensive than GNP alone.

The second Report, in 1991, took up the question of financing human development—and the role of governments. It looked at the potential for restructuring national budgets away from wasteful expenditure on the military and on loss-making public enterprises, for example—and towards more relevant priorities, such as basic education and primary health care.

The analysis used four ratios to highlight government spending priorities. These showed that developing countries spend more than 25% of their GNP through the budget, yet devote less than one-tenth of this to human development priorities. The 1991 Report also discovered similar imbalances in international aid: less than 7% of total aid is spent on human priority areas. It concluded that the world had an enormous opportunity to increase investments in human development—even with existing resources.

The 1992 Report extended the analysis by adding an international dimension. It focused specifically on global markets and on how they meet—or fail to meet—human needs. The Report discovered that global markets make developing countries lose

---

BOX 1.1

An agenda for peace

Worldwide, there have been more than 100 major conflicts in the past four decades, taking the lives of some 20 million people. The United Nations was often powerless to deal with these conflicts—paralysed by vetoes by major powers on both sides of the East-West divide.

Since May 1990, however, no such vetoes have been cast, and there has been a growing demand for UN support in dealing with such conflicts. In July 1992, responding to a request of the first-ever meeting of the Security Council at the level of heads of state and government, the UN Secretary-General prepared a report, *Agenda for Peace*, setting forth the organization's objectives for peace and security, quoted here:
- *To seek to identify, at the earliest possible stage, situations that could produce conflict, and to try through diplomacy to remove the sources of danger before violence results.*

- *Where conflict erupts, to engage in peacemaking aimed at resolving the issues that have led to conflict.*
- *Through peacekeeping, to work to preserve peace, however fragile, where fighting has been halted and to assist in implementing agreements achieved by the peacemakers.*
- *To stand ready to assist in peace-building in its differing contexts: rebuilding the institutions and infrastructures of nations torn by civil war and strife; and building bonds of peaceful mutual benefit among nations formerly at war.*
- *And in the largest sense, to address the deepest causes of conflict: economic despair, social injustice and political oppression. It is possible to discern an increasingly common moral perception that spans the world's nations and peoples, and which is finding expression in international laws, many owing their genesis to the work of this Organization.*

economic opportunities worth around $500 billion annually—ten times what they receive in foreign assistance. No wonder that the global income disparity has doubled during the past three decades: the richest 20% of the world's people now receive more than 150 times the income of the poorest 20%.

That Report suggested two priority areas for future action. First, developing countries should invest massively in their people to sharpen their competitive edge in international markets. Second, there should be a radical dismantling of trade barriers and a major reform of international institutions, including the United Nations and the Bretton Woods institutions, to establish a new vision of global cooperation for the 21st century.

The HDI has attracted much attention from the academic community and from policy-makers. Technical note 1 explains its construction, and our intention is to continue to refine the methodology of the HDI in the light of comments and to steadily improve the database. Technical note 2 presents a detailed discussion of the HDI's methodology, the criticisms received, the refinements contemplated and the methodological options for dealing with some of the issues raised. We include this note to elicit further comments so that a much improved methodology can be devised for the 1994 Report. This Report introduces no changes in the method of HDI measurement, enabling a comparison of country rankings with the 1992 Report.

This year's country rankings show that Japan has displaced Canada at the top because of its significant increase (23%) in real GDP per capita during 1989–90 (table 1.1). For the countries with the lowest levels of human development, there has not been much change in ranking (table 1.2 and figure 1.4).

An analysis of the HDI country rankings brings out some interesting policy conclusions:

1. *There is no automatic link between income and human development*—Several countries—such as Chile, China, Colombia, Costa Rica, Madagascar, Sri Lanka,

Tanzania and Uruguay—have done well in translating their income into the lives of their people: Their human development rank is way ahead of their per capita income rank (figure 1.5). Other societies—such as Algeria, Angola, Gabon, Guinea, Namibia, Saudi Arabia, Senegal, South Africa and United Arab Emirates—have income ranks

TABLE 1.1
HDI ranking for industrial countries

Country	HDI value	HDI rank	GNP per capita rank	GNP per capita rank minus HDI rank[a]
Japan	0.983	1	3	2
Canada	0.982	2	11	9
Norway	0.978	3	6	3
Switzerland	0.978	4	1	–3
Sweden	0.977	5	5	0
USA	0.976	6	10	4
Australia	0.972	7	20	13
France	0.971	8	13	5
Netherlands	0.970	9	17	8
United Kingdom	0.964	10	21	11
Iceland	0.960	11	9	–2
Germany	0.957	12	8	–4
Denmark	0.955	13	7	–6
Finland	0.954	14	4	–10
Austria	0.952	15	14	–1
Belgium	0.952	16	16	0
New Zealand	0.947	17	23	6
Luxembourg	0.943	18	2	–16
Israel	0.938	19	27	8
Ireland	0.925	21	29	8
Italy	0.924	22	18	–4
Spain	0.923	23	28	5
Greece	0.902	25	35	10
Czechoslovakia	0.892	26	49	23
Hungary	0.887	28	52	24
Malta	0.855	39	33	–6
Bulgaria	0.854	40	67	27
Portugal	0.853	41	38	–3
Poland	0.831	48	80	32
Romania	0.709	77	84	7
Albania	0.699	78	90	12
Other countries				
Lithuania	0.881	29	51	22
Estonia	0.872	34	42	8
Latvia	0.868	35	43	8
Russian Fed.	0.862	37	47	10
Belarus	0.861	38	50	12
Ukraine	0.844	45	58	13
Armenia	0.831	47	63	16
Georgia	0.829	49	72	23
Kazakhstan	0.802	54	55	1
Azerbaijan	0.770	62	82	20
Moldova, Rep.	0.758	64	61	–3
Turkmenistan	0.746	66	81	15
Uzbekistan	0.695	80	92	12
Kyrgyzstan	0.689	83	85	2
Tajikistan	0.657	88	94	6

a. A positive figure shows that the HDI rank is higher than the GNP rank, a negative the opposite.

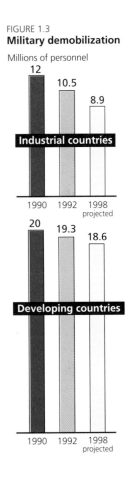

FIGURE 1.3
Military demobilization

Millions of personnel

Industrial countries

12 (1990) · 10.5 (1992) · 8.9 (1998 projected)

Developing countries

20 (1990) · 19.3 (1992) · 18.6 (1998 projected)

BOX 1.2

Balance sheet of human development—developing countries

PROGRESS	DEPRIVATION

LIFE EXPECTANCY

PROGRESS	DEPRIVATION
• Average life expectancy increased by over one-third during the past three decades; 23 countries have achieved a life expectancy of 70 years and more.	• Of the 300 million people above the age of 60, only 20% have any form of income security.

HEALTH AND SANITATION

PROGRESS	DEPRIVATION
• In the developing world, more than 70% of the population has access to health services. • Nearly 60% of the population has access to sanitation.	• About 17 million people die every year from infectious and parasitic diseases, such as diarrhoea, malaria and tuberculosis. • More than 80% of the 12–13 million HIV-infected people are in the developing world, and the cumulative direct and indirect cost of AIDS during the past decade was around $30 billion.

FOOD AND NUTRITION

PROGRESS	DEPRIVATION
• Between 1965 and 1990, the number of countries that met their daily per capita calorie requirements doubled—from about 25 to 50.	• Some 800 million people still do not get enough food.

EDUCATION

PROGRESS	DEPRIVATION
• Primary school enrolment increased in the past two decades—from less than 70% to well over 80%. In the same period, secondary enrolment almost doubled—from less than 25% to 40%.	• Nearly one billion people—35% of the adult population—are still illiterate, and the drop-out rate at the primary level is still as high as 30%.

INCOME AND POVERTY

PROGRESS	DEPRIVATION
• In South and East Asia, where two-thirds of the developing world's population live, the GNP growth averaged more than 7% a year during the 1980s.	• Almost one-third of the total population, or 1.3 billion people, are in absolute poverty.

CHILDREN

PROGRESS	DEPRIVATION
• During the past 30 years, infant and under-five mortality rates were more than halved.	• Each day, 34,000 young children still die from malnutrition and disease.

WOMEN

PROGRESS	DEPRIVATION
• The secondary enrolment ratio for girls increased from around 17% in 1970 to 36% in 1990.	• Two-thirds of illiterates are women.

HUMAN SECURITY

PROGRESS	DEPRIVATION
• With the end of the cold war, developing countries no longer have to serve as proxies for superpower rivalry, and in 1990, about 380,000 refugees returned to their homelands in Asia, Africa and Latin America.	• Internal conflicts afflict some 60 countries, and about 35 million people are refugees or internally displaced.

ENVIRONMENT

PROGRESS	DEPRIVATION
• The percentage of rural families with access to safe water has increased from less than 10% to almost 60% during the past two decades.	• More than 850 million people live in areas that are in various stages of desertification. • The rate of tropical forest destruction is about the equivalent of one soccer field per second.

BOX 1.3

Balance sheet of human development—industrial countries

PROGRESS	DEPRIVATION

LIFE EXPECTANCY AND HEALTH

• In 1960, life expectancy was more than 70 years in only 12 countries. Now, it is more than 70 years in all industrial countries.	• Nearly two million people are HIV-infected, and the direct and indirect cost during the 1980s was $210 billion.

EDUCATION

• The tertiary enrolment ratio more than doubled between 1965 and 1990.	• More than one-third of the adults lack any upper-secondary or higher education.

INCOME AND EMPLOYMENT

• The per capita GNP grew at an annual rate of 2.4% between 1965 and 1990.	• The average unemployment rate is about 7%, and a quarter of the more than 30 million unemployed have been out of work for more than two years.

SOCIAL SECURITY

• Social security expenditures now account for just under 15% of GDP.	• About 100 million people live below the poverty line.

WOMEN

• Women now account for more than 40% of total employment.	• Women hold fewer than 10% of parliamentary seats.

SOCIAL FABRIC

• There are now five library books and more than one radio for every person, and more than one telephone and one TV set for every two people. One in three people reads a newspaper.	• There are more than 15 suicides, more than 100 drug crimes and more than 15 deaths from road accidents per 100,000 people. • The number of divorces is now one-third the number of marriages contracted, and well over 5% of households are single-parent homes.

POPULATION AND ENVIRONMENT

• Energy requirements per unit of GDP fell by 40% between 1965 and 1990.	• People in industrial countries make up about one-fifth of world population but consume ten times more commercial energy than people in developing countries, and they account for 71% of the world's carbon monoxide emissions and 68% of the world's industrial waste.

far above their human development rank, showing their enormous potential for improving the lives of their people.

Several countries enjoying similar incomes per capita have very divergent human development experiences. Five countries with a GNP per capita of around $380 in 1990 had human accomplishments that could not be more dissimilar: Guyana, Kenya, Ghana, Pakistan and Haiti. Of this group, Guyana has the highest HDI value (0.541, rank 105), Haiti the lowest (0.275, rank 137). Ghana's average life expectancy is ten years shorter than Guyana's, and Pakistan's infant mortality rate is twice as high as Guyana's—and its illiteracy rate 16 times higher. Income alone is obviously a poor indicator of human development.

2. *The change in human development is as significant as its level*—Many countries started at a low level of human development three decades ago but have since made very rapid progress, particularly the Gulf States, whose real economic prosperity came in the mid-1970s after the steep increase in oil prices (figure 1.6). It clearly

TABLE 1.2
HDI ranking for developing countries

Country	HDI value	HDI rank	GNP rank	Country	HDI value	HDI rank	GNP rank	Country	HDI value	HDI rank	GNP rank
Barbados	0.928	20	34	Ecuador	0.646	89	108	Ghana	0.311	131	140
Hong Kong	0.913	24	24	Paraguay	0.641	90	97	Pakistan	0.311	132	136
Cyprus	0.890	27	30	Korea, Dem. Rep.	0.640	91	103	Cameroon	0.310	133	107
Uruguay	0.881	30	54	Philippines	0.603	92	114	India	0.309	134	146
Trinidad and Tobago	0.877	31	46	Tunisia	0.600	93	88	Namibia	0.289	135	98
Bahamas	0.875	32	25	Oman	0.598	94	36	Côte d'Ivoire	0.286	136	113
Korea, Rep. of	0.872	33	37	Peru	0.592	95	95	Haiti	0.275	137	143
Chile	0.864	36	75	Iraq	0.589	96	73	Tanzania, U. Rep. of	0.270	138	172
Costa Rica	0.852	42	76	Dominican Rep.	0.586	97	112	Comoros	0.269	139	129
Singapore	0.849	43	26	Samoa	0.586	98	109	Zaire	0.262	140	158
Brunei Darussalam	0.847	44	19	Jordan	0.582	99	91	Lao People's Dem. Rep.	0.246	141	161
Argentina	0.832	46	62	Mongolia	0.578	100	104	Nigeria	0.246	142	153
Venezuela	0.824	50	56	China	0.566	101	142	Yemen	0.233	143	124
Dominica	0.819	51	70	Lebanon	0.565	102	87	Liberia	0.222	144	127
Kuwait	0.815	52	15	Iran, Islamic Rep.	0.557	103	59	Togo	0.218	145	135
Mexico	0.805	53	60	Botswana	0.552	104	69	Uganda	0.194	146	167
Qatar	0.802	55	22	Guyana	0.541	105	141	Bangladesh	0.189	147	159
Mauritius	0.794	56	68	Vanuatu	0.533	106	96	Cambodia	0.186	148	168
Malaysia	0.790	57	66	Algeria	0.528	107	65	Rwanda	0.186	149	151
Bahrain	0.790	58	32	Indonesia	0.515	108	122	Senegal	0.182	150	115
Grenada	0.787	59	71	Gabon	0.503	109	44	Ethiopia	0.172	151	170
Antigua and Barbuda	0.785	60	41	El Salvador	0.503	110	102	Nepal	0.170	152	166
Colombia	0.770	61	93	Nicaragua	0.500	111	133	Malawi	0.168	153	162
Seychelles	0.761	63	39	Maldives	0.497	112	131	Burundi	0.167	154	160
Suriname	0.751	65	48	Guatemala	0.489	113	110	Equatorial Guinea	0.164	155	147
United Arab Emirates	0.738	67	12	Cape Verde	0.479	114	116	Central African Rep.	0.159	156	139
Panama	0.738	68	77	Viet Nam	0.472	115	156	Mozambique	0.154	157	173
Jamaica	0.736	69	86	Honduras	0.472	116	118	Sudan	0.152	158	138
Brazil	0.730	70	53	Swaziland	0.458	117	99	Bhutan	0.150	159	163
Fiji	0.730	71	78	Solomon Islands	0.439	118	121	Angola	0.143	160	126
Saint Lucia	0.720	72	64	Morocco	0.433	119	106	Mauritania	0.140	161	128
Turkey	0.717	73	83	Lesotho	0.431	120	123	Benin	0.113	162	145
Thailand	0.715	74	89	Zimbabwe	0.398	121	117	Djibouti	0.104	163	125
Cuba	0.711	75	101	Bolivia	0.398	122	119	Guinea-Bissau	0.090	164	165
Saint Vincent	0.709	76	79	Myanmar	0.390	123	152	Chad	0.088	165	164
Saint Kitts and Nevis	0.697	79	45	Egypt	0.389	124	120	Somalia	0.087	166	171
Syrian Arab Rep.	0.694	81	105	São Tomé and Principe	0.374	125	137	Gambia	0.086	167	148
Belize	0.689	82	74	Congo	0.372	126	100	Mali	0.082	168	154
Saudi Arabia	0.688	84	31	Kenya	0.369	127	144	Niger	0.080	169	150
South Africa	0.673	85	57	Madagascar	0.327	128	157	Burkina Faso	0.074	170	149
Sri Lanka	0.663	86	130	Papua New Guinea	0.318	129	111	Afghanistan	0.066	171	169
Libyan Arab Jamahiriya	0.658	87	40	Zambia	0.314	130	134	Sierra Leone	0.065	172	155
								Guinea	0.045	173	132

FIGURE 1.4

Human development varies by region

Human development index weighted by population

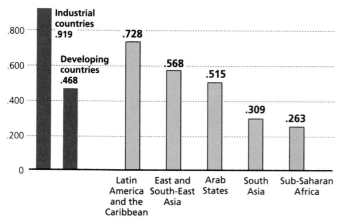

FIGURE 1.7

HDIs have diverged for countries with similar starting points

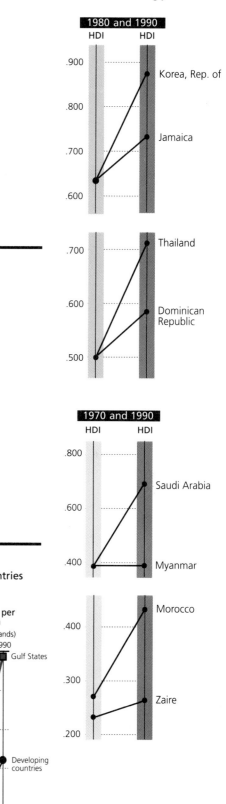

FIGURE 1.5

There is no automatic link between income and human development

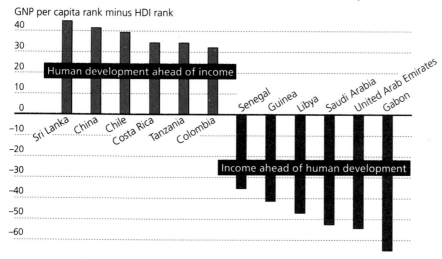

FIGURE 1.6

Human development progress in the Gulf States

■ Gulf States
● All developing countries

Life expectancy (years)	Infant mortality (per 1,000 live births)	Daily per capita calorie supply (percentage of requirement)	Adult literacy rate (percent)	Combined primary & secondary enrolment ratio	Real GDP per capita (PPP$ thousands)

TABLE 1.3
Gender-disparity-adjusted HDI

Country	HDI value	Gender-disparity-adjusted HDI	Difference between HDI and gender-disparity-adjusted ranks
Sweden	0.977	0.921	4
Norway	0.978	0.881	1
France	0.971	0.864	5
Denmark	0.955	0.860	8
Finland	0.954	0.859	8
Australia	0.972	0.852	1
New Zealand	0.947	0.844	9
Netherlands	0.970	0.826	1
USA	0.976	0.824	−3
United Kingdom	0.964	0.818	0
Canada	0.982	0.816	−9
Belgium	0.952	0.808	3
Austria	0.952	0.782	1
Switzerland	0.978	0.768	−10
Germany	0.957	0.768	−4
Italy	0.924	0.764	3
Japan	0.983	0.763	−16
Czechoslovakia	0.892	0.754	4
Ireland	0.925	0.720	−1
Luxembourg	0.943	0.713	−3
Greece	0.902	0.691	0
Portugal	0.853	0.672	3
Cyprus	0.890	0.656	0
Costa Rica	0.852	0.632	2
Hong Kong	0.913	0.618	−5
Singapore	0.849	0.585	1
Korea, Rep. of	0.872	0.555	−3
Paraguay	0.641	0.546	1
Sri Lanka	0.663	0.499	−1
Philippines	0.603	0.451	0
Swaziland	0.458	0.344	0
Myanmar	0.390	0.297	0
Kenya	0.369	0.241	0

A positive difference shows that the gender-disparity-adjusted HDI rank is higher than the unadjusted HDI rank, a negative the opposite.

FIGURE 1.8
Changes in rank with a gender-disparity-adjusted HDI

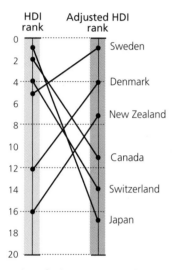

Ranks are for the 33 countries in table 1.3.

FIGURE 1.9
Difference between HDI and gender-disparity-adjusted HDI

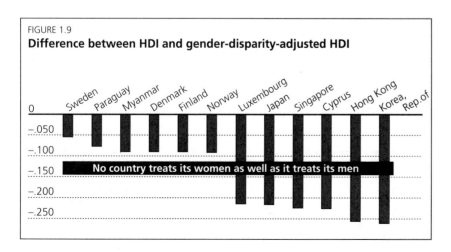

took time to invest the new income in people, but during the past 20 years, the Gulf States have made much faster progress than the average developing country. Saudi Arabia had the greatest change in its HDI value—from 0.386 in 1970 to 0.688 in 1990.

Several countries with similar HDIs in 1970 have since had dissimilar experiences. Myanmar and Saudi Arabia, for example, started with similar HDIs in 1970, as did Zaire and Morocco. For Myanmar and Zaire, the world has stood still in terms of human development—a factor which no doubt has contributed to the countries' present problems. But Saudi Arabia has since nearly doubled its HDI, and Morocco has raised its HDI by 60% (figure 1.7).

3. *The economies in transition have very high levels of human development*—Two-thirds of the 15 newly independent states of the former Soviet Union fall into the category of high human development, the other third into the medium. The formerly socialist countries have already made major investments in the education and health of their people—and thus have considerable human capital available for the transition ahead. The average life expectancy for these economies is 70 years, and the population per doctor is around 300, compared with 63 years and 5,000 respectively for developing countries.

4. *When the HDI is adjusted for gender disparity, no country improves its HDI value*—The meaning: no country treats its women as well as it treats its men, a disappointing result after so many years of debate on gender equality, so many struggles by women and so many changes in national laws (table 1.3 and figures 1.8 and 1.9). But some countries do better than others, so adjusting for gender disparity makes a big difference to the rankings: Japan falls from number 1 to 17, Canada from number 2 to 11 and Switzerland from number 4 to 14. By contrast, Sweden improves its rank from number 5 to 1, Denmark from number 12 to 4 and New Zealand from number 16 to 7.

In industrial countries, gender discrimination (measured by the HDI) is mainly in employment and wages, with women often

TABLE 1.4
Income-distribution-adjusted HDI

Country	HDI value	Income-distribution-adjusted HDI value	Difference between HDI and income-distribution-adjusted ranks
Japan	0.983	0.981	0
Netherlands	0.970	0.966	7
Switzerland	0.978	0.958	1
Sweden	0.977	0.958	1
Norway	0.978	0.956	–2
Canada	0.982	0.947	–4
Belgium	0.952	0.946	6
United Kingdom	0.964	0.945	2
USA	0.976	0.943	–3
France	0.971	0.938	–2
Australia	0.972	0.934	–4
Finland	0.954	0.932	0
Denmark	0.955	0.925	–2
Israel	0.938	0.912	1
New Zealand	0.947	0.909	–1
Ireland	0.925	0.908	0
Spain	0.923	0.898	1
Italy	0.924	0.892	–1
Korea, Rep. of	0.872	0.885	2
Hungary	0.887	0.873	0
Hong Kong	0.913	0.871	–2
Singapore	0.849	0.836	3
Costa Rica	0.852	0.829	1
Chile	0.864	0.818	–2
Portugal	0.853	0.802	–2
Argentina	0.832	0.791	0
Venezuela	0.824	0.771	0
Mauritius	0.794	0.745	1
Mexico	0.805	0.737	–1
Colombia	0.770	0.734	1
Malaysia	0.790	0.732	–1
Thailand	0.715	0.672	4
Panama	0.738	0.654	–1
Turkey	0.717	0.650	1
Syrian Arab Rep.	0.694	0.644	2
Jamaica	0.736	0.643	–3
Sri Lanka	0.663	0.634	1
Brazil	0.730	0.627	–4
Tunisia	0.600	0.583	1
Philippines	0.603	0.575	–1
Iran, Islamic Rep.	0.557	0.519	0
Indonesia	0.515	0.519	0
El Salvador	0.503	0.488	0
Honduras	0.472	0.419	0
Egypt	0.389	0.377	0
Kenya	0.369	0.344	0
Pakistan	0.311	0.303	1
Zambia	0.314	0.291	–1
India	0.309	0.289	0
Côte d'Ivoire	0.286	0.246	0
Bangladesh	0.189	0.172	0
Nepal	0.170	0.138	0

A positive difference shows that the income-distribution-adjusted HDI rank is higher than the unadjusted HDI rank, a negative the opposite.

getting less than two-thirds of the employment opportunities and about half the earnings of men.

In developing countries, the great disparities, besides those in the job market, are in health care, nutritional support and education. For instance, women make up two-thirds of the illiterate population. And South and East Asia, defying the normal biological result that women live longer than men, have more men than women. The reasons: high maternal mortality and infanticide and nutritional neglect of the girl-child. According to one estimate, some 100 million women are "missing".

5. *The poor distribution of income has a major impact on human development*—Income disparities are wide in many countries, particularly in the developing world. Brazil has one of the most unequal distributions of income—the richest 20% of the population receives 26 times the income of the poorest 20%. When the income component of its HDI is reduced to reflect this maldistribution, its HDI falls by 14% (figure 1.10). The same correction also causes a major drop in the HDI of many other countries, including Jamaica, Malaysia, Mexico, Panama and Turkey (figure 1.11). Table 1.4 gives the income-distribution-adjusted HDI for 52 countries having data. Among the industrial countries, the largest adjustments downwards are for Portugal, New Zealand, Australia, Canada, France, Italy and the United States.

6. *When the HDI is disaggregated by calculating the specific HDI for groups or regions in a country, there can be startling divergences*

FIGURE 1.10
Changes in rank with an income-distribution-adjusted HDI

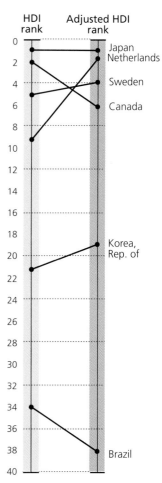

Ranks are for the 52 countries in table 1.4.

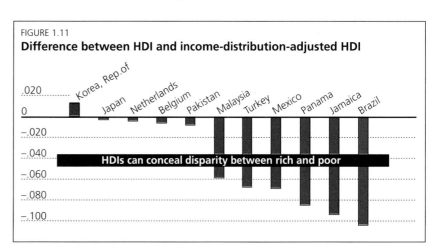

FIGURE 1.11
Difference between HDI and income-distribution-adjusted HDI

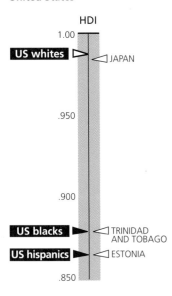

FIGURE 1.12

HDIs are higher for whites than for blacks and hispanics in the United States

from the national average—Disaggregating HDIs provides a group-specific or region-specific human development measure, whereas the gender-adjusted and income-distribution-adjusted HDIs are still national averages incorporating the extent of inequality. Five countries that have readily available data to undertake such a disaggregation: the United States, India, Mexico, Turkey and Swaziland. More countries should launch efforts to gather such data.

In the United States, with the HDIs of white, black and hispanic populations separated, whites rank number 1 in the world (ahead of Japan), blacks rank number 31 (next to Trinidad and Tobago) and hispanics rank number 35 (next to Estonia). This, even despite the fact that income levels are considerably discounted in the HDI calculations. So, full equality is a distant prospect in the United States (figures 1.12 and 1.13).

Similar disparities are obvious elsewhere. In India, the HDI in Uttar Pradesh is a third lower than the national average and 60% lower than that in Kerala (figure 1.14). In Mexico, the state of Oaxaca has an HDI 20% lower than the national average (figure 1.15). In Turkey, the HDI for rural females is 25% lower than that for rural males (figure 1.16). By contrast, Swaziland, with a smaller population of less than one million, is a more homogeneous society.

With so many inequalities in multiethnic and otherwise divided societies, a disaggregated HDI profile is essential to eventually understanding the underlying sources of tension and potential causes of future trouble.

The HDI is thus a useful and informative tool for analysing and assessing development. But it probably is still too early to use the HDI to evaluate a country's performance, or to allocate aid funds. That kind of application must await further improvements to the HDI.

A human development agenda

Since the *Human Development Report* appeared, it has attracted a great deal of international attention and debate. And many countries, going beyond discussions and policy statements, are putting human development ideas into practice. Bangladesh, Colombia, Ghana and Pakistan have already prepared comprehensive human development strategies, and more than 20 other countries are—with UNDP assistance—undertaking different types of human development initiatives. These efforts are likely to include ten significant steps.

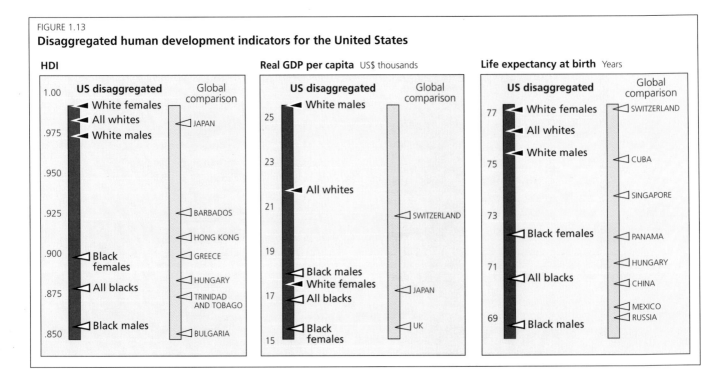

FIGURE 1.13

Disaggregated human development indicators for the United States

1. *Prepare a national human development report*—Since the *Human Development Report* must publish internationally comparable data, it often cannot use the most recent or most relevant information for countries. Some—including Cameroon, Côte d'Ivoire and Paraguay—have therefore produced their own reports reflecting their own circumstances, statistics and policy concerns.

2. *Prepare a human development country profile*—As a part of the national report, or as a separate initiative, a short statistical profile of human development can be prepared, showing the progress achieved and the distance yet to be travelled. This has already been done in Mozambique, Thailand, Papua New Guinea and elsewhere.

3. *Improve human development statistics*—Most countries put a lot of effort into publishing statistics on economic growth, but much less into those on the human condition—how many people are below the poverty line, for example, or are homeless. Often, the data are collected but not collated into usable form because of an apparent lack of demand. Priorities need to be re-established to ensure that data on human development are collected and made available to policy-makers, as has been found in Kenya, Mexico and the Philippines, among others.

4. *Set human development targets*—Human development targets are seldom quantitative—again because the underlying data are missing. The best progress in targeting has, often with UNICEF's assistance, been in the area of children's development, health and education. This experience needs to be extended to other areas to establish just what is to be achieved by which group—and when. To be kept in mind, though, is that human development objectives cannot be limited to quantifiable targets. Many important aspects of human development escape quantification and can be analysed only in qualitative terms. For example, people's education depends both on years of schooling and on the type of knowledge imparted.

5. *Cost the targets*—While the construction costs of roads or industrial plants are frequently estimated (if not very accurately), human development targets rarely are (even tentatively). This makes social expenditure vulnerable to economic cutbacks—since if nobody knows what good health costs, it is difficult to defend in the budget.

6. *Clarify who does what*—National strategies need to consider the most appropriate roles for central, regional and local governments—and for the private sector and NGOs. To be considered above all is how people can best participate and take charge of their own lives and the interests of their families and communities.

7. *Establish who will pay*—In some cases, the state will need to make the investment—in basic education or health. In oth-

---

FIGURE 1.14
Disparity among India's states

Percentage of national average

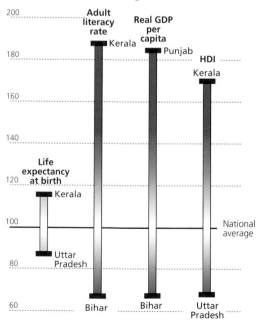

FIGURE 1.15
Disparity among Mexico's states

Percentage of national average

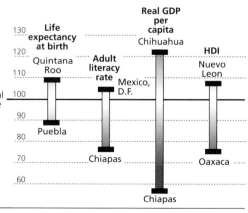

FIGURE 1.16
Gender differences in Turkey and Swaziland

Percentage of national average

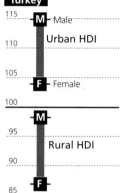

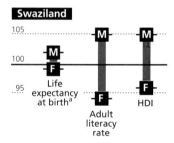

a. Adjusted to account for the biological differential.

---

ers, some segments of the population could be asked to pay for services through user charges. Or it might be better to concentrate on providing more employment and income-earning opportunities that would enable people to become more self-sufficient and independent.

8. *Design a national strategy*—To ensure that all the activities link together naturally, it might be useful to formulate a comprehensive country strategy for human development—a strategy concerning all the steps from the identification of priority areas to the implementation of policies and programmes and a monitoring of progress.

9. *Seek external cooperation*—Most governments of developing countries can improve levels of human development with the resources they already have. But more substantial achievements will also depend on international cooperation—through fairer access to international markets and through more effective technical assistance and financial aid (box 1.4). They should establish areas of common interest and common priority with industrial countries. For Bangladesh and Pakistan, human development has been an agenda item of consultative group meetings.

10. *Build political alliances*—Human development accelerates where people understand the benefits from a healthier and better-educated population. Governments can assist this process by working with natural allies, such as doctors and teachers, to promote these ideas. They can also target media campaigns at small businesses, for example, to extol the virtues of educating children better so that they can one day help manage businesses—or at men, to explain how all society benefits when women have better opportunities. To broaden support for human development country strategies, it is often useful to ensure full participation of all interested partners right from the start—of all concerned government entities, as well as the private sector, NGOs and people at large.

These ten steps are only schematic, and each country will decide on its agenda. The steps nevertheless highlight the value of approaching human development systematically. Remember that the struggle for human progress in the industrial countries is a continuous process (box 1.5). Clearly, reorienting development towards people—although doable—is a complex challenge.

BOX 1.4

Technical cooperation's high cost in Africa

Technical cooperation is an important way for developing countries to acquire skills, build up their capacity and pursue self-reliant development. About a quarter of all development assistance to Africa has been in this form—more than $3 billion a year. But this technical cooperation is under attack for being expensive and outmoded—serving the priorities of the donors rather than building up national capacity.

Such programmes often rely heavily on expatriate personnel. A study of ten African countries showed that around 75% of the resources are spent on personnel—as opposed to equipment and operating expenses. Relatively little use is made of national experts. In Mali in 1990, donors employed some 80 foreign doctors and medical personnel, even though 100 qualified Malian doctors were unemployed.

Donors often impose experts on reluctant national governments who feel this to be the price of financial assistance. When the experts come, they often run the programmes, with control over the purse strings. This is frustrating for African governments and for aspiring professionals in African institutions, who, using the expert-counterpart training system, find themselves "overshadowed" by a foreign expert.

Technical assistance is very expensive aid. Donor spending on technical cooperation is as large as the entire civil service bill—in Uganda, many times greater. The cost of one person-year of an expatriate expert can exceed a department's entire operating budget. In capital assistance projects, the situation may even be worse.

Proposals are beginning to be implemented that could help improve technical cooperation. One is to make greater use of local experts and to pass the management of programmes to recipient governments. Another is to include market elements in technical cooperation. If recipients were given the money—untied to any predetermined "package" from the donors—they would probably make very different decisions on how best to use it for human development.

BOX 1.5

Progress possible—though not inevitable—on three fronts

The more enlightened advanced societies have taken three centuries to achieve the civil, political and social dimensions of human development. The 18th century established *civil* rights: from freedom of thought, speech and religion to the rule of law. In the 19th century, *political* freedom and participation in the exercise of political power made major strides, as the right to vote was extended to more people. In the 20th century the welfare state extended human development to the *social* and *economic* spheres, by recognizing that minimum standards of education, health, nutrition, well-being and security are basic to a civilized life and to exercising the civil and political attributes of citizenship. These battles were not won easily or without resistance. Each progressive thrust was followed by reactionary counterthrusts and setbacks.

The struggle for *civil* liverty was opposed, after the French Revolution, by those fearful that it would lead only to tyranny—that the fight for political participation would enslave the masses. We are now witnessing one of these counterattacks on the economic liberties of the welfare state, and on some fronts partial retreat. The argument again is that the opposite of the intended result is achieved. Just as civil liverty was said to lead to tyranny, and political liberty to slavery, so compassionate concern for the poor, it is now said, can lead only to their continuing poverty. The *Human Development Reports* show that human progress is possible, though not inevitable, along all three fronts.

CHAPTER 2

People's participation

Participation means that people are closely involved in the economic, social, cultural and political processes that affect their lives (box 2.1). People may, in some cases, have complete and direct control over these processes—in other cases, the control may be partial or indirect. The important thing is that people have constant access to decision-making and power. Participation in this sense is an essential element of human development.

Participation, certainly not a new term, has been a part of the development vocabulary since the 1960s, or even before. But it has generally referred only to people's involvement in particular projects or programmes. In this Report, the critical difference is that participation is an overall development strategy—focusing on the central role that people should play in all spheres of life. Human development involves widening their choices, and greater participation enables people to gain for themselves access to a much broader range of opportunities.

People can participate as individuals or as groups. As individuals in a democracy, they may participate as voters or political activists—or in the market as entrepreneurs or workers. Often, however, they participate more effectively through group action—as members of a community organization, perhaps, or a trade union or a political party.

People everywhere are certainly demanding much greater access to political, economic and social opportunities. They might not expect "full participation"—but they do want a steady advance towards it. Participation is, after all, a process, not an event.

Since participation requires increased influence and control, it also demands in-

creased empowerment—in economic, social and political terms. In economic terms, this means being able to engage freely in any economic activity. In social terms, it means being able to join fully in all forms of community life, without regard to religion, colour, sex or race. And in political terms, it means the freedom to choose and change governance at every level, from the presidential palace to the village council.

All these forms of participation are intimately linked. Without one, the others will be incomplete and less effective.

Any proposal to increase people's participation must therefore pass the empowerment test—does it increase or decrease people's power to control their lives? This test applies to all institutions that organize or affect human lives—whether markets, governments or community organizations. Each must advance the cause of people.

Participation, from the human development perspective, is both a means and an end. Human development stresses the need to invest in human capabilities and then ensure that those capabilities are used for the benefit of all. Greater participation has an important part to play here: it helps maximize the use of human capabilities and

---

BOX 2.1

A checklist of effective participation

Do people have:
- Equitable access to health and other aspects of physical well-being?
- Equitable access to knowledge, skills, technology and information?
- Equal human rights?

If there are obstacles, do they lie in:
- The legal system?
- Administrative rules and procedures?
- Social norms and values?

- The distribution of income and assets?

What should be the priority concern for a strategy to promote people's participation?
- Increasing public expenditure on human development priorities?
- Dismantling market barriers?
- Improving democratic governance?
- Strengthening the elements of a civil society, such as people's organizations, NGOs and a free press?

---

is thus a *means* of increasing levels of social and economic development. But human development is also concerned with personal fulfilment. So, active participation, which allows people to realize their full potential and make their best contribution to society, is also an *end* in itself.

Forms of participation

Since participation can take place in the economic, social and political arenas, each person necessarily participates in many ways, at many levels. In economic life as a producer or a consumer, an entrepreneur or an employee. In social life as a member of a family, or of a community organization or ethnic group. And in political life as a voter, or as a member of a political party or perhaps a pressure group. All these roles overlap and interact, forming patterns of participation that interconnect with—and often reinforce—each other.

• *Household participation*—It is almost always women who rear the children and provide food and water, as well as ensure adequate health care for the family. And to fulfil such responsibilities, they also work outside the home, often in the informal sector.

This contribution of women to society remains unrecognized in economic statistics, and it does not give women even an equal say in decisions in the household. A survey in Uganda found that the management of household income was a joint responsibility for only a small minority. In most cases, the husband handed over only a small proportion of "housekeeping money" to the wife.

Where women do have control over household funds, they generally make much better use of them. In Malaysia, a case study of rubber tappers found that almost all income earned by women was directed to meeting household needs—while men tended to devote sums equivalent to 40% of household incomes to their personal requirements, such as tobacco. Most societies are still a long way from looking at household tasks as a shared responsibility of men and women.

The starkest example of gender discrimination in the household is revealed through child survival rates. In Bangladesh, nearly 15% more girls than boys die in the first few years of life. And under the age of five, the mortality rate for girls in many countries is higher than that of boys—5% higher in Nepal, 4% in Pakistan and India, and 2% in Bhutan—whereas, biologically, more girls should survive than boys.

• *Economic participation*—Most people spend a large part of their lives in economic activity. It is in the economic arena that people have a unique opportunity to use their capabilities and to gain a remunerative income, which in turn enables them, through increased purchasing power, to increase their range of choices. Participation in economic life also affords people a basis for self-respect and social dignity, attributes that are integral to participating in all dimensions of life.

The nature of economic participation can vary widely, from forms of drudgery to creative, productive and independent economic activity. Societies also vary greatly in the value they place on forms of work, ranging from the association of manual work with servitude to a respect for manual labour in more egalitarian societies. And closely related to this range of social attitudes is the nature of the work environment itself, which can be more or less participatory. But it is only in a democratic environment that people can derive full satisfaction from work and from the perception that they are making a valuable contribution to development.

• *Social and cultural participation*—All people, and all communities, have a right to create their culture in whatever way they wish—whether through language, through ritual, art, music and dance or through literature or storytelling—in any of the myriad forms of culture through which human beings the world over express themselves.

But globally there has been a tendency towards homogenization. The world today has around 4,000 languages, but thousands of languages have been lost over the past couple of centuries. In the 19th century, there were 1,000 Indian languages in South

America. Now there are fewer than 200. And dress has similarly become more uniform, with most traditional costumes being steadily replaced by a much smaller number of international styles.

Even the very form of expression can come under threat. Oral cultures are particularly at risk since the current trend is towards less emphasis on memory and more on literacy and mechanical reproduction—substituting books for the spoken word. This means, for example, that much traditional wisdom in health and medicine, not written down, has been lost.

Similarly, many communities have communicated from one generation to the next through such intricate skills as weaving and carving—skills constantly being eroded by mass industrial production.

Such changes are usually accepted, often welcomed, as "progress". Only now—with the threat that some languages and skills might disappear altogether—is the world becoming more concerned about the wealth of valuable human information that might be lost.

Cultures need to be respected and constantly asserted or they die. Hence the determination of many groups, particularly indigenous peoples, to participate actively to preserve and reassert their identity. This is a form of cultural participation to which they have a right—and from which the whole world gains.

But if these valuable elements of the human experience are to survive, all parts of society have to contribute—including people's organizations, non-governmental organizations (NGOs) and governments. Cultural riches must be available to all at reasonable prices, not limited to the wealthy or to tourists. UNESCO studies show how critical the decentralization of cultural institutions is for ensuring that they are readily accessible at the local level. And while new technologies can often diminish local cultures, used creatively they can also make them available to much wider audiences.

• *Political participation*—In recent years people have been struggling, individually and collectively, to have a much greater say in national life. In many cases, opposing au-tocratic regimes has demanded great courage—as with those who opposed the regimes in Argentina, the Philippines and South Africa, as well as in Eastern Europe and the former Soviet Union. In other cases, as in Zambia, the rulers have themselves recognized that, in the long term, stifling people's power and initiative would be counter-productive. And international pressures have also reinforced national forces for political change as ideas about human rights and democracy have spread around the globe.

Achieving meaningful and durable democracy is far from simple. It may include several aspects: guarantees of human rights, including freedom of speech and association; rule of law; free, fair and fully contested elections at periodic intervals; a multiparty system; orderly transition of government and elected representatives fully accountable to voters.

Democracy demands an effective and open political system, not just within governments but within political parties so that people have a real choice when nominating candidates for election. And if governments are to be kept free from undue influence from vested interests, democracy also demands strong institutions of civil society (such as a free press) and a diversity of non-governmental organizations (such as the environmental groups that have had such an impact in many countries in recent years).

Democracy cannot be achieved overnight. Just as economic growth means little unless it is translated into improvements in human lives, so democracy can be merely an empty ritual of periodic elections unless people participate, aware and empowered, in all the institutions of civil society. Elections are a necessary, but certainly not a sufficient, condition for democracy. Political participation is not just a casting of votes. It is a way of life.

New openings

Despite a number of violent conflicts, the world seems to be going through a period of positive change: participation of all kinds

Political participation is not just a casting of votes. It is a way of life

seems to be on the upswing—particularly in the formerly socialist countries and in the developing world.

- *Democracy*—has been extended to many parts of the world in the past decade. Close to two-thirds of humankind now live in countries that are moving towards, or are already enjoying, democratic forms of government.

- *The transition to market economies*—is also gathering pace all over the world as governments dismantle state controls and open new doors for participation and entrepreneurial activity. Most formerly socialist countries have by now committed themselves to more market-based strategies. And many developing countries are liberalizing their economies—removing restrictive regulations, establishing much greater transparency in business affairs and offering entrepreneurs greater opportunities for participation in economic activity.

- *Privatization*—is creating new avenues for participation in the economies of many countries. Since 1980, around 7,000 state-owned enterprises have been privatized, about 1,400 of them in developing countries.

Markets exclude those whose poverty renders them uncreditworthy

- *The information revolution*—is bringing reports of global events to everyone's home. Now, through radio and TV, people have a much greater sense of participation in international events—as they happen. And people now have many different ways of communicating within their own countries, not just through broadcast media, but also through newer media, from fax machines to videocassettes, that are much less vulnerable to censorship—making it much harder for governments to monopolize the flow of information.

- *Non-governmental organizations*—have increased substantially in recent years. In 1990, there were an estimated 50,000 non-governmental organizations (NGOs) in developing countries working in many different fields, from health care to informal education. And they have taken on an important advocacy role on such issues as gender discrimination, human rights and environmental concerns.

These changes, rapid and complex, have taken different directions in different countries. In some, the impetus has come from the government in power. In others, it has been the outcome of popular rebellion. And the results have been as diverse as the events. Some countries have succeeded in strengthening democratic institutions and enjoyed steady increases in efficiency. Others have suffered economic crisis, social chaos, ethnic disruptions and even civil war.

The groups excluded

Despite the accumulating forces for greater participation, large numbers of people continue to be excluded from the benefits of development: the poorest segments of society, people in rural areas, many religious and ethnic minorities—and, in almost every country, women. Also excluded are those millions, particularly children, whose preventable and premature deaths cut short their lives.

Many of these groups necessarily overlap but it is useful to identify some of them individually.

- *The poorest people*—find that their very poverty is a formidable barrier to entering many aspects of social, economic and polit-

---

BOX 2.2

Children of the streets

Millions of children live in the slums or on the streets of Third World cities, and their numbers grow daily as poverty in the rural areas drives people to the cities in the hope of a better life. Thirty years ago, the population of Brazil was 55% rural—now it is 75% urban. Around three-quarters of street children in Brazil are thought to be migrants.

Many street children do have homes and parents, but they may visit them only rarely, forced to earn their livelihood on the streets and driven from the squalor of one or two crowded rooms in the shantytowns. In Manila in the Philippines, three million people live in slums, about half of them children. Fewer than a quarter of families have piped water, and two-thirds have no sanitary facilities. Manila has about 75,000 street children.

India probably has the greatest number of street children. New Delhi, Bombay and Calcutta have around 100,000 street children each, and Bangalore about 45,000. There, as elsewhere, they must work to survive—collecting rags, shining shoes, selling newspapers, scavenging on rubbish dumps. Many also turn to crime. India's juvenile crime rate is 3.1 per 1,000 people.

Street children are also a growing problem in Africa. There, too, migration from the countryside is swelling the urban slums. Mathare Valley in Nairobi is the largest slum community in Kenya, with around 200,000 people. The majority are migrants and a high proportion are children. Four years ago, Nairobi had about 16,000 street children, today there are thought to be 25,000.

Street children are one of the most obvious signs of urban deprivation. Hungry, sick and often homeless children with little chance of a basic education are a sharp reminder of the human potential the world is wasting.

ical life. In many developing countries, income disparities are very wide. In Indonesia, the poorest 20% of the people receive only 8.8% of national income, in Sri Lanka 4.8%. And in many cases, the gaps between the poor and the rich are widening. In Chile between 1970 and 1988, the real income of the poorest 20% fell by 3%, while that of the richest 20% increased by 10%. Markets, in theory open to everyone, in practice exclude those whose poverty renders them uncreditworthy. In Bangladesh, the landless make up around half the rural households but receive only 17% of institutional credit.

Poverty has its greatest impact on children and is a denial to future generations. Infant mortality rates in the least developed countries are still 114 per 1,000 live births, and nearly 13 million children die each year before their fifth birthday. The HIV/AIDS pandemic will increase not only the number of child deaths but also the problem of orphans and hence child poverty.

And even children who do survive are deprived of the opportunity to participate fully in their countries' development. Some 200 million of today's children are having their potential for growth stunted by malnutrition. And well over 300 million children who should be in primary or secondary schools are missing their education, either because of the need to work or because schools are unavailable or too expensive. Many of these children spend their days at work in the fields or in the streets (box 2.2).

Poverty can also be harsh for the elderly. In the formerly socialist countries, the pensioners are among those who suffer most from the current reform process.

For millions of people all over the world, the daily struggle for survival absorbs so much of their time and energy that, even if they live in democratic countries, genuine political participation is, for all practical purposes, a luxury.

• *Women*—are the world's largest excluded group (box 2.3). Even though they make up half the adult population, and often contribute much more than their share to society, inside and outside the home, they are frequently excluded from positions of power. They make up just over 10% of the

world's parliamentary representatives, and consistently less than 4% of cabinet ministers or other positions of executive authority.

In many industrial countries, the female human development index is only around 80% that of males. Women participate inadequately in employment, and in some industrial countries, women's earnings are less than half those of men (box 2.4).

Many developing countries exclude women from both political participation and productive work—whether by tradition, discriminatory laws or withheld edu-

BOX 2.3

Women—the non-participating majority

Women, a majority of the world's population, receive only a small share of developmental opportunities. They are often excluded from education or from the better jobs, from political systems or from adequate health care.

• *Literacy*—Women are much less likely than men to be literate. In South Asia, female literacy rates are only around 50% those of males. And in many countries the situation is even worse: in Nepal 35%, Sierra Leone 37%, Sudan 27% and Afghanistan 32%. Women make up two-thirds of the world's illiterates.

• *Higher education*—Women in developing countries lag far behind men. In Sub-Saharan Africa, their enrolment rates for tertiary education are only a third of those of men. Even in industrial countries, women are very poorly represented in scientific and technical study: in Spain, the ratio of female to male third-level students in these fields is 28%, in Austria 25% and in Canada 29%.

• *Employment*—In developing countries women have many fewer job opportunities: the employment participation rates of women are on average only 50% those of men (in South Asia 29%, and in the Arab States only 16%). Even when they do find work, they tend to get paid much less: in the Republic of Korea, women's wages are only 47% those of men. Wage discrimination is also a feature of industrial countries: in Japan, women receive only 51% of male wages.

Women who are not in paid employment are, of course, far from idle. Indeed, they tend to work much longer

hours than men. The problem is that the work they do, in domestic chores and caring for children and the elderly, does not get the recognition it deserves in national income accounts.

• *Self-employment*—Women's opportunities for self-employment can be restricted in a number of ways. In some countries they are still not allowed to own property, or to offer collateral for bank loans or even to drive.

• *Politics*—In some countries, women are still not allowed to vote. And women almost everywhere are underrepresented in government: in 1980, they made up just over 10% of the world's parliamentarians and less than 4% of national cabinets. In 1993, only six countries had women as heads of government.

• *Health*—Women tend on average to live longer than men. But in some Asian and North African countries, the discrimination against women—through neglect of their health or nutrition—is such that they have a shorter life expectancy. Indeed, comparing the populations who should be alive, based on the global mortality patterns, it seems that 100 million Asian women are "missing".

One of the greatest health risks for women in poor countries is childbirth. Maternal mortality rates in the developing world are more than 15 times higher than in the industrial countries.

• *National statistics*—Women are often invisible in statistics. If women's unpaid housework were counted as productive output in national income accounts, global output would increase by 20–30%.

Women in Japan

Japan, despite some of the world's highest levels of human development, still has marked inequalities in achievement between men and women. The 1993 human development index puts Japan first. But when the HDI is adjusted for gender disparity, Japan slips to number 17. Here's why:

In education, the tertiary enrolment ratio for females is only two-thirds that of males.

Similarly in employment, women are considerably worse off. Women's average earnings are only 51% those of men, and women are largely excluded from decision-making positions: they hold only 7% of administrative and managerial jobs.

Their representation is even lower in the political sphere. Women obtained the right to vote, and to be elected to parliament, only after the Second World War. Yet today, only 2% of parliamentary seats are held by women, and at the ministerial level there are no women at all (compared with the 9% average for industrial countries and 13% for the other countries of Asia). Nevertheless, one or two women have achieved important political positions, and a number of women were among the founders of the Social Democratic Party.

In legal rights in general, Japan's patrilineal society is only gradually changing to offer women greater recognition and independence. Only in 1980 were the inheritance rights of Japanese women raised from one-third to one-half of their late husbands' property (the rest goes to the children). And in other aspects the law is still not gender-neutral. Thus, the legal age of marriage is 18 for men, but 16 for women. And after divorce, a man can remarry immediately, but a woman has to wait six months.

Japan now has political and non-governmental organizations pressing for change. The League of Women Voters, for instance, is lobbying for a correction in the disparity of seat distribution in parliament, and for a greater participation of women in policy-making.

One country, two nations

Almost every country has one or more ethnic groups whose level of human development falls far below the national average. One of the clearest, and best documented, cases is that of blacks in the United States.

Their disadvantage starts at birth. The infant mortality rate for whites is 8 per 1,000 live births, but for blacks it is 19. And black children are much more likely than white children to grow up in single-parent homes—in 1990, 19% of white children were growing up in single-parent households, compared with 54% of black children.

Children in black families are also more likely to grow up in poverty. The real GDP per capita for whites in 1990 was around $22,000, but for blacks it was around $17,000.

As Andrew Hacker, the author of *Two Nations* (1992), graphically records:

The statistics are dismaying. Nearly two-thirds of black babies are now born out of wedlock, and over half of black families are headed by women. The majority of black youngsters live only with their mother; and in over half of these households, she has never been married. At the last count, over half of all single black women have already had children, and among women in their mid to late thirties, less than half have intact marriages. These figures are from three to five times greater than for white households, and markedly higher than those recorded for black Americans a generation ago.... Black Americans are Americans yet they subsist as aliens in the only land they know. Other groups may remain outside the mainstream—some religious sects, for example—but they do so voluntarily. In contrast, blacks must endure a segregation that is far from freely chosen. So America may be seen as two separate nations.

Indeed, if the United States were divided into two "countries", the one with the white population would rank number one in the world, according to the human development index, while that with the black population would be only number 31.

cation. In the countries for which relevant data are available, the female human development index is only 60% that of males. Indeed, for decades, life has changed very little for 500 million rural women in the developing world.

• *Minorities and indigenous peoples*—often find it difficult to participate fully in societies that consistently operate in favour of the dominant groups. Sometimes this discrimination is embedded in the legal framework—denying minority groups equal access to education, to employment opportunities or to political representation. But exclusion is generally less a matter of official policy than everyday practice. In the United States, where everyone is "created free and equal", there is a marked difference between the white and black populations. As chapter 1 showed, if the US were divided into two "countries", the one with only the white population would be in first place in the human development index, while the one with the blacks would be number 31 (box 2.5). In Guatemala, the Indian population has an infant mortality rate 20% higher than the rest of the population. And in South Africa, the blacks are a marginalized majority (box 2.6).

An extreme form of discrimination and exclusion is through violence. Since the Second World War, 40 ethnic groups around the world have been persecuted or massacred, suffering millions of deaths.

• *People in rural areas*—have very restricted participation in economic and social life in the developing world. The rural per capita income in many countries is around half that in towns and cities. And rural people have much less access to government services. Despite making up around two-thirds of the population, they receive on average less than a quarter of the education, health, water and sanitation services. In Ethiopia, 87% of the people live in rural areas but only 11% of them have access to safe drinking water, compared with 70% of the urban population. In Bangladesh, 84% of the population is rural but only 4% of them have access to sanitation facilities, compared with 40% of the urban population. And in India, school attendance for children aged 5–14 is much lower in rural areas: 55% for boys and

35% for girls (compared with 74% and 52% in urban areas).

Urban biases are a predominant feature almost everywhere. But even when the parliaments of some developing countries are dominated by rural elites, this does not mean that they act on behalf of rural people. Most are composed of city-based absentee landlords with little personal interest in public services in rural areas. They often ensure their own access to electricity or water through private generators or tubewells, and send their children abroad for education. Meanwhile, rural people in developing countries remain a deprived and marginalized majority.

• *The disabled*—make up at least 10% of the world's population. They include all those who have experienced injury, trauma or disease that results in long-term physical or mental changes.

Disability is common to both industrial and developing countries, but the sources tend to be different: in the industrial countries, the principal causes are degenerative diseases associated with ageing, while in the developing world the causes are more likely to be disease, malnutrition and war. Of Cambodia's 8.5 million people, 150,000 have been disabled by mines.

Disability, even in industrial countries, is closely linked with poverty. In the United States, blacks and native Americans are twice as likely to be disabled as whites. And children in poor families are 13% more likely to be mentally retarded than those in middle- and upper-income families.

In developing countries, disability is more common in rural than in urban areas, and among the poor. In Bangladesh, those most likely to be disabled are the landless labourers.

The disabled face many barriers to participation. They tend, for example, to have less access to education: in Hong Kong in 1981, more than a quarter of the disabled population between 15 and 24 had received no schooling. And they are also more likely to be unemployed: in Japan in 1980, when 62% of the total population was employed, only 32% of the disabled were employed.

Some countries have taken measures to give the disabled greater opportunities. Germany has a quota for employment of the disabled of 6% in both government and private business. And the United States has far-reaching legislation: the 1992 Americans with Disabilities Act sets a large number of standards to be achieved in working life.

The disabled in the developing world have much more basic problems. In Zimbabwe in 1982, when 10% of the population was estimated to be disabled, only 2% had access to any kind of rehabilitation services. For most of the world's disabled, full participation is still a long way off.

• *Poor nations*—cannot participate on an equal footing in international markets or extend market opportunities to their own people. Poverty is a formidable barrier to participation, whether within or between nations. The very poverty of poor nations denies them international credit, and barriers on the movement of both goods and people cut their potential earnings. The 1992 *Human Development Report* estimated that poor nations are being denied $500 billion of market opportunities annually—

TABLE 2.1
Share of poorest 20% of world population in global opportunities
(percentage of global economic activity)

	1960–70	1990
Global GNP	2.3	1.3
Global trade	1.3	0.9
Global domestic investment	3.5	1.1
Global domestic savings	3.5	0.9
Global commercial credit	0.3	0.2

BOX 2.6
Blacks in South Africa—still a people apart

South Africa has officially abolished apartheid. Yet the country's black people continue to live in a world apart.
• *Assets*—The richest 5% of the population, mostly white, owns 88% of all private property.
• *Poverty*—Half the population, mostly black, lives below the poverty line.
• *Children*—Many poor black children are being stunted by malnutrition: 40% of rural children and 15% of urban children.
• *Literacy*—One-third of the black population over 15 (some three million people) is illiterate.
• *Education*—Three-quarters of black teachers are either unqualified, or underqualified, for their job. The education system thus perpetuates a vicious circle of deprivation and discrimination.

For South African blacks, the achievement of full political rights would be a vital step towards greater participation. But unravelling apartheid completely will be a complex and difficult task in the years ahead.

about ten times the annual flow of foreign assistance they receive. The poorest 20% of the world's population now receives only 0.2% of global commercial credit, 0.9% of global trade and only 1.3% of global income (table 2.1).

It would be short-sighted to assume that the growing demands for increased participation will stop at national frontiers. Millions of workers from developing countries have already voted with their feet and migrated, legally and illegally, to industrial countries or to neighbouring developing countries. And the process has only just started. Unless more people can begin to participate in global economic opportunities, the 21st century may witness an unprecedented migration across national borders.

Increased participation at a global level will require a radical readjustment of the international order—in particular a dismantling of international trade restrictions and a much more democratic system of global governance.

Taking these and other excluded groups together, it seems likely that fewer than 10% of the world's people participate fully in political, economic, social and cultural life. For the vast majority, real participation will require a long and persistent struggle.

Obstacles

Participation is a plant that does not grow easily in the human environment. Powerful vested interests, driven by personal greed, erect numerous obstacles to block off the routes to people's political and economic power. These obstacles include:

- *Legal systems*—Laws are often arbitrary and capricious and favour those with political influence or economic clout. In too many countries, legislation fails to measure up to ideals of transparency, accountability, fairness—and equality before the law. Some countries' laws exclude the participation of women, for example, or of religious or ethnic minorities, or deny certain rights to workers.
- *Bureaucratic constraints*—Many developing countries have shackled their people

with innumerable regulations and controls, demanding all sorts of permits and permissions for even the most modest business initiative. Fortunately, many governments have started to dismantle the most stifling of these controls and are opening new avenues for entrepreneurial activity.

- *Social norms*—Even when laws change, many old values and prejudices persist, whether against women or different tribes, castes or religious groups—and are often deeply embedded in everyday language and behaviour. Laws may promote equality, but it is usually left to the discriminated group to struggle against prejudice. Thus, working women, for example, even when they prove themselves better, are not given equal treatment.
- *Maldistribution of assets*—In developing countries, one of the most significant assets is land. A high proportion of the people struggle to make a living in agriculture, but their efforts are often thwarted by the dominance of feudal elites who exert an overwhelming control over land. In most Latin American countries, the land tenure systems are notoriously skewed in favour of the rich (table 2.2). Inequality is conventionally expressed by the "Gini coefficient", which varies from zero (equal assets for everybody) to 1 (one person owns everything). In most Latin American countries, the Gini coefficient for land distribution is around 0.8—in Panama 0.84, in Brazil 0.86 and in Paraguay 0.94.

Maldistribution of land is by no means confined to Latin America. In Egypt, the richest 20% of landowners still control 70% of the agricultural land. And in Bangladesh, small farmers (with less than 2.5 acres) account for 70% of farms but have only 29% of the land area.

In these countries, there can never be true participation in the rural areas without far-reaching land reforms—as well as the extension services, training and credit for smaller farmers that can help them become productive and self-reliant.

Whether in urban or rural areas, vested interests that currently enjoy economic, financial, political or social power are usually determined to defend their position—

either individually or through close-knit associations, well-financed lobbies and even violence.

Changing the power equation requires the organization of a countervailing force, or even a revolution. People's organizations—be they farmers' cooperatives, residents' associations or consumer groups—offer some of the most important sources of countervailing power. And they often exercise it most effectively through the sharing of information and ideas—it is ideas, not vested interests, that rule the world for good or evil.

Structure of the Report

Participation is an important element in these and many other aspects of human life. This Report concentrates on participation in development—through markets, government and community organizations.

Chapter 3 focuses on free and open markets as a dynamic form of participation for both producers and consumers, assessing the extent to which markets are accessible to wide popular participation—that is, whether they are "people-friendly". It also analyses the participation of people through work, especially their participation in labour markets. It shows how current strategies result in output growth without employment and argues for a fundamental change in development thinking. This chapter also reviews the experiences to date in liberating private enterprise and explores how participatory human development requires a new balance between the private and the public sectors.

Chapter 4 is devoted to people's participation in governance. It looks at political participation and at how governments reach out to people, particularly through decentralization as a technique for opening governance up to greater popular participation—examining the conditions for successful participation as well as highlighting the potential pitfalls, including the risk of creating even firmer power bases for entrenched local elites.

Chapter 5 examines people's participation in civil society, particularly the role of non-governmental organizations. Considering them from both a national and an international perspective, it shows how these organizations can oppose existing power structures and engineer practical changes—and through their advocacy bring millions of the world's marginalized people into the mainstream of social and economic life.

Changing the power equation requires the organization of a countervailing force

TABLE 2.2
Inequality in the distribution of landholdings in selected countries

Country	Year	Gini coefficient
Very high inequality (Gini above 0.75)		
Paraguay	1981	0.94
Brazil	1980	0.86
Panama	1981	0.84
Uruguay	1980	0.84
Saudi Arabia	1983	0.83
Madagascar	1984	0.80
Kenya	1981	0.77
High inequality (0.51 to 0.75)		
Colombia	1984	0.70
Dominican Rep.	1981	0.70
Ecuador	1987	0.69
Grenada	1981	0.69
Chile	1987	0.64
Honduras	1981	0.64
Yemen	1982	0.64
Sri Lanka	1982	0.62
Peru	1984	0.61
Nepal	1982	0.60
Uganda	1984	0.59
Turkey	1980	0.58
Jordan	1983	0.57
Pakistan	1980	0.54
Philippines	1981	0.53
Medium inequality (0.40 to 0.50)		
Bahrain	1980	0.50
Bangladesh	1980	0.50
Morocco	1982	0.47
Togo	1983	0.45
Ghana	1984	0.44
Low inequality (below 0.40)		
Malawi	1981	0.36
Mauritania	1981	0.36
Egypt	1984	0.35
Niger	1981	0.32
Korea, Rep. of	1980	0.30

The Gini coefficient is a measure of inequality in distribution. It ranges from zero to 1: the closer the value to 1, the greater the inequality.

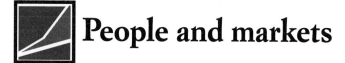

CHAPTER 3

People and markets

People-friendly markets allow people to participate fully in their operation and to share equitably in their benefits

Free markets provide the most efficient mechanism yet devised for the exchange of goods and services—impersonally matching supply and demand, bringing together buyers and sellers, employers and workers, and constantly setting and resetting prices so that the economy works at peak efficiency. Free enterprise provides a mechanism for unleashing human creativity and entrepreneurial ability.

Three critical questions: Are the markets really free? Are they accessible to all the people? And what is their impact on the distribution of income and other development opportunities and benefits?

Most markets are stifled by barriers—many raised by government regulations and some by powerful interest groups. And markets are not automatically or inevitably people-friendly. They make no value judgements. They reward those who have either substantial purchasing power or valuable commodities or services to sell. But people enter markets as unequal participants and often leave with unequal rewards, even when markets operate neutrally.

So, for all their efficiency at matching buyers and sellers, markets can also be associated with increasing inequality and poverty, as well as large-scale unemployment.

Markets may also place very little value on environmental concerns and the needs of future generations. Soil, water, fossil fuels and minerals are important inputs to the production process. But their market prices often fail to reflect their true scarcity value—leading to overexploitation and depletion. Company profit and loss accounts seldom register the true costs of pollution—which are passed on to the rest of society. Similarly, national income accounts fail to register the constant depletion of nat-

ural capital—and thus hide from policymakers the high cost of environmental neglect. Costa Rica during 1970–90 lost natural capital (such as soils and forests) amounting to more than 6% of its total GDP in that period. And in Indonesia during 1971–84, these losses were more than 9% of GDP. Yet their national income accounts were silent on this continuing haemorrhage.

Sustainable human development demands more of markets—that they continue to offer their advantages but that they do so in a more balanced way, combining efficiency, equity and sustainability. Markets are, after all, not an end in themselves. They are a means to human development. Markets should serve people—rather than people serving markets.

Making markets more people-friendly

People-friendly markets allow people to participate fully in their operation and to share equitably in their benefits. Making markets more people-friendly will require a strategy that maintains their dynamism but supplements them with other measures to allow many more people to capitalize on the advantages they offer.

Most markets suffer from three types of distortions. First, there are distortions in the workings of the markets themselves. Some may be due to monopoly power as well as to short-term business considerations that make the markets less competitive, less efficient or less respectful of environmental concerns. Others are due to controlled prices, fiscal disincentives and constant government intervention in the market.

Second, there are distortions in the form of disparities among people who enter the market. Many people lack the education, the assets, the credit or the skills to be competitive—or are excluded on the grounds of sex, race or ethnicity.

Third, markets often fail to reflect external costs and benefits—be it pollution (an external cost) or the prevention of communicable diseases (an external benefit). In addition, there are areas where markets are missing altogether. National income accounts do not, for example, include household work—nor do they measure the depreciation of natural capital assets over time. For both, a proper accounting should be made.

Traditional discussions of markets have focused more on their efficiency than on their equity aspects. But since markets are only a means towards human development, we must closely examine ways to build a bridge between markets and people—to make them more "people-friendly". The measures that would make such a radical transformation possible can be divided into four groups (box 3.1):
1. Preconditions
2. Accompanying conditions
3. Corrective actions
4. Social safety nets.

1. Preconditions

Certain conditions need to be met for markets to be kept free—and open to all those who seek to enter them.
• *Investment in people*—To compete effectively and to make a productive contribution, people need to have the health, the education and the skills to do so. The more dynamic developing countries have recognized the value of investing in their people. The newly industrializing countries of East Asia have sharpened their competitive edge, not just with lower-wage labour but with skill and entrepreneurship. Investments in human capital raise labour's productivity—and, if matched by the kind of technology best suited to the skills of the workforce, can have a multiplier effect throughout the economy. These investments can also help reduce social and economic disparities.

Consider this: labour productivity increased by 11% a year in the Republic of Korea between 1963 and 1979, and in Thailand by 63% between 1980 and 1985. Most of this increase came from a generous investment in the education and skills of people. And in Western Europe between 1970 and 1980, improvements in human capabilities accounted for 20–30% of the growth in income.
• *Access to assets*—If people are to participate freely in markets, they also need the physical and financial resources to do so. One of the greatest obstacles to a dynamic economy is an excessive concentration of land or business assets. But measures such as land reform may be only the start of the process. Many countries also have progressive fiscal regimes to ensure that income and wealth continue to be redistributed to the poorer members of society.

Steps towards people-friendly markets

People-friendly markets allow people to participate fully in their operations and to share equitably in their benefits. Having markets serve people, rather than people serve markets, requires concrete steps:

1. Preconditions
• Adequate investment in the education, health and skills of people to prepare them for the market
• An equitable distribution of assets, particularly land in poor agrarian societies
• Extension of credit to the poor
• Access to information, particularly about the range of market opportunities
• Adequate physical infrastructure, especially roads, electricity and telecommunications, and adequate support for R & D
• A legal framework to protect property rights
• No barriers to entry, irrespective of race, religion, sex or ethnic origin
• A liberal trade regime, supported by the dismantling of international trade barriers.

2. Accompanying conditions
• A stable macroeconomic environment, especially ensuring stability in domestic prices and external currency values

• A comprehensive incentive system, with correct price signals, a fair tax regime and adequate rewards for work and enterprise
• Freedom from arbitrary government controls and regulations.

3. Corrective actions
• Protection of competition, through antimonopoly laws and safeguards against financial malpractices
• Protection of consumers, especially through drug regulations, safety and hygiene standards and honest advertising
• Protection of workers, through regulated working conditions and minimum wage standards
• Protection of special groups, particularly women, children and ethnic minorities
• Protection of the environment, particularly through incentive systems and by banning pollution or making polluters pay.

4. Social safety nets
• Adequate arrangements to look after the temporary victims of market forces to bring them back into the markets, primarily through human investment, worker retraining and access to credit opportunities—as well as more permanent support for groups such as the disabled and the aged.

• *Extension of credit to the poor*—Much of the future growth in developing countries will have to come from small enterprises. But without adequate access to credit—and, where appropriate, to fiscal incentives and government contracts—small enterprises are unlikely to grow as rapidly as they might. So, the state should ensure, with private banks, that credit is available to smaller enterprises that can use it productively.

• *Access to information*—One of the essential characteristics of a people-friendly market is a good flow of information. The more widely information is available, the better the chances of fair competition and the equal sharing of benefits—information on global prices, efficient labour exchanges, transparent business contracts and honest advertising for consumers. Information is power: denying people information is a sure way of disempowering them and denying them equitable access to market opportunities.

• *Adequate infrastructure*—Private investment depends for its success on the existence of physical infrastructure such as roads and communications. Infrastructure is particularly important for rural areas, where roads, electricity and improved water supplies can enable people to participate in trade and industrialization and in increased employment opportunities. In many of the more successful developing economies, such as the Republic of Korea and Taiwan (province of China), the non-farm income of farm families now exceeds their income from agriculture.

There is also a need to ensure adequate funding for research and development (R & D) directed at human development. If R & D is left to the private sector alone, there may be little research directed at the needs of "excluded groups"—such as subsistence farmers and small-scale industries. There may also be too little funding for the development of more environment-friendly production technologies and alternative energy sources.

• *The rule of law*—Productive market participation demands clear and open transactions, primarily on the basis of mutual trust and respect but with the sanction of legal enforcement. At the same time, the legal system needs to protect property rights, both from illegal forced seizure in civil society and from capricious nationalization by the state.

In too many developing countries, however, business is conducted on the basis of contacts rather than contracts—and directed less by open competition than by bribes and corruption. This saps initiative, reduces output and distracts from the real challenge of productive investment. Closed markets permit exploitation by the few, rather than unleash the creativity of the many.

• *No barriers to entry*—Many people are also excluded from effective participation in markets by political or social discrimination. Women, ethnic minorities and the disabled are often excluded either by legal fiat or by social practice. Many "low-caste" people have paid a heavy price, sometimes with their lives, when they dared to challenge the market barriers that their societies erected against them. Governments can play a major role in ensuring that markets are open to all—irrespective of race, religion, sex or ethnic origin.

• *A liberal trade regime*—All countries need to exploit their comparative advantages, keeping their economies open to international trade. But liberal strategies in the South can succeed only if the North keeps dismantling its protectionist barriers and opening its restricted markets.

2. Accompanying conditions

Markets also need accompanying conditions to ensure that they are people-friendly and work as efficiently and equitably as possible.

• *A stable economic environment*—Markets function much better in a stable economic environment created by sound fiscal and monetary policies. High rates of inflation and violent fluctuations in exchange rates make it difficult for entrepreneurs to plan. Contracts entered into in good faith can become impossible to complete or enforce if conditions change drastically. Wild swings in exchange rates, although a delight to currency speculators, inhibit genuine entrepreneurs and restrict their decision-making to short-term visible horizons.

- *A comprehensive incentive system*—Correct price signals, a fair tax regime and adequate rewards for work and enterprise will ensure efficient resource allocation and utilization, including that of labour.
- *Freedom from arbitrary government actions*—Markets are greatly disturbed by sudden government intervention. Through changes in excise duties, tariffs or direct price controls, governments can distort markets such that prices reflect the interests of those in government, and their supporters, rather than the forces of the market. Government intervention is often essential to accelerate development. But it should follow three golden rules, as suggested by *World Development Report 1991*. First, intervene reluctantly: "let markets work unless it is demonstrably better to step in". Second, "put interventions continually to the discipline of the international and domestic markets": for instance, withdraw state subsidies when they are no longer needed. Third, intervene openly: "make interventions simple, transparent and subject to rules rather than official discretion"—preferring tariffs to quotas, for example.

3. Corrective actions

Where markets alone do not produce a desirable outcome, the state needs to regulate and correct. This should, of course, be done cautiously and only where necessary. But caution must not be confused with indecision. Corrective actions must be effective, though limited. This requires:

- *Protection of competition*—All governments need regulations to keep markets open and free. For instance, they need effective antimonopoly legislation—as well as regulations for banks and financial markets to ensure transparency and accountability in their operations. Such regulations are never villain-proof, as the savings and loan failures in the United States, the Recruit stock exchange scandal in Japan and the insider trading deals in the Bombay stock markets have shown. Regulations require energetic policing and swift reactions if the financially strong and powerful are not to reap unfair profits at the expense of the majority.

- *Protection of consumers*—The interests of responsible businesses, as well as those of consumers, are best served by clear sets of standards that the community expects producers to achieve. Regulations for the pharmaceutical industry, for example, require that drugs be tested over a certain period before they are released. Food manufacturers have to meet standards of health and hygiene. Car manufacturers must maintain standards of safety.
- *Protection of workers*—Less responsible employers are tempted to exploit their workers—among them, children (box 3.2). This requires action on two fronts. First, trade unions should be allowed to organize as a countervailing power to resist exploitation by employers. Second, governments need labour legislation to ensure good working conditions and minimum wages.
- *Protection of specific groups*—There are many cases where the natural workings of

---

BOX 3.2

Children without childhood

Child labourers are among the world's most exploited workers. Hundreds of millions of children work in fields and factories, on street corners and in garbage dumps all over the world. Most do some form of work from their earliest years, helping around the home or running errands. But the term "child labour" implies exploitation—that children are working long hours for low pay, sacrificing their health, their education and their childhood.

The largest numbers of child workers are in Asia, where in some countries they make up more than 10% of the labour force. But there are also large numbers in Africa, where several countries are reported to have up to 20% of their children working. And in Latin America, more than a quarter of children in some countries are thought to be working.

Industrial countries also have a substantial child workforce. In Europe, some of the largest numbers are in Italy and Spain. And there are believed to be large numbers in the United States, where between 1983 and 1990 there was a 250% increase in violations of child labour laws.

Poverty is the chief cause of child labour. When a family is poor, everyone has to work, every extra contribution helps. But many children work because of lack of other opportunities: schools might be unavailable, inadequate or just too expensive.

Others are forced to work. Pakistan, according to some reports, has millions of bonded child labourers, working long hours each day in all sorts of activities, from agriculture to carpet factories to brick kilns. And in Thailand, children are bought and sold to work in private houses, restaurants, factories and brothels.

While the long-term objective must be to eliminate child labour, much needs to be done for children who currently have to work—providing them with support through health services, feeding programmes or informal education schemes that they can fit in around their work. And children should be removed immediately from the most hazardous environments.

Improving educational opportunities is one of the most important steps—to make schooling a real and practical alternative for today's working children. But in the ultimate analysis, child labour will be eliminated only through alleviation of poverty—the real cause of child labour.

Stakeholders—consumers, workers, nature—should be given at least as much consideration as shareholders

an impersonal market would still ignore the potential participation of particular groups—women and ethnic minorities. They may require strong affirmative action (see box 3.5 on page 45).

• *Protection of the environment*—Many companies find that they can maximize short-term profits at the expense of the environment, through pollution and other forms of environmental degradation. The pricing of environmental resources—or more effective regulation—can ensure that everyone works under the same rules, and that today's production does not pass on some of its costs to society in general or deplete resources that need to be conserved for future generations. Making the polluter pay—or banning certain types of pollution—are among the most effective ways of ensuring sustainable development. Domestically, this requires antipollution legislation, as well as taxes on the consumption of non-renewable energy. Internationally, this would require tradable permits for carbon emissions and other forms of international taxation on polluting nations. If resources were properly priced and polluters were paying for environmental costs, the incentive structure would tend to stimulate development of technologies required to ensure more sustainable development. In short: stakeholders—consumers, workers, nature—should be given at least as much consideration as shareholders.

4. Social safety nets

Every country needs to establish effective social safety nets to catch the victims of the competitive struggle—such as the temporarily unemployed—and to protect the lowest income groups, the young, the old and the disabled. In the United States and the United Kingdom, around 25% of GNP is committed to social safety nets in the forms of health care, unemployment and social security benefits. In the Scandinavian countries, the figure is roughly 40%.

But there is always a debate over just how substantial these safety nets should be. If they are too firm and reassuring, they may discourage people from working. If they are too open or flimsy, they may let the gen-

uinely deprived fall through. The latter has more often been the problem than the former in developing countries. Where the need is greatest, the safety nets are often weakest—amounting generally to no more than 5% of GNP. Millions of people live in absolute poverty and lack the most basic social services. Most countries have some form of health care, though the delivery is very uneven—and often inadequate in rural areas. But few developing countries offer widespread social security in the form of pensions, and almost none pay unemployment benefits.

Governments in developing countries do offer some relief to the poor, for example, through the distribution of food supplements for children, and they may organize labour-intensive public works programmes to provide income—especially in times of disaster. But in practice, most people in developing countries have to rely on support from their families or communities in times of difficulty.

It should be clearly understood that the purpose of people-friendly markets is not to invite governments to introduce more discretionary controls, which rarely work. The basic idea is to protect the interests of everyone who seeks to enter the market. Correct price signals and an efficient incentive system are usually much more effective than direct controls in achieving this.

Encouraging participation through employment

For most people, the best form of market participation is through productive and remunerative work and through self-employment and wage employment. This empowers them not just economically but also socially and politically.

Employment empowers people economically by giving them purchasing power for goods and services. It empowers them socially by offering a productive role that enhances their dignity and self-esteem. And it can empower them politically if they begin to influence decision-making in the workplace and beyond.

The measures that lead to people-friendly markets can make a major contribution to employment creation. Land reform, for example, allows larger numbers of farmers to develop the land and results in more labour-intensive cultivation. And opening markets and credit to women and other so far excluded groups can help create many more small enterprises—and many more jobs, since smaller companies tend to be more labour-intensive. In Japan, small and medium-size businesses create 57% of value added to products but employ about 74% of the total industrial workforce.

Growth without employment

The need for a fresh approach is evident from the high unemployment throughout the world. In OECD countries, unemployment stayed above 6% throughout the 1980s, reaching a peak of 6.9% in 1991, which means more than 30 million jobless. Unemployment in the European members of OECD increased threefold from 3% in the mid-1970s to about 10% in 1992.

The situation in the developing countries is much worse. In Sub-Saharan Africa, not a single country had single-digit unemployment figures throughout this period. In Latin America, urban unemployment has been above 8%. And in Asia, countries like India and Pakistan, despite respectable GDP growth rates (more than 6% a year), had unemployment rates above 15%. Only the East Asian countries had low unemployment rates—below 3%.

A comparison of the growth in GDP and employment in various regions of the world during 1960–73 and 1973–87 shows that employment has consistently lagged behind economic growth (table 3.1). This is true in both industrial and developing countries. The industrial countries had fairly respectable GDP growth rates, but between 1973 and 1987, employment in countries like France, Germany and the United Kingdom actually fell (figure 3.1). The reason: three-quarters of the rise in output in these countries came from increases in total productivity, with the rest from increased capital investment—without creating new jobs.

The developing countries have had a similar problem, though they have experienced at least some employment growth. In 1960–73, GDP growth rates were fairly high (4–5% a year) but employment growth rates were less than half this. Less than a third of the increase in output in developing countries between 1960 and 1987 came from increased labour, more than two-thirds from increases in capital investment.

The pattern is similar for transnational corporations with subsidiaries in developing countries: they have made substantial investments without creating large numbers of jobs. In 1990, there were at least 35,000 transnational corporations with more than 150,000 foreign affiliates. Of the 22 million people they employ outside their home country, around seven million are directly employed in developing countries—less than 1% of their economically active population. In addition, probably an equal number are employed indirectly as

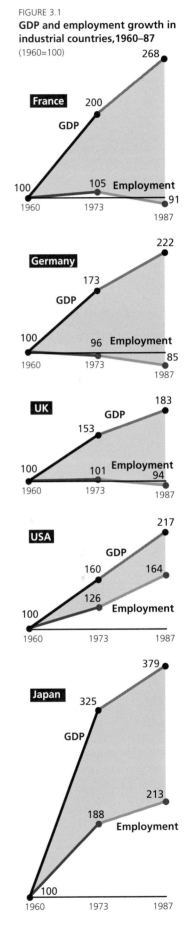

FIGURE 3.1

GDP and employment growth in industrial countries, 1960–87
(1960=100)

TABLE 3.1
Growth in GDP and employment, 1960–87
(percent)

Region or country	Average annual growth rate of GDP		Average annual growth rate of employment	
	1960–73	1973–87	1960–73	1973–87
Selected developing regions				
Africa	4.0	2.6	2.1	2.3
South Asia	3.8	5.0	1.8	2.3
Latin America	5.1	2.3	2.5	2.8
Selected industrial countries				
France	5.5	2.1	0.4	–1.0
Germany	4.3	1.8	–0.3	–0.9
Japan	9.5	4.6	1.2	0.9
United Kingdom	3.3	1.3	0.1	–0.5
USA	3.7	2.2	1.8	1.9

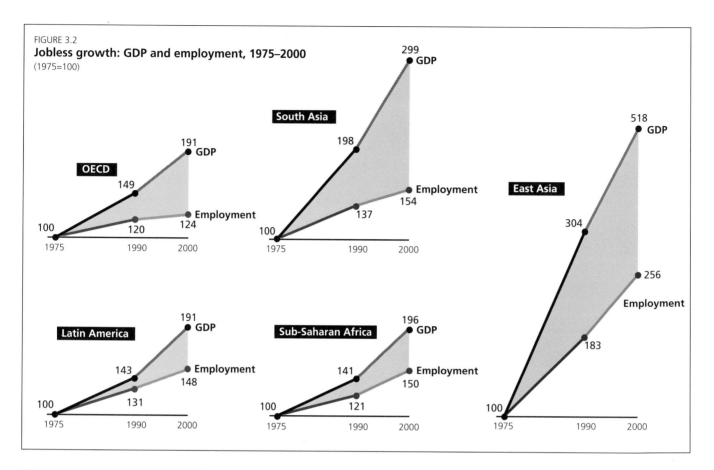

FIGURE 3.2
Jobless growth: GDP and employment, 1975–2000
(1975=100)

Box 3.3

Jobless growth

Many parts of the world are witnessing a new phenomenon—*jobless growth*. Even when output increases, increase in employment lags way behind.
• Developing countries experienced 4–5% growth in GDP during 1960–73, but employment grew only half as much.
• Industrial countries managed fairly respectable output growth during 1973–87, but in France, Germany and the United Kingdom, employment levels actually fell.
• Informal employment has increased sharply in developing countries, offering low-wage, non-permanent jobs, instead of remunerative employment.
• In the United States, the recent economic recovery has been a "jobless recovery".

Policy-makers all over the world are searching for strategies that combine a high GDP growth rate with more job opportunities. No comprehensive programme has emerged, but there are several measures that can contribute to an increase in employment:
• Invest generously in basic education, relevant skills and worker retraining.

• Liberate private enterprise and make markets more accessible to everyone.
• Support small-scale enterprises and informal sector employment, principally through reform of the credit system, fiscal incentives and proper legal framework.
• Create an efficient service economy for the future by investing in the new skills required and removing international barriers.
• Encourage labour-intensive technologies, especially through tax breaks.
• Extend employment safety nets through labour-intensive public works programmes in periods of major economic distress.

These measures could greatly help in both developing and industrial countries, but nagging questions remain: if new technologies continue to increase human productivity at a sharply accelerating rate, do people need to work such long hours? Is it not time to redefine the concept of employment? Can there be work sharing? Should we not redefine work to include what are unpaid tasks today, such as housework, community work or even political work?

suppliers, for example, or through service companies. This total number is still relatively small, however, and the proportion of the world's economically active population employed by transnationals appears to be falling.

Thus, in many parts of the world, we are beginning to witness a new phenomenon—*jobless growth* (figure 3.2 and box 3.3). In the United States, if job growth during the current recovery of the business cycle had matched the rate of eight previous recoveries, an additional 3.9 million jobs would have been created. In industrial countries, a major part of the output growth came from total productivity increases—primarily an outcome of labour-saving technological advancement.

There are four major causes of this phenomenon. First, the search for labour-saving technology was encouraged by the demographic situation of industrial countries, where stagnating population growth often led to growing labour shortages in the 1960s. Second, it was also enhanced by rising labour costs as well as an active trade union movement. Third, technological innovation in the civilian sphere often resulted as a by-product of military research and development, which usually has a preference for capital intensity. Finally, the prevalent technology reflects the existing pattern of income distribution—20% of the world's population has 83% of the world's income and, hence, five times the purchasing power of the poorer 80% of humankind. Clearly, technology will cater to the preferences of the richer members of the international society.

In developing countries, the total labour force increased by more than 400 million during 1960–90. This was due to rapid population growth (2.3% a year), an increase in the proportion of people of working age, and greater numbers of women joining the ranks of job-seekers.

Without substantial policy changes, the employment outlook for these people is bleak. The labour force in developing countries will continue to increase by 2.3% a year in the 1990s, requiring an additional 260 million jobs. Women's participation in the labour force is likely to increase. And there will be a steady migration of people to urban areas in search of work: the annual rate of net migration is likely to be about 4.6% by the year 2000.

Taking into account the number of people unemployed or underemployed, the total requirement for the next decade is around one billion new jobs. This would imply increasing total employment in developing countries by more than 4% a year in the 1990s, compared with less than 3% in the 1980s.

If present trends continue, it is extremely doubtful that countries will achieve such an increase in employment. The ILO estimates that the labour force for Sub-Saharan Africa will grow 3.3% a year in the 1990s, while productive employment will increase by only 2.4% a year. Even this employment growth assumes an acceleration of GDP growth from 3.7% to around 5%. The situation is unlikely to be any better in Latin America or South Asia (figure 3.3). And the capacity in industrial countries to absorb more economic migrants from developing countries may also be limited, given their own high unemployment.

Deteriorating job security

The problem of labour today is not only the discrepancy between demand and supply in quantitative terms. The problem is that there is also a change in the quality of the work available: job security is deteriorating.

In both industrial and developing countries, the composition of the labour force has been changing significantly. Enterprises have been reducing their reliance on a permanent labour force, engaging instead a highly skilled core group of workers surrounded by a periphery of temporary workers.

Some of these peripheral workers will be engaged under short-term contracts or as part-time, temporary or casual workers. In the United Kingdom by the early 1990s, almost 40% of jobs did not involve regular full-time wages or employment. Others among these workers may be self-employed individuals working from home. But a large number will be engaged through subcontractors. Medium-size and large firms in South and South-East Asia—particularly in garments, footwear and woodworking—are subcontracting a growing proportion of their production to smaller firms.

This problem exists in industrial countries but it is even more pronounced in the developing countries. Here, many subcontractors are small entrepreneurs—either microenterprises or enterprises in the informal sector.

The East Asian path

Maintaining competitive production and ensuring substantial increases in employment will be no easy task. But the experience of Japan and the East Asian industrializing countries indicates one potentially successful path.

One of the essential starting points was land reform. In the Republic of Korea between 1952 and 1954, the proportion of cultivators who were owners rather than tenants increased from about 50% to 94%. As a result, between 1954 and 1968, the labour used per hectare increased by 4.7% a year.

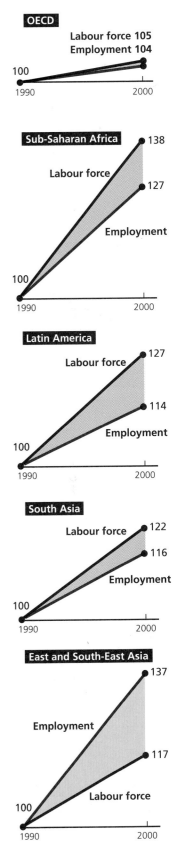

FIGURE 3.3
Labour force and employment projection, 1990–2000
(1990=100)

OECD
Labour force 105
Employment 104

Sub-Saharan Africa — Labour force 138; Employment 127

Latin America — Labour force 127; Employment 114

South Asia — Labour force 122; Employment 116

East and South-East Asia — Employment 137; Labour force 117

Land reform also had a very positive impact on employment in Taiwan (province of China). After the reform, the number of people involved in agriculture increased rapidly—from 400,000 to about two million between 1952 and 1968. There was a substantial increase in output, too, particularly from adding new crops. Using multiple-cropping techniques, accompanied by irrigation facilities and improved water management, the farmers were also able to grow fruits, pulses and vegetables. These opened up more job opportunities after harvesting since they required more processing—whether drying, pickling, canning, freezing or dehydrating. In Taiwan (province of China) in the 1960s, the number of workers in food processing rose

from 11,000 to 144,000. Such increases in employment led to enhanced income and purchasing power for the people. As a result, the domestic markets for goods and services also expanded, which in turn had positive effects on technology choices and on further increases in employment.

In addition to redistributing assets, these countries simultaneously invested in the health, education and skills of their people—so the workforce was ready and able to take advantage of the latest technologies and methods of production as they were introduced. These societies also established a comprehensive framework for the rapid growth of private enterprise and combined outward orientation of their economies and exposure to foreign competition with support for national economic capacity building.

Labour productivity in these countries has been increasing at an annual rate of 10% or more—half of which has been attributed to investment in education and technical skills. And during the 1980s, while unemployment was in double figures for most developing countries, and more than 6% in the OECD nations, it consistently stayed below 3% in Japan and East Asia.

In this connection, it may also be useful to look specifically at the Japanese experience. The Japanese entrepreneurial system has been based on three pillars, often referred to as the three sacred treasures—lifetime employment, seniority wage system and enterprise unions. It is primarily a community of people, rather than a piece of property belonging to the shareholders. It is made up of the people who work in it, not only for it. But according to recent reports, the system of lifetime employment is now coming under pressure and being abandoned, even for white-collar workers.

A participatory process in the workplace can also lead to significant productivity benefits. One investigation of a problem plant of the ASEA Brown Bovery Group in Sweden, for example, found women workers doing monotonous production-line work. Personnel turnover was about 40% annually, and productivity was low. The company decided to make a complete change in the production system—allowing

---

BOX 3.4

Education for life—addressing educated unemployment

Education and training are often put forward as the keys to employment, but in developing countries many remain unemployed despite, or because of, their high level of education. In Asian countries, the least educated often have the lowest recorded unemployment rates, because they are usually involved in informal subsistence activities. In India, while the unemployment rate in 1989 for people with no education was 2%, that for those with secondary education was 9% and for university graduates 12% (box table). In Bangladesh, about 40% of people with a master's degree are either unemployed or underemployed. In Thailand during 1973–83, unemployment rates among university graduates ranged from 20% to 35%.

In Africa, too, secondary school graduates are more likely to be unemployed than those with less education. Graduate unemployment, not yet as high as in some Asian countries, is expected to rise in the years ahead with cuts in recruitment to government service, where many graduates would previously have expected automatic employment.

The fundamental problem is the mismatch between supply and demand. This can be tackled in the short term by offering the unemployed more vocationally oriented training—and perhaps by offering the private sector greater incentives to employ them. But in the longer term, the educational and training systems of societies must be such that people can acquire relevant skills—skills that help them master their lives. This change has to come at all levels of learning—from literacy courses to university training.

BOX TABLE
Unemployment in selected countries by educational level
(percent)

Country	Year	No education	Primary	Secondary	Tertiary
Algeria	1989	9.2	24.2	28.9	5.8
Tunisia	1989	11.2	20.4	17.4	5.2
Ghana	1988	3.4	7.6	13.5	14.7
Kenya	1986	13.5	15.6	22.2	5.4
Zimbabwe	1987	1.6	6.8	11.6	..
Malaysia	1985	4.7	22.9	30.6	3.9
India	1989	2.0	3.0	9.0	12.0
Indonesia	1985	0.6	1.5	7.5	5.3
Sri Lanka	1981	4.5	14.5	15.1	4.2
Côte d'Ivoire	1985	1.0	5.2	21.7	13.7

workers to move among different tasks and take charge of many aspects of production, including material planning and quality control. This made a dramatic difference. Labour turnover was reduced virtually to zero, and while previously only about 10% of production was being delivered on time, afterwards the level rose to 98%.

Most developing countries, and many industrial countries, have been slow to pick up on this lesson. Many of their workers have skills that are out of date or inappropriate for the fast-changing environment of the 1990s. And in some cases, a striking mismatch between supply and demand leads to high unemployment even among the more educated (box 3.4).

It would be naive to assume that the experience of one group of countries can be easily replicated elsewhere. But if one message does emerge, it is that the solution is to focus not merely on capital or on production processes—but on people. Too often, human beings have had to fit into roles preordained by economic theorists, state planners and the developers of technology. A much more refreshing approach is to start with human beings, invest liberally in their education and technical skills, and see how their energy and creativity can best be released.

Working people need to be seen as creators of development rather than as one of its residuals. Employment should be seen as a deliberate process of empowerment, rather than as a mere by-product of production.

Promoting entrepreneurship and small enterprises

One of the surest ways of encouraging employment is to promote small businesses. The increasingly important role of small enterprises is evident from the extent of self-employment in industrial and developing countries (table 3.2). In the United States, for example, half of all private sector employees work for companies with fewer than 100 employees.

Developing countries also have increasing numbers of small enterprises. In Singapore in 1983, small and medium-size enterprises made up over 90% of all enterprises. In Kenya during the 1980s, more than 1,500 new private limited liability companies were registered each year.

Many productive enterprises are started on the initiative of one individual. A study in Malaysia found that 86% of a sample of firms were started by their owners, who were relatively young and well-educated—and often had experience in working in the same field with another company.

And an increasing proportion of new enterprises today are being started by women. In the United States, 22% of small businesses in 1982 were owned by women, while by 1987 the figure had risen to 30%. There seems to be a similar trend in developing countries. In Latin America as a whole, one-third of microentrepreneurs and their workers are women, and in some cases, as in rural Honduras, women entrepreneurs are now in the majority.

Of all the steps that governments can take to encourage entrepreneurs, probably

It would be naive to assume that the East Asian development experience can be easily replicated elsewhere

TABLE 3.2
Share of self-employment in selected countries

Developing countries	Year	Self-employment in total labour force (%)
Ghana	1984	68
Pakistan	1984	56
Ecuador	1981	56
Nigeria	1983	56
Mexico	1981	48
Indonesia	1986	44
Bangladesh	1987	41
Philippines	1987	36
India	1981	31
Korea, Rep. of	1987	30
Thailand	1982	29
Colombia	1987	28
Malaysia	1981	28
Brazil	1981	27

Industrial countries	Year	Self-employment in non-agricultural sector (%)
Italy	1987	22
Spain	1987	20
United Kingdom	1987	14
Australia	1987	13
Ireland	1987	12
France	1987	11
Netherlands	1987	8
Germany	1987	8
USA	1987	8
Canada	1987	7

Three groups find it difficult to get credit: small farmers, entrepreneurs in the informal sector in general and women in particular

none is more important than ensuring ready access to capital. The capital market is generally very unfriendly to the small entrepreneur—particularly the poorest ones. Banks are generally unwilling to lend to poorer people, partly because they cannot offer acceptable collateral and partly because the sums they require are often too small to be profitable. So, banks often ignore the needs of small-scale operators in agriculture, industry and services—or between 30% and 70% of the labour force in developing countries. In the Philippines in 1991, small enterprises received only 8% of institutional credit.

Lack of credit can be a significant brake on progress. In Ghana, small enterprises report that up to 50% of their capacity is idle because of a shortage of working capital. A 1989 survey found that almost 90% of the enterprises perceived the lack of credit as a serious constraint to new investments. And if they get credit, smaller firms tend to pay interest rates around one-third higher than larger firms. A similar situation was found in Tunisia.

Three important groups find it difficult to get access to credit: small farmers, entrepreneurs in the informal sector in general and women in particular. In Bangladesh, large owners of land, who constitute 7% of rural households, received 37% of institutional credit in 1989. In Kenya, less than 5% of the institutional credit goes to informal activities.

Women, in both the formal and the informal sectors, also have great trouble getting bank loans. Women account for about 18% of the self-employed in developing countries. But in the Philippines, only 10% of formal credit goes to women, and in Pakistan, the Agricultural Development Bank makes less than 0.1% of its loans to women.

Without access to formal credit, many poor people are forced to turn to moneylenders who charge usurious rates (in Bangladesh, 70% of total rural credit comes from moneylenders). One common mechanism in many countries is a "five-six" arrangement, in which a borrower receives five pesos in the morning and repays six pesos in the evening—20% interest a day.

In Sierra Leone, the trade and tariff regime is such that smaller firms pay 25% more than larger firms for capital goods. In Pakistan, they pay 38% more. And in the Philippines, sectors dominated by large-scale enterprise enjoy effective rates of tariff protection of 25–500%, while sectors providing two-thirds of small-scale employment have negative rates of effective protection. Similarly, the protective tariffs in Malaysia tend to be higher the larger the plant size.

Clearly, smaller enterprises should not face this discrimination. Indeed, it can be argued that governments should give preference to smaller enterprises.

In addition to giving greater assistance to smaller enterprises through fairer macroeconomic policies, such as protective tariffs and interest rates, governments can take specific measures to promote the development of small enterprises.

Experience shows that the best way to support small-scale enterprise is to combine improved availability of credit with measures aimed at enhancing competitiveness.

In western Guatemala, the weavers of Momostenango use almost 40% of the country's wool to weave ponchos, blankets and other products. But the quality of the wool had been low, and the weavers lacked credit to expand production. In 1986, a foundation with technical and financial support from the government and international donors was set up to help the farmers, the weavers and those marketing the finished products. A year later, 14 technical assistance centres were organized to help increase wool quantity and quality. Funds of up to $20,000 were available to offer credit to weavers to increase production. As a result of these and other measures, export volumes have increased substantially—11 weaver groups with 160 members have been formed to fill export orders.

In rural Cameroon, the extension of credit has been used with new basic technologies to offer new opportunities for women. The staple crop there is maize, chiefly grown by women but mostly ground by mechanical plate mills in towns and cities. The farmers could not afford either to buy the imported mills or to maintain them subsequently. But in the mid-1980s, some organizations came together to develop a cheaper locally made plate mill, and to help form rural groups that could buy and run them. By mid-1989, 28 such groups had received credit and gone into production. Each mill is owned on average by 50 women, serving 250 families and earning for the group the equivalent of $70 a month.

People-friendly capital markets would address the needs of those groups, who find it difficult to get credit. First, on preconditions, a better distribution of assets (such as land) would increase their chances of offering collateral. Second, the corrective actions would give special access to weaker groups—either through government action or through informal credit schemes, such as cooperatives, savings groups and credit unions. These have played an important role in many industrial countries, and in the developing world as well: in Togo, loans from credit unions grew by 33% in the past decade.

One of the most important forms of assistance to small enterprises is training—not just vocational training but an introduction to management skills. One interesting example of a more comprehensive approach is the Malawian Enterprise Development Institute, targeted mainly at educated unemployed youths. In addition to vocational training, the programme offers training in business management and entrepreneurship. At the end of the course, the graduates are rewarded with a tool set and loans, but they are not given a trade certificate, which might encourage them to go simply into wage employment.

There is also a need for a working system of enterprises with medium-size and large firms feeding off the smaller ones. In Europe, large enterprises such as General Electric, Olivetti and Philips have all developed broad-based technological cooperation networks for manufacturing new technologies available to smaller companies.

People-friendly markets should encourage and nurture small enterprises, for the profit not only of the individual entrepreneurs, but for society as a whole, through steady increases in output and employment.

Informal sector support

In the developing countries, the informal sector is growing almost everywhere. And small-scale enterprises are often part of this sector. In Latin America, 25% of all non-agricultural employment was in the informal sector at the beginning of the 1980s, 31% at the end.

In Sub-Saharan Africa, the informal sector increased by 6.7% a year between 1980 and 1989, substantially faster than the modern sector. Between 1980 and 1985, while the modern sector added only 500,000 jobs to the urban labour market, the informal sector created some six million new jobs. By 1990, the informal sector employed more than 60% of the urban workforce—more than twice the share employed by the modern sector.

In some Asian countries, including India, the Philippines and Sri Lanka, wage employment in the urban informal sector has been growing faster than in the formal sector. In India, twice as many jobs have been created in the unorganized manufacturing sector as in the organized.

Swollen by young people leaving school with nowhere else to go, the informal sector is also absorbing large numbers of workers who have lost their jobs in government or in the formal private sector. Some of those made redundant may have small sums they can invest in a new business, but most seek work from other people (the majority of people in the informal sector are wage-earners). Their reduced family income may mean that other members of the family have to work: when males lose jobs in the formal sector, it is often easier for women to replace some of the income with informal work. In Kenya, women's participation in the urban labour force rose from 39% in 1978 to 56% in 1986.

Support for small-scale enterprises should, therefore, not only focus on the formal sector. It must also extend to the informal sector without discouraging the courage and vibrancy of its enterprises. The objective must be to promote the transition from informal to formal.

In Sub-Saharan Africa, the informal sector employs 60% of the urban workforce

Developing a new industrial and service economy

The technological breakthroughs of the past two decades—particularly in informatics—have transformed traditional services. Human skills are now the most important input in modern banking, finance, advertising and communications, as well as business management and public administration.

The notion that manufacturing is the foundation for all other economic activity is an old illusion. The distinction between industry and services is now largely meaningless. In industrial countries today, over half the workers in a typical manufacturing firm do service jobs—design, distribution, financial planning; only a minority make things on the factory floor. Second, the productivity in services, which is difficult to measure, does not lag behind that in manufacturing. There are many signs that a productivity revolution is sweeping services. Third, services are also the fastest-growing part of international trade, accounting for 20% of total world trade. Services account for 40% of the stock of foreign direct investment by the five big industrial economies.

Generating about 60% of the GDP and two-thirds of the employment opportunities in the industrial countries, services dominate the world economy (figure 3.4). Manufacturing's share will continue to dwindle as more low-technology factories move to countries where labour-intensive assembly or other operations can be performed more cheaply. The United States has by far the biggest service sector, accounting for about 70% of its GDP and nearly 80% of its labour force. But the developing countries still lag behind with only 47% of their GDP and 25% of their labour force coming from services. So, there is increasing scope for these countries to generate employment in their service sectors.

Between 1980 and 1990, the trade in services increased by an average of 7.7% annually, reaching some $990 billion in 1990. By 2000, the trade in services could approach $2 trillion.

Most developing countries are still net importers of services. Their net deficit in services increased from $4 billion in 1970 to more than $17 billion in 1990.

This new global services economy shifts comparative advantage more in favour of people than natural resources. Developing countries have a majority of the world's people, but still only a small share of the global trade in services. The rapid expansion of trade in skill-intensive services thus offers a tremendous opportunity to developing countries—if they can impart new knowledge and skills to their people.

Employment safety nets

Even with all the positive measures just proposed, the employment situation might be so serious, and the role of employment in a human development strategy so important, that a structural reform in the form of a guaranteed employment scheme should be considered. The point of departure of such a scheme is the recognition of the right of everyone to work.

Thus, for those who cannot find work, some developing countries have designed employment guarantee schemes, generally offering work, however poorly paid, through public works programmes. These schemes serve a function similar to unemployment benefits in industrial countries but are much less expensive, since they are narrowly focused on those prepared to do hard manual work for very low pay or for small amounts of food. In Bangladesh during the 1980s, 90% of the participants in the Food for Work programme were below the poverty line. In Botswana and Cape Verde, public works programmes in the 1980s are estimated to have saved the lives of 60,000 to 90,000 people in each country. In Chile and Peru, such programmes helped soften the impact of recession during the 1980s, and in Egypt, the Productive Families Programme is benefiting one million people.

Public works programmes also have the advantage that they build assets, such as roads or irrigation schemes.

One of the largest public works programmes in the developing world is the Employment Guarantee Scheme of Maha-

FIGURE 3.4
Services' growing share in GDP, 1970–90
Percentage of GDP

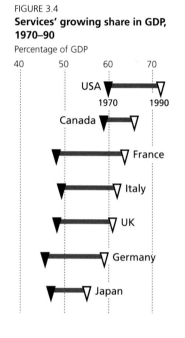

rashtra, in India. This was started in 1972 to provide employment on request at a stipulated wage, within 15 days, no more than five kilometres away from the participant's village home. During 1990–91, the scheme provided more than 90 million person-days of work, with nearly two-thirds of the workers from households below the poverty line. As well as providing work, the scheme has helped mobilize the rural poor as a political force and acted as a check on the power of local officials. The programme pays the official minimum wage, which is somewhat higher than the market wage (around $1 a day), and in 1991 cost Rs 2.4 billion ($103 million). It is one of the most cost-effective schemes anywhere for helping the poor.

The Maharashtra programme and other such schemes show that programmes need to be very carefully designed to ensure that they contribute useful assets and that they do not distort the local labour market. Above all, such schemes should enhance production, not just welfare.

In the future, it would also be desirable to consider whether employment guarantee schemes could not be expanded beyond their traditional, primarily public-works-oriented fields. Certainly, they could cover many environmental tasks that need to be done. They could also focus more on provision of social services, which would be critical to improved human development. They could include proposals for national service in exchange for a guaranteed education, as currently proposed by the new US administration. Too many societal activities remain undone while too many people remain unemployed. It does not take real genius to match unmet human needs with unemployed human resources.

Trade unions

When trade unions are closely in tune with their members and also with national needs, they can make the whole industrial process work more smoothly. Like many other institutions of a democratic society, trade unions help fuse the interests of different people so they form a coherent group. This can avoid disruptions and help increase productivity.

Germany has had powerful labour unions and its tripartite system of consultation and decision-making—involving employers, workers' representatives and government—has given the country almost the highest wages and the shortest working time of the OECD countries. Similarly, the Scandinavian countries have combined high standards of living with the highest "density levels" in the OECD (the density level is trade union members as a proportion of the total workforce). The five countries with the highest density levels are Sweden (85%), Iceland (78%), Denmark (73%), Finland (71%) and Norway (55%).

Trade union membership has been falling in most industrial countries in recent years. In the Netherlands, membership in unions fell from 39% in 1978 to 24% in 1991. And the United States has seen a three-decade slide in union membership from 30% to about 15%.

Trade unions in industrial countries have been undermined from different directions. Unemployment has reduced the number of workers and strengthened the hand of employers. And unions have also faced much tougher legislation from governments. Furthermore, enterprises and capital have moved from countries with powerful trade unions to low-wage, non-unionized countries. But a more fundamental problem is the fragmenting of the labour force, which is now much more resistant to mass organization. The shift to services and the growing numbers of part-time workers, or those adopting flexible working patterns, puts them beyond the reach of traditional methods of organization.

In the developing countries, a smaller proportion of the workforce tends to be unionized because there are fewer workers in the formal sector. In Latin America, around 20% of the workforce is unionized (rates are higher for Argentina, Brazil, Mexico and Venezuela). Singapore and Sri Lanka have some of the highest rates in Asia—up to 40%—while Malaysia and the Philippines have membership levels between 20% and 40%. In Africa, where only around 10% of the workforce is in the formal sector, union members are probably

Too many societal activities remain undone while too many people remain unemployed

only 1% or 2% of the total workforce. But unions are weakest of all in many Arab states. In most of these countries, governments restrict their activities—and in Bahrain, Oman, Qatar, Saudi Arabia and the United Arab Emirates, trade unions are banned.

Democratization may now offer the trade unions more freedom, but the accompanying process of economic liberalization is much more problematic. Trade unions often oppose privatizations since they frequently lead to job losses. Colombia, for example, was paralysed for a week in 1992 by a strike of telecommunications workers protesting privatization. Elsewhere, the process has been smoother: in Mexico, telecommunications workers were given credits of $325 million to help them purchase shares in the privatized company.

But a more basic problem for unions all over the world is a shift in the nature of the workforce, away from ranks of production-line workers towards the more fragmented workers in the service industries—as well as those on the precarious periphery, as discussed earlier in this chapter. As the ILO's *World Labour Report* points out in its 1993 survey of trade unions: "Working life today is very different from that in the old smoke-stack industries where trade union solidarity was originally forged. Today's workers in manufacturing are more likely to be operating complex equipment, often using computers and robots and developing skills which blur the traditional dividing lines between blue-collar and white."

Workers doing different jobs feel much less solidarity. And as they move out of manufacturing, their aspirations change and they tend to be even more individually oriented. Employers are capitalizing on this by adopting strategies of "human resource management" that deal with workers as individuals or small groups. This may or may not allow for greater participation by individual workers, but it certainly weakens the unions.

Unions also suffer from their relative neglect of women workers. Trade unions in many countries are very much a male preserve. In many sectors, women are now

more than half the workforce, yet in the largest international trade union organization, the International Confederation of Free Trade Unions, only 34% of members are women. In Latin America, only 3% of trade union officials are women. Many of the newer women entrants to the workforce are working part-time or in complex shift patterns, which makes them especially difficult to organize (box 3.5).

If trade unions are to be in the forefront of participation in the workplace in the years ahead, they clearly have to reinvent themselves to represent a new generation of workers.

Liberating private enterprise

About 80 countries are in the process of economic liberalization and privatization. Many industrial market economies have also made some movement in this direction, involving privatization not just of industrial production but also of some public services. There have been similar changes in developing countries, where programmes of economic adjustment have involved the state's withdrawing from some productive activities, as well as liberalizing the economy and opening to international trade.

Facing the most radical shifts are the countries of Eastern and Central Europe and the former Soviet Union as they move from command economies to more open markets. The country studies at the end of this chapter illustrate the diversity in the nature and pace of reforms, with details of the recent experiences of Argentina, Brazil, China, Ghana, Egypt, India, Kenya, Malaysia, Poland, Russia and Viet Nam.

Developing countries

Most developing countries moved towards more market-oriented policies in the 1980s and early 1990s—bringing domestic prices more into line with international market prices and offering greater encouragement to the private sector. A study of 47 developing countries by the International Finance Corporation shows that since the mid-1980s, private investment has been playing an increasingly important role. It

Trade unions must reinvent themselves to represent a new generation of workers

compensated for the slight decrease in public investment, increasing as a proportion of GDP from about 12% in 1985 to 15% in 1990 and 16% in 1991.

The trend is not universal, however. Even in some countries with liberalization measures, private sector investment actually declined as a proportion of GDP during the 1980s—as in Argentina, Bolivia, Colombia, Kenya, Peru and Trinidad and Tobago.

The changes have been greatest in developing countries, such as China and Viet Nam, that started from centrally planned economies. There, the basic reform was the legalization of private ownership and entrepreneurship, and—particularly significant for China—the breakup of agricultural communes. The new private sector has responded quickly and vigorously and helped increase output dramatically. Although the transition process has not been without social costs, millions in China have benefited from the new economic opportunities, and poverty reduction has progressed at an unprecedented pace. In Viet Nam, too, a large proportion of the population has already benefited from the reforms.

For other developing countries that already had a larger private sector, the shift has been less drastic. For them, the transition is usually referred to as "adjustment". The changes have usually included liberalizing trade and finance, reforming taxation systems, deregulating the labour market and reforming or privatizing public enterprises. These reforms have usually been preceded or accompanied by economic stabilization measures, such as sharp cuts in public spending.

In many countries, these reforms have yet to bear fruit in terms of human development. True, it is difficult to say whether their performance would have been worse without the reforms, but the fact is that three-quarters of adjusting countries in Sub-Saharan Africa have suffered declining per capita incomes, and in Latin America the declines were at least as bad.

It will be some years before any real balance sheet can be drawn up for the human development effects of liberalization and adjustment in developing countries. In

BOX 3.5

Affirmative action for women

By 1990, women's share of the total economically active population in the industrial countries increased dramatically to 42%. In East Asia, it had risen to 43%, in Latin America and the Caribbean to 32%, and in North Africa and the Arab States to 13%.

But women are generally employed in a restricted range of jobs—in low-paid, low-productivity work, where they are subject to discrimination and sometimes to sexual harassment. Added to this are the long hours of household work that frequently go unrecognized. According to a 1990 UN survey, if unpaid house and family care work were counted as productive output in national income accounts, global output would increase by 20–30%.

In developing countries, one of women's greatest contributions outside the home is to agriculture. In Africa, about 78% of economically active women work in agriculture (compared with 64% of men). And in Asia, 80% of post-harvest work is carried out by women.

Women also make up a significant proportion of the informal sector—often forced to combine work and child-care responsibilities. In Latin America, women make up 25–40% of informal sector employment.

Women in almost every country tend to be concentrated in lower-status jobs. In manufacturing, women often do much of the routine production-line work. In the export-processing zones of South-East Asia, in industries such as

electronics, food processing, textiles and footwear, women provide up to 80% of the workforce.

Low status is reflected in low productivity and low pay, with women's earnings frequently only 50–80% those of men (box table). Women are also more likely to be unemployed. In Colombia, men's unemployment in larger cities was 8.1% in 1990, women's 13.2%.

Many forms of discrimination against women arise because of the family responsibilities they have to shoulder. So, it is important that enterprises offer adequate parental leave and access to child-care facilities. But there may also be a need for specific legislation to ensure that discrimination in the workplace is illegal and for policies of affirmative action to redress persistent biases against women.

Affirmative action programmes are more common in industrial countries. A Department of Labor study in the United States has shown that women's employment increased by 15% in companies subject to affirmative action goals, compared with only 2% in other establishments.

There have been few affirmative action measures for women in developing countries, but there are some. In Bangladesh, 10–15% of government jobs are reserved for women. As a result, women's share of all government jobs increased from less than 3% in the early 1970s to 8% in 1990.

BOX TABLE
Disadvantageous position of women at work, 1990

Country	Unemployment rate (%)		Female earnings in non-agriculture (male pay=100)	Hours worked per week, including housework	
	Male	Female		Male	Female
Industrial countries					
Australia	9.8	9.1	88.0	48.3	46.9
Denmark	9.3	12.1	82.1	40.3	45.1
Germany	4.0	4.8	73.6	46.9	51.2
United Kingdom	11.8	5.1	67.4	47.2	51.9
Japan	2.0	2.2	50.7	50.6	45.4
Developing countries					
Kenya	15.6	18.6	80.5	40.1	47.2
Sri Lanka	10.8	24.3	78.5	52.4	56.7
Costa Rica	4.2	5.9	65.9	45.7	48.3
Korea, Rep. of	2.9	1.8	53.5	48.2	53.3

most countries, the reforms have yet to lead to improved economic performance. And social statistics usually lag far behind economic ones—particularly in the poorest countries.

Formerly socialist countries

The countries of Eastern and Central Europe and the former Soviet Union have been transformed in recent years—and not just in the economic, social and political spheres. They are also undergoing a democratic transition from autocratic rule to greater political freedom and participation, a sociocultural transition from a life without free movement and travel to one of open borders, and a psychological transition from a life of being provided for by the state to having individual and household living standards depend very much on private initiative and effort.

The economic reforms in these countries envisage a complete restructuring from a command economy to a market economy. This transition—much delayed—is likely to be traumatic. The economic mess has been accumulated over a long period: it cannot be sorted out very quickly or without pain. But the transition is necessary and inevitable. The only question is how skilfully it is carried out by various countries.

Many of the economic reforms are common throughout the region, but there are significant differences for individual countries. Some already had more of the elements of a market-based economy (such as private agriculture) or had started their reforms earlier than others—distinguishing such "early starters" as the Czech Republic, Hungary, Poland and the Slovak Republic from such "late starters" as Albania, Bulgaria, Romania and the newly independent states of the former Soviet Union. There have also been differences in the speed of reform—the "shock therapy" of Poland, compared with the more "institutional reformist" approach of Hungary.

All these countries started with distorted economic structures. Typically, they had a high proportion of the workforce working in large enterprises with obsolete technology. And many regions had a very narrow economic base, making them very vulnerable to the play of market forces. The service sectors were generally very small—and inadequate for the functioning of a modern economy. Agriculture was often very inefficient, particularly in the former Soviet Union.

THE REFORM PROCESS. Reforms throughout the region aim to change the balance between the private and public sectors—by allowing many new private enterprises to be created and by privatizing the state sector. Privatization will be an enormous undertaking. State-owned enterprises produced 60–90% of the GDP of these countries. Poland had more than 8,000 large industrial state enterprises, and the Soviet Union 47,000.

Private enterprise has, indeed, been growing on a significant scale in some of the early starting countries—generally through self-employment or the creation of small enterprises.

But the process of privatization has yet to get fully under way (box 3.6). One of the most important problems concerns the method of asset distribution. First, since few people owned much property, they now lack the money to purchase any new assets on offer. Second, there is the question of equity. Those who do have the money are often the "nomenklatura", who legally or il-

---

BOX 3.6

Unequal transitions—a tale of two cities

The transition to market-based economies in Eastern Europe will be long and difficult—and involve much more than just a shift from public to private sector industries. Its impact will be very different from one region or city to another—and require different policies.

This is illustrated by the varied experiences of two Polish cities, Krakow and Lodz. In both cities during the central planning period, large state-owned enterprises provided up to 80% of all industrial employment.

Today, unemployment in Lodz is around 18%, while in Krakow it is less than half this. Lodz is a textile city, hard hit by the collapse in trade with the former Soviet Union and by cheap imports from Asia. Krakow, a centre of metallur-

gy and metalworking, has managed to find new markets in Germany for its relatively cheap components.

This has a knock-on effect in the private sector. In Lodz, the private sector is largely in the retail and wholesale trade, leaving the city trapped in a downward spiral of low-paying jobs. In Krakow, a significant proportion of the growing private sector is based on subcontracting industrial services—a virtuous circle in which the growth in one firm feeds into that of another.

These two cities are a stark demonstration that the transition will have a different impact in different places—increasing inequalities and requiring special measures for those regions and cities that seem destined to lose out.

---

legally accumulated wealth under the old system and stand to make considerable further gains.

This problem is being tackled in different ways. One is through the distribution of property rights to all citizens in the form of vouchers that can either be traded or exchanged for stakes in one or more companies (as in Russia and the Czech Republic). Another way is through buyouts by management and employees (the common method in Hungary).

In Russia, when managers or workers are interested in buying a state enterprise, they are given financial assistance. They are allowed to use the net profits of the enterprise to establish funds for buying it. And if their bid for the company succeeds (through auction or competitive tender), they are entitled to a 30% discount off the sale price, with payment deferred for one year. In April 1992, more than 40% of the shops sold at a pilot auction in Nizhny Novgorod were purchased by workers taking advantage of such concessions. In Lviv, Ukraine, in the first pilot auction of shops in February 1993, nine of the 17 properties on offer were sold to the workers.

HUMAN COSTS OF REFORM. The long-term objectives of privatization may be to increase economic growth and promote human development, but the immediate effects have been traumatic. During 1990–92, the economies of all countries in the region were plunged into ever-deepening crises. Between 1988 and the first half of 1992, industrial production fell more than 40%. And in 1992 alone, output in Eastern Europe fell an estimated 10%, with much of the fall in defence industries (consumption did not fall as much). Also figuring heavily in the decline was the collapse of trade between the formerly socialist economies, which were also hit by the recession in the other industrial countries.

The human impact has been dramatic. In every country for which data are available, the proportion of the population living in poverty has increased. In Bulgaria, the Czech Republic, Poland, Romania and the Slovak Republic, the number of households living below the poverty line has risen sharply—and the available figures are probably considerable underestimates.

Millions of people all over the region have joined the "new working poor", whether through cuts in real wages, losses of social benefits or shorter working hours. Managers in Bulgaria, Romania and Russia are obliging many workers to take long periods of unpaid leave.

Millions more are unemployed. Current figures for unemployment are alarming enough, but even these are likely to be considerable underestimates. In Poland in 1992, when the official rate was 12%, the Polish Minister of Labour and Social Policy gave statistics for induced early retirements, and those with jobs but no work, suggesting the real figure to be nearer 20%. Eastern and Central Europe is entering an era of mass unemployment, at rates well above 15%, that could last for years.

Affecting almost the entire populations of these countries, the current crises hit some groups particularly hard: women, youths, older workers and ethnic minorities.

Women used to be reasonably well-integrated into the workforce. They had very high participation rates, even if they did not get the jobs they deserved. Now, however, it seems that they are treated more as "secondary workers", being displaced from enterprises more quickly than men, or seeing their wages and benefits fall more rapidly.

The youngest and oldest workers are also very vulnerable. Few companies are taking on new workers, so youth unemployment is becoming serious: in Poland in early 1992, one-third of all the unemployed were under 24. At the other end of the scale, the drive for efficiency is also eliminating the practice of keeping on workers beyond official retirement age to compensate them for miserable state pensions. In Czechoslovakia in the late 1980s, where the official retirement age for men was 60 years, more than 30% of men between 65 and 69 were still working.

Unemployment is also rising alarmingly among minority groups. In Slovakia in 1992, the official unemployment rate for gypsies was 30%—more than four times the rate for the rest of the population. And in Bulgaria, there are reports of unemploy-

Eastern and Central Europe is entering an era of unemployment that could last for years

ment of 50% for the Turkish minority and more than 80% for gypsies. These minorities tend either to be overrepresented in jobs that are eliminated, or to suffer direct discrimination in new recruitment.

In the face of rising unemployment and poverty, social security systems are finding it increasingly difficult to cope. State-owned enterprises used to distribute most social benefits, from child care to health care to pensions. But over the past three years, these widespread automatic benefits have been dramatically curtailed and are being replaced by "social safety nets" whose services are targeted much more narrowly—and thus risk missing millions of people in desperate need.

Experiences with privatization

Between 1980 and 1991, nearly 7,000 state enterprises were privatized, most in eastern states of Germany (4,500) and other countries with formerly centrally planned economies. Only around 1,400 were in de-veloping countries, of which 59% were in Latin America, 27% in Africa, 9% in Asia and 4% in the Arab States (table 3.3). Because most privatizations in the developing world have been recent, they do not appear fully in the 1991 data.

Public enterprises are being privatized mainly because of the belief that, in manufacturing and other productive sectors, private enterprise can deliver better results. But the final nail in the coffin of most public enterprises has been their demonstrable inefficiency, and above all, their enormous financial losses, which have drained the public purse of funds that could have been put to better use elsewhere.

Not all public enterprises lose money, and not all are always more inefficient than private sector firms. A recent study in Kenya found a number of public enterprise manufacturing companies performing better on a number of indicators than private sector firms. And the state-owned steel industry in the Republic of Korea is among the most efficient in the world. But in some countries, a high proportion of state enterprises do make losses. In China in 1991, despite substantial reforms, about a third of state enterprises were still operating at a loss. In Tanzania during the 1980s, about half the state-owned enterprises persistently made losses.

Such losses—equal to more than 3% of GDP in Bangladesh and Mexico in the 1980s, 4% in Turkey, 5% in Sub-Saharan Africa and 9% in Argentina and Poland—had to be covered by government subsidies. In Sri Lanka, those subsidies have accounted for 20% of government expenditure and 60% of the budget deficit. In Cameroon, the losses of state enterprises often exceeded the government's total revenue from oil.

The social opportunity cost has been staggering. If governments did not have to finance such losses, total expenditure on health and education in Bangladesh and Poland could have been doubled, and in Argentina almost tripled (table 3.4). According to the finance minister of Mexico, a small fraction of the $10 billion in losses of the state-owned steel complex could have brought drinking water, sewerage, hospitals

TABLE 3.3
Privatization of state-owned enterprises, 1980–91

Region	Enterprises privatized	Share of total privatizations (%)
Eastern Europe	5,305	78
Of which, former GDR	4,500	66
OECD countries	170	2
Latin America and the Caribbean	804	12
Sub-Saharan Africa	373	5
Asia	122	2
Arab States	58	1

TABLE 3.4
Social opportunity cost of public enterprise losses, 1988–90

Country or region	Estimated losses of public enterprises as % of GNP	Public education and health spending as % of GNP	Potential increase in education and health spending if public enterprise losses are eliminated (%)
Argentina	9	5.5	164
Poland	9	7.6	118
Bangladesh	3	3.1	97
Turkey	4	4.6	87
Egypt	3	11.0	27
Philippines	2	8.3	24
Sub-Saharan Africa	5	6.5	77

and education facilities to an entire region of his country.

Privatization is no panacea, however. Hastily conceived or executed, it might achieve very little. Privatization should thus be seen not as an end, but as a means to higher levels of human development.

The first task must be to ensure that companies are being privatized in an environment conducive to business. Newly privatized companies need to operate in an "enterprise culture" for there to be any real progress. Indeed, changing this culture—by providing adequate training for new entrepreneurs, for example, or ensuring a competitive environment—is probably more significant than changing ownership. And if the enterprise is still a monopoly after privatization, as is often the case with utilities, it must be subject to suitable controls—otherwise inefficiencies and monopoly power will merely be transferred to the private sector, with the costs being borne by consumers. Or monopolistic exploitation by efficient private owners replaces the inefficiencies of public ownership.

Clearly, the poorer countries, and those that have only recently adopted the principles of a mixed economy, will find it difficult to create such environments. They may also have limited capacity to manage the privatization process, and trouble finding suitable buyers for enterprises and ensuring that resources are distributed in an equitable way. Malawi and Papua New Guinea have struggled to achieve their privatization objectives because of the difficulty of mobilizing savings for equity investment.

The speed of privatization must also be a concern. Building a suitable framework of institutions and regulations takes time, so privatizations should not be rushed—even when there is pressure from financial institutions during structural adjustment programmes. And it may be better to gain experience by starting with smaller enterprises—as Chile, Jamaica, Mexico, Poland and Togo did—before moving on to larger ones.

Governments should also be realistic about the revenues that privatization can generate. In Malaysia, Papua New Guinea and Sri Lanka, privatizations in an average year produced less than 1% of GDP. Indeed, the taxes paid by the newly privatized enterprises have often generated more revenue than the original sale of the assets.

One of the most important issues—and the one usually given least attention—is what the impact of privatization will be on people. It is usually taken for granted that privatization has to be accompanied by unemployment, but this need not be so. With a better sequence of policy measures, much unemployment could be avoided. Restructuring many of the enterprises before they are privatized and making prior efforts to develop alternative employment in the private sector would be much more rational. And if layoffs are inevitable, governments should carry them out before the privatization. This would help ensure that workers get suitable compensation, with possible retraining or access to credit if they want to start their own enterprises.

Bear in mind that privatization may not be the only—or even the best—way to reduce losses from public enterprises. In Trinidad and Tobago between 1982 and 1988, reforms in state-owned enterprises reduced cumulative transfers to the state-owned sector over the period by more than 10% of GDP, compared with cumulative privatization receipts of only 2.3%. Similarly, in Sri Lanka between 1982 and 1988, reforms of state-owned enterprises reduced transfers by more than 6% of GDP, compared with privatization receipts of 0.2%. There can be competition among public enterprises as well as between public and private ones which keeps the public enterprise on its toes.

Seven sins of privatization

Privatization, conceived as one element of a total package, can stimulate private enterprise. Unfortunately, the process in many countries has been very different from this—more a "garage sale" of public enterprises to favoured individuals and groups than an integral part of a coherent strategy to encourage private investment.

Privatization in developing countries has therefore had very mixed results. In

If governments did not have to finance public enterprise losses, their social spending could increase manyfold

some cases, as in Mexico, it has been part of a process of fundamentally altering the organization of production—with benefits for consumers and the economy as a whole. In too many cases, however, privatization has taken place for the wrong reasons, under the wrong conditions and in the wrong way. Many countries seem to have been committing one or more of the seven deadly sins of privatization (box 3.7):

1. *For the wrong reason*—Many privatization strategies have aimed at maximizing short-term revenue rather than building competitive markets for the long term. For example, the sale of a telecommunications company as a monopoly would probably get a better price from a buyer who thought the company's activities would not be closely regulated: short-term revenue for the government but long-term losses for consumers and the efficiency of the economy as a whole. As the World Bank cautioned in its latest review of privatization experience: maximizing short-term revenues should not be the primary consideration. So, it could be better to create a competitive environment than to maximize revenue from sales into protected markets.

2. *In the wrong environment*—Privatization makes sense only if enterprises are released in an environment that allows them to become competitive and efficient. Where the market functions poorly and enterprises are still vulnerable to arbitrary government

edicts, transferring ownership to the private sector is unlikely to achieve much. It may merely transfer the ownership of rents from the public to the private sector. Similarly, creating private monopolies without an effective system of monitoring and control opens up the danger of exploitation of consumers.

3. *With non-transparent procedures*—Privatization has sometimes been accompanied by allegations of corruption, and claims that the process has enriched a few privileged cronies of the government. The disposal of assets should be so open and public that such allegations cannot arise. It should start with a publicity campaign explaining the rationale for the privatization and the method of selling and then proceed through competitive bidding, preferably through the stock exchange. The entire process of transferring ownership should be kept open to outside scrutiny—and should clearly state the national objectives that privatization hopes to accomplish. There should also be a detailed report on the sale to document if, and how, the objectives have been achieved.

4. *Only to finance budget deficits*—Harassed finance ministers are often tempted to sell state assets to cover their current budget deficits. The sale of public assets should be seen instead as a way of reducing the national debt—since these debts were often incurred in the first place for the establishment of such enterprises. Selling assets to meet current liabilities is mortgaging the options of future generations.

5. *With a poor financial strategy*—The best way to dispose of assets is through the capital markets selling shares to the public, difficult in many developing countries where capital markets are underdeveloped. Rather than take into account that stock exchanges are narrow and monopolized by a privileged minority, the financial strategies of many governments often make matters worse. A surprising number of governments have actually tried to privatize while at the same time issuing high-yield, low-risk, tax-free government bonds. Many governments have further narrowed their options by restricting sales of shares to foreigners. The aim instead should be a widespread distrib-

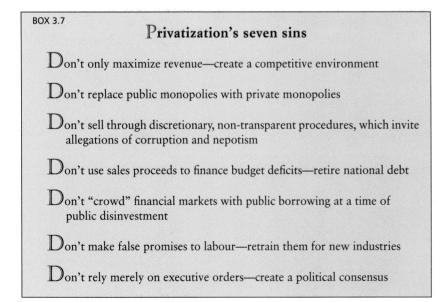

BOX 3.7

Privatization's seven sins

Don't only maximize revenue—create a competitive environment

Don't replace public monopolies with private monopolies

Don't sell through discretionary, non-transparent procedures, which invite allegations of corruption and nepotism

Don't use sales proceeds to finance budget deficits—retire national debt

Don't "crowd" financial markets with public borrowing at a time of public disinvestment

Don't make false promises to labour—retrain them for new industries

Don't rely merely on executive orders—create a political consensus

ution of shares to nationals and foreigners alike—with a timing and a distribution of shares that both maximize revenue and protect national interests.

6. *With unrealistic labour strategies*—Some governments have been so nervous about labour agitation in privatized industries that they have demanded guarantees from prospective buyers that no workers will subsequently be laid off. Others have "bought" labour cooperation by offering handshakes so golden that they exceed the asset's sale value. Employment is one of the most difficult and sensitive areas of privatization. But experience shows that it is better to have an open and free dialogue in advance. This should cover the possibilities of worker ownership and retraining schemes, as well as the inevitable job losses. False promises in the initial stages will create worse problems later.

7. *With no political consensus*—Privatization is not merely a technocratic exercise. It is also a political process. A hasty privatization forced through executive orders risks immediate conflict—and reversal after a change in government. There are many contending schools of thought on privatization, and unanimity is unlikely. But governments should still attempt to build as broad a consensus as possible and to use democratic parliamentary procedures to minimize violent lurches in policy.

The enumeration of these sins is a caution not against privatization, but against privatizing within the wrong framework and without a human development purpose in mind. Policy-makers can learn much from free and frank exchanges of experience—and from using information from the 80 countries that embarked on privatization strategies in the 1980s and early 1990s.

The enormous changes that have swept the world in recent years can be seen as a threat to the security and livelihoods of millions of people—or as a unique opportunity for people to shape new and different forms of social and economic participation. People-friendly markets have a vital role to play here—allowing people much broader opportunities to participate, and releasing some of the enormous human potential that remains untapped.

Markets and the state

The concept of people-friendly markets clearly envisages state and markets working in tandem. For this to happen, there must be a realistic assessment of the strengths and weaknesses of each.

Past discussions of the role of the state have generated more heat than light. Some believe in the benevolence of the state and the need for it constantly to correct the ill effects of the market. Others glorify the virtues of the market-place and argue that the economy should be liberated from the dead hand of state bureaucracy.

Changes in ideology have produced swings in policy backwards and forwards. Policy-makers in developing countries have highlighted the imperfections in markets. And they have been tempted to supplant them with state action, often in the mistaken belief that the public sector would necessarily do better.

Today, markets are much more popular. Indeed, some people claim that recent events prove the triumph of capitalism and the demise of socialism. This is too simplistic a view. If there is a triumph of capitalism, it need not be the triumph of personal greed. If there is a demise of socialism, it need not be the demise of all social objectives. Indeed, such labels inhibit creative thinking and risk repeating the mistakes of the past.

The issues are further clouded by three persistent myths about the roles of the public and private sectors in developing countries.

Myth 1: The public sector is too large in developing countries—As a proportion of GNP, public spending in developing countries is lower than that in industrial countries. In fact, to ensure that everyone has the basic education and health to benefit from people-friendly markets, and to maintain adequate and efficient social safety nets for their vulnerable groups, many countries will need to increase public spending.

Myth 2: After privatization, the balance between private and public investment will change dramatically—In fact, privatization will have very little effect on this balance. First, the number of enterprises that can be

Privatization is not merely a technocratic exercise. It is also a political process

privatized is not that great in most countries. And second, the state will simultaneously have to increase its investment in physical and social infrastructure since it had to be curtailed significantly in the 1980s. For the developing countries having data, the share of private investment in total investment fell from around 68% in 1970 to 57% in 1982 and then rose to 69% in 1991 (figure 3.5 and table 3.5). The share of private investment rebounded in the past few years but is still only a little higher than in the early 1970s. And a large part of the recent increase is a consequence not of privatization—but of governments decreasing their investment in infrastructure and of private sector growth from removed controls and regulations.

Myth 3: The activities of the state should be minimal—The real problem with the public sector in developing countries is not so much its size as its activities. Public enterprises have been overeager to engage in productive activities in industry and trade, which the private sector could have undertaken, often more efficiently. Consequently, governments have neither the time nor the resources for the job they should be doing. To quote Keynes: "The important thing for Governments is not to do things which individuals are doing already, and to do them a little better or a little worse; but to do those things which at present are not done at all."

Japan and the industrializing "tigers" of East Asia are powerful evidence of the value of such an approach. There, the state has played an enabling role for people-friendly markets—building the infrastructure, educating and training workers and providing a stable climate that enables enterprises to grow and flourish.

Entrepreneurs in developing countries have certainly been concerned about the role of government in economic activity. But they have been less bothered about government spending than about government control. Many forms of private investment demand numerous licences and permits before being allowed to go ahead—consuming valuable time and creating enormous uncertainty.

The central fallacy in the old ideological debate was that the state and the market are necessarily separate and even antagonistic—and that one is benevolent, and the

TABLE 3.5
Trends in private investment for selected developing countries

Country	Private share in total investment (average annual %)		Change in share (percentage points)
	1970–74	1987–91	
Mexico	65.2	77.1	+11.9
El Salvador	72.4	78.3	+5.9
Costa Rica	73.1	78.5	+5.4
Pakistan	46.6	51.3	+4.7
Tunisia	46.6	51.0	+4.4
Thailand	76.0	78.8	+2.8
Guatemala	78.2	80.6	+2.4
Ecuador	60.8	63.1	+2.3
Paraguay	78.1	80.2	+2.1
Korea, Rep. of	77.3	78.5	+1.2
Singapore	79.2	77.9	–1.3
Sri Lanka	60.7	58.4	–2.3
Kenya	60.4	57.2	–3.2
Turkey	58.2	54.2	–4.0
Malaysia	69.1	64.7	–4.4
India	58.7	53.7	–5.0
Belize	61.0	55.7	–5.3
Argentina	62.7	54.2	–8.5
Uruguay	75.7	65.6	–10.1
Zimbabwe	62.5	50.5	–12.0
Dominican Rep.	67.8	52.5	–15.3
Colombia	69.6	52.5	–17.1
Fiji	62.5	44.8	–17.7
Unweighted average	66.2	63.4	–2.8
Weighted average	63.2	65.0	+1.8

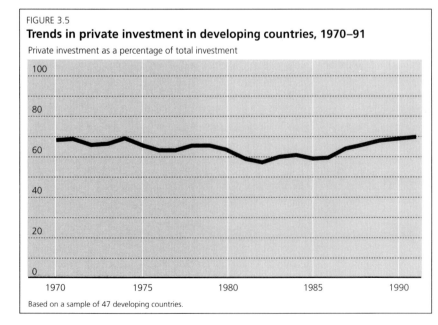

FIGURE 3.5
Trends in private investment in developing countries, 1970–91

Private investment as a percentage of total investment

Based on a sample of 47 developing countries.

other not. In practice, both state and markets are often dominated by the same power structures.

This suggests a more pragmatic third option: both state and market should be guided by the people. The two should work in tandem, and people should be sufficiently empowered to exert effective control over both. They may do so through participation in governance, as producers or consumers, or in many cases, through people's organizations or non-governmental organizations—an issue addressed in subsequent chapters.

Argentina

Argentina's liberalization programme seems to have stabilized the economy, and the government is pressing ahead with a massive privatization programme. Although this has yet to show demonstrable human development benefits, the long-term picture should be brighter.

Argentina's economic position deteriorated sharply in the 1980s. GNP per capita fell by an annual average of 1.8%. Investment, which in the 1970s was above 20% of GDP, dropped in 1990 to only 9%. And the economy was disrupted by hyperinflation. The government introduced shock programmes in both 1985 and 1987, including devaluations and wage and price controls, but neither stabilized the economy.

In 1989, the current government launched another stabilization programme. Since then, it has:
- Cut the government budget sharply
- Reformed the tax system and increased taxes
- Pegged the national currency to the US dollar
- Established large foreign currency reserves in the central bank and set a legal limit to printing money not backed by foreign currency
- Simplified government regulations
- Lowered tariff barriers
- Privatized many industries.

This time it seems the government has managed to stabilize the economy—and set it on the path to fundamental recovery. GDP grew by 6.5% in 1991, and at a similar rate for the first half of 1992. Investment also has risen significantly, and the tax base is increasing.

Argentina's privatization programme is massive: the plan is to divest almost the entire public sector. In the three years through 1992, the government privatized 51 companies, raising about $5.6 billion. Major privatizations included one of the telephone companies and an iron and steel company.

The process has not been entirely smooth, and in several cases the privatizations were in uncompetitive markets.

But the privatizations and the greater economic stability have attracted a large inflow of foreign investment—much of it the return of capital that fled in the 1980s. These capital inflows have financed the balance of payments deficit on the current account and helped build up international reserves.

Argentina's liberalization programme is relatively recent, but it does seem to be having a positive impact on the economy, with growth driven largely by an increased demand for private sector goods and services. In the long term, this should help increase levels of human development. But liberalization has yet to improve urban employment: in early 1992, unemployment in greater Buenos Aires was still more than 6.5%, and in other cities it was more than 10%.

HUMAN DEVELOPMENT RANK	46
GNP PER CAPITA RANK	62
GNP PER CAPITA ANNUAL GROWTH RATE (1980–90)	–1.8%
INFLATION RATE (1991)	128%
DEBT SERVICE RATIO (1990)	34%
CENTRAL GOVERNMENT EXPENDITURE AS % OF GNP (1990)	16%
TOTAL INVESTMENT AS % OF GDP (1990)	9%
PRIVATE SHARE OF TOTAL INVESTMENT (1970–74)	63%
PRIVATE SHARE OF TOTAL INVESTMENT (1990)	60%
FOREIGN DIRECT INVESTMENT INFLOWS AS % OF GROSS CAPITAL FORMATION (1986–89)	6.5%
LOSSES OF PUBLIC ENTERPRISES AS % OF GDP (1989–91)	9%
NUMBER OF PUBLIC ENTERPRISES SOLD (1990–92)	51
REVENUE FROM PUBLIC ENTERPRISE SALES AS % OF GNP (1989–91)	7%

Brazil

Brazil's liberalization programme started in earnest in the 1990s. Many measures have already been taken to liberalize trade and reform the financial system. Some public enterprises have already been privatized, but the process still has a long way to go, since privatization policy is only now being defined.

Brazil seems to have been riding an economic roller-coaster, switching between periods of fast and slow growth, occasionally dipping into contraction. The period between 1968 and 1974 was the "Brazilian miracle", with an average annual growth rate of 11%. The 1980s saw the country sink into recession, with widespread economic instability, high external debt, and rocketing inflation, which in 1989 and 1990 was over 1,500%.

Successive Brazilian governments have, since the mid-1980s, tried shock tactics to stabilize the economy, including attempts to freeze wages and prices. But they had little success—budget deficits and inflation continued to soar.

In 1990, the government introduced a major new set of reforms, which combined stabilization measures with trade liberalization and deregulation. Among other things, it:

- Reduced tariffs on imports, abolished non-tariff barriers and sped up import licencing, repealing part of Brazil's protectionist legislation
- Relaxed the conditions for foreign investment and technology transfer: since June 1991, direct foreign investment has been permitted on equal terms with domestic investment
- Let the currency float on the international exchanges
- Simplified some of the bureaucratic procedures
- Eliminated the single-retail-price structure, and removed the monopoly on domestic wheat distribution
- Launched a large-scale privatization programme.

The government had increased its direct participation in the economy from the 1940s onwards, launching some new industries and assuming control, or becoming a large investor, in others. Its involvement today includes banking, petroleum, mining, road and rail networks, ports and power generation, as well as distribution and storage.

HUMAN DEVELOPMENT RANK	70
GNP PER CAPITA RANK	53
GNP PER CAPITA ANNUAL GROWTH RATE (1980–90)	0.6%
INFLATION RATE (1991)	429%
DEBT SERVICE RATIO (1990)	21%
CENTRAL GOVERNMENT EXPENDITURE AS % OF GNP (1990)	36%
TOTAL INVESTMENT AS % OF GDP (1990)	22%
FOREIGN DIRECT INVESTMENT INFLOWS AS % OF GROSS CAPITAL FORMATION (1986–89)	2.4%
OPERATING DEFICIT OF PUBLIC ENTERPRISES AS % OF GDP (1986–88)	3%
NUMBER OF PUBLIC ENTERPRISES SOLD (UNTIL NOVEMBER 1992)	17
REVENUE FROM PUBLIC ENTERPRISE SALES AS % OF GNP	1%

Brazil has 159 public enterprises, some of them well-run and efficient. But on average they are less efficient than those in the private sector and often make losses. The operating deficit of public sector enterprises between 1986 and 1988 was about 3% of GDP, more than half the budget deficit. The state-owned enterprises hold about half of Brazil's total external debt. Broad support for privatization has developed.

Although privatization started in the 1980s, the current programme is the first to show any real results. Between 1990 and 1992, the government privatized 17 enterprises, with smaller shareholders, including employees, buying most of the shares (foreigners have so far bought very few). The revenue from future sales is unlikely to be significant in national terms—in 1990, the total market value of public enterprises was $25 billion, about 6% of annual GDP.

The government has yet to make much progress in dismantling monopolies. In telecommunications, it still monopolizes both local and long-distance services.

Liberalization, like privatization, is slow. Entrepreneurial activity remains stifled by numerous rules and regulations, and companies are uncertain about the direction of future government policies.

So far, there are few signs of a positive impact on human development. Poverty is widespread, and there are enormous income disparities, which the taxation system does little to reduce. Most revenues come from highly regressive payroll taxes, and neither personal income tax nor corporation tax is very progressive either.

High inflation continues to be a problem—particularly for those on fixed incomes and for the poor, who hold a large proportion of their assets in cash.

China

China's reforms have taken place gradually over 15 years. The most significant steps have been in agriculture, with the breakup of agricultural communes. Widespread deregulation also boosted industrial output and trade, and encouraged a new private sector to emerge. Although some major problems persist, the reduction of poverty has been unprecedented.

China's reforms have been carried out in two major stages. Between 1979 and 1984, they were concentrated in the rural areas, focusing on agriculture and rural industry, and from 1984 to the present, the emphasis has been on the urban sector and enterprise reform. Since 1979, the government has:
• Broken up the communes and turned the land over to household farming units
• Encouraged the growth of township- and village-owned enterprises, as well as non-public enterprises
• Introduced price reforms
• Decentralized state enterprise management and development planning.

The agricultural reforms between 1979 and 1984 broke up about 50,000 agricultural communes, distributing the land on the basis of a "household contract responsibility system". This meant that farmers had to produce agreed quotas of certain products for the state but were otherwise free to diversify to meet market demand. At the same time, most agricultural prices were freed to reach market clearing levels. By 1984, following these reforms, agricultural output almost doubled in value, and per capita consumption among the agricultural population increased by 68%.

As the agricultural reforms took place, the surplus rural labour and capital were encouraged to move into township-owned and village-owned enterprises. By 1991, these enterprises, which operate outside the influence of central planning, were the most rapidly expanding segment of the industrial sector—producing 31% of industrial output value and employing more than 22% of the labour force.

After 1984, the government encouraged the growth of non-public industrial enterprises. These included petty urban services, private enterprises, urban cooperatives and corporate enterprises, as well as foreign private investment in joint and wholly owned ventures—either in urban areas or in specially designated economic zones. By 1991, this sector accounted for 47% of total industrial output value.

To introduce greater competitiveness in the market-

HUMAN DEVELOPMENT RANK	**101**
GNP PER CAPITA RANK	**142**
GNP PER CAPITA ANNUAL GROWTH RATE (1980–90)	**7.9%**
INFLATION RATE (1991)	**3.5%**
DEBT SERVICE RATIO (1990)	**10.3%**
TOTAL INVESTMENT AS % OF GDP (1990)	**39%**

place, the government also reduced the number of products manufactured or distributed on the basis of state planning. Between 1982 and 1991, the number of these items had been reduced from 837 to 20. Most consumer products had been deregulated and were trading at market prices.

The state enterprises also underwent extensive reforms. Under the "contract responsibility system", managers were given shared responsibility for production planning, marketing, income distribution and investment decisions. The contracts specify production quotas and the amount of taxes and profits to be remitted to government. If the quotas are met, the enterprises can retain additional earnings. In 1992, further measures were introduced to separate state enterprise operations from government controls and financial subsidies. But labour productivity in these enterprises is still low, and around one-third are unprofitable.

Along with the economic reforms, there have been administrative ones—with a steady decentralization of responsibility for infrastructure and social services to lower levels of government.

China's reforms have been remarkably successful in many ways, but not without problems. The management of monetary and fiscal policy has been inadequate, and there have been economic fluctuations due to weakened planning and administrative controls. Some people are clearly benefiting more than others, with inequality increasing in favour of those employed in industry, trade and commercial agriculture. And there has been some deterioration in social services, especially in the poorer counties, since the services now rely more on local funding.

Pollution remains serious, both by state enterprises and by township- and village-owned enterprises unable or unwilling to comply with environmental regulations.

Most people in China are better off, with the number of rural people living in absolute poverty having fallen dramatically over the past two decades.

Egypt

*Egypt's economy faces some structural problems. High reliance on oil income
and overseas remittances have made it vulnerable to external shocks. The
government has a new reform programme. To protect human development in
the short term, it is also establishing a substantial social safety net.*

Egypt made considerable progress in human development in the 1970s and early 1980s. Between 1974 and 1981, GDP was growing 9% a year, spurred by rising oil production and prices as well as remittances from overseas workers. Since 1986, however, oil prices have fallen, Suez Canal revenues have declined and remittances have levelled off. As a result, annual GDP growth has been less than 5%, falling to about 2.5% in 1992.

The government, under pressure in the mid-1980s to repay the external debt, responded in 1987 with a reform package that included a liberalization of trade and domestic prices. But this did little to solve the underlying problems. And in the early 1990s, the economy was hard hit by the Gulf crisis—both by the fall in remittances from overseas workers and by the need to find jobs for returning workers when unemployment was already over 10%.

In 1991, the government adopted its Economic Reform and Structural Adjustment Programme—to move away from a reliance on the public sector, develop a stronger market economy and create more opportunities for the private sector. The programme:

- Freed interest rates
- Floated the currency
- Reduced subsidies on a wide range of items
- Curbed the growth in the money supply
- Overhauled the public enterprises and made plans for privatization.

These measures proved quite successful in restoring macroeconomic balances. Inflation fell below 10% in 1992. The balance of payments deficit was reduced, and the deficit in 1991/92 was brought down to its target figure of 7% of GDP. It is too early, however, to judge the long-term economic impact.

The public sector has dominated Egypt's economy since the 1960s, with large holding companies for textiles, food processing, electronics, chemicals, metals and engineering. In addition, the four public sector banks hold around 80% of all deposits and are major shareholders in companies run as joint ventures with the private sector. Public enterprises currently employ about 1.3 million people and account for 70% of the industrial sector and 80% of exports—but many operate at a loss.

The government is now seeking to privatize more than 70 state enterprises. Pilot programmes in the tourist industry have auctioned off two hotels, and another hotel company is to be floated on the stock market for about $300 million. In addition, a stake in one of the highly profitable joint-venture banks has been sold to employees. The first major privatizations were scheduled for early 1993, with one batch of ten companies for sale in January, and another ten in March.

One major problem for privatization is the small Cairo stock market, dormant since the 1960s. In 1990, it listed 500 companies, with shares traded in only around 20 companies a day. It is being revamped to make share-trading easier and more responsive to market fluctuations. The privatization programme is expected to increase Egypt's already high unemployment. It is estimated that 80,000 to 100,000 workers may have to move from the public sector to the private.

Egypt's reforms are a very promising step towards sustained economic growth and employment creation in the medium and long term. In the short term, however, they are likely to create several pressures for its people. The price of food and other basic goods is rising, and social services are deteriorating. Unemployment is still rising, particularly among youths and women. In response, the government has, with the assistance of such external donors as the World Bank and UNDP, established a Social Fund for Development to protect the most vulnerable groups, including displaced public enterprise workers, unemployed youth, Gulf crisis returnees and women-headed households.

HUMAN DEVELOPMENT RANK	**124**
GNP PER CAPITA RANK	**120**
GNP PER CAPITA ANNUAL GROWTH RATE (1980–90)	**2.1%**
INFLATION RATE (1991)	**22%**
DEBT SERVICE RATIO (1990)	**26%**
CENTRAL GOVERNMENT EXPENDITURE AS % OF GNP (1990)	**40%**
TOTAL INVESTMENT AS % OF GDP (1990)	**23%**
PRIVATE SHARE OF TOTAL INVESTMENT (1991)	**42%**
FOREIGN DIRECT INVESTMENT INFLOWS AS % OF GROSS CAPITAL FORMATION (1986–89)	**8.1%**

Ghana

*Ghana's liberalization started in 1983, and in 1987 the government began
to divest itself of some enterprises. But so far, private entrepreneurs have
been hesitant to take advantage of the new environment. Economic
growth has picked up, but people's living conditions have yet to improve.*

The Ghanaian economy declined in the 1970s and early 1980s, and real incomes and living standards fell. In the rural areas, cocoa farmers were hit particularly hard, with their real incomes falling sharply.

In 1983, the government adopted an Economic Recovery Programme. Since then it has:

- Liberalized consumer prices
- Reduced and rationalized import duties and trade taxes
- Devalued the currency several times
- Improved the banking system
- Established a stock exchange, which started trading in November 1990
- Liberalized the foreign exchange market
- Eliminated several subsidies
- Reformed the tax structure and increased revenue.

Investment, though increasing since the mid-1980s, is still low. By 1990, it had risen to 15% of GDP. But that is still very low considering that about 13% of GDP merely replaces depreciating capital.

HUMAN DEVELOPMENT RANK	**131**
GNP PER CAPITA RANK	**140**
GNP PER CAPITA ANNUAL GROWTH RATE (1980–90)	**–0.6%**
INFLATION RATE (1991)	**18.1%**
DEBT SERVICE RATIO (1990)	**35%**
CENTRAL GOVERNMENT EXPENDITURE AS % OF GNP (1990)	**14%**
TOTAL INVESTMENT AS % OF GDP (1990)	**15%**
PRIVATE SHARE OF TOTAL INVESTMENT (1991)	**50%**
FOREIGN DIRECT INVESTMENT INFLOWS AS % OF GROSS CAPITAL FORMATION (1986–89)	**0.9%**
NUMBER OF PUBLIC ENTERPRISES DIVESTED (1987–92)	**80**

The private sector is gradually responding to the improved economic environment. Between 1984 and 1990, private investment increased from 4% of GDP to 8%, and in 1991 it accounted for 50% of total investment. But most of the increase was in gold mining.

Entrepreneurs do not yet have much confidence in the government's economic management. Much of investment is seeking short-term profits, and many people are holding their savings in foreign currencies or outside the banking system. A 1989 survey of enterprises found that 38% considered economic uncertainty a problem, and most (particularly the larger ones) considered the regulatory framework still overly restrictive and cumbersome.

As formal sector employment and incomes declined, microenterprises and self-employment proliferated, driven mainly by excess labour.

For entrepreneurs without sufficient capital, credit is a major problem. About 90% of enterprises perceived the lack of credit as a serious constraint on new investment—even though the private sector's share of total credit rose from 30% in 1984 to 65% in 1989.

Public enterprises in Ghana have had low productivity and suffered substantial losses. In 1984, they had 28% of formal sector employment. In 1989, they commanded 12% of government expenditure—net of revenues.

As part of the structural adjustment programme, the government is aiming to improve the efficiency of many state enterprises and divest itself of others. From 1987 to late 1992, it disposed of 80 enterprises, through partial or total privatization or liquidation (26 cases). In the initial stages, almost all these enterprises were small (fewer than 60 employees), but larger enterprises have been privatized more recently. Delays in the implementation of the programme were partially due to technical matters in preparing for the sales. In 1992, the government still owned around 200 enterprises.

The divestiture programme has not yet been a financial success, and privatization has not yet adequately stimulated the local capital market or attracted the interest of domestic and foreign investors to the extent expected.

Economic growth in Ghana has picked up since 1984—averaging 5% annually. But considering the decline of the economy in the 1970s and early 1980s and the growth of the population, the recovery is only modest. And the recovery has not yet been translated into improved living conditions for the majority of people.

India

*India's reforms have encouraged some capital to return and stimulated
foreign investment and imports of technology. There also are extensive
privatization plans. But the benefits in efficiency have yet to appear
—and meanwhile, output growth in 1992 was only about 1%.*

India's recent efforts at economic reform started in 1985, when the government eliminated some licence regulations and other controls that had inhibited competition. But after this initial attempt, the process slowed.

In 1991, the new government, in response to a balance of payments crisis, initiated a fresh wave of reforms. Since June 1991, it has:

- Devalued the currency, and made it partially convertible
- Reduced quantitative restrictions on imports
- Reduced import duties on capital goods
- Cut a number of subsidies, including that on fertilizers
- Progressively liberalized interest rates
- Abolished production licences for most industries
- Eased restrictions on repatriating dividends and royalties
- Established a partial tax exemption on profits from export sales
- Allowed a partial sale of shares in selected public enterprises
- Reduced restrictions on foreign trading companies
- Revised the system of personal income tax.

HUMAN DEVELOPMENT RANK	**134**
GNP PER CAPITA RANK	**146**
GNP PER CAPITA ANNUAL GROWTH RATE (1980–90)	**3.2%**
INFLATION RATE (1991)	**12.8%**
DEBT SERVICE RATIO (1990)	**29%**
CENTRAL GOVERNMENT EXPENDITURE AS % OF GNP (1990)	**18.2%**
TOTAL INVESTMENT AS % OF GDP (1990)	**23%**
PRIVATE SHARE OF TOTAL INVESTMENT (1970–74)	**59%**
PRIVATE SHARE OF TOTAL INVESTMENT (1990)	**56%**
FOREIGN DIRECT INVESTMENT INFLOWS AS % OF GROSS CAPITAL FORMATION (1986–89)	**0.2%**
LOSSES OF PUBLIC ENTERPRISES AS % OF GDP	**0.4%**

Public enterprises account for about one-fifth of India's non-agricultural GDP and supply crucial inputs for the rest of the economy. They dominate the energy and financial sectors as well as the steel and fertilizer industries.

The privatization process in India is likely to be spread over about ten years. The first phase started in 1991, when the government sold shares in 31 state enterprises to mutual funds. In the second phase, in 1992, it started selling company shares through open auctions. Although the government intended to dispose of loss-making enterprises first, the pressure to earn revenues has caused it also to start selling some of the more profitable companies. Since the privatization process is still in its early stages, it is too soon to assess its impact.

The same is true for many other aspects of economic reform, but there are some early indications. On the positive side, capital has started to return to India. After the budget was announced in February 1992, the flow of private funds into India in the following weeks was estimated at $50 million a day. There also are signs of improved industrial efficiency, as liberalization has encouraged foreign investment and permitted the import of higher levels of technology. The electronics industry, for example, has received a major boost from the liberalization of technology and component imports, as well as from delicencing and cuts in excise duties. And a wider range of foreign goods —often of better quality than local goods—is now competing on the domestic market.

On the negative side, the reforms initially fuelled inflation, and the Bombay stock-market scam destabilized financial markets. In the year to July 1992, consumer prices for agricultural workers increased 20%, and those for industrial workers were up by 13%. At the same time, industrial output stagnated. The cold wind of foreign competition in a previously protected market has forced some companies out of business. The government established a fund to help soften the blow to workers affected by restructuring and to assist social sectors, especially primary education and basic health care, but this has not yet become operational.

The rural poor, more than a third of India's people, are paying a price for the reforms but not yet seeing many of the benefits: agricultural production fell more than 2% in 1992. It will therefore—at least during the period of reform—be important to improve the efficiency and coverage of social programmes.

It is too early to judge the course of India's economic reforms. What is apparent is that they are proceeding along the right lines but will need to cushion the adverse impact on the poor people, lest there be a major political backlash.

Kenya

*Kenya's liberalization programme has been slow. The government
has concentrated more on stabilization measures than on adjustment.
Privatization has been held back by political considerations. But the
privatization programme has recently been revived.*

Kenya experienced considerable economic growth in the 1960s and 1970s. During 1965–80, its average GDP growth was 6.8% a year. The 1980s were different, with economic growth only slightly higher than population growth (4% a year)—due in part to the effects of the second oil shock and the breakup of the East African Community. Kenya has a fairly open economy (exports and imports make up over 40% of GDP), and it has been hurt by sharply deteriorating terms of trade.

The government made several attempts in the 1980s to adjust the economy to changes in the external environment, focusing mainly on stabilization—devaluing the currency several times and exerting more control over public spending. But little was done to liberalize trade or stimulate production.

Some of the adjustment policies succeeded—particularly agricultural diversification. Horticultural exports doubled in the 1980s to become one of the top four export earners, along with coffee, tea and tourism.

The government has frequently expressed its intention to increase the private sector's role in the economy. But private investment has declined as a proportion of GDP—from 14% in 1970 to 10% in 1991, as total investment stayed at around 20% of GDP (except for a few years around 1980, when it was 25%).

Kenya's public enterprises are in a broad range of economic activities, including agriculture, finance, transport and trade. They produce about 11% of GDP and employ about 9% of the workforce. There is no clear evidence that public enterprises need be less efficient than private ones; the quality of management seems to be a more significant factor than ownership. But it has recently been calculated that the productivity of public enterprises declined by 2% annually during 1986–90, while that of the private sector rose 5% annually.

Kenya is thought to be the African country likely to benefit most from privatization. It has a relatively well-developed capital market, with a level of savings about twice as high as the average for Sub-Saharan Africa. And some of the markets in which public enterprises operate are quite competitive. But progress so far has been very limited. Indeed, between 1980 and 1990, only one enterprise was privatized. The problems seem to have been mainly political, with concerns that the assets, like much of Kenya's other commercial, financial and managerial capital, would be taken up by foreigners, and particularly privileged or enterprising ethnic groups. But the privatization programme has recently been revived, with the announcement in mid-1992 of the full or partial sale of 207 companies.

Even if privatization has been slow, the reforms in public enterprises and the threat of privatization have prevented the creation of more state enterprises.

If privatization does proceed, it is likely to lead to layoffs, which could cause considerable hardship, given Kenya's already high unemployment and underemployment. The government has already pledged to introduce redeployment programmes and social safety nets.

HUMAN DEVELOPMENT RANK	**127**
GNP PER CAPITA RANK	**144**
GNP PER CAPITA ANNUAL GROWTH RATE (1980–90)	**0.3%**
INFLATION RATE (1991)	**8.9%**
DEBT SERVICE RATIO (1990)	**34%**
CENTRAL GOVERNMENT EXPENDITURE AS % OF GNP (1990)	**31%**
TOTAL INVESTMENT AS % OF GDP (1990)	**24%**
PRIVATE SHARE OF TOTAL INVESTMENT (1970–74)	**60%**
PRIVATE SHARE OF TOTAL INVESTMENT (1991)	**55%**
FOREIGN DIRECT INVESTMENT INFLOWS AS % OF GROSS CAPITAL FORMATION (1986–89)	**1.4%**
NET OUTFLOW OF CENTRAL GOVERNMENT BUDGET TO PUBLIC ENTERPRISES AS % OF GDP (FISCAL 1991)	**1%**
NUMBER OF PUBLIC ENTERPRISES SOLD (1980–90)	**1**

Malaysia

Malaysia has a dynamic private sector and a large public sector. Fast economic growth has enabled substantial reductions in poverty. Privatization, so far not extensive, is likely to become more significant.

The exposure of Malaysia's dynamic private sector to a relatively liberal trade regime has ensured that it remains internationally competitive. The country has combined this with a relatively large public sector.

The government's major concern has been less the balance between private and public sectors than that between the levels of economic power of different ethnic groups. So, its New Economic Policy (NEP), adopted in 1971, was to promote economic growth while encouraging greater economic participation by the Bumiputras (Malays)—rather than by other Malaysians, mainly of Chinese and Indian origin. The Bumiputras are the indigenous people, forming the largest ethnic group and the largest number of poor. This effort included, for example, giving the Bumiputras preferential access to credit.

The policy appears to have been fairly successful at redistributing corporate assets. In 1980, foreigners owned 62%, other Malaysians 34% and Bumiputras 4%. By 1985, the figures had changed to foreigners 25%, other Malaysians 57% and Bumiputras 18%. Since 1990, the National Development Policy, successor to the NEP, has relaxed the quotas in favour of the Bumiputras but still aims at redistributing resources in their direction.

The government has also introduced more general economic liberalization measures. Since the early 1980s, it has:
- Liberalized investment licencing and foreign investment criteria
- Reformed the tax and tariff systems, increasing their simplicity and transparency
- Privatized state enterprises.

This has encouraged greater investment by the private sector—from 13% of GDP in 1970 to 24% in 1991. More than two-thirds of total investment is now private, though a significant proportion of this is foreign (one-third of paid-up capital in the industrial sector).

Even so, the state sector is still substantial—about 25% of GDP, among the highest proportions outside the world's (once) centrally planned economies. From 1970 onwards, the number of public enterprises grew rapidly as the state involved itself more in commerce and industry. In 1983, however, the government began to privatize these enterprises, starting with large enterprises in transport, infrastructure and telecommunications, such as the national airline and the container terminal. The privatization has also been managed to distribute ownership to Bumiputras and Bumiputra institutions, specifically reserving a part of all public share issues for them.

So far, the impact on the economy has been limited. Some enterprises have become more efficient, and privatization has helped develop the local capital market. But the volume remains small—between 1984 and 1989, total asset sales were less than 0.1% of GDP. And it is doubtful that the government has really decreased government control, since the assets merely passed to organizations of the ruling party. There is also the problem that government monopolies have in some cases, as with the container terminal, become private monopolies.

The process is nevertheless continuing. In 1991, 15 enterprises were privatized, including a cement factory and a shipyard. And some of the privatizations currently planned look much more significant—as with water and telecommunications, whose proceeds could be around 15% of GDP.

Malaysia is one of the world's fastest growing economies and has considerably reduced poverty—a demonstration that a sensible balance between private and public sectors can lead to rapid economic growth and good progress in human development.

HUMAN DEVELOPMENT RANK	57
GNP PER CAPITA RANK	66
GNP PER CAPITA ANNUAL GROWTH RATE (1980–90)	2.5%
INFLATION RATE (1991)	3.2%
DEBT SERVICE RATIO (1990)	11.7%
CENTRAL GOVERNMENT EXPENDITURE AS % OF GNP (1990)	31%
TOTAL INVESTMENT AS % OF GDP (1990)	34%
PRIVATE SHARE OF TOTAL INVESTMENT (1970–74)	69%
PRIVATE SHARE OF TOTAL INVESTMENT (1991)	68%
FOREIGN DIRECT INVESTMENT INFLOWS AS % OF GROSS CAPITAL FORMATION (1986–89)	9.6%
NUMBER OF PUBLIC ENTERPRISES SOLD (1980–90)	36

Poland

*Poland's three-year economic reform has in many ways been a remarkable
success. The economy has stabilized, and the private sector has enjoyed
sustained growth. But the benefits have not been shared equally: many
people in smaller towns and rural areas suffer from high unemployment.*

In the autumn of 1989, the Solidarity government inherited a catastrophic situation: declining output, widespread shortages and price increases close to hyperinflation. The new government acted quickly to stabilize the economy. At the beginning of 1990, it:

- Made drastic cuts in the budget, including reductions in consumer subsidies
- Increased interest rates to restrict credit growth
- Fixed the exchange rate to the US dollar
- Fully liberalized foreign trade.

External donors supported this package with a $1 billion stabilization loan and later wrote off a substantial part of Poland's external debt.

This "shock therapy" was the beginning of the transition towards a market economy. It brought a number of immediate benefits—significantly reducing inflation, eliminating shortages and stimulating an increase in exports to Western Europe and North America (which partly offset the collapse in trade with formerly socialist countries).

But the shock therapy also produced a sharp decline in economic activity. GDP fell by 12% in 1990 and by 7% in 1991. And during 1990–91, industrial output fell by 36% and employment by 14%.

More recently, the economy appears to be recovering. Inflation declined to about 43% in 1992. Economic growth in 1992 is estimated at about 1%, and growth in industrial production at 4%. Efficiency is on the increase in both the public and the private sectors, and industrial firms operate largely without subsidies. As an OECD study pointed out: "Except in the energy sector, the few subsidies that remain may be lower than those received on average by private firms in most OECD countries."

The Polish government has managed to build the infrastructure and legal framework for a market economy remarkably quickly. It has introduced laws to govern private property rights (in areas ranging from agricultural land transfer to urban land taxation) and developed bankruptcy legislation. But much still needs to be done to improve the financial system and the telecommunications infrastructure. And environmental standards are still low; for example, Polish industry is extremely inefficient in energy use.

Most of the privatization was initially concentrated on wholesale and retail trade. Lately, however, privatization has been carried out in broader areas, including manufacturing. By the end of 1992, around 97% of all shops were in private hands. And the availability of goods and the quality of service have increased dramatically.

The privatization process has generally been slower than expected. Most privatizations so far have been through liquidation methods, generally involving small and medium-size enterprises. About 50 enterprises have been privatized through capitalization methods (public offerings, trade sales and management and employee buyouts). The basic scheme for the Mass Privatization Programme has also been developed, but it has run into political obstacles.

Meanwhile, the urban private sector is growing rapidly under its own steam—particularly in services. By mid-1991, there were around 1.3 million individual private businesses in Poland (96% of which had fewer than five employees). During 1991–92, the number of domestic private companies rose by more than 20%. And about 58% of the employed workforce was in the private sector, including family farming.

In human development terms, most people are better off today than in the disastrous final days of central planning. But the gains have not been equally distributed. Most of the private sector growth has been in the big cities, where the younger and better-educated people have benefited most. Smaller towns have done less well, and in many agricultural regions unemployment is more than 20%.

HUMAN DEVELOPMENT RANK	**48**
GNP PER CAPITA RANK	**80**
GNP PER CAPITA ANNUAL GROWTH RATE (1980–90)	**1.2%**
INFLATION RATE (1991)	**65%**
DEBT SERVICE RATIO (1992)	**11.1%**
CENTRAL GOVERNMENT EXPENDITURE AS % OF GNP (1990)	**40%**
TOTAL INVESTMENT AS % OF GDP (1990)	**31%**
GOVERNMENT TRANSFERS AND SUBSIDIES TO PUBLIC ENTERPRISES AS % OF GDP (1989)	**9%**
NUMBER OF PUBLIC ENTERPRISES PRIVATIZED (1990–92)	**766**

Russia

Russia is undergoing a radical shift from a planned to a market economy in the midst of a deepening economic crisis. The government is going ahead with its privatization programme, distributing vouchers free to all citizens—though with unemployment widespread and increasing, most people are preoccupied with the struggle to survive.

The first serious attempt to open Russia's centrally planned economy to market forces was in 1987, when the former Soviet Union gave state-owned enterprises greater independence and more incentives to improve efficiency.

After Russia emerged as an independent nation, the government introduced "shock therapy" to stabilize the economy. At the beginning of 1992, it:
* Liberalized trade within the economy, removing price controls on almost all goods
* Sharply reduced government spending
* Introduced a value added tax
* Made the currency partly convertible.

Political considerations limited the extent of reform, which included almost no liberalization of foreign trade and continuing restrictions on access to hard currency. The government did cut the budget, but it failed to reach its deficit targets. At the same time, the central bank was making loans to industry at negative real interest rates, fuelling inflation and jeopardizing the stabilization programme.

Russia's economic situation deteriorated dramatically in 1992. Industrial output fell by at least 20% and inflation accelerated—by early 1993 it threatened to become hyperinflation.

The government is having to make radical changes to its economy at a time of economic crisis. It will, for example, have to find alternatives for much of the military industry, which accounts for 20% of employment and output. It will also have to use its resources more efficiently. At the end of 1992, oil was still being sold at only 20% of the world market price, encouraging inefficient use and adding to pollution. But raising the price sharply would be very painful for industries still inflexible in their use of technology.

In short, the government faces the stark choice between hyperinflation and mass unemployment. The external environment offers little help. Trade with the other newly independent states of the former Soviet Union has sharply declined, and trade with Eastern Europe has virtually disappeared. Unlike most of Eastern Europe, Russia has been unable to reorient its economy to western markets, and exports have fallen dramatically. Foreign donors have promised some assistance, but of the $24 billion pledged, less than half had been paid in 1992.

Despite the crisis, the government is still pursuing an ambitious privatization programme. This started with smaller enterprises, such as municipally owned shops. In the first half of 1992, nearly half the shops in Moscow and St. Petersburg were privatized. Now, it is moving on to larger undertakings. In 1993, the government plans to sell 5,000 large enterprises. To achieve this, it is distributing vouchers free to all citizens, who can sell them if they prefer cash in their hands today, or use them to buy privatized assets.

Agriculture is still dominated by state farms and large cooperatives—though management decisions and incentives for workers are increasingly being guided by market forces. And from the middle of 1992, it was planned that these farms would become joint-stock companies owned by the workers. As in the former Soviet Union, workers are also allowed their own small plots and can sell their produce on the open market. Private farming is increasing, but it still accounts for only about 3% of agricultural production.

Markets are developing very rapidly in Russia, but they are not proving very people-friendly. Studies by the ILO reveal massive poverty and deprivation. Real wages in 1992 fell by more than 40%—at the beginning of 1993 they were as low as $10 per month. Unemployment is expected to increase further because of the demobilization of much of the armed forces.

The Russian people now have great difficulty making ends meet. In late 1992, about 75% of family expenditure was going for food, and an estimated 80% of the population was below the poverty line.

HUMAN DEVELOPMENT RANK	37
GNP PER CAPITA RANK	47
INFLATION RATE (1991)	105%
CENTRAL GOVERNMENT EXPENDITURE AS % OF GNP (1990)	47%
TOTAL INVESTMENT AS % OF GDP (1990)	33%

Viet Nam

Viet Nam is undergoing a rapid transition, and many new enterprises have sprung up following its economic liberalization. Public enterprises are becoming more efficient, and some will be privatized. Most of the population has benefited from these changes, but unemployment has now become serious.

Viet Nam is changing rapidly. Since 1987, through its *doi moi* (renovation) policy, the government has started to transform the country into a socialist market economy. It introduced some agricultural reforms in 1988—giving farmers greater incentives to work land privately, lifting price controls and removing the requirement to deliver a quota of rice production to the government. Farmers were given long-term rights to land, but landownership is still vested in the state. Since 1989, the government has:

- Legalized private enterprise
- Liberalized prices
- Lifted controls on domestic trade
- Reorganized the tax system
- Introduced a managed float for the currency
- Given public enterprises greater autonomy and decreased their subsidies.

Viet Nam has recently faced a very hostile economic environment. Its major aid donor and trading partner, the Soviet Union, has disappeared (between 1988 and 1990, Soviet assistance amounted to 6% of GDP), and the United States sustains a trade and investment embargo. Nevertheless, Viet Nam's output grew about 4% in 1991 and growth in 1992 is estimated at 8%.

The non-state sector produces about 75% of GDP—in industry about 45%, and in agriculture (about half of GDP) 97%. Non-state industrial output comes from "households", cooperatives, private enterprises and "manufacturing groups".

Since private enterprise was legalized, family-based enterprises have restored many crafts, such as shoe making, tailoring and furniture making. And such cottage industries as silk weaving and ceramics have also revived. For some products, such as leather shoes for the domestic market, the non-state sector now dominates. All this has helped increase the supply of consumer products. The non-state sector has also increased its share of employment and now accounts for 88% of total employment. Most of these jobs (80%) are in agriculture, largely in cooperatives.

HUMAN DEVELOPMENT RANK	**115**
GNP PER CAPITA RANK	**156**
INFLATION RATE (1991)	**83%**
LOSSES OF PUBLIC ENTERPRISES AS % OF GDP (1987)	**5%**

Enterprises still find it difficult to get credit, however. Banks are relatively underdeveloped, and most of the loans go to state enterprises. Some foreign capital is arriving, particularly from other East Asian countries, and beginning to have a significant impact, particularly in urban areas.

State organizations still play an important role in wholesale trade, but the share of the state in domestic trade fell from 41% in 1987 to about 25% in 1991. Market prices prevail for more than 80% of state enterprises' output and for nearly all agricultural produce.

Although Viet Nam is a socialist country, its 12,000 state enterprises account for only one-quarter of GDP. Few of these are large: even in industry, the median size is 225 employees. About one-third of state enterprises were making losses in the late 1980s.

The government is increasing the efficiency of state enterprises by cutting their workforces. Between 1988 and 1990, their share of the total labour force fell from 14.2% to 11.9%.

Ownership of these enterprises may follow one of several paths. The state will retain ones related to state security, such as electricity and railways. It might also retain some of the more profitable ones, such as cigarette manufacturing and breweries (though there may also be joint ventures for these). Others will probably be converted into joint-stock companies in which the state retains some equity interest. Still others are likely to be liquidated when a new bankruptcy law comes into force.

Unemployment and underemployment have become very serious. People have been laid off from state enterprises, and half a million soldiers were demobilized after the withdrawal of forces from Cambodia. It will take some time for them to be absorbed into the economy.

Most of the population is, however, already gaining from the reforms. Over the past five years, income has increased about 6% a year, and the majority of the population has benefited from the liberalizations in agriculture.

CHAPTER 4

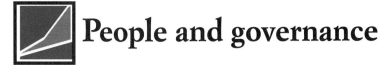 **People and governance**

The 1980s saw a move away from authoritarian rule towards greater political freedom and democracy. A positive trend, but there is still some way to go before people in developing countries are truly in command of their lives. Even where citizens can elect their leaders in regular, free and fair elections, they seldom have achieved full political participation. If people in developing countries are to influence development, the trend towards democracy will have to widen and deepen.

Participation in shaping governance

The movement towards democracy in the 1980s was partly a result of internal weaknesses in authoritarian regimes. Their claims to rule had been based on the promise of firm government that could establish order and promote economic growth. When growth faltered, particularly in Africa and Latin America, their legitimacy was undermined. In Brazil, the economic slowdown of the 1980s made it difficult for the military to justify what already was an unpopular rule. Internal disagreements on political and economic strategy further undermined the regime, and this enabled popular pressure to force a transition to democracy, as in other Latin American countries. Elsewhere, popular movements were the most significant element in forcing changes—most notably in Eastern Europe, Africa and the Philippines, where a broad coalition of popular organizations united against a corrupt regime.

These democratic movements are spreading. International media make people in the remotest areas aware of political unrest on the other side of the globe and inspire them to make similar demands—as many governments in Africa and the Arab States are now discovering. The reason in many cases is that governments are failing economically. But even where governments have been alleviating poverty, as in China and the Republic of Korea, people sooner or later want greater democracy.

There have also been attempts by outsiders to promote or encourage democracy—say, by making aid conditional on democratic reforms. While often an expression of shared concern for universal human rights, it can be counter-productive. It can antagonize people unnecessarily and undermine those pressing for democratic change—and it might not produce enduring change. Democracy is not a matter of one decision or of hastily organized elections. Democracy requires a long process of political development. And given the immense diversity of possible political forms, it is unlikely that the demands of outsiders will match another country's real needs.

People everywhere want to determine their own destiny. The kind of democracy they choose need not follow the models of Western Europe or North America—it usually has to be adapted to local circumstances. But the formal structure a country opts for, whatever it is, is only the starting point in a long process of facilitating effective forms of popular participation.

Democracy brings its own problems. One immediate difficulty is managing competing claims of different classes, ethnic groups and political actors. Developing countries are especially vulnerable because the state often controls a big part of the country's economic resources. When these resources are allocated by government decision, the rewards for influence can be very

Democracy is not a matter of one decision or of hastily organized elections

high. And if everyone makes claims at once, the outcome can be chaos.

The central problem for many developing countries is that they lack strong democratic institutions. Democracies, to work, need much more than voting booths. They also need stable political parties that can themselves draw together many diverse interests and weave them into a cohesive organization. And they need independent groups—farmers' organizations, trade unions, consumer groups, chambers of commerce, cultural and religious groups—and all the other elements of a civil society that systematically facilitate and regulate the process of articulating people's demands.

Building these institutions takes time—and constant renewal, if they are not to become instruments for a small elite to manipulate the levers of power.

Whether the leaders of new democracies always recognize the need for strong and democratic civil institutions is far from clear. In many countries, the prognosis is not good. Even in India, where political institutions were once strong and taken for granted, populist leaders pursuing their narrow goals have been weakening the instruments of democratic rule. Secularism, enshrined in the Indian constitution as the very foundation of the state, is now gravely threatened by the rising tide of communalism and fundamentalism.

There are also dangers from the other direction—from the creation of new forms of central control. Many countries are going through two difficult processes simultaneously—democratization and economic liberalization—straining the political capacities of many a newly elected leader. In Brazil and Russia, there is the risk of "two-track" democracy. Once elected, the government might want to be as free as possible from popular control in order to carry out unpopular reforms—negating the major goal of broadening political participation.

In many countries, it has therefore been found necessary to complement democratization with efforts aimed at enhanced transparency and accountability of government. Because it is one thing for people to be able to elect their representatives and another for them to be able to know and influence what policies the representatives pursue once they are elected.

In recent years, there has in many countries been a marked improvement in people's opportunities to take part in selecting governments. Yet governments still are quite removed and distant from people, especially in the case of their implementing arm—governmental bureaucracy and governmental programmes and projects. Many developing countries have, after gaining independence, initially emphasized efforts to build a nation-state. This has often had a highly centralizing effect. And external assistance, which in many countries forms a large part of the national budget, has only helped to reinforce these trends.

The following sections examine how governments reach out to people—and, in particular, how decentralization helps improve human development.

Decentralizing governance to increase local decision-making

Decentralizing governance—from capital cities to regions, towns and villages—can be one of the best means of promoting participation and efficiency. Local officials and politicians can be much more open to public scrutiny than national governments—and more accountable to the communities and individuals they are supposed to serve. And public projects—be they dams, roads, schools or health programmes—all become much more relevant and effective if the communities concerned have a real say in their planning and implementation.

Decentralization can take several forms: it might, for example, be horizontal or vertical. *Horizontal* decentralization disperses power among institutions at the same level—a government's spending decisions, rather than being concentrated in an all-powerful finance ministry, might be spread across different ministries. *Vertical* decentralization, which is more important, allows some of the powers of central government to be delegated downwards to lower tiers of authority—to states in federal countries, for example, and then further

Decentralizing governance is one of the best means of promoting participation and efficiency

down to regional and local governments, or even to village associations.

Vertical decentralization of government can itself take three forms:

• *Deconcentration*—This is limited to passing down only administrative discretion—to local offices of central government ministries, for example. Although it does result in some dispersal of power, few decisions can be taken without reference to the centre.

• *Delegation*—This involves passing some authority and decision-making powers to local officials. But central government retains the right to overturn local decisions and can, at any time, take these powers back.

• *Devolution*—The strongest form of decentralization: granting decision-making powers to local authorities and allowing them to take full responsibility without reference back to central government. This includes financial power as well as the authority to design and execute local development projects and programmes.

Why governance is not decentralized

In most developing countries, decentralization has generally been limited to deconcentration. Even Chile, Indonesia, Morocco and Zimbabwe have dispersed relatively little real power. All four have ostensibly autonomous levels of local government—the municipalities in Chile, the villages in Indonesia, the communes in Morocco and the district councils in Zimbabwe. But the resources they control are small, their decision-making powers narrow and many local appointments are imposed from above. (The country studies at the end of this chapter highlight the decentralization experience in these four countries. They are based on field studies and sample surveys, and their data do not always correspond to the tables in this chapter.)

In industrial countries, much social spending tends to be centralized—especially that for social security benefits. France, for example, spends nearly 20% of its GDP on social security. And other forms of social spending (such as education) may also be controlled centrally when there is a national consensus on the minimum standards that should prevail throughout the country. Nevertheless, local governments in many industrial countries do have considerable powers to raise revenue, and many spend substantial sums on social concerns.

The position is very different in developing countries. Social security systems are relatively weak, or non-existent, and so do not have the same centralizing influence. The explanations for concentration lie elsewhere.

1. *Centralization for nation-building*—Many countries lack democratic institutions and traditions—partly a legacy from colonial times. The colonial powers tried wherever possible to concentrate finance and decision-making in the capital. And the newly independent countries continued this practice, partly to enhance their political and economic control, but also because they were convinced that the state should assume the major responsibility for economic development and "nation building". This resulted in an overwhelming concentration of national power in the hands of central governments, as well as a massive accumulation of rules and regulations. Some countries have started to liberalize these controls, but there is still a long way to go.

2. *Weak democracy*—Many governments have been ruled in a non-democratic way with authoritarian structures. This perpetuates strong centralizing tendencies as central governments seek to maintain complete control. In the absence of democratic structures, local governments lack an effective political power base from which to generate local control over decision-making.

3. *Low social spending*—Many governments devote a high proportion of their budgets to centrally controlled military expenditure. Social spending, which has a greater potential for decentralization, tends to take up a smaller proportion of public allocations.

4. *Urban bias*—Most countries have a bias in social spending towards urban areas and more "prestigious" forms of service delivery: the city hospital rather than the rural health clinic, the elite university rather than

In the absence of democratic structures, local governments lack an effective power base

the provision of basic education for the mass of the people. These large and expensive items are usually the prerogative of central rather than local government.

5. *Foreign aid*—Also tending to have a centralizing influence, most forms of international assistance are negotiated by central governments which, when required, must also take responsibility for repayment of loans. This does not mean, however, that the aid need necessarily be spent centrally. Some countries do manage to delegate the implementation of development projects to local government. Indeed, some donors, particularly the Nordic countries, insist that management of projects, wherever appropriate, be executed by local governments or NGOs. But in practice, aid expenditure is still quite centralized. It would be useful if donors published annual estimates of the percentage of aid they channel through local governments.

The composition of aid also has a centralizing effect. Most aid is directed to large infrastructure projects, and only 15% goes to the social sectors—and less than half of this (6.5% of total official development assistance) is earmarked for human priority concerns that could normally be implemented locally. In addition, a large amount of assistance is for military purposes.

Measuring the decentralization of expenditure

It would be useful to compare the extent of decentralization between one country and another. This is difficult, however, primarily because there are no statistical measures for many aspects of decentralization. There could, for example, be substantial local autonomy in the way the judicial system works, or in the police force or in social and cultural affairs—all difficult to quantify. But the discussion here concentrates on financial flows between central and local government and on the distribution of government employees—which are more open to objective analysis. For many countries, even these data are unavailable or incomplete. The central government might appear to decentralize expenditure, but if it retains tight control over standards and priorities, such financial delegation may be meaningless.

Local spending should also take into account the contributions local people make to self-help projects "in kind"—through time and materials. Because this is often difficult to quantify, local spending is generally underestimated.

Cross-national comparisons of decentralization should, in addition, allow for the size of countries (table 4.1), with decentral-

Most foreign aid has a centralizing effect

TABLE 4.1
Governance structure in selected developing countries

Country	Total 1991 population (millions)	Largest state or province			Largest local body		
		Name	Population (millions)	Percentage of total	Name	Population (thousands)	Percentage of total
India	863	Uttar Pradesh	138.8	16.1	Midnapur	8,350	1.0
China	1,171	Sichuan	107.2	9.2	Ghao Yang	1,999	0.2
Pakistan	122	Punjab	62.3	51.3	Faisalabad	5,962	4.9
Indonesia	188	Jawa Barat	35.4	18.9	Lampung Tengah Regency	1,900	1.0
Bangladesh	116	Dhaka	32.3	27.7	Dhaka	5,775	5.0
Brazil	152	Sao Paulo	26.9	17.7	São Paulo	10,063	6.6
Mexico	86	Mexico	9.8	11.4	Guadalajara	1,629	1.9
Egypt	54	Cairo Governorate	6.5	12.1	..	..	..
Nigeria	112	Kano	5.6	5.0	Ojo	1,012	0.9
Zaire	39	Kivu	5.4	14.0	Word Kivu	2,434	6.3
Kenya	24	Eastern	4.4	18.0	..	..	..
Colombia	33	Antioquia	3.9	11.9	Medillin	1,468	4.5
Ecuador	11	Guayas	2.0	18.5	Guayaquil	1,328	12.3
Algeria	26	Algiers	1.7	6.6	Oran	610	2.4
Cameroon	12	Extreme-Nord	1.7	14.3	Douala III	399	3.4
Panama	3	Panama	1.1	44.0	Panama	585	23.4
Congo	2	Brazzaville	0.6	26.1	Pool	184	8.0

ization a higher priority for large countries than for small ones: the degree of decentralization acceptable for India would not be suitable for Jamaica. The population of one state in India, Uttar Pradesh, exceeds the populations of 168 member states of the United Nations. Larger countries need more layers of government than smaller ones—just to ensure that the smallest units are a manageable size.

All quantitative estimates of decentralization should thus be treated with caution, always to be complemented by a broader knowledge and understanding of the countries concerned.

With these qualifications, tables 4.2 to 4.4 express the financial decentralization using several statistical ratios.

1. *The expenditure decentralization ratio*—the percentage of total government expenditure spent by local governments.
2. *The modified expenditure decentralization ratio*—takes into account the fact that some government expenditure cannot be decentralized (specifically defence and debt servicing). Subtracting such expenditures gives a modified expenditure ratio that expresses the degree of decentralization of responsibilities that can, in practice, be decentralized.
3. *The revenue decentralization ratio*—assesses the significance of local taxation. It is the percentage of local government revenue in total government revenue.
4. *The financial autonomy ratio*—gives an indication of local government's independence from central government funding. It is the percentage of locally raised revenue in total local expenditure.

The ratios reveal some interesting contrasts between industrial and developing countries (tables 4.2 and 4.3). In industrial countries, local governments normally account for 20–35% of total government expenditure, and in some countries the expenditure decentralization ratios are even higher—45% in Denmark and 41% in Finland. In developing countries, however, the ratio is usually below 15%. Even modifying the ratio to exclude defence and debt servicing does not significantly improve the

position. Except for the Republic of Korea and Zimbabwe, the decentralization of public expenditure in developing countries is extremely limited.

A similar picture emerges from a comparison of revenue decentralization ratios. In industrial countries, local governments exert considerable taxation authority, and account for about 25% of total government revenue. In most developing countries,

TABLE 4.2
Financial decentralization in local government in selected countries

Country	Year	Expenditure decentralization ratio		Revenue decentralization ratio[c]	Financial autonomy ratio[d]
		Total[a]	Modified[b]		
Developing countries					
Korea, Rep. of	1987	33	..	31	99
Zimbabwe	1986	22	29	17	58
Nigeria	1988	17	..	..	..
Algeria	1986	14	..	16	101
Bangladesh	1987/88	12	..	8	39
South Africa	1988	10	11	10	79
Chile	1988	8	10	6	61
Brazil	1989	7	14	1	33
Thailand	1990	7	10	4	75
Philippines	1988	6	..	7	119
Morocco	1987	6	..	8	108
Paraguay	1989	4	5	3	88
Kenya	1989	4	5	7	134
Pakistan	1987/88	4	..	6	100
Costa Rica	1988	3	..	3	123
Ghana	1988	2	..	2	71
Côte d'Ivoire	1985	2	..	2	115
Industrial countries					
Denmark	1988	45	51	31	58
Finland	1989	41	43	29	63
Sweden	1989	37	42	30	78
Norway	1990	31	35	21	59
Poland	1988	27	27	23	78
United Kingdom	1989	26	31	16	55
Czechoslovakia	1990	26	27	19	61
Ireland	1989	23	28	10	33
Netherlands	1990	23	26	5	16
Iceland	1986	23	25	26	99
Switzerland	1984	22	24	22	87
USA	1989	21	26	16	65
Hungary	1990	19	21	11	53
France	1988	18	19	12	63
Germany	1988	17	18	14	73
Austria	1990	16	18	17	89
Canada	1989	16	18	11	53
Luxembourg	1988	15	16	7	42
Spain	1988	13	14	10	62
Belgium	1987	12	15	6	41
Romania	1989	9	10	8	103
Australia	1990	5	6	5	83

a. Local government expenditure as a percentage of total government expenditure.
b. Local government expenditure as a percentage of total government expenditure less defence expenditure less debt servicing.
c. Local government revenue as a percentage of total government revenue.
d. Local government revenue as a percentage of local government expenditure.

however, local authorities raise only around 6% (the Republic of Korea and Zimbabwe are again exceptions). Industrial countries have a wide range of local taxation options: property taxes, sales taxes, income taxes and user charges. Developing countries, by contrast, tend even at the national level to rely less on taxes on individuals and more on centralized sources like corporation tax or import duties, and the taxation options are fewer still at the local level.

International comparisons produce a curious result when it comes to financial autonomy ratios. The ratios for industrial and developing countries turn out to be much the same—in both cases, local governments control about 60% of local spending. But this covers two very different realities. In industrial countries, local governments have 60% control over a significant proportion of public spending. In developing countries, where local spending is smaller in the first place, local authorities control 60% of very little.

To discover the proportion of total expenditure controlled by local governments,

multiply the financial autonomy ratio by the decentralization ratio. For industrial countries, this produces a figure of about 25%, compared with 5% for developing countries. The available data do suggest, therefore, the limited decentralization in developing countries. Although several countries have, in recent years, attempted decentralization, few have made significant progress.

Industrial countries are also more decentralized than developing countries in the distribution of government employees. This can be expressed through the employment decentralization ratio: local government employees as a percentage of all government employees. A sample of 16 industrial and 31 developing countries for the late 1970s showed that in the industrial countries the ratio was 42%—compared with 21% in Asia, 19% in Latin America and only 10% in Africa.

Another key indicator of decentralization is control of social spending. It is generally presumed that when local governments are responsible for education or health, for example, they use the resources more efficiently and effectively, distribute the benefits more equitably and generally respond more sensitively than central governments to the needs of the local community (the validity of this presumption is discussed later).

The distribution of social spending can also be analysed through a series of ratios:

1. *The central government social allocation ratio*—the percentage of the central government budget devoted to social spending.
2. *The local government social allocation ratio*—the percentage of local government budgets devoted to social spending.
3. *The social expenditure decentralization ratio*—local government social spending as a proportion of total government social spending. This indicates the extent to which social spending is decentralized.
4. *The human priority ratios*—for both central and local governments, the percentage of their social spending devoted to social items that deserve first priority in most developing countries—basic education, primary health care, safe drinking water,

TABLE 4.3

Financial decentralization in provincial government in selected countries

Country	Year	Expenditure decentralization ratio		Revenue decentralization ratio[c]	Financial autonomy ratio[d]
		Total[a]	Modified[b]		
Developing countries					
Nigeria	1988	68	..	..	..
China	1991	60	..	61	96
Costa Rica	1988	48	..	40	96
India	1988	44	56	32	48
Argentina	1987	39	43	21	38
Pakistan	1987/88	24	..	18	50
Brazil	1989	21	42	8	80
Malaysia	1990	15	18	11	67
Bolivia	1990	13	15	10	65
South Africa	1988	11	12	2	17
Indonesia	1989	10	13	3	21
Mexico	1987	7	17	12	99
Algeria	1986	3	..	3	105
Industrial countries					
Canada	1989	41	47	41	79
Australia	1990	37	41	23	53
Switzerland	1984	30	32	25	74
Germany	1988	24	26	22	80
USA	1989	23	30	24	86
Austria	1990	13	15	10	67
Spain	1988	11	13	4	30

a. Provincial government expenditure as a percentage of total government expenditure.
b. Provincial government expenditure as a percentage of total government expenditure less defence expenditure less debt servicing.
c. Provincial government revenue as a percentage of total government revenue.
d. Provincial government revenue as a percentage of provincial government expenditure.

family planning services and nutrition programmes.

Social provision ultimately appears almost entirely at the local level in terms of clinics or schools or welfare services. So control over this could, in theory, be highly decentralized. In practice, this does not happen—in either industrial or developing countries (table 4.4). *Equity* considerations may well point to a critical role for the centre in social expenditure, especially in reallocating resources from better-off to worse-off regions—and in ensuring a *minimum* degree of participation.

For 15 industrial countries for which data are available, the social expenditure decentralization ratios are generally around 25%—significantly lower, in fact, than the 40% average for their decentralization ratio for total expenditure. Social spending is most highly centralized in Australia, France, Luxembourg and Romania. Denmark delegates more than half its budget to the local level.

The situation is worse in developing countries. In most, the social decentralization ratio is only around 5–6%, with central governments responsible for over 90% of total social spending.

The available statistical evidence is sketchy and inadequate because governments of developing countries do not make a concerted effort to collect and publish data on expenditure patterns at all significant levels: central, state, provincial and local. The World Bank and the International Monetary Fund (IMF) do little better—collecting and publishing only central government budgets, even though much of the social spending in large federal states such as Brazil or India is at the state or local level. Even their information on central budgets contains little useful detail on social spending priorities.

The lack of statistical evidence on decentralization means that this important issue is often subject to sweeping generalizations and unsustained assertions. A coherent reporting system is needed, with contributions from:
• *National governments*—which could publish all their central, provincial and local budgets, with details of social and human priority expenditure.
• *Donors*—which could give similar details on aid, indicating its distribution at the various levels of government as well as through NGOs.
• *The World Bank and the IMF*—which could collect and publish consolidated social expenditure budgets, subdivided into human priority expenditures, for each different level of government, in cooperation with other international agencies.

Such information would illuminate the links between decentralization and human development and permit a more thorough analysis than is currently possible.

Resources for decentralization

A shift to decentralization not only affects the way resources are spent—it affects the way money can be collected. It could, for example, allow more taxes to be raised locally if people are confident that their money will be used for the benefit of their own

TABLE 4.4
Social expenditure decentralization ratio in selected countries

Country	Year	Social allocation ratio[a]			Social decentralization ratio[b]	
		Central	Provincial	Local	Provincial	Local
Developing countries						
Chile	1988	46	..	31	..	6
Argentina	1987	41	35	..	36	..
Nigeria	1988	39	24	9	69	7
Zimbabwe	1986	32	..	34	..	23
Kenya	1989	25	..	22	..	3
Malawi	1984	21	..	22	..	6
Indonesia	1989	10	50	..	35	..
India	1988	5	35	..	85	..
Colombia	1984	..	67	35	85	15
Industrial countries						
Germany	1988	68	48	47	20	13
Austria	1990	67	62	..	15	..
France	1988	67	..	39	..	11
Switzerland	1984	66	55	46	28	18
Luxembourg	1988	59	..	24	..	7
United Kingdom	1989	49	..	43	..	23
Denmark	1988	48	..	81	..	58
Iceland	1986	48	..	49	..	24
Australia	1990	48	50	6	40	1
Canada	1989	44	62	50	49	15
USA	1989	41	68	59	31	24
Hungary	1990	40	..	55	..	25
Romania	1989	34	..	18	..	5
Czechoslovakia	1990	25	..	49	..	40

a. Central/provincial/local government social expenditure as a percentage of total central/provincial/local government expenditure.
b. Provincial/local government social expenditure as a percentage of total social sector expenditure.

communities. The main ways of increasing local revenue are through taxation, cost recovery, voluntary contributions and borrowing.

Taxation

Central governments tend to leave local governments relatively little flexibility when it comes to taxation—partly because central governments want to reserve for themselves the most buoyant and lucrative revenues, but also because they generally like to keep tight control over local government finances.

These controls determine, first of all, what kind of taxes can be raised. In Nigeria, local councils must get central approval before including any levy in their revenue estimates. Then there are controls over taxation rates. In Bangladesh, the rates of taxes levied by the *zila parishad* (district council) have to be approved by the district commissioner—a central government appointee.

Urban local authorities tend to be somewhat better off in this respect than rural ones. They generally have more political influence with the centre—as well as wealthier and more diverse communities to tax. In Zimbabwe, the urban councils usually manage to finance all their recurrent expenditure from their own revenue, while the rural district councils manage to finance only about 15%.

The most common form of local tax in both urban and rural areas is on property. In the Philippines, the property tax accounts for more than two-thirds of local tax revenues, and it is the mainstay of many other local taxation systems in Asia, including China, India, Pakistan and the Republic of Korea. It is such a significant source of revenue that in some cases, including Chile and Indonesia, the revenue is shared between central and local governments.

A World Bank survey of 14 major Third World cities in the mid-1970s showed that, for four of them, property taxes represented more than half of local revenue, and for five more, more than a third.

In the rural areas, the most significant property taxes are applied to land—and

produce substantial revenues. But they are often difficult to collect from rural elites and from other farmers who may resist payment when agricultural prices are low. Some countries have tried to index land taxes to crop prices, but since such indexation does not take productivity increases into account, revenue tends to lag behind agricultural incomes.

The next most common taxes are those based on motor vehicles and entertainment. And some of the poorer authorities also derive significant income from minor charges on local businesses, particularly through trading licences. Individual countries also produce many specific local taxes: in Indonesia, local taxes have been levied on cash-crop exports.

Even when local governments in developing countries are allowed to levy taxes, they often have great difficulty in collecting them, probably because of strong resistance from potential payers. In Zimbabwe between 1985 and 1988, local governments managed to collect only 16% of the "development levy", a type of poll tax that was widely resented.

A more common problem is that local governments lack the administrative capability. Property taxes, for example, require fairly regular surveys. In Baranquilla, Colombia, only three of the city's ten districts have had recent surveys—so the city collects revenues from less than half the taxable properties. And in Monrovia, Liberia, the land adjudication teams lack the necessary logistical support and have never been able to collect property taxes. Similar problems can arise in rural areas.

Local political influence can also reduce potential revenue. In Nigeria, local taxation has allegedly been used as a political weapon—supporters of the governing party are exempt, while members of opposition parties are overassessed. In Iloilo City, Philippines, the city's revenue has been undermined by the strong representation of property owners on the city's decision-making bodies—contributing to a gross underassessment of property values and the granting of numerous exemptions.

As administration systems improve, however, there have in places been consid-

More efficient collection and enforcement can also boost revenue

erable improvements in local tax collection. In Accra, Ghana, the city council computerized its budgeting and accounting procedures and restructured its Land Valuation Board—and so increased its revenue considerably in the second half of the 1980s.

More efficient forms of collection and enforcement can also boost revenue. New Delhi, India, with an improved management information system, can now offer rebates for those who pay on time and penalize those who pay late. Taxpayers also now have to pay their assessments before being allowed to appeal in court. These and other reforms produced significant increases in revenue, 16% in 1986 and 96% in 1987.

Revenue also rises as the opportunities for taxation increase. Car taxes are likely to prove a more important source of revenue in many developing countries. In Seoul, Republic of Korea, while total local tax revenue increased by 64% between 1982 and 1986, the automobile tax revenue more than doubled.

User charges

Local authorities can also raise revenue by charging users for services. In 25 countries surveyed by the World Bank, user charges accounted for nearly a third of all locally raised revenue.

Although businesses can reasonably be charged for many services, such as garbage collection, great care needs to be taken in charges for individuals, particularly for such social services as education or health care. Charges can deter many of the poorest users and cause considerable hardship—while raising relatively little money.

Human Development Report 1991 examined this issue at some length, concluding that some services should always be free: specifically primary health care (though there could in some cases be charges for drugs and hospital care) and basic education. The case is also strong for free secondary education. And for water and sanitation, the Report concluded that governments should bear the capital costs but that users might contribute to recurrent costs.

A slightly different kind of user charge can be levied on businesses that benefit from local authorities' investment in infrastructure. These "betterment levies" have been used extensively in Colombia, India and Indonesia as a way of recovering costs from landowners who benefit from public improvements on or near their property. In New Delhi, such charges have been used to recover 50% of the costs of public works. Sometimes these payments can be made in kind—often by giving some private land to the local authority—a system used successfully in the Republic of Korea, Taiwan (province of China) and Thailand.

Voluntary contributions

One advantage that local government has over central government is the ability to tap local voluntary contributions, in cash or in kind. This has proved valuable in the *harambee* movement in Kenya and the Tesito movement in the Gambia.

But such contributions are not always very effective, possibly because of poor coordination between voluntary groups and local authorities.

A common problem is that local people may be enthusiastic about building a school or a health centre, but the question of who is to finance the subsequent running costs is left open. In some countries, schools have been built with local labour on the understanding that they would then be supported by central government, and when this has not materialized they have stood empty for want of teachers.

There can also be questions about just how voluntary this labour is. In India, Indonesia and Nepal, university students are required to "volunteer" to help supervise and implement small-scale rural development projects. In some African countries, including Tanzania, local people can also be obliged to work on "self-help" development projects or suffer a fine or confiscation of property. Voluntary contributions should, however, be kept in proper perspective. One can never hope to finance projects having collective benefits entirely from individual voluntary contributions. Some element of social mobilization may be necessary and

Some services should always be free: specifically primary health care and basic education

acceptable, as long as it consists of encouragement and persuasion.

Borrowing

National governments are increasingly allowing local authorities to borrow to finance improvements in infrastructure, especially when local governments can subsequently be charged fees to recover costs.

An inherent danger here is that the central government could lose control over the national creation of credit—and macroeconomic management. So, the centre might have to either exert some kind of control over local government borrowing or adjust its fiscal and monetary policies to compensate.

An alternative way of financing local government investment is through special funds. In Jordan, the central government has an autonomous Cities and Villages Development Bank to provide investment finance and technical assistance to municipal and village councils. This has helped finance improvements throughout the country, bringing roads, schools, clinics and water supplies to even the smallest and most remote communities.

The same kind of arrangement can be made between lower levels of government. In Brazil, the state governments of Santa Catarina and Paraná have set up funds from which creditworthy municipalities can borrow for capital investment. There are some conditions, however. The municipalities have to be prepared to accept technical assistance to help them increase their capacity to raise revenue locally. And the federal government sets limits on the amount of debt and debt service that the municipalities can incur.

These types of funds have often been established with international aid. The Regional Development Fund in Chile is partly financed by the Inter-American Development Bank. This enables money to go straight to local authorities rather than passing through the central government—though generally, the central government still has to approve projects.

The fact that local authorities can raise their own funds could, in theory, expand to-

tal government expenditure. On the other hand, decentralizing public services might reduce costs and total expenditure. The fact is, however, that there is little conclusive evidence on the effect of decentralization on total public expenditure.

Decentralization in practice

One presumed benefit of decentralization is that local governments, being closer to the people and more responsive to local needs, make better use of resources—and that they will direct them at such human priority concerns as basic education and primary health care. But there's not enough data to test this hypothesis thoroughly. The discussion in this Report is based partly on four detailed case studies—Chile, Indonesia, Morocco and Zimbabwe—as well as a less systematic body of evidence. So, the conclusions reached can only be suggestive.

One issue the case studies highlight is that of choice. It was possible to investigate whether local governments that raised more of their own funds locally tended to use these more for social needs—that is, whether local bodies with greater financial autonomy ratios tended to have higher social allocation ratios. In Indonesia, this pattern appeared to be true at the provincial level, but the opposite was observed at the village level. In Zimbabwe, for a small sample of district councils, the results were also contrary to expectations: the higher the financial autonomy ratio, the lower the social allocation ratio. But this was largely due to the fact that central government transfers for basic education both reduced local financial autonomy and raised priority ratios.

The case studies suggest that decentralization would favour expenditure on human development. But this may not be true elsewhere. Many countries have local power structures dominated by elites little interested in human development. In Pakistan in 1985, members of parliament were each allocated a sum of money from the national budget to be devoted to development projects that met the needs of their constituencies. Most chose infrastructure priorities or more prestigious colleges and hospitals. Few chose primary schools or ba-

Many local power structures are dominated by elites little interested in human development

sic village health units. If the central government had not specified that at least 50% be devoted to basic education and primary health care, these concerns would have been neglected.

Since participation has thus far been quite limited, it is difficult to make a systematic assessment of its impact. This section therefore draws together some of the available information to help illustrate the major issues—showing what has happened in practice, what has worked and what has failed—summarized under efficiency, equity, economic participation and political participation.

Efficiency

In theory, decentralization should improve efficiency. At the outset, projects would be better able to match local needs. And with projects monitored locally, lines of communication should be shorter, with fewer delays due to conflicts between project staff and the beneficiaries.

One of the most important benefits of decentralization is the opportunity to cut costs, in several ways. First, if local people feel that it is their money being spent, they are likely to keep a tighter lid on expenditure and to use resources more efficiently. In the Philippines, schools that rely more heavily on local funding are more efficient, and operate with lower unit costs, than comparable schools financed centrally. Similarly, in the Indian state of Karnataka, the involvement of local people through the *gram sabhas* (village meetings) led to a notable improvement in the attendance of teachers when they became more accountable to the local community.

Involving local people can also result in a more appropriate structure of services, particularly in health care. In Tamil Nadu in India, local community health workers have proved superior to junior doctors and nurses on health projects. Not only are they more effective—they cost up to 75% less.

Local involvement also opens up the opportunity for people to add voluntary contributions to amplify a programme or project's impact. In Kenya, high levels of local participation in the Rural Access Roads Programme encouraged people to donate land to the project—and permitted the construction of 150 extra kilometres of roads, which would otherwise not have been built.

Some of the most effective contributions as a result of decentralization come from local labour and materials. In the Baglung district of Nepal, local committees working under the auspices of village councils built 62 bridges with little outside help, covering the whole district in five years. They used local materials and artisans, and no one was paid. Each bridge cost only a quarter of what the central government would have spent, and was built three to four times faster.

A final and lasting benefit of greater participation in the provision of local services is that they can be more efficiently run and maintained. In Guatemala, local involvement in the operation of 34 village water projects—villagers were trained in operation and maintenance—significantly increased their success rate. There, as in many other countries, the locally built systems have suffered fewer breakdowns, and the villages have had far fewer days without clean water.

Decentralization does not automatically produce gains in efficiency. If poorly planned and executed, decentralization can add to costs rather than reduce them. One common danger is duplicating layers of administration at national, regional and local levels. In Mexico and Venezuela, decentralizing the education systems increased costs because of the proliferation of different agencies.

Another risk is that the benefits of decentralization can be offset by losses in economy of scale. Some energy production, such as that through windmills, can be locally generated very efficiently. But the same may not be true of more conventional powerplants. In China in the 1980s, the construction of small local powerplants provided rural areas with much-needed energy. But the small plants proved much less efficient: for each unit of electricity, capital costs were about 30% higher and operating costs about 50% higher than those for centrally generated power—and they created more pollution.

One of the most important benefits of decentralization is the opportunity to cut costs

And while decentralization may in some cases help raise standards of service, there is also the danger of letting standards slip. In Kenya, the *harambee* schools built through local initiative are generally inferior to the central government schools. The teachers tend to be poorly qualified, and levels of pupil achievement are low—only 13% of the pupils reach the minimum standards, compared with 80% for government schools.

Above all, decentralization should not mean that higher levels of government completely withdraw support from, or neglect, social services. In Ecuador, decentralization of the rural public health programme meant that there was no effective supervision or logistical support, resulting in severe delays and supply shortages.

For decentralization to increase efficiency, a lot depends on the technical and financial support offered to local governments—and on how much it attracts local leadership and captures local enthusiasm.

Equity

Most countries, particularly those in the developing world, have very uneven levels of development, with marked disparities between different regions, between urban and rural areas or between different income and ethnic groups. Decentralization certainly alters some of these balances—though it can either improve equity or reduce it. In general, devolving greater power to regions, although promoting equity *within* individual regions, can increase disparities *among* them.

Within the region covered by a local authority, the effect can be positive. If decentralization produces more effective government services, the effect will be redistributive—since poor people generally make more use of local public services than rich ones. But unless the central government takes compensatory action, decentralization can increase the disparities between various regions and districts. Passing more responsibility for taxation and expenditure to local governments can benefit richer areas.

One reason for this is that richer areas have more political influence and can lobby more effectively for resources. In the Mexican state of Guerrero, decentralizing the health system allowed the wealthier areas to negotiate higher budgets. As a result, people living in the tourist areas and in the most important cities were better off, while the Indians and peasants living in small dispersed settlements suffered a significant decline in services.

Decentralization can also heighten inequalities if more of the services are funded locally—poorer areas can afford less. In Zambia, transferring some recurrent costs for primary education from the central government to the district level and to parents tended to increase interregional inequality. Parental spending on books and other materials in the six poorer regions was only half that in the three richer ones.

In general, decentralization causes interregional disparities to worsen unless the central government takes strong action. Some have done this through their systems of grants to local governments. Rather than just allocating funds on a per capita basis, they also take relative poverty levels into account. Brazil redistributes its tax revenue preferentially to the poorest states. In 1976, for every 100 cruzeiros it collected in taxes set aside by law for transfer to the states, the federal government returned only 25 cruzeiros to the richer states in the South and South-East while giving 75 cruzeiros to those in the poorer North.

The same principle can also be applied at lower levels of government, particularly for states in federal systems. In Uttar Pradesh, India, grants are distributed to districts on a criterion of "backwardness"—as indicated by the condition of their infrastructure and the proportion of their population in "scheduled castes". This arrangement, introduced in the process of decentralization, has helped reduce disparities between districts.

Another approach is to redistribute locally raised revenue. In Chile, the *Fondo Común Municipal* follows a set formula to pass revenue from the property and business taxes of the richer municipalities to spend in the poorer ones. In the metropolitan region of Santiago, this effectively reduces the per capita revenue of the three

Devolving power to regions, although promoting equity within *them, can increase disparities* among *them*

richest municipalities by 7–14%, while increasing that of the poorer ones by 35–50%.

Another way of containing interregional disparities is to set minimum national standards in various social services that the central government undertakes to finance and maintain—irrespective of local resources.

Economic participation

Decentralization can increase economic participation by facilitating local entrepreneurial activity, and thus increasing employment, in several ways.
- *Increased public expenditure*—The construction and maintenance of local infrastructure, such as roads, water supply and electricity, will directly employ local contractors and workers.
- *Higher-quality services*—Local facilities are likely to be more appropriate and better maintained if the local community influences their construction. They will thus be of more use to local entrepreneurs and help increase their profitability.
- *Better support for entrepreneurs*—Local governments might be able to offer better support to local business. They can offer management assistance and market information tailored to local needs. They are also in a much better position to cater to the needs of scattered rural enterprises.

In rural areas, one of the most important routes to increased economic participation is through land reform. In Taiwan (province of China), land reform in the 1950s and 1960s had a significant impact, not just on economic growth but on its spatial distribution—creating some 200,000 new owner-farmers as well as many new job opportunities in the rural areas. This, together with the decentralization of infrastructural improvements across the island, seems to have encouraged balanced growth of agriculture and industry and avoided overconcentration of population and economic activities in the metropolitan areas.

The distribution of government grants is another way of increasing economic opportunities in poorer regions. In Indonesia, the transfer of resources through block grants has probably promoted better growth rates in relatively poor regions, especially in the eastern islands.

Economic participation can also be increased by decentralized investment strategies that promote small-scale industries and make better use of local resources, raw materials and skills. In Tanzania, this has promoted local production of goods and services that would otherwise have had to be imported, using up scarce reserves of foreign exchange.

Nevertheless, there are many cases where decentralization does not seem to have produced tangible economic benefits—often because it has not been carried through with sufficient resources or conviction. In Zimbabwe, the government tried to promote regional industrialization through a "growth point" strategy. But the results, with a few exceptions, have been disappointing—perhaps because of the limited financial devolution, or the continuing centralizing tendency of government controls.

Similarly in the Philippines, the Regional Cities Development Project was designed to reduce some of the grave economic imbalances between regions—by developing urban infrastructure, and strengthening the management capabilities of the city governments. A 1988 study of the impact in Iloilo City concluded that the project had not yet induced economic growth. Some infrastructure had improved, particularly the port and the road system. But the city still lacked the adequate supplies of water and reasonably priced electricity that heavy industry needed.

Identifying a local economic effect specifically linked to decentralization is not easy. Economic development is, of course, subject to numerous other influences, from the government's macroeconomic policy and development strategy to its choices on investment in both infrastructure and human resources. But in general, there is little systematic hard evidence.

Political participation

If participation takes the form of deconcentration and delegation, the centre will retain effective control, and an increase in political participation is unlikely to result.

Decentralized investment strategies can increase economic participation

Devolution, by contrast, should lead to fuller political participation. But not necessarily, since power may merely be devolved to non-democratic and non-participatory local institutions. Indeed, devolution in some cases could require a strong central government to ensure that local administrations respect national standards on such matters as women's rights and civil liberties.

Three country case studies show the diversity of decentralization's possible outcomes.

Indonesia's central government, despite commendable decentralization, retains strong political control. Even where power is delegated to provinces or *kabupaten* (regions), it passes only into the hands of people appointed from above: the governors of provinces and the heads of *kabupaten,* who often come from the military. Both provinces and *kabupaten* also have legislative bodies, but their powers are largely advisory.

Chile's system of local government has passed through different stages in its recent turbulent history. The military government from 1973 onwards removed the elected local mayors and councils and replaced them with appointed mayors. The re-establishment of national democracy in the 1990s saw the return of local democracy: elections were reinstated for mayors, local councils and neighbourhood groups—and indirectly for regional councils.

Zimbabwe, since independence, has offered local people the opportunity to participate in the planning process through elected village and ward development committees, but this participation varies considerably. Some committees are dominated by traditional leaders, and there is relatively little participation. A 1985 survey discovered that many people did not know the name of their councillor or even that the committees existed. In some places, however, there is wide local participation and a high level of debate, particularly where there are substantive financial decisions to be made—on the revenue raised from wildlife, for example. But Zimbabwe also has separate rural councils in the white farming areas, which retain their pre-independence structure in that only tax-payers and their spouses have the right to vote.

Other developing countries show a diversity of experience. Decentralization has often merely taken the form of deconcentration and permitted the centre to retain strong political control. *Zambia,* for example, has had a policy of "deconcentration in centralism". Some political power has been passed to the district level but is exercised by party officials and political appointees. Whether the opening up to a multiparty system and the election of a new president have caused significant changes remains to be seen.

Peru, like Chile, has seen significant changes in the status of local government as central government regimes have changed. The authoritarian military regimes in the 1970s were determined to retain strong political control. But more recent democratic governments have emphasized political devolution. Indeed, before the recent setback to democracy, the previous government was attempting an extensive programme of devolution to regional and local levels.

The authoritarian regime in the *Philippines* up to 1985 also made a point of strengthening central power over local government. It created the new *barangays* as the main administrative unit of the country. While purportedly aimed at broadening local democracy, in practice these were led by people loyal to the regime and they primarily served to extend central control and political mobilization. More recently, the Philippines has adopted a promising local government code, which transfers responsibility for public works, agriculture, health and social welfare to the *municipios,* a level above the *barangays.* And for this purpose, the *municipios* will, over the next three years, be allocated 40% of all taxes. But exactly how this will be implemented has yet to be resolved.

Experience in many developing countries suggests that democratic regimes are the most likely to encourage genuine decentralization and popular participation. Authoritarian or single-party regimes, whether from the "right" or the "left", generally limit decentralization to deconcentration and aim to retain strong central control.

The shift towards multiparty democracy throughout the developing world is therefore a very promising sign.

The reality of decentralization

Decentralization of local government has the potential to improve government decisions with increasing democratic participation. As decisions are brought closer to the people they affect, expenditure on priorities often increases and efficiency of resource use improves. But this potential is realized only where there is genuine decentralization to democratic structures. We have found that:

1. *There is not much evidence of full devolution in many developing countries.* On average they are merely delegating less than 10% of total government expenditure to local governments, and less than 6% of total social expenditure. The taxation powers of most local authorities remain fairly limited.
2. *Where there has been some form of decentralization, it has generally increased efficiency.* This can be a result of lower costs, better maintenance, closer monitoring and supervision and the use of voluntary local labour. Decentralization also enables local people to insist that human priority concerns move to the top of the local development agenda.
3. *Where decentralization occurs, it often leads to better priority ratios.* This is partly the result of government rules allocating basic expenditure to the local level. But it also occurs as a result of choices made by democratic local governments. Care must be taken in non-democratic states, especially where local governments are dominated by elites who may neglect social priorities.
4. *Decentralization needs to be accompanied by central government action to reduce existing disparities among regions and districts.* Central governments need to devise innovative formulae to redistribute tax revenue from richer regions and districts to poorer ones. They can fund the implementation of minimum standards to be maintained throughout the country.
5. *Effective decentralization is not possible without the reform of existing power structures.* If power remains concentrated in the hands of elites—as is still the case in many developing countries—decentralization might further empower the elites rather than the people.

Many of the most effective forms of decentralization are not, however, based on the institutions of local government. Some of the most important local bodies, which can serve as a countervailing power to the influence of central government, are voluntary associations—including people's organizations and non-governmental organizations, the subject of the chapter that follows.

If power remains concentrated in the hands of elites, decentralization might further empower the elites rather than the people

Chile

CENTRAL GOVERNMENT EXPENDITURE AS % OF GNP (1990) **33%**

EXPENDITURE DECENTRALIZATION RATIO (1990) **8%**

REVENUE DECENTRALIZATION RATIO (1990) **5%**

FINANCIAL AUTONOMY RATIO (1990) **62%**

Chile's decentralization experience can be divided into three periods. First, the governments of Frei and Allende continued Chile's long democratic tradition of broadly based but centralized services. Next, the Pinochet dictatorship drew all political power to the centre but decentralized services. Then, the government of Aylwin restored local democracy, continuing with the decentralized services.

During the earlier democratic periods, there were elected municipal councils and various neighbourhood groups, which General Pinochet abolished, replacing them with a military hierarchy that included centrally appointed governors and mayors. He also gave municipal governments greater responsibilities for the delivery of services, particularly education and health. Municipal leaders thus became "service delivery agents" without local governing power.

Decentralization was initially accompanied by an increase in resources for local authorities. First, more of the locally raised property taxes could be spent locally. Before 1979, municipalities received only a fraction of the revenue—after, they got all of it. They could retain some 40% of the property tax and receive the rest through a redistribution among municipalities through a *Fondo Común Municipal*. This took 60% of the property tax, 50% of the vehicle tax and a proportion of the receipts from a tax on business in three high-income municipalities.

The second major new source of income took the form of flat subsidies to allow municipalities to provide basic education and primary health care. This payment system, intended to give municipalities an incentive to control costs, resulted in their subsidizing these services from elsewhere in their budgets—and running deficits.

For primary and secondary education, the central government has given a flat subsidy per pupil. This could go either to municipal schools or to new private (non-fee-charging) schools. But its real value fell through the 1980s, and municipal schools suffered because, while they lost pupils to the private sector, they could not readily cut their costs proportionally. In the health services, the flat payments to municipalities were in line with specific services provided. But these, too, failed to keep pace with costs and inflation.

The decentralization programme also dispersed some investment. A new Regional Development Fund was established in 1975 to finance projects in health and education, as well as minor infrastructure projects such as rural roads. These funds are distributed in response to project submissions by municipalities and regions, supposedly weighted towards the poorest communities.

This fund currently amounts to about 15% of the public sector investment budget, and there is a proposal to increase it by 25%. There is also an additional mechanism for sectoral ministries to allocate a small part of their funds (around 5%) to regional governments, which are free to select their own projects.

As a result of these reforms, Chile's revenue and expenditure decentralization ratios rose sharply during the 1980s. Municipal revenue rose to 6% of total government revenue, and the expenditure ratio to 8.3%. But since health and education are financed by transfers from the central government, the financial autonomy ratio fell sharply. Even so, municipalities in 1990 financed 60% of their activities from their own resources. There was nevertheless some decline in the decentralization ratios between 1988 and 1990. For investment, however, the municipalities depend more heavily on outside money. They finance only 16% of investment in their area (another 16% comes from the various regional funds, 68% from central ministries).

A major objective of Pinochet's policies was to increase the professional level of local government employees, and he seems to have succeeded. Professional and technical staff as a proportion of municipal employees rose from 8% to 33% between 1975 and 1988—a result of, among other things, increased staff training but also contracting out more of the unskilled work.

In the quality of services, the outcome of decentralization was mixed. The standards in municipal schools fell, and the differences between social groups widened. Private schools (which by 1986 had 31% of the school population) did rather better, though the differences were not so marked when controlled for socioeconomic status (the lower socioeconomic groups tended to do better in the municipal schools). The secondary enrolment ratio increased, and the number of years required for pupils to pass through the system fell.

In health, the resource picture is similar. Decentralization was accompanied by a cut in real resources and the introduction of some user charges. Public expenditure on health fell from 3.3% of GDP to 2.4% in 1988 (due to the privatization of contributions and services among the upper-income groups). But the outcome for health standards was generally positive with continuing (and marked) reductions in infant mortality rates and maternal mortality. In both health and education, the larger and richer municipalities did better than the others.

On balance, the outcome of decentralization in Chile seems to have been positive—and the situation should improve further as the present government combines it with more local democracy.

Indonesia

CENTRAL GOVERNMENT EXPENDITURE AS % OF GNP (1990)	**20%**
EXPENDITURE DECENTRALIZATION RATIO (1989)	**19%**
REVENUE DECENTRALIZATION RATIO (1989)	**8%**
FINANCIAL AUTONOMY RATIO (1989)	**25%**

Indonesia's widely dispersed territory argues both for a unifying central state to hold the country together—and for extensive decentralization to match government to local needs. The country's 188 million people live on more than 13,000 islands covering more than two million square kilometres—60% of the people live on the island of Java, with 7% of the land area. The government, in power since 1965, initially placed its emphasis on national unity and economic stabilization. But since the mid-1970s, it has paid increasing attention to economic growth, regional development and decentralization.

Indonesia is formally a parliamentary democracy, but authority for decisions is concentrated in the presidency. The elected assemblies at central, provincial and district levels can debate and advise, but the president and his ministers make most decisions. And though governors of the 27 provinces are elected by the provincial assemblies, the president has to confirm their appointment. In addition, the central government has officials dispersed throughout the country to assist with decisions. This has made Indonesia's planning system good at transferring commands from above, but not very sensitive to local priorities.

Local governments raise 25% of their financing from their own taxes and fees, with the rest coming from central government transfers and grants. Their largest source is the property tax, collected by the central government but given to districts. Local governments are responsible for the delivery of most health and education services, for which they receive direct transfers from the central government. These transfers come through the INPRES programme, Indonesia's principal means of decentralization. In the 1991 budget, these transfers accounted for 12% of total development expenditure and 51% of local government development expenditure.

INPRES funds, as block grants to each province or locality, come in two forms. First, there are the "general" funds intended to promote regional autonomy and improve local infrastructure. These are not centrally controlled, but they are subject to "general guidelines", strict for provinces though less so for districts. Another INPRES grant provides lump sums directly to each of Indonesia's nearly 67,000 villages. These grants are small but can be used for almost any purpose. Second, "specific" grants go only to the district level and are earmarked for specific purposes by the central government—say, for the construction of schools or their running costs. Districts have limited discretion on how to use these grants.

Indonesia's national budget, and the INPRES grants, are strongly influenced by the flow of oil revenue. Between 1975 and the mid-1980s, oil income rose to more than 50% of central government revenue—but then dropped to 41% in 1988–89, and INPRES grants also fell.

Provincial authorities do not, on average, have much financial autonomy, though the position varies considerably. At the provincial level, "own" funds as a percentage of the total range from 8% to 70%. At the district level, own funds controlled by local governments range from 4% to 56% of the total. Jakarta, with its diversified service and industrial economy, has plenty of scope for generating local revenues.

At both provincial and district levels, the proportion of total funds spent on development tends to rise as the financial autonomy ratio rises. And provincial governments spend a higher proportion of their funds on social investment than does the central government. In 1988–89, the local social allocation ratio was more than four times that of the central government, though the ratios are about the same when it comes to infrastructure investment. Again, however, there is considerable variation in the spending patterns. At the provincial level in 1983, social expenditure as a percentage of development expenditure varied between 8% and 43%, while infrastructure investment varied between 20% and 66% of development expenditure.

The system of decentralizing expenditure seems to have produced substantial improvements in basic services in health and education. In education, the government was generous with funding for investment in the 1970s, and although this dropped as oil revenues fell in the 1980s, education standards continued to improve. Government investment in education is also becoming more redistributive, as provinces with lower literacy rates receive a higher share of investment funds.

The picture is similarly positive for health. Resources declined in the 1980s, but standards continued to rise, probably reflecting increased investment in health by local governments. The number of health centres rose significantly, infant mortality fell by nearly 50% and life expectancy rose by eight years. The central government grants favour to areas with below-average health levels, and the variation in health standards between the regions decreased between 1976 and 1987.

A major problem is that many local authorities have proved ill-equipped to implement development projects. So far, the strengthening of local capacity has mostly entailed improving the professional standards of central officials stationed at lower levels of government, not those of local people. And since local government officials are paid out of central government allocations and their promotion and pay depend on central government decisions, any real devolution of decision-making is difficult.

By international standards, the real degree of decentralization in Indonesia is not high, but it is substantial for a large country with a unitary form of government. As the economy becomes more complex and regionally specialized, Indonesia will inevitably have to move towards greater decentralization and to improve the efficiency of local tax collection to provide local governments with additional revenue and autonomy.

Morocco

CENTRAL GOVERNMENT EXPENDITURE AS % OF GNP (1990)	**30%**
EXPENDITURE DECENTRALIZATION RATIO (1986)	**6%**
REVENUE DECENTRALIZATION RATIO (1988)	**8%**
FINANCIAL AUTONOMY RATIO (1988)	**108%**

Morocco has undergone a steady process of decentralization in recent decades. Until 1960, the country was organized through traditional assemblies—*Jmaa*—based on ethnic groups. These have been largely replaced by a system based on territory: seven regions, 60 *préfectures* or provinces, and 1,544 *communes* (1,297 rural and 247 urban).

Each commune has an elected president and assembly. The commune *councillors* in turn elect councillors for the *préfectures*.

The activities of the communes were greatly enlarged in 1976 to include responsibility for the management of a large number of local services, including water, sanitation, electricity and transport, as well as primary schools, health centres and vocational training. And the president of the commune was given considerable legal powers for local administration.

Alongside this increased responsibility went an increased flow of resources. In 1977, the revenue of the communes represented 5% of total public revenue, but by 1991 it had reached nearly 11%.

In 1988, the communes were given financial autonomy. Previously, the government made grants to help local authorities balance their budgets, but it has since decided to give them 30% of the proceeds of the value added tax (VAT). The local authorities do not consider this sufficient to meet the obligations placed on them. For capital expenditure, many have had to take loans from the *Fonds d'Équipement Communal*. They have therefore been pressing for an additional share of the VAT—to be distributed more on the basis of local needs and levels of development.

Decentralization has certainly changed the character of spending by local authorities. Between 1977 and 1987, the proportion of their budgets devoted to capital expenditure rose from 26% to 53%. And while the communes made 3.5% of total public capital expenditure in 1987, their share reached 17% by 1991.

The staff of local authorities has also increased—by 210% between 1977 and 1991. And to ensure an adequate supply of qualified personnel, several vocational and administrative training centres have been established. In 1991–92 alone, 1,571 people were being trained, 12.5% of those trained over the past 35 years. The rural communes were given special attention, being allocated university graduates such as doctors, veterinary surgeons and agronomists. Even so, there is a marked disparity in personnel between urban and rural areas. The urban areas have more than three times as many staff per 1,000 people as the rural ones.

The educational levels of the local councillors have also been a matter of concern. In 1983, a survey of the presidents of local councils found that 16% had no schooling, and of the rest, 39% had no more than primary education—let alone the experience in administration and finance that would allow them to work efficiently. Several political parties have organized training sessions for their members.

As far as the ordinary people are concerned, many features of the recent decentralization have offered considerable improvements. Administrative procedures have been speeded up—it now takes much less time to get many of the official certificates and licences. And people have plenty of opportunities to bring their complaints to the communal assemblies.

For services, it is too early to say whether education standards have been affected, but the health services have improved. One indicator is the substantial reduction in the time taken to walk to the nearest health centre. In 1979–80, 51% of households could reach a centre in less than an hour, and in 1990–91, 78%. And while more than half the patients previously had to wait more than an hour for a consultation, ten years later that proportion had dropped to less than a quarter.

The process of decentralization in Morocco is under constant review. So far, there have been five national conferences to bring together elected councillors, government officials, academics and representatives from the private sector. These allow for a critical assessment of the successes and failures of decentralization as well as a sharing of experience.

Zimbabwe

CENTRAL GOVERNMENT EXPENDITURE AS % OF GNP (1990) **41%**
EXPENDITURE DECENTRALIZATION RATIO (1986) **20%**
REVENUE DECENTRALIZATION RATIO (1986) **6%**
FINANCIAL AUTONOMY RATIO (1986) **27%**

The first democratic government inherited a highly centralized system in 1980 and has since established laws and procedures to devolve responsibility to lower levels of government—with limited impact. Although a government that grew out of a war of liberation with strong local roots might have had a headstart in establishing a decentralized state, Zimbabwe's restructuring of local government has essentially been a top-down initiative, partly due to the disarray of traditional structures in the wake of independence.

Before 1980, local government was divided on the basis of race. The whites elected their own urban and rural councils, while the black communal lands had African councils. After 1980, the government retained the white councils but consolidated the previously fragmented African councils into 55 district councils. Above both white and black councils, the eight provinces have appointed governors and provincial administrators.

The white rural councils and the black district councils were the subject of amalgamation legislation in 1988. But compromises undermined this effort to end the colonial legacy of separate development. The district councils are elected bodies, though they have some chiefs and headmen as ex officio members, with a district administrator responsible for overall planning, development and coordination.

The district councils raise only 15% of their total revenue—through taxes, fees and other charges. Secondary school fees are the most important component—and in 1984–85, they made up 60% of local revenue, with substantial variations among districts. Districts also apply a "development levy", a form of poll tax on all adults. Very unpopular, this has proved difficult to collect. Although the district councils have generally been raising an increasing proportion of their revenues, they still depend heavily on the central government. The urban councils do rather better. They receive a significant proportion of revenue from taxes on property, as well as a levy on beer, and manage to raise between 80% and 90% of recurrent revenue.

Local authorities raised only 6% of total government revenue in 1986, and they have almost no financial autonomy. In education, the ministry administers grants under the heading "tuition" and interprets this very narrowly to encompass only spending directly related to classroom learning, such as textbooks or chalkboards.

In 1984, the government established a hierarchy of representative bodies—development committees—at village, ward, district and provincial levels. The idea was to mesh bottom-up and top-down planning. These bodies were to draw up development plans and projects for central funding, but the links between national and local bodies have proved weak. The national plan, for example, is finalized before the regional ones, and in practice the key decisions for the operation of sector ministries have continued to emanate from Harare, where local efforts are often (literally) shelved.

In 1990, the social allocation ratio for central government expenditure was 36%. One possible indicator of local priorities is the preference expressed through requests for funding in the local plans—though these, too, may be influenced by central government, as districts might request funds for projects they believe the centre will fund. Analysis of a sample of development plans of district councils revealed that social development made up 39% of total bids, with agriculture next in importance at 30%. On the whole, the evidence suggests that more devolution of decision-making would focus public attention on infrastructure and priority social services.

Decentralization can also affect equity. The most striking inequalities in Zimbabwe are between the white minority and the black majority, but there are also wide divisions within the black communal areas. A 1991 sample survey indicated that the top 10% of households controlled 42% of measured income, the lower 50% only 15% and the bottom 25% less than 5%.

The clearest change in equity has been to focus attention on the communal lands. Since 1980, the school construction programme has increased the number of primary schools in communal lands by 86% and that of secondary schools by more than 700%. The number of village health workers increased 26-fold, and the share of the population with access to safe water has increased from 33% to 55%.

The distribution among the provinces has been less progressive. In fact, more public resources are directed at provinces with the highest per capita incomes. In health, Harare and Bulawayo, the two provinces with the four central hospitals, receive 1.4 to 2.7 times more per capita expenditure than the other provinces, even after adjusting for out-of-province patients. And the expenditure on water supplies is greater for those provinces that already have better facilities. Similarly, at the district level, a sample of 16 districts for 1982 and 1985 revealed that both central government grants and local government revenues were lowest in the neediest areas.

In principle, people can be involved at all levels of decision-making in Zimbabwe, from the village through wards and districts to the province. In practice, participation is much more constrained. Local decision-making is often dominated by central government employees: the village community workers, for example, often "tell" the community what its needs are, rather than allow for the people's participation. And local interests are often represented by a small elite: ward submissions to district councils are often prepared by the ward chairmen without consulting the local community. Overlaid on all this is the role of the ZANU (PF) party, which generally carries more weight than local government.

Zimbabwe has taken many significant steps towards decentralization in the short period since independence, but this has been constrained by the historical context of race and class.

CHAPTER 5

People in community organizations

People are more likely to be excluded than included in civil and political life

People's understanding of the world is formed and nurtured in face-to-face interactions in small social groups—first in the family, then the street, perhaps, or the neighbourhood or village. Such groups also serve a political purpose, for people generally gain greater benefits in groups than as individuals.

As people move outside such groups, however, they find the wider world organized on very different principles, and they are more likely to receive decisions handed down from on high. Whether in social services, in markets or in civil and political life, they are more likely to be excluded than included.

The problem is partly practical. Many facets of modern life cannot be confined to the home, village or street. The complexity and the sheer numbers of people involved reduce the possibilities for face-to-face interaction. The intrusion of market values also plays a part, with many more goods and services now obtained with hard cash than through mutual exchange within the community.

In time, countries develop the institutions of civil society—a fair judiciary, a responsive executive, a free press and traditions of transparency, accountability and fair play. Group action is often necessary for the evolution of such institutions and for ensuring that they continue to respond to people's aspirations for genuine participation.

But governments in developing countries often discourage such participation. Starting from a "top-down" development philosophy, they have generally concentrated on providing food, services or assets—rather than enabling people to do more for themselves. Governments have seen development as something to be done for, rather than by, people—stifling many grass-roots initiatives, holding them in check, rather than nurturing and extending them.

Things are changing. Many community groups now command the attention and respect of governments in many developing countries. The energy of the people who form them, and the creative solutions they demonstrate, have helped persuade governments of the value of involving participatory community groups. Donors, too—disillusioned with the performance of much official aid—are passing more of their money through non-governmental channels. As a result, there has been an explosion of participatory movements in most developing countries.

The community organizations driving those movements are by their nature difficult to classify and analyse. This Report refers to two broad types: people's organizations and non-governmental organizations (NGOs).

People's organizations can be defined as democratic organizations that represent the interests of their members and are accountable to them. They are formed by people who know each other, or who share a common experience, and their continued existence does not depend upon outside initiative or funding. In developing countries, many of them are small, locally based and loosely established. But they need not be confined to the grass roots—they can spread upwards and outwards from the local to the regional and national level, representing networks of community groups, or professional groups or trade unions.

Non-governmental organizations (NGOs) can be defined as voluntary organizations that work with and very often on behalf of others. Their work and their activities are focused on issues and people beyond their own staff and membership. NGOs often have close links with people's organizations, channelling technical advice or financial support as intermediate service organizations. But organizationally NGOs can be quite different from people's organizations, often having bureaucratic hierarchies without the democratic characteristics or accountability of most people's groups.

The distinction between the two is not rigid—many groups could reasonably fall into either category.

People's organizations in developing countries

The idea to form a people's organization can come from the people themselves—as with those traditional self-help groups in Asia and Sub-Saharan Africa in which people come together to pool their labour, to obtain credit, to buy goods in bulk or to promote and develop more sustainable forms of agriculture (boxes 5.1 and 5.2). Or the impetus can come from outside the group, perhaps from a dynamic individual who recognizes a community's needs and suggests ways they could meet them (box 5.3).

Sometimes, the groups are formed in response to a failure by government to provide infrastructure or services. The Cairo Public Housing Project was set up in the late 1970s as a result of prolonged government neglect of poor neighbourhoods. The aim was not just to provide some of their own housing, water and sewerage but also to induce the government to provide such services (box 5.4).

In other cases, it is what the government does that prompts groups to form. Police brutality, political oppression or the infringement of civil liberties has shown the need in most countries for groups that protect human rights, as with *Action Sociale et d'Organisation Paysanne* in Zaire.

People's organizations can also arise because the market fails to offer them the goods or services they need. The Self-Employed Women's Association in India is a striking example of how poor and disadvantaged people can enhance their bargaining strength through cooperation (box 5.5).

How many people's organizations are there? It is impossible even to come up with a reliable estimate, for a phenomenon so flexible and dynamic can never be captured in statistics. But here are some illustrative figures:
• *Kenya* has 23,000 women's groups alone.
• *Tamil Nadu* state in India has 25,000 registered grass-roots organizations.
• *Bangladesh* has at least 12,000 local groups that receive local and central government financial support (and many more that do not).

BOX 5.1

Self-help farming groups

Farmers all over the world have traditionally come together in self-help groups, particularly to share their labour. Neighbours might, for example, arrive on an appointed day to help work one farmer's land. Not paid, but fed, any of them can ask for similar help from the others.

In a more formal arrangement, farmers might, on a rotating basis, help each other prepare land for the cultivation of various crops. Widespread in Africa, this form of cooperation goes under the names *nhimbe* and *jangano* in Zimbabwe, *owe* and *are* in western Nigeria and *nnoboa* in south-eastern Ghana.

Self-help groups have also been formed to provide credit, normally among people with similar incomes, though individuals might join several groups if they meet the requirements. These groups also have a variety of names: *esusu* among the Yoruba people of western Nigeria, *susu* in Ghana, *ibimina* in the Kivuye commune in northern Rwanda, *tontines* or *njangis* in Cameroon, *cheetu* in Sri Lanka and *samabaya* in Bangladesh.

BOX 5.2

Mexico—Union de Ejidos Julio Sabines

In the 1970s, poor rural farmers migrated to the rainforest region of Marques de Comillas, near Mexico's border with Guatemala. Their shifting cultivation practices, combined with cattle ranching by more powerful groups, deforested some 40% of the area. In 1988, the Mexican government responded with a ban on the cutting of trees.

The ban drew a strong reaction from the farmers represented by the *Union de Ejidos Julio Sabines*. They held meetings with government agencies—discussing soil erosion, river flooding and changes in rainfall as a result of deforestation. They also discussed global warming—with some farmers pointing out that the international community should, if it wanted them to stop cutting trees, offer some compensation.

The majority, however, agreed to work with government agencies to develop sustainable forms of agriculture and look for alternative sources of income.

For the past four years, they have successfully developed farming techniques for both food and commercial crops, using natural fertilizers without using more land. They are also cultivating forest products for sale, as well as breeding some of the forest animals.

The government has provided medical and educational services and support for Indian communities—and created a special task force for community development.

As a result, the rainforest is being used and preserved—and the local community is flourishing.

- *The Philippines* has 18,000 registered NGOs, of which at least two-thirds might be considered people's organizations, such as community associations or cooperatives.
- The OECD suggests that there were up to 20,000 NGOs in developing countries in the 1980s, a considerable underestimate—the number is probably closer to 50,000 and could well be higher.
- The OECD's Directory of NGOs had information on more than 2,500 NGOs in the 25 OECD countries in 1990, up from 1,600 in 1980.

Among the largest people's organizations in both industrial and developing countries are the trade unions, which have offered the most significant form of group participation in the workplace. There might have been little that individual workers could do to influence the employer, but when individuals cooperated with the rest of the workforce—and with the ultimate threat of a mass strike—employers had no option but to listen and reach a compromise.

The wave of democratization of the 1980s received much of its impetus from trade unions. In Latin America, the unions in Argentina, Bolivia, Brazil, Ecuador and Uruguay—and most recently in Chile—were often the major source of opposition to dictatorships. In Asia, the unions have also been instrumental in democratization: in the Republic of Korea, it was a wave of strikes in 1986–87 that led to many democratic reforms.

In Africa, too, the trade union movement, though small in numbers, played a disproportionately large role in the moves towards multiparty democracy. In Mali, the National Union of Malian Workers organized nationwide strikes to bring down the government in 1981, and its secretary-general became vice-president of the transitional government that helped bring in a civilian administration in 1992. In Zambia, the Congress of Trade Unions was in the forefront of the opposition to the previous one-party state, and in the subsequent multiparty elections its leader was voted in as the new president.

In Eastern Europe and the Soviet Union, the new workers' organizations—Solidarity in Poland, Podkrepa in Bulgaria, Fratia in Romania, the miners' strike committees in the Soviet Union—propelled the moves towards democracy.

Non-governmental organizations in developing countries

NGOs cover a very wide spectrum, from small loose-knit local organizations to nationwide federations and international networks. And the issues they tackle might be anything from the human rights of one ethnic group to the entire mosaic of development concerns.

NGOs sometimes grow out of one people's organization, extending its principles

---

BOX 5.3

Pakistan—the Orangi Pilot Project

Orangi, a suburb of Karachi, Pakistan's largest city, has grown rapidly and now has more than 700,000 people crowded into it.

Akhtar Hameed Khan came to Orangi in 1980, a charismatic leader with considerable experience in organizing community self-help from his previous work in the Comilla project in Bangladesh. He found that housing was poor, sanitation and drainage facilities inadequate, health problems on the increase and epidemics frequent.

Khan was convinced that the best way to deal with Orangi's problems was to shun outside help and strengthen the capacity of local people to help themselves. The Orangi Pilot Project concentrated on five areas:
- Low-cost sanitation
- Low-cost housing
- Women's work centres
- Women's welfare programmes
- School education.

The results have been spectacular. The sanitation programme involves 28,000 families that have constructed some 430,000 feet of underground sewerage and built more than 28,000 latrines. They financed this with 30 million rupees ($1.2 million) of their own savings, at a cost of $66 per house—about one-quarter of what it would have cost local government.

BOX 5.4

Egypt—Cairo public housing project

Khalafaway, like many Cairo neighbourhoods, deteriorated greatly in the 1960s as a result of prolonged neglect by the government. Blocked sewage systems and piles of garbage in open areas were contaminating the drinking water and producing other serious health threats.

Disgusted by the deteriorating conditions, the Khalafaway neighbourhood started a self-help project in 1978 to improve its environment. Using their own money and volunteer labour, the people in the neighbourhood replaced broken water pipes, unblocked the sewage systems, cleared the garbage and organized regular collections. They also created a children's garden.

Three years later, these self-help efforts found a strong ally in Wafaa Ahmed Abdalla, a senior expert with the Institute for National Planning in Cairo. She developed a more scientific approach for community improvement and started training programmes for local people. As a result, five more self-help projects emerged in public housing neighbourhoods, enabling 5,000 residents to improve their environment.

and ideas to other places. Or they can be an amalgam of people's organizations coming together.

Or they can be offshoots of larger organizations, often churches that set up NGOs or task forces to tackle particular problems. In Chile, the Catholic Church established the *Vicaría de la Solidaridad* to expose atrocities and provide support to victims during the Pinochet regime. The Justice and Peace Commission in Rhodesia played a similar role under the Smith regime.

On other occasions, a group of likeminded people might set up a new NGO in response to a national problem. They might focus attention on women's issues, as in the Dominican Republic, where the *Centro de Investigación para la Acción Feminina* is committed to changing the status of women in the country (box 5.6). And in recent years, many new groups have been established around environmental concerns—as in the Philippines, where the Green Forum aims to raise the consciousness of local communities and the government on environmental protection.

Many NGOs have placed much of their emphasis on empowerment. The formal purpose of a programme might be improvements in health or literacy or agriculture, but NGOs have also been concerned with how much each project enhances people's power. And they have been particularly determined to empower the poor and marginalized—many say that their prime constituency is the "poorest of the poor".

Most NGOs work with, and through, people's organizations, offering financial and other support. The links can be established in different ways. In much of Africa, NGOs usually provide assistance to existing people's organizations. In Bangladesh and India, the NGOs often take the initiative to form new people's organizations. In Latin America, both approaches are common.

Other NGOs confine themselves to advocacy—mobilizing the public to put pressure on the government to act on a particular issue. Human rights is a common focus, as with the *Foro Nacional por Colombia* and the Shuar Federation in Ecuador.

Many others take on both roles—material help and advocacy—and their links with people's organizations give them unique sources of information and authority. The *Comissão Pastoral da Terra* in Brazil offers support to landless groups and argues for their rights at both national and international levels.

At a final level of cooperation, NGOs also link up with other NGOs in networks to enable them to present a common front to regional or national governments and to international agencies like the UN. In India, individual states have networks of NGOs—such as the Federation of Voluntary Organizations for Rural Development in Karnataka, and the Association of Volun-

---

BOX 5.5

India—Self-Employed Women's Association

The Self-Employed Women's Association (SEWA) is a trade union of poor women in Ahmedabad, India (in Hindi, *sewa* means service).

SEWA draws its membership from three types of workers: petty vendors and hawkers, home-based producers and those who provide casual labour and other services. Although it started in response to the needs of urban women, SEWA now also covers rural women in agriculture and other sectors.

SEWA's aim is to enhance women's income-earning opportunities as well as their working environment. It does this in several ways:
• Savings and credit cooperatives provide working capital to hawkers, vendors and home-based workers.
• Producer cooperatives help women get better prices for their goods.
• Training courses impart such skills as bamboo work, block printing, plumbing, carpentry, radio repair and accounting and management.
• Legal services enable women to obtain the benefits of national labour legislation. Until SEWA was formed in 1972, the women in the informal sector were not recognized as workers, either in law or by society.

SEWA has also developed a welfare component. It now gives assistance to its members through a maternal protection scheme, widows' benefits, child care and the training of midwives.

BOX 5.6

Dominican Republic—Centro de Investigación para la Acción Feminina

The *Centro de Investigación para la Acción Feminina* (CIPAF), a women's NGO in the Dominican Republic, is promoting lasting social change in the status of women. It tries to engineer basic changes in attitude through programmes of research, education, training and public information. By mobilizing the energies of middle-class women, it has organized over 200 workshops, trained thousands of workers and issued 31 publications.

One of CIPAF's major studies has been *Mujeres Rurales*—a report on the condition of peasant women. It followed this up with a nationwide information campaign to highlight the findings of the report and seek concrete changes in government policy. It is now completing a sequel on the problems of urban women.

CIPAF publishes a monthly newsletter that is reproduced in a nationwide daily newspaper, and it has conducted graduate seminars in the Dominican Republic, Honduras and Panama.

---

tary Agencies in Tamil Nadu. And at the national level, NGOs come together in the Voluntary Action Network India.

Some NGOs are not as non-governmental as they seem. Although formally independent, they might have links to government. In Zimbabwe, three NGOs are intimately linked with the ruling party: the President's Fund, Child Survival (under the patronage of the president's late wife) and the Zimbabwe Development Trust (under the tutelage of one of the country's vice-presidents). The Philippines similarly has government-inspired NGOs, known as GRINGOs, some of which were set up to further the aims of national and local politicians, and others to serve as recipients for foreign donors that required that a certain portion of their aid be channelled through NGOs. And while the vast majority of NGOs have a voluntary non-profit ethos, some are really commercial companies in disguise. For example, several NGOs in India have set themselves up as consultancies working (for a fee) with the voluntary sector.

In some cases, the most effective way for NGOs to operate is at the international level—as the remarkable success of Amnesty International and Greenpeace has demonstrated (box 5.7).

Northern NGOs in the South

All the industrial countries have a wide range of NGOs working on development issues, and their numbers are growing. These northern NGOs send large sums to developing countries. As with the various national Save the Children organizations, they do this in addition to helping in their home countries. Or as with the Oxfams, they spend their funds almost exclusively in developing countries.

On average, two-thirds of the funds northern NGOs raise for spending in the South come from private contributions. The highest per capita private contributions to NGOs were in Sweden, followed by Switzerland, Norway and Germany (above $13 per capita in all cases). Between 1970 and 1990, grants by northern NGOs to projects and programmes in developing countries increased from just over $1 billion to $5 billion. The country raising the most, however, is the United States—$2.7 billion, almost half the total in 1991.

Northern NGOs also serve as channels for government funds. On average, a third of their funds comes from governments, though the proportions vary widely—from 10% in Austria, Ireland and the United Kingdom to more than 80% in Belgium and Italy. Between 1970 and 1990, such funds increased from less than $200 million to $2.2 billion (table 5.1).

Taking private and government contributions together, the total transferred by and through northern NGOs increased from $1.0 billion in 1970 to $7.2 billion in 1990—in real terms twice the rate of increase for international development assistance. Indeed, government funding of northern NGOs has grown faster over the past ten years than support from the general public.

Many northern NGOs still execute their own programmes in the South—as with CARE, Plan International and World Vision in the United States, and ActionAid, Save the Children and Oxfam in the United Kingdom. But the trend is away from hands-on involvement and towards working in partnership with NGOs and people's organizations in developing countries. In

---

BOX 5.7

International advocacy by NGOs

Many of the issues that concern NGOs are truly global—and can often be best addressed by truly international NGOs. One of the best-known and respected of these is Amnesty International. By tirelessly recording and publicizing human rights violations, it has amply demonstrated the power of information to protect the rights of individuals and groups.

Amnesty has more than 6,000 groups of volunteers in more than 70 countries. Through their reports and letter-writing campaigns in 1990, these groups publicized the cases of 4,500 prisoners and contributed to the release of 1,296 of them.

A new organization—Transparency International—also plans to operate through international investigation and

publicity by identifying and exposing corruption in international business transactions and documenting its political, social and economic effects. The globalization of world trade increases the potential for large-scale corruption—as the Bofors arms sales scandal has shown only too vividly. Transparency International is unlikely to be short of work.

Another new international advocacy agency—in this case on environmental issues—is the Earth Council. It draws the lesson from the Rio environmental summit that people's continuing international participation is vital to the solution of environmental problems. It will provide a continuing global non-governmental forum for debate and action on sustainable development.

the United Kingdom, this is common for some of the largest NGOs, like Christian Aid and CAFOD—similarly with NOVIB in the Netherlands, and the church agencies in Germany and Scandinavia.

Most large NGOs in the South depend heavily on those in the North for finance. The northern NGOs typically refer to this as "partnership". But seen from the South, this relationship is often far removed from the equality the term implies.

The partnership clearly works best if donor and recipient agencies share a common perspective on development. And relations are smoother if the northern agencies provide a steady flow of funds and the southern agencies are willing and able to meet the reporting, management and accounting standards that the northern donors require.

In practice, these conditions do not always obtain. A central question that often remains unanswered is who defines the development agenda at the grass roots. The northern agencies can rarely guarantee long-term funding—and those in the South often resent the administrative demands on them. Agencies that receive money from child sponsorship organizations, for example, have to spend much of their time collecting copious quantities of personal information about the sponsored children—and employ large teams of "social workers" for this.

The donor agencies are thus in a position to set the conditions of the relationship. These may or may not be onerous, but they do restrict the freedom of the agencies they are placed on.

An additional complication in recent years has been that northern governments have been channelling aid through northern NGOs to NGOs in the South. While governments may find this attractive, they often ignore some fundamental incompatibilities. First, on the type of project: governments prefer programmes that produce tangible results, so they place a major emphasis on economic projects. NGOs, by contrast, prefer projects with stronger social or political elements that empower the poor.

Second are conflicts in time. Governments like their funds disbursed quickly, so

they are not too keen on long preproject assessments. NGOs, however, know only too well that participatory projects can be implemented only gradually—and after painstaking assessment and consultation with the people concerned.

The effect: northern NGOs have to persuade those in the South to generate economic projects with quick results—adding to the tensions between donor and recipient agencies. In response, there has been, as in the Philippines and Thailand with Canadian NGOs, the emergence of a collective dialogue between groups of NGOs, and the creation of consortia, as with the Bangladesh Rural Advancement Committee.

NGOs and people

Participation is a central tenet for almost all NGOs. Do they promote participation in practice? Mostly, it seems they do. Many studies have shown participation to be a dominant feature of their operations. And governments of developing countries, as well as donor agencies, concur that participation is the feature that distinguishes NGOs most sharply from the "top-down" approach of many official programmes.

NGOs' support for people's organizations, where face-to-face contact is the normal style of working, opens an ongoing debate on the form that interventions should take—sometimes with disconcerting results. In Bangladesh in the 1970s, Save the Children Fund (SCF) began working with the poorest women and children in the city slums. SCF wanted to concentrate on immunization and family planning, but the Slum Committees rejected this approach, insisting that the most urgent need was for curative health programmes. So that was the project's initial emphasis, and it was two years before SCF's preventive aspects were introduced.

But it should not be assumed that NGO contacts with people's organizations necessarily enhance participation. Sometimes, external assistance can discourage participation—or even repress it. This can happen when the NGOs feel under pressure to demonstrate concrete achievements quickly—to spend money fast. In the Philippines,

TABLE 5.1	
ODA flows through NGOs, 1983–86 (% of total)	
Switzerland	19.4
USA	11.1
Canada	10.8
Netherlands	7.0
Belgium	6.6
West Germany	6.5
Sweden	4.6
Italy	1.9
Japan	1.6
United Kingdom	1.3
France	0.3

the Ecosystems Research and Development Bureau, a quasi-autonomous agency, is working with local people's organizations to help improve livestock production in upland areas. Where people's organizations do not exist, the agency encourages people to form them, merely to take delivery of predetermined technologies.

Indeed, potential recipients might be tempted to form temporary or superficial groups if they sense that this is an easy way to obtain more goods or services. They tell the NGO "what it wants to hear" to gain access to the inputs they require. There is also the danger that people's organizations, after successfully attracting funds, are taken over by local elites who want to steer the inputs their way.

How far NGOs really enhance participation is impossible to say. But one recent Dutch study—with evidence from Brazil, Burkina Faso, Chile, India, Indonesia and Zimbabwe—concluded that NGOs had broadly increased empowerment, even if it could not offer quantitative evidence. It reported that people in the target groups now "... act more often as partners in discussions with organizations outside the village, have the courage to lodge complaints with civil servants of the local government, move freer and travel more. These are seemingly small changes but of essential importance for the people themselves."

A lesson many NGOs have learned is that efforts to promote participation and empowerment cannot be divorced from concrete economic achievements. If they are not simultaneously offering such improvements, efforts to promote empowerment come under strain.

An example: The Development Education and Leadership Training programme, initiated in Kenya in the early 1970s, has been adapted in Ghana, Nigeria, Sierra Leone, South Africa and Zimbabwe. The approach is to encourage communities to reflect on their place in society and their power to bring about change. But unless this awareness raising is matched by efforts to meet the immediate tangible needs of the groups involved, the result can be frustration and the group's disintegration.

The need for tangible outcomes is also an issue in Latin America now. For many years, NGO support of popular movements offered an outlet for people's democratic aspirations. Now that these have in many cases been fulfilled, people are focusing more on other matters. The poor and marginalized in people's organizations are demanding that empowerment efforts be complemented by activities that also address their pressing social and economic needs.

NGOs, like people's organizations, tend to be "value-driven" rather than profit-oriented or bureaucratically propelled. But this does not necessarily mean that they themselves work in a participatory fashion. While certainly open to a broad range of internal debate and discussion, many large organizations develop conventional bureaucratic characteristics.

Who exactly should be allowed to participate in the running of NGOs? Their trustees, their staff, their donors or the people they help? The order of priority today is probably staff, trustees, donors and, finally, beneficiaries. Many organizations refer not to "beneficiaries" but to "partners", though the equality of this partnership is sometimes open to doubt.

With such concerns so widespread, a statement at the end of a colloquy between NGOs and people's organizations in Sri Lanka in 1992 concluded that "NGOs must, as an objective, strive to increase the capability of people's organizations to articulate their concerns directly at the highest levels."

NGOs and government

NGOs have complex relations with governments, sometimes cooperating, sometimes in conflict—and often both simultaneously over different issues.

The NGOs' ability to promote participatory development is strongly influenced by the nature of the government. Where governments have been strong and authoritarian, one of the major contributions of NGOs has been to keep participatory democracy alive. In many countries in Latin America, and in the Philippines under

Efforts to promote participation and empowerment cannot be divorced from concrete economic achievements

Marcos, NGOs nurtured and supported a range of popular movements to oppose the excesses of national security states and to address poverty issues at the local level.

Where governments are hostile but weaker, there are many opportunities for NGOs to promote participatory development through social and economic projects. If the central government does not exert strong control, regional and district governments might be more able and willing to work with NGOs, especially where their interventions are successful and have the support of the people. Zaire in recent years falls into this category.

Strong governments that welcome NGOs may sound ideal, but not necessarily. Strong governments have strong views on what NGOs should be doing, and they commonly see NGOs as "gap-fillers" for inadequate social services rather than as champions of a different kind of development. But NGOs that have demonstrated successes with people's organizations may still be able to influence government approaches to development—as in Thailand and Zambia.

In recent years, the question of how NGOs and governments should work together has been sharpened by the widespread adoption of structural adjustment programmes. NGOs around the globe have been called upon to help mitigate the worst effects of these programmes, as well as take over some of the social services that governments can no longer finance. In most cases—such as the Gambia, Ghana, Guatemala and Uganda—NGOs have agreed to cooperate, often because this qualified them for government and external funds. In others—Bolivia is a striking example—NGOs have responded with greater reluctance. But in both cases, NGOs have been forced to reflect on how their approach meshes, or conflicts, with national policy. And governments for their part are realizing that NGOs and the participatory methods they promote have a role in national development.

The key issue now is how best to promote the strengths and interests of both governments and NGOs. Governments, seeing NGOs as widening their activities, will want to monitor, or probably control, them more closely. But they will have to find ways of doing this without nullifying the benefits they bring—introducing cumbersome procedures, for example, which inhibit NGOs or delay the speedy implementation of their programmes. And NGOs increasingly recognize that if they are not to be marginalized in national debates on the participatory approach to development, they have to engage more constructively with governments.

Governments and NGOs have to interact at three levels: line ministries, local government and national forums.

• *Central line ministries*—Government ministries need to know what NGOs are doing and devise mechanisms for using the insights that emerge from NGO interventions, and, where appropriate, include the activities of NGOs in future planning. They also need to encourage greater NGO involvement where the government is not involved.

The NGOs, for their part, need to carry out more rigorous assessment of their projects, cooperate and coordinate more closely among themselves and provide governments with more information on their activities and provide critiques and proposals on policy and legislation.

In many instances, it will be useful to have some form of government-NGO liaison body. These already exist in some countries, such as in the Philippines for agricultural research, and in Tanzania for health issues.

• *Local government*—NGO activities often challenge the local power structure. Indeed, that is often the intention. If the local power structure is elitist and oppresses the poor, this is something that NGOs will seek to change. But this attitude can spill over into arrogance and antagonism towards local politicians and administrators. NGOs need to be more sympathetic to the real problems facing local politicians and administrators.

And local governments for their part need to look beyond merely eliminating or controlling NGOs—to see them more as an opportunity for local gain than as a threat to local alliances. It ought to be possible in

The key issue is how best to promote the strengths and interests of both governments and NGOs

each district to establish a forum that provides for some interchange of ideas between the administration and NGOs, covering local development problems and the best ways of tackling them.

• *National forums*—In the past, NGOs have often had only a minimal impact on national debates about the form and content of development strategies. This is partly because most NGOs have concentrated on grass-roots activities and pursued only informal contacts with government officials. And in part it is also because governments have chosen not to discuss overall policy issues with NGOs. A major exception has been Latin America, where both NGOs and people's organizations have had a major role in the democratic movement, and in the Philippines, where NGOs constitute one-third of the membership of the Philippine Council for Sustainable Development, established in September 1992 to guide national followup to the Earth Summit.

But NGOs now recognize more the limits on what can be achieved at the grass-roots level and aim at having greater influence on national debates. This will require them to present a more united front and to devote more resources to having a much greater voice at the national level. If NGOs achieve that, the contribution they already make to participatory development at the grass-roots level could well be seen as only a relatively small part of their larger struggle to widen the opportunities for participatory development at the national level. In other words, the indirect impact of NGOs is often much wider than their direct contribution. Some specific country experiences are discussed below.

• *Bangladesh*—has one of the largest and most diversified NGO sectors in the world. No one knows the precise number, but at the start of the 1990s at least 12,000 groups were receiving financial and technical support. More than 550 local NGOs were registered with the Association for Development Agencies, and more than 300 national and foreign NGOs were getting funds from abroad. Around $100 million is channelled to NGOs from external sources (about 5% of total aid flows). Most are local and small, but some employ thousands of people.

Thought to reach 10–20% of the poor, NGOs in Bangladesh generally focus on the rural poor through a wide range of activities, which include both emergency assistance and long-term development. Credit has been one of their most important activities, and they have also been concentrating on income generation.

Most NGOs aim at empowering the poor, and particularly women, and they have had significant success. In some cases, however, groups have fallen apart, and there have been violent clashes when NGO programmes have encouraged people to confront local power blocs.

NGO relations with the government are complex and contradictory. On the one hand, they are welcomed to "supplement and complement government's development programmes". But the government has also at times seen them as a threat, undermining its legitimacy, and as a growing competitor for development finance, and has responded by placing obstacles in their way, including a restrictive process of registration and approval.

NGOs in Bangladesh do have an influence on government development policy, and the government has given some leading NGO figures important advisory positions. This could be seen as an endorsement of the value of NGOs—or as a way of co-opting potential opposition.

• *Chile*—showed a more rapid proliferation of NGOs in the 1970s than any other country in Latin America, a direct response to repression by the military regime. Large numbers of middle- and senior-level personnel were forced to leave government. Some were killed, and some fled abroad. But a high proportion moved to the voluntary sector, joining or creating NGOs sustained both by the church and by a massive injection of funds from overseas, governmental and non-governmental supporters.

The NGO movement worked in two ways. It was the focus of political opposition to the government, giving rise to an array of popular movements. But it was also working to mitigate the worst effects of pover-

The indirect impact of NGOs is often much wider than their direct contribution

ty—though here, too, popular education was always an important part of the process. NGOs were thus able to keep democratic ideals alive.

When a democratic government was elected in 1990, the participatory approach that NGOs had fostered became an important aspect of government policy—indeed, many people who spent time in NGOs now hold key government positions. In addition, the government has accepted that NGOs have an important role.

But this leaves the NGOs in something of a dilemma. Previously, their role was clear: they were united in opposition to General Pinochet. Now they have to develop a new role, which could take one of roughly three forms. Some groups are likely to draw back from popular education and participatory development to focus more on the delivery of services. Others, less certain of the durability of democracy, will maintain their distance from government. And a third group will probably combine its promotion of grass-roots participation with attempts to work with, and influence, the government.

Chile in the years ahead should be an interesting demonstration of participatory development being promoted simultaneously by the government from the top down, and by the NGOs from the bottom up.

• *Uganda*—is one of the poorest countries in Africa, and for most of its post-colonial history has been ravaged by war and civil unrest. Since 1986, the government has been attempting to create working state institutions. And alongside them are at least 250 local NGOs and 24 foreign-based ones with an emphasis thus far on emergency assistance and health programmes. More than $25 million in foreign funds went to local NGOs in 1990.

The government has been broadly supportive of NGOs, and the controls it applies to them are usually only administrative. This gives NGOs considerable freedom, but it has also meant that their services often run in parallel with those of the government and sometimes overlap. It means too that, with the possible exception of health care, NGOs have had little impact on public policy.

One significant area of NGO overlap with the government is in personnel. Since government salaries are inadequate, some NGOs, particularly the foreign ones, have been poaching government staff. Others have been "supplementing" the salaries of government workers and thus drawing them away from government projects and programmes. Either way, the effect has been to substitute NGO programmes for government ones.

Most Ugandan NGOs espouse participation, but this is not always evident in practice. Perhaps understandably, there is very little participation in emergency relief programmes. But even in long-term development programmes, the beneficiaries may have little involvement in planning. And when it comes to evaluation, the NGOs (like official aid organizations and developing country governments) often consider themselves more accountable to their donors than to the beneficiaries.

Effectiveness of NGOs

NGOs have certainly increased their outreach in recent years. Both the funds they spend and the numbers of people they deal with have been rising dramatically. In the early 1980s, one rough estimate suggested that NGO activity "touched" 100 million people in developing countries—60 million in Asia, 25 million in Latin America and some 12 million in Africa. Today, the total is probably nearer 250 million—and will rise considerably in the years ahead.

But NGO activity needs to be placed in perspective. The flows from northern NGOs and northern governments to NGOs in the South have been increasing. But the $7.2 billion in 1990 was still a small proportion of overall flows from North to South, equivalent to 13% of net disbursements of official aid, and only 2.5% of total resource flows to developing countries. Even if NGOs were to treble their spending by the year 2000, they would still account for less than 20% of official aid flows. But if ODA flows stagnate or shrink in real terms, the percentage will be higher.

It is difficult to judge how effective NGOs have been, whether in increasing ef-

NGO activities today touch the lives of about 250 million people in developing countries

ficiency, relieving poverty or promoting participation. There has been very little systematic analysis by the NGOs themselves or by independent organizations. Any general assessment of the impact of NGOs can thus be based only on partial evidence. This chapter considers:

1. Tackling poverty
2. Providing credit to the poor
3. Reaching the poorest
4. Empowering marginal groups
5. Challenging gender discrimination
6. Delivering emergency relief.

Tackling poverty

Many people judge NGOs primarily by their success in improving the living standards of the poor, and there are plenty of individual success stories. The landless have obtained land. Farmers are growing more food. Wells and boreholes have been sunk. Children have been inoculated against killer diseases. In these and countless other ways, NGOs have transformed the lives of millions of people all over the world.

The results have often been outstanding. In Zimbabwe, the agricultural groups supported by Silveira House increased crop yields sevenfold to tenfold, enabling farmers to break out of subsistence agriculture and move into the cash economy. In Burkina Faso, the *Groupements Naam* are helping 160,000 people to improve their communities and protect the environment (box 5.8). In south India, the Kanyakumari District Fisherman Sangam have significantly improved the lives of fishing communities by increasing the fish catches and by cutting out the merchants, giving the communities a fairer reward for their efforts.

But there have also been failures. An evaluation of income-generating activities supported by the Ford Foundation in Africa in the late 1980s concluded that there were "very few successes to talk about, especially in terms of post-intervention sustainability". Likewise, a mid-1980s study of projects supported by the European Community found that even projects selected for analysis because they had been "successful" failed to satisfy the evaluation criteria in a surprisingly large number of cases. Of the seven microprojects visited, six had quite serious problems.

More successes than failures? Nobody really knows.

What seems clear is that even people helped by successful projects still remain poor. NGO interventions do not generally help people escape from structural poverty, but they do reduce some of the worst forms of poverty. This might seem a modest achievement, but for the people helped, it can be very significant. If they are less preoccupied with the daily drudgery of making ends meet, or have a little cash to spend on items other than the barest necessities, they are in a much better position to focus on the next stage of the struggle to improve their lives.

Any assessment of NGOs' results should also take into account their operating circumstances. Compared with official aid donors (whose success rate is also unknown), NGOs take on much tougher tasks in very inhospitable environments. In Africa, where per capita incomes are falling almost everywhere, if NGOs can help people hold their incomes steady, this is a considerable accomplishment. And NGOs do this with very little money—less than 60 cents per person assisted, according to one Dutch study.

In addition, the benefits of NGO activity can often be indirect. Successful NGO interventions can induce other agencies to follow suit and replicate their experience elsewhere. In Zimbabwe, the experience of

TABLE 5.2
Shares of NGO credit in total credit advanced
(percent)

Country	Year	NGO credit share
Kenya	1990	1.6
Bangladesh	1990	0.6
Costa Rica	1992	0.2
Philippines	1990	0.1

BOX 5.8

Burkina Faso—Groupements Naam

The *Naam* groups started in 1967, in the Yatenga province of Burkina Faso, as a revival of traditional work groups. The basic idea is for the community to accumulate a production surplus and invest it in community development.

During the rainy season, group activities include cultivating market-garden plots and planting millet, cotton, sesame and groundnuts in communal fields. In the dry season, the focus shifts to soap making, textile production, animal husbandry and building fuel-efficient ovens. After provision is made for depreciation and the capital needed for new investments, the proceeds are shared among group members.

The *Naam* groups also undertake various community works, digging ditches, building rainwater storage tanks and small dams and tending community forests. The groups also promote sports and cultural activities and run literacy programmes.

In 1989, there were some 2,800 groups with more than 160,000 members. Their motto is "development without damage".

the Silveira House groups has been used by the government as the model for a major rural development initiative across the country. NGO successes can also induce other groups to form—and produce a ripple effect across communities or beyond, as has happened in Bangladesh and Sri Lanka (box 5.9).

Providing credit to the poor

One of the most important ways NGOs have made up for failures of the market is by providing credit. Poor people are often regarded as bad credit risks, and banks seldom are prepared to deal in the small sums that the poor need.

Many NGO credit schemes have taken over and adapted traditional self-help initiatives—known as *susu* in Ghana and *cheetu* in Sri Lanka. In Bangladesh, the traditional *samabaya* scheme was upgraded to the Swanirvar Movement. One of the best-known larger credit initiatives is also in Bangladesh—the Grameen Bank—which has an international reputation as an efficient rural credit scheme (box 5.10).

These schemes have often been highly successful—reaching the poorest people and giving them small amounts of low-cost credit. They have also had very high repayment rates—frequently in excess of 90%. They have shown that the poor are bankable—that their problem is lack of access to credit.

In some cases, however, administrative costs have been high, so that what had been intended as "revolving funds" have remained dependent on top-ups from donors. And on occasion, too many loans have been granted for consumption rather than investment.

A major concern for NGOs must be that their schemes—though generally useful, efficient and effective—are unlikely ever to be a major source of funds for poor people. In Costa Rica, where the *Fundación Costarricense de Desarrollo* is a significant source of credit for the poor, the NGOs provide only 0.2% of total credit. And in Bangladesh, even the impressive activities of the Grameen Bank account for only 0.1% of national credit. And all the NGOs

in Bangladesh combined provide only 0.6% of total credit (table 5.2).

This is not a criticism of the performance of NGOs, but a candid commentary on the situation. NGOs are in no position

BOX 5.9

Sri Lanka—Sarvodaya Sharamadana Movement

The Sarvodaya Sharamadana Movement (SSM) was founded in the late 1950s under the charismatic leadership of A. T. Ariyaratne to integrate low-caste families into the mainstream of national life. Now, it has more than 7,700 staff and covers 8,000 villages (more than a third of the total in Sri Lanka) in both Singhalese and Tamil parts of the country.

SSM takes its inspiration from Buddhist and Gandhian sources. It aims to help people mobilize their own resources, especially their labour, through forms of participation and self-sufficiency in tune with the country's cultural traditions.

It runs a variety of income-generating programmes, including batik and sewing shops, workshops for mechanical repairs and carpentry, printing presses and activities for farmers. On the welfare side, it has programmes for the deaf and disabled, relief and rehabilitation programmes (particularly for the victims of ethnic conflict), and nutrition programmes aimed especially at preschool children.

A recent survey of SSM and non-SSM villages in the same region found that people in SSM villages were much more likely to have overcome apathy and mutual suspicion. SSM's participatory approach has encouraged a new leadership, enabling people to bypass the inegalitarian structures associated with the temples, mutual aid committees and political parties.

SSM has also begun to work at the national level. Through seminars and discussion groups with lawyers, the police, the judiciary and various action groups, it is challenging the idea of development as a purely economic issue—and arguing that it should give greater priority to human concerns.

BOX 5.10

Bangladesh—the Grameen Bank

The Grameen Bank in Bangladesh is one of the most successful experiments in extending credit to the landless poor.

It started in 1976 in the village of Jobra. Professor Muhammad Yunus saw that it was impossible for landless people to get loans from commercial banks since they could offer no collateral. He decided personally to guarantee bank loans to the poor. This proved very successful: repayment rates were above 99%. The poor were bankable.

In 1983, the project became a full-fledged bank. The Bangladesh government contributed 60% of the initial paid-up capital, and the rest came from the savings of the borrowers themselves. International support has been considerable, but dependence on foreign funding has declined from 83% to 60%.

The bank's most significant innovation is to organize people into groups of five, and ask each person to guarantee the repayment of a loan to any of the other four members. The chair of each group has a weekly review meeting with a staff member of the bank. This combination of collective collateral, close supervision and peer group pressure has resulted in very high repayment rates (currently around 95%).

By 1991, the bank had extended its services to more than 23,000 villages through its nearly 900 branches. Around one million households have received credit. The average loan is $60, and the interest rate (16%) contains no subsidy. Primarily for working capital, the loans have generated a great deal of employment, especially for rural women.

Borrowers are also required to add one taka per week to their savings account. By 1991 this compulsory savings fund had accumulated Tk. 962 million—62% of outstanding loans.

to replace governments or commercial markets in the provision of credit. So, one of the most important roles of NGOs in this area must be to put pressure on governments to change their policies and priorities.

Reaching the poorest

NGOs often manage to reach groups that governments find most difficult to help, tending to work with people in rural areas, where government services are usually weak or non-existent. But many are now also focusing on urban areas, as in Bangladesh, Chile, South Africa and Zambia.

Whether they reach the *very* poorest, however, is another matter. If government and official aid programmes usually fail to reach the poorest 20% of income groups, most NGO interventions probably miss the poorest 5–10%. This would include, for example, the sick and the elderly as well as those with few assets and little or no education—as well as the high proportion of households headed by women. Such people are often dispersed and difficult to form into groups. And because they often live in remote and inaccessible regions, reaching them can be very expensive. On the whole, it is easier for NGOs to reach the not-so-poor than the very poorest.

When helping in rural areas, it is usually easier to assist those who have some productive land. In the Gambia, NGOs participating in the Farmer Innovation and Technology Testing Programme focus on the middle-income farmers. And in Kenya, a local NGO has an Agroforestry Plots for Rural Kenya Project, funded by the Ford Foundation, which has rarely contained representatives from the poorest households.

Many interventions do, however, reach such people. NGOs in Latin America and South Asia in particular have often worked with landless labourers. One way even the poorest can be reached is to have the activity embrace everybody in a given area, as with the various Campfire projects run by the Zimbabwe Trust and the Worldwide Fund for Nature in the Zambezi Valley—projects that generate income through the hunting and care of wildlife.

Until the early 1980s, most NGO interventions were gender-blind

Empowering marginal groups

In most developing countries, poverty is often caused less by an absolute shortage of resources than by their skewed distribution. The NGOs' emphasis on empowerment is partly a reflection of this, and their interventions do indeed occasionally enable poor people to resist local elites and claim their rights. In such cases, they are likely to come up against official opposition—as well as opposition from powerful local interests.

Some of the sharpest conflicts have been over land rights. In many countries, especially in Asia and Latin America, NGOs have been defending the land rights of minorities, pressuring governments to provide land for the landless and to embark on agrarian reform. In Ecuador, Indian federations have been formed to help the indigenous people gain secure title to their land. This has not only helped them materially, it has also strengthened their communities and helped challenge myths about Indian social and intellectual inferiority.

In several countries, NGOs have helped empower people in rural areas by organizing them into groups. For instance, in Zimbabwe, networking among groups has increased their effectiveness (box 5.11).

Challenging gender discrimination

Until the early 1980s, most NGO interventions were gender-blind, like those of other development agencies. Although there was always a small number of projects and programmes assisting grass-roots women's groups, the specific needs of women in general antipoverty programmes were often ignored. Today, NGOs are much more sensitive to such issues and often attempt to include gender- and women-focused elements in many of their initiatives. In part, this has been in response to pressures from the growing women's movement in many developing countries. And some NGOs have been established specifically to enhance the power of women in the family and in society.

In Cameroon, the Women's Networking Association brings together 50 women's groups. It carries out literacy campaigns and gives women other practical help—such as establishing a cooperative to purchase the produce that village women bring to market but are unable to sell at the end of the day. The association also organizes seminars and conferences to raise women's concerns at the national level.

In Kenya, the Green Belt Movement, tackling the intertwined problems of environmental degradation and poverty, is encouraging women to use soil rehabilitation measures and natural fertilizers. With the involvement of 50,000 women, it has planted ten million trees in Kenya. Also responsive to the needs of the women in the poorest families, the movement has established training centres to increase women's employment opportunities.

NGOs in many countries concentrate on advocacy on behalf of women. The Alliance of Costa Rican Women provides legal and health services to more than 4,000 low-income women. But it also campaigns to improve the status of poor women and publishes information on legal and heath issues, and on violence against women.

Even so, too many NGO projects still fail to challenge prevailing patterns of gender discrimination. Too often, the attempts to incorporate gender issues into projects have been only superficial, resulting in little empowerment of women. In other cases, project successes have been eclipsed by the more powerful forces in society.

Delivering emergency relief

One great strength of NGOs is their ability to respond quickly and effectively to emergencies. Indeed, a high proportion of NGOs were founded in response to emergencies from famines, wars or earthquakes—and only later did they extend their activities to long-term development. NGOs can bring five main strengths to emergency and relief work:

1. *Warning of disaster*—With an extended network of contacts on the ground, NGOs are in a good position to draw the attention of the international community to existing or impending emergencies, particularly vital when the government chooses to downplay the emergency or exclude bilateral or multilateral agencies. NGOs often make powerful use of the news media for this purpose—as with the Bangladesh cyclone in 1970, the Maharashtra drought in 1974 in India, the Ethiopian famine in the early 1970s and the Sub-Saharan crisis of 1984–85. Their dramatic efforts can also attract international attention—as Oxfam did in 1979, when it chartered a boat, filled it with food and medical supplies and sailed it from Hong Kong to Kompon Som in Cambodia.

2. *Advocacy for international action*—Following their warnings, the NGOs can lobby governments and international organizations to increase their resources for emergencies, sometimes through international consortia. Agencies in the European Community, for example, lobbied the EC to raise food aid to Africa from 1.5 million tons in 1990 to 2.1 million tons in 1991.

3. *Speedy response*—Untrammelled by bureaucratic and political constraints, NGOs can usually act much faster than official agencies. And since they are less susceptible to political pressures, they sometimes work where governments forbid interventions from government or multilateral agencies—as in Cambodia in the late 1970s and in Eritrea and Tigray in the early 1980s. In Somalia in the most recent

Attempts to incorporate gender issues into projects have too often been superficial

---

BOX 5.11
Zimbabwe—Organization of Rural Associations for Progress

The Organization of Rural Associations for Progress (ORAP), an indigenous NGO in Zimbabwe, acts as an umbrella organization for local groups, each with five to 30 rural families. These are often traditional work groups that managed to survive the paternalist and racist practices of the colonial period. ORAP provides funds and technical assistance, but the groups and their regional associations make the key decisions.

Most group members are farmers, so ORAP focused initially on generating income in agriculture. Lately, it has also been engaged in education, sanitation and extension services—and in food security and drought relief. Current projects include grinding mills, gardens, irrigation schemes, sewing and savings clubs, animal husbandry and horticulture.

Now operating in three provinces, ORAP employed 60 people directly in 1990, had an annual budget of around $1 million and covered more than 1,000 groups (80,000 families), which were also organized into 16 higher associations.

Also operating in the same areas as ORAP, the government is essentially delivering services, while ORAP puts the emphasis on participation and social mobilization. ORAP's approach is being studied by other groups in Zimbabwe, since it seems successfully to have blended an efficient service organization with a popular grass-roots movement.

---

emergency, such organizations as the Red Cross, Save the Children, CARE, Concern and *Médecins Sans Frontières* stayed on after the international agencies had left, even during periods of intense fighting. Today, they are responsible for much of the food distribution and, along with the International Committee of the Red Cross, are bringing in nearly 20,000 tons of food a month and running 800 kitchens for more than a million people.

4. *Cooperation with indigenous organizations*—Emergency aid is generally better administered by local organizations more sensitive to local needs. NGOs have been able to use their existing contacts to good effect and to help boost the capacity of local groups where needed. In the Sudan recently, the only NGO permitted by the government to visit the urban slums around Khartoum has been the Sudan Council of Churches, through which northern NGOs have been able to channel funds.

5. *Disaster preparedness*—Most disasters hit the poor hardest, the people living on marginal land liable to flooding or in mud houses that collapse in earthquakes. Local NGOs can try to ensure that the poor are better able to anticipate problems. In Bangladesh, the Ganges-Kobadak cooperatives monitor embankment breaches to warn of danger. And the NGO emphasis on participation and empowerment puts local communities in a stronger position to pick themselves up again more quickly after a disaster strikes.

It would be wrong, however, to assume that NGO responses to disaster are always beneficial. They can also create problems by poorly coordinating many agencies and by bringing in inexperienced workers—as with the Karamoja drought in Uganda in the late 1970s. And there have also been occasions when foreign NGOs have moved in and undermined local agencies and government efforts—as in Mozambique in the late 1980s.

Another common NGO failing in emergencies is that there is little evaluation of their work, so that mistakes are repeated in one emergency after another.

The future of NGOs

Many northern NGOs, but increasingly also southern NGOs, have joined in debates of such issues as the debt crisis, international trade, structural adjustment, the environment, women in development and peace. They now often employ or commission economists and other specialists to monitor such matters and produce detailed reports as well as campaigning materials.

NGOs have become accepted by people, governments and business as a legitimate voice, lobbying not just their own governments or enterprises, but also many international gatherings. And it seems clear that the voices of NGOs have prompted many actors to reassess their policies, as with the impact of structural adjustment on the poor. They have also enforced changes in the behaviour of multinational corporations, as in the marketing of infant formula and the use of fertilizers and pharmaceutical drugs in developing countries. And at the time of the Earth Summit in Rio de Janeiro in June 1992, NGOs kept up constant pressure on their governments for real changes in policy. Advocacy clearly is—and probably will continue to be—the NGOs' greatest strength.

NGOs affect relatively small (but growing) numbers of people: 250 million is less than 20% of the 1.3 billion people living in absolute poverty in developing countries. And by the end of the 1990s, optimistic assumptions suggest that they will reach nearly 30%.

In eradicating poverty and providing social services, NGOs are unlikely ever to play more than a complementary role. Much more significant is their ability to demonstrate participatory models that governments might follow—and to keep pressure on governments, in both the North and the South, encouraging them to focus more on the human development of the world's poorest people. Again, their importance lies more in making the point that poverty can be tackled rather than tackling it to any large extent. This, too, will continue to be a critical role for NGOs.

Advocacy clearly is the NGOs' greatest strength

Encouraging participation means responding sensitively to the felt needs of people and communities—and responding in ways that meet those needs without "taking over". There is always the risk of placing too much emphasis on effective delivery and too little on nurturing and strengthening participation. This tendency is likely to be heightened as NGOs open themselves up as channels for government funds. Government aid departments are used to demanding regular quantitative results and reports, and many have yet to accept fully that NGO projects need to be treated (somewhat) differently.

There is also the possibility that NGOs could "crowd out" governments. In some cases, they can offer local people better salaries and draw experienced people out of government service. Already happening in Mozambique and Uganda, this is likely to increase.

None of these concerns is new to the NGO community. Their "growing pains", evident for some years now, have been the subject of considerable internal debate. As their responsibilities and activities increase further, they will no doubt respond to this new challenge with their usual energy, creativity and commitment.

The increasing numbers of people's organizations and NGOs is a clear demonstration of how people all over the world are demanding greater participation in civil society.

These demands are likely to gather strength in the years ahead. Once set in motion, democratic movements are difficult to stop—they develop a rhythm and momentum of their own. People who know more, earn more and can do more will be raising their voices ever more loudly for greater participation in every process that affects their lives. And they will be requiring that governments, markets and all the institutions of a civil society respond to their real needs.

Authoritarian regimes might still stifle and repress. And new forms of intolerance, such as fundamentalism, might suddenly capture attention and power. But history is not on their side. The steady trend towards the dispersal of power, information and ideas cannot be reversed.

If states are to survive, they will have to establish new relationships with their people. Governments that have been able to respond sensitively and flexibly have so far been able to keep their countries intact. Others have not, and their states have come under increasing pressure.

Greater people's participation is no longer a vague ideology based on the wishful thinking of a few idealists. It has become an imperative—a condition of survival.

Greater people's participation has become an imperative—a condition of survival

Technical notes

1. The human development index

Construction of the human development index (HDI)
The HDI includes three key components—longevity, knowledge and income, which are combined to arrive at an average deprivation index (for a full technical description, see *Human Development Report 1991*, technical note 1, pp. 88–89). Longevity is measured by life expectancy at birth as the sole unadjusted indicator. Knowledge is measured by two educational stock variables: adult literacy and mean years of schooling. The measure of educational achievement is adjusted by assigning a weight of two-thirds to literacy and one-third to mean years of schooling:

$$E = a_1 \text{ LITERACY} + a_2 \text{ YEARS OF SCHOOLING}$$
$$a_1 = \frac{2}{3} \text{ and } a_2 = \frac{1}{3}$$

For income, the HDI is based on the premise of diminishing returns from income for human development using an explicit formulation for the diminishing return. A well-known and frequently used form is the Atkinson formulation for the utility of income:

$$W(y) = \frac{1}{1-\epsilon} \times y^{1-\epsilon}$$

Here, $W(y)$ is the utility or well-being derived from income, and the parameter measures the extent of diminishing returns. It is the elasticity of the marginal utility of income with respect to income. If $\epsilon = 0$ there are no diminishing returns. As ϵ approaches 1, the equation becomes:

$$W(y) = \log y$$

The value of ϵ rises slowly in the HDI as income rises. For this purpose, the full range of income is divided into multiples of the poverty line y^*. Thus, most countries are between 0 and y^*, some between y^* and $2y^*$, even fewer between $2y^*$ and $3y^*$ and so on. For all countries for which $y < y^*$—that is, the poor countries—ϵ is set equal to 0. There are no diminishing returns here. For income between y^* and $2y^*$, ϵ is set equal to 1/2. For income between $2y^*$ and $3y^*$, ϵ is set at 2/3. In general, if $ay^* \leq y \leq (a+1)y^*$, then $\epsilon = a/(a+1)$. This gives:

$$W(y) = y \text{ for } 0 < y \leq y^*$$
$$= y^* + 2(y - y^*)^{\frac{1}{2}} \text{ for } y^* \leq y \leq 2y^*$$
$$= y^* + 2(y^*)^{\frac{1}{2}} + 3(y - 2y^*)^{\frac{1}{3}} \text{ for } 2y^* \leq y \leq 3y^*$$

So, the higher the income relative to the poverty level, the more sharply the diminishing returns affect the contribution of income to human development. Income above the poverty line thus has a marginal effect, but not a full dollar-for-dollar effect. This marginal effect is enough, however, to differentiate significantly among industrial countries. This method does not take $\epsilon = 1$, but allows it to vary between 0 and 1.

For example, Singapore has a real GDP per capita of $15,880. With the poverty line set at $4,829, there are four terms in the equation to determine the well-being of Singapore:

$$W(y) = y^* + 2(y^*)^{\frac{1}{2}} + 3(y^*)^{\frac{1}{3}} + 4(y - 3y^*)^{\frac{1}{4}}$$
$$= 4,829 + 2(4,829)^{\frac{1}{2}}$$
$$+ 3(4,829)^{\frac{1}{3}}$$
$$+ 4(15,880 - 14,487)^{\frac{1}{4}}$$
$$= 4,829 + 139 + 51 + 24 = \$5,043$$

In calculating the HDI of Singapore using the improved variables and applying the methods described here, the following steps are taken:

Maximum country life expectancy	=	78.6
Minimum country life expectancy	=	42.0
Maximum country educational attainment	=	3.00
Minimum country educational attainment	=	0.00
Maximum country adjusted real GDP per capita	=	5,075
Minimum country adjusted real GDP per capita	=	367
Singapore life expectancy	=	74.0
Singapore educational attainment	=	2.04
Singapore adjusted GDP per capita	=	5,043
Singapore life expectancy deprivation = (78.6 – 74.0)/(78.6 – 42.0)	=	0.126

Singapore educational attainment deprivation
$$= (3.00 - 2.04)/(3.00 - 0.00) \qquad = 0.320$$
Singapore GDP deprivation
$$= (5,075 - 5,043)/(5,075 - 367) \qquad = 0.007$$
Singapore average deprivation
$$= (0.126 + 0.320 + 0.007)/3 \qquad = 0.151$$
Singapore human development index
$$= 1 - 0.151 \qquad = 0.849$$

Making the HDI gender-sensitive

For 33 countries we have comparable data on the relative wages and the relative rates of labour force participation for men and women (technical note table 1.1). These data reveal a remarkable pattern of discrimination. The female-male wage ratio for these 33 countries ranges from a low of 51% (Japan) to a high of 89% (Sweden). In labour force participation, the lowest female-male ratio is 40% (Costa Rica) and the highest is 92% (Sweden). Multiplying these two ratios gives the female-male wage-income ratio.

This wage-income ratio combines two identifiable correlates of gender discrimination. There is a gap between male and female wages, and an even greater gap in labour force participation rates. When this is translated into absolute income levels, we see the profound consequences. To do this, a basic assumption has to be made that is clearly gender-biased: that the ratio of non-wage income to wage income is the same for men and women. This ratio therefore understates the inequality.

In adjusted real GDP per capita, female incomes as a percentage of male incomes range from a low of 26% (Costa Rica) to a high of 82% (Sweden). But of the 33 countries for which we have comparable data, only nine have a ratio of 60% or above, while ten have a ratio below 40%. So, even in a statistic that understates the inequality, the differences are stark.

The female HDI gains from the near-equal or better ratio in life expectancy but loses from women's unequal access to education, particularly in the developing countries. In education, the industrial countries show very little gender difference: though the value for female achievement as a proportion of male achievement never goes above 104%, in seven countries it goes below 96%. In poorer countries the differences become substantial.

The overall HDI calculated separately for men and women reflects this pattern. Of the 33 countries for which the data are available, 22 are industrial countries. So, technical note table 1.1 does not capture the full extent of gender inequality.

How should this inequality be reflected in the overall HDI for any country? A simple approach is to multiply the overall HDI for any country by the ratio of the female HDI to the male HDI.

Adjusting the HDI for income distribution

The HDI is a national average, just like real income per capita, one of its components. The HDI therefore needs to be made sensitive to these distributions. It has the advantage that two of its three basic variables—life expectancy and educational attainment—are naturally distributed much less unequally than is income, the third

variable. A rich person cannot live a thousand times longer than a poor person, though their incomes may be in that ratio. Across countries, the range of life expectancy is 42 to 79, less than 2:1. Similarly, the percentage of adults who are literate ranges from 18% to 99%, a ratio of under 6:1. Mean years of schooling range from 0.1 to 12.3, revealing greater differences than in life expectancy.

All the variables used in the HDI have an obvious maximum, except for per capita income, which has no upper bound. For GNP per capita, the range among countries is $80 to $32,250, a ratio of 403:1. For real GDP per capita, the range is $367 (PPP) to $21,449 (PPP), or 58:1. Such inequalities in income are reproduced just as sharply within countries.

The ranking of countries by per capita income could be adjusted if per capita income were multiplied by a factor indicating distributional inequality—1 minus the Gini coefficient. For 41 countries data are available on the ra-

TECHNICAL NOTE TABLE 1.1
Gender-disparity-adjusted HDI

Country	HDI value	Female as % of male			Average female-male ratio for the three HDI components (percent)	Gender-disparity-adjusted HDI	Percentage difference between HDI and gender-disparity-adjusted HDI	Difference between HDI and gender-disparity-adjusted ranks[b]
		Life expectancy[a]	Educational attainment	Adjusted real GDP				
Sweden	0.977	101.1	100.0	81.9	94.3	0.921	−5.7	4
Norway	0.978	102.1	98.3	69.5	90.0	0.881	−10.0	1
France	0.971	104.2	101.7	61.0	88.9	0.864	−11.1	5
Denmark	0.955	101.2	98.4	70.6	90.1	0.860	−9.9	8
Finland	0.954	103.8	97.9	68.3	90.0	0.859	−10.0	8
Australia	0.972	102.3	98.5	62.3	87.7	0.852	−12.3	1
New Zealand	0.947	101.5	103.9	61.7	89.0	0.844	−11.0	9
Netherlands	0.970	102.1	103.8	49.7	85.2	0.826	−14.8	1
USA	0.976	103.0	101.6	48.7	84.4	0.824	−15.6	−3
United Kingdom	0.964	101.0	101.8	51.6	84.8	0.818	−15.2	0
Canada	0.982	102.5	96.7	50.1	83.1	0.816	−16.9	−9
Belgium	0.952	102.3	100.0	52.5	84.9	0.808	−15.1	3
Austria	0.952	103.1	89.7	53.6	82.1	0.782	−17.9	1
Switzerland	0.978	102.1	93.0	40.7	78.6	0.768	−21.4	−10
Germany	0.957	102.1	90.4	48.4	80.3	0.768	−19.7	−4
Italy	0.924	102.2	98.6	47.3	82.7	0.764	−17.3	3
Japan	0.983	100.8	98.1	33.9	77.6	0.763	−22.4	−16
Czechoslovakia	0.892	103.8	88.4	61.4	84.5	0.754	−15.5	4
Ireland	0.925	100.9	102.3	30.4	77.9	0.720	−22.1	−1
Luxembourg	0.943	102.5	95.1	29.2	75.6	0.713	−24.4	−3
Greece	0.902	102.7	89.0	38.2	76.6	0.691	−23.4	0
Portugal	0.853	102.7	75.8	57.7	78.7	0.672	−21.3	3
Cyprus	0.890	100.1	85.5	35.5	73.7	0.656	−26.3	0
Costa Rica	0.852	99.8	96.6	26.3	74.2	0.632	−25.8	2
Hong Kong	0.913	100.6	62.8	39.8	67.7	0.618	−32.3	−5
Singapore	0.849	101.1	66.1	39.5	68.9	0.585	−31.1	1
Korea, Rep. of	0.872	102.4	60.9	27.5	63.6	0.555	−36.4	−3
Paraguay	0.641	100.0	88.1	67.4	85.2	0.546	−14.8	1
Sri Lanka	0.663	99.6	79.7	46.5	75.3	0.499	−24.7	−1
Philippines	0.603	99.5	89.3	35.4	74.7	0.451	−25.3	0
Swaziland	0.458	100.7	81.8	43.2	75.2	0.344	−24.8	0
Myanmar	0.390	99.3	71.8	57.7	76.3	0.297	−23.7	0
Kenya	0.369	100.2	41.8	54.0	65.3	0.241	−34.7	0

a. Adjusted for natural biological life expectancy advantage for females.
b. A positive figure shows that the gender-disparity-adjusted HDI rank is higher than the unadjusted HDI rank, a negative the opposite.

tio of the income share of the highest 20% to the lowest 20%. Of these, 17 have data on the Gini coefficient as well, and there was found to be a very strong association between the two—the logarithm of the ratio being a good predictor of the Gini coefficient. This regression result was used to interpolate the Gini coefficient for another 11 countries, for a total of 52 countries (technical note table 1.2).

TECHNICAL NOTE TABLE 1.2
Income-distribution-adjusted HDI

Country	HDI value	Income-distribution-adjusted HDI value	Percentage difference between HDI and income-distribution-adjusted HDI	Difference between HDI and income-distribution-adjusted ranks[a]
Japan	0.983	0.981	–0.20	0
Netherlands	0.970	0.966	–0.41	7
Switzerland	0.978	0.958	–2.05	1
Sweden	0.977	0.958	–1.95	1
Norway	0.978	0.956	–2.25	–2
Canada	0.982	0.947	–3.56	–4
Belgium	0.952	0.946	–0.63	6
United Kingdom	0.964	0.945	–1.98	1
USA	0.976	0.943	–3.38	–3
France	0.971	0.938	–3.41	–2
Australia	0.972	0.934	–3.91	–4
Finland	0.954	0.932	–2.31	0
Denmark	0.955	0.925	–3.15	–2
Israel	0.938	0.912	–2.77	1
New Zealand	0.947	0.909	–4.01	–1
Ireland	0.925	0.908	–1.85	0
Spain	0.923	0.898	–2.71	1
Italy	0.924	0.892	–3.47	–1
Korea, Rep. of	0.872	0.885	1.49	2
Hungary	0.887	0.873	–1.68	0
Hong Kong	0.913	0.871	–4.60	–2
Singapore	0.849	0.836	–1.53	3
Costa Rica	0.852	0.829	–2.61	1
Chile	0.864	0.818	–5.33	–2
Portugal	0.853	0.802	–6.00	–2
Argentina	0.832	0.791	–4.92	0
Venezuela	0.824	0.771	–6.43	0
Mauritius	0.794	0.745	–6.18	1
Mexico	0.805	0.737	–8.46	–1
Colombia	0.770	0.734	–4.75	1
Malaysia	0.790	0.732	–7.35	–1
Thailand	0.715	0.672	–5.99	4
Panama	0.738	0.654	–11.35	–1
Turkey	0.717	0.650	–9.39	1
Syrian Arab Rep.	0.694	0.644	–7.22	2
Jamaica	0.736	0.643	–12.60	–3
Sri Lanka	0.663	0.634	–4.30	1
Brazil	0.730	0.627	–14.07	–4
Tunisia	0.600	0.583	–2.75	1
Philippines	0.603	0.575	–4.67	–1
Iran, Islamic Rep. of	0.557	0.519	–6.76	0
Indonesia	0.515	0.519	0.81	0
El Salvador	0.503	0.488	–3.01	0
Honduras	0.472	0.419	–11.21	0
Egypt	0.389	0.377	–3.12	0
Kenya	0.369	0.344	–6.83	0
Pakistan	0.311	0.303	–2.62	1
Zambia	0.314	0.291	–7.30	–1
India	0.309	0.289	–6.40	0
Côte d'Ivoire	0.286	0.246	–13.84	0
Bangladesh	0.189	0.172	–9.19	0
Nepal	0.170	0.138	–19.05	0

a. A positive figure shows that the income-distribution-adjusted HDI rank is higher than the unadjusted HDI rank, a negative the opposite.

Adjusted income was multiplied by $(1 - G)$, with G being the Gini coefficient, to modify income even further. Because this was done for the adjusted income, $W(y)$, rather than for the actual income, the diminishing return effect could be incorporated before the distributional adjustment modifies incomes further. This modified income $W(y)[1 - G]$ is then used as the third variable in addition to life expectancy and educational attainment to compute a distribution-adjusted HDI.

Measuring progress in human development over time
The human development index ranks countries relative to each other for a particular year. The maximum and minimum values that define the maximum distance to be travelled for each variable are specific to that year. Over time, the actual achieved values of life expectancy, literacy and income change, as will the maximum and minimum values of these variables across all countries.

So, improvements in the components of human development in any country over time may be reflected as a decline in its HDI value, if in the meantime its relative position has deteriorated. To combine a measure of progress over time with comparisons among countries at one point of time, the HDI has to be modified.

The way to tackle this problem, without changing the logic of the HDI, is to say that the minimum and maximum should be defined, not for each point of time, but over a period of time, using fixed goalposts. Thus, if we are measuring progress between 1970 and 1990, the minimum would be the minimum of all values of, say, life expectancy for all countries over the 20 years. Similarly for the maximum. The distance to be travelled is thus stretched out as the maximum over the 20-year period.

With this adaptation, the human development index becomes comparable over time as well as across countries. The difference in the value of the human development index over time can be shown to be a weighted sum of the growth rates in the three variables: the weights are given by the ratio of the initial value of a variable to the maximum range.

To express this algebraically—with X_1 as life expectancy, X_2 as literacy and X_3 as income—the contribution of each variable to the HDI can be written as Z_i, where:

$$Z_{ijt} = \frac{[X_{ijt} - \min_{j,t} X_{ijt}]}{[\max_{j,t} X_{ijt} - \min_{j,t} X_{ijt}]}$$

In the formula, j denotes the country, t the time period. Note now that the denominator will remain unchanged for all time periods and for all countries.

$$MHDI_{jt} = \frac{1}{3} \sum Z_{ijt}$$

$MHDI$ stands for the modified HDI since we have a new definition of the maximum and minimum. Countries are ranked by the size of the difference between the 1970 and 1990 values for the $MHDI$. These differences range from 0.302 for Saudi Arabia to –0.089 for Romania. For Romania, however, the HDI in 1970 was already quite high (0.798), and the lack of change does not necessarily reflect absolute deterioration (technical note table 1.3).

Disaggregating the HDI within a country

Within each country, there are very significant disparities: among ethnic groups, among subregions, between urban and rural areas and between the sexes. Unfortunately, there are not sufficient readily available data to present these disaggregations for most countries. They are illustrated in chapter 1 for five countries, one industrial country, the United States, and one from each of the developing regions, Mexico, India, Turkey and Swaziland. These countries have been used for illustrative purposes because reliable disaggregated data are available for them, and it is to their credit that such internal human development analyses are possible. The same disparities occur to a greater or lesser degree in other countries for which reliable disaggregated data are not available.

Disaggregated HDIs are arrived at by using the data for the HDI components pertaining to each of the groups into which the HDI is disaggregated, treating each group as if it were a separate country. The methodology is exactly the same as for the national HDIs. A country HDI using the same data components as the subnational HDIs is also calculated, and the country figure is adjusted to equal the figure for the national HDI found in indicator table 1 on the human development index. All group calculations are then adjusted proportionately so that the disaggregated HDIs are comparable to the national HDIs of this *Human Development Report.* In this way, it is possible to say where disaggregated groups of a particular country would rank among the other countries in indicator table 1 on the human development index.

TECHNICAL NOTE TABLE 1.3
Changing HDI over time

Country	HDI 1970	HDI 1990	Difference 1970–90	Country	HDI 1970	HDI 1990	Difference 1970–90	Country	HDI 1970	HDI 1990	Difference 1970–90
Saudi Arabia	0.386	0.688	0.302	Norway	0.870	0.978	0.108	Nepal	0.126	0.170	0.044
Korea, Rep. of	0.589	0.872	0.283	Belgium	0.846	0.952	0.106	Bulgaria	0.815	0.854	0.039
Mauritius	0.525	0.794	0.269	Ecuador	0.542	0.646	0.104	Panama	0.703	0.738	0.035
Tunisia	0.335	0.600	0.265	Sweden	0.873	0.977	0.104	Madagascar	0.292	0.327	0.035
Syrian Arab Rep.	0.432	0.694	0.262	Netherlands	0.866	0.970	0.104	Paraguay	0.607	0.641	0.034
Malaysia	0.538	0.790	0.252	Egypt	0.286	0.389	0.103	Zimbabwe	0.365	0.398	0.033
Botswana	0.319	0.552	0.233	Luxembourg	0.841	0.943	0.102	Burundi	0.135	0.167	0.032
Turkey	0.492	0.717	0.225	Spain	0.821	0.923	0.102	Zaire	0.232	0.262	0.030
Indonesia	0.316	0.515	0.199	Iraq	0.489	0.589	0.100	Mali	0.054	0.082	0.028
Thailand	0.535	0.715	0.180	New Zealand	0.848	0.947	0.099	Liberia	0.194	0.222	0.028
Algeria	0.358	0.528	0.170	Congo	0.278	0.372	0.094	Somalia	0.061	0.087	0.026
Morocco	0.268	0.433	0.165	Italy	0.830	0.924	0.094	Niger	0.054	0.080	0.026
Brazil	0.569	0.730	0.161	Trinidad and Tobago	0.784	0.877	0.093	Central African Rep.	0.138	0.159	0.021
Jordan	0.428	0.582	0.154	Iceland	0.867	0.960	0.093	El Salvador	0.483	0.503	0.020
Colombia	0.617	0.770	0.153	Iran, Islamic Rep. of	0.464	0.557	0.093	Malawi	0.149	0.168	0.019
Hong Kong	0.762	0.913	0.151	Costa Rica	0.759	0.852	0.093	Bolivia	0.383	0.398	0.015
Portugal	0.710	0.853	0.143	Denmark	0.864	0.955	0.091	Bangladesh	0.174	0.189	0.015
Yemen Arab Rep.	0.093	0.233	0.140	Sri Lanka	0.574	0.663	0.089	Myanmar	0.384	0.390	0.006
Gabon	0.370	0.503	0.133	Honduras	0.385	0.472	0.087	Chad	0.083	0.088	0.005
Israel	0.806	0.938	0.132	Ireland	0.840	0.925	0.085	Sierra Leone	0.060	0.065	0.005
Mexico	0.675	0.805	0.130	Pakistan	0.226	0.311	0.085	Poland	0.829	0.831	0.002
Japan	0.853	0.983	0.130	Cameroon	0.228	0.310	0.082	Burkina Faso	0.073	0.074	0.001
Chile	0.736	0.864	0.128	Uruguay	0.799	0.881	0.082	Rwanda	0.185	0.186	0.001
USA	0.848	0.976	0.128	Haiti	0.200	0.275	0.075	Peru	0.595	0.592	−0.003
Australia	0.849	0.972	0.123	Côte d'Ivoire	0.212	0.286	0.074	Sudan	0.155	0.152	−0.003
Canada	0.860	0.982	0.122	Dominican Rep.	0.513	0.586	0.073	Angola	0.147	0.143	−0.004
Singapore	0.730	0.849	0.119	Guatemala	0.416	0.489	0.073	Benin	0.117	0.113	−0.004
France	0.854	0.971	0.117	Ghana	0.246	0.311	0.065	Zambia	0.320	0.314	−0.006
Kenya	0.253	0.369	0.116	Philippines	0.542	0.603	0.061	Afghanistan	0.083	0.066	−0.017
Finland	0.838	0.954	0.116	Senegal	0.124	0.182	0.058	Papua New Guinea	0.342	0.318	−0.024
Switzerland	0.863	0.978	0.115	Hungary	0.830	0.887	0.057	Guinea	0.074	0.045	−0.029
Austria	0.838	0.952	0.114	Nigeria	0.189	0.246	0.057	Uganda	0.241	0.194	−0.047
United Kingdom	0.850	0.964	0.114	Czechoslovakia	0.836	0.892	0.056	Nicaragua	0.549	0.500	−0.049
Lesotho	0.317	0.431	0.114	India	0.258	0.309	0.051	Mozambique	0.205	0.154	−0.051
Venezuela	0.714	0.824	0.110	Argentina	0.784	0.832	0.048	Jamaica	0.797	0.736	−0.061
Greece	0.793	0.902	0.109	Togo	0.170	0.218	0.048	Romania	0.798	0.709	−0.089

2. Human development index: a survey of recent reviews

The human development index (HDI) was first published in *Human Development Report 1990*. It immediately attracted a lot of attention in the print and visual media. It has also received academic scrutiny. Although the process of critical review has been slow, sufficient material now exists to enable us to review these criticisms and assess their usefulness for future work. That is the purpose of this note.

Even before these reviews began to appear, the process of revising and improving the HDI was already under way, and the 1991 Report included a survey of improvements made. Some of the criticisms were thus already allowed for in the second version of the HDI, sometimes even before the reviews of the 1990 Report appeared. Nevertheless, the task of responding to and incorporating the criticisms remains as necessary as ever. The HDI should be seen as evolving and improving rather than as something cast in stone. It is also an exercise in which as many of its users as possible should actively participate.

The HDI is an unweighted average of the relative distances measured in longevity, education and resources. The proximate variables that measure these dimensions are life expectancy, literacy and (since the 1991 Report) mean years of schooling, and some modified measure of income per capita purporting to measure the "utility" or the welfare-generating capacity of income. The measure of distance is the difference between the actual value of the variable in a country (or a region or a subgroup—for example, women) and a minimum value divided by the range of the variable—that is, the difference between the maximum and the minimum.

It should be made clear at the outset that the *concept* of human development is broader than the *measure* of human development. Thus, although the HDI is a constantly evolving measure, it will never perfectly capture human development.

What does the HDI measure?

A question that immediately arises is: What does the HDI measure? Is it a normative measure of a desirable *standard of living* or a measure of the *level of living*? Does it measure *quality of life* or, as the British newspaper *The Daily Mail* said in its editorial on the 1992 Report, is it a *happiness* index?

A distinction needs to be made between the conceptual basis of the HDI and the measurement. Because for each dimension—longevity, educational attainment, access to resources—a relative distance is calculated that has a value between 0 and 1, it would seem that the HDI represents a normative measure. An overall value of 1 should represent a summit—bliss—if this were true.

But if human development is a process of expanding choice, there can be no limit, no bliss point. The index is best seen as a measure of people's ability to live a long and healthy life, to communicate and to participate in the life of the community and to have sufficient resources to obtain a decent living. It is a *minimal* measure. For a country that has achieved a high value of the HDI, the question then arises about other dimensions in which people can grow.

It is good to be in a country or group that enjoys high life expectancy, or to be literate and to have attended school for a certain number of years, but that is not the sum-total of human development. Similarly for income. Income is a means to a better life, and a higher income indicates less binding material constraints than a lower income. Income indicates the possibilities open to a person—but not the use the person makes of those possibilities: "It is the lives that [human beings] lead that is of intrinsic importance, not the commodities or income that they possess" (Anand and Sen 1992).

The *Human Development Report* made this aspect clear in its original definition of human development:

Human development is a process of enlarging people's choices. In principle, these choices can be infinite and change over time. But at all levels of development, the three essential ones are for people to lead a long and healthy life, to acquire knowledge and to have access to resources needed for a decent standard of living. If these choices are not available, many other opportunities remain inaccessible.

Thus, human development goes beyond the essential choices that the HDI captures. As noted earlier, the concept of human development is larger than the measure contained in the index.

Much of the criticism and discussion of the index has overlooked this crucial distinction. Thus, the HDI has often been compared with the neoclassical concept of consumer utility. In standard welfare economics, the lifetime utility of consumption for an individual consumer is the measure of that consumer's welfare (Ferroni and Kanbur 1991). Under some simplifying assumptions, this can be reduced to life expectancy times the logarithm of income. Because this captures at least two of the three dimensions, it is superficially similar to the HDI. But the neoclassical exercise makes sense only on the assumptions that an individual knows at birth the (constant) level of lifetime income to expect and that, far from representing the minimum, essential choice, the welfare measure captures the entire sum of human satisfaction. Income (or consumption) is an essential ingredient in human development, but it is not the sole end or even a principal measure of that process.

Human development and the HDI have also been compared with other measures. Principal among these is the basic needs approach proposed by the ILO as a measure of the adequacy of a development process (ILO 1976, referred to by Pyatt 1991b and Smith 1992). These basic needs are health, education, food, water supply, sanitation and housing (Hicks and Streeten 1979). Again,

---

This survey is a response to the many comments on the HDI during the last three years. The survey draws heavily on a special analysis prepared by Sudhir Anand and Amartya K. Sen (1992) for the Human Development Report Office, which will appear separately as an Occasional Paper of UNDP, and major contributions by Meghnad Desai.

there is overlap with the HDI. The HDI moves away from a commodities-based approach though at the same time it constructs a scalar measure. What is more, human development goes beyond basic needs, as the 1990 Report made clear when it said the basic needs approach "focuses on the provision of goods and services rather than the issue of human choices."

The extensive literature on social indicators of development has attempted similar exercises to capture development. Three approaches frequently contrasted are (1) the use of a monetary measure—income, (2) objective social indicators and (3) subjective social indicators (Baster 1985 and Smith 1992). There is overlap between the HDI and the first two of the three approaches. A problem with the objective social indicators approach has always been how to weight them. This has also been frequently the issue in the debate about the HDI.

The questions to address here are:

1. Why only three dimensions? Are these too many or too few?

2. Are the variables (indicators) chosen to measure the dimensions adequate? And for each dimension, are the associated variables too many or too few?

3. Are the measures subject to measurement errors, and, if so, do such errors invalidate the results? A subsidiary question is how up to date are the data used to construct the index.

4. Is the choice of the minimum and the maximum justifiable, or is it arbitrary? In any case, how robust is the measure to alternative maximum and minimum values?

5. Why choose equal weights? How sensitive is the measure to other weighting schemes?

The choice of dimensions

The three dimensions of the HDI relate to one or many capabilities that they are expected to capture. Thus, *longevity* captures the capability of leading a long and healthy life. *Educational attainment* captures the capability of acquiring knowledge, communicating and participating in the life of the community. *Access to resources* needed for a decent standard of living captures the capability of leading a healthy life, guaranteeing physical and social mobility, communicating and participating in the life of the community (including consumption).

An important omission frequently pointed out by critics is the dimension of freedom. Dasgupta has criticized the HDI for neglecting human rights: "As a measure of *human* development, it is quite incomplete; it is oblivious of what is commonplace to call human rights" (Dasgupta 1990; also Pyatt 1991b).

The 1991 Report made an effort to remedy this omission by constructing a human freedom index (HFI) based on the work of Charles Humana (1986). But a decision was made to keep the HDI separate from the HFI. As the 1991 Report argued, in addition to the lack of data on political freedom, there was another difficulty:

A second difficulty is political volatility. The human development index is based on relatively stable indicators, which don't change dramatically from year to year. Political freedom, by contrast, can appear or vanish abruptly. A military coup, for example, would cause a sudden drop in the index, even though many aspects of life might remain unchanged.

Human Development Report 1992 continued to consider political freedom separately, emphasizing an adequate methodology for constructing an index of political freedom or of human rights performance. This task is clearly essential but incomplete even at this stage. It would be premature to rush to include inadequate measures of political freedom in a development index. Further work is needed, preferably by academics who can look at this question in an environment free from international political pressures.

A different line of criticism has been that there are too many dimensions, that there is redundancy in the HDI. But this criticism relates to the variables used to measure the dimensions and the empirical correlations among them. This has to be considered next.

The choice of indicators

For longevity, life expectancy at birth has been chosen as the variable. This measure has been widely accepted as an indicator of development. But it has been suggested that infant mortality, life expectancy at one year, or under-five mortality would be desirable alternatives or complements to life expectancy. Pyatt (1991a) has argued that life expectancy is explained by income and infant mortality. If income is included in the HDI, infant mortality gives the extra information.

But although infant mortality and associated measures of mortality at a young age are good indicators of the quality of public health in developing countries, these variables fail to discriminate among the industrial countries. And the variable for life expectancy shows less difference between the group of industrial countries and the rest than the variable for infant mortality or under-five mortality. As a *universal* index, the HDI needs variables that discriminate among countries. Among the industrial countries as a group, maternal mortality is a better measure for this purpose.

Life expectancy at birth is an average for an entire group (nation, region, ethnic group), however, not the characteristic property of an individual, as income can be. In principle, for each person of a specific age, depending on the person's other characteristics (class, region of residence, race), a conditional expectation of remaining lifetime can be calculated. Such a variable potential lifetime (PLT) has been proposed as an alternative to life expectancy (Desai 1989). Although the PLT is a useful disaggregation, it is not suitable for comparisons between countries, however. The PLT computed for entire populations favours countries with growing populations and moderate life expectancy over those with static populations and high life expectancy. In a sense, the PLT as a measure for comparisons among countries has a "natalist" bias.

Life expectancy at birth has the further advantage that its true variance across individuals within a country is likely to be much smaller than that of income. Thus, as an indicator of the level of development, a group average for life expectancy is less misleading than one for income. A problem that remains, however, is that life expectancy is a quantitative measure. The quality of life is an issue that invites more attention than it has yet received.

For educational achievement, there are two indicators—the adult literacy rate and the mean years of schooling for individuals over 25 years of age. The 1990 Report used only the adult literacy rate, but this variable failed to discriminate among industrial countries, which often fail to report this statistic to UNESCO. It was for this reason that mean years of schooling was added to adult literacy.

There have been two strands of criticism of this choice. First, it has been argued that literacy is difficult to measure and that it takes different amounts of effort to achieve in different languages. Thus, a Chinese or a Japanese person has to put in much more effort to acquire literacy than a person whose language script is not ideographic (Lind 1991). But the definition of literacy is country-specific, and each culture appreciates the effort expended to acquire literacy. The relative difficulty of achieving literacy in different cultures would matter only if a universal definition were applied. Second, functional literacy is often much lower than recorded literacy, especially in industrial countries, which often claim an impossibly high 99% rate. As literacy is no longer the sole indicator of educational achievement, there is some correction to these biases, but a better definition of literacy would clearly be helpful. This is once again a question of the quality of the variable we are measuring, which is not captured by a simple quantitative measure.

One critic has urged that vocational education, on-the-job training and non-traditional modes of acquiring education be incorporated into the HDI (Nübler 1992a and 1992b). But it would be difficult to acquire reliable data across countries, and some of these variables relate more to human capital formation—and thus to income generation—than to the essential choices captured by the HDI.

Both life expectancy and educational attainment are *stock* variables; they change slowly. One strand of criticism says that school enrolment or university enrolment figures would capture recent educational advance better than the variables now used. In many developing countries, a substantial portion of the growing population is under 18, and often the majority is under 25. Measures that relate to adults or those over 25 cannot capture the *flow* of educational attainment being achieved (Smith 1992). This again is an argument for using a different indicator for the developing economies than that used for the industrial countries. This would make sense if the HDI were to be further developed for specific subgroups, but it is less plausible for a universal HDI (see below).

It is the third variable—income—that invites the most discussion. It is also the variable that has been subjected to revised treatment over the three Reports. The indicator used is real per capita GDP in purchasing power parity (PPP) dollars. Thus, there is already an adjustment for such factors as the degree of openness of an economy, the relative sizes of tradable and non-tradable sectors, and possible overvaluation of exchange rates. For income, the maximum difference is between per capita income as a group average and individual or household income as an indicator of access to resources. Income is notoriously unequally distributed but is nevertheless a misleading indicator of differences in well-being between people and households.

The many reservations concerning income as a measure of well-being have been trenchantly expressed by Anand and Sen (1992):

Income, commodities ("basic" or otherwise), and wealth do of course have instrumental importance but they do not constitute a direct measure of the living standard itself. A person's income level, for example, does not reveal what expectation of life the person has, whether he or she is presently healthy (or suffering from a disease), is disabled and incapable of moving about freely, etc. Even for those features of the living standard where the instrumental significance of private income is likely to be greater, such as adequate nutrition, there is enormous variation in converting income into achieved well-being. People's metabolic rates vary, as do their activity levels and the climatic conditions in which they live. People living in mountainous areas need more energy from food and fuel because they lose more energy in the colder ambient temperature. A handicapped person with a physical disability needs more income to achieve the same degree of mobility than a normal person does. The same is true of elderly and infirm people.

To some extent, one can adjust private household incomes for differences in certain very specific and limited needs. For example, a child needs less food to achieve the same level of nutrition as an adult. A large household needs more income than a small household to achieve the same level of consumption of goods and services, though not quite in proportion to the number of its members because of "economies of scale" in such consumption. A household living in a high-price region needs more income to purchase the same food and other commodities than one living in a low-price area. For these differences in needs, and only these, we can adjust household income to take them into account. We do this through so-called "equivalence scales" which correct household income for the size and age-sex composition of its members. And we use price indices to correct for regional and temporal price differences. But it is simply not possible, through income, to account for individual differences in morbidity, mortality or disability—and these features would seem to deserve priority in any assessment of the living standard. There are also other, non-private, economic goods and services which cannot be captured adequately through household incomes. These are the standard public or publicly-provided goods—the environment, infrastructure (such as roads), electricity, transport and communication facilities, epidemiological protection, etc. Thus private incomes fail to capture even some very basic instrumental features of the standard of living in developing countries.

In incorporating income in the HDI, two major variants were tried. First, in the 1990 Report, the logarithm of income was used rather than the actual value. Second, the poverty level of 17 industrial countries was averaged and converted to real PPP dollars. The logarithm of this poverty-level income was taken as a cut-off point. If a country had per capita income above this level, it was given no extra weight. The first of these two adjustments incorporated the principle of diminishing marginal utility, and the second was designed to emphasize the interest of the *Human Development Report* in poverty alleviation.

In general, the logarithmic transformation, though admitted as "analytically appropriate", was still thought to be "necessarily arbitrary". When combined with a poverty "cap", it was thought that "this implicitly provides greater weight to literacy and longevity than to" income. The treating of income differently than the other two variables was questioned also on the ground that "there is plausibly diminishing marginal utility to health and educational expenditure as well" (Kelley 1991).

The poverty cap by itself makes little difference, however, and removing it can be shown to have little effect on relative ranking among the rich countries. Kelley took a much higher value ($12,952, the average real per capita GDP of industrial countries) than the poverty level used in the 1990 Report ($4,861). He concluded that "the HDI does not appear to be particularly sensitive to the poverty line cut-off, a disquieting finding. It is difficult to believe that such a large increase in income per capita...would have only a small impact on 'enlarging people's choices'" (Kelley 1991).

This conclusion was reached independently in the 1991 Report, which explored a number of alternative treatments. The crucial transformation was to use the logarithm of income rather than the poverty cap. This transformation, though somewhat arbitrary, commands much support (McGillivray 1991 and McGillivray and White 1992a and 1992b).

In the 1991 and 1992 Reports, a different approach was tried. First, the logarithmic transformation was dropped. A modified way of allowing for diminishing marginal utility was introduced. Income up to the poverty level was not discounted at all; dollar for dollar, it was assumed to enhance well-being and to extend choice. Above the poverty level, a progressively severe correction for diminishing marginal utility was introduced through the use of a modified version of Atkinson's formula. Thus, for per capita income between the poverty level and twice the poverty level, the Atkinson parameter (the elasticity of marginal utility of income with respect to income) was taken to be one-half; for per capita income between two and three times the poverty level, the elasticity was taken to be two-thirds, and so on.

The logarithmic transformation over the entire range of income incorporates an elasticity of 1. A poverty cap imposes an infinite elasticity. The formula used in the 1991 Report and subsequently starts with zero elasticity below the poverty level and then gradually increases it. Thus, the capacity of income to produce diminishing marginal utility is taken to be progressive.

This modification has come in for some criticism. It is more complicated than a simple logarithmic transformation because it is a variable elasticity function rather than a constant elasticity one. But its functional form generates an anomaly at the boundary points. An extra dollar has a much higher marginal utility just above a multiple of the poverty level than just below it. Thus, above twice the poverty level, a dollar has a marginal utility of two. This "spike" is hardly visible in the final result but it is an anomaly (Trabold-Nübler 1991).

The main criticism has been that the transformation reduces the weight of extra income above poverty just as severely as the logarithmic transformation. Thus, between the United States and Brazil, the absolute difference in income was $15,230, but after adjustment the difference was $450 (Trabold-Nübler 1991).

Treating income above and below the poverty level differently is defensible. Our measure is per capita income, which is a group average rather than personal income. If we consider the poverty level the minimal cost of providing for the essential choices, it is difficult to argue that extra income within that range is somehow less effective in increasing well-being. Indeed, it can be argued that, until a minimum level of income is reached, it is inappropriate to speak of *utility* in the sense of positive satisfaction derived from income or consumption. In economic theory, the Linear Expenditure System provides us with an example of a utility function that has exactly this property. There is no utility calculable until a minimum level of consumption is achieved with respect to each good in a set of goods. It is only extra consumption—above subsistence—that yields *utility* (Desai 1990).

That said, the issue is still under scrutiny, and later in this technical note alternatives are offered. A logarithmic transformation of income remains a strong challenge to the current approach.

On income, the suggestion has been not that it be replaced (except perhaps by consumption) or supplemented, but that it be retained as the sole variable. It has been argued that, conceptually, income covers the other two variables and that, empirically, these variables are so highly correlated that the other two variables are *redundant.*

With regard to the conceptual issue—whether income captures or encompasses the other two variables—the *Human Development Report*'s approach is unambiguously and strongly in disagreement. The important question concerns the lives that people lead—what they succeed in being or doing rather than the goods they consume. The questions of interest are succinctly put by Anand and Sen (1992):

Do they have the capability to live long? Can they avoid mortality during infancy and childhood? Can they escape preventable morbidity? Do they avoid illiteracy? Are they free from hunger and undernourishment? Do they enjoy personal liberty and freedom?

These are the basic features of well-being which derive from looking at people as the center of all development activity. Enhancing their capabilities to function in these elementary ways is what lies at the core of human development. The achievements of people—be it in terms of long life or functional literacy—are valued as ends in themselves. This should be contrasted with more mainstream economic approaches which discuss human resource development. Here the focus is on human beings as a resource—an input into production activities. The development of human resources is seen in terms of their contribution to income generation—as an investment, like any other, in enhancing the productive potential.

Whereas the human development approach values capabilities related to, say, health, nutrition, and basic education as ends in themselves—and income as only a means to achieve these—human resource development (like "human capital" investment) is based on precisely the opposite valuation. This approach assesses investment in human capital—including health, nutrition, and education—entirely in terms of the extra income or output the investment generates, judging it to be worthwhile if the rate of return exceeds the capital cost. By contrast, proponents of the human development approach would argue for the enhancement of people's ability to read and write, or to be well-nourished and healthy, even if the conventionally measured economic return to investment in literacy, or improved food intake and health care, were zero (though, of course, they are typically quite high anyway).

The empirical issue of redundancy is best tackled in terms of the weights assigned to the different variables, because redundancy implies that the weights should be unequal—one for income, zero for the other two.

Measurement errors

A major problem with economic statistics at national and international levels is their accuracy. Very often, official statistics are estimates or projections based on past data. They frequently contain conceptual definitions that are inappropriate or not comparable with other countries' data, and errors due to faulty or inadequate sampling and to errors in recording and transmission. And the data are often not up to date. (Srinivasan 1992 offers a comprehensive overview of these problems.)

It has been pointed out that life expectancy data convey a spurious accuracy. These data should ideally be based on decennial censuses and then revised in the light of annual birth and death registrations. But seven of 180 developing countries have still not conducted a popular census, and for 22 others the most recent census dates to before 1975. For as many as 57 of 117 developing countries, reliable data on life expectancy are not yet available (Srinivasan 1992, citing Chamie 1992).

Data on literacy also depend on decennial censuses and are reported by countries to UNESCO. There may also be at least three widely accepted alternative definitions of literacy that UNESCO must try to reconcile in producing measures of literacy.

The measurement of income has a well-documented history of conceptual and statistical problems. For countries with substantial subsistence farming, there are formidable problems in estimating income. In many countries, industrial and developing, there is the problem of estimating informal sector and "black" income. In the transitional economies of Eastern Europe, the prices of many commodities have stabilized at levels that could be considered as reflecting relative scarcities, and pretransition prices have been exposed as misleading signals. This has led to drastic revisions in the estimated levels of income in pretransition years as well as to problems in gauging the challenges in maintaining incomes and living standards during the transition.

These problems are not easily overcome, but they need to be acknowledged more comprehensively. Ideally, all values should be interval estimates rather than point estimates. But while this remains a distant prospect, there is clearly a need for caution in taking HDI values (or any similar estimates) as firm guides in decision-making. At the same time, more resources can profitably be used in improving statistics.

On the issue of the robustness of HDI to measurement errors, McGillivray and White have tested the sensitivity of the HDI rankings to measurement errors in the underlying data. They considered two possibilities: first, that each variable was measured with an error of between –5% and +5%, and, second, that the errors lay between –10% and +10%. They generated random errors within this range and then added them to variables for different countries and calculated simulated HDIs. They found that

for the vast majority of countries, changes in ranking are relatively minor…If we calculate rank correlation coefficients between the HDI and its observed counterpart based on a measurement error within the range of –5 and +5 percent, we find coefficients of 0.996 and 0.995 in 1990 and 1991 respectively. Given the closeness of these coefficients to 1, we draw the conclusion that the HDI is extremely *robust to measurement error within this range.*

When they tried errors between –10% and +10%, the resulting correlation between the "true" and the simulated HDI was 0.993 for 1990 and 0.990 for 1991. Even when they tried a different range of errors for the poor and the rich countries, the conclusions were not altered. But none of this should detract from the need to improve the quality of the statistics.

Choice of minimum and maximum values

Each dimension of the HDI is measured by one or more variables and then reduced to a measure of relative distance. This distance measure is taken as the actual value minus the minimum value relative to the range—that is, maximum less minimum. Thus, for a dimension i for a country j

$$H_{ij} = \frac{X_{ij} - \min_{k} X_{ik}}{\max_{k} X_{ik} - \min_{k} X_{ik}}$$

where j and k are indexes for country. Then the overall index is

$$H_j = \frac{1}{3} \sum H_{ij}$$

In every *Human Development Report,* the maximum and the minimum for life expectancy have been defined by the sample. Thus, the actual maximum and minimum for all countries in any year enter the calculation of H_{ij}, labelling life expectancy as i.

If the maximum and minimum values were to change over time, this might lead to an anomaly in which a country's actual life expectancy could go up while its score goes down. This may happen because the minimum has gone up or the range has widened over time, or both. Thus, "moving the goalposts" makes comparing the HDI over time more difficult.

The 1991 Report considered trends in human development for the first time. For this purpose a modified HDI was introduced in which the maximum and minimum were defined not separately for each year but for the entire period 1960–90. Although this was good for each period, it fails to deal with the problem over time, because in the future—say, for 1960–95—the maximum and minimum values could move again.

TECHNICAL NOTE TABLE 2.1
Maximum and minimum values

	1990		1991		1992	
	Max	Min	Max	Min	Max	Min
Life expectancy	78	42	78.6	42	78.6	42
Literacy	99	12	99	13.3	99	18.2
Mean years of schooling	..	..	12.2	0.1	12.3	0.1

Before considering the alternative of normatively fixed maximum and minimum values, it may be of interest to examine the extent of the shift over time. As technical note table 2.1 shows, the movements in life expectancy are very slight. Indeed, the improvement from 78 to 78.6 can be thought of as the correction of a rounding error. Only the minimum value for literacy shows a sudden jump, from 12 to 13.3 to 18.2. This continues the earlier discussion about the difficulty of measuring literacy. One cannot of course discount the possibility that once it is known that literacy rates enter the HDI, their measurement may become subject to policy manipulation (a problem known in macroeconomics as "Goodhart's law"). The problem of fixing normative constant maximum and minimum values has been discussed by Anand and Sen (1992):

Granted that the "goalposts" need to be fixed if the HDI is to be comparable over time, we need to ask how the goalposts should be determined. It will not be enough to fix the range of values for each X by simply looking at the minimum and maximum levels achieved retrospectively, say in the period from 1960 to 1990. We also need to look prospectively at the projections for each X and ensure that individual country levels will remain inside the range forecast in the future, in other words, over the entire period—backward and forward—during which intertemporal comparisons are required to be undertaken.

In the main this affects the range for the longevity variable. Looking back in time to a point when sufficient data were available for intercountry comparisons (e.g. the year 1960), the minimum level of life expectancy at birth achieved was about 35 years. For comparisons in the future going as far as 2050, national life expectancy at birth has been projected to reach 85 years for some countries. Thus keeping to the basis definition of HDI, we could choose as our fixed endpoints for X a minimum value of 35 years and a maximum value of 85 years. This range encompasses the lower and upper bound of life expectancy estimates over which both cross-country and intertemporal comparisons of HDI are envisaged.

As far as the literacy variable is concerned we may choose the natural range of 0 to 100 percent. Although the lower end of the range is at the present time unlikely to be experienced at a national level, there are disaggregations we are proposing for which literacy rates even today fall below 10 percent (e.g. the female adult literacy rate in Burkina Faso or Somalia). Moreover, if intertemporal comparisons were to start back from 1960, we would indeed be approaching the lower end of the 0 to 100 percent range in some cases. Hence, we take 0 to 100 percent as the min-max interval for adult literacy.

The final component of HDI is the logarithm of per capita GDP in 1987 PPP dollars truncated at the average official poverty line income in nine developed countries. The logarithmic transform of income is taken in order to reflect diminishing returns to transforming income into human capabilities. The ceiling on income at the poverty line is imposed because of the particular relevance of poverty removal in human development (Desai 1991:355). The upper bound of the max-min range for the income variable is kept constant over time at the logarithm of PPP$4,861 in 1987 prices. The lower bound for the variable again poses a slight difficulty: we choose a value of 0 to reflect negligible human develop-

ment beyond the minimal levels of life expectancy and literacy achieved in the past in some countries.

Weights
The equal weighting afforded to the three variables has led to much debate. In an ideal world, the "meta production function" of human development would be specified, and the contribution of each variable to human development would be its weight. Objecting to equal weights, Allen Kelley (1991) wrote:

The greatest problem occurs with the relatively low weight accorded to GDP/N (per capita real income) in moderate to high income countries since the variable measured by this particular indicator (income) can be used to acquire and/or produce either of the other two indicators (improved health or education). Possibly a weight roughly reflecting the acquisition/production-transformation would have been appropriate under the premise that in some countries individuals may well have elected to use their income to expand choices in ways that do not result in, say, improved education or health. Indeed, it might be argued that the capacity to choose among many dimensions of human development accorded by increased income in particular merits giving a relatively higher weight to this indicator.

Of course, in the long run, causality can run from education and health to income as well as the other way around. Because higher per capita real income can lead to better provision of public goods as well as higher consumption, it is misleading to think of income simply in terms of personal choice.

Lacking a meta production function, investigators have explored the pattern of correlation among variables. One approach has been to carry out a principal component analysis (PCA) on the data (Tatlidil 1992). There is, of course, a high degree of simple correlation among the variables. For the three variables—life expectancy, educational attainment and (adjusted) income—and the data from the 1992 Report, the pattern of correlation was as in technical note table 2.2. But the PCA shows that the principal eigenvalue explains 88% of total variance in the data, obviously a very high measure of commonality in the data (technical note table 2.3).

TECHNICAL NOTE TABLE 2.2
Correlation matrix of variables

	Life expectancy	Adjusted GDP	Educational attainment
Life expectancy	1.000		
Adjusted income	0.848	1.000	
Educational attainment	0.871	0.729	1.000

TECHNICAL NOTE TABLE 2.3
Principal component analysis results

Eigenvalues	2.633	0.272	0.095
Explained variance	87.769	9.080	3.151
Component loadings			
Life expectancy	0.969	0.030	-0.246
Adjusted income	0.916	-0.386	0.113
Educational attainment	0.925	0.350	0.146

But it is interesting to see that the eigenvector corresponding to the leading eigenvalue puts virtually equal weight on the three variables—life expectancy (0.969), adjusted income (0.916) and educational attainment (0.925). The second and third eigenvalues, which explain relatively less (9% and 3%), have radically different eigenvectors, including some negative ones. Thus, although an HDI based on the eigenvalues of the principal eigenvector would give results identical to those of the present HDI, one based on the second eigenvalue would give a negative weight to income (–0.386) roughly equal to the positive weight attached to life expectancy. An HDI based on these weights would yield a very different interpretation. Because of the low explanatory power of such an HDI, it would be unwise to put more faith in it.

Thus, the PCA confirms the equal weights but also points to the high degree of correlation. There is no presumption about causality in the PCA. Thus, it does not advocate omitting or downgrading a variable. In another exercise, McGillivray and White correlated a combination of two of the three variables with the third. But rather than the actual values of the variables, they used the ranks. This weakens their point, but they did find high correlations for both the 1990 and the 1991 HDI for all countries as well as for developing countries and industrial countries. When they carried out the same exercise for high, medium and low levels of human development, they found a much lower correlation. Such a change in correlation would not occur if the actual values of the original variables had been used, but it does with the ranks because the ranks are shuffled differently in classifying countries by levels of HDI.

Because of the symmetry of the three variables and the lack of causality ordering, it is difficult to decide which of the three variables dominates; McGillivray and White prefer income over the others. The results of the PCA, which advocates equal weight on the same database, seem persuasive.

But the equal weights are partly misleading. Because each variable is relative to its range and the ranges are very different, the actual effective weights are also very different. This can be seen by asking the following question:

How much does a country's HDI change for a unit change in an indicator?

The ranges—that is, the difference between the maximum and minimum—were 36.6 (=78.6 – 42) years for life expectancy, 80.8 (=99 – 18.2) percentage points for literacy, 12.2 (=12.3 – 0.1) years for mean years of schooling and $5,074 dollars for adjusted income for 1992. Thus, a one-year improvement in life expectancy, a one-percentage-point increase in adult literacy, a one-year improvement in mean years of schooling and a $1 increase in per capita income would represent the following changes in the HDI:

One unit change in	Change in HDI
Life expectancy	1/108
Literacy	1/365
Mean years of schooling	1/108
Income	1/15,222

It would be tempting to interpret the relative coefficients as trade-offs, but a note of caution should be introduced. Superficially, it would be easy to say that one extra year of life expectancy is "worth" $150 of income, but these are not choices open to an optimizing economic agent. Take a poor country with per capita income as high as $1,500 (only 17 of the 65 countries with low human development in 1992 had income this high). An extra year of life expectancy (above a median value of about 50 years) would be the same as 10% growth in real per capita income. Neither of these two outcomes is likely in the short run, nor are they independent of each other in the real world. Thus, it would be wrong to interpret the coefficients as reflecting a "menu of policy choices".

The real importance of the calculations is to show that what are frequently seen as equal weights (and were even reflected in the principal component analysis) miss the unequal ranges of the variables. In the 1990 Report, the actual effective weight of income, after the log transformation and the capping at the poverty level, was variable at different levels of income. Thus, an increase in income from $400 to $450 improved the logarithmic value by 0.06 relative to the range of 3.68—by 1/60—and hence the actual effective weight was 1/180. At $2,000, an increase of $250 would be required to get the same effect. Above the poverty cap no amount of improvement was sufficient. Even in the context of the present transformation of income, an extra dollar of per capita income is not the same above as below the poverty line. The higher the income, the steeper the trade-off is in actual dollars.

There is another reason to be cautious in treating the ratios of actual effective weights as trade-offs: the HDI is not a cardinal index to be maximized, but an ordinal measure for relative ranking among countries. This is well expressed by Anand and Sen (1992):

Some commentators on the Human Development Report 1990 *have been disconcerted by this normalization of each component* H_{ij} *of the aggregate index* H_j. *They point out, for example, that an improvement in the achievement of the lowest-achieving country in the sample would decrease the HDI for country j, and this is not the sort of externalities that one wants in an index. But the human development index in the 1990 (and subsequent) Reports was constructed expressly as a measure of* relative performance *across countries at a point in time. No special significance is attached to the absolute value of the index, the entire analysis being conducted in terms of the* ranking *of countries relative to one another. Thus although a higher value of min* $\{X_{ik}\}$ *or of max* $\{X_{ik}\}$ *would indeed decrease for* H_{ij} *for country j, it would also do so for all other countries l too, and in proportion to the gap* ($H_{ij} - H_{il}$) *between countries j and l. This, of course, has the effect—given the basic information—of leaving the relative ranking of countries unchanged.*

As defined, the human development index H *for country j is invariant to positive affine transformations of the underlying variables* X_i, *i = 1,2,3. Thus if one were to substitute for each i = 1, 2, 3,* $Z_i = a_i X_i + b_i$ *where* $a_i > 0$, *the absolute value of each* H_{ij}, *and therefore also of* H_j, *would remain the same. In particular, if one changed the units of* *measurement of X_i by either scale changes ($a_i > 0$) or level changes ($b_i \neq 0$), the indices H_{ij} and H_j would have the same numerical values as before.*

Disaggregation of the HDI

In previous *Human Development Reports,* there has been an attempt to disaggregate the HDI for women and men. In a way, this disaggregation preserves the universality of the HDI while allowing for disaggregation. Gender is, after all, a univeral classifier. But other such classifiers can also be used. Thus, disaggregation by urban versus rural residence, by ethnicity, or by region or continent is possible. In *Human Development Report 1993,* a disaggregation by ethnic groups has been carried out for a small number of countries.

Disaggregation by gender raises some interesting issues. Anand and Sen (1992) discuss this in detail, and their analysis bears quoting in full:

…there is considerable evidence of anti-female bias in some countries in the world. This takes the form of unequal treatment in access to food, health care, education, employment and income-earning opportunities—and is reflected in different achievements of women relative to men. Gender bias exists both within the household and outside the household, for example, in the labour market or the provision of public health services. We should like to use the HDI to illuminate gender disparities that result from such unequal treatment.

Unlike conventional measures of development, such as those based on income or the possession of commodities, the HDI is particularly well-suited to examining gender inequalities. The reason is that the informational requirements of resource-use measures such as income—especially when estimation of their allocation within the household is involved—make them very problematic in shedding light on inter-individual differences. By contrast, the consequences of female disadvantage and gender bias, both intra- and extra-household, will be reflected in the achievements of the individuals concerned in terms of their life expectancy, literacy, survival chances, and so on. Data on these achievements are colllected not at the household level through household income and expenditure surveys, but at the individual level through demographic surveys and population censuses. There is, thus, a strong practical reason—in addition to concern for what is intrinsically important—in adopting the HDI to examine gender and other inter-individual disparities.

In considering the disaggregation of HDI by gender, we must take note…of the higher potential life expectancy of females vis-à-vis males. The separate goalposts of life expectancy for females and males are taken to be 37.5 and 87.5 years for women, and 32.5 and 82.5 years for men. Thus the life expectancy range is 50 years for both women and men; this implies that a unit increase in longevity for either sex (over time) will contribute the same increment to the overall HDI…

The range for adult literacy is the same for females and males, as is that for the logarithm of per capita GDP truncated at the poverty line income. While separate adult literacy figures are in general available by gender, sex-specific estimates of income-use are difficult, if not impossible, to establish with any accuracy even for the advanced industrial countries (for the reasons mentioned earlier). Thus if F and M refer to females and males, respectively, the female and male HDIs for country j are given by

$$H_j(F) = \frac{1}{3}\left[\frac{X_{ij}(F) - 37.5}{50} + \frac{X_{2j}(F)}{100} + \frac{X_{3j}(F)}{3.687}\right]$$

and

$$H_j(M) = \frac{1}{3}\left[\frac{X_{ij}(M) - 32.5}{50} + \frac{X_{2j}(M)}{100} + \frac{X_{3j}(M)}{3.687}\right]$$

HDI: universal or specialized

A constant concern in constructing the HDI has been to preserve its universality—to retain a single index for both the rich and the poor countries. This makes clear that human development is not a concern solely for poor countries. In the 1990 Report, the deformations caused in rich societies by a number of adverse developments—drug addiction, crime, family breakup—were remarked upon.

There has also been a search for variables that will help discriminate among rich countries that might otherwise all cluster near the top of the HDI ranking. Thus, mean years of schooling was introduced to allow fine distinction at the top. A similar motivation was behind the decision to remove the zero weight to income above the poverty line in the 1991 Report.

But if the HDI is taken to be a measure of the minimum necessary—of the essential choices—there is obviously scope for human development beyond the top value for the HDI. And at lower levels of human development, there may be a need to emphasize indicators that can be ignored at higher levels. The universality of the HDI would then be an obstacle to constructing subindices for special groups of countries.

One set of suggestions in this respect has been made by Anand and Sen. They propose using the distinction currently made among high, medium and low levels of development. Then, for each group they propose a specific group of indicators. Thus, for the low level, they would drop mean years of schooling and revert to the 1990 Report's definition of the HDI. For the medium level, they propose adding under-five mortality to life expectancy, secondary school enrolment to literacy and incidence of poverty to log of per capita income. For the high level, they propose further adding maternal mortality, tertiary enrolment and Gini-corrected mean national income; these suggestions are summarized in technical note table 2.4. Anand and Sen do not discuss the question of the weights to be assigned to these indices in each use, however.

Suggestions for future improvements

This survey of the many critical papers written on the HDI shows that in many instances the criticisms have been implemented, and in some cases (for example, the treatment of income) there is scope for further change. No change has been incorporated in the 1993 Report, in part to avoid inconvenience caused to the users of the HDI by frequent revisions. But it is also the intention of the *Human Development Report* team to invite suggestions from readers about the future course of the HDI.

Following are possible improvements that have been discussed:

• Keeping the maximum and minimum normatively fixed rather than variable. Thus, for longevity, the maximum would be 85 years and the minimum 35 years. With an adjustment for gender to construct separate indices for women and men, the maximum would be 87.5 years for women and 82.5 for men; the minimum would be similarly adjusted. For literacy, the limits would be 100 and 0 and for mean years of schooling, 15 and 0. For income, the upper limit can be taken to be $35,000 in real income per capita (PPP), which would require 2% growth for 50 years for the richest country to reach.

• Taking the logarithm of income over the entire range rather than the present variable elasticity approach. This would also mean removing the poverty cap.

• Constructing supplementary indices for specific groups of countries with low, medium and high human development. The suggestions by Anand and Sen were described above, but there is clearly scope for other suggestions here.

• Disaggregating the HDI within each country. The HDI is already disaggregated by gender, though only for a limited number of countries. Disaggregation by region and by ethnic group has been introduced in this Report. There is no doubt scope for further disaggregation—for example, by immigrants within a country, the elderly and the disabled.

• Adding dimensions. The possibility of adding new dimensions has not been explored beyond refining the number of variables used for each of the three dimensions. The small number of dimensions has been helpful in preserving the simplicity of the HDI, which has been a strong factor in its transparency and the ease of communicating its meaning to a wide audience. Any additional dimension will have to have strong grounds for inclusion.

It is hoped that some of the suggestions will be commented upon by our readers and by those who use the HDI—whether in academia, in policy-making circles or in the private sector. The participatory mode is desirable not only for the process of human development but for its measurement as well.

TECHNICAL NOTE TABLE 2.4
Suggestions for special human development indices for specific groups of countries

Human development level	Low	Medium	High
Human development indicators	1.1 Life expectancy	1.1 Life expectancy 1.2 Under-five mortality	1.1 Life expectancy 1.2 Under-five mortality 1.3 Maternal mortality
	2.1 Adult literacy	2.1 Adult literacy 2.2 Secondary school enrolment	2.1 Adult literacy 2.2 Secondary school enrolment 2.3 Tertiary enrolment
	3.1 Log per capita GDP (up to international poverty line)	3.1 Log per capita GDP (up to international poverty line) 3.2 Incidence of poverty	3.1 Log per capita GDP (up to international poverty line) 3.2 Incidence of poverty 3.3 Gini-corrected mean national income

Source: Anand and Sen 1992.

Bibliography

Adelman, Irma. 1975. "Development Economics: A Reassessment of Goals." *American Economic Review: Papers and Proceedings* 65 (2): 302–09.

Anand, Sudhir. 1983. *Inequality and Poverty in Malaysia: Measurement and Decomposition.* New York: Oxford University Press.

———. 1991. "Poverty and Human Development in Asia and the Pacific." UNDP, New York.

Anand, Sudhir, and Martin Ravallion. Forthcoming. "Human Development in Poor Countries: On the Role of Private Incomes and Public Services." *Journal of Economic Perspectives.*

Anand, Sudhir, and Amartya Sen. 1992. "Human Development Index: Methodology and Measurement." Background paper for *Human Development Report 1993.* UNDP, New York.

Atkinson, Anthony B. 1983. *Social Justice and Public Policy.* Cambridge, Mass.: MIT Press.

Baster, Nancy. 1985. "Social Indicator Research: Some Issues and Debates." In Hilhorst and Klatter 1985.

Brewster, Havelock R. 1991. "Review of UNDP's *Human Development Report 1991:* Medicine Without Cures for Life Without Growth." UNCTAD, New York. Mimeo.

Caldwell, John C. 1986. "Routes to Low Mortality in Poor Countries." *Population and Development Review* 12 (2): 171-220.

Chamie, Joseph. 1992. "Population Databases in Development Analysis." The Conference on Database of Development Analysis, May 15–16, Yale University, New Haven, Conn.

Chenery, Hollis B., Montek S. Ahluwalia, Clive L.G. Bell, John H. Duloy and Richard Jolly. 1974. *Redistribution with Growth.* New York: Oxford University Press.

Chenery, Hollis B., and T.N. Srinivasan, eds. 1988. *Handbook of Development Economics.* Vol. I. Amsterdam: Elsevier Science Publishers.

Das, Tarun Kanti. 1992. "UNDP Human Development Index: Some Methodological Issues and Alternative Measures." UNDP, New York.

Dasgupta, Partha. 1990. "Well-Being in Poor Countries." *Economic and Political Weekly* (August 4): 1713–20.

Dasgupta, Partha, and Martin Weale. 1992. "On Measuring the Quality of Life." *World Development* 20 (1): 119–31.

Deaton, Angus S. 1987. "The Allocation of Goods within the Household: Adults, Children and Gender." Princeton University, Princeton, N.J. Mimeo.

Deaton, Angus S., and John N.J. Muellbauer. 1980. *Economics and Consumer Behavior.* Cambridge: Cambridge University Press.

———. 1986. "On Measuring Child Costs: With Applications to Poor Countries." *Journal of Political Economy* 94 (4): 720–44.

Desai, Meghnad. 1989. "Potential Lifetime (PLT): A Proposal for an Index of Social Welfare." In *Towards a New Way to Measure Development.* Caracas: Office of the South Commission.

———. 1990. "Poverty and Capability: Towards an Empirically Implementable Measure." Development Economics Research Programme Discussion Paper 27. London School of Economics, STICERD, London.

———. 1991. "Human Development: Concepts and Measurement." *European Economic Review* 35: 350–57.

Desai, Meghnad, and A.R. Shah. 1988. "An Econometric Approach to the Measurement of Poverty." *Oxford Economic Papers* 40 (November).

Drewnowski, J., and W. Scott. 1966. "The Level of Living Index." Report 4 (September). United Nations Research Institute for Social Development, Geneva.

Drèze, Jean P., and Amartya K. Sen. 1989. *Hunger and Public Action.* Oxford: Clarendon Press.

Ferroni, Marco, and Ravi Kanbur. 1990. *Poverty-Conscious Restructuring of Public Expenditure.* Social Dimensions of Adjustment in Sub-Saharan Africa Working Paper 9. Washington, D.C.: World Bank.

Genné, Marcelle. 1992. "Réflexion sur le Indicateurs de Développement Humain." *Canadian Journal of Development Studies* 13 (1): 81–90.

Goldstein, Joshua S. 1985. "Basic Human Needs: The Plateau Curve." *World Development* 13 (5): 595–609.

Grant, James P. 1978. *Disparity Reduction Rates in Social Indicators.* Washington, D.C.: Overseas Development Council.

Hammond, Peter J. 1978. "Economic Welfare with Rank-Order Price Weighting." *Review of Economic Studies* 45.

Henderson, Hazel. "New Indicators for Culturally Specific, Sustainable Development." *IFDA Dossier* 75/76 (January/April): 68–76.

Hicks, John R. 1939. *Value and Capital.* Oxford: Clarendon Press.

Hicks, Norman, and Paul Streeten. 1979. "Indicators of Development: The Search for a Basic Needs Yardstick." *World Development* 7: 567–80.

Hilhorst, J.G.M., and M. Klatter, eds. 1985. *Social Development in the Third World.* London: Croom Helm.

Hopkins, Michael. 1991. "Human Development Revisited: A New UNDP Report." *World Development* 19 (10): 1469–73.

Humana, Charles. 1986. *The World Guide to Human Rights.* New York: Facts on File.

International Labour Office. 1976. *Employment, Growth and Basic Needs: A One-World Problem.* Geneva.

Kanbur, Ravi. 1990. "Poverty and Development: The *Human Development Report* and *The World Development Report, 1990.*" Pensamiento Iberoameri-cano. University of Warwick. Mimeo.

Kelley, Allen C. 1991. "The Human Development Index: 'Handle with Care'." *Population and Development Review* 17 (2): 315–24.

Klein, Lawrence R. 1991. Personal communication to Inge Kaul.

Larson, D.A., and W.T. Wilford. 1979. "The Physical Quality of Life Index: A Useful Social Indicator?" *World Development* 7: 581–84.

Lind, Niels C. 1991. "Some Thoughts on the Human Development Index." University of Waterloo, Institute for Risk Research, Waterloo, Ontario.

Lisk, F. 1979. "Indicators of Basic Needs-Oriented Development Planning." *Labour and Society* 4(3).

Marx, Karl. 1938. *Capital.* Vol. I. London: Allen and Unwin.

McGillivray, Mark. 1991. "The Human Development Index: Yet Another Redundant Composite Development Indicator?" *World Development* 19 (10): 1461–68.

McGillivray, Mark, and Howard White. 1992a. "Inter-Country Quality of Life Comparison: Does Measurement Error Really Matter?" Deakin University, Geelong, Australia. Mimeo.

———. 1992b. "Measuring Development: The UNDP's Human Development Index." Paper prepared for the ESRC Development Economics Study Group Annual Conference, March 27–28, University of Leicester.

McGranahan, D.V., and P. Pizarro. 1985. *Measurement and Analysis of Socio-Economic Development.* Geneva: United Nations Research Institute for Social Development.

McGranahan, D.V., C. Richaud-Proust, N.V. Sovani and M. Subramanian. 1972. *Contents and Measurement of Socio-economic Development.* New York: Praeger.

Meade, James E. 1976. *The Just Economy.* London: Allen and Unwin.

Moon, M., and E. Smolensky, eds. 1977. *Improving Measures of Economic Well-Being.* New York: Academic Press.

Morris, Morris D. 1979. *Measuring the Condition of the World's Poor: The Physical Quality of Life Index.* New York: Pergamon.

Moss, M., ed. 1973. *The Measurement of Economic and Social Performance.* Studies in Income and Wealth 38. New York: National Bureau of Economic Research.

Nübler, Irmgard. 1992a. "Capturing Non-Formal Vocational Education and Training Through Statistics." UNDP, New York.

———. 1992b. "The Knowledge Dimension in the Human Development Index: In Search of a Broader Concept." UNDP, New York.

Nübler, Irmgard, and Harald Trabold-Nübler. 1992. "Income and Income Distribution-Adjustment in the HDI." UNDP, New York.

Phelps, Edmund S. 1973. *Economic Justice.* Harmonds-worth: Penguin.

Pomfret, R. 1992. *Diverse Paths of Economic Development.* Hemel Hempstead, UK: Harvester/Wheatsheaf.

Preston, Samuel H. 1975. "The Changing Relation Between Mortality and Level of Economic Development." *Population Studies* 29 (2): 231–48.

Pyatt, F. Graham. 1976. "On the Interpretation and Disaggregation of Gini Coefficients." *Economic Journal* 86.

———. 1987. "Measuring Welfare, Poverty and Inequality." *Economic Journal* 97.

———. 1991a. Personal communication to Inge Kaul.

———. 1991b. "Poverty: A Wasted Decade." *European Economic Review* 35: 358–65.

———. 1992. "There is Nothing Wrong With the HDI, but...." University of Warwick, Department of Economics. Mimeo.

Quetelet, Lambert-Adolphe-Jacques. 1842. *Sur l'Homme et le Développement de ses Facultés, on Essai de Physique Sociale* (A Treatise on Man and the Development of His Faculties). Translated by Robert Knox. Edinburgh: Chambers.

———. 1870. *Anthropométrie oui Mesure des Différentes Facultés de l'Homme.* Brussels: C. Muquardt.

Rao, V.V. Bhanoji. 1991. "*Human Development Report 1990:* Review and Assessment." *World Development* 19 (10): 1451–60.

Rawls, John. 1971. *A Theory of Justice.* Cambridge, Mass.: Harvard University Press.

Roberts, Kevin W.S. 1980. "Price-Independent Welfare Prescriptions." *Journal of Public Economics* 13.

Rowett Research Institute. 1991. "Body Mass Index: An Objective Measure for the Estimation of Chronic Energy Deficiency in Adults." Aberdeen.

Sandhu, K.S., and P. Wheatley. 1989. *The Management of Success: The Moulding of Modern Singapore.* Singapore: Institute of Southeast Asian Studies.

Sen, Amartya K. 1973. *On Economic Inequality.* Oxford: Clarendon Press.

———. 1976. "Real National Income." *Review of Economic Studies* 43.

———. 1981. "Public Action and the Quality of Life in Developing Countries." *Oxford Bulletin of Economics and Statistics* 43 (4): 287–319.

———. 1984. "The Living Standard." *Oxford Economic Papers* 36 (supplement): 74–90.

———. 1985. *Commodities and Capabilities.* Amsterdam: North Holland.

———. 1987. *The Standard of Living.* The Tanner Lectures. Cambridge: Cambridge University Press.

———. 1992a. *Inequality Reexamined.* Cambridge, Mass.: Harvard University Press.

———. 1992b. "Missing Women." *British Medical Journal.*

———. Forthcoming. *Life Expectancy and Inequality: Some Conceptual Issues.* New York: Oxford University Press.

Smith, Adam S. 1910. *An Inquiry into the Nature and Causes of the Wealth of Nations.* Reprint. London: Home University.

Smith, Peter. 1992. "Measuring Human Development." University of Southampton. Mimeo.

Srinivasan, T.N. 1992. "Data Base for Development Analysis: An Overview." The Conference on Database of Development Analysis, May 15–16, Yale University, New Haven, Conn.

Srinivasan, T.N., and Pranab K. Bardhan, eds. 1974. *Poverty and Income Distribution in India.* Calcutta: Statistical Publishing Society.

———. 1988. *Rural Poverty in South Asia.* New York: Columbia University Press.

Stewart, Frances J. 1985. *Planning to Meet Basic Needs.* London: Macmillan.

Streeten, Paul P. 1984. "Basic Needs: Some Unsettled Questions." *World Development* 12 (9): 973–1780.

Streeten, Paul P., S. Javed Burki, Mahbub ul Haq, Norman Hicks and Frances J. Stewart. 1981. *First Things First: Meeting Basic Human Needs in the Developing Countries.* New York: Oxford University Press.

Tatlidil, Huseyin. 1992. "A New Approach for Human Development: Human Development Scores." IDS, Sussex. Mimeo.

Trabold-Nübler, Harald. 1991. "The Human Development Index: A New Development Indicator?" *Intereconomics* (September/October): 236–43.

———. 1992. "Making the Human Development Index Comparable Over Time." German Institute for Economic Research (DIW), Berlin. Mimeo.

UNDP. 1990. *Human Development Report 1990.* New York: Oxford University Press.

———. 1991. *Human Development Report 1991.* New York: Oxford University Press.

———. 1992. *Human Development Report 1992.* New York: Oxford University Press.

UNICEF. 1993. *The State of the World's Children 1993.* Oxford: Oxford University Press.

Yotopoulos, Pan A. 1989. "Distributions of Real Income: Within Countries and by World Income Class." *Review of Income and Wealth* 35 (4): 357–75.

———. 1977. "The Population Problem and the Development Solution." *Food Research Institute Studies* 16 (1): 1–22.

Bibliographic note

Chapter 1 draws on the following: Ajab, Gankou and Mathonnat 1991, Akder 1990, Barrett 1992, Bouassami 1990, Boutros-Ghali 1992, Brown, Flavin and Kane 1992, Deger and Sen 1990, de Graft-Johnson 1992, Fundación para la Educación Superior y el Desarrollo 1992, Gay and others 1991, Griffin and McKinley forthcoming, Henry 1991, Hewett 1991, International Monetary Fund 1992, Kaul 1993a, Khatib 1990, Kouidhi and Ramamonjisoa 1991, McNamara 1991, Menezes 1992, Shiva Kumar 1990, Stockholm International Peace Research Institute 1992, Svasti, Chaiyasoot, Suvachittanont and Masnee 1991, UNDP 1990, 1991b, 1992a, 1992c, 1992d and 1992e, United Nations 1992b and 1992c, World Bank 1992b and Wulf 1992a and 1992b.

References for the the boxes are as follows: box 1.1, Boutros-Ghali 1992; box 1.2, Barrett 1992, Menezes 1992, UNESCO 1991, UNHCR 1991, UNICEF 1992 and WHO 1992; box 1.3, Organisation for Economic Co-operation and Development 1991; box 1.4, UNDP 1993.

References for the figures are as follows: figure 1.2, Brown, Flavin and Kane 1992; figure 1.3, Wulf 1992a.

Chapter 2 draws on the following: Acharya and Bennett 1982, Adepoju 1991, Ahmadullah 1981, Balisacan 1992, Barlett and Steele 1992, Black 1991, Boraine 1991, Bose 1992, Bruce and Dwyer 1988, Chamie 1991, Chatterji 1992, Children's Defense Fund 1992, Espiell 1990, Food and Agriculture Organization of the United Nations 1988, Girard and Gentil 1983, Hacker 1992, Jaynes and Williams 1989, Kanbargi 1991, Krongkaew, Tinakorn and Suphachlasai 1992, Lewenhak 1992, McIvor 1990, Munachonga 1986, Munyakho 1992, Nobel 1981, Ramaga 1992, Rizzini and others 1992, Stavenhagen 1990, Swift 1991, UNESCO 1981, 1986 and 1990, UNICEF 1990, 1991 and 1992, United Nations 1989, 1990a, 1990c and 1992e, United Nations Economic Commission for Africa 1990 and White 1987.

References for the boxes are are follows: box 2.2, Black 1991, Bose 1992, Chatterji 1992, Munyakho 1992, Rizzini and others 1992 and Swift 1991; box 2.3, Inter-Parliamentary Union 1992, Lewenhak 1992 and United Nations 1992e; box 2.4, Inter-Parliamentary Union 1992 and White 1987; box 2.5, Hacker 1992 and Jaynes and Williams 1989; box 2.6; Boraine 1991.

References for the tables are as follows: table 2.2, Food and Agriculture Organization of the United Nations 1988 and Jazairy, Alamgir and Panuccio 1992.

Chapter 3 draws on the following: Abell 1992, Aslund 1985, Aspe 1991, Baumol 1990, Bayliss 1990, Blanchard, Froot and Sachs forthcoming, Brush 1990, Candoy-Sekse and Palmer 1990, Central and Eastern European Privatization Network 1992, Corbo, Fischer and Webb 1992, Cornia, van der Hoeven and Mkandawire 1992, Cowan 1990, Danns 1989, de Soto 1990, Demery and Demery 1992, de Wilde, Schreurs and Richman 1991, Dore, Bounine-Cabale and Tapioli 1989, Elkan 1988, Galal 1991, Galal and others 1992, Getubig and Oshima 1991, Grosh 1992, Haggard and Kaufman 1992, International Finance Corporation 1992, International Labour Office 1990a, 1990b, 1991a, 1991b, 1991c, 1992 and 1993, International Monetary Fund 1992, Jahan 1991, Johnson 1992 and 1993, Kikeri, Nellis and Shirley 1992, Klitgaard 1991, Labazée 1988, Leipziger 1992, Leonard and others 1989, Lipton and Sachs 1990, Lubell 1991, Mahendra Dev 1992, Marinakis 1992, Marsden 1990, Moghadam 1992, Muralidharan 1992, Ohiorhenuan 1992, Onn 1990, Organisation for Economic Co-operation and Development 1990b, 1990c, 1992c and 1992d, Parker 1992, Perkins 1992, Perkins and Roemer 1991, Pfeffermann and Madarassy 1992a and 1992b, Remenyi 1991, Roemer and Jones 1991, Rohwer 1992, Salome 1989, Shapiro and Taylor 1990, Sherif forthcoming, Siegal 1990, Singh 1992, Sipos 1992, Smyth 1992, Standing 1992, Standing and Tokman 1991, Steel and Webster 1992, Stewart 1991, Stewart, Thomas and de Wilde 1990, Swedish International Development Authority 1993, Turnham, Salome and Schwarz 1990, UNDP 1992d, UNIDO 1992, United Nations 1990b, 1991b, 1992c and 1992d, United Nations Economic Commission for Europe 1992, United Nations Economic Commission for Latin America and the Caribbean 1992, US Department of Commerce 1986, van de Walle 1989, Wade 1990, Walker 1992, and World Bank 1989, 1990, 1991a, 1991b, 1991c, 1991d, 1991e, 1992a, 1992c, 1992d, 1992e and 1992f.

References for the boxes are as follows: box 3.2, International Labour Office 1992; box 3.3, World Bank 1991e; box 3.4, Getubig and Oshima 1991, International Labour Office 1991a and Jahan 1991; box 3.5, International Labour Office 1991a, 1991b, 1991c and 1992, Jahan 1991, United Nations 1991b and 1992c and US Department of Commerce 1986; box 3.6, Johnson 1993.

References for the tables are as follows: table 3.1, World Bank 1991e; table 3.2, Bayliss 1990 and International Labour Office 1990b; tables 3.3 and 3.4, Kikeri, Nellis and Shirley 1992; table 3.5, Pfeffermann and Madarassy 1992b.

References for the figures are as follows: figure 3.1, World Bank 1991e; figure 3.2, UNIDO 1992 and World Bank 1991e; figure 3.3, United Nations 1990b and International Labour Office 1991a and 1991b; figure 3.4, Organisation for Economic Co-operation and Development 1992d; figure 3.5, Pfeffermann and Madarassy 1992b.

Country studies in the annex draw on national statistics in addition to, for Argentina, United Nations Economic Commission for Latin America and the Caribbean 1992; for Brazil, United Nations Economic Commission for Latin America and the Caribbean 1992, Perkins 1992 and World Bank 1989 and 1991a; for China, Rohwer 1992, Singh 1992 and World Bank 1992a; for Egypt, Walker 1992 and World Bank 1991b; for Ghana, Pfeffermann and Madarassy 1992b, Sherif forthcoming, Steel and Webster 1992 and World Bank 1991c; for India, Muralidharan 1992 and World Bank 1992c; for Kenya, Adam, Cavendish and Mistry 1992 and World Bank 1992d; for Malaysia, Adam, Cavendish and Mistry 1992, Demery and Demery 1992 and Galal and others 1992; for Poland, Johnson 1992, Organisation for Economic Co-operation and Development 1992c and Standing 1992; for Russia, Johnson 1992, Parker 1992 and Standing 1992; and for Viet Nam, Leipziger 1992 and World Bank 1992e.

Chapter 4 draws on the following: Ananta, Taufik and Yosephine 1990, Benazzon 1992, Bird and Oldman 1990, Brass 1991, Cheema 1986, Chowdhury 1990, Conyers 1983, Gish, Malik and Sudharto 1988, Gonzalez-Block and others 1989, Greffe 1992, Guzmán 1990, Hyden and Bratton 1992, International Monetary Fund 1991, Klugman, Stewart and Helmsing 1992, Lisk 1985, MacAndrews 1986, Nellis 1983, Ranis and Stewart 1992a, 1992b and 1992c, Rondinelli, Nellis and Cheema 1983, Sundararajan 1990, Tordoff 1988, Tri 1988, United Nations Centre for Human Settlements 1991, Wunsch and Olowu 1990 and Yao 1990.

References for the tables are as follows: table 4.1, UN Population Division (national data) and country censuses (subnational data); tables 4.2–4.4, International Monetary Fund 1991 and studies commissioned by UNDP/HDRO in 1990.

References for the country studies in the annex are as follows: for Chile, Ranis and Stewart 1992a; for Indonesia, Ranis and Stewart 1992a; for Morocco, Benazzon 1992; and for Zimbabwe, Klugman, Stewart and Helmsing 1992.

Chapter 5 draws on the following: Amnesty International 1990 and 1991, Annis 1987, Annis and Hankim 1988, Archer 1992, Ashe and Cosslett 1989, Badejo 1992, Bebbington and Thiele 1993, Beets, Neggers and Wils 1988, Borton 1992, Brown and Korten 1989, Carroll 1992, Cernea 1988, Chambers 1989, Clark 1990, Constantino-David 1992, de Coninck 1992, de Crombrugghe, Howes and Nieuwkerk 1985, Dietz and Moyo 1991, Ekins 1992, Farrington and others 1993, Gemeenschappelijk Overleg Medefinanciering 1992, Ghai 1989, Goulet 1989, Green 1992, *Groots Network News* 1993, Harsch 1993, Hirschman 1984, Khan 1983, Korten 1990, Lecomte 1992, Lehmann 1990, Loveman 1991, Marsden and Oakley 1990, Muir 1992, Oakley and others 1991, Organisation for Economic Co-operation and Development 1988, 1990a and 1992a, Overseas Development Administration 1992, Paul and Israel 1991, People's Organizations and NGOs in Asia 1991, Rahman 1991, Remenyi 1991, Ribe and others 1990, Riddell 1992, Riddell and Robinson 1992 and 1993, Ringrose 1992, Robinson 1992, Schmitz and Gillies 1992, Schneider 1988, Smith 1990, Sollis 1992, Tendler 1987, Theunis 1992, UNEP 1991, United Nations Economic Commission for Africa 1990, Uphoff 1992, White 1992, Wils and Mindlin 1991, and World Bank 1992f.

References for the boxes are as follows: box 5.1, Badejo 1992; box 5.2, Khan 1983 and Cernea 1988; box 5.3, Arizpe 1992; box 5.4, UNEP 1991; box 5.5, Ghai 1989; box 5.6, Theunis 1992; box 5.7, Amnesty International 1991; box 5.8, United Nations Economic Commission for Africa 1990; box 5.9, Goulet 1989; box 5.10, Ashe and Cosslett 1989 and UNDP 1992c; box 5.11, United Nations Economic Commission for Africa 1990 and Ghai 1989.

References for the tables are as follows: table 5.1, Clark 1990; table 5.2, country studies commissioned by UNDP/HDRO.

References

Abell, Derek F. 1992. *Turnaround in Eastern Europe: In-depth Studies.* New York: UNDP, Management Development Programme.

Acharya, M., and Lynn Bennett. 1982. *Women and the Subsistence Sector: Economic Participation and Household Decision-Making in Nepal.* World Bank Staff Working Paper 526. Washington, D.C.

Adam, Christopher, William Cavendish and Percy Mistry. 1992. *Adjusting Privatization: Case Studies from Developing Countries.* London: James Currey.

Adepoju, Aderanti. 1991. *Africa Recovery Briefing Paper 3.* New York: United Nations.

Ahmadullah, M. 1981. "The Situation of Handicapped Children in Bangladesh." Assignment Children 53/54. UNICEF, New York.

Ajab, A., J-M Gankou and J. Mathonnat. 1991. "Cameroun: Evolution du Profile du Développement Humain." Paper prepared for UNDP. Doula.

Akder, Halis. 1990. "Turkey: Country Profile; Human Development Indices for All Turkish Provinces." Middle East Technical University, Department of Economics. UNDP, Ankara. Mimeo.

Amnesty International. 1990. *Amnesty International Report 1990.* London.

———. 1991. *Amnesty International Report 1991.* London.

Ananta, Aris, Salman Taufik and Susanne Yosephine. 1990. "Financial Aspect of Human Development: A Case Study in Indonesia." UNDP, New York.

Annis, Sheldon. 1987. "Can Small-Scale Development Be a Large-Scale Policy? The Case of Latin America." *World Development* 15, supplement (Autumn).

Annis, Sheldon, and Peter Hankim, eds. 1988. *Direct to the Poor: Grassroots Development in Latin America.* Boulder, Colo.: Lynne Rienner.

Archer, Robert. 1992. "Development, Democracy and Hope?" Policy Unit Report. Christian Aid, London. Mimeo.

Arizpe, Lourdes. 1992. "Ethnicity, Nations and Culture." *Development 1992* 4.

Ashe, Jeffrey, and Christopher E. Cosslett. 1989. *Credit for the Poor: Past Activities and Future Directions for the United Nations Development Programme.* New York: UNDP, Policy Division, Bureau for Programme Policy and Evaluation.

Asian Development Bank. 1991. *Key Indicators of Developing Asian and Pacific Countries.* Economics and Development Resource Center, Manila.

Aslund, Anders. 1985. *Private Enterprise in Eastern Europe.* New York: St. Martin's Press.

Aslund, Anders, and Richard Layard. 1993. *Changing Economic System in Russia.* London: Pinter Publishers.

Aspe, Pedro. 1991. "Thoughts on the Structural Transformation of Mexico: The Case of Privatization of Public Sector Enterprises." Address to Los Angeles World Affairs Council, June 21.

Avramovic, Dragoslav. 1992. "Developing Countries in the International Economic System: Their Problems and Prospects in the Markets for Finance, Commodities, Manufactures and Services." HDRO Occasional Paper 3. UNDP, New York.

Badejo, Babafemi A. 1992. "Non-Governmental Organizations." Background paper for *Human Development Report 1993.* UNDP, New York. Mimeo.

Balisacan, Arsenio. 1992. "Rural Poverty in the Philippines: Incidence, Determinants and Policies." *Asian Development Review* 10 (1): 125–63.

Barlett, Donald L., and James B. Steele. 1992. *America: What Went Wrong.* Kansas City: Andrews and McMeel.

Barrett, Bill. 1992. "AIDS Pandemic Affects Rio Process." *The Earth Times,* December 1, p. 3.

Baumol, William J. 1990. "Entrepreneurship: Productive, Unproductive and Destructive." *Journal of Political Economy* 98 (5): 893–921.

Bayliss, Fernando J. 1990. *Self-Employment in Industrialised Market Economy Countries.* Labour Market Analysis and Employment Planning Working Paper 38. Geneva: ILO.

Bebbington, Anthony, and Graham Thiele. 1993. *Non-Governmental Organisations and the State in Asia: Rethinking Roles in Sustainable Agricultural Development.* London: Routledge.

Beets, Nico, Jan Neggers and Fritz Wils. 1988. *"Big and Still Beautiful": Enquiry in the Efficiency and Effectiveness of Three Big NGOs (BINGO's) in South Asia.* Programme Evaluation 32. The Netherlands: DGIS/NOVIB.

Benazzon, Chaouk. 1992. "Le Decentralisation Cas du Maroc." Background paper for *Human Development Report 1993.* UNDP, New York.

Bird, R., and O. Oldman, eds. 1990. *Taxation in Developing Countries.* Baltimore: Johns Hopkins University Press.

Black, Maggie. 1991. "Philippines: Children of the Runaway Cities." Innocenti Studies. UNICEF, Florence.

Blanchard, Olivier J., Kenneth A. Froot and Jeffrey D. Sachs, eds. Forthcoming. *The Transition in Eastern*

Europe. Chicago: The University of Chicago Press and National Bureau of Economic Research.

Boraine, Alex. 1991. "Demokratie Will Gelernt Sein." *Der Überblick* (Hamburg) 4/91 (December): 14–16.

Borton, John. 1992. "The Enhanced Role of NGOs in Relief Operations." In *Development Research Insights.* Sussex: Overseas Development Institute and the Institute of Development Studies.

Bose, A.B. 1992. "The Disadvantaged Urban Child in India." Innocenti Occasional Paper 1. The Urban Child Series. UNICEF, Florence.

Bouassami, Mohammed. 1990. "Indicateur de Développement Humain: Cas du Maroc, IDH par Province." Paper prepared for UNDP, Rabat.

Boutros-Ghali, Boutros. 1992. "An Agenda for Peace: Peacemaking and Peace-Keeping." Report of the Secretary-General Pursuant to the Statement Adopted by the Summit Meeting of the Security Council on January 31, 1992. United Nations, New York. DPI/1247.

Brass, Paul R. 1991. *Ethnicity and Nationalism: Theory and Comparison.* New Delhi: Sage Publications.

Brown, David L., and David C. Korten. 1989. "Understanding Voluntary Organizations: Guidelines for Donors." Policy Research Working Paper 258. World Bank, Washington, D.C.

Brown, Lester R., Christopher Flavin and Hal Kane. 1992. *Vital Signs 1992.* New York: W.W. Norton.

Bruce, J., and D. Dwyer. 1988. *A Home Divided: Women and Income in the Third World.* Palo Alto, Calif.: Stanford University Press.

Brush, Candida. 1990. "Women and Enterprise Creation." OECD, Paris.

Buhmann, Brigitte, Lee Rainwater, Guenther Schmaus and Timothy M. Smeeding. 1988. "Equivalence Scales, Well-Being, Inequality, and Poverty: Sensitivity Estimates Across Ten Countries Using the Luxembourg Income Study LIS Database." *Review of Income and Wealth* 34 (2): 115–42.

Candoy-Sekse, Rebecca, and Anne Ruiz Palmer. 1990. *Techniques of Privatization of State-Owned Enterprises:* Vol. III, *Inventory of Country Experience and Reference Materials.* World Bank Technical Paper 90. Washington, D.C.

Carlson, Beverley A., and Tessa M. Wardlaw. 1990. "A Global, Regional and Country Assessment of Child Malnutrition." UNICEF Staff Working Paper 7. New York.

Carroll, Thomas F. 1992. *Intermediary NGOs: The Supporting Links in Grassroots Development.* West Hartford, Conn.: Kumarian Press.

Central and Eastern European Privatization Network. 1992. "Country Privatization Report 1992: Poland." Ljubljana.

Cernea, Michael M. 1988. *Nongovernmental Organizations and Local Development.* World Bank Discussion Paper 40. Washington, D.C.

Chambers, Robert, ed. 1989. "Vulnerability: How the Poor Cope." *IDS Bulletin* 20 (2): 39–47.

Chamie, Mary. 1991. "Aging, Disability and Gender." United Nations, New York.

Chatterji, Amrita. 1992. "India: The Forgotten Child of the Cities." Innocenti Studies. UNICEF, Florence.

Cheema, G. Shabbir, ed. 1986. *Reaching the Urban Poor: Project Implementation in Developing Countries.* Boulder, Colo.: Westview Press.

Children's Defense Fund. 1992. *The State of America's Children.*

Chowdhury, Omar. 1990. "UNDP Country Report on Bangladesh." UNDP, Dhaka.

Clark, John. 1990. *Democratizing Development: The Role of Voluntary Organizations.* West Hartford, Conn.: Kumarian Press.

Commonwealth Secretariat. 1989. *Engendering Adjustment for the 1990s: Report of a Commonwealth Expert Group on Women and Structural Adjustment.* London.

Constantino-David, Karina. 1992. "The Caucus of Development NGO Networks: The Philippine Experience in Scaling-up NGO Impact." University of Manchester, Institute for Development Policy and Management, Manchester.

Conyers, D. 1983. "Decentralisation: The Latest Fashion in Development Administration?" *Public Administration and Development* 3: 197–220.

Corbo, Vittorio, Stanley Fischer and Steven B. Webb. 1992. *Adjustment Lending Revisited: Policies to Restore Growth.* A World Bank Symposium. Washington, D.C.: World Bank.

Cornia, G. Andrea, Rolph van der Hoeven and Thandika Mkandawire. 1992. *Africa's Recovery in the 1990s.* A UNICEF Study. London: Macmillan.

Cowan, L. Gray. 1990. *Privatization in the Developing World.* New York: Praeger Publishers.

Dalal, K.L., ed. 1991. *Human Development: An Indian Perspective.* New Delhi: Vikas Publishing House for UNDP.

Danns, George K. 1989. "The Entrepreneur in Development." *Caribbean Affairs* 2 (3): 152–60.

de Coninck, John. 1992. *Evaluating the Impact of NGOs in Rural Poverty Alleviation: Uganda Country Study.* Working Paper 51. London: Overseas Development Institute.

de Crombrugghe, G., M. Howes and R. Nieuwkerk. 1985. *An Evaluation of EC Small Development Projects.* Brussels: Le Collectif d'Echanges pour la Technologie Appropriée (COTA).

Deger, Saadet, and Somnath Sen. 1990. *Military Expenditure: The Political Economy of International Security.* New York: Oxford University Press.

de Graft-Johnson, K.T. 1992. "Interagency Programme to Monitor Progress Towards the Attainment of Social Goals in the 1990s: A Synthesis of Five Pilot Studies in Ecuador, Kenya, Mali, Mexico and Philippines." Interagency Working Group, Accra. Mimeo.

Demery, David, and Lionel Demery. 1992. *Adjustment and Equity in Malaysia.* Development Centre Studies. OECD, Paris.

de Soto, Hernando. 1990. *The Other Path.* New York: Perennial Library.

de Wilde, Ton, Stijntje Schreurs and Arleen Richman, eds. 1991. *Opening the Market Place to the Small Enterprise: Where Magic Ends and Development Begins.* West Hartford, Conn.: Kumarian Press.

Dietz, Ton, and Sam Moyo. 1991. *Zimbabwe: Organisation of Rural Associations for Progress (ORAP).* The Netherlands: Veldonderzoek, Impactstudie Medefinancieringsprogramma.

Dore, Ronald, Jean Bounine-Cabale and Kari Tapioli, eds. 1989. *Japan at Work: Markets, Management and Flexibility.* OECD, Paris.

Drèze, Jean, and Amartya K. Sen. 1989. *Hunger and Public Action.* Oxford: Oxford University Press.

Ekins, Paul. 1992. *A New World Order: Grassroots Movements for Global Change.* London: Routledge.

Elkan, Walter. 1988. "The Background of African Entrepreneurs." *World Bank Research Observer* 3 (2).

Espiell, Hector Gros. 1990. *Report by the Expert on Guatemala.* New York: UN Economic and Social Council. E/CN.4/1990/45/Add.1. December 12.

Farrington, John, Anthony Bebbington, David J. Lewis and Kate Wellard. 1993. *Reluctant Partners? Non-Governmental Organisations, the State and Sustainable Agricultural Development.* London: Routledge.

Food and Agriculture Organization of the United Nations. 1988. *Rural Poverty in Latin America and the Caribbean.* Proceedings of the World Conference on Agrarian Reform and Rural Development. Rome.

Fundación para la Educación Superior y el Desarrollo. 1992. *Un Plan de Desarrollo Humano de Largo Plazo para Colombia.* Bogotá.

Galal, Ahmed. 1991. *Public Enterprise Reform: Lessons from the Past and Issues for the Future.* World Bank Discussion Paper 119. Washington, D.C.

Galal, Ahmed, Leroy Jones, Pankaj Tandon and Ingo Vogelsang. 1992. "Welfare Consequences of Selling Public Enterprises: Case Studies from Chile, Malaysia, Mexico and the U.K." Conference Papers. World Bank, Country Economics Department, Public Sector Management and Private Sector Development Division, Washington, D.C.

Gay, John, Debby Gill, Thuso Green, David Hall, Mike Mhlanga and 'Manthastisi Mohapi. 1991. "Poverty in Lesotho: A Mapping Exercise." Paper prepared for UNDP. Sechaba Consultants, Maseru.

Gemeenschappelijk Overleg Medefinanciering. 1992. *Significance of the Co-financing Programme: An Exploration.* Final Report of the Steering Group, Impact Co-financing Programme. The Hague.

Getubig, Ismael, Jr., and Harry T. Oshima, eds. 1991. *Towards a Full Employment Strategy for Accelerated Economic Growth.* Kuala Lumpur: Asian and Pacific Development Centre.

Ghai, Dharam. 1989. "Participatory Development: Some Perspective from Grass-Roots Experiences." *Journal of Development Planning* (19): 215–46.

Girard, Augustin, and Genevieve Gentil. 1983. *Cultural Development: Experience and Policies.* 2nd edition. Paris: UNESCO.

Gish, O., R. Malik and P. Sudharto. 1988. "Who Gets What? Utilisation of Health Services in Indonesia." *International Journal of Health Planning and Management* 5: 41–52.

Gonzalez-Block, N., and others. 1989. "Health Services Decentralization in Mexico: Formulation, Implementation and Results of Policy." *Health Policy and Planning* 4: 301–15.

Goulet, Denis. 1989. "Participation in Development: New Avenues." *World Development* 17(2): 169–71.

Green, Reginald H. 1992. "Transformation, Poverty and Civil Society in Sub-Saharan Africa: What Roles for NGOs?" Nineteenth Forum Internazionale, Europa Universo. Cuneo, Italy. Mimeo.

Greffe, Xavier. 1992. "Les Conditions de Reussite de la Decentralisation dans les Pays en Développement." Background paper for *Human Development Report 1993.* UNDP, New York. Mimeo.

Griffin, Keith. 1991. "Foreign Aid After the Cold War." *Development and Change* 22: 645–85.

Griffin, Keith, and Azizur Rahman Khan. 1992. "Globalization and the Developing World: An Essay on the International Dimensions of Development in the Post–Cold War Era." HDRO Occasional Paper 2. UNDP, New York.

Griffin, Keith, and John Knight, eds. 1990. *Human Development and the International Development Strategy for the 1980s.* London: Macmillan.

Griffin, Keith, and Terry McKinley. Forthcoming. "Guidelines for Implementing a Human Development Strategy." HDRO Occasional Paper. UNDP, New York.

Groots Network News (New York). 1993. February.

Grosh, Barbara. 1992. *Public Enterprise in Kenya.* Boulder, Colo.: Lynne Rienner.

Guzmán, Generoso de. 1990. "Human Development Report: Philippines Case Study." UNDP, New York.

Hacker, Andrew. 1992. *Two Nations: Black and White, Separate, Hostile, Unequal.* New York: Macmillan.

Haggard, Stephan, and Robert R. Kaufman, eds. 1992. *The Politics of Economic Adjustment.* Princeton, N.J.: Princeton University Press.

Halperin, Morton H., David J. Scheffer and Patricia L. Small. 1992. *Self-Determination in the New World Order.* Washington, D.C.: Carnegie Endowment for Peace.

Haq, Mahbub ul. 1992a. "Human Development in a Changing World." HDRO Occasional Paper 1. UNDP, New York.

———. 1992b. "New Analysis: Bridges on the 'Road to Rio'." *Earth Summit Times*, special edition, July 21, pp. 1 and 12.

———. 1992c. "Reinterpreting Human Development." *Choices* (March).

———. 1992d. "Towards Sustainable Human Development." Opening Statement at The Hague Symposium on Sustainable Development: From Concept to Action, November 25–27, The Hague.

Harsch, Ernest. 1992. "Strengthened Somalia Relief Effort Threatened by Continued Fighting." *Africa Recovery* 6 (3): 6–9.

———. 1993. "Somalia Restoring Hope." Africa Recovery Briefing Paper 7. United Nations, New York.

Henry, Ralph M. 1991. "Trinidad and Tobago: Human Development Indicators." Paper prepared for UNDP, Port-of-Spain.

Hewett, Daniel P. 1991. "Military Expenditures in the Developing World." *Finance and Development* 28 (3).

Hirschman, Albert O. 1984. *Getting Ahead Collectively: Grassroots Development in Latin America.* New York: Pergamon Press.

Hyden, Goran, and Michael Bratton, eds. 1992. *Governance and Politics in Africa.* Boulder, Colo.: Lynne Rienner.

International Finance Corporation. 1992. *1992 Annual*

Report. Washington, D.C.: World Bank.

International Labour Office. 1990a. *Employment and Equity: The Challenge of the 1990s.* Programa Regional del Empleo para America Latina y el Caribe. Santiago: ILO World Employment Programme.

———. 1990b. *The Promotion of Self-Employment.* International Labour Conference, 77th Session, Report VII. Geneva.

———. 1991a. *African Employment Report.* Addis Ababa: Jobs and Skill Programme for Africa.

———. 1991b. "Labour Market Adjustment in Latin America: An Appraisal of the Social Effects in the 1980s." Programa Regional para el Empleo en la América Latina y el Caribe, Santiago.

———. 1991c. *Yearbook of Labour Statistics.* Geneva.

———. 1992. *World Labour Report.* Geneva.

———. 1993. *World Labour Report.* Geneva.

International Labour Organisation. 1989. "Farm Redeployment to Sustained Employment Generation: Challenges for Ghana's Programme for Economic Recovery and Development." WFP/JASPA Report. ILO, Addis Ababa.

International Monetary Fund. 1991. *Government Financial Statistics.* Washington, D.C.

———. 1992. *World Economic Outlook.* Washington, D.C. October.

Inter-Parliamentary Union. 1992. *Women and Political Power.* Reports and Documents Series 19. Geneva.

Jahan, Selim. 1991. *Female Employment Opportunities and Job Entry Qualifications in Bangladesh.* Dhaka: ILO.

Jaynes, Gerald David, and Robin M. Williams, Jr., eds. 1989. *A Common Destiny: Blacks and American Society.* Washington, D.C.: National Academy Press.

Jazairy, Idris, Mohiuddin Alamgir and Theresa Panuccio. 1992. *The State of World Rural Poverty: An Inquiry into Its Causes and Consequences.* International Fund for Agricultural Development. New York: New York University Press.

Johnson, Simon. 1992. "Private Business and Human Development: The Evidence After Communism." Background paper for *Human Development Report 1993.* UNDP, New York. Mimeo.

———. 1993. "A Tale of Two Cities: Krakow and Lodz." Background paper for *Human Development Report 1993.* UNDP, New York. Mimeo.

———. Forthcoming. "Private Business in Eastern Europe." In Blanchard, Froot and Sachs forthcoming.

Kanbargi, Ramesh, ed. 1991. *Child Labour in the Indian Subcontinent: Dimensions and Implications.* New Delhi: Sage Publications.

Kaul, Inge. 1993a. "Making the Human Development Concern Operational: A 10-Point Agenda." UNDP, New York. Mimeo.

———. 1993b. "A New Approach to Aid." UNDP, New York. Mimeo.

Kelley, Allen C. 1991. "The Human Development Index: Handle With Care." *Population and Development Review* 17(2): 315–24.

Kennedy, Paul. 1993. *Preparing for the Twenty-First Century.* New York: Random House.

Khan, Akhtar Hameed. 1983. "Orangi Project: A Task Bigger than Colombo." *Pakistan and Gulf Economist* 2 (24): 12–18.

Khatib, H. 1990. "*Human Development Report 1990*: Jordan: a Follow-up." Paper prepared for UNDP, Amman.

Kikeri, Sunita, John Nellis and Mary Shirley. 1992. *Privatization: The Lessons of Experience.* Washington, D.C.: World Bank.

Kingma, Kees. 1993. "Can Development Be Measured?" *The Courier* 137:70–72.

Klitgaard, Robert. 1991. *Adjusting to Reality: Beyond "State versus Market" in Economic Development.* An International Center for Economic Growth Publication. San Francisco: ICS Press.

Klugman, Jeni. 1992. "Decentralization: A Survey of Literature." Background paper for *Human Development Report 1993.* UNDP, New York. Mimeo.

Klugman, Jeni, Frances Stewart and A.H. Helmsing. 1992. "Decentralization in Zimbabwe." Background paper for *Human Development Report 1993.* UNDP, New York. Mimeo.

Korten, David C. 1990. *Getting to the 21st Century: Voluntary Action and the Global Agenda.* West Hartford, Conn.: Kumarian Press.

Kouidhi, Moncef, and Joselyne Ramamonjisoa. 1991. "Développement Humain et Identification des Zones Prioritaires d'Intervention." Paper prepared by Dirassat (Tunisie) for UNDP. Antananarivo.

Krongkaew, Medhi, Pranee Tinakorn and Suphat Suphachlasai. 1992. "Rural Poverty in Thailand: Policy Issues and Responses." *Asian Development Review* 10 (1): 199–225.

Kühne, Winrich. 1992. "Blauhelme in Einer Turbulenten Welt: Neue Aufgaben für die Vereinten Nationen." *Der Überblick* (Hamburg) 4/92 (September): 5–10.

Labazée, Pascal. 1988. *Entreprises et Entrepreneurs du Burkina Faso.* Paris: Karthala Éditions.

Lecomte, Bernard. 1992. "Report on Human Development." Background paper for *Human Development Report 1993.* UNDP, New York. Mimeo.

Lehmann, David. 1990. *Democracy and Development in Latin America: Economics, Politics and Religion in the Post-War Period.* Philadelphia: Temple University Press.

Leipziger, Danny M. 1992. *Awakening the Market: Viet Nam's Economic Transition.* World Bank Discussion Paper 157. Washington, D.C.

Leonard, H. Jeffrey, and others. 1989. *Environment and the Poor: Development Strategies for a Common Agenda.* U.S. Third World Policy Perspectives 11. Overseas Development Council. New Brunswick, N.J.: Transaction Books.

Lewenhak, Sheila. 1992. *The Revaluation of Women's Work.* London: Earthscan Publications Ltd.

Lipton, David, and Jeffrey Sachs. 1990. "Creating a Market Economy in Eastern Europe: The Case of Poland." *Brookings Papers on Economic Activity* 1: 75–147.

Lisk, F., ed. 1985. *Popular Participation in Planning for Basic Needs.* Aldershot, U.K.: Gower.

Loveman, Brian. 1991. "NGOs and the Transition to Democracy in Chile." *Grassroots Development* 15 (2).

Lubell, Harold. 1991. *The Informal Sector in the 1980s and 1990s.* Paris: OECD Development Centre.

MacAndrews, C., ed. 1986. *Central Government and Local Development in Indonesia.* New York: Oxford University Press.

Mahbubani, Kishore. 1992. "The West and the Rest." UNDP Development Study Programme, New York. Mimeo.

Mahendra Dev, S. 1992. *Poverty Alleviation Programmes: A Case Study of Maharashtra with Emphasis on the Employment Guarantee Scheme.* Discussion Paper 37. Bombay: Indira Gandhi Institute of Development Research.

Mamdani, Mahmood. 1992. "Africa: Democratic Theory and Democratic Struggles." *Economic and Political Weekly,* October 10.

Marinakis, Andrés E. 1992. "Public Sector Employment in Developing Countries: An Overview of Past and Present Trends." Occasional Paper 3, Interdepartmental Project on Structural Adjustment. ILO, Geneva.

Marsden, David, and Peter Oakley, eds. 1990. *Evaluating Social Development Projects.* Development Guidelines 5. Oxford: Oxfam.

Marsden, Keith. 1990. *African Entrepreneurs: Pioneers of Development.* Washington, D.C.: World Bank.

McIvor, C. 1990. "A New Approach to the Disabled in Africa." *The Courier* 124.

McNamara, Robert S. 1991. "Reducing Military Expenditures in the Third World." *Finance and Development* 28 (3).

Menezes, Rohit. 1992. "Panos AIDS Study Warns of Economic Implications." *The Earth Times*, December 1, p. 16.

Millman, Sara R., and others. 1991. *The Hunger Report: Update 1991.* The Alan Shawn Feinstein World Hunger Program. Providence, R.I.: Brown University.

Moghadam, Valentine M., ed. 1992. *Privatization and Democratization in Central and Eastern Europe and the Soviet Union: The Gender Dimension.* Helsinki: WIDER.

Muir, Ann. 1992. *Evaluating the Impact of NGOs in Rural Poverty Alleviation: Zimbabwe Country Study.* Working Paper 52. London: Overseas Development Institute.

Munachonga, M. 1986. "Impact of Economic Adjustment on Women in Zambia." In *UNDP Restructuring and Development in Zambia: Roles for Technical Cooperation.* New York: UNDP.

Munyakho, Dorothy. 1992. "Kenya: Child Newcomers in the Urban Jungle." Innocenti Studies. UNICEF, Florence.

Muralidharan, Sukumar. 1992. "Inflationary Impulse." *Frontline*, October 23, pp. 114–15.

Nellis, J. 1983. "Tutorial Decentralisation in Morocco." *Journal of Modern African Studies* 21 (3): 423–35.

Nobel, J.H. 1981. "Social Inequality and the Prevalence of Disability in the Disabled Child." UNICEF, New York.

Oakley, Peter, and others. 1991. *Projects with People.* Geneva: ILO.

Ohiorhenuan, Lily. 1992. "People's Participation in the Markets." Background paper for *Human Development Report 1993.* UNDP, New York. Mimeo.

Onn, Fong Chan. 1990. "Small and Medium Industries in Malaysia: Economic Efficiency and Entrepreneurship." *The Developing Economies* 28 (2): 152–79.

Organisation for Economic Co-operation and Development. 1988. *Voluntary Aid for Development: The Role of Non-Governmental Organisations.* Paris.

———. 1990a. *Directory of Non-Governmental Development Organisations in OECD Member Countries.* Paris.

———. 1990b. *Implementing Change: Entrepreneurship and Local Initiative.* Paris.

———. 1990c. *OECD Economic Outlook: Historical Statistics 1960–1988.* Paris.

———. 1991. *The State of the Environment.* Paris.

———. 1992a. *Development Co-operation: Efforts and Policies of the Members of the Development Assistance Committee.* Paris.

———. 1992b. *Development Cooperation 1992 Report.* Paris.

———. 1992c. *Industry in Poland: Structural Adjustment Issues and Policy Options.* Centre for Co-operation with European Economies in Transition. Paris.

———. 1992d. "Structural Shifts in Major OECD Countries." Industrial Policy in OECD Countries: Annual Review, 1992. Paris.

Overseas Development Administration. 1992. "Report on the ODA/NGO Seminar on Popular Participation." London.

Parker, John. 1992. "Russia Reborn: A Survey of Russia." *The Economist,* December 5.

Paul, Samuel. 1985. "Privatization and the Public Sector." *Finance and Development* 22 (4).

Paul, Samuel, and Arturo Israel, eds. 1991. *Nongovernmental Organizations and the World Bank: Cooperation for Development.* Washington, D.C.: World Bank.

People's Organizations and NGOs in Asia. 1991. *Colombo Statement of People's Empowerment.* Colombo.

Perkins, Dwight H., and Michael Roemer, eds. 1991. *Reforming Economic Systems in Developing Countries.* Cambridge, Mass.: Harvard Institute for International Development.

Perkins, Liza M. 1992. "The Brazilian Privatization Program: Procedures, Impediments, and Implications." New York University, Center for Latin American and Caribbean Studies, New York. Mimeo.

Pfeffermann, Guy P., and Andrea Madarassy. 1992a. *Trends in Private Investment in Developing Countries, 1992 edition.* IFC Discussion Paper 14. Washington, D.C.: World Bank.

———. 1992b. *Trends in Private Investment in Developing Countries 1993.* IFC Discussion Paper 16. Washington, D.C.: World Bank.

Picciotto, Robert. 1992. "Participatory Development: Myths and Dilemmas." Policy Research Working Paper 930. World Bank, Washington, D.C.

Porter, Michael E. 1990. *The Competitive Advantage of Nations.* New York: Free Press.

Pronk, Jan, and Mahbub ul Haq. 1992. "Sustainable Development: From Concept to Action." The Hague Report. Ministry of Development Cooperation, The Hague; and UNDP, New York.

Rahman, Rushidan Islam. 1991. "Poor Women's Access to Economic Gain from Grameen Bank Loans." Working Paper 91/2. Australian National University Research School of Pacific Studies, National Centre for

Development Studies, Canberra.

Ramaga, Philip Vuciri. 1992. "Relativity of the Minority Concept." *Human Rights Quarterly* 14: 104–19.

Ranis, Gustav, and Frances Stewart. 1992a. "Decentralization in Chile." Background paper for *Human Development Report 1993.* UNDP, New York. Mimeo.

———. 1992b. "Decentralization in Indonesia." Background paper for *Human Development Report 1993.* UNDP, New York. Mimeo.

———. 1992c. "Participation and Human Development." Background paper for *Human Development Report 1993.* UNDP, New York. Mimeo.

Remenyi, Joe. 1991. *Where Credit Is Due: Income-Generating Programs for the Poor in Developing Countries.* Boulder, Colo.: Westview Press.

Repetto, Robert, and M. Gillis, eds. 1988. *Public Policies and the Misuse of Forest Resources.* Cambridge: Cambridge University Press.

Ribe, Helen, Soniya Carvalho, Robert Liebenthal, Peter Nicholas and Elaine Zuckerman. 1990. *How Adjustment Programs Can Help the Poor: The World Bank's Experience.* Washington, D.C.: World Bank.

Riddell, Roger. 1992. "Grassroots Participation and the Role of NGOs." Background paper for *Human Development Report 1993.* UNDP, New York. Mimeo.

Riddell, Roger, and Mark Robinson. 1992. *The Impact of NGO Poverty Alleviation Projects: Results of the Case Study Evaluations.* Working Paper 68. London: Overseas Development Institute.

———. 1993. *Working with the Poor: NGOs and Rural Poverty Alleviation.* London: Overseas Development Institute.

Ringrose, Nigel. 1992. "Increasing UNDP's Impact on Poverty Alleviation and Grassroots Development." UNDP, New York. Mimeo.

Rizzini, Irene, Irma Rizzini, Monica Munhoz and Lidia Galeano. 1992. "Childhood and Urban Poverty in Brazil: Street and Working Children and Their Families." Innocenti Occasional Papers, The Urban Child Series, No. 3. UNICEF, Florence.

Robinson, Mark. 1992. *Evaluating the Impact of NGOs in Rural Poverty Alleviation: India Country Study.* Working Paper 49. London: Overseas Development Institute.

Roemer, Michael, and Christine Jones, eds. 1991. *Markets in Developing Countries.* San Francisco: ICS Press.

Rohwer, Jim. 1992. "When China Wakes: A Survey of China." *The Economist,* November 28.

Rondinelli, D., J. Nellis and G. Chabbir Cheema. 1983. *Decentralization in Developing Countries: A Review of Recent Experience.* World Bank Staff Working Paper 581. Washington, D.C..

Salome, Bernard. 1989. *Fighting Urban Unemployment in Developing Countries.* Paris: OECD Development Centre.

Schmitz, Gerald J., and David Gillies. 1992. *The Challenge of Democratic Development: Sustaining Democratization in Developing Societies.* Ottawa: The North-South Institute.

Schneider, Bertrand. 1988. *The Barefoot Revolution: A Report to the Club of Rome.* London: Intermediate Technology Publications.

Sen, Amartya K. 1981. *Poverty and Famines: An Essay on Entitlement and Deprivation.* Oxford: Oxford University Press.

———. 1990a. "Development as Capability Expansion." In Griffin and Knight 1990.

———. 1990b. "More than 100 Million Women Are Missing." *New York Review of Books* 37 (20): 61–66.

Shapiro, Helen, and Lance Taylor. 1990. "The State and Industrial Strategy." *World Development* 18 (6): 861–78.

Sherif, Khaled. Forthcoming. *Regional Study on Public Enterprise Reform and Privatization in Africa.* Washington, D.C.: World Bank.

Shiva Kumar, A.K. 1990. "The UNDP's Human Development Index: A Computation for 17 Indian States." Harvard Center for Population Studies, Cambridge, Mass. Mimeo.

Siegal, Beth. 1990. "Business Creation and Local Economic Development: Why Entrepreneurship Should Be Encouraged." *Enterprising Women.* Paris: OECD.

Singer, Hans. 1992. "Beyond the Debt Crisis." *Development,* No. 1.

Singh, Inderjit. 1992. *China: Industrial Policies for an Economy in Transition.* World Bank Discussion Paper 143. Washington, D.C.

Sipos, Sandos. 1992. "Poverty Measurement in Central and Eastern Europe Before the Transition to the Market Economy." Innocenti Occasional Papers, Economic Policy Series 29. UNICEF, Florence.

Smith, Brian. 1990. *More than Altruism: The Politics of Private Foreign Aid.* Princeton, N.J.: Princeton University Press.

Smyth, Ines. 1992. "Collective Efficiency and Selective Benefits: The Growth of the Rattan Industry of Tegalwangi (Indonesia)." *IDS Bulletin* 23 (3): 51–56.

Sollis, Peter. 1992. "Multilateral Agencies, NGOs and Policy Reform." *Development in Practice* 2 (3).

South Commission. 1990. *The Challenge of the South: The Report of the South Commission.* New York: Oxford University Press.

Sridhar, V. 1993. "A Global Crisis: Commodity Trade at the Crossroads." *Frontline,* January 1, pp. 98–100.

Standing, Guy. 1992. "Human Development in Eastern and Central Europe." Background paper for *Human Development Report 1993.* UNDP, New York. Mimeo.

Standing, Guy, and Victor Tokman. 1991. *Towards Social Adjustment: Labour Market Issues in Structural Adjustment.* Geneva: ILO.

Stavenhagen, Rudolfo. 1990. *The Ethnic Question: Conflicts, Development and Human Rights.* Tokyo: United Nations University Press.

Steel, William F., and Leila M. Webster. 1992. "How Small Enterprises in Ghana Have Responded to Adjustment." *World Bank Economic Review* 6 (3): 423–38.

Stewart, Frances. 1991. "The Many Faces of Adjustment." *World Development* 19 (12): 1847–64.

Stewart, Frances, Henk Thomas and Ton de Wilde, eds. 1990. *The Other Policy.* London: Intermediate Technology Publications.

Stockholm International Peace Research Institute. 1992. *SIPRI Yearbook 1992: World Armaments and Disarmament.* New York: Oxford University Press.

Streeten, Paul. 1992. "Global Governance for Human

Development." HDRO Occasional Paper 4. UNDP, New York.

Strong, Maurice F. 1992. "Earth Inc. Needs Better Management." *The Earth Times,* December 1, p. 8.

Subbarao, K. 1985. "State Policies and Regional Disparity in Indian Agriculture." *Development and Change* 16 (4).

Summers, Robert, and Alan Heston. 1988. "A New Set of International Comparisons of Real Product and Prices: Estimates for 130 Countries, 1950–1985." *Review of Income and Wealth* 34 (1): 1-26.

———. 1991. "Pann World Table (Mark 5): An Expanded Set of International Comparisons, 1950–88." *Quarterly Journal of Economics* 106 (2): 327–68.

Summers, Robert, Irving B. Kravis and Alan Heston. 1984. "Changes in the World Income Distribution." *Journal of Policy Modelling* 6 (2): 237–69.

Sundararajan, C.R. 1990. "Resources for Human Development: Country Study: India." UNDP, New York.

Svasti, Pongsvas, Naris Chaiyasoot, Waraporn Suvachittanont and Paranee Masnee. 1991. "Human Development Indicators in Thailand." Paper prepared for UNDP. Bangkok.

Svasti, Pongsvas, and others. 1991. "Human Development Indicators." UNDP, Bangkok.

Swedish International Development Authority (SIDA). 1993. *Redefining the Role of the State and Market in the Development Process.* Stockholm.

Swift, Anthony. 1991. "Brazil: The Fight for Childhood in the City." Innocenti Studies. UNICEF, Florence.

Tendler, Judith. 1987. *Whatever Happened To Poverty Alleviation?* Report for the Mid-Decade Review of the Ford Foundation's Programs on Livelihood, Employment and Income Generation. New York: Ford Foundation.

Theunis, Sjef, ed. 1992. *Non-Governmental Development Organizations of Developing Countries: and the South Smiles...* Dordrecht, The Netherlands: Martinus Nijhoff.

Tordoff, W. 1988. "Local Administration in Botswana." *Public Administration and Development* 8: 183–202.

Treagust, Steven. 1990. "Improving the Quality of Education in Developing Countries." In Griffin and Knight 1990.

Tri, Huynh Cao, ed. 1988. *Participative Administration and Endogenous Development.* Paris: UNESCO.

Turnham, David, Bernard Salome and Antoine Schwarz. 1990. *The Informal Sector Revisited.* Paris: OECD Development Centre.

UNCTAD. 1990a. *The Least Developed Countries 1990 Report.* New York: United Nations.

———. 1990b. *Trade and Development Report, 1990.* Report by the Secretariat of the United Nations Conference on Trade and Development. New York: United Nations.

———. 1991a. *The Least Developed Countries 1991 Report.* New York: United Nations.

———. 1991b. *Trade and Development Report, 1991.* Report by the Secretariat of the United Nations Conference on Trade and Development. New York: United Nations.

UNDP. 1990. *Human Development Report 1990.* New York: Oxford University Press.

———. 1991a. "Cities, People and Poverty, Urban Development Cooperation for the 1990s." A UNDP Strategy Paper. New York.

———. 1991b. *Human Development Report 1991.* New York: Oxford University Press.

———. 1991c. "Poverty Alleviation in Asia and the Pacific: The UNDP Response." Report of a Regional Workshop, May 26–28, 1991. Kuala Lumpur.

———. 1992a. *Balanced Development: An Approach to Social Action in Pakistan.* Islamabad.

———. 1992b. "Bucharest Statement on Change: Systems and People." Proceedings of a Round Table on Global Development Challenges, held in Bucharest, Romania, September 4–6.

———. 1992c. *Human Development in Bangladesh: Local Action Under National Constraints.* Dhaka.

———. 1992d. *Human Development Report 1992.* New York: Oxford University Press.

———. 1992e. *Making People Matter: Introductory Comment on a Human Development Strategy for Ghana.* Accra.

———. 1992f. "NGO Perspectives on Poverty, Environment and Development." Environment and Natural Resources Group and NGO Programme. New York.

———. 1993. *Rethinking Technical Cooperation: Reforms for Capacity Building in Africa.* New York.

UNEP. 1991. *Success Stories of Women and the Environment.* Washington, D.C.: UNEP and WorldWIDE, Inc.

UNESCO. 1981. *Cultural Development: Some Regional Experiences.* Paris.

———. 1986. *Participation in Cultural Activities: Three Case Studies.* Paris.

———. 1990. *Tradition and Development in Africa Today.* Paris.

———. 1991. *World Education Report 1991.* Paris.

UNFPA. 1991. *The State of World Population.* New York.

———. 1992. *The State of World Population.* New York.

UNHCR. 1991. *Refugees: The Global Outlook 1990.* No.18. Geneva.

UNICEF. 1990. *The State of the World's Children 1991.* New York: Oxford University Press.

———. 1991. *The State of the World's Children 1992.* New York: Oxford University Press.

———. 1992. *The State of the World's Children 1993.* New York: Oxford University Press.

———. 1993. *Indicators Concerning Children in the Countries of the Former Soviet Union: A Statistical Review.* Programme Division Working Paper.

UNIDO. 1992. *Industry and Development: Global Report 1992/93.* Vienna.

United Nations. 1989. "Report on National Legislation for the Equalisation of Opportunities for People with Disabilities." New York.

———. 1990a. *Disability Statistics Compendium.* New York.

———. 1990b. *Global Outlook 2000.* New York.

———. 1990c. *A Global Strategy for the Prevention and Control of Iodine Deficiency Disorders.* New York.

———. 1991a. *World Economic Survey 1991: Current Trends and Policies in the World Economy.* Department of International Economic and Social Affairs. New York. E/91/75/ST/ESA/222.

———. 1991b. *The World's Women 1970–1990: Trends and Statistics.* New York.

———. 1992a. "Report of the Secretary-General on the Work of the Organization." New York. A/47/1.

———. 1992b. "Study on Defensive Security Concepts and Policies." Report of the Secretary-General. New York. A/47/394.

———. 1992c. *World Economic Survey 1992: Current Trends and Policies in the World Economy.* Department of Economic and Social Development. New York. E/1992/40. ST/ESA/231.

———. 1992d. *World Investment Report 1992.* New York.

———. 1992e. *The World's Women.* New York.

United Nations Centre for Human Settlements (Habitat). 1991. *Human Settlements: Development Through Community Participation.* Nairobi.

United Nations Conference on Environment and Development. 1992. "The Rio Declaration on Environment and Development." New York. A/CONF.151/5/Rev.1.

United Nations Economic Commission for Africa. 1990. "African Charter for Popular Participation in Development and Transformation." Proceedings of the International Conference on Popular Participation in the Recovery and Development Process in Africa, held in Arusha, Tanzania, February 12–16. Addis Ababa: UNECA. E/ECA/CM.16/11.

United Nations Economic Commission for Europe. 1992. *Economic Survey in Europe in 1991–1992.* Geneva.

United Nations Economic Commission for Latin America and the Caribbean. 1992. *Economic Panorama of Latin America 1992.* Santiago.

Uphoff, Norman. 1992. *Local Institutions and Participation for Sustainable Development.* Gatekeeper Series 31. London: International Institute for Environment and Development.

US Department of Commerce. 1986. *Women and Business Ownership.* Washington, D.C.

van de Walle, Nicolas. 1989. "Privatization in Developing Countries: A Review of the Issues." *World Development* 17 (5): 601–16.

Wade, Robert. 1990. *Governing the Market: Economic Theory and the Role of Government in East Asian Industrialization.* Princeton, N.J.: Princeton University Press.

Walker, Tony. 1992. "Public Sector Liability for Egypt." *Financial Times,* August 12.

Weiner, Myron. 1992. "Peoples and States in a New Ethnic Order." *Third World Quarterly* 13 (2): 317–32.

White, David. 1991. "East Asia Arms Build-Up is Other Side of Peace Dividend Coin." *Financial Times,* March 13, p. 4.

White, Merry. 1987. "The Virtue of Japanese Mothers: Cultural Definitions of Women's Lives." *Daedalus* 116 (3): 149–64.

White, Sarah C. 1992. *Evaluating the Impact of NGOs in Rural Poverty Alleviation: Uganda Country Study.* Working Paper 50. London: Overseas Development Institute.

WHO. 1992. "Global Health Situation and Projections: Estimates." Division of Epidemiological Surveillance and Health Situation and Trend Assessment. Geneva.

WHO/HST/92.1.

Wils, Fritz, and Lielson Antonia de Almeida Coelho. 1991. *Brazil: Coordenadora Ecumência De Servício (CESE).* The Netherlands: Veldonderzoek, Impactstudie Medefinancieringsprogramma.

Wils, Fritz, and Betty Mindlin. 1991. *Brazil: Commissão Pastoral da Terra, Norte (II).* The Netherlands: Veldonderzoek, Impactstudie Medefinancieringsprogramma.

World Bank. 1989. "Brazil: Prospects for Privatization." Latin America and the Caribbean Country Department I, Finance and Industry Division. Washington, D.C.

———. 1990. *World Development Report 1990.* New York: Oxford University Press.

———. 1991a. "Brazil: Economic Stabilization and Structural Reforms." Latin America and the Caribbean, Country Department I, Country Operations Division. Washington, D.C.

———. 1991b. *Egypt: Alleviating Poverty during Structural Adjustment.* A World Bank Country Study. Washington, D.C.

———. 1991c. "Ghana: Progress and Adjustment." Western Africa Department. Washington, D.C.

———. 1991d. *Global Economic Prospects and the Developing Countries.* Washington, D.C.

———. 1991e. *World Development Report 1991.* New York: Oxford University Press.

———. 1991f. *World Tables 1991.* Washington, D.C.

———. 1992a. *China: Reform and the Role of the Plan in the 1990s.* A World Bank Country Study. Washington, D.C.

———. 1992b. *Global Economic Prospects in Developing Countries.* Washington, D.C.

———. 1992c. "India: Stabilizing and Reforming the Economy." South Asia Country Department II. Washington, D.C.

———. 1992d. *Kenya: Reinvesting in Stabilization and Growth through Public Sector Adjustment.* A World Bank Country Study. Washington, D.C.

———. 1992e. "Viet Nam: Restructuring Public Finance and Public Enterprises." East Asia and Pacific Country Department I. Washington, D.C.

———. 1992f. *World Development Report 1992.* New York: Oxford University Press.

World Resources Institute. 1992. *World Resources 1992.* In collaboration with the United Nations Environment Programme and the United Nations Development Programme. New York: Oxford University Press.

Wulf, Herbert. 1992a. "The Demobilization of Military Personnel as a Problem and a Potential for Human Development." Background paper for *Human Development Report 1993.* UNDP, New York. Mimeo.

———. 1992b. "Disarmament as a Chance for Human Development: Is There a Peace Dividend?" HDRO Occasional Paper 5. UNDP, New York.

Wunsch, J., and D. Olowu, eds. 1990. *The Failure of the Centralized State.* Boulder, Colo.: Westview Press.

Yao, Joseph Y. 1990. "Resources for Human Development: Case Study of Côte d'Ivoire." UNDP, New York.

HUMAN
DEVELOPMENT
INDICATORS

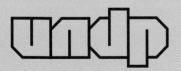

KEY TO INDICATORS

Indicator	Indicator tables[a]	Original international source
A		
Agricultural production	13,26,49	FAO,WBANK
Aid for social priority	19,41	OECD*
Aid social allocation ratio	19,41	OECD*
Aid social priority ratio	19,41	OECD*
Aid human expenditure ratio	19,41	OECD*
AIDS	35	WHO
Air pollution	48	WRI
Armed forces, % of population	21,43	WPI*
per doctor	21,43	WPI*
per teacher	21,43	WPI*
Arms exports, total	43	SIPRI
% of global exports	43	SIPRI*
Arms imports, total	21	SIPRI
% of national imports	21	SIPRI*
B		
Birth-weight, low	11	WHO
Births attended by health personnel	11	WHO
Births outside marriage	30	EUROSTAT
Book titles published	16,37	UNESCO
Breast-feeding	11	MACRO
Budget surplus/deficit	27,50	IMF
C		
Calorie supply per capita	2,4,13	FAO,UNICEF*
South-North gap	6	FAO,UNICEF*
Cereal imports	13	FAO
Cinema attendances	16,37	UNESCO
Circulatory system diseases	35	WHO
Consumption, government	26,49	WBANK*
private	26,49	WBANK*
Contraceptive prevalence	23,45	MACRO,UNFPA
Current account balance	20,42	IMF
D		
Debt	20	WBANK,OECD
Debt service	20	WBANK,OECD
Deforestation	24	FAO,WRI
Dependency ratio	45	UNPOP
Divorces	30	EUROSTAT
Doctors	12,28,35	WHO
Drug crimes	29,30	UNCSDHA
E		
Earnings per employee	17,38	UNIDO,WBANK
Education expenditure, total	31,36,40	OECD
public	15,18	UNESCO
% of all public expenditure	15	UNESCO
primary and secondary combined	15	UNESCO*
tertiary	15,36	UNESCO,OECD
Education, free and compulsory	36	OECD
Educational attainment, secondary	29	OECD
Energy consumption, total	25,47	UNSTAT,WBANK
per capita	25,47	UNSTAT,WBANK
share of world consumption	47	UNSTAT,WBANK*
rate of change	25,47	UNSTAT,WBANK
Enrolment, overall, South-North gap	7	UNESCO*
Enrolment, primary total	14	UNESCO
primary, female	8	UNESCO
primary, female-male gap	9	UNESCO*
primary and secondary, combined	2,4	UNESCO*
Enrolment, secondary total	14	UNESCO
secondary, female	8	UNESCO
secondary, female-male gap	9	UNESCO*
secondary technical	15,36	UNESCO,OECD*
upper secondary	36	OECD
upper secondary, female	33	OECD
upper secondary, female-male gap	34	OECD*
Enrolment, tertiary total	14,31	UNESCO,OECD
tertiary, female	8	UNESCO
tertiary, female-male gap	9	UNESCO*
tertiary science	15,36	UNESCO,OECD*
tertiary science, female	8,33	UNESCO,OECD*
tertiary science, female-male gap	34	OECD*
tertiary full-time equivalent	28,36	OECD
female	28,33	OECD
female-male gap	34	OECD*
tertiary students abroad	15	UNESCO*
Export to import growth rate	42	UNSTAT*
Export-import ratio	20,42	UNSTAT*
Exports, % of GDP	26,49	UNSTAT*
% of GDP growth rate	27,50	UNSTAT*

Indicator	Indicator tables[a]	Original international source
F		
Fertility, total	23,45	UNPOP
South-North gap	7	UNPOP*
rates of change	23,45	UNPOP*
Food aid, US dollars	13	WFP
Food import dependency ratio	13	FAO*
Food production per capita	13	FAO
Fuelwood production	24	FAO,WRI
G		
GDP, total	26,49	WBANK
GDP, real per capita (PPP$)	1,2,4,18,28, 31,40	PENN
GDP, real per capita (PPP$), South-North gap	7	PENN*
GNP, total	27,50	WBANK
annual growth rate	27,50	WBANK
ind. market economies, country share	40	WBANK*
GNP per capita	2,18,28,31,40	WBANK
GNP per capita annual growth rate	27,50	WBANK
Government expenditure, central	26,49	IMF,WBANK
Graduates, upper secondary, total	36	OECD*
upper secondary, female	33	OECD*
upper secondary, female-male gap	34	OECD*
Graduates, tertiary	5,32	UNESCO,OECD*
tertiary sciences	5,32	UNESCO,OECD*
H		
Health care expenditure, price index	35	OECD
Health care institutions, occupancy rate	35	OECD
Health expenditure, total	31,35,40	OECD
public	12,18	WHO
private	35	OECD
Health insurance, public, eligibility	35	OECD
public, bills paid by	35	OECD
Health services, % with access	2,12	WHO
population without access	3	WHO*
rural/urban access	10	WHO
rural-urban gap	10	WHO*
Holidays and annual leave days	38	ILO
Homicides	30	UNCSDHA
Human development index	1	UNDP
I, J, K		
Illiterates, total/female	3	UNESCO*
Immunization	11	WHO,UNICEF
Imports, % of GDP	26,49	UNSTAT*
Income share, lowest 40% of households	18,40	WBANK*
highest 20%/lowest 20%	18,29,40	WBANK*
Gini coefficient	18	WBANK*
Industrial production	26,49	UNSTAT,WBANK
Infant mortality rate	4,11	UNPOP
Inflation rate	27,29,50	IMF,WBANK
International reserves, gross	20,42	IMF
Investment, gross domestic	26,49	WBANK
L		
Labour force, total	17,38	ILO
agriculture	17,38	ILO
industry	17,38	ILO
services	17,38	ILO
% female	8,17,38	ILO*
female-male gap	9,34	ILO*
future replacement ratio	39	UNPOP*
Labour market programmes, expenditure	38	OECD
Land area, total	24,46	FAO
arable	24,46	FAO
irrigated	24,46	FAO
forest	24,46	FAO
Library books	37	UNESCO
Life expectancy, total	1,2,4,28,31	UNPOP
South-North gap	6	UNPOP*
female	8,33	UNPOP
female-male gap	9,34	UNPOP*
at age 60	45	OECD
Literacy, total	1,2,4,5	UNESCO
South-North gap	6	UNESCO*
female/male	5	UNESCO
female-male gap	9	UNESCO*
age 15-19	5	UNESCO
female, age 15-24	8	UNESCO
M		
Malnourished children, underweight	3,11	MACRO,UNICEF*
underweight, rural-urban gap	10	MACRO,UNICEF*
stunting and wasting	11	MACRO,UNICEF

Indicator	Indicator tables[a]	Original international source
Maternal mortality rate	8,12,28, 33,35	WHO
Military expenditure, % of GDP	21,43	SIPRI
% of education and health	21,43	SIPRI*
Museum attendances	37	UNESCO
N		
Newspaper circulation	2,16,28,37	UNESCO
Nuclear fuel inventories, spent	48	WRI
Nurses per population	12	WHO
Nurses per doctor	12	WHO*
O		
ODA given, total	41	OECD
% of GNP	41	OECD
per capita	41	OECD
to least developing countries	41	OECD*
% of central government budget	41	OECD
% of military expenditure	43	OECD*
% of military exports	41	OECD*
ODA received, total	19	OECD
% of GNP	19	OECD
per capita	19	OECD*
per poor person	19	OECD*
Out-of-school children, primary and secondary	3	UNESCO*
P, Q		
Passenger cars	16,37	UNSTAT
Population, total	23,45	UNPOP
annual growth rate	23,45	UNPOP
rates of change	23	UNPOP*
doubling date	23	UNPOP
female-male gap	9,34	UNPOP
rural	10	UNPOP
urban	22,44	UNPOP
urban annual growth rate	22,44	UNPOP
cities	22,44	ICUS
Population density	23,46	UNPOP
Post offices	16,37	UNESCO
Poverty, people in, total/rural	3	WBANK*
% population, total/rural/urban	18	WBANK
Prenatal care	11	WHO
Primary education, intake, total/female	14	UNESCO
repeaters	14	UNESCO
completers	14	UNESCO
transition to secondary	14	UNESCO*
Primary entrants to secondary	14	UNESCO*
Primary pupil-teacher ratio	15	UNESCO
Prisoners, total	30	UNCSDHA
juvenile	30	UNCSDHA
R		
Radios	16,37	UNESCO
Rapes	30	UNSTAT
Research and development, scientists and technicians	5,32	UNESCO
expenditure	32	UNESCO
Road accidents, deaths	29	UNEP
Road traffic noise	44	OECD
S		
Safe water, % with access	2,4,12	WHO
population without access	3	WHO*
% with access, South-North gap	6	WHO*
rural/urban access	10	WHO
rural-urban gap	10	WHO*
Sanitation, % with access	2,12	WHO
population without access	3	WHO*
rural/urban access	10	WHO
rural-urban gap	10	WHO*
Savings, gross domestic	26,49	WBANK
Schooling, mean years, total	1,5,32	UNESCO*
South-North gap	7	UNESCO*
female/male	5,32	UNESCO*
female-male gap	9,34	UNESCO*
Scientists and technicians	5,28,32	UNESCO
Secondary repeaters	14	UNESCO
Services	26,49	UNSTAT,WBANK
Single-parent homes	30	OECD
Social security expenditure	18,40	ILO
Suicides	29,30	WHO
Sulfur emissions, major cities	48	WRI

Indicator	Indicator tables[a]	Original international source
T		
Tax revenue, % of GNP	26,49	IMF*
% of GNP growth	27,50	IMF*
Taxes, direct	27,50	IMF*
Telephones	16,37	UNSTAT
South-North gap	7	UNSTAT
Televisions	2,16,28,37	UNESCO
Trade dependency	20,42	UNSTAT*
Trade, terms of	20,42	UNSTAT
Travel time to and from work	44	OECD
U, V		
Under-five mortality rate	3,11	UNPOP,UNICEF
South-North gap	6	UNPOP,UNICEF*
Unemployment, total	29,39	OECD
female	39	OECD
female-male gap	34	OECD*
youth	29,39	OECD*
long-term, more than 6 months	39	OECD
long-term, more than 12 months	39	OECD
long-term, more than 24 months	39	OECD
regional disparity	39	OECD*
educational attainment disparity	39	OECD*
Unionization	38	OECD
W, X, Y, Z		
Waste, industrial	48	OECD
hazardous, generation	29,48	WRI
municipal	48	OECD
water treatment plants	48	OECD
Waste paper recycled	48	UNEP
Water per capita, internal renewable	24,46	WRI
Water withdrawals, fresh	24,46	WRI
Women, employment	33	ILO
wages	29,34	ILO*
administrative and managerial	8,33	UNSTAT
parliament	8,33	IPU
average age at first marriage	8,33	UNPOP
Workers remittances from abroad	20,42	IMF*
Working hours	38	ILO

a. In addition to being shown in the tables as listed, all indicators in tables 2 to 27 are also shown in aggregated form in tables 51 and 52. The aggregates include global, regional, HDI and income aggregates. A few of these aggregates are also included in the subject tables themselves. The industrial subregional aggregates for all indicators in tables 28 to 50 are shown in the industrial subject tables themselves.

* The first source listed is the main international source for the indicator. Whenever data come originally from more than one international source or when a second agency has published the data in a more convenient form, the leading secondary source follows the main source. When the original data have been specially commissioned, or have not been published by the original international source or have been reanalysed by the Human Development Report team with the assistance of Leo Goldstone, World Statistics Ltd., the original international source is followed by an asterisk.

Key to international source abbreviations

EUROSTAT	Statistical Office of the European Communities
FAO	Food and Agriculture Organization of the United Nations
ICUS	International Centre for Urban Studies
ILO	International Labour Organisation
IMF	International Monetary Fund
IPU	Inter-Parliamentary Union
MACRO	Macro International, Inc. (DHS)
OECD	Organisation for Economic Co-operation and Development
PENN	University of Pennsylvania
SIPRI	Stockholm International Peace Research Institute
UNDP	United Nations Development Programme
UNEP	United Nations Environment Programme
UNESCO	United Nations Educational, Scientific and Cultural Organization
UNFPA	United Nations Population Fund
UNICEF	United Nations Children's Fund
UNIDO	United Nations Industrial Development Organization
UNPOP	United Nations Population Division
UNCSDHA	United Nations Centre for Social Development and Humanitarian Affairs
UNSTAT	United Nations Statistical Division
WBANK	World Bank
WFP	World Food Programme
WHO	World Health Organization
WPI	World Priorities, Inc.
WRI	World Resources Institute

171	Afghanistan	12	Germany	3	Norway
78	Albania	131	Ghana	94	Oman
107	Algeria	25	Greece	132	Pakistan
160	Angola	59	Grenada	68	Panama
60	Antigua and Barbuda	113	Guatemala	129	Papua New Guinea
46	Argentina	173	Guinea	90	Paraguay
47	Armenia	164	Guinea-Bissau	95	Peru
7	Australia	105	Guyana	92	Philippines
15	Austria	137	Haiti	48	Poland
62	Azerbaijan	116	Honduras	41	Portugal
32	Bahamas	24	Hong Kong	55	Qatar
58	Bahrain	28	Hungary	77	Romania
147	Bangladesh	11	Iceland	37	Russian Federation
20	Barbados	134	India	149	Rwanda
38	Belarus	108	Indonesia	79	Saint Kitts and Nevis
16	Belgium	103	Iran, Islamic Rep. of	72	Saint Lucia
82	Belize	96	Iraq	76	Saint Vincent
162	Benin	21	Ireland	98	Samoa
159	Bhutan	19	Israel	125	São Tomé and Principe
122	Bolivia	22	Italy	84	Saudi Arabia
104	Botswana	69	Jamaica	150	Senegal
70	Brazil	1	Japan	63	Seychelles
44	Brunei Darussalam	99	Jordan	172	Sierra Leone
40	Bulgaria	54	Kazakhstan	43	Singapore
170	Burkina Faso	127	Kenya	118	Solomon Islands
154	Burundi	91	Korea, Dem. Rep. of	166	Somalia
148	Cambodia	33	Korea, Rep. of	85	South Africa
133	Cameroon	52	Kuwait	23	Spain
2	Canada	83	Kyrgyzstan	86	Sri Lanka
114	Cape Verde	141	Lao People's Dem. Rep.	158	Sudan
156	Central African Rep.	35	Latvia	65	Suriname
165	Chad	102	Lebanon	117	Swaziland
36	Chile	120	Lesotho	5	Sweden
101	China	144	Liberia	4	Switzerland
61	Colombia	87	Libyan Arab Jamahiriya	81	Syrian Arab Rep.
139	Comoros	29	Lithuania	88	Tajikistan
126	Congo	18	Luxembourg	138	Tanzania, U. Rep. of
42	Costa Rica	128	Madagascar	74	Thailand
136	Côte d'Ivoire	153	Malawi	145	Togo
75	Cuba	57	Malaysia	31	Trinidad and Tobago
27	Cyprus	112	Maldives	93	Tunisia
26	Czechoslovakia	168	Mali	73	Turkey
13	Denmark	39	Malta	66	Turkmenistan
163	Djibouti	161	Mauritania	6	USA
51	Dominica	56	Mauritius	146	Uganda
97	Dominican Rep.	53	Mexico	45	Ukraine
89	Ecuador	64	Moldova, Rep. of	67	United Arab Emirates
124	Egypt	100	Mongolia	10	United Kingdom
110	El Salvador	119	Morocco	30	Uruguay
155	Equatorial Guinea	157	Mozambique	80	Uzbekistan
34	Estonia	123	Myanmar	106	Vanuatu
151	Ethiopia	135	Namibia	50	Venezuela
71	Fiji	152	Nepal	115	Viet Nam
14	Finland	9	Netherlands	143	Yemen
8	France	17	New Zealand	140	Zaire
109	Gabon	111	Nicaragua	130	Zambia
167	Gambia	169	Niger	121	Zimbabwe
49	Georgia	142	Nigeria		

In the human development indicators, the countries and areas are ranked in descending order of their human development index (HDI). The reference numbers, indicating that rank, are in the alphabetical list of countries provided here.

Official government data received by the responsible United Nations system agencies or other international organizations have been used whenever possible. In other cases, where there are no reliable official figures, estimates by the responsible agency have been used if available. In some cases, UNDP has made its own estimates, based on field information or comparable country data. Only comprehensive or representative national data have been used. The data in the human development indicators, derived from so many sources, inevitably cover a wide range of data reliability.

To help the reader use these tables, all the indicators are indexed alphabetically with table locations and sources.

Unless otherwise stated, the summary measures for the various human development, income and regional groups of countries are the appropriately weighted values for each group (see the lists following the indicators for the composition of each group). Where the summary measure is a total, the letter T appears after the figure. In the absence of the phrase "annual", "annual rate" or "growth rate", a hyphen between two years indicates that the data refer to a range of years, and a slash between two years indicates an average for that period. The following signs have been used:

..   Data not available
(.)   Less than half the unit shown
T   Total
Italicized figures are UNDP estimates.

Contents

HDI rank	Life expectancy at birth (years) 1990	Adult literacy rate (%) 1990	Mean years of schooling 1990	Literacy index	Schooling index	Educational attainment 1990	Real GDP per capita (PPP$) 1990	Adjusted real GDP per capita	Human development index 1990	GNP per capita rank minus HDI rank[a]
High human development										
1 Japan	78.6	99.0	10.7	1.00	0.87	2.87	17,616	5,049	0.983	2
2 Canada	77.0	99.0	12.1	1.00	0.98	2.98	19,232	5,052	0.982	9
3 Norway	77.1	99.0	11.6	1.00	0.95	2.95	16,028	5,044	0.979	3
4 Switzerland	77.4	99.0	11.1	1.00	0.90	2.90	20,874	5,074	0.978	-3
5 Sweden	77.4	99.0	11.1	1.00	0.90	2.90	17,014	5,047	0.977	0
6 USA	75.9	99.0	12.3	1.00	1.00	3.00	21,449	5,075	0.976	4
7 Australia	76.5	99.0	11.5	1.00	0.94	2.94	16,051	5,044	0.972	13
8 France	76.4	99.0	11.6	1.00	0.94	2.94	17,405	5,048	0.971	5
9 Netherlands	77.2	99.0	10.6	1.00	0.86	2.86	15,695	5,042	0.970	8
10 United Kingdom	75.7	99.0	11.5	1.00	0.94	2.94	15,804	5,043	0.964	11
11 Iceland	77.8	99.0	8.9	1.00	0.72	2.72	16,496	5,045	0.960	-2
12 Germany	75.2	99.0	11.1	1.00	0.90	2.90	18,213	5,050	0.957	-4
13 Denmark	75.8	99.0	10.4	1.00	0.84	2.84	16,781	5,046	0.955	-6
14 Finland	75.5	99.0	10.6	1.00	0.86	2.86	16,446	5,045	0.954	-10
15 Austria	74.8	99.0	11.1	1.00	0.90	2.90	16,504	5,045	0.952	-1
16 Belgium	75.2	99.0	10.7	1.00	0.87	2.87	16,381	5,045	0.952	0
17 New Zealand	75.2	99.0	10.4	1.00	0.84	2.84	13,481	5,015	0.947	6
18 Luxembourg	74.9	99.0	10.0	1.00	0.81	2.81	19,244	5,052	0.943	-16
19 Israel	75.9	95.0	10.0	0.95	0.81	2.71	10,840	5,000	0.938	8
20 Barbados	75.1	99.0	8.9	1.00	0.72	2.72	8,304	4,947	0.928	14
21 Ireland	74.6	99.0	8.7	1.00	0.70	2.70	10,589	4,997	0.925	8
22 Italy	76.0	97.1	7.3	0.98	0.59	2.54	15,890	5,043	0.924	-4
23 Spain	77.0	97.5	6.8	0.96	0.54	2.46	11,723	5,006	0.923	5
24 Hong Kong	77.3	90.0	7.0	0.89	0.57	2.34	15,595	5,042	0.913	0
25 Greece	76.1	93.2	6.9	0.93	0.56	2.41	7,366	4,930	0.902	10
26 Czechoslovakia	71.8	97.0	9.0	0.98	0.73	2.68	7,300	4,928	0.892	23
27 Cyprus	76.2	87.0	7.0	0.85	0.57	2.27	9,953	4,988	0.890	3
28 Hungary	70.9	97.0	9.6	0.98	0.78	2.73	6,116	4,901	0.887	24
29 Lithuania	71.5	96.0	9.0	0.96	0.73	2.66	4,913	4,847	0.881	22
30 Uruguay	72.2	96.2	7.8	0.97	0.63	2.56	5,916	4,895	0.881	24
31 Trinidad and Tobago	71.6	96.0	8.0	0.96	0.65	2.58	6,604	4,913	0.877	15
32 Bahamas	71.5	99.0	6.2	1.00	0.50	2.50	11,235	5,003	0.875	-7
33 Korea, Rep. of	70.1	96.3	8.8	0.97	0.72	2.65	6,733	4,916	0.872	4
34 Estonia	70.0	96.0	9.0	0.96	0.73	2.66	6,438	4,909	0.872	8
35 Latvia	69.6	96.0	9.0	0.96	0.73	2.66	6,457	4,910	0.868	8
36 Chile	71.8	93.4	7.5	0.93	0.61	2.47	5,099	4,862	0.864	39
37 Russian Federation	69.3	94.0	9.0	0.94	0.73	2.61	7,968	4,941	0.862	10
38 Belarus	71.3	95.0	7.0	0.95	0.57	2.47	5,727	4,889	0.861	12
39 Malta	73.4	87.0	6.1	0.85	0.50	2.20	8,732	4,954	0.855	-6
40 Bulgaria	72.6	93.0	7.0	0.93	0.57	2.42	4,700	4,700	0.854	27
41 Portugal	74.0	85.0	6.0	0.83	0.48	2.13	8,770	4,955	0.853	-3
42 Costa Rica	74.9	92.8	5.7	0.92	0.46	2.31	4,542	4,542	0.852	34
43 Singapore	74.0	88.0	3.9	0.86	0.31	2.04	15,880	5,043	0.849	-17
44 Brunei Darussalam	73.5	86.0	5.0	0.84	0.40	2.08	14,000	5,017	0.847	-25
45 Ukraine	70.5	95.0	6.0	0.95	0.48	2.38	5,433	4,878	0.844	13
46 Argentina	71.0	95.3	8.7	0.95	0.71	2.61	4,295	4,295	0.832	16
47 Armenia	71.8	93.0	5.0	0.93	0.40	2.25	4,741	4,741	0.831	16
48 Poland	71.8	96.0	8.0	0.96	0.65	2.57	4,237	4,237	0.831	32
49 Georgia	72.8	93.0	5.0	0.93	0.40	2.25	4,572	4,572	0.829	23
50 Venezuela	70.0	88.1	6.3	0.87	0.51	2.24	6,169	4,902	0.824	6
51 Dominica	76.0	97.0	4.7	0.98	0.38	2.33	3,910	3,910	0.819	19
52 Kuwait	73.4	73.0	5.4	0.68	0.43	1.79	15,178	5,039	0.815	-37
53 Mexico	69.7	87.6	4.7	0.86	0.38	2.10	5,918	4,895	0.805	7
54 Kazakhstan	68.8	93.0	5.0	0.93	0.40	2.25	4,716	4,716	0.802	1
55 Qatar	69.2	82.0	5.6	0.79	0.45	2.03	11,400	5,004	0.802	-33
Medium human development										
56 Mauritius	69.6	86.0	4.1	0.84	0.33	2.00	5,750	4,890	0.794	12
57 Malaysia	70.1	78.4	5.3	0.75	0.43	1.92	6,140	4,901	0.790	9
58 Bahrain	71.0	77.4	3.9	0.73	0.31	1.78	10,706	4,998	0.790	-26
59 Grenada	71.5	96.0	4.7	0.96	0.38	2.30	4,081	4,081	0.787	12
60 Antigua and Barbuda	72.0	96.0	4.6	0.96	0.37	2.29	4,000	4,000	0.785	-19
61 Colombia	68.8	86.7	7.1	0.85	0.58	2.27	4,237	4,237	0.770	32
62 Azerbaijan	71.0	93.0	5.0	0.93	0.40	2.25	3,977	3,977	0.770	20
63 Seychelles	70.0	89.0	4.6	0.88	0.37	2.12	4,191	4,191	0.761	-24
64 Moldova, Rep. of	68.7	95.0	6.0	0.95	0.48	2.38	3,896	3,896	0.758	-3
65 Suriname	69.5	94.9	4.2	0.95	0.33	2.23	3,927	3,927	0.751	-17
66 Turkmenistan	66.4	93.0	5.0	0.93	0.40	2.25	4,230	4,230	0.746	15
67 United Arab Emirates	70.5	55.0	5.1	0.46	0.41	1.32	16,753	5,046	0.738	-55
68 Panama	72.4	88.1	6.7	0.87	0.54	2.27	3,317	3,317	0.738	9
69 Jamaica	73.1	98.4	5.3	0.99	0.42	2.41	2,979	2,979	0.736	17
70 Brazil	65.6	81.1	3.9	0.78	0.31	1.87	4,718	4,718	0.730	-17

HDI rank	Life expectancy at birth (years) 1990	Adult literacy rate (%) 1990	Mean years of schooling 1990	Literacy index	Schooling index	Educational attainment 1990	Real GDP per capita (PPP$) 1990	Adjusted real GDP per capita	Human development index 1990	GNP per capita rank minus HDI rank[a]
71 Fiji	64.8	87.0	5.1	0.85	0.41	2.11	4,427	4,427	0.730	7
72 Saint Lucia	70.5	93.0	3.9	0.93	0.31	2.16	3,470	3,470	0.720	-8
73 Turkey	65.1	80.7	3.5	0.77	0.28	1.82	4,652	4,652	0.717	10
74 Thailand	66.1	93.0	3.8	0.93	0.31	2.16	3,986	3,986	0.715	15
75 Cuba	75.4	94.0	7.6	0.94	0.62	2.49	2,200	2,200	0.711	26
76 Saint Vincent	70.0	84.0	4.6	0.81	0.37	2.00	3,647	3,647	0.709	3
77 Romania	70.8	95.0	7.0	0.95	0.57	2.47	2,800	2,800	0.709	7
78 Albania	72.2	85.0	6.0	0.83	0.48	2.14	3,000	3,000	0.699	12
79 Saint Kitts and Nevis	67.5	92.0	6.0	0.91	0.48	2.31	3,300	3,300	0.697	-34
80 Uzbekistan	69.5	93.0	5.0	0.93	0.40	2.25	3,115	3,115	0.695	12
81 Syrian Arab Rep.	66.1	64.5	4.2	0.57	0.33	1.48	4,756	4,756	0.694	24
82 Belize	69.5	95.0	4.6	0.95	0.37	2.27	3,000	3,000	0.689	-8
83 Kyrgyzstan	68.8	93.0	5.0	0.93	0.40	2.25	3,114	3,114	0.689	2
84 Saudi Arabia	64.5	62.4	3.7	0.55	0.30	1.39	10,989	5,001	0.688	-53
85 South Africa	61.7	70.0	3.9	0.64	0.31	1.59	4,865	4,841	0.673	-28
86 Sri Lanka	70.9	88.4	6.9	0.87	0.56	2.29	2,405	2,405	0.663	44
87 Libyan Arab Jamahiriya	61.8	63.8	3.4	0.56	0.27	1.40	7,000	4,922	0.658	-47
88 Tajikistan	69.6	93.0	5.0	0.93	0.40	2.25	2,558	2,558	0.657	6
89 Ecuador	66.0	85.8	5.6	0.84	0.45	2.12	3,074	3,074	0.646	19
90 Paraguay	67.1	90.1	4.9	0.89	0.39	2.17	2,790	2,790	0.641	7
91 Korea, Dem. Rep. of	70.4	95.0	6.0	0.95	0.48	2.38	2,000	2,000	0.640	12
92 Philippines	64.2	89.7	7.4	0.88	0.60	2.37	2,303	2,303	0.603	22
93 Tunisia	66.7	65.3	2.1	0.58	0.16	1.33	3,579	3,579	0.600	-5
94 Oman	65.9	35.0	0.9	0.21	0.06	0.48	9,972	4,988	0.598	-58
95 Peru	63.0	85.1	6.4	0.83	0.52	2.17	2,622	2,622	0.592	0
96 Iraq	65.0	59.7	4.8	0.51	0.39	1.41	3,508	3,508	0.589	-23
97 Dominican Rep.	66.7	83.3	4.3	0.81	0.34	1.96	2,404	2,404	0.586	15
98 Samoa	66.5	92.0	5.7	0.91	0.46	2.29	1,900	1,900	0.586	11
99 Jordan	66.9	80.1	5.0	0.77	0.40	1.93	2,345	2,345	0.582	-8
100 Mongolia	62.5	93.0	7.0	0.93	0.57	2.42	2,100	2,100	0.578	4
101 China	70.1	73.3	4.8	0.68	0.39	1.75	1,990	1,990	0.566	41
102 Lebanon	66.1	80.1	4.4	0.77	0.35	1.88	2,300	2,300	0.565	-15
103 Iran, Islamic Rep. of	66.2	54.0	3.9	0.44	0.31	1.19	3,253	3,253	0.557	-44
104 Botswana	59.8	73.6	2.4	0.69	0.19	1.56	3,419	3,419	0.552	-35
105 Guyana	64.2	96.4	5.1	0.97	0.41	2.35	1,464	1,464	0.541	36
106 Vanuatu	69.5	67.0	3.7	0.60	0.29	1.50	2,005	2,005	0.533	-10
107 Algeria	65.1	57.4	2.6	0.49	0.20	1.17	3,011	3,011	0.528	-42
108 Indonesia	61.5	81.6	3.9	0.78	0.32	1.88	2,181	2,181	0.515	14
109 Gabon	52.5	60.7	2.6	0.53	0.21	1.26	4,147	4,147	0.503	-65
110 El Salvador	64.4	73.0	4.1	0.68	0.33	1.68	1,950	1,950	0.503	-8
111 Nicaragua	64.8	81.0	4.3	0.78	0.35	1.90	1,497	1,497	0.500	22
Low human development										
112 Maldives	62.5	95.0	4.5	0.95	0.36	2.26	1,200	1,200	0.497	19
113 Guatemala	63.4	55.1	4.1	0.46	0.33	1.24	2,576	2,576	0.489	-3
114 Cape Verde	67.0	66.5	2.2	0.60	0.17	1.37	1,769	1,769	0.479	2
115 Viet Nam	62.7	87.6	4.6	0.86	0.37	2.09	1,100	1,100	0.472	41
116 Honduras	64.9	73.1	3.9	0.68	0.31	1.67	1,470	1,470	0.472	2
117 Swaziland	56.8	72.0	3.7	0.67	0.29	1.62	2,384	2,384	0.458	-18
118 Solomon Islands	69.5	24.0	1.0	0.07	0.07	0.22	2,689	2,689	0.439	3
119 Morocco	62.0	49.5	2.8	0.39	0.22	1.00	2,348	2,348	0.433	-13
120 Lesotho	57.3	78.0	3.4	0.74	0.27	1.75	1,743	1,743	0.431	3
121 Zimbabwe	59.6	66.9	2.9	0.60	0.23	1.44	1,484	1,484	0.398	-4
122 Bolivia	54.5	77.5	4.0	0.73	0.32	1.79	1,572	1,572	0.398	-3
123 Myanmar	61.3	80.6	2.5	0.77	0.20	1.74	659	659	0.390	29
124 Egypt	60.3	48.4	2.8	0.37	0.22	0.97	1,988	1,988	0.389	-4
125 São Tomé and Principe	65.5	63.0	2.3	0.55	0.18	1.29	600	600	0.374	12
126 Congo	53.7	56.6	2.1	0.48	0.16	1.11	2,362	2,362	0.372	-26
127 Kenya	59.7	69.0	2.3	0.63	0.18	1.43	1,058	1,058	0.369	17
128 Madagascar	54.5	80.2	2.2	0.77	0.17	1.70	704	704	0.327	29
129 Papua New Guinea	54.9	52.0	0.9	0.42	0.07	0.90	1,786	1,786	0.318	-18
130 Zambia	54.4	72.8	2.7	0.68	0.21	1.57	744	744	0.314	4
131 Ghana	55.0	60.3	3.5	0.52	0.28	1.32	1,016	1,016	0.311	9
132 Pakistan	57.7	34.8	1.9	0.21	0.14	0.55	1,862	1,862	0.311	4
133 Cameroon	53.7	54.1	1.6	0.44	0.13	1.01	1,646	1,646	0.310	-26
134 India	59.1	48.2	2.4	0.37	0.19	0.93	1,072	1,072	0.309	12
135 Namibia	57.5	40.0	1.7	0.27	0.13	0.67	1,400	1,400	0.289	-37
136 Côte d'Ivoire	53.4	53.8	1.9	0.44	0.15	1.03	1,324	1,324	0.286	-23
137 Haiti	55.7	53.0	1.7	0.43	0.13	0.99	933	933	0.275	6
138 Tanzania, U. Rep. of	54.0	65.0	2.0	0.58	0.16	1.32	572	572	0.270	34
139 Comoros	55.0	61.0	1.0	0.53	0.07	1.13	721	721	0.269	-10
140 Zaire	53.0	71.8	1.6	0.66	0.12	1.45	367	367	0.262	18
141 Lao People's Dem. Rep.	49.7	54.0	2.9	0.44	0.23	1.11	1,100	1,100	0.246	20

HDI rank	Life expectancy at birth (years) 1990	Adult literacy rate (%) 1990	Mean years of schooling 1990	Literacy index	Schooling index	Educational attainment 1990	Real GDP per capita (PPP$) 1990	Adjusted real GDP per capita	Human development index 1990	GNP per capita rank minus HDI rank[a]
142 Nigeria	51.5	50.7	1.2	0.40	0.09	0.89	1,215	1,215	0.246	11
143 Yemen	51.5	38.6	0.8	0.25	0.06	0.56	1,562	1,562	0.233	-19
144 Liberia	54.2	39.5	2.0	0.26	0.16	0.68	857	857	0.222	-17
145 Togo	54.0	43.3	1.6	0.31	0.12	0.74	734	734	0.218	-10
146 Uganda	52.0	48.3	1.1	0.37	0.08	0.83	524	524	0.194	21
147 Bangladesh	51.8	35.3	2.0	0.21	0.16	0.58	872	872	0.189	12
148 Cambodia	49.7	35.2	2.0	0.21	0.16	0.58	*1,100*	1,100	0.186	20
149 Rwanda	49.5	50.2	1.1	0.40	0.08	0.87	657	657	0.186	2
150 Senegal	48.3	38.3	0.8	0.25	0.06	0.56	1,248	1,248	0.182	-35
151 Ethiopia	45.5	*66.0*	1.1	0.59	0.08	1.26	369	369	0.172	19
152 Nepal	52.2	25.6	2.1	0.09	0.16	0.35	920	920	0.170	14
153 Malawi	48.1	*47.0*	1.7	0.36	0.13	0.85	640	640	0.168	9
154 Burundi	48.5	50.0	0.3	0.39	0.02	0.80	625	625	0.167	6
155 Equatorial Guinea	47.0	50.2	0.8	0.40	0.06	0.85	*700*	700	0.164	-8
156 Central African Rep.	49.5	37.7	1.1	0.24	0.08	0.56	768	768	0.159	-17
157 Mozambique	47.5	32.9	1.6	0.18	0.13	0.49	1,072	1,072	0.154	16
158 Sudan	50.8	27.1	0.8	0.11	0.05	0.27	949	949	0.152	-20
159 Bhutan	48.9	38.4	0.2	0.25	0.01	0.51	*800*	800	0.150	4
160 Angola	45.5	41.7	1.5	0.29	0.11	0.70	840	840	0.143	-34
161 Mauritania	47.0	34.0	0.3	0.20	0.02	0.41	1,057	1,057	0.140	-33
162 Benin	47.0	23.4	0.7	0.06	0.05	0.18	1,043	1,043	0.113	-17
163 Djibouti	48.0	*19.0*	0.3	0.01	0.02	0.04	*1,000*	1,000	0.104	-38
164 Guinea-Bissau	42.5	36.5	0.3	0.23	0.02	0.47	841	841	0.090	1
165 Chad	46.5	29.8	0.2	0.14	0.01	0.30	559	559	0.088	-1
166 Somalia	46.1	24.1	0.2	0.07	0.01	0.16	836	836	0.087	5
167 Gambia	44.0	27.2	0.6	0.11	0.04	0.26	913	913	0.086	-19
168 Mali	45.0	32.0	0.3	0.17	0.02	0.36	572	572	0.082	-14
169 Niger	45.5	28.4	0.1	0.13	0.00	0.25	645	645	0.080	-19
170 Burkina Faso	48.2	18.2	0.1	0.00	0.00	0.00	618	618	0.074	-21
171 Afghanistan	42.5	29.4	0.8	0.14	0.06	0.33	714	714	0.066	-2
172 Sierra Leone	42.0	20.7	0.9	0.03	0.07	0.13	1,086	1,086	0.065	-17
173 Guinea	43.5	24.0	0.8	0.07	0.06	0.20	501	501	0.045	-41

a. A positive figure shows that the HDI rank is higher than the GNP rank, a negative the opposite.

Note: Figures in italics are UNDP estimates.

Profile of human development

HDI rank	Life expectancy at birth (years) 1990	Population with access to			Daily calorie supply (as % of requirements) 1988-90	Adult literacy rate (%) 1990	Combined primary and secondary enrolment ratio 1987-90	Daily newspaper circulation (per 1,000 people) 1988-90	Tele-visions (per 1,000 people) 1990	GNP per capita (US$) 1990	Real GDP per capita (PPP$) 1990
		Health services (%) 1987-90	Safe water (%) 1988-90	Sanitation (%) 1988-90							
High human development	**70.6**	**94**	**79**	**85**	**123**	**91**	**88**	**197**	**184**	**3,470**	**6,290**
20 Barbados	75.1	100	99	100	128	..	99	118	267	6,460	8,304
24 Hong Kong	77.3	..	100	..	125	..	87	632	274	11,700	15,595
27 Cyprus	76.2	95	100	100	..	..	97	111	150	8,230	9,953
30 Uruguay	72.2	..	84	..	101	96	92	233	233	2,620	5,916
31 Trinidad and Tobago	71.6	99	96	99	114	..	90	..	302	3,460	6,604
32 Bahamas	71.5	100	..	..	..	..	..	138	225	11,550	11,235
33 Korea, Rep. of	70.1	100	78	99	120	96	97	280	210	5,450	6,733
36 Chile	71.8	95	86	83	102	93	90	455	205	1,950	5,099
42 Costa Rica	74.9	97	94	97	121	93	77	102	149	1,900	4,542
43 Singapore	74.0	100	100	96	136	..	87	280	376	11,200	15,880
44 Brunei Darussalam	73.5	96	..	..	..	..	..	38	233	..	..
46 Argentina	71.0	..	..	89	131	95	96	124	222	2,380	4,295
50 Venezuela	70.0	..	89	92	99	88	83	142	167	2,560	6,169
51 Dominica	76.0	100	..	..	100	..	..	..	61	2,220	3,910
52 Kuwait	73.4	100	100	98	130	73	94	221	285	..	15,178
53 Mexico	69.7	91	78	74	131	88	82	127	139	2,490	5,918
55 Qatar	69.2	100	91	97	..	..	94	217	516	15,870	..
Medium human development	**68.0**	..	**73**	**84**	**114**	**76**	**86**	..	**67**	**940**	**2,710**
Excluding China	**65.4**	**68**	**75**	**65**	**116**	**79**	**84**	**55**	**114**	**1,690**	**3,660**
56 Mauritius	69.6	100	100	98	128	..	77	74	215	2,310	5,750
57 Malaysia	70.1	88	78	94	120	78	75	140	148	2,330	6,140
58 Bahrain	71.0	100	100	100	..	77	99	56	403	6,830	10,706
59 Grenada	71.5	..	..	..	..	..	..	..	353	2,130	4,081
60 Antigua and Barbuda	72.0	100	..	..	..	..	..	79	303	4,290	..
61 Colombia	68.8	87	92	68	106	87	79	61	115	1,260	4,237
63 Seychelles	70.0	99	99	65	100	..	..	46	87	4,820	4,191
65 Suriname	69.5	91	84	57	..	95	87	95	130	3,350	3,927
67 United Arab Emirates	70.5	90	100	95	151	..	94	157	110	19,870	16,753
68 Panama	72.4	82	83	84	98	88	83	70	165	1,900	3,317
69 Jamaica	73.1	..	72	91	114	98	80	63	130	1,500	2,979
70 Brazil	65.6	..	96	78	114	81	91	54	213	2,680	4,718
71 Fiji	64.8	99	79	75	108	..	90	35	14	1,780	4,427
72 Saint Lucia	70.5	100	..	..	102	..	..	..	167	2,350	3,470
73 Turkey	65.1	..	92	..	127	81	81	72	175	1,640	4,652
74 Thailand	66.1	59	72	62	103	93	59	72	112	1,420	3,986
75 Cuba	75.4	100	..	..	135	94	95	124	207	..	..
76 Saint Vincent	70.0	80	..	..	99	..	..	..	129	1,710	3,647
79 Saint Kitts and Nevis	67.5	100	..	..	..	..	..	..	205	3,540	..
81 Syrian Arab Rep.	66.1	99	79	63	126	65	83	22	59	1,000	4,756
82 Belize	69.5	95	..	..	114	..	..	..	166	1,960	..
84 Saudi Arabia	64.5	98	95	86	121	62	65	42	283	7,070	10,989
85 South Africa	61.7	..	..	..	128	..	..	38	105	2,530	4,865
86 Sri Lanka	70.9	90	60	50	101	88	88	32	35	470	2,405
87 Libyan Arab Jamahiriya	61.8	100	97	98	140	64	..	15	99	..	..
89 Ecuador	66.0	80	58	56	105	86	89	87	83	960	3,074
90 Paraguay	67.1	..	33	58	116	90	72	39	59	1,090	2,790
91 Korea, Dem. Rep. of	70.4	100	..	..	121	..	..	230	15	..	..
92 Philippines	64.2	..	81	70	104	90	97	54	48	730	2,303
93 Tunisia	66.7	91	65	45	131	65	80	37	80	1,450	3,579
94 Oman	65.9	89	57	51	..	..	82	41	766	5,650	9,972
95 Peru	63.0	..	58	49	87	85	..	79	97	1,100	2,622
96 Iraq	65.0	98	93	72	128	60	75	34	69	..	3,508
97 Dominican Rep.	66.7	..	62	60	102	83	92	32	84	830	2,404
98 Samoa	66.5	100	82	94	..	..	..	..	37	920	1,900
99 Jordan	66.9	90	99	100	110	80	..	56	81	1,340	2,345
100 Mongolia	62.5	100	66	76	97	..	95	74	41	..	..
101 China	70.1	..	71	96	112	73	88	..	31	370	1,990
102 Lebanon	66.1	95	98	78	127	80	92	118	330	..	..
103 Iran, Islamic Rep. of	66.2	73	89	71	125	54	83	27	70	2,490	3,253
104 Botswana	59.8	86	56	38	97	74	88	14	15	2,230	3,419
105 Guyana	64.2	96	81	90	108	96	82	..	38	380	1,464
106 Vanuatu	69.5	80	71	42	..	..	..	..	9	1,100	2,005
107 Algeria	65.1	..	69	59	123	57	79	51	74	2,330	3,011
108 Indonesia	61.5	43	42	44	121	82	81	28	60	560	2,181
109 Gabon	52.5	87	72	..	104	61	..	17	37	3,550	4,147
110 El Salvador	64.4	..	41	61	102	73	67	87	90	1,000	1,950
111 Nicaragua	64.8	..	53	27	99	..	73	65	62	420	1,497

HDI rank	Life expectancy at birth (years) 1990	Population with access to			Daily calorie supply (as % of requirements) 1988-90	Adult literacy rate (%) 1990	Combined primary and secondary enrolment ratio 1987-90	Daily newspaper circulation (per 1,000 people) 1988-90	Tele-visions (per 1,000 people) 1990	GNP per capita (US$) 1990	Real GDP per capita (PPP$) 1990
		Health services (%) 1987-90	Safe water (%) 1988-90	Sanitation (%) 1988-90							
Low human development	56.5	..	62	20	98	49	58	..	28	360	1,110
Excluding India	54.4	65	50	27	96	50	49	13	25	360	1,140
112 Maldives	62.5	75	70	28	80	..	..	7	25	450	..
113 Guatemala	63.4	60	60	57	103	55	52	21	52	910	2,576
114 Cape Verde	67.0	82	74	16	125	67	77	..	..	680	1,769
115 Viet Nam	62.7	97	50	53	103	88	69	9	39	..	1,470
116 Honduras	64.9	62	52	33	98	73	75	39	72	640	1,470
117 Swaziland	56.8	55	30	32	105	..	85	13	20	1,030	2,384
118 Solomon Islands	69.5	80	61	..	84	..	..	..	..	590	2,689
119 Morocco	62.0	62	73	65	125	50	50	13	74	970	2,348
120 Lesotho	57.3	80	46	22	93	..	78	11	6	540	1,743
121 Zimbabwe	59.6	71	36	42	94	67	88	21	31	650	1,484
122 Bolivia	54.5	..	46	34	84	78	68	55	..	630	1,572
123 Myanmar	61.3	48	33	36	114	81	62	5	2	..	659
124 Egypt	60.3	99	86	54	132	48	90	57	109	610	1,988
125 São Tomé and Principe	65.5	88	..	..	103	..	..	..	..	400	..
126 Congo	53.7	..	20	..	103	57	..	7	6	1,000	2,362
127 Kenya	59.7	..	28	46	89	69	72	15	9	370	1,058
128 Madagascar	54.5	65	..	..	95	80	53	4	20	230	704
129 Papua New Guinea	54.9	96	33	56	114	52	43	13	2	850	1,786
130 Zambia	54.4	75	59	55	87	73	67	12	30	420	744
131 Ghana	55.0	76	56	30	93	60	58	13	15	390	1,016
132 Pakistan	57.7	85	50	22	99	35	29	15	17	400	1,862
133 Cameroon	53.7	15	34	..	95	54	65	7	29	960	1,646
134 India	59.1	..	75	13	101	48	68	..	32	360	1,072
135 Namibia	57.5	..	..	..	..	..	72	..	17	1,080	..
136 Côte d'Ivoire	53.4	60	83	36	111	54	..	8	61	750	1,324
137 Haiti	55.7	45	42	21	89	53	53	7	5	370	933
138 Tanzania, U. Rep. of	54.0	93	52	77	95	..	40	7	2	110	572
139 Comoros	55.0	82	..	83	90	..	52	..	(.)	480	721
140 Zaire	53.0	59	34	14	96	72	54	..	1	220	367
141 Lao People's Dem. Rep.	49.7	67	28	11	111	..	65	3	7	200	..
142 Nigeria	51.5	67	46	13	93	51	49	16	32	290	1,215
143 Yemen	51.5	..	..	..	..	39	56	11	31	540	1,562
144 Liberia	54.2	34	50	11	98	40	..	14	18	..	857
145 Togo	54.0	..	71	23	99	43	64	3	6	410	734
146 Uganda	52.0	71	15	13	93	48	51	2	10	180	524
147 Bangladesh	51.8	74	78	12	88	35	42	6	5	210	872
148 Cambodia	49.7	..	..	13	96	35	..	..	9	170	..
149 Rwanda	49.5	..	64	61	82	50	47	(.)	..	310	657
150 Senegal	48.3	40	53	..	98	38	38	7	36	710	1,248
151 Ethiopia	45.5	55	18	17	73	..	28	1	2	120	369
152 Nepal	52.2	..	37	6	100	26	60	8	2	180	920
153 Malawi	48.1	80	53	..	88	..	52	3	1	200	640
154 Burundi	48.5	80	38	57	84	50	39	4	1	210	625
155 Equatorial Guinea	47.0	..	..	..	..	50	..	6	9	340	..
156 Central African Rep.	49.5	13	12	20	82	38	41	1	4	390	768
157 Mozambique	47.5	30	22	19	77	33	32	5	3	80	1,072
158 Sudan	50.8	70	..	12	87	27	36	24	71	400	949
159 Bhutan	48.9	80	34	..	128	38	18	..	..	190	..
160 Angola	45.5	24	38	22	80	42	45	11	6	..	840
161 Mauritania	47.0	30	66	..	106	34	35	1	23	500	1,057
162 Benin	47.0	50	50	41	104	23	37	3	5	360	1,043
163 Djibouti	48.0	..	43	78	..	..	32	..	56	..	..
164 Guinea-Bissau	42.5	80	25	21	97	37	38	6	..	180	841
165 Chad	46.5	26	..	..	73	30	33	(.)	1	180	559
166 Somalia	46.1	20	56	12	81	24	14	1	14	120	836
167 Gambia	44.0	90	77	..	103	27	42	2	..	340	913
168 Mali	45.0	..	49	23	96	32	16	1	1	280	572
169 Niger	45.5	30	59	9	95	28	18	1	5	310	645
170 Burkina Faso	48.2	70	67	10	94	18	21	(.)	5	330	618
171 Afghanistan	42.5	49	21	..	72	29	19	11	8	..	714
172 Sierra Leone	42.0	36	43	43	83	21	34	2	10	250	1,086
173 Guinea	43.5	32	33	..	97	24	24	..	7	440	501
All developing countries	62.8	72	68	55	107	65	73	50	55	810	2,170
Least developed countries	51.0	62	47	22	90	45	42	6	9	240	740
Sub-Saharan Africa	51.8	60	41	26	93	47	46	11	23	490	1,200
Industrial countries	74.5	..	..	..	..	..	..	304	545	14,580	14,440
World	64.7	..	..	..	..	..	..	130	148	4,010	4,890

Note: Data for industrial countries for this subject area are in table 28.

3 Profile of human deprivation

		Millions (unless otherwise stated)								
HDI rank	Without access to health services 1991	Without access to safe water 1991	Without access to sanitation 1991	Children dying before age five (thousands) 1990	Mal-nourished children under five 1991	Children not in primary or secondary school 1991	Illiterate adults (15+) 1991	Illiterate females (15+) 1991	People in absolute poverty	
									Total 1991	Rural 1991
High human development	..	..	..	..	..	..	..	..	..	..
20 Barbados	(.)	(.)	(.)	(.)	..	(.)	..	..	..	..
24 Hong Kong	..	(.)	..	1	..	0.1	..	..	..	..
27 Cyprus	(.)	(.)	(.)	(.)	..	(.)	..	..	..	..
30 Uruguay	..	0.5	..	1	(.)	(.)	0.1	0.1	..	..
31 Trinidad and Tobago	(.)	0.1	(.)	1	(.)	(.)	..	..	..	0.2
32 Bahamas	(.)	..	..	..	..	..	..	..	..	..
33 Korea, Rep. of	(.)	9.5	0.3	20	..	0.2	1.2	1.1	5.7	1.4
36 Chile	0.7	1.9	2.2	8	(.)	0.3	0.6	0.3	..	..
42 Costa Rica	0.1	0.2	0.1	2	(.)	0.2	0.1	0.1	..	..
43 Singapore	(.)	(.)	0.1	(.)	(.)	0.1	..	..	..	..
44 Brunei Darussalam	(.)	..	..	..	..	..	..	..	..	..
46 Argentina	..	..	3.6	24	..	0.3	1.1	0.6	..	..
50 Venezuela	..	2.1	1.5	25	0.2	0.9	1.5	0.6	..	..
51 Dominica	(.)	..	..	(.)	..	..	..	..	..	..
52 Kuwait	(.)	(.)	(.)	1	(.)	(.)	0.4	0.2	..	..
53 Mexico	7.8	19.4	22.8	122	1.7	4.3	6.2	3.9	..	..
55 Qatar	(.)	(.)	(.)	(.)	..	(.)	..	..	..	..
Medium human development	..	..	..	..	..	..	..	..	..	..
Excluding China	..	..	..	..	..	..	..	..	..	..
56 Mauritius	(.)	(.)	(.)	1	(.)	(.)	..	..	..	..
57 Malaysia	2.2	4.0	1.2	16	..	1.3	2.4	1.6	5.8	4.0
58 Bahrain	(.)	(.)	(.)	(.)	..	(.)	0.1	(.)	..	..
59 Grenada	..	..	..	(.)	..	..	..	..	..	..
60 Antigua and Barbuda	(.)	..	..	(.)	..	..	..	..	..	..
61 Colombia	4.3	2.7	10.5	44	0.4	1.8	2.7	1.4	..	..
63 Seychelles	(.)	(.)	(.)	(.)	..	(.)	(.)	(.)	..	..
65 Suriname	(.)	0.1	0.2	(.)	..	(.)	(.)	(.)	..	..
67 United Arab Emirates	0.2	(.)	0.1	1	..	(.)	..	..	..	..
68 Panama	0.4	0.4	0.4	2	(.)	0.1	0.2	0.1	0.6	0.3
69 Jamaica	..	0.7	0.2	1	(.)	0.1	(.)	(.)	..	..
70 Brazil	..	5.9	32.9	..	1.2	3.5	18.4	9.9	..	..
71 Fiji	(.)	0.2	0.2	1	..	(.)	..	..	..	0.1
72 Saint Lucia	(.)	..	..	(.)	..	..	..	..	..	..
73 Turkey	..	4.6	..	134	..	2.7	7.1	5.1	..	..
74 Thailand	22.7	15.5	20.8	39	1.5	5.2	3.4	2.2	17.5	14.6
75 Cuba	(.)	..	..	3	..	0.1	0.5	0.3	..	..
76 Saint Vincent	(.)	..	..	(.)	..	..	..	..	..	..
79 Saint Kitts and Nevis	(.)	..	..	(.)	..	..	..	..	..	..
81 Syrian Arab Rep.	0.1	2.7	4.7	33	..	0.8	2.6	1.9	..	..
82 Belize	(.)	..	..	(.)	..	..	..	..	..	..
84 Saudi Arabia	0.3	0.8	2.1	54	..	1.8	2.9	1.7	..	..
85 South Africa	..	..	..	98	..	..	..	..	..	..
86 Sri Lanka	1.7	7.0	8.8	13	0.5	0.5	1.4	1.0	..	..
87 Libyan Arab Jamahiriya	(.)	0.1	0.1	22	..	..	0.9	0.6	..	..
89 Ecuador	2.2	4.6	4.7	28	0.3	0.3	0.9	0.5	6.1	3.1
90 Paraguay	..	2.9	1.9	9	(.)	0.4	0.3	0.2	1.7	1.1
91 Korea, Dem. Rep. of	(.)	..	..	18	..	..	..	..	..	..
92 Philippines	..	12.1	19.1	138	3.2	0.6	3.9	2.0	37.3	23.1
93 Tunisia	0.7	2.9	4.5	15	0.1	0.4	1.8	1.1	1.4	0.6
94 Oman	0.2	0.7	0.8	3	..	0.1	..	..	..	..
95 Peru	..	9.2	11.2	75	0.4	(.)	2.0	1.5	..	..
96 Iraq	0.4	1.4	5.2	68	0.4	1.6	4.1	2.5	..	..
97 Dominican Rep.	..	2.8	3.0	17	0.1	0.2	0.7	0.4	3.2	1.2
98 Samoa	(.)	(.)	(.)	(.)	..	..	..	..	..	..
99 Jordan	0.4	(.)	(.)	8	(.)	..	0.4	0.3	0.7	0.2
100 Mongolia	(.)	0.8	0.6	7	..	(.)	..	..	..	..
101 China	..	336.0	42.1	900	25.3	28.4	224.0	156.0	..	..
102 Lebanon	0.1	0.1	0.6	5	..	0.1	0.4	0.3	..	..
103 Iran, Islamic Rep. of	16.2	6.7	17.4	36	5.0	3.5	15.5	9.0	..	10.4
104 Botswana	0.2	0.6	0.8	5	(.)	0.1	0.2	0.1	0.7	0.5
105 Guyana	(.)	0.2	0.1	1	..	(.)	(.)	(.)	..	..
106 Vanuatu	(.)	(.)	0.1	1	..	..	..	..	..	..
107 Algeria	..	7.9	10.5	86	0.4	1.7	6.0	3.9	..	..
108 Indonesia	107.6	110.0	106.0	..	9.4	9.1	20.9	14.4	31.1	20.9
109 Gabon	0.2	0.3	..	8	..	..	0.3	0.2	..	..
110 El Salvador	..	3.1	2.1	17	..	0.5	0.8	0.5	1.4	0.9
111 Nicaragua	..	1.8	2.8	1	0.1	0.4	..	..	0.8	0.3

HDI rank	Without access to health services 1991	Without access to safe water 1991	Without access to sanitation 1991	Children dying before age five (thousands) 1990	Mal-nourished children under five 1991	Children not in primary or secondary school 1991	Illiterate adults (15+) 1991	Illiterate females (15+) 1991	People in absolute poverty Total 1991	People in absolute poverty Rural 1991
Low human development	..	..	..	..	..	..	..	..	..	..
Excluding India	..	..	..	..	..	..	..	..	..	..
112 Maldives	0.1	0.1	0.2	(.)	..	..	..	..	..	..
113 Guatemala	3.8	3.8	4.1	34	0.6	1.5	2.3	1.3	6.8	4.2
114 Cape Verde	0.1	0.1	0.3	1	..	(.)	0.1	..	..	..
115 Viet Nam	2.0	33.9	31.8	134	4.0	6.0	5.1	3.5	..	..
116 Honduras	2.0	2.6	3.6	17	0.2	0.4	0.8	0.4	2.4	1.6
117 Swaziland	0.3	0.5	0.5	6	..	(.)	..	..	0.4	0.3
118 Solomon Islands	0.1	0.1	..	..	..	..	..	..	..	..
119 Morocco	9.7	7.0	15.6	96	0.6	3.8	7.5	4.7	7.9	4.3
120 Lesotho	0.4	1.0	1.4	9	(.)	0.1	..	..	1.0	0.8
121 Zimbabwe	3.0	6.6	6.0	35	0.2	0.4	1.8	1.1	..	..
122 Bolivia	..	3.9	4.8	50	0.2	0.7	0.9	0.6	..	3.0
123 Myanmar	22.2	28.8	27.6	111	2.1	4.5	5.1	3.7	..	..
124 Egypt	..	7.4	24.9	148	0.8	1.6	16.5	10.5	12.6	7.2
125 São Tomé and Principe	(.)	..	..	(.)	..	..	..	..	..	..
126 Congo	..	1.8	..	12	0.1	..	0.5	0.3	..	..
127 Kenya	..	17.5	13.2	122	0.7	2.4	..	..	12.6	10.3
128 Madagascar	4.3	..	..	96	0.9	2.0	..	..	..	..
129 Papua New Guinea	0.2	2.7	1.8	10	0.2	0.7	1.1	0.7	2.9	2.5
130 Zambia	2.1	3.4	3.8	53	0.5	1.0	..	..	5.9	3.4
131 Ghana	3.7	6.9	10.8	93	0.8	2.2	3.3	2.0	6.5	3.8
132 Pakistan	18.2	60.9	94.4	..	9.0	27.9	43.5	25.0	36.0	24.0
133 Cameroon	10.1	7.8	..	83	0.4	1.3	2.9	2.0	4.3	2.8
134 India	..	220.0	754.0	..	73.1	72.9	281.0	174.0	423.0	321.0
135 Namibia	..	..	..	13	0.1	0.1	..	..	..	..
136 Côte d'Ivoire	5.0	2.1	8.0	82	0.3	..	..	..	..	..
137 Haiti	3.6	3.9	5.2	30	0.4	0.9	1.9	1.1	4.9	3.7
138 Tanzania, U. Rep. of	1.9	12.9	6.3	235	2.9	5.6	..	..	15.5	10.8
139 Comoros	0.1	..	0.1	4	..	(.)	..	..	..	..
140 Zaire	15.8	25.4	33.2	211	..	6.2	..	..	..	18.5
141 Lao People's Dem. Rep.	1.4	3.1	3.8	28	0.3	0.5	..	..	..	..
142 Nigeria	37.0	60.7	98.1	..	8.4	19.9	28.7	18.0	..	..
143 Yemen	..	..	..	113	1.4	2.0	2.6	1.7	..	..
144 Liberia	1.8	1.3	2.4	25	..	..	0.8	0.5	..	..
145 Togo	..	1.1	2.8	23	0.2	0.4	1.1	0.7	..	..
146 Uganda	5.3	15.4	15.8	161	0.9	3.1	4.9	3.2	..	..
147 Bangladesh	30.3	25.3	102.2	..	13.0	20.2	42.0	24.6	..	..
148 Cambodia	..	..	7.4	62	0.3	..	..	..	..	..
149 Rwanda	..	2.6	2.8	73	0.6	1.4	1.8	1.2	..	..
150 Senegal	4.5	3.6	3.6	61	0.3	1.5	2.5	1.6	..	..
151 Ethiopia	23.1	42.4	42.9	..	4.3	12.2	..	..	..	..
152 Nepal	..	12.7	18.9	137	..	2.6	8.2	4.7	12.2	11.1
153 Malawi	2.0	4.7	..	125	0.6	1.7	..	..	8.2	7.5
154 Burundi	1.1	3.5	2.4	50	0.5	1.2	1.5	9.3	4.8	4.5
155 Equatorial Guinea	..	..	..	3	..	..	..	..	..	0.2
156 Central African Rep.	2.7	2.7	2.5	23	..	0.6	1.0	0.7	..	..
157 Mozambique	10.1	11.4	11.7	208	..	3.3	5.9	3.5	..	..
158 Sudan	7.8	..	22.7	191	1.0	5.4	10.1	6.1	..	17.2
159 Bhutan	0.3	1.0	..	11	0.1	0.3	..	..	..	..
160 Angola	7.2	5.9	7.5	138	..	1.8	3.2	2.0	..	..
161 Mauritania	1.5	0.7	..	20	0.2	0.5	0.7	0.5	..	..
162 Benin	2.4	2.4	2.8	34	..	1.0	1.9	1.1	..	1.9
163 Djibouti	..	0.3	0.1	3	..	(.)	..	..	..	..
164 Guinea-Bissau	0.2	0.7	0.8	10	(.)	0.2	0.4	0.2	..	..
165 Chad	4.2	..	..	54	..	1.2	..	..	3.1	2.2
166 Somalia	7.1	3.9	7.8	77	..	2.7	3.0	1.9	..	4.0
167 Gambia	0.1	0.2	..	9	..	(.)	0.4	0.2	..	0.3
168 Mali	..	4.9	7.3	134	0.7	2.8	3.4	2.0	4.3	3.7
169 Niger	5.6	3.2	7.3	89	0.9	2.3	2.7	1.6	..	2.2
170 Burkina Faso	2.8	3.0	8.3	97	..	2.4	4.1	2.3	..	..
171 Afghanistan	9.0	14.0	..	260	1.6	4.5	6.8	4.0	6.1	5.2
172 Sierra Leone	2.7	2.4	2.4	52	0.2	0.9	1.8	1.1	..	1.9
173 Guinea	4.0	4.0	..	70	..	1.5	..	..	..	..
All developing countries	1,200T	1,300T	2,000T	12,600T	200T	330T	920T	600T	1,300T	1,000T
Least developed countries	200T	250T	350T	420T	40T	100T	170T	150T	300T	250T
Sub-Saharan Africa	..	..	..	3,600T	..	..	140T	..	..	..
Industrial countries	..	..	..	300T	..	..	..	..	..	..
World	..	..	..	12,900T	..	..	..	..	..	..

Trends in human development

HDI rank	Life expectancy at birth (years)		Infant mortality (per 1,000 live births)		Population with access to safe water (%)		Daily calorie supply (as % of requirements)		Adult literacy rate (%)		Combined primary and secondary enrolment ratio		Real GDP per capita (PPP$)	
	1960	1990	1960	1991	1975-80	1988-90	1965	1988-90	1970	1990	1970	1987-90	1960	1990
High human development	58.5	70.6	83	31	68	79	107	123	83	91	73	88	3,140	6,290
20 Barbados	64.3	75.1	74	11	98	99	..	..	..	..	..	..	3,443	8,304
24 Hong Kong	66.2	77.3	44	6	99	100	..	..	..	..	76	87	2,323	15,595
27 Cyprus	68.6	76.2	30	10	100	100	..	..	..	..	..	..	2,039	9,953
30 Uruguay	67.7	72.2	51	21	..	..	106	101	93	96	87	92	4,401	5,916
31 Trinidad and Tobago	63.5	71.6	56	20	93	96	103	114	..	..	83	90	4,754	6,604
32 Bahamas	63.2	71.5	51	25	..	..	..	..	..	..	..	..	..	..
33 Korea, Rep. of	53.9	70.1	85	22	66	78	96	120	88	96	76	97	..	..
36 Chile	57.1	71.8	114	17	70	86	108	102	89	93	87	90	3,103	5,099
42 Costa Rica	61.6	74.9	85	15	72	94	104	121	88	93	76	77	2,160	4,542
43 Singapore	64.5	74.0	36	7	..	..	87	136	..	..	77	87	2,409	15,880
44 Brunei Darussalam	62.3	73.5	63	9	..	..	..	..	..	..	..	..	..	..
46 Argentina	64.9	71.0	60	30	..	..	119	131	93	95	81	96	3,381	4,295
50 Venezuela	59.5	70.0	81	34	79	89	94	99	75	88	70	83	3,899	6,169
51 Dominica	..	..	..	..	..	..	..	..	..	..	..	..	..	..
52 Kuwait	59.5	73.4	89	14	..	..	..	..	54	73	67	94	..	..
53 Mexico	57.0	69.7	92	37	62	78	111	131	74	88	67	82	2,870	5,918
55 Qatar	53.0	69.2	145	28	..	..	..	..	..	..	..	..	..	..
Medium human development	48.5	68.0	139	42	42	73	88	114	60	76	64	86	1,010	2,710
Excluding China	50.4	65.4	124	53	42	75	92	116	60	79	61	84	1,680	3,660
56 Mauritius	59.1	69.6	70	22	99	100	103	128	..	..	62	77	2,113	5,750
57 Malaysia	53.9	70.1	73	15	..	..	101	120	60	78	62	75	1,783	6,140
58 Bahrain	55.5	71.0	130	14	100	100	..	..	..	..	83	99	..	..
59 Grenada	..	..	..	..	..	..	..	..	..	..	..	..	..	..
60 Antigua and Barbuda	..	..	..	..	..	..	..	..	..	..	..	..	..	..
61 Colombia	56.5	68.8	99	38	64	92	94	106	78	87	82	79	1,874	4,237
63 Seychelles	..	..	..	..	79	99	..	..	..	..	..	..	..	..
65 Suriname	60.2	69.5	70	30	88	84	..	..	..	..	..	..	2,234	3,927
67 United Arab Emirates	53.0	70.5	145	23	..	..	..	..	..	..	63	94	..	..
68 Panama	60.7	72.4	69	22	77	83	98	98	81	88	75	83	1,533	3,317
69 Jamaica	62.7	73.1	63	15	86	72	100	114	97	98	75	80	1,829	2,979
70 Brazil	54.6	65.6	116	59	62	96	100	114	66	81	65	91	1,404	4,718
71 Fiji	59.0	64.8	71	24	..	..	..	..	..	..	..	..	2,354	4,427
72 Saint Lucia	..	..	..	..	..	..	..	..	..	..	..	..	..	..
73 Turkey	50.1	65.1	190	60	68	92	105	127	52	81	67	81	1,669	4,652
74 Thailand	52.3	66.1	103	28	25	72	95	103	79	93	58	59	985	3,986
75 Cuba	63.8	75.4	65	14	..	..	102	135	87	94	76	95	..	..
76 Saint Vincent	..	..	..	..	..	..	..	..	..	..	..	..	..	..
79 Saint Kitts and Nevis	..	..	..	..	..	..	..	..	..	..	..	..	..	..
81 Syrian Arab Rep.	49.7	66.1	135	42	..	..	89	126	40	65	61	83	1,787	4,756
82 Belize	..	..	..	..	..	..	..	..	..	..	..	..	..	..
84 Saudi Arabia	44.4	64.5	170	33	64	95	79	121	9	62	31	65	7,612	10,989
85 South Africa	49.0	61.7	89	55	..	..	107	128	..	..	..	..	2,984	4,865
86 Sri Lanka	62.0	70.9	71	25	19	60	100	101	77	88	71	88	1,389	2,405
87 Libyan Arab Jamahiriya	46.7	61.8	160	72	87	97	83	140	37	64	..	..	..	..
89 Ecuador	53.1	66.0	124	59	36	58	83	105	72	86	63	89	1,461	3,074
90 Paraguay	63.8	67.1	66	48	13	33	112	116	80	90	67	72	1,200	2,790
91 Korea, Dem. Rep. of	53.9	70.4	85	25	..	..	99	121	..	..	..	..	..	..
92 Philippines	52.8	64.2	80	42	..	..	82	104	83	90	85	97	1,183	2,303
93 Tunisia	48.3	66.7	159	45	35	65	94	131	31	65	64	80	1,394	3,579
94 Oman	40.1	65.9	214	32	..	..	..	..	..	..	25	82	..	..
95 Peru	47.7	63.0	142	80	..	..	98	87	71	85	..	..	2,130	2,622
96 Iraq	48.5	65.0	139	60	66	93	89	128	34	60	49	75	..	..
97 Dominican Rep.	51.8	66.7	125	59	55	62	85	102	67	83	63	92	1,227	2,404
98 Samoa	..	..	..	..	95	82	..	..	..	..	..	..	..	..
99 Jordan	46.9	66.9	135	38	..	..	93	110	47	80	..	..	1,328	2,345
100 Mongolia	46.7	62.5	128	62	..	..	106	97	..	..	..	..	..	..
101 China	47.1	70.1	150	29	..	..	86	112	..	..	66	88	723	1,990
102 Lebanon	59.6	66.1	68	36	..	..	99	127	69	80	77	92	..	..
103 Iran, Islamic Rep. of	49.5	66.2	169	44	51	89	87	125	29	54	52	83	1,985	3,253
104 Botswana	45.5	59.8	116	62	..	..	88	97	41	74	46	88	474	3,419
105 Guyana	56.1	64.2	100	50	72	81	..	..	..	..	80	82	1,630	1,464
106 Vanuatu	..	..	..	..	55	71	..	..	..	..	..	..	..	..
107 Algeria	47.0	65.1	168	65	77	69	72	123	25	57	46	79	1,676	3,011
108 Indonesia	41.2	61.5	139	68	11	42	81	121	54	82	49	81	..	..
109 Gabon	40.8	52.5	171	97	..	..	81	104	33	61	..	..	1,373	4,147
110 El Salvador	50.5	64.4	130	50	53	41	80	102	57	73	60	67	1,305	1,950
111 Nicaragua	47.0	64.8	140	58	46	53	107	99	..	..	54	73	1,756	1,497

HDI rank	Life expectancy at birth (years)		Infant mortality (per 1,000 live births)		Population with access to safe water (%)		Daily calorie supply (as % of requirements)		Adult literacy rate (%)		Combined primary secondary enrolment ratio			
	1960	1990	1960	1991	1975-80	1988-90	1965	1988-90	1970	1990	1970	198_		
Low human development	42.6	56.5	165	96	30	62	89	98	31	49	41	..	670	1,740
Excluding India	41.4	54.4	166	99	28	50	89	96	28	50	34	49	740	1,140
112 Maldives	43.6	62.5	158	58	..	..	..	..	..	..	..	..	..	..
113 Guatemala	45.6	63.4	125	51	39	60	93	103	44	55	35	52	1,667	2,576
114 Cape Verde	52.0	67.0	110	44	40	74	..	..	..	..	..	..	..	..
115 Viet Nam	44.2	62.7	147	39	..	..	97	103	..	..	69	69	..	..
116 Honduras	46.5	64.9	160	62	41	52	87	98	53	73	58	75	901	1,470
117 Swaziland	40.2	56.8	157	76	43	30	..	..	..	..	63	85	1,182	2,384
118 Solomon Islands	50.3	69.5	132	28	27	61	..	..	..	..	..	..	..	..
119 Morocco	46.7	62.0	163	72	..	..	92	125	22	50	32	50	854	2,348
120 Lesotho	42.9	57.3	149	82	17	46	89	93	..	..	61	78	346	1,743
121 Zimbabwe	45.3	59.6	110	61	..	..	87	94	55	67	47	88	937	1,484
122 Bolivia	42.7	54.5	167	89	34	46	77	84	57	78	61	68	1,142	1,572
123 Myanmar	43.8	61.3	158	85	17	33	89	114	71	81	54	62	341	659
124 Egypt	46.1	60.3	179	59	75	86	97	132	35	48	55	90	557	1,988
125 São Tomé and Principe	..	..	..	..	..	..	..	..	..	..	..	..	..	..
126 Congo	41.6	53.7	143	83	38	20	101	103	35	57	..	..	1,092	2,362
127 Kenya	44.7	59.7	124	68	17	28	98	89	32	69	41	72	635	1,058
128 Madagascar	40.7	54.5	220	113	..	..	108	95	50	80	50	53	1,013	704
129 Papua New Guinea	40.6	54.9	165	56	20	33	72	114	32	52	32	43	1,136	1,786
130 Zambia	41.6	54.4	135	85	42	59	91	87	52	73	61	67	1,172	744
131 Ghana	45.0	55.0	132	84	35	56	87	93	31	60	52	58	1,049	1,016
132 Pakistan	43.1	57.7	163	101	25	50	76	99	21	35	26	29	820	1,862
133 Cameroon	39.2	53.7	163	66	..	..	89	95	33	54	50	65	736	1,646
134 India	44.0	59.1	165	90	31	75	89	101	34	48	49	68	617	1,072
135 Namibia	42.5	57.5	146	73	..	..	..	..	..	..	..	..	..	..
136 Côte d'Ivoire	39.2	53.4	166	93	..	..	102	111	18	54	..	..	1,021	1,324
137 Haiti	42.2	55.7	182	89	12	42	88	89	22	53	36	53	921	933
138 Tanzania, U. Rep. of	40.5	54.0	147	104	39	52	85	95	..	..	24	40	272	572
139 Comoros	42.5	55.0	165	92	..	..	..	..	..	..	19	52	..	..
140 Zaire	41.3	53.0	158	96	19	34	98	96	42	72	..	..	379	367
141 Lao People's Dem. Rep.	40.4	49.7	155	101	..	..	86	111	..	..	29	65	..	..
142 Nigeria	39.5	51.5	190	99	..	..	95	93	25	51	21	49	1,133	1,215
143 Yemen	36.4	51.5	214	110	..	..	..	..	8	39	..	..	..	..
144 Liberia	41.2	54.2	184	131	..	..	94	98	18	40	..	..	967	857
145 Togo	39.3	54.0	182	88	16	71	101	99	17	43	39	64	411	734
146 Uganda	43.0	52.0	133	105	35	15	96	93	41	48	25	51	371	524
147 Bangladesh	39.6	51.8	156	111	..	..	91	88	24	35	37	42	621	872
148 Cambodia	42.4	49.7	146	120	..	..	98	96	..	..	..	..	..	..
149 Rwanda	42.3	49.5	150	112	68	64	73	82	32	50	42	47	538	657
150 Senegal	37.2	48.3	172	82	36	53	104	98	12	38	24	38	1,136	1,248
151 Ethiopia	36.0	45.5	175	125	8	18	77	73	..	..	11	28	262	369
152 Nepal	38.3	52.2	187	102	8	37	87	100	13	26	19	60	584	920
153 Malawi	37.8	48.1	207	144	51	53	91	88	..	..	23	52	423	640
154 Burundi	41.3	48.5	153	108	29	38	103	84	20	50	18	39	473	625
155 Equatorial Guinea	36.8	47.0	188	120	..	..	..	..	..	..	..	..	..	..
156 Central African Rep.	38.5	49.5	175	106	..	..	91	82	16	38	36	41	806	768
157 Mozambique	37.3	47.5	190	149	..	..	86	77	22	33	28	32	1,368	1,072
158 Sudan	38.7	50.8	170	102	..	..	79	87	17	27	24	36	975	949
159 Bhutan	37.3	48.9	203	133	..	..	..	..	..	..	4	18	..	..
160 Angola	33.0	45.5	208	128	17	38	81	80	12	42	..	..	1,308	840
161 Mauritania	35.3	47.0	191	120	..	..	88	106	..	..	9	35	930	1,057
162 Benin	35.0	47.0	185	88	34	50	88	104	16	23	23	37	1,075	1,043
163 Djibouti	36.0	48.0	186	115	42	43	..	..	..	..	..	..	..	..
164 Guinea-Bissau	34.0	42.5	201	143	10	25	..	..	..	..	29	38	..	..
165 Chad	34.8	46.5	195	125	..	..	99	73	11	30	19	33	785	559
166 Somalia	36.0	46.1	175	125	38	56	92	81	3	24	7	14	891	836
167 Gambia	32.3	44.0	213	135	..	..	..	..	..	..	16	42	411	913
168 Mali	34.8	45.0	210	162	..	..	83	96	8	32	15	16	541	572
169 Niger	35.3	45.5	192	127	..	..	85	95	4	28	8	18	604	645
170 Burkina Faso	36.2	48.2	205	120	25	67	91	94	8	18	18	21	..	..
171 Afghanistan	33.4	42.5	215	165	9	21	90	72	8	29	19	19	775	714
172 Sierra Leone	31.5	42.0	219	146	14	43	79	83	13	21	22	34	871	1,086
173 Guinea	33.6	43.5	203	137	14	33	81	97	14	24	24	24	444	501
All developing countries	46.2	62.8	149	71	36	68	90	107	46	65	55	73	950	2,170
Least developed countries	39.0	51.0	170	114	21	47	88	90	29	45	29	42	580	740
Sub-Saharan Africa	40.0	51.8	165	103	25	41	92	93	28	47	26	46	..	..
Industrial countries	69.0	74.5	35	14	..	..	..	..	..	..	..	..	..	..
World	53.4	64.7	128	64	..	..	..	..	..	..	..	..	..	..

Note: Data for industrial countries for this subject area are in table 31.

uman capital formation

HDI rank	Adult literacy rate (as % of age 15+)			Literacy rate (as % of age 15-19) 1990	Mean years of schooling (25+)			Scientists and technicians (per 1,000 people) 1986-90	R & D scientists and technicians (per 10,000 people) 1986-89	Tertiary graduate ratio (as % of corresponding age group) 1987-90	Science graduates (as % of total graduates) 1988-90
	Total 1990	Male 1990	Female 1990		Total 1990	Male 1990	Female 1990				
High human development	91	93	91	97	6.6	7.1	6.1	49.8	9.4	2.9	32
20 Barbados	..	..	..	..	8.9	9.2	8.6	11.6	..	..	11
24 Hong Kong	..	..	..	..	7.0	8.6	5.4	41.0	..	6.7	39
27 Cyprus	..	..	..	..	7.0	7.6	6.5	61.1	2.0	..	21
30 Uruguay	96	97	96	99	7.8	7.4	8.2	..	..	..	44
31 Trinidad and Tobago	..	..	..	..	8.0	8.0	8.1	..	4.5	1.2	33
32 Bahamas	..	..	..	..	6.2	6.4	6.0	..	..	..	33
33 Korea, Rep. of	96	99	94	100	8.8	11.0	6.7	47.3	22.0	..	29
36 Chile	93	94	93	98	7.5	7.8	7.2	..	5.9	3.1	27
42 Costa Rica	93	93	93	97	5.7	5.8	5.6	..	..	2.7	20
43 Singapore	..	..	..	..	3.9	4.7	3.1	23.6	18.7	5.8	53
44 Brunei Darussalam	..	..	..	..	5.0	5.5	4.5	27.0	6.3	..	0
46 Argentina	95	96	95	97	8.7	8.5	8.9	29.1	5.4	..	32
50 Venezuela	88	87	90	97	6.3	6.4	6.2	95.3	4.4	2.7	32
51 Dominica	..	..	..	..	4.7	4.9	4.5	..	..	..	33
52 Kuwait	73	77	67	82	5.4	6.0	4.7	64.4	12.7	4.2	18
53 Mexico	88	90	85	96	4.7	4.8	4.6	..	6.1	2.5	32
55 Qatar	..	..	..	..	5.6	5.8	5.4	26.6	9.3	4.3	13
Medium human development	76	84	67	93	4.8	5.8	3.8	10.8	..	1.2	31
Excluding China	79	85	74	93	4.8	5.4	4.2	15.2	..	2.4	26
56 Mauritius	..	..	..	..	4.1	4.8	3.3	16.2	3.4	0.7	26
57 Malaysia	78	87	70	94	5.3	5.6	5.0	..	4.0	1.4	28
58 Bahrain	77	82	69	93	3.9	4.7	3.2	43.3	..	2.3	52
59 Grenada	..	..	..	..	4.7	4.9	4.5	..	..	..	26
60 Antigua and Barbuda	..	..	..	..	4.6	5.1	4.1	..	..	..	24
61 Colombia	87	88	86	94	7.1	6.9	7.3	..	0.8	2.6	28
63 Seychelles	..	..	..	..	4.6	4.8	4.4	..	3.8	..	..
65 Suriname	95	95	95	..	4.2	4.3	4.0	..	..	..	3
67 United Arab Emirates	..	..	..	..	5.1	5.1	5.2	..	..	1.7	12
68 Panama	88	88	88	95	6.7	6.5	6.9	8.0	..	2.3	42
69 Jamaica	98	98	99	100	5.3	5.3	5.2	6.2	0.1	2.0	19
70 Brazil	81	83	80	92	3.9	4.0	3.8	29.5	..	2.5	19
71 Fiji	..	..	..	..	5.1	5.6	4.6	13.0	1.8	1.1	22
72 Saint Lucia	..	..	..	..	3.9	4.0	3.8	..	10.4	..	0
73 Turkey	81	90	71	91	3.5	4.7	2.3	27.5	3.7	2.1	36
74 Thailand	93	95	91	99	3.8	4.3	3.3	1.2	1.6	5.0	18
75 Cuba	94	95	93	100	7.6	7.5	7.7	..	19.8	3.8	26
76 Saint Vincent	..	..	..	..	4.6	4.7	4.5	..	..	..	37
79 Saint Kitts and Nevis	..	..	..	..	6.0	6.1	5.9	..	..	..	0
81 Syrian Arab Rep.	65	..	..	82	4.2	5.2	3.1	3.6	..	4.0	33
82 Belize	..	..	..	..	4.6	4.8	4.4	..	..	..	..
84 Saudi Arabia	62	73	48	..	3.7	5.9	1.5	..	..	2.5	14
85 South Africa	..	..	..	..	3.9	4.1	3.7	..	..	..	..
86 Sri Lanka	88	93	84	96	6.9	7.7	6.1	..	2.2	1.4	12
87 Libyan Arab Jamahiriya	64	75	50	89	3.4	5.5	1.3	11.6	..	..	..
89 Ecuador	86	88	84	95	5.6	5.8	5.3	9.1	..	2.3	..
90 Paraguay	90	92	88	96	4.9	5.2	4.6	..	..	..	31
91 Korea, Dem. Rep. of	..	..	..	..	6.0	7.4	4.6	..	..	..	..
92 Philippines	90	90	90	96	7.4	7.8	7.0	..	1.3	6.7	30
93 Tunisia	65	74	56	95	2.1	3.0	1.2	1.4	..	0.9	36
94 Oman	..	..	..	..	0.9	1.4	0.3	6.6	..	..	24
95 Peru	85	92	79	96	6.4	7.1	5.7	21.2	..	..	38
96 Iraq	60	70	49	85	4.8	5.7	3.9	3.6	..	..	20
97 Dominican Rep.	83	85	82	94	4.3	4.6	4.0	..	..	..	..
98 Samoa	..	..	..	..	5.7	6.4	5.0	..	..	..	..
99 Jordan	80	89	70	97	5.0	6.0	4.0	..	1.3	5.6	25
100 Mongolia	..	..	..	..	7.0	7.2	6.8	0.9	..	..	44
101 China	73	84	62	93	4.8	6.0	3.6	8.5	..	0.5	43
102 Lebanon	80	88	73	..	4.4	5.3	3.5	..	..	2.9	24
103 Iran, Islamic Rep. of	54	65	43	79	3.9	4.6	3.1	8.5	1.1	0.9	61
104 Botswana	74	84	65	..	2.4	2.5	2.4	1.2	..	0.6	3
105 Guyana	96	98	95	100	5.1	5.4	4.9	2.3	3.5	1.1	19
106 Vanuatu	..	..	..	..	3.7	4.3	3.1	..	..	..	30
107 Algeria	57	70	46	88	2.6	4.4	0.8	..	..	2.2	42
108 Indonesia	82	88	75	95	3.9	5.0	2.9	10.1	..	0.6	11
109 Gabon	61	74	49	..	2.6	3.9	1.3	..	..	0.8	20
110 El Salvador	73	76	70	88	4.1	4.1	4.1	1.4	3.4	1.7	9
111 Nicaragua	..	..	..	..	4.3	4.1	4.5	..	2.9	0.9	37

HDI rank	Adult literacy rate (as % of age 15+)			Literacy rate (as % of age 15-19)	Mean years of schooling (25+)			Scientists and technicians (per 1,000 people)	R & D scientists and technicians (per 10,000 people)	Tertiary graduate ratio (as % of corresponding age group)	Science graduates (as % of total graduates)
	Total 1990	Male 1990	Female 1990	1990	Total 1990	Male 1990	Female 1990	1986-90	1986-89	1987-90	1988-90
Low human development	49	63	39	66	2.3	3.3	1.3	2.9	2.4	0.6	..
Excluding India	50	64	43	66	2.2	3.1	1.4	1.7	2.1	..	20
112 Maldives	..	..	..	..	4.5	5.1	3.9			..	38
113 Guatemala	55	63	47	67	4.1	4.4	3.8	1.4	2.1		
114 Cape Verde	67	..	..	..	2.2	3.2	1.3			..	..
115 Viet Nam	88	92	83	93	4.6	5.8	3.4			..	..
116 Honduras	73	76	71	90	3.9	4.0	3.7	1.9		0.5	36
117 Swaziland	..	..	..	..	3.7	4.0	3.3			0.7	16
118 Solomon Islands					1.0	1.2	0.8				
119 Morocco	50	61	38	80	2.8	4.1	1.5			1.1	27
120 Lesotho	..	..	..	..	3.4	2.7	4.0			0.7	5
121 Zimbabwe	67	74	60	81	2.9	4.2	1.7			0.5	12
122 Bolivia	78	85	71	94	4.0	5.0	3.0			..	..
123 Myanmar	81	89	72	90	2.5	3.0	2.1			..	..
124 Egypt	48	63	34	65	2.8	3.9	1.6		6.0	3.8	19
125 São Tomé and Principe					2.3	3.3	1.3				33
126 Congo	57	70	44	..	2.1	3.1	1.1		12.4	1.2	20
127 Kenya	69	..	..	..	2.3	3.2	1.3	1.4		0.2	24
128 Madagascar	80	88	73	..	2.2	2.6	1.7		1.1	0.4	32
129 Papua New Guinea	52	65	38	..	0.9	1.2	0.6	3.2		0.6	23
130 Zambia	73	81	65	90	2.7	3.7	1.7	4.4		0.2	10
131 Ghana	60	70	51	88	3.5	4.8	2.2	1.5			23
132 Pakistan	35	47	21	50	1.9	3.0	0.7	4.1	1.5	..	..
133 Cameroon	54	67	43	77	1.6	2.5	0.8			0.3	..
134 India	48	62	34	66	2.4	3.5	1.2	3.6	2.5	..	20
135 Namibia	..	..	..	..	1.7	1.7	1.7				
136 Côte d'Ivoire	54	67	40	..	1.9	2.9	0.9			..	..
137 Haiti	53	59	47	..	1.7	2.0	1.3	4.9		0.2	..
138 Tanzania, U. Rep. of	..	..	..	..	2.0	2.8	1.3			0.1	20
139 Comoros	..	..	..	..	1.0	1.2	0.8				
140 Zaire	72	84	61	91	1.6	2.4	0.8			0.2	27
141 Lao People's Dem. Rep.	..	..	..	..	2.9	3.6	2.1			0.5	17
142 Nigeria	51	62	40	78	1.2	1.8	0.5	0.9	0.7	0.3	23
143 Yemen	39	53	27	..	0.8	1.3	0.2	0.2		0.2	3
144 Liberia	40	50	29	67	2.0	3.2	0.8			0.3	17
145 Togo	43	56	31	63	1.6	2.4	0.8	0.2		..	18
146 Uganda	48	62	35	..	1.1	1.6	0.6			0.1	26
147 Bangladesh	35	47	22	46	2.0	3.1	0.9	0.5		0.6	16
148 Cambodia	35	48	22	..	2.0	2.3	1.7			..	..
149 Rwanda	50	64	37	65	1.1	1.6	0.5	0.2	0.2	0.1	25
150 Senegal	38	52	25	..	0.8	1.3	0.4			1.0	22
151 Ethiopia	..	..	..	..	1.1	1.5	0.7			0.2	24
152 Nepal	26	38	13	39	2.1	3.2	1.0	0.6		0.3	13
153 Malawi	..	..	..	..	1.7	2.4	1.1			0.1	23
154 Burundi	50	61	40	80	0.3	0.5	0.2		0.6	0.2	31
155 Equatorial Guinea	50	..	..	..	0.8	1.3	0.3			..	..
156 Central African Rep.	38	52	25	..	1.1	1.6	0.5		2.2	0.4	16
157 Mozambique	33	45	21	53	1.6	2.1	1.2			0.0	21
158 Sudan	27	43	12	37	0.8	1.1	0.5	0.4		0.4	3
159 Bhutan	38	..	..	..	0.2	0.3	0.1			0.1	..
160 Angola	42	56	29	..	1.5	2.0	1.0			..	45
161 Mauritania	34	47	21	..	0.3	0.5	0.1			..	..
162 Benin	23	32	16	41	0.7	1.1	0.3		2.3	..	19
163 Djibouti	..	..	..	..	0.3	0.5	0.2	0.1		..	4
164 Guinea-Bissau	37	50	24	..	0.3	0.5	0.1			..	..
165 Chad	30	42	18	..	0.2	0.3	0.1			0.1	11
166 Somalia	24	36	14	..	0.2	0.3	0.1			..	13
167 Gambia	27	39	16	..	0.6	0.9	0.2			..	..
168 Mali	32	41	24	67	0.3	0.5	0.1			0.2	9
169 Niger	28	20	17	..	0.1	0.2	0.1			0.2	4
170 Burkina Faso	18	28	9	33	0.1	0.1	0.1			0.3	28
171 Afghanistan	29	44	14	51	0.8	1.4	0.2			0.2	32
172 Sierra Leone	21	31	11	..	0.9	1.4	0.4			..	..
173 Guinea	24	35	13	..	0.8	1.3	0.3		4.2	0.3	62
All developing countries	65	75	55	82	3.7	4.6	2.7	8.9	3.2	1.2	29
Least developed countries	45	56	33	59	1.6	2.3	0.9	..	..	0.3	18
Sub-Saharan Africa	47	58	36	..	1.6	2.2	1.0			0.2	23
Industrial countries	..	..	..	..	10.0	10.4	9.6	81.0	40.5	9.4	35
World	..	..	..	..	5.0	5.8	4.3	22.2	12.2	3.7	30

Note: Data for industrial countries for this subject area are in table 32.

6 Narrowing South-North gaps

HDI rank	Life expectancy		Under-five mortality		Daily calorie supply		Adult literacy		Access to safe water	
	1960	1990	1960	1990	1965	1988-90	1970	1990	1975	1988-90
High human development	85	95	92	98	86	92	87	92	68	79
20 Barbados	93	100+	96	100+	..	..	..	..	98	99
24 Hong Kong	96	100+	98	100+	..	..	..	..	99	100+
27 Cyprus	99	100+	100+	100+	..	..	..	..	100+	100+
30 Uruguay	98	97	99	99	85	78	94	97	..	..
31 Trinidad and Tobago	92	96	98	100+	83	90	..	..	93	96
32 Bahamas	91	96	..	..	..	..	..	..	..	..
33 Korea, Rep. of	78	94	93	99	77	90	88	97	66	78
36 Chile	83	96	90	99	87	79	90	94	70	86
42 Costa Rica	89	100+	92	100+	84	92	88	94	72	94
43 Singapore	93	99	100+	100+	70	94	..	..	..	..
44 Brunei Darussalam	90	99	..	..	..	..	..	..	..	..
46 Argentina	94	95	97	98	96	99	94	96	..	..
50 Venezuela	86	94	93	98	76	78	76	89	79	89
51 Dominica	..	..	..	..	..	..	..	..	..	..
52 Kuwait	86	98	92	100+	..	..	54	74	..	..
53 Mexico	83	94	84	96	90	100+	74	88	62	78
55 Qatar	77	93	86	95	..	..	..	..	..	..
Medium human development	70	91	84	96	71	85	63	77	42	73
Excluding China	73	88	86	95	74	87	63	80	42	75
56 Mauritius	86	93	94	99	83	88	..	..	99	100+
57 Malaysia	78	94	94	99	81	89	60	79	..	..
58 Bahrain	80	95	84	100+	..	..	..	..	..	100+
59 Grenada	..	..	..	..	..	..	..	..	..	..
60 Antigua and Barbuda	..	..	..	..	..	..	..	..	..	..
61 Colombia	82	92	89	97	76	83	78	88	64	92
63 Seychelles	..	..	..	..	..	..	..	..	79	99
65 Suriname	87	93	95	98	..	..	..	..	88	84
67 United Arab Emirates	77	95	81	99	..	..	..	..	..	..
68 Panama	88	97	94	99	79	80	82	89	77	83
69 Jamaica	91	98	96	100+	81	86	97	99	86	72
70 Brazil	79	88	89	94	81	84	67	82	62	96
71 Fiji	85	87	95	99	..	..	..	..	..	..
72 Saint Lucia	..	..	..	..	..	..	..	..	..	..
73 Turkey	73	87	79	94	85	89	52	82	68	92
74 Thailand	76	89	90	98	77	77	80	94	25	72
75 Cuba	92	100+	96	100+	82	100+	87	95	..	..
76 Saint Vincent	..	..	..	..	..	..	..	..	..	..
79 Saint Kitts and Nevis	..	..	..	..	..	..	..	..	..	..
81 Syrian Arab Rep.	72	89	83	96	72	95	40	65	..	..
82 Belize	..	..	..	..	..	..	..	..	..	..
84 Saudi Arabia	64	87	75	93	64	88	9	63	64	95
85 South Africa	71	83	85	93	86	93	..	..	..	..
86 Sri Lanka	90	95	93	98	81	79	78	89	19	60
87 Libyan Arab Jamahiriya	68	83	78	91	67	100+	37	64	87	97
89 Ecuador	77	89	86	94	67	75	72	87	36	58
90 Paraguay	92	90	91	96	90	91	81	91	13	33
91 Korea, Dem. Rep. of	78	95	93	98	80	100+	..	..	..	..
92 Philippines	76	86	91	95	66	74	83	91	..	..
93 Tunisia	70	90	79	96	76	91	31	66	35	65
94 Oman	58	88	67	97	..	..	..	..	..	..
95 Peru	69	85	81	90	79	70	71	86	..	..
96 Iraq	70	87	82	93	72	94	34	60	66	93
97 Dominican Rep.	75	89	85	94	69	77	68	84	55	62
98 Samoa	..	..	..	..	..	..	..	..	95	82
99 Jordan	68	90	83	97	75	88	47	81	..	..
100 Mongolia	68	84	86	93	85	87	..	..	..	..
101 China	68	94	84	98	69	83	..	..	..	..
102 Lebanon	86	89	95	96	80	93	69	81	..	..
103 Iran, Islamic Rep. of	72	89	79	96	70	96	29	55	51	89
104 Botswana	66	80	87	93	71	74	41	74	..	..
105 Guyana	81	86	92	95	..	..	..	..	72	81
106 Vanuatu	..	..	..	..	..	..	..	..	55	71
107 Algeria	68	87	78	92	58	84	25	58	77	69
108 Indonesia	60	83	82	92	65	90	55	82	11	42
109 Gabon	59	71	76	85	65	76	33	61	..	..
110 El Salvador	73	86	84	93	65	78	58	74	53	41
111 Nicaragua	68	87	84	94	86	78	..	..	46	53

Index: North=100 (see note)

	Life expectancy		Under-five mortality		Daily calorie supply		Adult literacy		Access to safe water	
HDI rank	1960	1990	1960	1990	1965	1988-90	1970	1990	1975	1988-90
Low human development	**62**	**76**	**76**	**86**	**72**	**73**	**32**	**49**	**30**	**62**
Excluding India	60	73	77	86	72	72	29	51	28	50
112 Maldives	63	84	..	..		..	..	..	39	60
113 Guatemala	66	85	82	92	75	80	44	56	39	60
114 Cape Verde	75	90	88	96	..	..	..	..	40	74
115 Viet Nam	64	84	81	95	78	76	..	..	..	..
116 Honduras	67	87	81	93	70	72	53	74	41	52
117 Swaziland	58	76	82	85	..	..	..	..	43	30
118 Solomon Islands	73	93	..	..	..	..	..	..	27	61
119 Morocco	68	83	78	91	74	85	22	50	..	..
120 Lesotho	62	77	84	89	72	76	..	..	17	46
121 Zimbabwe	65	80	86	93	70	70	56	68	..	..
122 Bolivia	62	73	76	86	62	65	58	78	34	46
123 Myanmar	63	82	82	93	72	88	72	81	17	33
124 Egypt	67	81	74	93	78	95	35	49	75	86
125 São Tomé and Principe	..	..	..	..	..	..	..	..	..	..
126 Congo	60	72	80	91	81	84	35	57	38	20
127 Kenya	65	80	84	91	79	66	32	70	17	28
128 Madagascar	59	73	68	84	87	68	50	81	25	..
129 Papua New Guinea	59	74	80	94	58	72	32	53	20	33
130 Zambia	60	73	82	90	73	69	52	74	42	59
131 Ghana	65	74	82	88	70	71	31	61	35	56
132 Pakistan	62	78	77	86	61	69	21	35	25	50
133 Cameroon	57	72	77	87	72	70	33	55	..	..
134 India	64	79	76	88	72	70	34	49	31	75
135 Namibia	61	77	78	85	..	..	..	..	..	..
136 Côte d'Ivoire	57	72	78	88	82	76	18	54	..	..
137 Haiti	61	75	78	89	71	63	22	54	12	42
138 Tanzania, U. Rep. of	59	72	80	85	69	70	..	..	39	52
139 Comoros	62	74	77	87	..	..	..	..	..	..
140 Zaire	60	71	78	89	79	69	42	73	19	34
141 Lao People's Dem. Rep.	58	67	81	87	69	86	..	..	..	..
142 Nigeria	57	69	73	85	77	64	25	51	..	..
143 Yemen	53	69	..	..	..	71	9	39	..	..
144 Liberia	60	73	74	81	76	73	18	40	..	..
145 Togo	57	72	74	87	81	70	17	44	16	71
146 Uganda	62	70	82	85	77	61	41	49	35	15
147 Bangladesh	57	70	78	84	73	62	24	36	..	..
148 Cambodia	61	67	83	83	79	73	..	..	68	64
149 Rwanda	61	66	80	82	59	59	32	51	68	64
150 Senegal	54	65	75	83	84	63	12	39	36	53
151 Ethiopia	52	61	75	80	62	50	..	..	8	18
152 Nepal	55	70	75	83	70	70	13	26	8	37
153 Malawi	55	65	68	77	73	66	..	..	51	53
154 Burundi	60	65	79	83	83	70	20	51	29	38
155 Equatorial Guinea	53	63	73	81	..	..	..	..	..	..
156 Central African Rep.	56	66	74	85	73	65	16	38	..	..
157 Mozambique	54	64	71	72	69	53	22	33	..	..
158 Sudan	56	68	75	85	64	59	17	27	..	..
159 Bhutan	54	66	75	83	..	..	..	..	..	..
160 Angola	48	61	70	73	65	56	12	42	17	38
161 Mauritania	51	63	72	80	71	75	..	..	..	..
162 Benin	51	63	74	87	71	70	16	24	34	50
163 Djibouti	52	64	..	..	..	..	..	..	42	43
164 Guinea-Bissau	49	57	71	77	..	..	..	..	10	25
165 Chad	50	62	72	80	80	55	11	30	..	..
166 Somalia	52	62	75	80	74	54	3	24	38	56
167 Gambia	47	59	67	78	..	..	..	..	..	..
168 Mali	50	60	68	73	67	68	8	32	..	..
169 Niger	51	61	72	80	69	72	4	29	..	..
170 Burkina Faso	52	65	68	79	73	62	8	18	25	67
171 Afghanistan	48	57	66	73	73	70	8	30	9	21
172 Sierra Leone	46	56	71	76	64	59	13	21	14	43
173 Guinea	49	58	71	78	65	66	14	24	14	33
All developing countries	**67**	**84**	**80**	**90**	**72**	**80**	**41**	**66**	**36**	**68**
Least developed countries	57	68	75	83	71	67	29	45	21	47
Sub-Saharan Africa	58	75	84	70	74	70	28	47	25	41
Industrial countries	100	100	100	100	100	100	100	100	100	100
World	..	..	..	..	..	..	..	..	..	..

Note: All figures are expressed in relation to the North average, which is indexed to equal 100. The smaller the figure the bigger the gap, the closer the figure is to 100 the smaller the gap, and a figure above 100 indicates that the country is better than the North average.

7 Widening South-North gaps

	Real GDP per capita		Mean years of schooling		Overall enrolment		Fertility		Telephones	
HDI rank	1960	1990	1980	1990	1980	1987-90	1965	1991	1980	1986-88
High human development	**50**	**44**	**59**	**66**	**62**	**66**	**63**	**68**	**48**	**27**
20 Barbados	37	58	69	89	58	47	..	..	97	88
24 Hong Kong	37	100+	68	70	42	35	67	100+	46	100+
27 Cyprus	36	69	76	74	16	41	..	..	44	94
30 Uruguay	70	41	67	78	65	100+	100+	80	92	35
31 Trinidad and Tobago	..	..	67	80	17	16	70	67	..	..
32 Bahamas	..	..	68	62	..	..	..	..	99	100+
33 Korea, Rep. of	15	47	73	88	59	100+	61	100+	33	64
36 Chile	62	35	68	75	50	48	62	71	38	15
42 Costa Rica	35	31	62	57	84	69	48	61	19	31
43 Singapore	33	100+	38	39	..	..	64	100+	63	98
44 Brunei Darussalam	..	..	55	50	..	..	..	..	30	39
46 Argentina	66	30	66	87	86	100+	97	66	98	25
50 Venezuela	100	43	58	63	83	75	49	52	93	20
51 Dominica	..	..	52	47	..	..	..	..	18	18
52 Kuwait	..	..	49	54	46	48	41	52	37	41
53 Mexico	46	41	44	47	53	39	45	57	28	21
55 Qatar	..	..	49	56	41	65	..	..	58	75
Medium human development	**19**	**18**	**49**	**48**	**15**	**13**	**48**	**66**	**10**	**5**
Excluding China	**24**	**25**	**42**	**48**	**33**	**31**	**54**	**53**	**21**	**9**
56 Mauritius	21	40	41	41	4	5	62	98	35	15
57 Malaysia	23	43	44	53	16	19	48	51	14	21
58 Bahrain	..	..	22	39	21	47	..	..	66	61
59 Grenada	..	..	52	47	..	..	..	..	42	14
60 Antigua and Barbuda	..	..	51	46	..	..	..	..	..	..
61 Colombia	29	29	57	71	38	37	46	63	27	17
63 Seychelles	..	..	51	46	..	..	..	..	34	45
65 Suriname	33	27	44	42	26	25	..	..	64	22
67 United Arab Emirates	..	..	34	51	12	29	44	42	23	53
68 Panama	27	23	65	67	82	59	53	63	36	22
69 Jamaica	31	21	56	53	23	13	53	76	..	..
70 Brazil	21	33	36	39	44	31	54	57	32	21
71 Fiji	38	31	54	51	9	11	..	..	75	19
72 Saint Lucia	..	..	43	39	..	..	..	..	..	..
73 Turkey	27	32	31	35	22	37	53	55	26	25
74 Thailand	15	28	38	38	51	44	48	79	20	4
75 Cuba	..	..	63	76	66	56	..	..	41	11
76 Saint Vincent	..	..	51	46	..	..	..	..	62	18
79 Saint Kitts and Nevis	..	..	66	60	..	..	..	..	..	..
81 Syrian Arab Rep.	26	33	33	42	62	54	39	29	49	12
82 Belize	..	..	51	46	..	..	..	..	..	..
84 Saudi Arabia	77	76	30	37	29	35	41	27	32	34
85 South Africa	56	34	41	39	..	..	49	44	23	31
86 Sri Lanka	21	17	60	69	11	11	61	74	13	2
87 Libyan Arab Jamahiriya	..	..	30	34	30	27	41	28	..	..
89 Ecuador	24	21	59	56	..	..	44	47	..	..
90 Paraguay	21	19	51	49	33	22	45	43	17	6
91 Korea, Dem. Rep. of	..	..	66	60	..	..	..	..	..	..
92 Philippines	19	16	73	74	..	..	44	46	10	4
93 Tunisia	18	25	20	21	20	23	43	51	20	9
94 Oman	43	69	6	9	..	..	42	27	4	11
95 Peru	37	18	63	64	69	96	45	50	34	7
96 Iraq	..	..	44	48	35	37	42	31	..	..
97 Dominican Rep.	20	17	47	43	..	..	43	54	..	..
98 Samoa	..	..	55	57	..	..	..	..	..	..
99 Jordan	24	16	55	50	..	..	38	33	..	..
100 Mongolia	..	..	66	74	51	59	51	39	..	..
101 China	15	14	53	48	5	5	47	81	4	2
102 Lebanon	..	..	48	44	..	..	48	53	..	..
103 Iran, Islamic Rep. of	39	23	38	39	..	..	42	38	16	9
104 Botswana	10	24	22	24	5	8	43	28	8	5
105 Guyana	30	10	55	51	10	14	..	..	..	..
106 Vanuatu	..	..	41	37	..	..	..	..	31	5
107 Algeria	28	21	14	26	24	28	41	37	47	9
108 Indonesia	10	15	34	39	14	23	55	58	5	1
109 Gabon	17	29	27	26	12	11	73	37	..	..
110 El Salvador	23	14	37	41	16	46	45	41	42	6
111 Nicaragua	34	10	38	43	52	23	42	36	..	..

Index: North=100 (see note)

HDI rank	Real GDP per capita		Mean years of schooling		Overall enrolment		Fertility		Telephones	
Index: North=100 (see note)	1960	1990	1980	1990	1980	1987-90	1965	1990	1980	1986-88
Low human development	11	8	23	22	23	15	47	38	8	2
Excluding India	11	8	22	21	13	11	45	33	14	3
112 Maldives	..	..	49	45	..	..	..	..	..	..
113 Guatemala	27	18	44	41	32	23	45	34	..	..
114 Cape Verde	..	..	22	22	..	..	..	..	5	2
115 Viet Nam	..	..	35	46	..	..	..	..	15	20
116 Honduras	16	10	33	39	30	25	41	36	11	3
117 Swaziland	9	17	33	37	14	11	..	..	19	6
118 Solomon Islands	..	..	11	10	..	..	..	..	16	3
119 Morocco	11	16	20	28	24	28	42	42	16	3
120 Lesotho	5	12	30	34	6	11	52	33	1	3
121 Zimbabwe	13	10	22	29	5	12	38	34	7	7
122 Bolivia	19	11	44	40	47	62	45	32	..	..
123 Myanmar	7	5	27	25	18	15	52	49	..	..
124 Egypt	11	14	19	28	69	52	44	45	35	6
125 São Tomé and Principe	..	..	25	23	..	..	..	..	21	5
126 Congo	12	16	22	21	22	15	53	30	..	..
127 Kenya	10	7	22	23	4	4	38	28	6	3
128 Madagascar	14	5	22	22	11	10	45	29	21	1
129 Papua New Guinea	21	12	10	9	7	5	48	38	9	4
130 Zambia	16	5	29	27	6	5	45	26	5	3
131 Ghana	11	7	36	35	6	4	44	30	21	1
132 Pakistan	12	13	19	19	10	8	43	31	12	2
133 Cameroon	11	11	15	16	6	9	58	28	7	1
134 India	11	7	24	24	..	..	48	45	5	1
135 Namibia	..	..	19	17	..	..	49	32	..	..
136 Côte d'Ivoire	16	9	19	19	..	..	41	26	..	..
137 Haiti	13	6	16	17	4	3	49	39	..	..
138 Tanzania, U. Rep. of	4	4	22	20	1	1	45	27	..	..
139 Comoros	..	..	11	10	..	..	..	..	..	..
140 Zaire	7	3	16	16	4	6	50	31	8	(.)
141 Lao People's Dem. Rep.	..	..	27	29	2	4	49	28	..	..
142 Nigeria	12	8	11	12	8	9	43	28	..	..
143 Yemen	..	..	8	8	8	8	43	25	..	..
144 Liberia	10	6	18	20	10	7	47	28	..	..
145 Togo	9	5	16	16	8	7	46	29	..	..
146 Uganda	7	4	11	11	2	3	43	26	5	1
147 Bangladesh	9	6	22	20	11	9	44	36	..	..
148 Cambodia	..	..	22	20	..	..	48	42	..	..
149 Rwanda	5	5	11	11	1	2	40	23	2	(.)
150 Senegal	16	9	8	8	11	8	47	30	4	..
151 Ethiopia	6	3	11	11	2	2	52	28	4	1
152 Nepal	10	6	20	21	11	17	50	33	..	..
153 Malawi	5	4	19	17	2	2	38	25	6	1
154 Burundi	9	4	3	3	2	2	47	28	..	..
155 Equatorial Guinea	..	..	9	8	..	..	..	..	..	..
156 Central African Rep.	13	5	11	11	4	4	67	31	6	1
157 Mozambique	17	7	18	16	(.)	1	44	30	3	1
158 Sudan	14	7	8	8	7	8	45	30	23	1
159 Bhutan	..	..	2	2	..	..	51	34	..	..
160 Angola	19	6	16	15	1	2	47	30	..	..
161 Mauritania	9	7	3	3	..	..	46	29	..	..
162 Benin	13	7	7	7	6	8	44	27	..	..
163 Djibouti	..	..	3	3	..	..	..	..	12	5
164 Guinea-Bissau	..	..	3	3	..	..	..	..	..	..
165 Chad	11	4	2	2	..	..	50	33	..	..
166 Somalia	10	6	2	2	..	..	45	29	..	..
167 Gambia	9	6	5	6	..	..	..	..	..	..
168 Mali	9	4	3	3	3	2	46	27	..	..
169 Niger	6	4	1	1	1	2	42	27	4	(.)
170 Burkina Faso	6	4	1	1	1	2	47	29	4	(.)
171 Afghanistan	14	5	9	8	6	5	42	28	..	..
172 Sierra Leone	6	8	9	9	2	4	47	29	..	..
173 Guinea	9	3	9	8	15	4	51	27	..	..
All developing countries	17	15	38	37	20	18	50	49	12	5
Least developed countries	9	5	17	16	8	7	47	31	7	1
Sub-Saharan Africa	14	8	17	16	6	5	46	29	10	3
Industrial countries	100	100	100	100	100	100	100	100	100	100
World	..	..	..	..	..	..	..	..	..	..

Note: All figures are expressed in relation to the North average, which is indexed to equal 100. The smaller the figure the bigger the gap, the closer the figure is to 100 the smaller the gap, and a figure above 100 indicates that the country is better than the North average.

HDI rank		Life expectancy at birth (years) 1990	Maternal mortality rate (per 100,000 live births) 1988	Average age at first marriage (years) 1980-85	Literacy rate (age 15-24 only) 1980-89	Enrolment ratio			Tertiary science and engineering enrolment (% female) 1987-88	Administrative and managerial staff (% female) 1980-89	Women in labour force (% of total) 1990	Parliament (% of seats occupied by women) 1991
						Primary (net) 1988-90	Secondary (gross) 1988-90	Tertiary (gross) 1988-90				
High human development		73.8	120	22.0	93	..	65	23	..	13	29	8
20	Barbados	77.4	35	..	..	96	83	21	..	31	48	4
24	Hong Kong	80.1	6	25.3	..	..	75	9	..	12	36	..
27	Cyprus	78.6	10	24.4	..	..	91	16	24	7	37	5
30	Uruguay	75.5	50	22.4	99	..	..	54	32	25	31	6
31	Trinidad and Tobago	74.1	120	22.3	99	90	82	5	28	..	27	17
32	Bahamas	..	..	..	..	..	..	..	..	..	47	4
33	Korea, Rep. of	73.1	80	24.1	..	100	86	28	13	3	34	2
36	Chile	75.3	67	23.6	97	..	77	16	25	18	31	6
42	Costa Rica	77.3	36	22.7	98	87	43	..	..	22	29	12
43	Singapore	76.9	14	26.2	96	100	71	..	..	22	39	5
44	Brunei Darussalam	..	..	..	93	..	..	..	..	6	..	..
46	Argentina	74.4	140	22.9	97	..	78	44	35	..	21	5
50	Venezuela	73.2	130	21.2	94	62	41	27	..	15	22	10
51	Dominica	..	..	..	..	..	..	..	(.)	24	42	17
52	Kuwait	76.0	30	22.9	76	84	..	20	43	4	14	..
53	Mexico	73.0	150	20.6	91	..	53	12	..	15	31	12
55	Qatar	72.6	140	..	..	..	94	43	34	..	7	..
Medium human development		69.8	170	22.0	82	98	44	4	..	11	39	16
Excluding China		67.5	220	21.0	81	..	50	10	23	13	33	8
56	Mauritius	72.2	130	21.7	..	94	53	1	24	15	35	7
57	Malaysia	72.3	120	23.5	83	..	58	7	29	8	31	5
58	Bahrain	73.5	80	..	82	92	..	21	32	4	10	..
59	Grenada	..	..	..	..	..	..	..	..	..	49	..
60	Antigua and Barbuda	..	..	..	..	..	..	..	(.)	..	..	..
61	Colombia	71.7	150	20.4	..	..	57	14	28	21	41	..
63	Seychelles	..	..	..	..	..	..	..	(.)	12	42	16
65	Suriname	72.1	120	..	..	100	57	10	16	..	..	..
67	United Arab Emirates	73.5	130	18.0	56	100	72	21	54	1	6	(.)
68	Panama	74.5	60	21.2	93	92	62	26	39	22	27	8
69	Jamaica	75.3	120	25.2	..	96	63	4	48	..	31	5
70	Brazil	68.4	230	22.6	85	..	..	12	..	..	35	6
71	Fiji	67.1	150	21.6	91	98	53	3	27	9	19	..
72	Saint Lucia	..	..	..	..	..	..	..	6	19	..	(.)
73	Turkey	67.0	200	20.6	75	..	42	10	26	3	33	1
74	Thailand	68.1	180	22.7	96	..	32	..	..	21	47	4
75	Cuba	77.3	54	19.9	99	95	94	25	39	..	32	34
76	Saint Vincent	..	..	..	..	..	..	..	17	20	..	..
79	Saint Kitts and Nevis	..	..	..	..	..	..	..	1	14	..	7
81	Syrian Arab Rep.	68.1	200	22.1	..	93	43	17	24	33	15	8
82	Belize	..	..	..	..	..	..	..	(.)	12	33	(.)
84	Saudi Arabia	66.5	220	..	..	56	41	11	31	..	7	..
85	South Africa	64.7	250	..	..	..	..	..	..	17	33	..
86	Sri Lanka	73.1	180	24.4	90	..	77	4	20	7	37	5
87	Libyan Arab Jamahiriya	63.7	200	..	..	..	..	..	..	..	9	..
89	Ecuador	68.2	200	22.1	93	..	57	23	15	15	30	6
90	Paraguay	69.3	200	22.1	94	94	31	8	39	..	41	6
91	Korea, Dem. Rep. of	73.3	130	..	..	..	..	..	..	..	46	20
92	Philippines	66.2	250	22.4	92	98	75	..	..	25	37	9
93	Tunisia	67.5	200	24.3	63	91	40	7	24	..	13	4
94	Oman	67.8	220	..	..	82	48	5	..	..	8	..
95	Peru	65.0	300	22.7	90	..	..	..	..	8	33	6
96	Iraq	66.1	250	20.8	..	78	37	11	28	..	6	11
97	Dominican Rep.	68.9	200	20.5	..	73	..	..	..	21	15	..
98	Samoa	..	..	..	..	..	..	..	..	19	..	..
99	Jordan	68.8	200	22.6	77	..	..	..	31	14	10	(.)
100	Mongolia	63.8	250	..	..	..	96	26	45	..	45	2
101	China	71.8	130	22.4	82	..	41	1	..	11	43	21
102	Lebanon	68.0	200	..	..	..	..	..	..	..	27	(.)
103	Iran, Islamic Rep. of	66.6	250	19.7	42	90	45	4	10	..	18	2
104	Botswana	62.8	300	26.4	..	93	47	3	..	36	35	5
105	Guyana	67.1	200	20.7	..	..	58	4	15	13	21	37
106	Vanuatu	..	..	..	68	..	..	..	..	..	46	4
107	Algeria	66.1	210	21.0	60	83	53	6	16	..	4	2
108	Indonesia	63.3	300	20.0	82	96	41	..	21	7	40	12
109	Gabon	54.2	600	..	..	..	..	3	..	..	38	..
110	El Salvador	67.7	200	..	71	71	26	14	12	16	45	8
111	Nicaragua	66.2	200	..	..	77	44	9	48	..	34	16

HDI rank	Life expectancy at birth (years) 1990	Maternal mortality rate (per 100,000 live births) 1988	Average age at first marriage (years) 1980-85	Literacy rate (age 15-24 only) 1980-89	Enrolment ratio Primary (net) 1988-90	Enrolment ratio Secondary (gross) 1988-90	Enrolment ratio Tertiary (gross) 1988-90	Tertiary science and engineering enrolment (% female) 1987-88	Administrative and managerial staff (% female) 1980-89	Women in labour force (% of total) 1990	Parliament (% of seats occupied by women) 1991
Low human development	57.3	590	19.0	41	..	26	4	20	3	26	7
Excluding India	55.6	610	19.0	42	..	20	3	16	..	27	7
112 Maldives	..	..	..	87	..	..	..	..	10	20	4
113 Guatemala	65.9	250	20.5	..	..	..	..	..	16	26	..
114 Cape Verde	67.9	200	..	..	93	20	(.)	..	..	29	6
115 Viet Nam	64.8	400	..	94	..	40	..	..	..	47	18
116 Honduras	67.0	220	..	94	94	..	7	..	..	18	12
117 Swaziland	58.6	400	..	75	84	49	3	..	..	40	..
118 Solomon Islands	..	..	..	..	..	..	..	..	..	..	(.)
119 Morocco	63.7	270	21.3	..	45	30	8	25	..	20	(.)
120 Lesotho	61.8	350	19.6	..	76	31	6	20	..	44	..
121 Zimbabwe	61.4	330	20.4	..	..	46	2	..	15	35	12
122 Bolivia	56.9	600	22.1	76	75	31	..	..	..	24	7
123 Myanmar	63.0	600	22.4	81	..	23	..	..	..	37	..
124 Egypt	61.5	300	21.3	38	..	69	13	26	14	11	2
125 São Tomé and Principe	..	..	..	74	..	..	..	..	9	..	11
126 Congo	56.3	900	..	..	..	..	2	8	..	39	..
127 Kenya	61.7	400	20.4	..	..	19	1	14	..	40	1
128 Madagascar	56.0	600	20.3	..	63	18	3	30	..	40	7
129 Papua New Guinea	55.7	700	..	..	67	10	..	8	..	39	(.)
130 Zambia	55.5	600	19.4	..	79	14	1	5	11	29	5
131 Ghana	56.8	700	19.3	..	..	31	1	9	9	40	..
132 Pakistan	57.8	600	19.8	25	..	13	2	..	..	11	1
133 Cameroon	55.3	550	17.5	59	69	21	..	..	6	30	14
134 India	59.3	550	18.7	40	..	33	4	22	2	26	7
135 Namibia	58.8	400	..	..	..	38	..	..	..	24	7
136 Côte d'Ivoire	55.2	680	17.8	..	..	12	..	..	..	34	5
137 Haiti	57.4	600	23.8	51	44	19	1	12	33	40	..
138 Tanzania, U. Rep. of	55.7	600	..	54	48	4	..	8	..	48	11
139 Comoros	55.5	500	19.5	55	50	15	(.)	10	..	41	(.)
140 Zaire	54.7	700	20.1	..	53	16	..	..	..	36	5
141 Lao People's Dem. Rep.	51.3	750	..	..	..	21	1	17	..	45	9
142 Nigeria	53.3	750	18.7	..	..	17	2	..	..	20	..
143 Yemen	52.0	800	17.8	..	..	10	..	..	..	13	3
144 Liberia	55.5	600	..	..	..	..	1	10	..	31	..
145 Togo	55.8	600	..	36	58	10	1	3	8	37	4
146 Uganda	53.7	700	..	..	50	..	1	11	..	41	12
147 Bangladesh	51.5	650	16.7	27	61	11	1	16	2	7	10
148 Cambodia	51.2	800	..	..	..	..	..	4	..	39	..
149 Rwanda	51.2	700	21.2	45	65	6	(.)	10	..	48	17
150 Senegal	49.3	750	17.7	..	41	11	1	11	..	26	13
151 Ethiopia	47.1	900	..	..	24	12	(.)	11	..	42	..
152 Nepal	51.6	850	17.9	15	43	17	..	..	..	34	3
153 Malawi	48.7	500	17.8	..	52	3	(.)	16	..	42	10
154 Burundi	50.2	800	20.8	..	46	4	(.)	13	..	..	..
155 Equatorial Guinea	48.6	800	..	..	..	..	..	8	..	36	..
156 Central African Rep.	52.0	650	..	18	43	6	1	..	..	46	4
157 Mozambique	49.2	800	17.6	25	37	4	(.)	17	..	48	16
158 Sudan	52.0	700	21.3	..	..	17	2	27	..	29	(.)
159 Bhutan	48.2	800	..	..	..	2	..	..	..	32	(.)
160 Angola	47.1	900	..	..	..	..	0	..	..	39	15
161 Mauritania	48.7	800	19.2	..	..	10	1	15	..	22	..
162 Benin	48.7	800	18.2	18	36	6	1	10	..	24	6
163 Djibouti	49.7	740	..	..	33	12	(.)	..	..	..	(.)
164 Guinea-Bissau	44.1	1,000	..	18	32	4	(.)	8	..	42	..
165 Chad	48.1	800	..	..	23	3	..	..	..	17	..
166 Somalia	47.6	900	20.1	..	8	7	1	10	..	39	..
167 Gambia	45.6	1,000	..	..	45	10	(.)	..	15	41	8
168 Mali	46.6	850	18.1	14	14	4	(.)	9	..	16	..
169 Niger	47.1	850	..	..	19	4	(.)	6	..	47	5
170 Burkina Faso	49.9	750	17.4	7	23	5	(.)	10	..	49	..
171 Afghanistan	43.0	1,000	17.8	11	13	5	1	..	..	8	3
172 Sierra Leone	43.6	1,000	..	..	..	12	1	..	..	33	..
173 Guinea	44.0	1,000	..	..	17	5	(.)	10	..	30	..
All developing countries	64.2	420	20.7	65	86	36	5	20	8	33	12
Least developed countries	52.0	740	18.9	36	45	12	1	14	..	29	9
Sub-Saharan Africa	53.6	690	19.1	37	42	14	2	12	..	34	..
Industrial countries	77.9	26	23.5	99	..	..	..	22	24	42	9
World	67.3	370	21.2	69	..	..	..	21	12	34	11

Note: Data for industrial countries for this subject area are in table 33.

	Females as a percentage of males (see note)									
	Life expectancy	Population	Literacy		Mean years of schooling	Primary enrolment		Secondary enrolment	Tertiary enrolment	Labour force
HDI rank	1990	1990	1970	1990	1990	1960	1988-90	1988-90	1988-90	1990
High human development	110	100	90	98	86	95	100	99	80	42
20 Barbados	107	109	..	..	93	..	98	92	..	92
24 Hong Kong	107	94	71	..	63	85	99	106	56	57
27 Cyprus	107	101	..	..	86	..	100	102	114	60
30 Uruguay	109	103	100	99	110	100	98	..	114	45
31 Trinidad and Tobago	107	101	94	..	101	98	100	104	68	38
32 Bahamas	..	106	..	..	94	..	..	..	..	90
33 Korea, Rep. of	109	100	86	94	61	90	100	97	53	51
36 Chile	110	102	98	100	92	96	92	108	82	45
42 Costa Rica	106	98	99	101	97	98	100	105	68	40
43 Singapore	108	97	60	..	66	93	100	104	..	64
44 Brunei Darussalam	..	94	..	..	83	..	..	..	..	..
46 Argentina	110	102	98	100	105	101	107	113	117	27
50 Venezuela	109	98	90	103	97	100	103	..	91	27
51 Dominica	..	..	..	..	91	..	..	..	..	72
52 Kuwait	106	76	65	87	79	78	98	94	129	16
53 Mexico	110	100	88	94	96	94	97	102	76	46
55 Qatar	107	60	..	..	93	..	98	112	..	8
Medium human development	105	96	59	80	65	83	99	82	57	66
Excluding China	105	99	..	87	75	..	95	88	75	54
56 Mauritius	108	102	77	..	68	90	102	100	52	54
57 Malaysia	106	98	68	81	91	77	100	105	95	45
58 Bahrain	106	73	..	84	67	..	98	101	..	11
59 Grenada	..	..	..	..	93	..	..	..	..	94
60 Antigua and Barbuda	..	..	..	..	80	..	..	..	..	..
61 Colombia	109	99	96	98	106	100	103	119	108	69
63 Seychelles	..	101	..	..	92	..	99	100	..	74
65 Suriname	107	102	..	100	92	..	100	119	113	41
67 United Arab Emirates	106	48	29	..	101	..	100	114	..	7
68 Panama	106	97	100	100	106	96	106	109	..	37
69 Jamaica	106	101	101	100	97	101	98	111	75	45
70 Brazil	109	101	91	97	94	96	..	90	100	54
71 Fiji	107	99	..	..	83	..	101	104	57	23
72 Saint Lucia	..	106	..	..	96	..	..	..	..	..
73 Turkey	105	95	49	79	50	64	93	64	55	49
74 Thailand	106	99	84	96	76	90	..	97	..	88
75 Cuba	105	97	101	98	103	100	99	112	..	46
76 Saint Vincent	..	..	..	..	95	..	..	..	..	..
79 Saint Kitts and Nevis	..	..	..	..	97	..	..	..	..	..
81 Syrian Arab Rep.	106	98	33	..	60	44	93	72	72	18
82 Belize	..	..	..	..	93	..	98	..	..	49
84 Saudi Arabia	106	84	13	66	26	..	81	75	73	8
85 South Africa	110	101	..	..	90	90	..	..	..	50
86 Sri Lanka	106	99	81	89	80	90	100	107	71	59
87 Libyan Arab Jamahiriya	106	91	22	67	23	26	90	..	..	10
89 Ecuador	107	99	91	95	92	91	98	104	68	43
90 Paraguay	107	97	88	96	88	86	99	107	88	70
91 Korea, Dem. Rep. of	110	101	..	..	63	..	..	100	..	85
92 Philippines	106	99	96	99	89	95	98	104	..	59
93 Tunisia	103	98	39	76	41	49	91	80	67	15
94 Oman	106	91	..	..	22	..	94	81	80	9
95 Peru	106	99	74	86	80	75	96	..	24	49
96 Iraq	103	96	36	71	69	38	87	64	64	6
97 Dominican Rep.	107	97	94	96	87	99	100	..	..	17
98 Samoa	..	..	..	..	78	..	..	..	..	..
99 Jordan	106	95	45	79	66	63	..	..	..	11
100 Mongolia	104	99	85	..	95	99	103	110	..	83
101 China	105	94	..	73	60	..	100	77	50	76
102 Lebanon	106	106	73	83	66	94	92	71	44	37
103 Iran, Islamic Rep. of	101	97	43	67	68	48	91	73	45	21
104 Botswana	111	109	..	78	97	..	106	..	76	55
105 Guyana	109	99	..	98	91	..	100	105	76	27
106 Vanuatu	..	92	..	..	71	..	..	..	..	86
107 Algeria	103	100	28	65	18	67	88	80	44	5
108 Indonesia	106	101	64	85	58	67	96	84	..	66
109 Gabon	107	103	51	66	33	..	..	..	41	61
110 El Salvador	111	104	87	92	98	..	103	100	73	81
111 Nicaragua	104	100	98	..	110	102	104	..	121	51

			Females as a percentage of males (see note)							
	Life expectancy	Population	Literacy		Mean years of schooling	Primary enrolment		Secondary enrolment	Tertiary enrolment	Labour force
HDI rank	1990	1990	1970	1990	1990	1960	1988-90	1988-90	1988-90	1990
Low human development	103	97	44	59	39	50	99	62	41	39
Excluding India	105	100	45	65	43	50	81	63	35	42
112 Maldives	..	..	..	..	77	..	..	..	..	25
113 Guatemala	108	98	73	75	86	78	85	68	..	34
114 Cape Verde	103	112	..	..	39	..	95	100	..	41
115 Viet Nam	107	104	..	91	59	..	94	93	28	88
116 Honduras	107	98	91	94	93	99	106	..	65	22
117 Swaziland	107	103	..	..	82	..	105	96	68	67
118 Solomon Islands	..	..	..	..	70	..	..	..	..	..
119 Morocco	106	100	29	62	36	40	68	70	59	26
120 Lesotho	117	108	..	..	..	..	119	..	..	78
121 Zimbabwe	106	102	75	82	40	..	100	85	36	54
122 Bolivia	109	103	68	83	60	64	90	84	..	31
123 Myanmar	106	101	67	81	72	85	98	92	..	60
124 Egypt	104	97	40	54	42	65	79	75	53	12
125 São Tomé and Principe	..	..	..	..	39	..	..	..	..	..
126 Congo	110	103	38	63	35	51	..	..	20	64
127 Kenya	107	100	43	..	42	47	96	70	45	67
128 Madagascar	106	102	77	83	65	78	98	90	82	66
129 Papua New Guinea	103	93	62	58	50	12	85	63	38	64
130 Zambia	104	103	56	81	45	67	98	56	37	40
131 Ghana	107	101	42	73	46	48	81	65	26	67
132 Pakistan	100	92	37	45	25	28	55	45	41	13
133 Cameroon	106	103	40	64	33	49	86	68	..	42
134 India	101	93	43	55	34	50	97	61	47	34
135 Namibia	104	101	..	..	..	..	..	..	..	31
136 Côte d'Ivoire	107	97	38	60	31	35	..	44	27	52
137 Haiti	106	104	65	80	63	84	100	95	35	67
138 Tanzania, U. Rep. of	107	102	38	..	45	55	104	80	33	93
139 Comoros	102	102	..	..	65	..	83	75	..	69
140 Zaire	107	102	36	73	33	36	79	50	..	56
141 Lao People's Dem. Rep.	106	99	76	..	59	47	80	68	50	81
142 Nigeria	107	102	40	63	26	59	93	77	38	25
143 Yemen	101	108	15	50	18	..	..	20	..	15
144 Liberia	105	98	30	58	26	40	..	55	31	44
145 Togo	107	102	26	54	31	38	68	30	15	58
146 Uganda	107	102	58	56	41	..	88	44	36	71
147 Bangladesh	99	94	33	47	30	39	88	50	22	7
148 Cambodia	106	101	..	46	71	..	..	..	..	64
149 Rwanda	107	102	49	58	31	..	100	67	20	92
150 Senegal	104	102	28	48	29	..	75	52	26	35
151 Ethiopia	107	102	..	..	43	27	75	71	23	71
152 Nepal	98	95	13	35	32	5	51	40	..	51
153 Malawi	103	103	43	..	46	..	95	50	27	72
154 Burundi	107	104	34	65	33	33	84	67	33	..
155 Equatorial Guinea	107	103	..	..	20	..	..	..	..	56
156 Central African Rep.	111	106	23	48	32	23	65	35	20	86
157 Mozambique	107	103	48	47	54	60	82	44	33	92
158 Sudan	105	99	21	27	45	40	71	74	68	41
159 Bhutan	97	93	..	..	32	..	65	29	..	48
160 Angola	107	103	44	51	52	..	82	..	15	64
161 Mauritania	107	102	..	45	29	23	70	45	14	28
162 Benin	107	103	35	49	29	39	52	38	15	31
163 Djibouti	107	98	..	..	33	..	73	67	..	..
164 Guinea-Bissau	108	105	..	48	27	..	55	44	..	72
165 Chad	107	103	10	42	31	14	44	25	11	21
166 Somalia	107	110	20	39	31	..	57	58	22	64
167 Gambia	108	103	..	41	23	..	73	45	..	69
168 Mali	107	106	36	59	27	43	58	44	14	20
169 Niger	107	102	33	82	40	43	61	44	17	89
170 Burkina Faso	107	102	23	32	54	42	64	56	27	96
171 Afghanistan	102	94	15	32	12	13	52	45	18	9
172 Sierra Leone	108	104	44	37	26	..	75	57	20	49
173 Guinea	102	102	33	38	20	36	50	36	12	43
All developing countries	104	96	54	72	58	61	94	74	51	52
Least developed countries	104	100	38	58	43	44	81	58	28	48
Sub-Saharan Africa	107	102	42	64	46	52	85	64	32	55
Industrial countries	110	106	..	..	99	..	..	..	..	77
World	106	99	..	..	72	..	..	..	..	56

Note: All figures are expressed in relation to the male average, which is indexed to equal 100. The smaller the figure the bigger the gap, the closer the figure to 100 the smaller the gap, and a figure above 100 indicates that the female average is higher than the male. Data for industrial countries for this subject area are in table 34.

	Rural population (as % of total) 1991	Population with access to services (%)						Rural-urban disparity (100=rural-urban parity: see note)			
		Health		Water		Sanitation		Health	Water	Sanitation	Child nutrition
HDI rank		Urban 1987-90	Rural 1987-90	Urban 1988-90	Rural 1988-90	Urban 1988-90	Rural 1988-90	1987-90	1988-90	1988-90	1980-90
High human development	25	100	..	88	48	..	..	..	55	..	..
20 Barbados	55	100	100	100	99	100	100	100	99	100	..
24 Hong Kong	6	..	..	..	..	..	..	..	..	..	..
27 Cyprus	47	95	95	100	100	100	100	100	100	100	..
30 Uruguay	14	..	..	95	27	..	..	..	28	..	..
31 Trinidad and Tobago	31	..	..	100	87	100	97	..	87	97	97
32 Bahamas	..	100	100	..	..	..	..	100	..	..	..
33 Korea, Rep. of	28	100	100	91	49	99	100	100	54	101	..
36 Chile	14	..	..	100	21	100	6	..	21	6	..
42 Costa Rica	53	..	..	100	84	100	93	..	84	93	..
43 Singapore	(.)	100	100	100	100	..	..	100	100	..	..
44 Brunei Darussalam	..	..	..	..	..	..	..	..	..	..	..
46 Argentina	14	..	..	..	..	100	29	..	..	29	..
50 Venezuela	9	..	..	89	89	97	70	..	99	72	..
51 Dominica	59	100	100	..	..	77	36	100	..	47	..
52 Kuwait	4	100	100	100	100	98	100	100	100	102	..
53 Mexico	27	..	..	89	49	100	12	..	55	12	..
55 Qatar	11	100	100	100	48	100	85	100	48	85	..
Medium human development	58	..	81	90	59	90	72	..	66	80	..
Excluding China	42	..	..	92	56	81	52	..	61	73	..
56 Mauritius	59	100	100	100	100	100	96	100	100	96	92
57 Malaysia	57	..	..	96	66	94	94	..	69	100	..
58 Bahrain	17	100	100	100	100	100	100	100	100	100	..
59 Grenada	..	..	..	..	..	..	..	..	..	..	..
60 Antigua and Barbuda	69	100	100	..	..	100	100	100	..	100	..
61 Colombia	30	..	..	100	76	96	13	..	76	14	95
63 Seychelles	..	..	..	100	98	..	..	..	98	..	..
65 Suriname	53	100	100	82	94	64	36	100	114	56	..
67 United Arab Emirates	22	..	..	100	100	100	77	..	100	77	..
68 Panama	47	..	..	100	66	100	68	..	66	68	..
69 Jamaica	48	..	..	95	46	92	90	..	48	98	98
70 Brazil	25	..	..	100	86	89	48	..	86	54	94
71 Fiji	61	..	..	96	69	91	65	..	72	71	..
72 Saint Lucia	..	100	100	..	..	..	..	100	..	..	..
73 Turkey	39	..	..	..	..	..	..	..	..	..	..
74 Thailand	77	..	..	..	..	84	86	..	..	102	81
75 Cuba	25	100	100	..	..	..	..	100	..	..	..
76 Saint Vincent	73	..	..	..	..	78	78	..	..	100	..
79 Saint Kitts and Nevis	59	100	100	100	100	..	..	100	100	..	..
81 Syrian Arab Rep.	50	100	99	91	68	72	55	99	75	76	..
82 Belize	50	100	90	100	38	67	28	90	38	42	..
84 Saudi Arabia	23	100	78	100	74	100	30	78	74	30	..
85 South Africa	..	..	..	..	..	..	..	..	..	..	..
86 Sri Lanka	79	..	..	80	55	68	45	..	69	66	85
87 Libyan Arab Jamahiriya	30	100	100	100	80	100	85	100	80	85	..
89 Ecuador	44	..	..	75	37	75	34	..	49	46	..
90 Paraguay	52	..	..	..	..	55	60	..	..	110	..
91 Korea, Dem. Rep. of	40	..	..	..	..	..	..	..	..	..	..
92 Philippines	57	..	..	93	72	79	63	..	78	80	..
93 Tunisia	46	100	80	95	31	72	15	80	33	21	92
94 Oman	89	100	85	87	47	100	34	85	54	34	..
95 Peru	30	..	..	78	22	67	17	..	29	25	83
96 Iraq	29	100	96	100	72	95	18	96	72	19	..
97 Dominican Rep.	40	..	..	..	..	77	36	..	..	47	92
98 Samoa	79	100	100	100	77	100	92	100	77	92	..
99 Jordan	32	..	..	100	98	100	100	..	98	100	..
100 Mongolia	48	100	100	78	50	100	43	100	64	43	..
101 China	67	..	..	87	68	100	81	..	78	81	86
102 Lebanon	16	..	..	..	..	94	18	..	..	19	..
103 Iran, Islamic Rep. of	43	100	70	100	75	100	35	70	75	35	..
104 Botswana	72	..	..	98	46	98	20	..	47	20	..
105 Guyana	65	..	..	94	74	97	86	..	79	89	..
106 Vanuatu	79	100	75	100	64	82	33	75	64	40	..
107 Algeria	48	100	80	85	55	80	40	80	65	50	..
108 Indonesia	69	..	..	65	32	40	45	..	49	113	76
109 Gabon	54	..	..	90	50	..	..	..	55	..	..
110 El Salvador	56	..	..	76	10	86	39	..	13	45	..
111 Nicaragua	40	..	..	78	19	35	16	..	24	46	..

HDI rank	Rural population (as % of total) 1991	Population with access to services (%)						Rural-urban disparity (100=rural-urban parity: see note)			
		Health		Water		Sanitation		Health 1987-90	Water 1988-90	Sanitation 1988-90	Child nutrition 1980-90
		Urban 1987-90	Rural 1987-90	Urban 1988-90	Rural 1988-90	Urban 1988-90	Rural 1988-90				
Low human development	72	98	..	78	56	47	11	..	72	23	75
Excluding India	71	94	59	77	40	54	18	63	52	33	..
112 Maldives	70	..	..	77	68	95	4	..	88	4	..
113 Guatemala	61	..	..	91	41	72	48	..	45	67	85
114 Cape Verde	71	..	..	87	65	35	9	..	75	26	..
115 Viet Nam	78	..	..	70	33	..	..	..	47	..	..
116 Honduras	56	..	..	56	49	..	..	..	88	..	..
117 Swaziland	67	..	..	100	7	100	10	..	7	10	..
118 Solomon Islands	91	..	..	82	58	73	..	..	70	..	..
119 Morocco	52	100	30	100	50	100	19	30	50	19	87
120 Lesotho	80	..	..	59	45	..	..	..	75	..	92
121 Zimbabwe	72	..	..	..	14	100	22	..	..	22	91
122 Bolivia	49	..	..	77	15	55	13	..	20	23	91
123 Myanmar	75	..	..	43	29	39	34	..	69	88	93
124 Egypt	53	100	99	96	82	100	34	99	85	34	91
125 São Tomé and Principe	67	..	..	..	..	..	..	..	..	..	..
126 Congo	59	..	..	42	7	..	..	..	17	..	..
127 Kenya	76	..	..	61	21	75	39	..	34	52	89
128 Madagascar	76	..	..	81	10	12	..	..	12	..	88
129 Papua New Guinea	84	100	96	94	20	54	56	96	21	104	..
130 Zambia	50	100	50	76	43	77	34	50	56	44	..
131 Ghana	67	..	..	93	39	63	15	..	42	24	89
132 Pakistan	68	100	50	84	35	56	8	50	42	13	..
133 Cameroon	59	..	..	47	27	35	16	..	57	46	..
134 India	73	..	..	79	73	38	4	..	92	10	..
135 Namibia	72	..	..	..	..	..	..	..	..	..	..
136 Côte d'Ivoire	60	..	..	100	75	69	20	..	75	29	96
137 Haiti	72	..	..	56	36	42	15	..	66	35	..
138 Tanzania, U. Rep. of	67	94	73	75	46	76	77	78	62	102	..
139 Comoros	72	..	..	..	..	90	80	..	..	89	..
140 Zaire	60	..	..	59	17	14	14	..	29	104	..
141 Lao People's Dem. Rep.	81	..	..	47	25	30	8	..	53	27	..
142 Nigeria	65	87	62	100	20	30	5	71	20	17	42
143 Yemen	71	..	..	..	..	..	..	..	..	..	58
144 Liberia	54	..	..	93	22	24	8	..	24	34	..
145 Togo	74	60	60	100	61	42	16	100	61	38	86
146 Uganda	90	..	..	45	12	40	10	..	27	25	87
147 Bangladesh	84	..	..	..	..	40	4	..	..	11	77
148 Cambodia	88	..	..	..	..	..	..	..	..	..	..
149 Rwanda	92	..	..	66	64	..	..	..	96	..	..
150 Senegal	62	..	..	79	38	..	..	..	48	..	88
151 Ethiopia	87	..	..	70	11	97	7	..	16	7	..
152 Nepal	90	..	..	66	34	34	3	..	51	9	..
153 Malawi	88	..	..	82	50	..	..	..	61	..	89
154 Burundi	94	..	..	100	34	80	..	..	34	..	77
155 Equatorial Guinea	71	..	..	..	..	..	..	..	..	..	..
156 Central African Rep.	53	..	..	14	11	36	9	..	81	25	..
157 Mozambique	73	..	..	44	17	61	11	..	39	18	..
158 Sudan	78	..	..	..	..	40	5	..	..	13	..
159 Bhutan	95	..	..	60	30	80	7	..	50	9	..
160 Angola	72	..	..	75	19	25	20	..	25	80	..
161 Mauritania	53	..	..	67	65	34	..	..	98	..	91
162 Benin	62	..	..	79	35	60	31	..	44	52	..
163 Djibouti	19	..	..	50	21	94	20	..	42	21	..
164 Guinea-Bissau	80	..	..	..	..	30	18	..	..	60	..
165 Chad	70	..	..	..	..	..	..	..	..	..	..
166 Somalia	64	50	15	58	55	41	5	30	95	13	..
167 Gambia	77	..	..	92	73	..	..	..	79	..	..
168 Mali	81	..	..	100	36	94	5	..	36	5	..
169 Niger	80	..	17	100	52	39	3	..	52	8	66
170 Burkina Faso	91	..	..	..	..	35	6	..	..	16	..
171 Afghanistan	82	65	45	39	17	..	..	69	44	..	..
172 Sierra Leone	68	88	..	83	22	59	35	..	26	59	89
173 Guinea	74	..	..	56	25	..	..	..	44	..	..
All developing countries	63	90	..	85	60	76	40	..	71	77	82
Least developed countries	80	85	..	61	45	45	15	..	74	33	80
Sub-Saharan Africa	69	87	..	79	28	47	18	..	35	38	67
Industrial countries	77	..	..	..	..	..	..	..	..	..	..
World	55	..	..	..	..	..	..	..	..	..	..

Note: The figures in the last four columns are expressed in relation to the urban average, which is indexed to equal 100. The smaller the figure the bigger the gap, the closer the figure to 100 the smaller the gap, and a figure above 100 indicates that the rural average is higher than the urban.

HDI rank	Pregnant women with prenatal care (%) 1988-90	Births attended by health personnel (%) 1988-90	Low-birth-weight babies (%) 1986-90	Infant mortality rate (per 1,000 live births) 1991	Children breast-fed at 12-15 months (%) 1986-91	One-year-olds immunized (%) 1989-91	Children suffering from malnutrition (%) 1980-91 Under-weight (under five)	Wasting (12-23 months)	Stunting (24-59 months)	Under-five mortality rate (per 1,000 live births) 1990
High human development	72	70	6	31	27	80	11	..	..	..
20 Barbados	98	98	..	11	..	89	..	..	..	12
24 Hong Kong	..	100	..	6	..	81	..	..	..	7
27 Cyprus	100	100	..	10	..	85	..	..	..	13
30 Uruguay	56	100	8	21	..	89	7	..	16	25
31 Trinidad and Tobago	95	95	13	20	30	80	7	5	4	17
32 Bahamas	100	100	..	25	..	85	..	..	..	..
33 Korea, Rep. of	96	95	4	22	27	79	..	..	..	30
36 Chile	91	98	7	17	20	98	3	1	10	27
42 Costa Rica	91	97	7	15	24	93	6	3	8	22
43 Singapore	95	100	7	7	..	89	14	..	..	9
44 Brunei Darussalam	100	97	..	9	..	91	..	..	..	..
46 Argentina	..	92	6	30	14	92	..	..	..	35
50 Venezuela	74	82	10	34	30	65	6	4	7	43
51 Dominica	96	96	11	16	..	94	..	..	..	..
52 Kuwait	99	99	7	14	12	95	6	2	14	19
53 Mexico	60	45	..	37	32	78	14	6	22	49
55 Qatar	100	100	6	28	..	85	..	..	..	36
Medium human development	..	80	8	42	..	91	24	8	38	..
Excluding China	60	66	11	53	57	86	26	9	31	..
56 Mauritius	90	91	8	22	40	90	24	16	22	28
57 Malaysia	84	92	8	15	19	93	..	6	..	29
58 Bahrain	99	99	..	14	..	92	..	..	..	17
59 Grenada	..	81	..	30	..	78	..	..	..	..
60 Antigua and Barbuda	..	86	..	19	..	96	..	..	..	..
61 Colombia	59	51	7	38	39	89	10	5	18	50
63 Seychelles	99	99	10	17	..	88	..	..	..	..
65 Suriname	100	91	13	30	..	76	..	..	..	38
67 United Arab Emirates	76	97	6	23	26	85	..	..	..	30
68 Panama	83	85	8	22	55	87	16	7	24	31
69 Jamaica	67	88	11	15	43	86	7	6	7	20
70 Brazil	75	73	15	59	25	83	7	2	15	83
71 Fiji	100	98	18	24	..	94	..	..	..	31
72 Saint Lucia	95	..	10	18	..	89	..	..	..	..
73 Turkey	..	83	..	60	63	82	..	..	..	80
74 Thailand	53	71	10	28	58	91	26	10	28	34
75 Cuba	100	100	7	14	..	95	..	1	..	14
76 Saint Vincent	..	..	..	22	..	96	..	..	..	..
79 Saint Kitts and Nevis	..	..	9	36	..	99	..	..	..	..
81 Syrian Arab Rep.	40	80	8	42	41	90	..	..	..	59
82 Belize	92	87	13	23	..	81	..	..	..	..
84 Saudi Arabia	70	82	7	33	..	94	..	..	..	91
85 South Africa	..	..	..	55	..	71	..	..	..	88
86 Sri Lanka	86	85	22	25	71	88	29	21	39	35
87 Libyan Arab Jamahiriya	76	..	..	72	..	82	..	..	..	112
89 Ecuador	47	26	..	59	51	71	17	4	39	83
90 Paraguay	57	30	..	48	40	78	4	..	17	60
91 Korea, Dem. Rep. of	..	..	..	25	..	99	..	..	..	35
92 Philippines	77	76	15	42	53	89	34	14	45	69
93 Tunisia	60	60	..	45	57	92	10	4	23	62
94 Oman	98	90	8	32	76	95	..	..	..	49
95 Peru	60	78	..	80	57	73	13	3	43	116
96 Iraq	65	74	15	60	58	77	12	..	..	86
97 Dominican Rep.	43	44	14	59	23	81	13	3	26	78
98 Samoa	52	52	..	46	..	74	..	..	..	..
99 Jordan	75	86	10	38	61	90	6	3	21	52
100 Mongolia	98	..	..	62	..	87	..	..	..	84
101 China	..	94	6	29	..	98	21	8	41	42
102 Lebanon	85	..	10	36	15	68	..	..	..	56
103 Iran, Islamic Rep. of	25	70	12	44	51	91	43	23	55	59
104 Botswana	71	78	8	62	77	85	15	..	..	85
105 Guyana	95	93	12	50	..	80	..	..	..	71
106 Vanuatu	..	67	..	68	..	79	..	..	..	..
107 Algeria	..	..	..	65	..	90	10	4	13	98
108 Indonesia	47	44	8	68	82	89	40	..	..	97
109 Gabon	70	..	10	97	..	82	..	..	..	164
110 El Salvador	69	66	8	50	55	72	..	3	36	87
111 Nicaragua	87	42	8	58	..	79	11	..	22	78

HDI rank		Pregnant women with prenatal care (%) 1988-90	Births attended by health personnel (%) 1988-90	Low-birth-weight babies (%) 1986-90	Infant mortality rate (per 1,000 live births) 1991	Children breast-fed at 12-15 months (%) 1986-91	One-year-olds immunized (%) 1989-91	Children suffering from malnutrition (%) 1980-91			Under-five mortality rate (per 1,000 live births) 1990
								Under-weight (under five)	Wasting (12-23 months)	Stunting (24-59 months)	
Low human development		64	55	23	96	..	76	47	..	..	..
	Excluding India	59	42	19	99	80	66	36	..	..	..
112	Maldives	47	..	20	58	..	94	..	..	..	..
113	Guatemala	34	23	..	51	82	68	34	3	68	94
114	Cape Verde	..	49	..	44	..	88	..	..	..	56
115	Viet Nam	73	90	17	39	49	88	42	12	49	65
116	Honduras	78	63	9	62	24	83	21	2	34	84
117	Swaziland	76	67	7	76	..	90	..	..	..	167
118	Solomon Islands	92	85	20	28	..	77	..	..	..	..
119	Morocco	25	31	9	72	62	84	16	6	34	112
120	Lesotho	50	40	10	82	76	81	16	7	23	129
121	Zimbabwe	83	65	6	61	90	71	12	2	31	87
122	Bolivia	38	29	9	89	73	48	13	2	51	160
123	Myanmar	90	94	13	85	94	72	32	..	..	88
124	Egypt	..	24	12	59	77	87	10	4	32	85
125	São Tomé and Principe	76	63	7	68	..	71	..	..	..	..
126	Congo	..	..	..	83	90	81	24	13	33	110
127	Kenya	..	28	15	68	83	71	14	5	32	108
128	Madagascar	77	71	10	113	85	48	33	17	56	176
129	Papua New Guinea	68	20	23	56	..	74	35	..	..	80
130	Zambia	80	43	..	85	93	83	25	10	59	122
131	Ghana	65	42	..	84	94	64	27	15	39	140
132	Pakistan	70	70	30	101	78	82	40	11	60	158
133	Cameroon	56	25	13	66	..	61	17	2	43	148
134	India	70	75	30	90	..	92	63	27	65	142
135	Namibia	82	71	14	73	73	58	29	9	30	167
136	Côte d'Ivoire	..	50	15	93	78	50	12	17	20	136
137	Haiti	43	40	15	89	29	46	37	17	51	130
138	Tanzania, U. Rep. of	..	60	16	104	70	86	48	..	..	170
139	Comoros	76	24	13	92	..	94	..	..	..	151
140	Zaire	..	..	10	96	86	40	..	..	..	130
141	Lao People's Dem. Rep.	..	..	30	101	..	21	37	20	44	152
142	Nigeria	86	45	17	99	86	66	36	16	54	167
143	Yemen	..	..	9	110	..	88	53	15	..	..
144	Liberia	50	..	..	131	67	43	..	..	..	205
145	Togo	83	56	32	88	95	68	24	10	37	147
146	Uganda	86	..	..	105	86	82	23	4	25	164
147	Bangladesh	..	7	34	111	82	66	66	16	65	180
148	Cambodia	..	..	..	120	72	42	20	..	..	193
149	Rwanda	82	28	16	112	74	86	33	1	34	198
150	Senegal	21	40	10	82	93	69	22	8	28	185
151	Ethiopia	40	10	10	125	95	46	38	19	43	220
152	Nepal	9	6	26	102	82	80	..	..	..	189
153	Malawi	76	41	11	144	96	84	24	8	61	253
154	Burundi	80	26	..	108	96	86	38	10	60	192
155	Equatorial Guinea	15	58	10	120	..	85	..	..	..	206
156	Central African Rep.	38	66	18	106	..	86	..	..	..	169
157	Mozambique	54	29	11	149	..	52	..	..	..	297
158	Sudan	40	60	15	102	80	64	20	13	32	172
159	Bhutan	..	11	..	133	90	95	38	4	56	189
160	Angola	27	16	15	128	..	33	..	..	..	292
161	Mauritania	39	20	10	120	89	41	48	18	65	214
162	Benin	69	51	10	88	76	74	..	..	..	147
163	Djibouti	76	79	9	115	..	88	..	..	..	..
164	Guinea-Bissau	29	39	12	143	98	52	23	..	..	246
165	Chad	22	21	..	125	..	33	..	..	..	216
166	Somalia	..	..	..	125	54	24	..	..	..	215
167	Gambia	72	65	10	135	..	89	..	..	..	238
168	Mali	11	14	10	162	90	52	31	16	34	284
169	Niger	33	21	20	127	15	24	49	23	38	221
170	Burkina Faso	49	33	12	120	97	50	..	..	..	228
171	Afghanistan	8	8	19	165	61	25	38	..	..	292
172	Sierra Leone	30	..	13	146	92	85	23	14	..	257
173	Guinea	36	76	11	137	85	26	..	..	..	237
All developing countries		63	66	16	71	68	83	36	14	48	104
	Least developed countries	51	31	18	114	82	60	42	15	50	..
	Sub-Saharan Africa	66	38	13	103	84	61	31	13	44	165
Industrial countries		..	..	..	14	..	..	..	..	..	16
World		..	..	..	64	..	..	..	..	..	93

12 Health profile

HDI rank	Population with access to			Population per doctor (1984-89)	Population per nurse (1984-89)	Nurses per doctor (1984-89)	Maternal mortality rate (per 100,000 live births) 1988	Public expenditure on health (as % of GNP)	
	Health services (%) 1987-90	Safe water (%) 1988-90	Sanitation (%) 1988-90					1960	1988-90
High human development	94	79	85	1,010	740	1.7	120	1.2	4.6
20 Barbados	100	99	100	1,120	220	5.0	35	3.0	..
24 Hong Kong	..	100	..	1,080	240	4.5	6		..
27 Cyprus	95	100	100	750	270	2.7	10	0.6	4.2
30 Uruguay	..	84	..	510			50	2.6	..
31 Trinidad and Tobago	99	96	99	940	250	3.7	120	1.7	2.6
32 Bahamas	100	..	..	1,060	210	5.1	..	..	3.5
33 Korea, Rep. of	100	78	99	1,160	580	2.0	80	0.2	6.4
36 Chile	95	86	83	1,230	370	3.3	67	2.0	..
42 Costa Rica	97	94	97	960	450	2.1	36	3.0	5.6
43 Singapore	100	100	96	1,410	340	..	14	1.0	2.9
44 Brunei Darussalam	96	..	..	1,460	260	5.6	..		2.2
46 Argentina	..	..	89	370	980	0.4	140	1.3	..
50 Venezuela	..	89	92	700	..	..	130	2.6	..
51 Dominica	100	..	..	2,950	..	..	..	..	..
52 Kuwait	100	100	98	690	220	3.2	30	..	..
53 Mexico	91	78	74	1,240	880	1.4	150	1.9	2.9
55 Qatar	100	91	97	530	200	2.6	140	..	3.1
Medium human development	..	73	84	2,210	1,270	2.0	170	0.8	3.7
Excluding China	68	75	65	3,760	1,090	3.7	220	0.7	3.9
56 Mauritius	100	100	98	1,900	580	3.3	130	1.5	2.0
57 Malaysia	88	78	94	1,940	1,010	1.9	120	1.1	1.6
58 Bahrain	100	100	100	930	420	2.2	80	..	6.0
59 Grenada	..	..	..	2,120	..	..	..	..	..
60 Antigua and Barbuda	100	..	..	..	..	..	..	..	..
61 Colombia	87	92	68	1,230	650	1.9	150	0.4	3.0
63 Seychelles	99	99	65	2,170	..	..	..	..	..
65 Suriname	91	84	57	1,260	280	4.6	120	..	5.7
67 United Arab Emirates	90	100	95	1,020	390	2.6	130	..	9.0
68 Panama	82	83	84	1,000	390	2.6	60	3.0	..
69 Jamaica	..	72	91	2,040	490	4.2	120	2.0	2.9
70 Brazil	..	96	78	1,080	1,210	0.9	230	0.6	3.9
71 Fiji	99	79	75	2,030	490	4.1	150	..	..
72 Saint Lucia	100	..	..	3,830	..	..	..	..	..
73 Turkey	..	92	..	1,370	1,030	1.3	200	0.8	2.8
74 Thailand	59	72	62	6,290	710	8.8	180	0.4	5.6
75 Cuba	100	..	..	530	290	1.9	54	3.0	3.4
76 Saint Vincent	80	..	..	3,760	..	..	..	..	..
79 Saint Kitts and Nevis	100	..	..	2,180	..	..	..	..	..
81 Syrian Arab Rep.	99	79	63	1,290	890	1.5	200	0.4	..
82 Belize	95	..	..	2,220	500	4.5	..	..	2.2
84 Saudi Arabia	98	95	86	740	350	2.1	220	0.6	2.1
85 South Africa	..	..	..	..	..	..	250	0.5	..
86 Sri Lanka	90	60	50	5,520	1,290	4.3	180	2.0	2.3
87 Libyan Arab Jamahiriya	100	97	98	690	350	2.0	200	1.3	..
89 Ecuador	80	58	56	820	610	1.3	200	0.4	..
90 Paraguay	..	33	58	1,460	1,000	1.5	200	0.5	3.2
91 Korea, Dem. Rep. of	100	..	..	..	..	..	130	0.5	..
92 Philippines	..	81	70	6,570	2,680	2.4	250	0.4	5.3
93 Tunisia	91	65	45	2,160	370	5.9	200	1.6	2.4
94 Oman	89	57	51	1,100	390	2.8	220	..	2.1
95 Peru	..	58	49	1,040	..	..	300	1.1	2.4
96 Iraq	98	93	72	1,810	1,720	1.1	250	1.0	..
97 Dominican Rep.	..	62	60	1,770	1,210	1.5	200	1.3	..
98 Samoa	100	82	94	3,570	410	8.7	..	..	5.6
99 Jordan	90	99	100	860	980	0.9	200	0.6	6.0
100 Mongolia	100	66	76				250	..	..
101 China	..	71	96	1,010	1,410	0.7	130	1.3	3.1
102 Lebanon	95	98	78	670	..	..	200	..	..
103 Iran, Islamic Rep. of	73	89	71	2,950	1,150	2.6	250	0.8	3.2
104 Botswana	86	56	38	6,900	700	9.8	300	1.5	3.2
105 Guyana	96	81	90	6,220	890	7.0	200	..	..
106 Vanuatu	80	71	42	5,000	450	11.2	..	..	2.9
107 Algeria	..	69	59	2,330	330	7.1	210	1.2	6.0
108 Indonesia	43	42	44	9,410	1,260	7.5	300	0.3	2.5
109 Gabon	87	72	..	2,790	270	10.3	600	0.5	3.2
110 El Salvador	..	41	61	2,830	940	3.0	200	0.9	..
111 Nicaragua	..	53	27	1,560	540	2.9	200	0.4	..

HDI rank	Population with access to			Population per doctor 1984-89	Population per nurse 1984-89	Nurses per doctor 1984-89	Maternal mortality rate (per 100,000 live births) 1988	Public expenditure on health (as % of GNP)	
	Health services (%) 1987-90	Safe water (%) 1988-90	Sanitation (%) 1988-90					1960	1988-90
Low human development	..	62	20	8,490	2,550	3.6	590	0.6	3.2
Excluding India	65	50	27	13,600	3,270	5.5	610	0.7	3.3
112 Maldives	75	70	28	15,000	610	24.5	..	..	5.0
113 Guatemala	60	60	57	2,180	850	2.6	250	0.6	1.1
114 Cape Verde	82	74	16	5,130	720	7.2	200	..	..
115 Viet Nam	97	50	53	950	590	1.6	400	..	..
116 Honduras	62	52	33	1,510	670	2.2	220	1.0	..
117 Swaziland	55	30	32	18,820	1,050	17.9	400	..	5.8
118 Solomon Islands	80	61	..	7,420	..	..	..	..	5.0
119 Morocco	62	73	65	4,760	1,050	4.5	270	1.0	3.2
120 Lesotho	80	46	22	18,610	..	..	350	1.0	1.2
121 Zimbabwe	71	36	42	7,180	1,000	7.2	330	1.2	5.5
122 Bolivia	..	46	34	1,530	2,470	0.6	600	0.4	2.2
123 Myanmar	48	33	36	3,740	900	4.1	600	0.7	0.8
124 Egypt	99	86	54	770	780	1.0	300	0.6	5.0
125 São Tomé and Principe	88	..	..	1,940	280	6.9	..	..	..
126 Congo	..	20	..	8,320	590	14.2	900	1.6	3.0
127 Kenya	..	28	46	10,130	950	10.7	400	1.5	2.1
128 Madagascar	65	..	..	9,780	1,720	5.7	600	1.4	0.9
129 Papua New Guinea	96	33	56	6,070	880	6.9	700	..	3.2
130 Zambia	75	59	55	7,150	740	9.6	600	1.0	5.1
131 Ghana	76	56	30	20,460	1,670	12.3	700	1.1	1.2
132 Pakistan	85	50	22	2,940	5,040	0.6	600	0.3	4.5
133 Cameroon	15	34	..	..	..	..	550	1.0	..
134 India	..	75	13	2,520	1,700	1.5	550	0.5	3.2
135 Namibia	..	..	..	..	..	..	400	..	5.0
136 Côte d'Ivoire	60	83	36	..	..	..	680	1.5	3.0
137 Haiti	45	42	21	7,140	2,280	3.1	600	1.0	..
138 Tanzania, U. Rep. of	93	52	77	24,990	5,490	4.6	600	0.5	..
139 Comoros	82	..	83	12,290	2,270	5.4	500	..	3.3
140 Zaire	59	34	14	13,540	1,880	7.2	700	..	5.6
141 Lao People's Dem. Rep.	67	28	11	1,360	530	2.6	750	0.5	2.0
142 Nigeria	67	46	13	6,420	900	7.1	750	0.3	(.)
143 Yemen	..	..	..	..	1,940	..	800	..	..
144 Liberia	34	50	11	9,340	1,380	6.8	600	0.8	3.5
145 Togo	..	71	23	8,700	1,240	7.0	600	1.3	3.5
146 Uganda	71	15	13	21,830	2,050	10.7	700	0.7	..
147 Bangladesh	74	78	12	6,890	9,530	0.7	650	..	0.9
148 Cambodia	..	..	13	..	..	..	800	..	..
149 Rwanda	..	64	61	74,950	4,300	17.4	700	0.5	0.6
150 Senegal	40	53	..	13,060	2,030	6.4	750	1.5	1.8
151 Ethiopia	55	18	17	78,780	5,390	14.6	900	0.7	2.0
152 Nepal	..	37	6	30,220	4,680	6.5	850	0.2	0.7
153 Malawi	80	53	..	11,340	3,110	3.6	500	0.2	..
154 Burundi	80	38	57	21,000	4,380	4.8	800	0.8	6.0
155 Equatorial Guinea	..	..	..	..	..	..	800	..	..
156 Central African Rep.	13	12	20	23,510	2,210	10.6	650	1.3	..
157 Mozambique	30	22	19	37,970	5,760	6.6	800	..	1.4
158 Sudan	70	..	12	10,190	1,260	8.1	700	1.0	0.3
159 Bhutan	80	34	..	9,730	2,990	3.3	800	..	4.2
160 Angola	24	38	22	17,750	1,010	17.5	900	..	1.8
161 Mauritania	30	66	..	11,900	1,180	10.1	800	0.5	5.5
162 Benin	50	50	41	15,940	1,760	9.1	800	1.5	5.1
163 Djibouti	..	43	78	4,180	510	8.3	740	..	..
164 Guinea-Bissau	80	25	21	7,260	1,130	6.4	1,000	..	1.3
165 Chad	26	..	..	38,360	3,400	11.3	800	0.5	..
166 Somalia	20	56	12	19,950	1,900	10.5	900	0.6	..
167 Gambia	90	77	..	11,690	..	..	1,000	..	1.6
168 Mali	..	49	23	23,510	1,350	17.4	850	1.0	0.5
169 Niger	30	59	9	53,610	3,680	14.6	850	0.2	1.8
170 Burkina Faso	70	67	10	57,330	1,680	34.1	750	0.6	..
171 Afghanistan	49	21	..	6,430	8,900	0.7	1,000	..	1.6
172 Sierra Leone	36	43	43	13,620	1,090	12.5	1,000	..	..
173 Guinea	32	33	..	46,420	5,160	9.0	1,000	1.0	2.0
All developing countries	72	68	55	5,080	1,870	2.7	420	1.0	3.7
Least developed countries	62	47	22	22,590	4,620	6.9	740	0.7	2.4
Sub-Saharan Africa	60	41	26	24,380	2,400	9.9	690	0.7	3.1
Industrial countries	..	..	..	380	150	3.1	26	4.2	..
World	..	..	..	4,090	1,510	2.8	370	..	..

Note: Data for industrial countries for this subject area are in table 35.

HDI rank	Food production per capita index (1979-81=100) 1988-90	Agricultural production (as % of GDP) 1990	Daily calorie supply per capita 1988-90	Daily calorie supply (as % of requirements) 1988-90	Food import dependency ratio (%) 1969/71	Food import dependency ratio (%) 1988/90	Cereal imports (1,000 metric tons) 1990	Food aid (US$ millions) 1991
High human development	**99**	**9**	**2,900**	**123**	**19.2**	**36.4**	**21,680T**	**..**
20 Barbados	..	..	3,217	128	68.8	71.7	..	..
24 Hong Kong	80	(.)	2,860	125	104.6	141.8	754	..
27 Cyprus	..	..	..	..	..	..	498	..
30 Uruguay	109	11	2,668	101	9.2	8.8	55	..
31 Trinidad and Tobago	87	3	2,770	114	70.7	80.8	295	..
32 Bahamas	..	..	2,777	..	71.7	63.5	..	..
33 Korea, Rep. of	..	9	2,826	120	26.2	50.8	9,087	..
36 Chile	113	..	2,484	102	23.1	10.5	247	1.5
42 Costa Rica	91	16	2,711	121	23.4	30.2	326	0.4
43 Singapore	69	(.)	3,121	136	223.4	417.0	737	..
44 Brunei Darussalam	..	..	2,858	..	81.2	93.5	..	..
46 Argentina	93	13	3,068	131	1.3	0.4	4	..
50 Venezuela	96	6	2,443	99	32.3	43.2	1,603	..
51 Dominica	..	..	2,911	100	50.1	66.4	..	0.3
52 Kuwait	..	1	3,043	130	110.6	97.3	427	..
53 Mexico	102	9	3,062	131	3.2	24.8	7,648	5.3
55 Qatar	..	..	..	..	..	..	..	..
Medium human development	**122**	**16**	**2,660**	**114**	**6.1**	**10.4**	**62,590T**	**210T**
Excluding China	**108**	**13**	**2,680**	**116**	**12.2**	**18.0**	**48,870T**	**190T**
56 Mauritius	100	12	2,897	128	57.0	95.3	210	2.4
57 Malaysia	147	..	2,671	120	46.1	51.3	2,582	..
58 Bahrain	..	..	..	..	..	..	..	..
59 Grenada	..	..	2,400	..	61.3	77.5	..	0.3
60 Antigua and Barbuda	..	..	2,307	..	83.0	83.4	..	..
61 Colombia	104	17	2,453	106	9.3	10.2	880	2.9
63 Seychelles	..	..	2,356	100	83.1	86.8	..	0.1
65 Suriname	..	..	2,436	..	32.6	39.6	..	..
67 United Arab Emirates	..	2	3,285	151	93.2	136.5	576	..
68 Panama	90	10	2,269	98	19.2	24.8	125	0.4
69 Jamaica	95	5	2,558	114	59.9	63.7	262	3.2
70 Brazil	115	10	2,730	114	4.6	3.1	3,421	12.5
71 Fiji	..	..	2,769	108	50.6	70.1	..	..
72 Saint Lucia	..	..	2,424	102	52.0	75.7	..	..
73 Turkey	97	18	3,196	127	3.4	10.9	3,177	1.4
74 Thailand	106	12	2,280	103	1.4	3.8	387	..
75 Cuba	..	..	3,129	135	..	..	..	12.5
76 Saint Vincent	..	..	2,460	99	56.8	113.1	..	..
79 Saint Kitts and Nevis	..	..	2,435	..	56.8	86.4	..	..
81 Syrian Arab Rep.	80	28	3,122	126	31.8	31.7	2,091	12.0
82 Belize	..	..	2,575	114	46.8	40.4	..	..
84 Saudi Arabia	189	8	2,929	121	57.3	72.4	5,273	..
85 South Africa	87	5	3,133	128	6.5	9.7	876	..
86 Sri Lanka	87	26	2,246	101	37.8	30.4	996	1.9
87 Libyan Arab Jamahiriya	78	..	3,293	140	69.1	77.9	2,290	..
89 Ecuador	100	13	2,399	105	7.1	13.9	474	8.4
90 Paraguay	116	28	2,684	116	6.0	1.1	..	2.2
91 Korea, Dem. Rep. of	106	..	2,843	121	9.1	8.0	..	..
92 Philippines	84	22	2,341	104	8.6	11.4	2,545	3.9
93 Tunisia	87	16	3,122	131	38.8	59.9	1,439	3.4
94 Oman	..	3	..	..	..	..	338	..
95 Peru	100	7	2,037	87	17.5	27.1	1,562	8.2
96 Iraq	92	..	..	128	30.7	64.5	2,834	30.5
97 Dominican Rep.	90	17	2,310	102	16.1	38.3	662	0.4
98 Samoa	..	..	2,695	..	31.7	31.2	..	1.1
99 Jordan	100	8	..	110	61.0	87.2	1,491	12.6
100 Mongolia	86	17	2,361	97	21.3	12.2	57	..
101 China	133	27	2,641	112	1.7	4.7	13,719	21.6
102 Lebanon	135	..	..	127	80.7	74.9	356	3.7
103 Iran, Islamic Rep. of	104	21	..	125	10.1	31.6	6,250	29.5
104 Botswana	75	3	2,260	97	47.5	74.8	87	2.4
105 Guyana	..	..	2,495	108	28.9	22.6	53	0.7
106 Vanuatu	..	..	2,736	..	27.8	16.6	..	..
107 Algeria	96	13	2,944	123	34.2	76.8	5,185	3.7
108 Indonesia	123	22	2,605	121	4.7	5.7	1,828	8.0
109 Gabon	84	9	..	104	19.5	32.8	57	..
110 El Salvador	97	11	..	102	15.9	24.5	176	13.4
111 Nicaragua	58	..	..	99	11.3	26.9	177	7.0

HDI rank	Food production per capita index (1979-81=100) 1988-90	Agricultural production (as % of GDP) 1990	Daily calorie supply per capita 1988-90	Daily calorie supply (as % of requirements) 1988-90	Food import dependency ratio (%) 1969/71	Food import dependency ratio (%) 1988/90	Cereal imports (1,000 metric tons) 1990	Food aid (US$ millions) 1991
Low human development	108	30	2,250	98	5.9	7.8	25,540T	900T
Excluding India	100	29	2,270	96	8.5	12.9	25,090T	850T
112 Maldives	..	..	..	80	61.9	68.6	..	15.5
113 Guatemala	91	26	2,254	103	11.0	18.5	383	5.9
114 Cape Verde	..	..	2,778	125	75.7	71.3	..	16.6
115 Viet Nam	127	..	..	103	19.3	1.8	204	5.5
116 Honduras	83	23	2,210	98	11.4	13.7	162	
117 Swaziland	..	..	2,634	105	25.9	30.5	..	2.0
118 Solomon Islands	..	..	2,278	84	15.4	29.8	..	
119 Morocco	128	16	3,031	119	18.1	21.1	1,578	17.0
120 Lesotho	86	24	2,121	93	30.5	59.0	97	10.0
121 Zimbabwe	94	13	2,256	94	5.0	4.6	83	4.2
122 Bolivia	109	24	2,013	84	20.0	11.6	147	6.2
123 Myanmar	93	..	2,454	114	1.0	0.9	..	13.5
124 Egypt	118	17	3,310	132	19.8	42.6	8,580	
125 São Tomé and Principe	..	..	2,153	103	51.6	40.1	..	2.0
126 Congo	94	13	2,295	103	13.2	25.1	94	1.2
127 Kenya	106	28	2,064	89	7.4	9.6	188	10.4
128 Madagascar	88	33	2,156	95	4.5	5.2	183	7.8
129 Papua New Guinea	103	29	..	114	19.7	27.5	222	..
130 Zambia	103	17	2,016	87	22.0	7.0	100	2.7
131 Ghana	97	48	2,144	93	12.4	11.3	337	14.5
132 Pakistan	101	26	2,280	99	3.5	14.1	2,048	95.4
133 Cameroon	89	27	2,208	95	6.7	17.7	398	6.7
134 India	119	31	2,229	101	2.8	1.8	447	52.7
135 Namibia	93	11	..	..	36.4	30.8	..	2.5
136 Côte d'Ivoire	101	47	2,568	111	14.7	18.4	502	5.5
137 Haiti	94	..	2,005	89	7.2	26.2	236	0.7
138 Tanzania, U. Rep. of	88	59	2,195	95	4.9	3.3	73	6.3
139 Comoros	..	..	1,760	90	27.2	37.5	25	0.8
140 Zaire	97	30	2,130	96	4.9	4.8	336	2.2
141 Lao People's Dem. Rep.	114	..	..	111	9.8	5.6	54	4.1
142 Nigeria	106	36	2,200	93	2.6	3.7	502	
143 Yemen	..	20	..	..	29.4	66.0	2,001	15.1
144 Liberia	84	..	2,259	98	18.6	23.9	70	75.0
145 Togo	88	33	2,269	99	5.5	21.0	111	1.3
146 Uganda	95	67	2,178	93	2.2	1.4	..	17.7
147 Bangladesh	96	38	2,037	88	8.3	12.3	1,726	58.6
148 Cambodia	165	..	..	96	1.8	3.2	20	..
149 Rwanda	77	38	1,913	82	2.3	7.4	21	2.1
150 Senegal	102	21	2,322	98	31.4	38.1	534	8.9
151 Ethiopia	84	41	..	73	1.1	9.4	687	170.6
152 Nepal	115	60	2,205	100	0.3	2.3	21	2.5
153 Malawi	83	33	2,049	88	4.4	5.6	115	59.0
154 Burundi	92	56	1,948	84	2.0	3.3	11	1.6
155 Equatorial Guinea	..	..	..	..	..	..	11	2.2
156 Central African Rep.	91	42	1,846	82	6.1	9.4	37	3.2
157 Mozambique	81	65	1,805	77	7.3	21.9	416	32.6
158 Sudan	71	..	2,043	87	9.5	14.8	586	29.8
159 Bhutan	93	43	..	128	..	..	11	4.0
160 Angola	81	13	..	80	9.8	35.9	272	19.4
161 Mauritania	85	26	2,447	106	33.4	59.4	205	10.7
162 Benin	112	37	2,383	104	5.8	12.0	126	2.1
163 Djibouti	..	..	..	..	90.9	87.7	44	2.5
164 Guinea-Bissau	..	..	..	97	24.6	26.6	52	2.1
165 Chad	85	38	..	73	3.8	4.8	36	11.4
166 Somalia	94	65	1,874	81	12.7	17.0	194	11.3
167 Gambia	..	..	2,290	103	18.8	64.2	95	7.6
168 Mali	97	46	2,259	96	6.6	7.7	61	6.2
169 Niger	71	36	2,239	95	2.0	9.9	86	10.0
170 Burkina Faso	114	32	2,219	94	3.8	8.9	145	7.7
171 Afghanistan	85	..	..	72	7.4	14.3	322	6.7
172 Sierra Leone	89	32	1,899	83	15.3	19.0	146	2.4
173 Guinea	87	28	2,242	97	4.8	17.2	210	3.8
All developing countries	115	17	2,490	107	6.7	10.5	109,480T	1,100T
Least developed countries	93	37	2,130	90	..	11.3	8,770T	600T
Sub-Saharan Africa	95	22	2,250	93	6.5	10.2	7,850T	500T
Industrial countries	..	..	..	..	..	..	..	..
World	..	..	..	..	..	..	..	..

161

14 Education flows

HDI rank	Primary intake rate first grade (%) Total 1988	Female 1988	Primary enrolment ratio (net) 1988-90	Primary repeaters (as % of primary enrolment) 1988-91	Completing primary level (as % of grade one entrants) 1988	Transition to secondary level (as % of primary completers) 1988	Primary entrants who proceed to secondary schooling (%) 1988	Secondary enrolment ratio (gross) 1988-90	Secondary repeaters (as % of secondary enrolment) 1988-90	Tertiary enrolment ratio (gross) 1988-90
High human development	..	..	92	..	78	..	..	61	..	24
20 Barbados	..	..	97	..	..	..	..	87	..	17
24 Hong Kong	..	..	..	2	97	..	..	73	..	13
27 Cyprus	85	86	..	..	99	99	98	90	2	15
30 Uruguay	97	96	88	9	93	..	..	77	..	..
31 Trinidad and Tobago	..	..	90	3	96	73	70	80	2	6
32 Bahamas	..	..	..	..	..	..	..	..	..	..
33 Korea, Rep. of	100	100	100	..	99	99	98	88	..	41
36 Chile	..	..	86	..	73	..	..	74	..	18
42 Costa Rica	100	100	87	11	79	61	48	42	12	26
43 Singapore	100	100	100	..	98	..	..	69	..	..
44 Brunei Darussalam	..	..	..	..	..	..	..	..	..	..
46 Argentina	..	..	..	..	..	..	..	74	..	..
50 Venezuela	100	100	61	11	73	88	64	35	7	28
51 Dominica	..	..	..	5	79	79	62	..	5	..
52 Kuwait	92	90	85	5	90	70	63	..	..	18
53 Mexico	100	..	98	9	72	81	58	53	3	14
55 Qatar	70	72	..	7	96	84	81	..	16	24
Medium human development	99	..	96	8	75	65	52	50	..	7
Excluding China	97	96	92	10	69	72	57	52	..	13
56 Mauritius	99	100	93	8	98	48	47	53	13	2
57 Malaysia	100	100	..	..	96	..	..	56	..	7
58 Bahrain	95	92	93	5	97	95	92	..	6	18
59 Grenada	..	..	..	..	..	..	..	..	..	..
60 Antigua and Barbuda	..	..	..	..	..	..	..	..	..	..
61 Colombia	100	100	73	11	57	60	34	52	8	14
63 Seychelles	..	..	..	..	98	..	..	..	..	..
65 Suriname	100	100	100	23	..	..	..	53	..	9
67 United Arab Emirates	100	100	100	7	94	94	88	67	10	11
68 Panama	100	100	92	10	72	85	61	59	8	22
69 Jamaica	94	94	94	4	93	..	..	60	2	5
70 Brazil	..	..	88	19	20	..	..	39	..	12
71 Fiji	100	100	98	3	51	29	15	52	7	4
72 Saint Lucia	..	..	..	..	..	34	..	..	3	..
73 Turkey	98	96	98	7	96	47	45	54	26	14
74 Thailand	85	..	..	3	59	..	..	32	..	16
75 Cuba	100	100	95	4	89	96	85	89	3	21
76 Saint Vincent	..	..	..	..	..	..	..	..	..	..
79 Saint Kitts and Nevis	..	..	..	..	88	..	..	..	..	..
81 Syrian Arab Rep.	100	100	98	7	88	72	63	52	15	20
82 Belize	..	..	..	..	67	..	..	..	..	..
84 Saudi Arabia	73	70	62	10	90	..	..	48	13	13
85 South Africa	..	..	..	..	..	..	..	..	..	..
86 Sri Lanka	100	100	..	8	94	92	86	74	13	4
87 Libyan Arab Jamahiriya	..	..	..	..	..	..	..	..	..	10
89 Ecuador	100	100	..	6	63	..	..	56	..	29
90 Paraguay	100	100	95	9	56	..	..	30	..	8
91 Korea, Dem. Rep. of	..	..	..	..	..	..	..	..	..	..
92 Philippines	100	100	99	2	70	93	65	73	2	27
93 Tunisia	95	93	95	20	79	43	34	45	16	9
94 Oman	95	93	84	11	91	86	78	54	13	5
95 Peru	100	100	95	..	..	..	..	67	10	..
96 Iraq	91	87	84	19	58	56	32	47	32	14
97 Dominican Rep.	100	..	73	17	33	..	..	74	..	19
98 Samoa	..	..	..	..	..	..	..	..	..	..
99 Jordan	..	..	..	5	84	91	76	..	7	..
100 Mongolia	..	..	94	..	..	..	..	92	..	22
101 China	100	..	100	6	80	62	50	48	2	2
102 Lebanon	..	..	..	..	..	..	..	67	..	..
103 Iran, Islamic Rep. of	100	100	94	9	89	74	66	54	14	6
104 Botswana	100	100	91	5	87	45	39	46	1	3
105 Guyana	69	69	..	6	..	..	..	57	11	5
106 Vanuatu	..	..	..	..	..	..	..	..	..	..
107 Algeria	92	87	88	9	88	82	72	60	14	11
108 Indonesia	100	..	98	10	79	..	..	45	1	8
109 Gabon	..	..	..	31	44	37	16	..	25	4
110 El Salvador	100	100	70	8	35	..	..	26	1	17
111 Nicaragua	100	100	75	17	36	94	34	38	6	8

HDI rank	Primary intake rate first grade (%) Total 1988	Primary intake rate first grade (%) Female 1988	Primary enrolment ratio (net) 1988-90	Primary repeaters (as % of primary enrolment) 1988-91	Completing primary level (as % of grade one entrants) 1988	Transition to secondary level (as % of primary completers) 1988	Primary entrants who proceed to secondary schooling (%) 1988	Secondary enrolment ratio (gross) 1988-90	Secondary repeaters (as % of secondary enrolment) 1988-90	Tertiary enrolment ratio (gross) 1988-90
Low human development	..	..	67	9	..	..	..	31	..	5
Excluding India	69	59	..	14	61	47	23	23	15	4
112 Maldives	..	..	..	..	..	..	..	..	..	9
113 Guatemala	100	..	..	4	36	..	..	21	20	(.)
114 Cape Verde	100	100	95	19	45	45	20	20	20	(.)
115 Viet Nam	..	..	..	..	57	..	..	42	..	..
116 Honduras	100	100	91	..	43	..	..	32	..	9
117 Swaziland	100	100	82	15	66	70	46	50	8	4
118 Solomon Islands	..	..	..	..	..	..	..	..	..	..
119 Morocco	64	53	55	15	63	61	38	36	17	10
120 Lesotho	100	100	70	22	53	59	31	26	6	4
121 Zimbabwe	..	..	..	1	75	..	..	50	..	5
122 Bolivia	..	..	79	3	43	..	..	34	5	23
123 Myanmar	..	..	..	..	..	..	..	24	..	5
124 Egypt	87	79	..	3	95	..	..	82	..	19
125 São Tomé and Principe	..	..	..	29	88	..	..	..	42	6
126 Congo	..	..	..	36	62	62	38	23	..	6
127 Kenya	..	..	..	..	44	..	..	23	..	2
128 Madagascar	..	..	64	35	31	38	12	19	17	3
129 Papua New Guinea	92	85	73	..	59	..	..	13	..	..
130 Zambia	..	..	80	2	80	..	..	20	..	2
131 Ghana	..	..	..	..	..	..	..	39	..	2
132 Pakistan	..	..	..	..	57	..	..	22	..	3
133 Cameroon	95	90	75	29	68	30	20	26	11	4
134 India	..	..	..	4	..	..	..	44	..	7
135 Namibia	..	..	64	..	..	..	..	34	..	..
136 Côte d'Ivoire	61	53	..	28	73	23	17	20	19	..
137 Haiti	..	..	44	11	32	61	20	19	8	1
138 Tanzania, U. Rep. of	69	69	48	5	68	..	..	4	..	(.)
139 Comoros	68	59	55	37	31	30	9	17	33	(.)
140 Zaire	81	75	60	21	64	..	..	24	..	2
141 Lao People's Dem. Rep.	100	..	69	30	..	..	..	26	10	1
142 Nigeria	..	..	..	..	84	..	..	20	..	3
143 Yemen	..	..	..	..	74	..	..	31	..	3
144 Liberia	..	..	..	..	..	..	..	..	..	3
145 Togo	92	83	72	37	46	27	12	22	35	3
146 Uganda	84	80	53	14	..	..	..	13	..	1
147 Bangladesh	..	..	65	7	46	..	..	17	..	3
148 Cambodia	..	..	..	..	..	4	2	7	6	1
149 Rwanda	94	94	65	11	46	39	32	16	11	3
150 Senegal	52	46	48	16	81	78	34	15	13	1
151 Ethiopia	59	45	28	11	44	..	..	15	13	1
152 Nepal	100	..	64	21	..	..	..	30	9	6
153 Malawi	..	..	54	21	47	7	3	4	2	1
154 Burundi	80	76	51	22	87	10	9	5	14	1
155 Equatorial Guinea	..	..	..	..	..	..	..	11	29	2
156 Central African Rep.	62	52	55	31	48	31	15	11	..	2
157 Mozambique	75	70	41	27	34	34	12	7	27	(.)
158 Sudan	58	46	..	..	76	..	..	20	..	3
159 Bhutan	29	31	..	17	26	..	..	5	6	..
160 Angola	..	..	..	..	..	..	..	11	..	1
161 Mauritania	48	41	..	20	68	26	18	16	17	4
162 Benin	71	49	52	26	40	38	15	11	32	3
163 Djibouti	44	..	39	14	89	27	24	15	8	(.)
164 Guinea-Bissau	56	42	45	42	8	73	6	7	20	(.)
165 Chad	54	39	38	33	30	40	12	7	20	1
166 Somalia	..	..	11	..	37	..	..	10	..	3
167 Gambia	54	43	53	18	64	32	20	16	2	(.)
168 Mali	23	17	19	27	40	44	18	6	33	1
169 Niger	32	24	25	14	75	31	23	7	19	1
170 Burkina Faso	36	28	29	18	63	33	21	7	19	1
171 Afghanistan	28	19	19	6	63	..	..	8	4	2
172 Sierra Leone	..	..	..	..	..	..	..	16	..	2
173 Guinea	32	21	26	20	48	58	28	9	23	1
All developing countries	91	76	83	8	69	63	48	40	7	7
Least developed countries	65	54	49	15	53	47	21	16	15	2
Sub-Saharan Africa	67	59	46	18	62	44	21	17	17	2
Industrial countries	..	..	..	..	..	..	..	..	..	45
World	..	..	..	..	..	..	..	..	..	16

HDI rank	Primary pupil-teacher ratio 1988-90	Secondary technical enrolment (as % of total secondary) 1987-88	Tertiary science enrolment (as % of total tertiary) 1987-88	Tertiary students abroad (as % of those at home) 1987-88	Public expenditure on				
					Education (as % of GNP)		Education (as % of total public expenditure) 1988-90	Primary and secondary education (as % of all levels) 1987-90	Higher education (as % of all levels) 1987-90
					1960	1988-90			
High human development	29	12.8	33	2.7	2.2	3.5	11.9	63	20
20 Barbados	18	..	39	12.6	..	8.0	20.5	75	19
24 Hong Kong	27	10.0	43	32.2	..	2.7	15.9	70	29
27 Cyprus	21	7.8	33	..	..	3.6	11.3	85	4
30 Uruguay	23	14.1	48	0.6	3.7	3.3	15.1	65	22
31 Trinidad and Tobago	26	0.8	43	61.7	2.8	4.1	11.6	79	12
32 Bahamas	20	..	..	..	..	..	..	..	..
33 Korea, Rep. of	34	15.9	31	1.9	2.0	3.7	22.4	78	7
36 Chile	29	18.1	17	1.4	2.7	2.9	10.4	70	20
42 Costa Rica	32	21.9	41	1.8	4.1	4.6	20.8	45	36
43 Singapore	26	..	29	25.3	2.8	3.4	11.5	65	31
44 Brunei Darussalam	17	5.8	..	..	..	4.9	11.8	50	10
46 Argentina	19	..	37	0.3	2.1	1.5	10.9	48	47
50 Venezuela	23	5.1	26	1.1	3.7	4.1	18.8	..	..
51 Dominica	29	1.1	..	..	..	5.8	10.6	86	3
52 Kuwait	18	0.3	35	16.4	..	5.0	12.1	69	17
53 Mexico	31	12.6	36	0.6	1.2	4.1	..	56	17
55 Qatar	11	3.5	10	19.7	..	3.4	7.2	..	..
Medium human development	24	9.4	25	3.7	2.2	3.3	12.9	65	18
Excluding China	25	12.4	36	4.3	2.5	3.6	13.6	64	17
56 Mauritius	21	1.3	..	..	3.0	3.5	10.5	81	7
57 Malaysia	20	1.7	34	38.1	2.9	5.5	18.3	69	20
58 Bahrain	..	18.0	..	44.6	..	5.4	10.3	76	13
59 Grenada	26	..	..	..	..	..	12.5	70	3
60 Antigua and Barbuda	..	..	..	..	..	..	14.4	..	..
61 Colombia	30	20.8	36	1.3	1.7	2.9	21.4	60	21
63 Seychelles	19	31.0	..	..	..	9.1	11.9	69	10
65 Suriname	23	26.5	..	..	..	9.7	22.8	75	9
67 United Arab Emirates	18	0.8	46	24.8	..	1.9	14.6	..	..
68 Panama	20	25.9	32	3.4	3.6	5.7	14.3	60	21
69 Jamaica	32	3.5	37	21.5	2.3	5.9	12.8	68	21
70 Brazil	23	..	40	0.5	1.9	3.9	17.7	60	18
71 Fiji	30	9.1	35	53.6	..	5.0	15.4	88	9
72 Saint Lucia	29	..	40	..	..	7.2	..	74	10
73 Turkey	30	21.9	..	3.2	2.6	1.8	10.5	68	24
74 Thailand	18	16.2	25	0.9	2.3	3.8	20.0	78	15
75 Cuba	12	29.0	25	0.6	5.0	6.7	12.8	59	14
76 Saint Vincent	18	3.7	..	..	..	6.9	13.8	96	(.)
79 Saint Kitts and Nevis	22	..	14	..	..	3.0	12.0	89	2
81 Syrian Arab Rep.	25	6.9	31	8.8	2.0	4.4	13.1	74	23
82 Belize	25	1.2	..	..	..	..	15.0	..	..
84 Saudi Arabia	16	1.9	34	5.7	3.2	5.8	16.7	..	..
85 South Africa	..	..	47	0.7	3.0	..	..	..	..
86 Sri Lanka	14	..	37	5.6	3.8	2.7	8.1	84	13
87 Libyan Arab Jamahiriya	19	..	..	6.7	2.8	9.6	20.8	..	..
89 Ecuador	31	33.8	21	0.6	1.9	2.7	19.1	64	14
90 Paraguay	25	7.1	50	1.0	1.3	1.0	12.1	66	24
91 Korea, Dem. Rep. of	26	..	34	..	..	..	..	..	..
92 Philippines	33	..	..	0.3	2.3	3.0	11.2	73	15
93 Tunisia	28	13.3	31	24.5	3.3	6.0	14.1	83	17
94 Oman	28	5.1	34	..	..	3.7	11.1	91	7
95 Peru	28	..	25	0.8	2.3	3.5	15.7	..	..
96 Iraq	23	13.7	33	3.3	5.8	5.1	6.4	75	21
97 Dominican Rep.	47	..	..	0.7	2.1	1.5	10.0	63	20
98 Samoa	27	..	..	..	..	..	..	..	..
99 Jordan	28	8.0	..	41.4	3.0	4.4	8.5	64	33
100 Mongolia	28	..	56	0.7	..	..	..	..	..
101 China	22	7.9	18	3.2	1.8	2.4	12.4	66	19
102 Lebanon	..	..	45	21.3	..	..	16.8	..	..
103 Iran, Islamic Rep. of	28	4.9	39	16.2	2.4	4.1	22.4	72	14
104 Botswana	32	5.9	26	23.8	2.7	5.6	16.3	76	20
105 Guyana	36	3.4	41	30.8	..	8.8	8.1	55	18
106 Vanuatu	29	..	..	..	..	4.4	24.6	86	3
107 Algeria	28	4.9	14	6.6	5.6	9.1	27.0	54	17
108 Indonesia	23	10.6	39	1.6	2.5	0.9	4.3	52	20
109 Gabon	46	20.6	22	26.2	2.1	5.7	9.4	..	..
110 El Salvador	40	..	50	1.9	2.3	1.8	12.5	68	14
111 Nicaragua	33	18.8	43	9.9	1.5	2.5	12.0	..	..

						Public expenditure on				
HDI rank		Primary pupil-teacher ratio 1988-90	Secondary technical enrolment (as % of total secondary) 1987-88	Tertiary science enrolment (as % of total tertiary) 1987-88	Tertiary students abroad (as % of those at home) 1987-88	Education (as % of GNP) 1960	Education (as % of GNP) 1988-90	Education (as % of total public expenditure) 1988-90	Primary and secondary education (as % of all levels) 1987-90	Higher education (as % of all levels) 1987-90
Low human development		43	..	32	6.6	2.3	3.5	10.3	71	18
	Excluding India	41	6.0	31	11.7	2.3	3.9	12.2	72	19
112	Maldives	..	..	..	..	..	6.9	8.5	..	..
113	Guatemala	35	..	39	1.9	1.4	..	12.4	..	..
114	Cape Verde	33	8.3	..	..	..	2.9	..	69	1
115	Viet Nam	34	..	..	4.3	..	..	..	..	..
116	Honduras	39	32.6	29	3.7	2.2	4.6	15.9	73	21
117	Swaziland	32	1.4	..	11.5	..	7.2	22.5	62	21
118	Solomon Islands	23	17.3	..	..	..	..	12.4	..	..
119	Morocco	25	1.4	59	13.9	3.1	7.4	25.5	84	16
120	Lesotho	55	3.7	16	10.7	3.2	4.0	14.8	76	18
121	Zimbabwe	36	1.7	32	8.3	0.5	8.2	15.0	88	8
122	Bolivia	25	..	21	1.8	1.5	2.4	20.1	88	3
123	Myanmar	34	1.2	32	0.3	2.2	1.9	..	86	13
124	Egypt	23	21.8	38	1.5	4.1	6.0	..	70	30
125	São Tomé and Principe	35	1.4	..	..	..	4.3	18.8	..	..
126	Congo	66	11.9	8	28.3	2.5	5.5	14.4	66	34
127	Kenya	33	1.6	21	17.3	4.6	6.4	27.0	77	15
128	Madagascar	40	4.3	20	11.5	2.3	1.9	..	..	..
129	Papua New Guinea	32	11.2	11	5.7	2.5	..	..	..	..
130	Zambia	44	..	..	14.2	1.6	2.9	8.7	66	17
131	Ghana	27	1.9	30	15.3	3.8	3.4	23.4	65	12
132	Pakistan	41	1.6	..	9.0	1.1	3.4	5.0	70	18
133	Cameroon	51	22.5	35	40.3	1.7	3.3	18.7	66	23
134	India	46	..	32	0.5	2.3	3.2	8.5	71	17
135	Namibia	..	..	9	..	..	..	4.1	56	33
136	Côte d'Ivoire	36	9.8	28	20.2	4.6	..	22.6	83	17
137	Haiti	35	..	..	31.1	1.4	1.8	20.0	72	9
138	Tanzania, U. Rep. of	35	..	9	31.4	2.1	5.8	11.4	74	17
139	Comoros	36	1.4	..	..	..	4.3	13.2	70	21
140	Zaire	37	23.1	34	14.7	2.4	0.9	6.4	65	35
141	Lao People's Dem. Rep.	28	5.1	42	13.5	..	1.1	6.6	..	..
142	Nigeria	39	..	30	6.8	1.5	1.7	12.0	57	..
143	Yemen	35	..	12	33.2	..	..	23.5	65	4
144	Liberia	..	..	..	18.0	0.7	5.7	24.3	..	..
145	Togo	5	5.9	52	26.2	1.9	5.2	21.2	64	14
146	Uganda	35	2.5	41	9.9	3.2	3.4	22.5	81	13
147	Bangladesh	63	0.7	34	0.8	0.6	2.2	10.5	87	8
148	Cambodia	..	..	..	..	..	..	..	..	..
149	Rwanda	57	..	25	37.7	0.3	4.2	25.4	82	16
150	Senegal	58	2.9	31	23.0	2.4	..	..	60	23
151	Ethiopia	43	0.5	37	17.0	0.8	4.8	9.4	81	13
152	Nepal	37	..	30	1.8	0.4	2.9	10.8	56	33
153	Malawi	64	3.5	37	13.9	2.1	3.5	8.8	57	22
154	Burundi	66	19.1	45	18.6	2.4	3.5	16.7	76	22
155	Equatorial Guinea	..	..	..	..	..	1.7	3.9	..	..
156	Central African Rep.	90	4.4	34	45.3	2.0	2.8	16.8	67	22
157	Mozambique	58	8.0	25	11.1	..	..	..	..	..
158	Sudan	35	..	27	27.3	1.9	4.8	9.1	87	(.)
159	Bhutan	37	..	6	19.8	..	3.7	..	..	..
160	Angola	33	..	26	29.5	0.3	7.3	13.8	96	4
161	Mauritania	49	3.1	12	33.6	2.1	..	..	66	24
162	Benin	35	6.0	18	25.2	2.5	..	..	..	..
163	Djibouti	43	25.3	..	..	..	2.5	10.5	80	12
164	Guinea-Bissau	25	8.8	..	..	..	2.8	..	92	..
165	Chad	67	7.0	12	50.2	0.9	..	..	..	..
166	Somalia	19	..	18	9.8	0.9	0.4	2.8	..	..
167	Gambia	31	..	..	..	..	5.2	11.0	63	18
168	Mali	38	11.5	3	38.5	2.0	3.3	17.3	71	13
169	Niger	42	1.4	24	27.9	0.5	3.1	9.0	83	..
170	Burkina Faso	57	6.4	21	30.2	1.5	2.3	17.5	68	32
171	Afghanistan	37	..	22	9.7	..	..	4.0	88	12
172	Sierra Leone	34	..	..	48.8	..	1.4	12.4	53	35
173	Guinea	40	6.3	..	19.5	1.5	1.4	21.5	42	31
All developing countries		34	9.8	32	2.9	2.2	3.4	11.9	65	18
	Least developed countries	45	4.7	31	7.9	1.3	2.8	11.5	73	18
	Sub-Saharan Africa	41	7.5	29	14.2	2.4	3.4	13.9	68	20
Industrial countries		..	..	39	..	..	..	..	..	..
World		..	..	36	..	..	..	..	..	..

Note: Data for industrial countries for this subject area are in table 36.

165

HDI rank	Radios (per 1,000 people) 1990	Televisions (per 1,000 people) 1990	Daily newspaper circulation (per 1,000 people) 1988-90	Telephones (per 1,000 people) 1986-88	Passenger cars (per 1,000 people) 1985-89	Book titles published (per 100,000 people) 1988-90	Annual cinema attendances (per person) 1987-90	Average number of people served by one post office 1986-88
High human development	510	180	200	160	71	32	2.1	13,310
20 Barbados	882	267	118	408	145	30	..	15,900
24 Hong Kong	649	274	632	504	29	..	12.2	..
27 Cyprus	292	150	111	439	238	99	..	900
30 Uruguay	603	233	233	163	72	26	2.1	..
31 Trinidad and Tobago	468	302	..	174	208	..	..	5,200
32 Bahamas	542	225	138	525	..	..	..	1,600
33 Korea, Rep. of	1,006	210	280	296	27	92	1.2	14,500
36 Chile	342	205	455	68	49	18	1.0	10,600
42 Costa Rica	259	149	102	143	53	8	..	7,900
43 Singapore	643	376	280	456	100	..	12.5	19,800
44 Brunei Darussalam	259	233	38	182	..	9	13.0	16,900
46 Argentina	681	222	124	115	125	..	1.7	5,400
50 Venezuela	436	167	142	92	94	..	0.8	..
51 Dominica	512	61	..	86	..	..	..	..
52 Kuwait	343	285	221	189	227	41	0.6	..
53 Mexico	243	139	127	96	65	4	..	10,900
55 Qatar	514	516	217	349	233	..	1.9	10,400
Medium human development	210	71	..	29	15	6	1.7	17,190
Excluding China	240	120	62	59	39	7	1.7	11,790
56 Mauritius	356	215	74	71	41	7	8.5	9,500
57 Malaysia	429	148	140	97	91	26	..	2,800
58 Bahrain	531	403	56	282	185	..	..	..
59 Grenada	635	353	..	64	..	..	..	..
60 Antigua and Barbuda	342	303	79	..	185	..	..	..
61 Colombia	170	115	61	81	28	5	2.0	17,200
63 Seychelles	464	87	46	209	54	..	..	..
65 Suriname	635	130	95	101	85	..	..	..
67 United Arab Emirates	324	110	157	245	..	18	..	15,600
68 Panama	223	165	70	104	65	..	..	6,800
69 Jamaica	411	130	63	..	..	..	..	2,800
70 Brazil	379	213	54	96	104	..	0.7	11,900
71 Fiji	576	14	35	87	48	..	..	3,200
72 Saint Lucia	667	167	..	121	42	..	..	1,900
73 Turkey	161	175	72	117	26	11	0.5	800
74 Thailand	185	112	72	19	15	14	..	13,100
75 Cuba	345	207	124	52	22	21	7.6	12,300
76 Saint Vincent	638	129	..	85	47	..	..	2,600
79 Saint Kitts and Nevis	614	205	..	76	..	7	..	..
81 Syrian Arab Rep.	251	59	22	58	11	..	1.1	19,100
82 Belize	583	166	..	..	..	..	..	1,500
84 Saudi Arabia	318	283	42	158	..	..	..	15,800
85 South Africa	326	105	38	146	96	14	..	..
86 Sri Lanka	197	35	32	11	..	14	2.3	4,300
87 Libyan Arab Jamahiriya	224	99	15	..	..	3	..	10,900
89 Ecuador	315	83	87	36	15	..	..	18,300
90 Paraguay	171	59	39	27	..	..	..	7,500
91 Korea, Dem. Rep. of	119	15	230	..	..	..	9.2	..
92 Philippines	138	48	54	17	6	2	..	..
93 Tunisia	196	80	37	43	23	4	..	11,000
94 Oman	646	766	41	53	..	..	..	14,600
95 Peru	253	97	79	31	19	2	1.9	7,700
96 Iraq	205	69	34	..	15	..	..	..
97 Dominican Rep.	170	84	32	..	23	..	..	..
98 Samoa	440	37	..	..	..	..	..	..
99 Jordan	254	81	56	..	58	..	..	3,600
100 Mongolia	132	41	74	..	..	33	..	..
101 China	184	31	..	9	2	6	..	20,800
102 Lebanon	840	330	118	..	..	..	..	..
103 Iran, Islamic Rep. of	247	70	27	41	2	12	0.6	12,400
104 Botswana	115	15	14	23	15	..	..	7,500
105 Guyana	486	38	101	41	..	6	..	6,500
106 Vanuatu	278	9	..	23	18	..	..	..
107 Algeria	233	74	51	40	..	..	0.9	10,500
108 Indonesia	147	60	28	5	7	(.)	..	9,900
109 Gabon	141	37	17	..	16	..	..	..
110 El Salvador	404	90	87	27	28	(.)	..	13,500
111 Nicaragua	249	62	65	..	14	..	1.8	..

HDI rank	Radios (per 1,000 people) 1990	Televisions (per 1,000 people) 1990	Daily newspaper circulation (per 1,000 people) 1988-90	Telephones (per 1,000 people) 1986-88	Passenger cars (per 1,000 people) 1985-89	Book titles published (per 100,000 people) 1988-90	Annual cinema attendances (per person) 1987-90	Average number of people served by one post office 1986-88
Low human development	110	31	..	10	5	2	5.1	15,680
Excluding India	130	25	15	15	10	2	1.6	28,080
112 Maldives	116	25	7	14	..	..	..	7,000
113 Guatemala	65	52	21	16	..	..	1.0	..
114 Cape Verde	159	..	..	8	..	3	..	..
115 Viet Nam	108	39	9	93	..	..	5.9	..
116 Honduras	385	72	39	14	9	..	..	..
117 Swaziland	155	20	13	29	32	..	..	..
118 Solomon Islands	119	..	..	19	..	..	..	..
119 Morocco	209	74	13	16	24	..	1.9	20,100
120 Lesotho	70	6	11	12	4	..	..	11,500
121 Zimbabwe	85	31	21	32	30	4	0.6	24,300
122 Bolivia	599	..	55	29	5	6	..	..
123 Myanmar	82	2	5	2	2	..	..	..
124 Egypt	324	109	57	28	20	3	0.7	5,500
125 São Tomé and Principe	264	..	..	24	24	..	..	9,600
126 Congo	110	6	7	12	13	..	..	14,400
127 Kenya	125	9	15	15	..	1	..	20,900
128 Madagascar	200	20	4	4	..	1	..	1,200
129 Papua New Guinea	72	2	13	20	5	..	..	34,200
130 Zambia	77	30	12	12	..	..	..	15,200
131 Ghana	266	15	13	6	..	..	0.3	12,200
132 Pakistan	87	17	15	7	5	..	..	8,100
133 Cameroon	139	29	7	6	8	..	..	33,800
134 India	79	32	..	6	2	2	6.5	4,700
135 Namibia	135	17	..	..	..	6	..	..
136 Côte d'Ivoire	142	61	8	..	16	..	..	8,600
137 Haiti	46	5	7	9	4	5	0.4	..
138 Tanzania, U. Rep. of	24	2	7	6	..	1	0.2	30,300
139 Comoros	125	(.)	..	..	..	..	..	..
140 Zaire	103	1	..	1	..	..	..	..
141 Lao People's Dem. Rep.	126	7	3	..	..	3	..	..
142 Nigeria	172	32	16	3	4	1	0.1	28,400
143 Yemen	33	31	11	15	..	..	2.5	65,800
144 Liberia	225	18	14	..	..	..	..	30,400
145 Togo	211	6	3	..	1	..	..	8,100
146 Uganda	101	10	2	4	2	..	..	36,100
147 Bangladesh	42	5	6	..	(.)	1	..	13,200
148 Cambodia	113	9	..	..	..	..	..	..
149 Rwanda	62	..	(.)	2	1	..	..	24,300
150 Senegal	113	36	7	..	1	..	..	..
151 Ethiopia	191	2	1	3	1	1	..	87,000
152 Nepal	34	2	8	..	..	1	..	..
153 Malawi	238	..	3	6	2	2	..	23,800
154 Burundi	58	1	4	..	2	..	(.)	..
155 Equatorial Guinea	423	9	6	..	..	5	..	20,500
156 Central African Rep.	66	4	1	3	..	..	..	32,300
157 Mozambique	42	3	5	4	2	..	0.7	43,800
158 Sudan	250	71	24	4	4	..	0.6	27,300
159 Bhutan	16	..	..	..	..	..	..	..
160 Angola	54	6	11	..	..	..	0.4	64,700
161 Mauritania	144	23	1	..	6	..	..	..
162 Benin	90	5	3	4	6	..	0.4	24,000
163 Djibouti	90	56	..	23	..	..	..	..
164 Guinea-Bissau	39	..	6	..	4	..	..	..
165 Chad	238	1	(.)	2	2	..	..	..
166 Somalia	43	14	1	..	..	..	..	..
167 Gambia	170	..	2	10	..	5	..	..
168 Mali	43	1	1	..	3	..	..	66,300
169 Niger	60	5	1	2	..	..	..	28,100
170 Burkina Faso	26	5	(.)	2	1	..	0.5	37,000
171 Afghanistan	105	8	11	..	..	17	..	..
172 Sierra Leone	223	10	2	..	..	..	..	..
173 Guinea	42	7	..	..	..	..	0.4	..
All developing countries	180	55	50	28	13	6	..	16,330
Least developed countries	100	9	6	4	2	2	..	39,390
Sub-Saharan Africa	150	23	11	18	15	3	0.3	40,620
Industrial countries	1,130	545	304	590	390	61	3.0	4,200
World	360	148	130	130	87	12	..	14,170

Note: Data for industrial countries for this subject area are in table 37.

167

HDI rank	Labour force (as % of total population) 1989-91	Women in labour force (as % of total labour force) 1990	Percentage of labour force in						Earnings per employee annual growth rate (%)	
			Agriculture		Industry		Services		1970-80	1980-89
			1965	1989-91	1965	1989-91	1965	1989-91		
High human development	36	29	28	16	32	33	40	51	..	..
20 Barbados	46	48	..	4	..	26	..	70	..	..
24 Hong Kong	50	36	6	1	53	35	41	64	6.4	4.4
27 Cyprus	48	37	..	14	..	37	..	49	..	..
30 Uruguay	40	31	20	15	29	18	51	67	..	0.8
31 Trinidad and Tobago	38	27	20	10	35	41	45	49	..	-0.7
32 Bahamas	51	47								
33 Korea, Rep. of	42	34	55	16	15	34	30	50	10.0	6.3
36 Chile	37	31	27	18	29	30	44	52	8.2	-1.0
42 Costa Rica	37	29	47	24	19	30	34	46	..	..
43 Singapore	56	39	6	(.)	27	40	67	60	3.0	5.0
44 Brunei Darussalam	..	..	..	..	..	..	..	..	..	..
46 Argentina	38	21	18	13	34	34	48	53	-1.5	-0.8
50 Venezuela	37	22	30	12	24	32	46	56	3.8	-2.9
51 Dominica	38	42	..	..	..	..	..	..	..	..
52 Kuwait	39	14	2	..	34	..	64	..	..	3.8
53 Mexico	30	31	49	22	22	31	29	47	1.2	-3.9
55 Qatar	42	7	..	3	..	28	..	69	..	..
Medium human development	51	39	73	61	11	16	16	23	..	..
Excluding China	40	33	54	38	18	19	29	43	..	..
56 Mauritius	39	35	37	19	25	31	38	50	1.8	-0.6
57 Malaysia	38	31	58	31	13	27	29	42	2.0	3.2
58 Bahrain	27	10	..	3	..	35	..	62	..	..
59 Grenada	40	49	..	..	..	..	..	..	..	..
60 Antigua and Barbuda	..	..	..	..	..	..	..	..	..	..
61 Colombia	45	41	45	1	21	31	34	68	-0.2	1.7
63 Seychelles	44	42								
65 Suriname	..	..	..	20	..	20	..	60	..	..
67 United Arab Emirates	50	6	21	5	32	38	47	57	..	..
68 Panama	36	27	46	12	16	21	38	67	0.2	2.1
69 Jamaica	45	31	37	25	20	12	43	63	-0.2	-0.8
70 Brazil	43	35	49	28	20	25	31	47	4.0	7.1
71 Fiji	31	19	..	44	..	20	..	36	..	..
72 Saint Lucia	..	..	..	..	..	..	..	..	..	..
73 Turkey	38	33	75	46	11	22	14	32	6.1	-3.1
74 Thailand	56	47	82	70	5	11	13	19	1.0	6.5
75 Cuba	44	32	33	24	25	29	42	47	..	..
76 Saint Vincent	..	..	..	..	..	..	..	..	..	..
79 Saint Kitts and Nevis	..	..	..	..	..	..	..	..	..	..
81 Syrian Arab Rep.	26	15	52	22	20	36	28	42	2.8	-5.6
82 Belize	31	33	..	..	..	..	..	..	..	..
84 Saudi Arabia	29	7	68	48	11	14	21	37	..	..
85 South Africa	39	33	32	14	30	24	38	62	2.7	(.)
86 Sri Lanka	43	37	56	49	14	12	30	45	..	2.1
87 Libyan Arab Jamahiriya	24	9	41	18	21	29	38	53	..	..
89 Ecuador	35	30	55	30	19	24	26	46	3.3	-0.2
90 Paraguay	45	41	54	48	20	21	26	31	..	..
91 Korea, Dem. Rep. of	45	46	57	43	23	30	20	27	..	..
92 Philippines	36	37	58	41	16	19	26	40	-3.7	6.4
93 Tunisia	30	13	50	22	21	16	29	62	4.2	..
94 Oman	28	8	62	49	15	22	23	29	..	..
95 Peru	40	33	49	35	19	12	32	53	..	-3.0
96 Iraq	24	6	50	13	20	8	30	79	..	..
97 Dominican Rep.	30	15	59	46	14	15	27	39	-1.1	-4.4
98 Samoa	..	..	..	..	..	..	..	..	..	..
99 Jordan	23	10	37	10	26	26	37	64	..	-1.0
100 Mongolia	46	45	54	40	20	21	26	39	..	..
101 China	59	43	81	73	8	14	11	13	..	4.2
102 Lebanon	30	27	29	14	24	27	47	59	..	..
103 Iran, Islamic Rep. of	26	18	49	25	26	28	25	47	..	-8.2
104 Botswana	35	35	88	43	4	5	8	52	2.6	-5.7
105 Guyana	36	21	..	27	..	26	..	47	..	..
106 Vanuatu	47	46	..	68	..	8	..	24	..	..
107 Algeria	24	4	57	14	17	11	26	75	-1.0	..
108 Indonesia	43	40	70	54	9	8	21	38	5.0	5.9
109 Gabon	48	38	..	75	..	11	..	14	..	..
110 El Salvador	41	45	58	10	16	35	26	55	2.4	-9.4
111 Nicaragua	35	34	56	46	16	16	28	38	..	-10.0

HDI rank	Labour force (as % of total population) 1989-91	Women in labour force (as % of total labour force) 1990	Percentage of labour force in						Earnings per employee annual growth rate (%)	
			Agriculture		Industry		Services			
			1965	1989-91	1965	1989-91	1965	1989-91	1970-80	1980-89
Low human development	37	26	74	63	10	11	16	26	..	..
Excluding India	36	27	75	64	9	11	16	25	..	..
112 Maldives	27	20	..	25	..	32	..	43		
113 Guatemala	34	26	64	48	15	23	21	29	-3.2	-1.9
114 Cape Verde	34	29	..	52	..	23	..	25		
115 Viet Nam	49	47	79	67	6	12	15	21	..	..
116 Honduras	39	18	68	36	12	17	20	47	..	1.5
117 Swaziland	24	40	..	74	..	9	..	17	..	..
118 Solomon Islands	..	..	..	..	..	..	..	..		
119 Morocco	31	20	61	46	15	25	24	29	..	-3.6
120 Lesotho	46	44	91	23	3	33	6	44	..	..
121 Zimbabwe	41	35	79	64	8	6	13	30	1.6	(.)
122 Bolivia	31	24	54	47	20	19	26	34	(.)	-4.8
123 Myanmar	41	37	63	64	14	9	23	27	..	..
124 Egypt	28	11	55	34	15	22	30	44	4.1	-2.1
125 São Tomé and Principe	..	..	..	..	..	..	..	..		
126 Congo	40	39	66	62	11	12	23	26	..	..
127 Kenya	40	40	86	81	5	7	9	12	-3.4	0.1
128 Madagascar	43	40	85	81	4	6	11	13	-0.9	-8.3
129 Papua New Guinea	47	39	87	76	6	10	7	14	2.9	-1.9
130 Zambia	32	29	79	38	8	8	13	54	-3.2	6.5
131 Ghana	38	40	61	59	15	11	24	30		7.8
132 Pakistan	28	11	60	44	18	25	22	31	3.4	6.1
133 Cameroon	39	30	87	73	4	5	9	22	..	..
134 India	38	26	73	62	12	11	15	27	0.4	3.0
135 Namibia	29	24	..	43	..	22	..	35	..	..
136 Côte d'Ivoire	39	34	80	65	5	8	15	27	-0.9	
137 Haiti	41	40	77	50	7	6	16	44	-3.3	4.6
138 Tanzania, U. Rep. of	47	48	91	85	3	5	6	10	..	-12.7
139 Comoros	38	41	..	83	..	6	..	11	..	..
140 Zaire	37	36	82	71	9	13	9	16	..	..
141 Lao People's Dem. Rep.	55	45	80	76	5	7	15	17	..	..
142 Nigeria	31	20	72	43	10	13	18	44	-0.8	..
143 Yemen	25	13	73	63	8	11	19	26	..	..
144 Liberia	36	31	79	75	10	9	11	16	..	1.7
145 Togo	41	37	78	65	9	6	13	29	..	..
146 Uganda	45	41	91	86	3	4	6	10	..	..
147 Bangladesh	30	7	84	56	5	10	11	34	-3.0	0.9
148 Cambodia	47	39	80	74	4	7	16	19	..	..
149 Rwanda	46	48	95	90	2	4	3	6	..	..
150 Senegal	34	26	83	81	6	6	11	13	-4.9	..
151 Ethiopia	41	42	86	80	5	8	9	12	-4.6	0.1
152 Nepal	40	34	94	93	2	1	4	6	..	..
153 Malawi	42	42	92	82	3	3	5	15	..	-0.8
154 Burundi	53	..	94	92	2	2	4	6	-7.5	..
155 Equatorial Guinea	39	36	..	66	..	11	..	23	..	..
156 Central African Rep.	48	46	88	83	3	3	9	14	..	..
157 Mozambique	55	48	87	85	6	7	7	8	..	..
158 Sudan	35	29	81	62	5	10	14	28	..	..
159 Bhutan	46	32	94	92	2	3	4	5	..	..
160 Angola	41	39	79	73	8	10	13	17	..	..
161 Mauritania	33	22	89	69	3	9	8	22	..	..
162 Benin	35	24	83	70	5	7	12	23	..	..
163 Djibouti	..	..	..	..	..	..	..	..	..	..
164 Guinea-Bissau	30	42	..	82	..	4	..	14	..	..
165 Chad	37	17	92	83	3	5	5	12	..	..
166 Somalia	29	39	81	76	6	8	13	16	-5.1	..
167 Gambia	36	41	..	84	..	7	..	9	..	..
168 Mali	32	16	91	85	1	2	8	13	..	..
169 Niger	51	47	95	85	1	3	4	12	..	0.4
170 Burkina Faso	51	49	90	87	3	4	7	9	..	..
171 Afghanistan	30	8	69	61	11	14	20	25	..	..
172 Sierra Leone	35	33	78	70	11	14	11	16	..	..
173 Guinea	39	30	87	78	6	1	7	21	..	..
All developing countries	44	33	72	61	11	14	17	25	1.3	4.0
Least developed countries	38	29	83	72	6	8	11	20	..	..
Sub-Saharan Africa	39	34	79	67	8	9	13	24	-1.5	..
Industrial countries	49	42	22	7	36	26	42	67	2.2	1.4
World	45	34	57	48	19	17	24	35	1.6	3.5

Note: Data for industrial countries for this subject area are in table 38.

18 Wealth, poverty and social investment

HDI rank	Real GDP per capita (PPP$) 1990	GNP per capita (US$) 1990	Income share: Lowest 40% of households (%) 1985-89	Income share: Ratio of highest 20% to lowest 20% 1985-89	Gini coefficient 1975-88	People in absolute poverty: Total (%) 1977-89	People in absolute poverty: Urban (%) 1977-89	People in absolute poverty: Rural (%) 1977-89	Public expenditure on Education (as % of GNP) 1988-90	Public expenditure on Health (as % of GNP) 1988-90	Social security benefits expenditure (as % of GDP) 1980-89
High human development	6,290	3,470	..	..	..	..	..	..	3.5	4.6	..
20 Barbados	8,304	6,460							8.0		0.9
24 Hong Kong	15,595	11,700	16.2	8.7	0.45				2.7	..	
27 Cyprus	9,953	8,230							3.6	4.2	2.3
30 Uruguay	5,916	2,620							3.3		7.5
31 Trinidad and Tobago	6,604	3,460						39	4.1	2.6	2.1
32 Bahamas	11,235	11,550								3.5	0.5
33 Korea, Rep. of	6,733	5,450			0.36	13	18	11	3.7	6.4	..
36 Chile	5,099	1,950	..		0.46				2.9		9.9
42 Costa Rica	4,542	1,900	11.6	16.5	0.42				4.6	5.6	6.3
43 Singapore	15,880	11,200	15.0	9.6	0.42				3.4	2.9	7.1
44 Brunei Darussalam									4.9	2.2	
46 Argentina	4,295	2,380							1.5		
50 Venezuela	6,169	2,560	13.9	10.8					4.1		1.1
51 Dominica	3,910	2,220							5.8		
52 Kuwait	15,178								5.0		
53 Mexico	5,918	2,490			0.50				4.1	2.9	1.5
55 Qatar		15,870							3.4	3.1	
Medium human development	2,710	940	..	..	..	..	..	..	3.3	3.7	..
Excluding China	3,660	1,690	..	..	..	..	..	..	3.6	3.9	..
56 Mauritius	5,750	2,310							3.5	2.0	5.6
57 Malaysia	6,140	2,330	13.9	11.1	0.48	32	13	38	5.5	1.6	0.5
58 Bahrain	10,706	6,830							5.4	6.0	0.1
59 Grenada	4,081	2,130									
60 Antigua and Barbuda		4,290									
61 Colombia	4,237	1,260	12.7	13.3	0.45		34		2.9	3.0	1.5
63 Seychelles	4,191	4,820							9.1		1.7
65 Suriname	3,927	3,350							9.7	5.7	0.6
67 United Arab Emirates	16,753	19,870							1.9	9.0	
68 Panama	3,317	1,900			0.57	26	21	30	5.7		9.4
69 Jamaica	2,979	1,500	15.3	9.1	0.66				5.9	2.9	1.2
70 Brazil	4,718	2,680	8.1	26.1	0.57				3.9	3.9	4.6
71 Fiji	4,427	1,780						30	5.0		0.6
72 Saint Lucia	3,470	2,350							7.2		
73 Turkey	4,652	1,640			0.51				1.8	2.8	4.5
74 Thailand	3,986	1,420			0.47	32	15	34	3.8	5.6	
75 Cuba									6.7	3.4	7.1
76 Saint Vincent	3,647	1,710							6.9		
79 Saint Kitts and Nevis		3,540					40		3.0		
81 Syrian Arab Rep.	4,756	1,000							4.4		
82 Belize		1,960								2.2	
84 Saudi Arabia	10,989	7,070							5.8	2.1	1.4
85 South Africa	4,865	2,530									
86 Sri Lanka	2,405	470	13.3	11.7	0.45				2.7	2.3	2.0
87 Libyan Arab Jamahiriya									9.6		
89 Ecuador	3,074	960				56	40	65	2.7		1.6
90 Paraguay	2,790	1,090				39	19	50	1.0	3.2	
91 Korea, Dem. Rep. of											
92 Philippines	2,303	730	15.2	8.7	0.45	58	48	63	3.0	5.3	0.7
93 Tunisia	3,579	1,450			0.40	17	20	15	6.0	2.4	3.6
94 Oman	9,972	5,650							3.7	2.1	
95 Peru	2,622	1,100	12.9	11.8	0.31		49		3.5	2.4	
96 Iraq	3,508								5.1		
97 Dominican Rep.	2,404	830				44	45	43	1.5		0.5
98 Samoa	1,900	920								5.6	
99 Jordan	2,345	1,340				16	14	17	4.4	6.0	(.)
100 Mongolia											
101 China	1,990	370							2.4	3.1	3.4
102 Lebanon											1.2
103 Iran, Islamic Rep. of	3,253	2,490			0.46			40	4.1	3.2	
104 Botswana	3,419	2,230	9.0	23.6		50	40	55	5.6	3.2	
105 Guyana	1,464	380							8.8		0.8
106 Vanuatu	2,005	1,100							4.4	2.9	
107 Algeria	3,011	2,330					20		9.1	6.0	
108 Indonesia	2,181	560	21.2	4.7	0.31	17	20	16	0.9	2.5	
109 Gabon	4,147	3,550							5.7	3.2	2.0
110 El Salvador	1,950	1,000			0.40	27	20	32	1.8		1.0
111 Nicaragua	1,497	420				20	21	19	2.5		1.5

HDI rank	Real GDP per capita (PPP$) 1990	GNP per capita (US$) 1990	Income share Lowest 40% of households (%) 1985-89	Income share Ratio of highest 20% to lowest 20% 1985-89	Gini coefficient 1975-88	People in absolute poverty Total (%) 1977-89	Urban (%) 1977-89	Rural (%) 1977-89	Public expenditure on Education (as % of GNP) 1988-90	Health (as % of GNP) 1988-90	Social security benefits expenditure (as % of GDP) 1980-89
Low human development	1,110	360	..	..	..	..	..	..	3.5	3.2	..
Excluding India	1,140	360	..	..	..	..	..	..	3.9	3.3	..
112 Maldives	..	450	..	..	..	..	..	..	6.9	5.0	..
113 Guatemala	2,576	910	14.1	10.0	..	71	66	74	..	1.1	0.8
114 Cape Verde	1,769	680	..	..	..	..	..	..	2.9	..	..
115 Viet Nam	..	..	..	..	..	..	..	..	..	..	..
116 Honduras	1,470	640	..	..	0.62	46	14	55	4.6	..	..
117 Swaziland	2,384	1,030	..	..	..	48	45	50	7.2	5.8	..
118 Solomon Islands	2,689	590	..	..	..	..	..	..	..	5.0	..
119 Morocco	2,348	970	22.8	4.0	0.40	31	28	32	7.4	3.2	1.5
120 Lesotho	1,743	540	..	..	..	54	50	55	4.0	1.2	..
121 Zimbabwe	1,484	650	..	..	..	..	..	..	8.2	5.5	0.1
122 Bolivia	1,572	630	..	..	..	..	..	85	2.4	2.2	2.3
123 Myanmar	659	..	..	..	..	..	..	..	1.9	0.8	..
124 Egypt	1,988	610	..	..	0.38	23	21	25	6.0	5.0	1.1
125 São Tomé and Principe	..	400	..	..	..	..	..	..	4.3	..	..
126 Congo	2,362	1,000	..	..	..	..	..	..	5.5	3.0	..
127 Kenya	1,058	370	..	..	..	52	10	55	6.4	2.1	0.6
128 Madagascar	704	230	..	..	..	..	..	..	1.9	0.9	..
129 Papua New Guinea	1,786	850	..	..	..	73	10	75	..	3.2	..
130 Zambia	744	420	..	..	..	71	26	80	2.9	5.1	..
131 Ghana	1,016	390	18.6	6.2	..	42	59	37	3.4	1.2	..
132 Pakistan	1,862	400	19.0	5.8	0.36	30	32	29	3.4	4.5	..
133 Cameroon	1,646	960	..	..	..	37	15	40	3.3	..	..
134 India	1,072	360	20.4	5.1	0.42	49	40	51	3.2	3.2	0.5
135 Namibia	..	1,080	..	..	..	..	..	..	..	5.0	..
136 Côte d'Ivoire	1,324	750	13.0	10.5	0.55	..	..	..	..	3.0	0.5
137 Haiti	933	370	..	..	..	74	55	78	1.8	..	..
138 Tanzania, U. Rep. of	572	110	..	..	..	58	10	60	5.8	..	..
139 Comoros	721	480	..	..	..	..	..	..	4.3	3.3	..
140 Zaire	367	220	..	..	..	..	..	80	0.9	5.6	..
141 Lao People's Dem. Rep.	..	200	..	..	..	..	..	..	1.1	2.0	..
142 Nigeria	1,215	290	..	..	..	..	..	..	1.7	(.)	..
143 Yemen	1,562	540	..	..	..	..	..	..	..	..	..
144 Liberia	857	..	..	..	..	..	23	..	5.7	3.5	..
145 Togo	734	410	..	..	..	..	42	..	5.2	3.5	0.8
146 Uganda	524	180	..	..	..	..	..	..	3.4	..	..
147 Bangladesh	872	210	23.7	3.7	0.34	..	..	..	2.2	0.9	2.1
148 Cambodia	..	170	..	..	..	..	..	..	..	..	..
149 Rwanda	657	310	..	..	..	..	30	..	4.2	0.6	0.3
150 Senegal	1,248	710	..	..	..	..	..	..	..	1.8	1.4
151 Ethiopia	369	120	..	..	..	..	..	..	4.8	2.0	1.4
152 Nepal	920	180	..	..	0.53	60	55	61	2.9	0.7	..
153 Malawi	640	200	..	..	..	82	25	85	3.5	..	..
154 Burundi	625	210	..	..	..	84	55	85	3.5	6.0	0.7
155 Equatorial Guinea	..	340	..	..	..	64	60	65	1.7	..	..
156 Central African Rep.	768	390	..	..	..	..	..	..	2.8	..	..
157 Mozambique	1,072	80	..	..	..	..	..	..	..	1.4	..
158 Sudan	949	400	..	..	..	..	..	85	4.8	0.3	(.)
159 Bhutan	..	190	..	..	..	..	..	..	3.7	4.2	..
160 Angola	840	..	..	..	..	..	..	..	7.3	1.8	..
161 Mauritania	1,057	500	..	..	..	..	..	..	..	5.5	..
162 Benin	1,043	360	..	..	..	..	..	65	..	5.1	0.6
163 Djibouti	..	..	..	..	..	..	..	..	2.5	..	1.4
164 Guinea-Bissau	841	180	..	..	..	..	..	..	2.8	1.3	..
165 Chad	559	180	..	..	..	54	30	56	..	..	..
166 Somalia	836	120	..	..	..	..	..	70	0.4	..	..
167 Gambia	913	340	..	..	..	..	..	40	5.2	1.6	..
168 Mali	572	280	..	..	..	46	27	48	3.3	0.5	0.5
169 Niger	645	310	..	..	..	..	..	35	3.1	1.8	0.3
170 Burkina Faso	618	330	..	..	..	..	..	..	2.3	..	0.4
171 Afghanistan	714	..	..	..	..	35	18	36	..	1.6	..
172 Sierra Leone	1,086	250	..	..	0.59	..	..	65	1.4	..	..
173 Guinea	501	440	..	..	..	..	..	..	1.4	2.0	..
All developing countries	2,170	810	..	..	..	32	25	36	3.4	3.7	..
Least developed countries	740	240	..	..	..	70	62	72	2.8	2.4	..
Sub-Saharan Africa	1,200	490	..	..	..	..	..	..	3.4	3.1	..
Industrial countries	14,400	14,580	..	..	..	..	..	..	..	..	..
World	4,890	4,010	..	..	..	..	..	..	..	..	..

Note: Data for industrial countries for this subject area are in table 40.

HDI rank	Official development assistance (ODA) received				Aid social allocation ratio (%) 1988/90	Aid social priority ratio (%) 1988/90	Aid human expenditure ratio (%) 1988/91	Social priority aid (as % of total aid) 1988/90
	US$ millions 1991	As % of GNP 1991	Per capita (US$) 1991	Per poor person (US$) 1991				
High human development	**1,050T**	**0.2**	**5**	**..**	**22.7**	**20.5**	**0.009**	**4.7**
20 Barbados	4	0.2	13	..	..	..	..	..
24 Hong Kong	34	0.1	6	..	58.1	..	..	..
27 Cyprus	50	0.9	71	..	84.2	..	..	..
30 Uruguay	59	0.7	19	..	26.3	22.0	0.043	5.8
31 Trinidad and Tobago	9	0.2	8	..	21.0	..	..	..
32 Bahamas	3	0.1	10	..	..	..	..	..
33 Korea, Rep. of	64	(.)	1	..	27.5	16.8	0.001	4.6
36 Chile	122	0.5	9	..	39.0	24.4	0.045	9.5
42 Costa Rica	193	3.6	62	..	11.3	19.9	0.082	2.3
43 Singapore	..	..	..	..	..	..	..	..
44 Brunei Darussalam	..	..	..	..	..	..	..	..
46 Argentina	255	0.3	8	..	6.6	20.8	0.005	1.4
50 Venezuela	81	0.2	4	..	36.9	..	..	..
51 Dominica	19	9.5	190	..	41.3	48.4	1.897	20.0
52 Kuwait	..	..	..	..	..	..	..	..
53 Mexico	183	0.1	2	..	12.0	14.4	0.001	1.7
55 Qatar	..	..	..	..	..	..	..	..
Medium human development	**14,120T**	**0.8**	**7**	**..**	**14.7**	**34.7**	**0.041**	**5.1**
Excluding China	**11,950T**	**0.9**	**14**	**..**	**14.6**	**37.6**	**0.049**	**5.5**
56 Mauritius	95	4.0	86	..	6.9	0.9	0.002	0.1
57 Malaysia	459	1.1	25	97	36.9	76.3	0.311	28.1
58 Bahrain	46	..	92	..	..	..	..	..
59 Grenada	17	8.5	170	..	13.8	56.4	0.660	7.8
60 Antigua and Barbuda	7	1.8	70	..	..	..	..	..
61 Colombia	143	0.4	4	..	16.1	33.4	0.019	5.4
63 Seychelles	20	6.7	200	..	9.3	14.9	0.092	1.4
65 Suriname	40	2.9	100	..	20.5	31.0	0.182	6.4
67 United Arab Emirates	..	..	..	..	..	..	..	..
68 Panama	112	2.5	45	184	7.5	..	..	..
69 Jamaica	197	5.5	82	..	14.8	15.9	0.129	2.3
70 Brazil	196	(.)	1	6	35.8	25.4	0.004	9.1
71 Fiji	46	3.5	66	..	21.0	60.8	0.451	12.7
72 Saint Lucia	20	6.7	200	..	48.3	7.8	0.252	3.8
73 Turkey	1,640	1.8	29	..	5.5	58.5	0.058	3.2
74 Thailand	738	0.9	13	45	10.2	15.5	0.015	1.6
75 Cuba	42	..	4	..	12.8	2.7	..	0.3
76 Saint Vincent	16	8.0	160	..	..	..	..	..
79 Saint Kitts and Nevis	7	7.0	175	..	51.4	..	..	..
81 Syrian Arab Rep.	219	1.8	17	..	43.8	4.1	0.032	1.8
82 Belize	28	7.0	140	..	33.5	46.6	1.093	15.6
84 Saudi Arabia	..	..	..	..	..	..	..	..
85 South Africa	..	..	..	..	..	..	..	..
86 Sri Lanka	651	8.1	37	..	24.8	46.6	0.939	11.5
87 Libyan Arab Jamahiriya	19	..	4	..	..	..	..	..
89 Ecuador	208	2.1	19	38	17.5	48.5	0.174	8.5
90 Paraguay	111	2.3	25	74	3.6	5.9	0.005	0.2
91 Korea, Dem. Rep. of	8	..	(.)	..	..	..	..	..
92 Philippines	1,231	2.8	19	34	9.9	45.0	0.124	4.4
93 Tunisia	312	2.7	38	216	9.0	15.0	0.036	1.3
94 Oman	15	0.1	9	..	11.2	..	..	..
95 Peru	339	..	15	..	12.9	72.5	..	9.3
96 Iraq	417	..	22	..	..	..	..	..
97 Dominican Rep.	95	1.6	13	30	17.1	45.4	0.127	7.8
98 Samoa	52	52.0	260	..	15.6	15.7	1.273	2.4
99 Jordan	668	17.1	163	..	16.9	53.7	1.553	9.1
100 Mongolia	18	..	8	..	89.9	6.8	..	6.1
101 China	2,166	0.5	2	18	14.7	19.3	0.015	2.8
102 Lebanon	138	..	49	..	23.3	6.4	..	1.5
103 Iran, Islamic Rep. of	81	0.1	1	..	6.8	..	..	..
104 Botswana	131	5.0	101	200	40.2	38.5	0.781	15.5
105 Guyana	125	41.7	156	..	1.5	..	..	..
106 Vanuatu	48	24.0	240	..	21.0	19.2	0.971	4.0
107 Algeria	351	0.7	14	..	8.5	0.8	0.005	0.1
108 Indonesia	1,733	1.7	9	25	13.1	19.9	0.045	2.6
109 Gabon	142	3.8	118	..	6.9	8.8	0.023	0.6
110 El Salvador	290	5.0	55	207	20.0	20.4	0.204	4.1
111 Nicaragua	680	..	179	..	11.8	54.1	..	6.4

HDI rank	Official development assistance (ODA) received				Aid social allocation ratio (%) 1988/90	Aid social priority ratio (%) 1988/90	Aid human expenditure ratio (%) 1988/91	Social priority aid (as % of total aid) 1988/90
	US$ millions 1991	As % of GNP 1991	Per capita (US$) 1991	Per poor person (US$) 1991				
Low human development	29,900T	4.7	16	..	17.6	49.7	0.411	8.7
Excluding India	28,230T	9.1	28	..	18.0	49.9	0.817	9.0
112 Maldives	28	28.0	140	..	38.0	6.8	0.719	2.6
113 Guatemala	189	2.3	20	29	16.7	51.4	0.196	8.6
114 Cape Verde	107	35.7	268	..	13.4	54.5	2.599	7.3
115 Viet Nam	218	..	3	..	40.0	29.8	..	11.9
116 Honduras	332	11.1	63	174	22.8	34.2	0.862	7.8
117 Swaziland	48	8.0	60	124	50.8	33.1	1.346	16.8
118 Solomon Islands	40	20.0	133	..	16.5	44.8	1.475	7.4
119 Morocco	1,203	5.1	47	130	5.6	43.5	0.124	2.4
120 Lesotho	125	15.6	69	131	30.1	50.4	2.368	15.2
121 Zimbabwe	376	6.0	37	..	9.9	40.4	0.240	4.0
122 Bolivia	540	12.0	74	..	15.3	41.7	0.766	6.4
123 Myanmar	167	..	4	10	8.2	58.8	..	4.8
124 Egypt	4,638	14.8	87	371	18.0	79.4	2.109	14.3
125 São Tomé and Principe	48	..	480	..	26.6	69.1	..	18.4
126 Congo	134	5.8	58	..	25.9	76.1	1.150	19.7
127 Kenya	884	9.8	36	79	21.2	31.3	0.651	6.6
128 Madagascar	358	13.3	29	60	8.5	53.4	0.602	4.5
129 Papua New Guinea	381	11.2	95	147	43.5	18.0	0.875	7.8
130 Zambia	587	17.3	70	..	16.2	63.9	1.784	10.3
131 Ghana	603	10.4	39	91	11.4	17.8	0.212	2.0
132 Pakistan	1,183	2.8	10	32	19.1	44.9	0.237	8.5
133 Cameroon	507	4.5	43	152	20.2	37.7	0.345	7.6
134 India	1,657	0.6	2	4	10.3	44.6	0.026	4.6
135 Namibia	179	..	119	..	19.2	36.5	..	7.0
136 Côte d'Ivoire	597	6.7	48	172	6.1	56.4	0.232	3.5
137 Haiti	197	8.2	30	40	30.9	63.1	1.603	19.5
138 Tanzania, U. Rep. of	1,038	37.1	39	..	19.4	52.9	3.796	10.2
139 Comoros	53	26.5	88	..	11.7	41.4	1.283	4.8
140 Zaire	505	6.2	13	..	10.4	26.6	0.172	2.8
141 Lao People's Dem. Rep.	161	20.1	37	..	16.8	42.1	1.426	7.1
142 Nigeria	293	0.9	3	..	15.1	3.8	0.005	0.6
143 Yemen	244	..	20	..	16.0	45.5	..	7.3
144 Liberia	143	..	53	..	18.6	58.1	..	10.8
145 Togo	201	13.4	56	..	6.2	45.1	0.374	2.8
146 Uganda	566	14.9	31	..	21.3	52.2	1.661	11.2
147 Bangladesh	2,142	9.5	18	22	14.7	83.4	1.159	12.2
148 Cambodia	62	..	7	..	..	..	..	..
149 Rwanda	328	14.9	45	53	28.0	64.9	2.708	18.2
150 Senegal	769	14.5	103	..	17.7	58.1	1.488	10.3
151 Ethiopia	951	15.9	19	32	14.7	42.4	0.991	6.3
152 Nepal	403	12.2	20	35	19.7	34.5	0.829	6.8
153 Malawi	494	29.1	50	75	13.8	16.7	0.673	2.3
154 Burundi	249	20.8	44	55	18.3	41.1	1.560	7.5
155 Equatorial Guinea	60	60.0	150	..	20.6	64.6	7.968	13.3
156 Central African Rep.	225	18.8	73	..	8.2	70.5	1.078	5.7
157 Mozambique	1,022	85.2	70	..	16.8	35.7	5.121	6.0
158 Sudan	836	..	32	..	15.8	50.2	..	7.9
159 Bhutan	55	18.3	34	..	39.0	53.7	3.837	20.9
160 Angola	250	..	26	..	23.1	16.3	..	3.8
161 Mauritania	208	20.8	99	..	12.5	45.2	1.172	5.6
162 Benin	270	15.9	56	..	40.9	36.6	2.376	15.0
163 Djibouti	102	..	204	..	10.6	25.5	..	2.7
164 Guinea-Bissau	123	61.5	123	..	26.1	70.8	11.381	18.5
165 Chad	269	24.5	47	98	27.5	20.3	1.364	5.6
166 Somalia	282	31.3	31	63	22.6	42.4	3.008	9.6
167 Gambia	95	47.5	106	..	28.7	24.1	3.292	6.9
168 Mali	408	17.7	43	99	21.7	40.2	1.549	8.7
169 Niger	418	17.4	52	..	22.8	60.4	2.396	13.8
170 Burkina Faso	379	12.6	41	..	27.0	49.4	1.683	13.3
171 Afghanistan	521	..	29	..	36.9	13.9	..	5.1
172 Sierra Leone	108	10.8	25	..	13.0	66.1	0.926	8.6
173 Guinea	331	11.8	56	..	22.3	43.2	1.140	9.6
All developing countries	45,100T	1.5	11	..	16.9	44.9	0.114	7.6
Least developed countries	14,810T	15.1	29	..	18.9	47.8	1.364	9.0
Sub-Saharan Africa	15,100T	10.0	31	..	18.0	43.3	0.779	7.8
Industrial countries	..	..	..	..	..	..	..	..
World	..	..	..	..	..	..	..	..

Note: Data for industrial countries for this subject area are in table 41.

HDI rank	Total debt (as % of GNP) 1990	Debt service ratio (as % of exports of goods and services) 1970	Debt service ratio (as % of exports of goods and services) 1990	Net workers' remittances from abroad (as % of GNP) 1990	Export-import ratio 1990	Trade dependency (exports plus imports as % of GDP) 1990	Terms of trade (1987=100) 1990	Gross international reserves (months of import coverage) 1990	Current account balance (US$ millions) 1990
High human development	**38**	**..**	**19.1**	**..**	**125**	**63**	**107**	**3.8**	**11,400T**
20 Barbados	..	..	..	..				..	..
24 Hong Kong	..	..	..	..	35	187	100	..	..
27 Cyprus	..	..	..	..				..	..
30 Uruguay	47	21.7	41.0	..	120	38	104	8.1	216
31 Trinidad and Tobago	51	4.6	14.5	0.1	165	70	110	3.3	434
32 Bahamas	..	..	..	..				..	..
33 Korea, Rep. of	14	19.5	10.7	(.)	93	57	108	2.2	-2,181
36 Chile	74	19.2	25.9	..	122	56	131	7.1	-935
42 Costa Rica	70	10.0	24.5	..	72	61	114	2.3	-679
43 Singapore	..	..	..	..	87	327	100	4.8	2,445
44 Brunei Darussalam								..	..
46 Argentina	62	21.6	34.1	(.)	303	18	112	5.6	1,789
50 Venezuela	71	2.9	20.7	-1.2	271	49	164	12.2	8,221
51 Dominica	..	..	..	..				..	..
52 Kuwait	..	..	..	..	173	56	77	4.3	8,656
53 Mexico	42	23.6	27.8	0.9	95	23	110	2.4	-6,521
55 Qatar	..	..	..	..				..	..
Medium human development	**32**	**11.0**	**20.0**	**..**	**114**	**37**	**101**	**4.0**	**-9,100T**
Excluding China	**39**	**..**	**23.0**	**..**	**113**	**38**	**101**	**3.2**	**-21,100T**
56 Mauritius	38	3.2	8.7	..	73	134	114	4.7	-128
57 Malaysia	48	3.8	11.7	..	101	138	94	3.5	-1,733
58 Bahrain	..	..	..	..				..	..
59 Grenada	..	..	..	..				..	..
60 Antigua and Barbuda	..	..	..	..				..	..
61 Colombia	45	12.0	38.9	1.2	121	30	92	5.6	406
63 Seychelles	..	..	..	..				..	..
65 Suriname	..	..	..	..				..	..
67 United Arab Emirates	..	..	..	..				..	..
68 Panama	155	7.7	4.3	..	21	39	138	0.9	-27
69 Jamaica	132	2.8	31.0	..	80	76	88	0.7	-386
70 Brazil	25	12.5	20.8	..	139	13	123	2.8	-2,983
71 Fiji	..	..	..	..				..	..
72 Saint Lucia	..	..	..	..				..	..
73 Turkey	46	21.9	28.2	3.5	58	37	98	3.1	-3,778
74 Thailand	33	3.3	17.2	0.1	69	70	99	4.4	-7,235
75 Cuba	..	..	..	..				..	..
76 Saint Vincent	..	..	..	..				..	..
79 Saint Kitts and Nevis	..	..	..	..				..	..
81 Syrian Arab Rep.	118	11.3	26.9	3.0	174	45	87	..	1,747
82 Belize	..	..	..	..				..	..
84 Saudi Arabia	..	..	..	..	129	68	95	3.6	294
85 South Africa	..	..	..	..	129	46	93	1.2	2,243
86 Sri Lanka	73	11.0	13.8	5.0	74	64	90	1.7	-474
87 Libyan Arab Jamahiriya	..	..	..	..	359		97	9.2	2,239
89 Ecuador	121	8.6	33.2	..	146	42	109	3.5	-236
90 Paraguay	41	11.8	11.0	..	86	39	110	4.6	102
91 Korea, Dem. Rep. of	..	..	..	..				..	..
92 Philippines	69	7.5	21.2	0.6	66	50	93	1.5	-3,052
93 Tunisia	62	19.7	25.8	5.1	64	81	99	1.6	-715
94 Oman	..	..	13.0	..	18	40	..	5.5	1,153
95 Peru	59	11.6	11.0	..	101	18	78	4.3	-921
96 Iraq	..	..	..	..	390		..	..	..
97 Dominican Rep.	63	4.5	10.3	5.4	36	38	98	0.3	-114
98 Samoa	..	..	..	..				..	..
99 Jordan	221	3.6	23.0	12.7	43	114	112	3.3	-1,147
100 Mongolia	..	..	..	..				..	-647
101 China	14	..	10.3	(.)	116	32	111	7.4	11,935
102 Lebanon	..	..	..	..				..	..
103 Iran, Islamic Rep. of	8	..	3.5	..	115	24	72	..	-385
104 Botswana	21	1.0	4.4	-1.6	..	..	..	17.0	-179
105 Guyana	..	..	..	..	..	..	..	..	..
106 Vanuatu	..	..	..	..				..	..
107 Algeria	53	4.0	59.4	0.6	146	61	99	2.6	1,419
108 Indonesia	66	7.0	30.9	0.2	117	44	111	3.2	-2,430
109 Gabon	86	5.7	7.6	-3.9	325	68	96	0.2	236
110 El Salvador	40	3.6	17.1	6.0	46	32	114	4.4	-360
111 Nicaragua	..	10.6	4.1	..	51	..	110	..	-571

HDI rank	Total debt (as % of GNP) 1990	Debt service ratio (as % of exports of goods and services) 1970	1990	Net workers' remittances from abroad (as % of GNP) 1990	Export-import ratio 1990	Trade dependency (exports plus imports as % of GDP) 1990	Terms of trade (1987=100) 1990	Gross international reserves (months of import coverage) 1990	Current account balance (US$ millions) 1990
Low human development	58	11.3	25.2	2.0	81	28	97	2.2	-27,200T
Excluding India	94	9.0	23.7	3.6	86	40	97	2.3	-17,400T
112 Maldives	..	..	..	..	..	..	..	..	..
113 Guatemala	38	7.4	13.3	0.8	74	37	102	2.1	-335
114 Cape Verde	..	..	..	..	..	..	..	..	..
115 Viet Nam	..	..	..	..	..	..	..	..	-323
116 Honduras	141	2.8	40.0	..	89	82	104	0.4	-397
117 Swaziland	..	..	..	..	..	..	..	..	..
118 Solomon Islands	..	..	..	..	..	..	..	..	..
119 Morocco	97	8.7	23.4	8.4	62	44	86	3.2	-520
120 Lesotho	40	4.5	2.4	47.0	..	..	..	1.2	-148
121 Zimbabwe	54	2.3	22.6	..	..	..	..	1.5	-266
122 Bolivia	101	11.3	39.8	(.)	129	37	97	4.5	-339
123 Myanmar	..	..	..	..	119	..	127	4.7	-204
124 Egypt	127	38.0	25.7	11.9	29	40	76	2.7	-2,535
125 São Tomé and Principe	..	..	..	..	..	..	..	..	..
126 Congo	204	11.5	20.7	-1.8	198	59	99	0.2	-197
127 Kenya	81	6.0	33.8	(.)	49	42	103	0.9	-684
128 Madagascar	134	3.7	47.2	-0.4	70	30	102	3.7	-324
129 Papua New Guinea	84	1.1	36.0	1.5	89	74	75	2.6	-566
130 Zambia	261	6.4	12.3	-0.7	..	..	..	0.9	-490
131 Ghana	57	5.5	34.9	0.1	62	31	75	2.3	-442
132 Pakistan	52	23.8	22.8	4.6	76	37	95	1.2	-1,902
133 Cameroon	57	3.2	21.5	(.)	92	22	91	0.5	-278
134 India	25	22.2	28.8	0.7	76	16	96	1.9	-9,828
135 Namibia	..	..	..	..	..	..	..	..	..
136 Côte d'Ivoire	205	7.1	38.6	-6.1	124	62	80	0.1	-1,210
137 Haiti	36	7.2	9.5	2.0	51	15	97	0.3	-158
138 Tanzania, U. Rep. of	282	5.3	25.8	(.)	32	60	108	1.4	-955
139 Comoros	..	..	..	..	..	..	..	..	..
140 Zaire	141	4.4	15.4	..	113	25	163	1.0	-860
141 Lao People's Dem. Rep.	123	..	12.1	..	..	..	..	2.9	-148
142 Nigeria	111	4.3	20.3	(.)	240	56	100	5.1	5,027
143 Yemen	97	..	5.4	..	..	..	..	1.2	503
144 Liberia	..	8.0	..	..	111	..	111	..	..
145 Togo	82	3.1	14.1	0.3	43	62	114	5.3	-208
146 Uganda	92	2.9	54.5	..	33	22	88	0.7	-434
147 Bangladesh	54	..	25.4	3.4	46	23	95	1.8	-1,541
148 Cambodia	..	..	..	..	..	..	..	..	..
149 Rwanda	35	1.5	14.5	-0.6	40	18	98	1.4	-224
150 Senegal	67	2.9	20.4	0.6	48	41	106	0.1	-481
151 Ethiopia	54	11.4	33.0	..	27	25	84	0.6	-308
152 Nepal	53	3.2	18.2	(.)	30	24	..	5.4	-316
153 Malawi	86	7.8	22.5	..	72	60	93	2.4	-162
154 Burundi	83	2.3	43.6	..	32	31	70	4.3	-205
155 Equatorial Guinea	..	..	..	..	..	..	..	..	..
156 Central African Rep.	71	5.1	11.9	..	76	25	109	3.6	-260
157 Mozambique	385	..	14.4	3.7	..	..	..	..	-784
158 Sudan	..	10.6	5.8	..	67	..	100	0.1	-1,217
159 Bhutan	32	..	6.8	(.)	..	..	..	7.4	-38
160 Angola	..	..	..	..	250	55	..	..	..
161 Mauritania	227	3.4	13.9	(.)	189	75	107	1.0	-199
162 Benin	..	2.5	3.4	4.1	19	32	..	1.4	-153
163 Djibouti	..	..	..	..	..	..	..	..	..
164 Guinea-Bissau	..	..	..	..	..	..	..	..	..
165 Chad	45	4.2	5.1	(.)	44	59	..	3.5	-298
166 Somalia	277	2.1	11.7	..	36	55	111	0.5	-346
167 Gambia	..	..	..	..	..	..	..	..	..
168 Mali	101	1.4	11.5	3.0	54	40	97	2.7	-364
169 Niger	74	4.0	24.1	0.5	189	26	77	4.6	-247
170 Burkina Faso	26	7.1	6.4	2.8	33	21	100	4.2	-383
171 Afghanistan	..	..	..	..	..	..	..	10.3	-454
172 Sierra Leone	146	10.8	15.9	(.)	95	34	80	0.2	-136
173 Guinea	98	..	8.3	..	..	..	..	..	-283
All developing countries	39	13.3	20.4	1.1	111	42	101	3.7	-20,900T
Least developed countries	96	4.5	20.5	2.3	58	29	101	2.1	-11,500T
Sub-Saharan Africa	107	4.7	21.3	-0.4	127	46	100	1.9	-4,100T
Industrial countries	..	..	..	..	94	..	100	..	..
World	..	..	..	..	97	..	101	..	..

Note: Data for industrial countries for this subject area are in table 42.

HDI rank	Military expenditure (as % of GDP)		Military expenditure (as % of combined education and health expenditure)		Armed forces			Annual average imports of major conventional arms	
	1960	1990	1977	1990	As % of total population 1987	Per teacher 1987	Per doctor 1987	US$ millions 1987-91	As % of national imports 1990
High human development	**1.9**	**2.5**	**96**	**..**	**0.60**	**0.8**	**6**	**1,930T**	**1.0**
20 Barbados	..	..	2	..	..	..	..	..	..
24 Hong Kong	..	0.4	..	..	..	..	..	..	..
27 Cyprus	..	1.2	49	25	1.91	2.6	14	114	..
30 Uruguay	2.5	2.1	45	51	0.88	1.0	5	22	1.5
31 Trinidad and Tobago	..	..	4	33	0.16	0.2	2	..	..
32 Bahamas	..	..	..	..	..	..	..	..	..
33 Korea, Rep. of	6.0	4.0	201	110	1.49	2.5	19	710	1.0
36 Chile	2.8	5.0	67	..	0.78	1.0	10	212	3.0
42 Costa Rica	1.2	0.5	8	4	..	..	..	..	..
43 Singapore	0.4	5.0	158	109	2.14	2.8	19	255	0.4
44 Brunei Darussalam	..	..	..	..	1.66	1.3	20	7	..
46 Argentina	2.1	3.3	78	..	0.25	0.2	1	137	3.4
50 Venezuela	2.5	2.0	20	23	0.27	0.3	18	107	1.7
51 Dominica	..	..	..	..	..	..	..	1	..
52 Kuwait	..	6.5	88	83	0.81	0.5	5	223	4.6
53 Mexico	0.7	0.4	13	8	0.16	0.2	2	67	0.2
55 Qatar	..	..	53	..	2.15	1.2	10	74	..
Medium human development	**6.9**	**3.7**	**86**	**230**	**0.50**	**0.6**	**9**	**11,280T**	**3.1**
Excluding China	**2.6**	**3.7**	**80**	**..**	**0.70**	**0.9**	**15**	**11,120T**	**3.7**
56 Mauritius	0.2	0.2	2	5	..	..	..	6	0.3
57 Malaysia	1.9	3.6	59	65	0.70	0.7	19	21	0.1
58 Bahrain	..	5.0	32	134	0.65	0.6	5	182	..
59 Grenada	..	..	..	..	..	..	..	..	..
60 Antigua and Barbuda	..	..	..	..	..	..	..	..	..
61 Colombia	1.2	2.7	29	..	0.22	0.3	3	80	1.4
63 Seychelles	..	..	..	..	..	..	..	(.)	..
65 Suriname	..	..	..	..	..	..	..	..	..
67 United Arab Emirates	..	4.7	149	174	2.96	2.7	23	358	..
68 Panama	0.1	2.5	10	23	0.22	0.2	2	6	0.4
69 Jamaica	..	..	8	9	0.08	0.1	2	..	..
70 Brazil	1.8	1.7	35	22	0.21	0.2	2	250	1.1
71 Fiji	..	2.5	7	9	0.42	0.4	8	1	..
72 Saint Lucia	..	..	..	..	..	..	..	..	..
73 Turkey	5.2	4.9	90	118	1.25	2.1	17	1,277	5.7
74 Thailand	2.6	3.2	77	74	0.48	0.6	27	674	2.0
75 Cuba	5.1	10.0	41	118	1.75	1.2	8	102	..
76 Saint Vincent	..	..	..	..	..	..	..	..	..
79 Saint Kitts and Nevis	..	..	..	..	..	..	..	..	..
81 Syrian Arab Rep.	7.9	13.0	243	204	3.63	3.0	47	689	28.7
82 Belize	..	..	..	..	..	..	..	(.)	..
84 Saudi Arabia	5.7	17.7	137	177	0.59	0.5	4	2,119	8.8
85 South Africa	0.9	4.3	121	..	0.29	0.3	4	13	0.1
86 Sri Lanka	1.0	4.8	15	62	0.13	0.2	10	55	2.0
87 Libyan Arab Jamahiriya	1.2	8.6	29	56	1.86	1.0	14	220	5.5
89 Ecuador	2.4	1.5	60	33	0.37	0.4	3	78	4.2
90 Paraguay	1.7	1.0	74	72	0.43	0.5	7	7	0.6
91 Korea, Dem. Rep. of	11.0	8.7	277	..	3.92	..	..	926	..
92 Philippines	1.2	1.8	110	47	0.18	0.3	12	29	0.2
93 Tunisia	2.2	3.2	35	58	0.55	0.6	11	13	0.2
94 Oman	..	15.8	..	268	1.65	1.7	18	120	4.6
95 Peru	2.0	2.1	69	70	0.55	0.6	6	188	5.8
96 Iraq	8.7	20.0	212	511	5.86	6.3	105	2,064	47.8
97 Dominican Rep.	5.0	0.8	55	25	0.31	0.5	6	2	0.1
98 Samoa	..	..	..	..	..	..	..	(.)	..
99 Jordan	16.7	10.9	183	128	2.11	2.1	26	123	4.6
100 Mongolia	4.2	10.0	95	..	1.68	1.9	7	..	..
101 China	12.0	..	107	97	0.30	0.4	5	159	0.3
102 Lebanon	..	..	..	..	0.58	0.4	5	17	..
103 Iran, Islamic Rep. of	4.5	..	147	..	1.27	1.4	39	572	4.4
104 Botswana	..	2.5	..	16	0.26	0.3	15	18	..
105 Guyana	..	1.9	19	53	0.51	0.8	50	..	..
106 Vanuatu	..	..	..	..	..	..	2	(.)	..
107 Algeria	2.1	1.5	26	18	0.73	0.7	17	220	2.1
108 Indonesia	5.8	1.6	94	143	0.16	0.1	13	286	1.3
109 Gabon	..	4.5	16	63	0.28	0.5	8	33	4.4
110 El Salvador	1.1	2.9	37	121	0.95	1.9	28	..	..
111 Nicaragua	1.9	28.3	57	318	2.20	3.5	31	89	11.8

HDI rank	Military expenditure (as % of GDP)		Military expenditure (as % of combined education and health expenditure)		Armed forces			Annual average imports of major conventional arms	
					As % of total population	Per teacher	Per doctor	US$ millions	As % of national imports
	1960	1990	1977	1990	1987	1987	1987	1987-91	1990
Low human development	2.2	3.6	100	105	0.30	0.7	27	8,490T	7.9
Excluding India	2.5	3.9	124	123	0.40	1.0	44	4,980T	5.2
112 Maldives	..	..	..	..	..	..	..	..	..
113 Guatemala	0.9	1.2	47	87	0.47	0.9	11	..	..
114 Cape Verde	..	..	..	..	..	..	..	..	..
115 Viet Nam	..	..	356	..	2.01	2.9	..	1	..
116 Honduras	1.2	6.9	34	102	0.36	0.7	6	15	1.4
117 Swaziland	..	..	5	20	..	..	..	..	..
118 Solomon Islands	..	..	..	..	..	..	..	(.)	..
119 Morocco	2.0	4.5	88	52	0.88	1.3	46	110	1.6
120 Lesotho	..	..	..	..	..	..	..	1	..
121 Zimbabwe	..	7.3	116	65	0.53	0.6	..	58	3.1
122 Bolivia	2.0	3.2	36	144	0.42	0.5	7	23	3.2
123 Myanmar	7.0	3.5	147	..	0.48	1.2	17	54	19.9
124 Egypt	5.5	4.6	341	57	0.89	1.1	7	1,092	10.6
125 São Tomé and Principe	..	..	..	..	..	..	..	..	..
126 Congo	0.3	3.2	51	50	0.49	0.8	45	0	0.1
127 Kenya	0.5	2.4	52	31	0.06	0.1	6	43	2.0
128 Madagascar	0.3	1.4	44	34	0.19	0.4	18	..	..
129 Papua New Guinea	..	..	15	..	0.11	0.3	13	5	0.4
130 Zambia	1.1	3.2	140	43	0.21	0.5	..	..	..
131 Ghana	1.1	0.6	14	13	0.08	0.1	6	11	0.9
132 Pakistan	5.5	6.6	214	239	0.43	1.5	10	460	6.2
133 Cameroon	1.7	2.1	36	51	0.12	0.3	17	4	0.3
134 India	1.9	3.3	73	80	0.16	0.3	4	3,512	14.8
135 Namibia	..	..	..	..	..	..	..	..	..
136 Côte d'Ivoire	0.5	1.2	10	14	0.06	0.1	12	12	0.6
137 Haiti	2.4	1.5	93	45	0.13	0.3	10	..	..
138 Tanzania, U. Rep. of	0.1	6.9	58	108	0.16	0.4	33	..	..
139 Comoros	..	..	..	..	..	..	..	..	..
140 Zaire	..	1.2	54	67	0.08	0.2	..	..	..
141 Lao People's Dem. Rep.	5.8	..	300	..	1.48	1.9	93	27	..
142 Nigeria	0.2	0.9	92	65	0.09	0.2	7	75	1.3
143 Yemen	..	..	207	..	0.68	..	..	73	..
144 Liberia	1.1	..	18	29	0.09	0.9	30	..	..
145 Togo	..	3.2	28	46	0.19	0.4	30	5	0.7
146 Uganda	(.)	0.8	63	..	0.12	0.2	33	..	..
147 Bangladesh	..	1.6	88	57	0.10	0.3	6	110	3.0
148 Cambodia	..	..	..	..	0.65	1.8	100	64	..
149 Rwanda	..	1.7	77	35	0.08	0.3	25	1	0.5
150 Senegal	0.5	2.0	51	..	0.15	0.6	20	6	0.4
151 Ethiopia	1.6	13.5	121	239	0.73	4.2	533	121	11.2
152 Nepal	0.4	1.7	47	61	0.17	0.4	33	2	0.4
153 Malawi	..	1.5	50	31	0.07	0.3	25	2	0.3
154 Burundi	..	2.2	65	65	0.14	0.7	35	..	..
155 Equatorial Guinea	..	..	125	..	0.24	0.5	..	..	..
156 Central African Rep.	..	1.8	36	41	0.15	0.7	20	1	0.7
157 Mozambique	..	..	132	..	0.22	1.4	107	..	..
158 Sudan	1.5	2.0	94	..	0.25	0.8	25	46	7.6
159 Bhutan	..	..	..	..	..	..	..	..	..
160 Angola	..	20.0	..	..	0.57	2.3	106	721	60.1
161 Mauritania	..	..	154	..	0.80	3.0	75	..	..
162 Benin	1.1	2.0	22	..	0.09	0.2	13	1	0.2
163 Djibouti	..	..	..	..	..	..	..	1	..
164 Guinea-Bissau	..	..	..	..	..	..	..	..	..
165 Chad	..	..	150	..	0.32	2.4	170	14	3.0
166 Somalia	..	3.0	91	500	0.95	5.9	130	..	..
167 Gambia	..	..	..	..	0.13	0.3	10	..	..
168 Mali	1.7	3.2	62	83	(.)	0.5	23	6	1.0
169 Niger	0.3	0.8	18	21	0.05	0.3	15	..	..
170 Burkina Faso	0.6	2.8	92	85	0.11	1.0	45	..	..
171 Afghanistan	..	..	100	..	0.34	2.3	20	1,686	..
172 Sierra Leone	..	0.7	18	11	0.08	0.2	10	2	1.4
173 Guinea	1.3	..	27	..	0.16	0.9	100	5	..
All developing countries	4.2	3.4	91	169	0.40	0.6	18	21,330T	3.1
Least developed countries	2.1	2.8	89	146	0.30	1.1	77	2,260T	3.3
Sub-Saharan Africa	0.7	3.8	86	108	0.20	0.9	76	1,180T	2.6
Industrial countries	6.3	..	..	..	0.80	1.0	3	..	..
World	6.0	..	..	..	0.50	0.7	15	..	..

Note: Data for industrial countries for this subject area are in table 43.

HDI rank	Urban population (as % of total)			Urban population annual growth rate (%)		Population in cities of more than 1 million (as % of urban)	Population in largest city (as % of urban)	Major city with highest population density	
	1960	1991	2000	1960-91	1991-2000	1990	1980	City	Population per km² 1980-88
High human development	52	75	80	3.6	2.2	51	..	..	..
20 Barbados	35	45	51	1.1	1.7	..	..	..	..
24 Hong Kong	89	94	96	2.4	1.0	100	100	Hong Kong	5,048
27 Cyprus	36	53	60	2.0	2.1	..	..	..	..
30 Uruguay	80	86	87	0.9	0.8	45	..	Montevideo	6,952
31 Trinidad and Tobago	23	69	75	5.3	2.3	..	..	..	..
32 Bahamas	..	..	..	..	..	..	..	..	..
33 Korea, Rep. of	28	72	81	5.1	2.1	69	41	Seoul	15,932
36 Chile	68	86	89	2.6	1.8	42	..	Santiago	9,878
42 Costa Rica	37	47	53	3.9	3.2	72	64	..	..
43 Singapore	100	100	100	1.7	1.0	100	100	Singapore	4,160
44 Brunei Darussalam	..	..	..	..	..	..	..	..	..
46 Argentina	74	86	89	2.0	1.4	49	45	Buenos Aires	14,615
50 Venezuela	67	91	94	4.3	2.6	29	26	..	..
51 Dominica	..	41	..	..	..	..	..	..	..
52 Kuwait	72	96	97	7.9	2.8	55	30	..	..
53 Mexico	51	73	77	4.1	2.6	45	32	Guadalajara	10,286
55 Qatar	73	89	91	8.0	3.3	..	..	..	..
Medium human development	25	42	54	4.0	4.0	33	13	..	..
Excluding China	36	58	65	4.2	3.1	40	23	..	..
56 Mauritius	33	41	42	2.3	1.3	..	..	Port Louis	3,795
57 Malaysia	25	43	51	4.5	3.9	22	..	Kuala Lumpur	3,772
58 Bahrain	83	83	85	4.1	3.1	..	..	..	..
59 Grenada	..	..	..	..	..	..	..	..	..
60 Antigua and Barbuda	..	31	..	..	..	..	..	..	..
61 Colombia	48	70	75	3.7	2.5	39	26	Medellin	3,106
63 Seychelles	..	..	..	..	..	..	..	..	..
65 Suriname	47	47	54	1.3	3.0	..	..	..	..
67 United Arab Emirates	40	78	78	12.5	2.1	..	..	..	..
68 Panama	41	53	59	3.4	2.8	..	66	Panama	3,890
69 Jamaica	34	52	59	2.9	2.2	..	66	..	..
70 Brazil	45	75	81	4.2	2.5	47	15	Recife	6,232
71 Fiji	30	39	43	3.2	2.3	..	..	..	..
72 Saint Lucia	..	..	..	..	..	..	..	..	..
73 Turkey	30	61	74	4.9	3.7	35	24	Ankara	3,438
74 Thailand	13	23	29	4.6	4.0	57	..	Bangkok	3,486
75 Cuba	55	75	80	2.5	1.5	..	..	Havana	2,749
76 Saint Vincent	..	27	..	..	..	..	..	..	..
79 Saint Kitts and Nevis	..	41	..	..	..	..	..	..	..
81 Syrian Arab Rep.	37	50	56	4.5	4.6	60	33	..	..
82 Belize	..	50	..	..	..	..	..	..	..
84 Saudi Arabia	30	77	82	7.6	4.5	29	18	..	..
85 South Africa	47	..	66	3.2	3.2	30	13	..	..
86 Sri Lanka	18	21	24	2.5	2.5	..	16	..	..
87 Libyan Arab Jamahiriya	23	70	76	8.1	4.5	65	65	..	..
89 Ecuador	34	56	64	4.6	3.7	49	29	..	..
90 Paraguay	36	48	54	4.0	4.0	..	44	..	..
91 Korea, Dem. Rep. of	40	60	63	3.7	2.4	..	..	..	..
92 Philippines	30	43	49	3.9	3.6	32	30	Manila	45,839
93 Tunisia	36	54	59	3.6	2.7	37	30	..	..
94 Oman	4	11	15	7.5	7.5	..	..	..	..
95 Peru	46	70	75	4.1	2.7	41	39	Lima	1,379
96 Iraq	43	71	75	5.2	3.9	29	..	Baghdad	5,384
97 Dominican Rep.	30	60	68	5.1	3.1	51	..	..	..
98 Samoa	..	21	..	..	..	..	..	..	..
99 Jordan	43	68	74	4.5	4.2	36	36	Amman	11,104
100 Mongolia	36	52	55	4.1	3.2	..	..	..	..
101 China	19	33	47	3.8	4.9	27	6	Beijing	4,039
102 Lebanon	40	84	87	3.8	2.5	..	..	..	..
103 Iran, Islamic Rep. of	34	57	63	5.0	3.5	41	28	Mashhad	21,132
104 Botswana	2	28	42	13.5	7.9	..	..	..	..
105 Guyana	29	35	42	1.7	3.1	..	..	..	..
106 Vanuatu	..	21	..	..	..	..	..	..	..
107 Algeria	30	52	60	4.7	4.3	23	12	Algiers	7,930
108 Indonesia	15	31	40	4.7	4.4	33	..	..	..
109 Gabon	17	46	54	6.3	4.9	..	..	..	..
110 El Salvador	38	44	50	2.9	3.6	..	..	..	..
111 Nicaragua	40	60	66	4.7	4.1	44	..	..	..

HDI rank		Urban population (as % of total)			Urban population annual growth rate (%)		Population in cities of more than 1 million (as % of urban)	Population in largest city (as % of urban)	Major city with highest population density	
		1960	1991	2000	1960-91	1991-2000	1990	1980	City	Population per km² 1980-88
Low human development		16	28	34	4.2	4.5	34	17	..	..
	Excluding India	15	29	36	4.7	4.9	36	27	..	..
112	Maldives	..	30	..	..	..	..	..	..	..
113	Guatemala	32	39	44	3.5	4.0	..	..	..	..
114	Cape Verde	16	29	36	4.1	5.6	..	..	..	..
115	Viet Nam	15	22	27	3.6	4.3	30	21	..	..
116	Honduras	23	44	52	5.6	4.7	..	33	..	..
117	Swaziland	4	33	45	10.5	6.7	..	..	..	..
118	Solomon Islands	..	9	..	..	..	..	..	..	..
119	Morocco	29	48	55	4.3	3.8	36	26	Casablanca	12,133
120	Lesotho	3	20	28	8.6	6.3	..	..	..	..
121	Zimbabwe	13	28	35	5.9	5.4	..	50	..	..
122	Bolivia	39	51	58	3.5	4.2	33	..	Cochabamba	6,558
123	Myanmar	19	25	28	3.0	3.5	32	23	..	..
124	Egypt	38	47	54	3.1	3.6	52	39	Cairo	29,393
125	São Tomé and Principe	..	33	..	..	..	..	..	..	..
126	Congo	32	41	47	3.6	4.9	..	56	..	..
127	Kenya	7	24	32	7.7	7.0	27	..	Nairobi	1,587
128	Madagascar	11	24	31	5.6	6.0	..	36	..	..
129	Papua New Guinea	3	16	20	8.6	4.8	..	25	..	..
130	Zambia	17	50	59	7.1	5.5	..	35	..	..
131	Ghana	23	33	38	3.9	4.6	22	..	..	..
132	Pakistan	22	32	38	4.3	4.6	42	21	Karachi	3,990
133	Cameroon	14	41	51	6.5	5.7	..	21	..	..
134	India	18	27	32	3.6	3.9	32	6	Calcutta	88,135
135	Namibia	15	28	34	4.8	5.4	..	..	..	..
136	Côte d'Ivoire	19	40	47	6.5	5.5	45	34	Abidjan	3,030
137	Haiti	16	28	34	3.8	4.1	56	56	Port-au-Prince	6,985
138	Tanzania, U. Rep. of	5	33	47	10.3	7.5	18	..	..	..
139	Comoros	10	28	34	6.8	5.8	..	..	..	..
140	Zaire	22	40	46	4.8	5.0	25	..	..	..
141	Lao People's Dem. Rep.	8	19	25	5.1	5.9	..	48	..	..
142	Nigeria	14	35	43	6.3	5.4	24	17	..	..
143	Yemen	9	29	37	5.8	6.2	..	33	..	..
144	Liberia	19	46	57	6.2	5.5	..	..	..	..
145	Togo	10	26	33	6.2	6.0	..	60	..	..
146	Uganda	5	10	14	6.1	6.6	..	52	..	..
147	Bangladesh	5	16	23	6.8	6.2	47	30	Dhaka	9,930
148	Cambodia	10	12	15	1.8	4.3	..	..	..	..
149	Rwanda	2	8	11	7.4	7.6	..	..	..	..
150	Senegal	32	38	45	3.5	4.4	53	..	..	..
151	Ethiopia	6	13	17	4.8	5.8	30	..	..	..
152	Nepal	3	10	14	6.3	6.5	..	27	..	..
153	Malawi	4	12	16	6.5	6.5	..	19	..	..
154	Burundi	2	6	7	5.5	6.1	..	..	..	..
155	Equatorial Guinea	25	29	33	1.5	4.0	..	..	..	..
156	Central African Rep.	23	47	55	4.8	4.6	..	36	..	..
157	Mozambique	4	27	41	9.5	7.2	38	..	..	..
158	Sudan	10	22	27	5.4	4.8	35	31	..	..
159	Bhutan	3	5	8	4.4	6.3	..	..	..	..
160	Angola	10	28	36	5.9	5.4	61	..	..	..
161	Mauritania	6	47	59	9.8	5.3	..	39	..	..
162	Benin	9	38	45	7.4	5.0	..	63	..	..
163	Djibouti	50	81	84	7.3	3.5	..	..	..	..
164	Guinea-Bissau	14	20	25	3.2	4.7	..	..	..	..
165	Chad	7	30	39	7.1	5.4	..	39	..	..
166	Somalia	17	36	44	5.8	4.7	..	34	..	..
167	Gambia	13	23	30	5.2	5.3	..	..	..	..
168	Mali	11	19	23	4.4	5.2	..	24	..	..
169	Niger	6	20	27	7.4	6.7	..	31	..	..
170	Burkina Faso	5	9	12	4.6	6.3	..	41	..	..
171	Afghanistan	8	18	22	4.3	6.9	..	..	..	..
172	Sierra Leone	13	32	40	5.2	5.1	..	47	..	..
173	Guinea	10	26	33	5.3	5.8	88	80	Conakry	6,912
All developing countries		22	37	45	4.0	4.0	36	18	..	..
	Least developed countries	8	20	26	5.3	5.8	35	34	..	..
	Sub-Saharan Africa	15	31	38	5.2	5.3	29	28	..	..
Industrial countries		61	73	75	1.4	0.8	34	..	..	..
World		34	45	60	2.9	2.8	35	..	..	..

Note: Data for industrial countries for this subject area are in table 44.

HDI rank	Estimated population (millions) 1960	1991	2000	Annual population growth rate (%) 1960-91	1991-2000	Ratio of population growth rate 1985-90 to 1955-60	Population doubling date (at current rate)	Total fertility rate 1991	Ratio of 1991 fertility rate to 1960	Contraceptive prevalence rate (%) 1985-90	Population density (per 1,000 hectares) 1991
High human development	**110T**	**220T**	**250T**	**2.2**	**1.4**	**62**	**..**	**2.8**	**53**	**62**	**330**
20 Barbados	0.2	0.3	0.3	0.4	0.4	90	2100+	1.7	39	55	6,000
24 Hong Kong	3.1	5.8	6.1	2.0	0.7	21	2081	1.4	28	81	58,121
27 Cyprus	0.6	0.7	0.8	0.7	0.8	69	2064	2.3	66	..	767
30 Uruguay	2.5	3.1	3.3	0.7	0.6	42	2100+	2.4	82	..	178
31 Trinidad and Tobago	0.8	1.3	1.4	1.3	1.0	41	2055	2.8	54	53	2,439
32 Bahamas	0.1	0.3	0.3	2.8	1.4	43	2033	2.1	54	..	260
33 Korea, Rep. of	25.0	43.8	46.9	1.8	0.8	40	2076	1.7	30	77	4,435
36 Chile	7.6	13.4	15.3	1.8	1.5	71	2036	2.7	51	60	179
42 Costa Rica	1.2	3.1	3.8	3.0	2.2	74	2020	3.2	46	70	610
43 Singapore	1.6	2.7	3.0	1.7	0.9	26	2058	1.7	32	74	44,902
44 Brunei Darussalam	0.1	0.3	0.3	3.8	2.1	49	2021	3.2	46	..	501
46 Argentina	20.6	32.7	36.2	1.5	1.1	74	2050	2.8	91	..	120
50 Venezuela	7.5	19.8	23.6	3.1	2.0	59	2024	3.2	50	..	224
51 Dominica	0.1	0.1	0.1	0.6	-0.2	..	..	2.5	..	50	960
52 Kuwait	0.3	2.1	1.7	6.5	-2.2	66	..	3.8	52	..	1,171
53 Mexico	36.5	86.3	102.6	2.8	1.9	72	2025	3.3	49	53	452
55 Qatar	0.1	0.4	0.5	7.4	2.3	70	2016	4.5	65	..	400
Medium human development	**1,110T**	**2,120T**	**2,440T**	**2.1**	**1.6**	**92**	**..**	**2.9**	**47**	**64**	**530**
Excluding China	**450T**	**950T**	**1,130T**	**2.4**	**1.9**	**85**	**..**	**3.6**	**57**	**53**	**260**
56 Mauritius	0.7	1.1	1.2	1.6	1.0	36	2060	2.0	35	75	5,870
57 Malaysia	8.1	18.4	22.3	2.6	2.1	88	2020	3.7	55	51	561
58 Bahrain	0.2	0.5	0.7	3.9	2.6	105	2016	3.8	54	..	7,618
59 Grenada	0.1	0.1	0.1	(.)	0.4	19	2100+	4.9	..	31	2,676
60 Antigua and Barbuda	0.1	0.1	0.1	0.6	0.7	56	2068	1.7	..	53	1,500
61 Colombia	15.9	32.9	37.8	2.3	1.6	62	2033	2.7	41	66	316
63 Seychelles	(.)	0.1	0.1	1.7	0.9	58	2075	2.6	..	..	2,630
65 Suriname	0.3	0.4	0.5	1.3	1.7	65	2028	2.8	42	..	28
67 United Arab Emirates	0.1	1.6	2.0	9.3	2.1	126	2021	4.6	66	..	195
68 Panama	1.1	2.5	2.9	2.5	1.8	82	2027	3.0	50	58	325
69 Jamaica	1.6	2.4	2.7	1.3	1.0	84	2059	2.5	46	55	2,256
70 Brazil	72.6	151.6	172.8	2.4	1.5	64	2035	2.9	47	66	179
71 Fiji	0.4	0.7	0.8	2.0	1.0	24	2063	3.0	48	..	401
72 Saint Lucia	0.1	0.1	0.2	1.5	1.3	197	2044	3.3	..	47	2,213
73 Turkey	27.5	57.2	68.2	2.4	2.0	75	2025	3.6	56	63	743
74 Thailand	26.4	55.4	61.2	2.4	1.1	45	2046	2.3	36	66	1,084
75 Cuba	7.0	10.7	11.5	1.4	0.8	60	2069	1.9	45	70	975
76 Saint Vincent	0.1	0.1	0.1	1.0	0.9	52	2067	2.6	..	58	2,769
79 Saint Kitts and Nevis	(.)	(.)	(.)	-0.6	-0.3	..	..	2.5	..	41	1,167
81 Syrian Arab Rep.	4.6	12.8	17.5	3.3	3.5	127	2010	6.3	87	..	696
82 Belize	0.1	0.2	0.2	2.4	1.8	84	2025	4.5	..	47	85
84 Saudi Arabia	4.1	15.4	20.7	4.3	3.3	146	2012	6.5	90	..	72
85 South Africa	17.4	38.9	47.9	2.6	2.3	99	2020	4.2	64	48	318
86 Sri Lanka	9.9	17.4	19.4	1.8	1.2	53	2046	2.5	48	62	2,698
87 Libyan Arab Jamahiriya	1.3	4.7	6.4	4.0	3.4	101	2011	6.5	92	..	27
89 Ecuador	4.4	10.8	13.1	2.9	2.1	84	2021	3.8	55	53	390
90 Paraguay	1.8	4.4	5.5	2.9	2.6	110	2017	4.4	65	48	111
91 Korea, Dem. Rep. of	10.8	22.2	25.9	2.3	1.7	52	2028	2.4	42	..	1,843
92 Philippines	27.6	63.8	76.1	2.7	2.0	84	2024	4.0	59	44	2,140
93 Tunisia	4.2	8.2	9.8	2.2	1.9	116	2025	3.6	50	50	530
94 Oman	0.5	1.6	2.2	3.7	3.5	180	2010	6.8	96	..	74
95 Peru	9.9	22.0	26.3	2.6	2.0	77	2025	3.7	54	59	172
96 Iraq	6.8	18.7	24.8	3.2	3.1	113	2013	5.8	81	..	427
97 Dominican Rep.	3.2	7.3	8.6	2.6	1.8	67	2026	3.5	47	50	1,513
98 Samoa	0.1	0.2	0.2	1.2	0.3	..	2100+	4.7	..	..	558
99 Jordan	1.7	4.1	5.6	2.9	3.4	103	2011	5.8	76	35	466
100 Mongolia	1.0	2.2	2.8	2.7	2.6	114	2017	4.7	79	..	14
101 China	657.5	1,170.7	1,309.7	1.9	1.2	97	2040	2.3	40	71	1,255
102 Lebanon	1.9	2.8	3.3	1.3	1.9	19	2026	3.2	51	..	2,721
103 Iran, Islamic Rep. of	21.6	59.9	77.9	3.3	2.9	140	2017	6.1	85	..	366
104 Botswana	0.5	1.3	1.7	3.1	2.9	141	2015	5.2	76	33	22
105 Guyana	0.6	0.8	0.9	1.1	1.1	..	2065	2.6	41	..	41
106 Vanuatu	0.1	0.2	0.2	2.8	2.5	106	2020	5.4	..	..	126
107 Algeria	10.8	25.6	32.7	2.8	2.7	128	2017	5.0	69	36	108
108 Indonesia	96.2	187.7	218.0	2.2	1.7	91	2030	3.2	58	50	1,036
109 Gabon	0.5	1.2	1.6	2.9	3.3	870	2012	5.2	129	..	46
110 El Salvador	2.6	5.3	6.4	2.3	2.2	59	2023	4.2	61	47	2,549
111 Nicaragua	1.5	3.8	5.2	3.0	3.4	84	2010	5.2	70	27	321

HDI rank	Estimated population (millions)			Annual population growth rate (%)		Ratio of population growth rate 1985-90 to 1955-60	Population doubling date (at current rate)	Total fertility rate 1991	Ratio of 1991 fertility rate to 1960	Contraceptive prevalence rate (%) 1985-90	Population density (per 1,000 hectares) 1991
	1960	1991	2000	1960-91	1991-2000						
Low human development	910T	1,920T	2,360T	2.4	2.3	107	..	5.0	77	31	590
Excluding India	470T	1,050T	1,340T	2.6	2.7	122	..	5.8	87	19	380
112 Maldives	0.1	0.2	0.3	2.6	2.9	159	2014	6.3	90	..	7,333
113 Guatemala	4.0	9.5	12.2	2.8	2.8	100	2015	5.5	80	23	873
114 Cape Verde	0.2	0.4	0.5	2.1	2.8	77	2015	4.4	64	..	926
115 Viet Nam	34.7	68.1	81.5	2.2	2.0	131	2025	4.0	66	53	2,092
116 Honduras	1.9	5.3	6.8	3.2	2.8	96	2014	5.1	71	41	474
117 Swaziland	0.3	0.8	1.0	2.8	2.7	115	2017	5.0	77	20	448
118 Solomon Islands	0.1	0.3	0.4	3.3	3.3	117	2012	5.5	86	..	118
119 Morocco	11.6	25.7	31.7	2.6	2.3	94	2020	4.5	63	36	576
120 Lesotho	0.9	1.8	2.2	2.3	2.5	139	2019	4.8	82	..	590
121 Zimbabwe	3.8	10.3	13.2	3.2	2.8	110	2014	5.5	73	43	265
122 Bolivia	3.4	7.3	9.0	2.5	2.3	112	2020	4.7	70	30	68
123 Myanmar	21.7	42.7	51.6	2.2	2.1	102	2023	4.3	71	5	650
124 Egypt	25.9	53.6	64.8	2.3	2.1	100	2023	4.2	60	38	539
125 São Tomé and Principe	0.1	0.1	0.1	2.1	2.1	364	2022	5.4	..	..	1,260
126 Congo	1.0	2.3	3.0	2.7	2.9	140	2014	6.3	107	..	67
127 Kenya	8.3	24.4	32.8	3.5	3.3	116	2012	6.4	81	27	428
128 Madagascar	5.3	12.4	16.6	2.7	3.2	135	2012	6.6	100	..	213
129 Papua New Guinea	1.9	4.0	4.9	2.3	2.3	118	2021	5.0	79	..	88
130 Zambia	3.1	8.4	10.7	3.2	2.7	129	2015	6.5	98	15	113
131 Ghana	6.8	15.5	20.2	2.7	2.9	97	2014	6.1	88	13	673
132 Pakistan	50.0	121.5	154.8	2.9	2.7	130	2017	6.3	92	12	1,576
133 Cameroon	5.3	11.9	15.3	2.6	2.8	162	2016	5.8	101	16	255
134 India	442.3	862.7	1,018.7	2.2	1.8	87	2027	4.0	67	43	2,902
135 Namibia	0.6	1.5	2.0	2.8	3.1	137	2013	6.0	100	26	18
136 Côte d'Ivoire	3.8	12.4	17.1	3.8	3.5	113	2010	7.4	103	3	391
137 Haiti	3.8	6.6	8.0	1.8	2.0	124	2025	4.9	77	10	2,402
138 Tanzania, U. Rep. of	10.2	26.9	35.9	3.1	3.2	127	2012	6.8	100	10	304
139 Comoros	0.2	0.6	0.8	3.1	3.6	172	2010	7.1	104	..	2,529
140 Zaire	15.3	38.6	51.0	3.0	3.1	139	2013	6.7	112	29	170
141 Lao People's Dem. Rep.	2.2	4.3	5.6	2.2	2.8	138	2014	6.7	109	..	188
142 Nigeria	42.3	112.1	147.7	3.1	3.1	126	2013	6.6	96	6	1,231
143 Yemen	5.2	12.1	16.4	2.7	3.4	175	2011	7.3	97	..	229
144 Liberia	1.0	2.7	3.6	3.0	3.2	123	2012	6.8	103	6	276
145 Togo	1.5	3.6	4.8	2.8	3.1	225	2013	6.6	100	34	670
146 Uganda	6.6	18.1	23.4	3.3	2.8	93	2014	7.3	106	5	908
147 Bangladesh	51.4	116.4	144.3	2.6	2.4	98	2020	4.8	73	31	8,946
148 Cambodia	5.4	8.6	10.6	1.5	2.4	112	2019	4.5	72	..	485
149 Rwanda	2.7	7.3	9.8	3.1	3.3	120	2011	8.5	113	10	2,947
150 Senegal	3.2	7.5	9.6	2.8	2.7	111	2017	6.2	89	11	391
151 Ethiopia	24.2	51.4	67.2	2.4	3.0	133	2014	7.0	104	2	467
152 Nepal	9.4	20.1	24.9	2.4	2.4	165	2019	5.6	97	14	1,467
153 Malawi	3.5	10.0	12.6	3.4	2.6	248	2012	7.6	110	7	1,061
154 Burundi	2.9	5.7	7.2	2.1	2.7	161	2015	6.8	100	9	2,205
155 Equatorial Guinea	0.3	0.4	0.5	1.2	2.5	211	2018	5.9	107	..	128
156 Central African Rep.	1.5	3.1	3.9	2.3	2.5	164	2017	6.2	110	..	50
157 Mozambique	7.5	14.5	19.4	2.1	3.3	47	2015	6.5	103	..	185
158 Sudan	11.2	25.9	33.2	2.7	2.7	151	2016	6.2	92	9	109
159 Bhutan	0.9	1.6	1.9	2.0	2.3	137	2021	5.9	98	..	335
160 Angola	4.8	9.5	13.1	2.2	3.5	173	2010	7.2	113	..	76
161 Mauritania	1.0	2.1	2.7	2.4	2.8	143	2015	6.5	100	1	20
162 Benin	2.2	4.8	6.3	2.4	3.0	257	2013	7.1	103	9	431
163 Djibouti	0.1	0.5	0.6	5.6	3.0	99	2014	6.6	100	..	195
164 Guinea-Bissau	0.5	1.0	1.2	1.9	2.1	264	2023	5.8	114	..	350
165 Chad	3.1	5.7	7.3	2.0	2.8	132	2017	5.9	99	..	45
166 Somalia	3.8	8.9	11.9	2.8	3.2	91	2013	7.0	100	1	142
167 Gambia	0.4	0.9	1.1	3.0	2.5	123	2018	6.2	97	..	884
168 Mali	4.4	9.5	12.6	2.5	3.1	136	2013	7.1	100	5	78
169 Niger	3.0	8.0	10.6	3.1	3.2	132	2012	7.1	100	1	63
170 Burkina Faso	4.5	9.2	11.8	2.4	2.7	127	2016	6.5	102	..	338
171 Afghanistan	10.8	17.7	26.8	1.6	4.6	129	2001	6.9	99	..	271
172 Sierra Leone	2.2	4.3	5.4	2.1	2.6	168	2017	6.5	104	4	595
173 Guinea	3.1	5.9	7.8	2.1	3.0	138	2014	7.0	100	..	241
All developing countries	2,070T	4,160T	4,930T	2.3	1.9	98	2025	3.8	60	49	541
Least developed countries	240T	520T	680T	2.5	3.0	126	2015	6.1	92	16	285
Sub-Saharan Africa	210T	520T	680T	2.9	2.8	129	2015	6.5	97	15	245
Industrial countries	940T	1,220T	1,290T	0.8	0.6	..	..	2.0	65	59	225
World	3,010T	5,380T	6,220T	1.9	1.6	..	..	3.4	61	52	409

Note: Data for industrial countries for this subject area are in table 45.

HDI rank	Land area (million hectares)	Arable land (as % of land area) 1989-90	Irrigated land (as % of arable land area) 1989-90	Forest area (as % of land area) 1989-90	Internal renewable water resources per capita (1,000 m³ per year) 1990	Annual rate of deforest-ation (%) 1981-85	Annual change in production of fuelwood (%) 1979-90	Annual fresh water withdrawals As % of water resources 1980-87	Per capita (m³) 1980-87
High human development	**700T**	**9.0**	**14**	**..**	**12.6**	**..**	**0.6**	**14**	**762**
20 Barbados	(.)	76.7	..	(.)	0.2	..	..	51	117
24 Hong Kong	0.1	6.1	29	12.1	..	..	..	..	..
27 Cyprus	0.9	11.3	21	13.3	1.3	..	-2.4	60	807
30 Uruguay	17.5	7.2	8	3.8	18.9	..	2.4	1	241
31 Trinidad and Tobago	0.5	14.4	18	43.1	4.0	0.4	3.8	3	149
32 Bahamas	1.0	0.8	..	32.4	..	..	..	..	..
33 Korea, Rep. of	9.9	20.1	64	65.7	1.4	..	-3.4	17	298
36 Chile	74.9	5.7	29	11.8	35.5	0.7	1.8	4	1,625
42 Costa Rica	5.1	5.6	22	32.1	31.5	3.6	3.3	1	779
43 Singapore	0.1	1.6	..	4.9	0.2	..	..	32	84
44 Brunei Darussalam	0.5	0.6	14	44.6	..	..	..	..	..
46 Argentina	273.7	9.5	5	21.7	21.5	..	-2.5	3	1,059
50 Venezuela	88.2	3.6	7	34.5	43.4	0.7	3.3	(.)	387
51 Dominica	0.1	9.3	..	41.3	..	..	..	..	..
52 Kuwait	1.8	0.2	50	0.1	(.)	..	..	..	238
53 Mexico	190.9	12.1	21	22.5	4.0	1.3	2.7	15	901
55 Qatar	1.1	0.5	..	..	0.1	..	..	663	415
Medium human development	**3,390T**	**8.0**	**23**	**29.9**	**7.2**	**..**	**1.9**	**16**	**493**
Excluding China	**2,440T**	**7.0**	**16**	**35.1**	**13.2**	**..**	**1.9**	**16**	**532**
56 Mauritius	0.2	54.1	16	30.8	2.0	3.3	-1.4	16	415
57 Malaysia	32.9	3.2	7	58.1	26.3	1.2	2.6	2	765
58 Bahrain	0.1	1.5	..	5.9	(.)	..	..	..	609
59 Grenada	(.)	14.7	..	8.8	..	..	..	..	..
60 Antigua and Barbuda	(.)	18.2	..	11.4	..	..	..	..	..
61 Colombia	103.9	3.7	10	48.7	33.6	1.7	2.4	(.)	179
63 Seychelles	(.)	3.7	..	18.5	..	..	..	..	..
65 Suriname	15.6	0.4	84	95.2	496.3	(.)	-4.3	(.)	1,181
67 United Arab Emirates	8.4	0.3	13	(.)	0.2	..	..	299	565
68 Panama	7.6	5.8	5	44.0	59.6	0.9	0.8	1	744
69 Jamaica	1.1	19.1	13	17.2	3.3	3.0	8.6	4	157
70 Brazil	845.7	7.9	3	65.4	34.5	0.5	2.5	1	212
71 Fiji	1.8	8.3	..	64.9	38.1	0.2	11.8	(.)	37
72 Saint Lucia	0.1	8.2	..	13.1	..	..	..	..	..
73 Turkey	77.0	32.3	8	26.2	3.5	..	-3.1	8	317
74 Thailand	51.1	37.2	20	27.9	2.0	2.5	2.1	18	599
75 Cuba	11.0	23.7	26	25.1	3.3	0.1	2.1	23	868
76 Saint Vincent	(.)	10.3	..	35.9	..	..	..	..	..
79 Saint Kitts and Nevis	(.)	22.2	..	16.7	..	..	..	..	..
81 Syrian Arab Rep.	18.4	26.6	12	3.9	0.6	..	0.4	9	449
82 Belize	2.3	1.9	4	44.4	..	0.6	6.4	(.)	..
84 Saudi Arabia	215.0	0.5	36	0.6	0.2	..	..	164	255
85 South Africa	122.1	10.1	9	3.7	1.4	..	(.)	18	404
86 Sri Lanka	6.5	14.3	29	27.0	2.5	3.5	1.8	15	503
87 Libyan Arab Jamahiriya	176.0	1.0	11	0.4	0.2	..	0.1	404	623
89 Ecuador	27.7	6.1	20	40.5	29.1	2.3	3.9	2	561
90 Paraguay	39.7	5.3	3	36.1	22.0	1.1	2.6	(.)	111
91 Korea, Dem. Rep. of	12.0	14.1	50	74.5	2.9	..	1.6	21	1,649
92 Philippines	29.8	15.3	19	35.4	5.2	1.0	3.1	9	693
93 Tunisia	15.5	19.5	6	4.1	0.5	1.7	2.9	53	325
94 Oman	21.2	0.1	85	..	1.4	..	..	24	325
95 Peru	128.0	2.7	33	53.6	1.8	0.4	3.0	15	294
96 Iraq	43.7	12.0	47	4.3	1.8	..	3.7	43	4,575
97 Dominican Rep.	4.8	20.7	15	12.8	2.8	0.6	10.6	15	453
98 Samoa	0.3	19.4	..	47.3	..	..	..	..	..
99 Jordan	8.9	3.5	15	0.8	0.2	..	4.4	41	173
100 Mongolia	156.7	0.9	3	8.9	11.0	..	(.)	2	272
101 China	932.6	10.3	46	13.6	2.5	..	1.9	16	462
102 Lebanon	1.0	20.3	29	7.8	1.6	..	0.2	16	271
103 Iran, Islamic Rep. of	163.6	8.6	39	11.0	2.1	0.5	0.6	39	1,362
104 Botswana	56.7	2.4	..	19.3	0.8	0.1	4.2	1	98
105 Guyana	19.7	2.4	26	83.2	231.7	(.)	5.1	2	7,616
106 Vanuatu	1.2	1.6	..	75.0	..	..	..	..	..
107 Algeria	238.2	3.0	5	2.0	0.7	2.3	3.6	16	161
108 Indonesia	181.2	8.7	35	62.6	14.0	0.5	2.1	1	96
109 Gabon	25.8	1.1	..	77.6	140.1	0.1	4.9	(.)	51
110 El Salvador	2.1	27.3	16	5.0	3.6	3.2	1.5	5	241
111 Nicaragua	11.9	9.3	7	29.4	45.2	2.7	3.8	1	370

HDI rank	Land area (million hectares)	Arable land (as % of land area) 1989-90	Irrigated land (as % of arable land area) 1989-90	Forest area (as % of land area) 1989-90	Internal renewable water resources per capita (1,000 m³ per year) 1990	Annual rate of deforestation (%) 1981-85	Annual change in production of fuelwood (%) 1979-90	Annual fresh water withdrawals As % of water resources 1980-87	Per capita (m³) 1980-87
Low human development	3,480T	12	17	28.6	5.8	0.8	2.9	17	536
Excluding India	3,190T	7	15	29.1	8.9	0.7	3.4	16	472
112 Maldives	(.)	10.0	..	3.3	..	..	..	..	..
113 Guatemala	10.8	12.8	4	35.3	12.6	2.0	3.3	1	139
114 Cape Verde	0.4	9.2	5	0.2	0.5	..	..	20	148
115 Viet Nam	32.5	17.5	28	30.1	5.6	0.6	2.5	1	81
116 Honduras	11.2	14.3	5	29.9	19.9	2.3	4.1	1	508
117 Swaziland	1.7	9.3	38	6.3	8.8	..	1.0	4	414
118 Solomon Islands	2.8	1.4	..	91.5	149.0	(.)	3.9	(.)	18
119 Morocco	44.6	19.4	14	17.8	1.2	0.4	3.6	37	501
120 Lesotho	3.0	10.5	..	65.9	2.3	..	3.2	1	34
121 Zimbabwe	38.7	7.0	8	49.7	2.4	0.4	3.1	5	129
122 Bolivia	108.4	3.0	5	51.3	41.0	0.2	3.1	(.)	184
123 Myanmar	65.8	14.5	10	49.3	26.0	0.3	2.3	(.)	103
124 Egypt	99.5	2.3	100	(.)	(.)	..	3.1	97	1,202
125 São Tomé and Principe	0.1	2.1	..	(.)	..	..	..	..	..
126 Congo	34.2	0.4	2	62.0	90.8	0.1	3.1	(.)	20
127 Kenya	57.0	3.4	2	4.1	0.6	1.7	4.7	7	48
128 Madagascar	58.2	4.4	29	27.0	3.3	1.2	3.6	41	1,675
129 Papua New Guinea	45.3	0.1	..	84.4	199.7	0.1	0.8	(.)	25
130 Zambia	74.3	7.1	1	38.9	11.4	0.2	4.4	(.)	86
131 Ghana	23.0	5.0	..	35.4	3.5	0.8	7.1	1	35
132 Pakistan	77.1	26.3	75	4.5	2.4	0.4	4.3	33	2,053
133 Cameroon	46.5	12.8	..	53.0	18.5	0.4	3.1	(.)	30
134 India	328.7	55.6	25	22.4	2.2	0.3	2.4	18	612
135 Namibia	82.3	0.8	1	22.0	..	0.2	..	2	77
136 Côte d'Ivoire	31.8	7.6	2	24.0	5.9	5.2	5.2	1	68
137 Haiti	2.8	20.1	8	1.5	1.7	3.7	2.0	(.)	46
138 Tanzania, U. Rep. of	88.6	4.7	3	46.3	2.8	0.3	4.4	1	36
139 Comoros	0.2	35.0	..	15.7	2.0	3.1	..	1	15
140 Zaire	226.8	3.2	..	77.0	28.3	0.2	3.7	(.)	22
141 Lao People's Dem. Rep.	23.1	3.8	13	55.5	66.3	1.0	2.3	(.)	228
142 Nigeria	91.1	31.6	3	13.4	2.3	2.7	4.0	1	44
143 Yemen	52.8	2.6	..	7.7	..	..	3.1	..	1,167
144 Liberia	9.6	1.3	1	18.3	90.8	2.3	3.0	(.)	54
145 Togo	5.4	25.3	..	29.6	3.3	0.7	3.4	1	40
146 Uganda	20.0	25.1	..	28.1	3.6	0.8	4.0	(.)	20
147 Bangladesh	13.0	69.3	24	15.0	11.7	0.9	3.1	1	211
148 Cambodia	17.7	16.5	3	75.8	10.7	0.2	2.2	(.)	69
149 Rwanda	2.5	34.4	..	22.6	0.9	2.2	1.2	2	23
150 Senegal	19.3	27.1	3	30.9	3.1	0.5	2.4	4	201
151 Ethiopia	110.1	12.0	1	24.7	2.4	0.3	2.1	2	48
152 Nepal	13.7	19.1	28	18.1	8.9	4.0	2.9	2	155
153 Malawi	9.4	25.3	1	39.8	1.1	3.5	3.7	2	22
154 Burundi	2.6	43.7	5	2.6	0.7	2.7	3.1	3	20
155 Equatorial Guinea	2.8	4.6	..	46.2	68.2	0.2	1.0	(.)	11
156 Central African Rep.	62.3	3.1	..	57.5	48.4	0.2	2.9	(.)	27
157 Mozambique	78.4	3.7	4	18.3	3.7	0.8	3.3	1	53
158 Sudan	237.6	5.2	15	19.0	1.2	1.1	3.6	14	1,089
159 Bhutan	4.7	2.4	26	55.4	62.7	0.1	0.7	(.)	15
160 Angola	124.7	2.4	..	42.5	15.8	0.2	3.1	(.)	43
161 Mauritania	102.5	0.2	6	4.8	0.2	2.4	4.0	10	473
162 Benin	11.1	12.7	..	31.8	5.5	1.7	3.5	(.)	26
163 Djibouti	2.3	..	..	0.3	0.7	..	..	2	28
164 Guinea-Bissau	2.8	10.7	..	38.1	31.4	2.7	0.2	(.)	18
165 Chad	125.9	2.5	..	10.2	6.8	0.6	2.6	(.)	35
166 Somalia	62.7	1.6	11	14.5	1.5	0.1	4.7	7	167
167 Gambia	1.0	17.8	7	16.2	3.5	2.4	0.6	(.)	33
168 Mali	122.0	1.7	10	5.7	6.6	0.5	3.2	2	159
169 Niger	126.7	2.8	1	1.6	2.0	2.6	3.3	1	44
170 Burkina Faso	27.4	13.0	..	24.3	3.1	1.7	2.9	1	20
171 Afghanistan	65.2	12.1	33	2.9	3.0	..	-0.6	52	1,436
172 Sierra Leone	7.2	23.1	2	28.9	38.5	0.3	2.6	(.)	99
173 Guinea	24.6	2.5	3	59.5	32.9	0.8	2.6	(.)	115
All developing countries	7,550T	16	20	28.7	6.8	1.1	2.3	16	523
Least developed countries	1,540T	6	10	28.5	11.4	0.6	3.0	6	259
Sub-Saharan Africa	2,040T	6	6	29.5	7.4	0.5	3.6	5	120
Industrial countries	5,360T	13	7	30.1	7.6	..	6.5	21	1,204
World	12,910T	11	16	29.1	7.0	..	3.0	17	645

Note: Data for industrial countries for this subject area are in table 46.

HDI rank	Commercial energy consumption per capita (kg of oil equivalent)		Total commercial energy consumption (billion kg of oil equivalent)		Annual rate of change in commercial energy consumption (%)		Commercial energy consumed in kg of oil equivalent per $100 GDP	
	1965	1990	1965	1990	1960-74	1980-90	1990	Indexed (1965=100)
High human development	**810**	**1,718**	**102T**	**363T**	**8.4**	**3.4**	**46**	**31**
20 Barbados	..	..	..	..	..	..	..	..
24 Hong Kong	584	1,717	2	10	6.8	3.9	16	24
27 Cyprus	..	..	..	..	..	..	..	..
30 Uruguay	765	821	2	3	3.1	0.5	31	14
31 Trinidad and Tobago	4,492	5,940	4	7	4.8	1.4	155	42
32 Bahamas	..	..	..	..	..	..	..	..
33 Korea, Rep. of	238	1,898	7	82	13.2	8.1	35	15
36 Chile	652	887	6	12	6.1	2.9	42	45
42 Costa Rica	267	622	(.)	2	10.4	3.8	33	49
43 Singapore	2,214	5,685	4	15	16.8	5.8	45	35
44 Brunei Darussalam	..	..	..	..	..	..	..	..
46 Argentina	975	1,801	22	58	5.7	3.5	62	47
50 Venezuela	2,319	2,582	21	50	6.6	2.1	103	48
51 Dominica	..	..	..	..	..	..	..	..
52 Kuwait	16,781	6,414	8	14	6.7	5.0	58	..
53 Mexico	605	1,300	26	110	7.7	1.2	46	36
55 Qatar	..	..	..	..	..	..	..	..
Medium human development	**229**	**703**	**547T**	**1,480T**	**5.8**	**5.4**	**81**	**50**
Excluding China	**316**	**848**	**417T**	**786T**	**8.9**	**4.9**	**51**	**33**
56 Mauritius	160	394	(.)	(.)	..	3.5	20	32
57 Malaysia	313	974	3	17	11.1	7.8	41	43
58 Bahrain	..	..	..	..	..	..	..	..
59 Grenada	..	..	..	..	..	..	..	..
60 Antigua and Barbuda	..	..	..	..	..	..	..	..
61 Colombia	412	811	8	26	6.3	3.3	64	49
63 Seychelles	..	..	..	..	..	..	..	..
65 Suriname	..	..	..	..	..	..	..	..
67 United Arab Emirates	126	10,874	(.)	17	..	13.9	61	..
68 Panama	3,065	1,694	4	4	10.5	(.)	86	74
69 Jamaica	703	931	1	2	11.2	-1.5	57	45
70 Brazil	286	915	24	136	8.6	4.9	33	27
71 Fiji	..	..	..	..	..	..	..	..
72 Saint Lucia	..	..	..	..	..	..	..	..
73 Turkey	258	857	8	48	9.9	6.9	50	47
74 Thailand	82	352	3	19	16.9	7.2	24	41
75 Cuba	..	..	..	..	4.4	..	..	..
76 Saint Vincent	..	..	..	..	..	..	..	..
79 Saint Kitts and Nevis	..	..	..	..	..	..	..	..
81 Syrian Arab Rep.	212	913	1	11	9.0	4.0	77	98
82 Belize	..	..	..	..	..	..	..	..
84 Saudi Arabia	1,759	5,033	8	75	14.4	9.3	93	25
85 South Africa	1,744	2,447	35	93	..	3.1	102	31
86 Sri Lanka	106	179	1	3	6.2	5.1	43	63
87 Libyan Arab Jamahiriya	222	3,399	(.)	15	17.9	7.1	..	..
89 Ecuador	162	678	1	7	8.3	4.4	66	89
90 Paraguay	84	232	(.)	1	8.5	5.1	19	48
91 Korea, Dem. Rep. of	..	..	..	..	9.1	..	..	..
92 Philippines	158	215	5	13	9.6	2.3	31	35
93 Tunisia	170	520	1	4	9.5	4.6	38	42
94 Oman	14	2,648	(.)	4	..	10.7	52	388
95 Peru	395	509	5	11	6.2	1.5	30	33
96 Iraq	399	774	3	14	5.9	5.3	..	..
97 Dominican Rep.	127	336	(.)	2	14.6	2.4	33	60
98 Samoa	..	..	..	..	..	..	..	..
99 Jordan	393	994	1	4	6.5	5.8	120	..
100 Mongolia	461	1,277	1	3	7.3	3.1	..	..
101 China	178	598	130	690	3.6	5.6	189	96
102 Lebanon	713	968	2	3	6.3	4.1	..	..
103 Iran, Islamic Rep. of	524	1,026	259	60	15.6	4.5	52	24
104 Botswana	191	425	(.)	1	..	3.1	19	9
105 Guyana	..	..	..	..	..	..	..	..
106 Vanuatu	..	..	..	..	..	..	..	..
107 Algeria	226	1,956	3	49	12.2	17.8	116	..
108 Indonesia	91	272	10	50	4.2	4.1	47	18
109 Gabon	153	1,158	(.)	1	..	2.5	28	86
110 El Salvador	140	233	(.)	1	7.7	2.3	22	41
111 Nicaragua	172	261	(.)	1	10.0	2.9	..	..

	HDI rank	Commercial energy consumption per capita (kg of oil equivalent)		Total commercial energy consumption (billion kg of oil equivalent)		Annual rate of change in commercial energy consumption (%)		Commercial energy consumed in kg of oil equivalent per $100 GDP	
		1965	1990	1965	1990	1960-74	1980-90	1990	Indexed (1965=100)
	Low human development	96	182	90T	335T	6.4	5.0	59	74
	Excluding India	91	140	41T	140T	7.9	4.3	44	70
112	Maldives	..	..	..	..	..	..	..	..
113	Guatemala	150	171	1	2	6.1	0.6	21	40
114	Cape Verde	..	..	..	..	..	..	..	..
115	Viet Nam	97	100	4	7	..	2.6	..	..
116	Honduras	111	198	(.)	1	8.9	2.1	43	78
117	Swaziland	..	..	..	..	..	..	..	..
118	Solomon Islands	..	..	..	..	..	..	..	..
119	Morocco	124	247	2	6	7.7	2.9	25	43
120	Lesotho	(.)	(.)	(.)	(.)	..	..	(.)	..
121	Zimbabwe	441	525	2	5	..	1.2	98	47
122	Bolivia	156	257	1	2	7.0	-0.4	41	48
123	Myanmar	39	82	1	3	3.6	4.8	..	..
124	Egypt	313	598	9	31	2.7	5.0	94	47
125	São Tomé and Principe	..	..	..	..	..	..	..	..
126	Congo	90	213	(.)	(.)	5.2	3.4	17	33
127	Kenya	110	100	1	2	4.2	1.1	31	26
128	Madagascar	34	40	(.)	(.)	8.9	1.8	17	64
129	Papua New Guinea	56	233	(.)	1	..	2.4	28	77
130	Zambia	464	379	2	3	..	1.1	99	62
131	Ghana	76	68	1	1	6.6	-4.1	16	57
132	Pakistan	135	233	8	28	5.9	6.5	78	54
133	Cameroon	67	147	(.)	2	4.0	4.5	15	31
134	India	100	231	50	195	4.9	5.9	77	78
135	Namibia	..	..	..	..	..	..	..	..
136	Côte d'Ivoire	101	173	(.)	2	15.5	2.7	27	44
137	Haiti	23	53	(.)	(.)	2.8	2.0	12	44
138	Tanzania, U. Rep. of	37	38	(.)	1	10.4	2.0	48	87
139	Comoros	..	..	..	..	..	..	..	..
140	Zaire	75	71	1	3	4.3	1.7	35	113
141	Lao People's Dem. Rep.	24	39	(.)	(.)	13.4	1.8	19	..
142	Nigeria	34	138	2	15	10.2	4.8	43	150
143	Yemen	6	234	(.)	3	12.7	23.8	41	..
144	Liberia	179	169	(.)	(.)	19.3	-4.1	..	..
145	Togo	27	51	(.)	(.)	12.5	0.7	11	44
146	Uganda	36	27	(.)	(.)	9.5	4.7	17	63
147	Bangladesh	..	57	..	6	..	7.9	28	..
148	Cambodia	19	59	(.)	(.)	-0.1	2.5	..	..
149	Rwanda	8	41	(.)	(.)	..	3.1	14	78
150	Senegal	342	156	1	1	4.6	-0.5	20	55
151	Ethiopia	10	20	(.)	1	14.7	3.5	18	78
152	Nepal	6	25	(.)	(.)	12.3	9.2	17	197
153	Malawi	25	41	(.)	(.)	..	1.0	24	52
154	Burundi	5	21	(.)	(.)	..	7.3	12	107
155	Equatorial Guinea	..	..	..	..	..	..	..	..
156	Central African Rep.	22	30	(.)	(.)	7.4	3.5	7	28
157	Mozambique	81	85	1	1	5.7	2.4	91	..
158	Sudan	67	58	1	1	13.2	0.7	..	..
159	Bhutan	..	13	..	(.)	..	..	7	..
160	Angola	114	203	1	2	8.8	2.5	24	..
161	Mauritania	48	114	(.)	(.)	16.8	0.2	24	73
162	Benin	21	46	(.)	(.)	8.8	3.8	12	50
163	Djibouti	..	..	..	..	..	..	..	..
164	Guinea-Bissau	..	..	..	..	..	..	..	..
165	Chad	12	17	(.)	(.)	7.2	0.3	9	..
166	Somalia	11	64	(.)	1	7.4	2.0	62	297
167	Gambia	..	..	..	..	..	..	..	..
168	Mali	14	24	(.)	(.)	5.5	2.1	9	34
169	Niger	8	40	(.)	(.)	14.3	2.3	12	286
170	Burkina Faso	7	17	(.)	(.)	6.5	1.1	5	50
171	Afghanistan	30	90	(.)	1	9.4	8.3	..	..
172	Sierra Leone	109	77	(.)	(.)	10.3	-0.1	38	46
173	Guinea	64	73	(.)	(.)	3.2	1.5	15	..
	All developing countries	204	517	709T	2,084T	6.2	5.1	68	50
	Least developed countries	42	63	9T	32T	9.0	4.7	27	89
	Sub-Saharan Africa	204	282	49T	140T	9.1	2.7	58	61
	Industrial countries	3,387	4,937	2,521T	4,443T	6.0	1.4	..	..
	World	936	1,316	7,230T	6,527T	6.2	4.5	..	..

Note: Data for industrial countries for this subject area are in table 47.

HDI rank	Total GDP (US$ billions) 1990	Agricultural production (as % of GDP) 1990	Industrial production (as % of GDP) 1990	Services (as % of GDP) 1990	Consumption Private (as % of GDP) 1990	Consumption Government (as % of GDP) 1990	Gross domestic investment (as % of GDP) 1990	Gross domestic savings (as % of GDP) 1990	Tax revenue (as % of GNP) 1990	Central government expenditure (as % of GNP) 1990	Exports (as % of GDP) 1990	Imports (as % of GDP) 1990
High human development	**780T**	**9**	**38**	**53**	**66**	**10**	**25**	**27**	**14**	**18**	**30**	**36**
20 Barbados	..	..	..	..	..	..	..	..	..	..	..	..
24 Hong Kong	59.7	(.)	26	73	59	8	28	33	..	..	44	124
27 Cyprus	..	..	..	..	..	..	..	..	..	..	..	..
30 Uruguay	8.2	11	34	55	67	13	12	19	27	28	21	18
31 Trinidad and Tobago	4.8	3	48	49	52	16	17	33	..	..	47	28
32 Bahamas	..	..	..	..	..	..	..	..	..	..	..	..
33 Korea, Rep. of	236.4	9	45	46	63	..	37	37	14	16	28	30
36 Chile	27.8	..	..	..	67	10	20	23	24	33	34	28
42 Costa Rica	5.7	16	26	58	60	18	29	22	21	27	27	38
43 Singapore	34.6	(.)	37	63	45	11	39	45	17	23	157	181
44 Brunei Darussalam	..	..	..	..	..	..	..	..	..	..	..	..
46 Argentina	93.3	13	41	46	79	5	9	16	12	16	16	5
50 Venezuela	48.3	6	49	45	62	9	9	29	17	23	34	13
51 Dominica	..	..	..	..	..	..	..	..	..	..	..	..
52 Kuwait	23.5	1	56	43	..	..	..	..	1	31	..	..
53 Mexico	237.8	9	30	61	70	11	20	19	14	18	12	13
55 Qatar	..	..	..	..	..	..	..	..	..	..	..	..
Medium human development	**1,710T**	**16**	**39**	**45**	**59**	**12**	**28**	**29**			**17**	**17**
Excluding China	**1,350T**	**13**	**38**	**49**	**62**	**13**	**25**	**25**	**16**	**27**	**18**	**18**
56 Mauritius	2.1	12	33	55	66	12	30	21	22	24	49	67
57 Malaysia	42.4	..	..	..	54	13	34	33	22	31	71	70
58 Bahrain	..	..	..	..	..	..	..	..	..	..	..	..
59 Grenada	..	..	..	..	..	..	..	..	..	..	..	..
60 Antigua and Barbuda	..	..	..	..	..	..	..	..	..	..	..	..
61 Colombia	41.1	17	32	51	64	10	19	25	12	15	17	14
63 Seychelles	..	..	..	..	..	..	..	..	..	..	..	..
65 Suriname	..	..	..	..	..	..	..	..	..	..	..	..
67 United Arab Emirates	28.3	2	55	43	..	..	..	..	1	13	..	..
68 Panama	4.8	10	9	81	62	22	16	16	18	32	7	35
69 Jamaica	4.0	5	46	49	56	15	30	30	..	..	37	47
70 Brazil	414.1	10	39	51	61	16	22	23	..	36	8	6
71 Fiji	..	..	..	..	..	..	..	..	..	..	..	..
72 Saint Lucia	..	..	..	..	..	..	..	..	..	..	..	..
73 Turkey	96.5	18	33	49	68	14	23	18	16	25	14	24
74 Thailand	80.2	12	39	49	57	10	37	34	18	15	29	42
75 Cuba	..	..	..	..	..	..	..	..	..	..	..	..
76 Saint Vincent	..	..	..	..	..	..	..	..	..	..	..	..
79 Saint Kitts and Nevis	..	..	..	..	..	..	..	..	..	..	..	..
81 Syrian Arab Rep.	14.7	28	22	50	72	14	14	14	19	28	34	19
82 Belize	..	..	..	..	..	..	..	..	..	..	..	..
84 Saudi Arabia	80.9	8	45	47	..	..	..	..	..	..	..	..
85 South Africa	90.7	5	44	51	56	19	19	25	28	35	26	20
86 Sri Lanka	7.3	26	26	48	76	9	22	15	19	28	25	34
87 Libyan Arab Jamahiriya	..	..	..	..	..	..	..	..	..	..	..	..
89 Ecuador	10.9	13	42	45	70	8	19	22	17	16	27	18
90 Paraguay	5.3	28	23	49	70	6	22	23	9	9	20	23
91 Korea, Dem. Rep. of	..	..	..	..	..	..	..	..	..	..	..	..
92 Philippines	43.9	22	35	43	75	9	22	16	14	20	20	30
93 Tunisia	11.1	16	32	52	64	16	27	19	25	37	30	47
94 Oman	7.7	3	79	18	..	..	..	..	10	49	..	..
95 Peru	36.6	7	37	56	71	6	23	23	5	10	13	13
96 Iraq	..	..	..	..	..	..	..	..	..	..	..	..
97 Dominican Rep.	7.3	17	27	56	82	7	15	11	14	15	13	35
98 Samoa	..	..	..	..	..	..	..	..	..	..	..	..
99 Jordan	3.3	8	26	66	85	24	19	-9	16	39	29	68
100 Mongolia	..	17	34	49	73	24	30	3	..	..	..	..
101 China	364.9	27	42	31	49	8	39	43	..	..	15	13
102 Lebanon	..	..	..	..	..	..	..	..	..	..	..	..
103 Iran, Islamic Rep. of	116.0	21	21	58	69	11	21	20	6	17	11	9
104 Botswana	2.7	3	57	40	..	..	..	..	33	42	..	..
105 Guyana	..	..	..	..	..	..	..	..	..	..	..	..
106 Vanuatu	..	..	..	..	..	..	..	..	..	..	..	..
107 Algeria	42.2	13	46	41	44	18	33	38	..	..	30	20
108 Indonesia	107.3	22	40	38	54	9	36	37	17	20	25	22
109 Gabon	4.7	9	49	42	43	20	19	37	..	..	68	21
110 El Salvador	5.4	11	21	68	88	11	12	1	10	10	10	21
111 Nicaragua	..	..	..	..	73	29	20	-2	..	..	..	..

HDI rank	Total GDP (US$ billions) 1990	Agricultural production (as % of GDP) 1990	Industrial production (as % of GDP) 1990	Services (as % of GDP) 1990	Consumption Private (as % of GDP) 1990	Consumption Government (as % of GDP) 1990	Gross domestic investment (as % of GDP) 1990	Gross domestic savings (as % of GDP) 1990	Tax revenue (as % of GNP) 1990	Central government expenditure (as % of GNP) 1990	Exports (as % of GDP) 1990	Imports (as % of GDP) 1990
Low human development	540T	30	28	42	71	13	20	16	13	21	11	15
Excluding India	290T	29	27	44	73	13	18	13	15	25	17	22
112 Maldives	..	..	..	..	..	..	..	..	..	..	..	..
113 Guatemala	7.6	26	19	55	85	7	12	8	8	12	15	20
114 Cape Verde	..	..	..	..	..	..	..	..	..	..	..	..
115 Viet Nam	..	..	..	..	..	..	..	..	..	..	30	34
116 Honduras	2.4	23	24	53	80	15	13	6	..	..	..	..
117 Swaziland	..	..	..	..	..	..	..	..	..	..	..	..
118 Solomon Islands	..	..	..	..	..	..	..	..	..	..	18	29
119 Morocco	25.2	16	33	51	65	16	26	20	..	..	..	..
120 Lesotho	0.3	24	30	46	118	24	71	-41	19	25	..	..
121 Zimbabwe	5.3	13	40	47	53	26	21	21	32	41	..	29
122 Bolivia	4.5	24	32	44	77	15	11	8	9	19	20	16
123 Myanmar	..	..	..	..	..	..	..	..	..	..	..	..
124 Egypt	33.2	17	29	54	80	10	23	10	23	40	10	33
125 São Tomé and Principe	..	..	..	..	..	..	..	..	..	..	..	..
126 Congo	2.9	13	39	48	51	19	16	31	..	..	49	25
127 Kenya	7.5	28	21	51	63	18	24	18	20	31	12	24
128 Madagascar	2.8	33	13	54	83	9	17	8	..	..	12	18
129 Papua New Guinea	3.3	29	31	40	66	24	25	10	19	29	34	38
130 Zambia	3.1	17	54	29	68	15	14	17	11	22	..	..
131 Ghana	6.3	47	16	37	82	8	15	11	13	14	13	21
132 Pakistan	35.5	26	25	49	73	15	19	12	14	24	13	17
133 Cameroon	11.1	27	28	45	70	12	17	19	17	21	11	12
134 India	254.5	31	29	40	68	12	23	20	12	18	6	8
135 Namibia	..	11	38	51	..	..	..	..	39	43	29	24
136 Côte d'Ivoire	7.6	47	27	26	68	18	10	14	..	..	..	..
137 Haiti	2.8	..	..	..	90	9	11	1	..	..	6	11
138 Tanzania, U. Rep. of	2.1	59	12	29	95	10	25	-6	..	..	11	34
139 Comoros	..	..	..	..	..	..	..	..	..	..	..	..
140 Zaire	7.5	30	33	37	..	..	11	..	11	13	12	11
141 Lao People's Dem. Rep.	0.9	..	..	..	89	12	12	-2	..	..	..	..
142 Nigeria	34.8	36	39	25	59	11	15	29	..	..	44	18
143 Yemen	6.7	20	33	47	66	26	15	8	..	..	..	..
144 Liberia	..	..	..	..	..	..	..	..	17	..	..	..
145 Togo	1.6	33	22	45	70	19	22	11	..	..	20	47
146 Uganda	2.8	67	7	26	94	7	12	-1	5	..	4	12
147 Bangladesh	22.9	38	15	47	89	9	12	2	9	15	7	16
148 Cambodia	..	..	..	..	..	..	..	..	..	..	..	..
149 Rwanda	2.1	38	22	40	78	18	12	4	..	..	5	13
150 Senegal	5.8	21	18	61	77	14	13	9	..	..	15	31
151 Ethiopia	5.5	41	17	42	68	26	13	6	..	..	5	18
152 Nepal	2.9	60	14	26	80	12	18	8	8	20	5	17
153 Malawi	1.7	33	20	47	75	15	19	10	21	29	25	35
154 Burundi	1.0	56	15	29	84	15	19	1	..	..	7	20
155 Equatorial Guinea	..	..	..	..	..	..	..	..	..	..	..	..
156 Central African Rep.	1.2	42	17	41	88	14	11	-2	12	26	11	14
157 Mozambique	1.3	64	15	21	92	20	37	-12	..	..	..	..
158 Sudan	..	..	..	..	..	..	..	..	..	..	..	..
159 Bhutan	0.3	44	27	29	58	20	36	22	6	44	..	..
160 Angola	7.7	13	44	43	..	..	..	..	..	..	47	25
161 Mauritania	1.0	26	29	45	88	10	15	3	20	34	..	..
162 Benin	1.8	37	15	48	87	11	12	2	..	..	5	28
163 Djibouti	..	..	..	..	..	..	..	..	..	..	..	..
164 Guinea-Bissau	..	..	..	..	..	..	..	..	..	..	..	..
165 Chad	1.1	38	17	45	92	23	10	-15	..	..	19	42
166 Somalia	0.9	65	9	26	78	..	16	22	..	..	14	38
167 Gambia	..	..	..	..	..	..	..	..	..	..	..	..
168 Mali	2.5	46	13	41	80	10	26	10	16	29	15	28
169 Niger	2.5	36	13	51	..	..	9	..	..	..	18	10
170 Burkina Faso	3.1	32	24	44	83	13	20	5	..	..	5	16
171 Afghanistan	..	..	..	..	..	..	..	..	..	..	..	..
172 Sierra Leone	0.8	32	13	55	85	10	11	5	9	11	14	15
173 Guinea	2.8	28	33	39	71	8	20	21	14	25	..	..
All developing countries	3,000T	17	36	47	63	12	26	26	15	..	19	21
Least developed countries	86T	36	22	42	82	13	15	5	12	..	10	18
Sub-Saharan Africa	240T	22	35	43	63	16	17	21	24	..	25	21
Industrial countries	16,200T	4	37	59	..	..	..	..	24	28	..	..
World	19,200T	7	37	56	..	..	..	..	23	..	..	..

Note: Data for industrial countries for this subject area are in table 49.

HDI rank	Total GNP (US$ billions) 1990	Total GNP (% annual growth rate) 1980-90	GNP per capita annual growth rate (%) 1965-80	1980-90	Average annual rate of inflation (%) 1980-90	1991	Exports as % of GDP (% annual growth rate) 1980-90	Tax revenue as % of GNP (% annual growth rate) 1972-90	Direct taxes as % of total taxes 1972	1990	Overall budget surplus/deficit (as % of GNP) 1972	1990
High human development	**730T**	**4.5**	**3.9**	**2.9**	**94.4**	**35.1**	**-5.7**	**1.4**	**38**	**43**	**-2.3**	**0.1**
20 Barbados	1.7	1.7	3.5	1.4	..	..	..	..	..	..	..	..
24 Hong Kong	66.7	7.0	6.2	5.5	7.2	..	-7.7	..	..	..	..	..
27 Cyprus	5.6	6.0	..	4.9	..	..	..	..	..	..	..	..
30 Uruguay	7.9	-0.3	2.5	-0.9	61.4	1.6	5.5	0.3	5	7	-2.7	0.4
31 Trinidad and Tobago	4.5	-4.3	3.1	-6.0	6.3	16.5	-4.9	..	..	..	..	..
32 Bahamas	2.9	3.6	1.0	1.7	..	..	..	..	..	..	..	..
33 Korea, Rep. of	231.1	10.1	7.3	8.9	5.1	10.9	-9.3	0.9	33	38	..	-0.7
36 Chile	25.5	2.8	(.)	1.1	20.5	21.7	7.0	0.8	17	31	-13.0	-0.2
42 Costa Rica	5.3	3.0	3.3	0.6	23.5	29.3	3.2	2.9	20	11	-4.5	-3.3
43 Singapore	33.5	7.0	8.3	5.7	1.7	..	-1.6	2.1	36	40	1.3	10.5
44 Brunei Darussalam	..	..	..	..	..	..	..	..	..	..	..	..
46 Argentina	76.5	-0.5	1.7	-1.8	395.1	127.8	10.1	..	..	5	0.3	-2.7
50 Venezuela	50.6	0.7	2.3	-2.0	19.3	21.2	-0.1	0.7	73	75	-0.2	-1.2
51 Dominica	0.2	4.3	-0.8	3.0	..	..	..	..	..	..	-0.2	..
52 Kuwait	..	2.2	0.6	-2.2	-2.9	..	..	13.7	76	18	17.4	-7.2
53 Mexico	214.5	1.1	3.6	-0.9	70.4	19.2	3.1	2.2	40	40	-2.9	0.8
55 Qatar	7.0	-6.6	..	-11.4	..	..	..	..	..	..	..	..
Medium human development	**1,750T**	**4.7**	**4.0**	**2.5**	**32.4**	**62.0**	**3.9**	**..**	**..**	**..**	**-2.4**	**..**
Excluding China	**1,330T**	**3.2**	**3.8**	**0.8**	**68.7**	**149.6**	**2.6**	**2.9**	**37**	**41**	**-2.4**	**-6.6**
56 Mauritius	2.4	6.4	3.7	5.4	8.8	7.4	..	2.5	25	15	-1.2	-0.5
57 Malaysia	41.5	5.1	4.7	2.5	1.6	3.2	1.9	2.3	32	41	-9.4	-2.8
58 Bahrain	..	-0.1	..	-4.2	..	..	..	..	..	..	..	..
59 Grenada	0.2	5.8	0.1	5.1	..	..	..	..	..	..	..	..
60 Antigua and Barbuda	0.4	5.2	-1.4	4.7	..	..	..	..	..	..	(.)	..
61 Colombia	40.8	3.1	3.7	1.1	24.8	29.7	2.3	1.3	40	30	-2.5	-2.0
63 Seychelles	0.3	3.2	4.6	2.5	..	4.7	..	..	..	..	..	..
65 Suriname	1.4	-2.6	5.5	-5.0	..	..	..	..	..	..	..	..
67 United Arab Emirates	31.6	-3.1	0.6	-7.2	1.1	..	..	..	..	0	0.3	-0.6
68 Panama	4.4	0.1	2.8	-2.0	2.4	1.4	-3.4	1.4	28	20	-6.5	-8.2
69 Jamaica	3.6	0.7	-0.1	-0.4	18.3	60.7	0.5	..	..	..	..	..
70 Brazil	402.8	2.7	6.3	0.6	284.4	428.5	-0.8	..	..	..	-0.3	-16.6
71 Fiji	1.3	1.3	4.2	-0.4	..	4.0	..	..	..	..	..	..
72 Saint Lucia	0.3	6.3	2.7	4.2	..	..	..	..	..	..	..	..
73 Turkey	91.7	5.5	3.6	3.0	43.2	56.7	10.1	-0.5	37	51	-2.2	-4.2
74 Thailand	79.0	7.6	4.4	5.6	3.3	5.6	4.1	2.4	14	26	-4.2	4.9
75 Cuba	..	..	0.6	..	..	..	..	..	..	..	..	..
76 Saint Vincent	0.2	6.9	0.2	5.7	..	..	..	..	..	..	..	..
79 Saint Kitts and Nevis	0.1	4.8	4.0	6.0	..	..	..	..	..	..	..	..
81 Syrian Arab Rep.	12.4	1.4	5.1	-2.1	14.7	..	7.5	-2.5	15	40	-3.5	-0.7
82 Belize	0.4	5.3	3.4	2.5	..	..	..	..	..	..	..	..
84 Saudi Arabia	..	-0.8	0.6	-5.6	-5.2	..	..	..	..	..	..	..
85 South Africa	90.4	1.5	3.2	-0.9	14.4	..	-2.9	1.6	63	53	-4.4	-2.5
86 Sri Lanka	8.0	3.9	2.8	2.4	11.0	11.6	0.1	0.3	21	12	-5.3	-7.9
87 Libyan Arab Jamahiriya	..	-5.4	0.6	-9.2	0.2	..	..	..	..	..	..	..
89 Ecuador	10.1	1.9	5.4	-0.8	36.7	47.7	2.4	1.4	20	58	0.2	2.0
90 Paraguay	4.8	1.9	4.1	-1.3	24.4	14.6	11.0	1.3	10	13	-1.7	2.9
91 Korea, Dem. Rep. of	..	..	0.6	..	..	..	..	..	..	..	-3.9	..
92 Philippines	44.0	0.9	3.2	-1.5	14.9	16.5	1.6	1.3	15	32	-2.1	-3.5
93 Tunisia	11.6	3.4	4.7	0.9	7.4	6.5	(.)	2.2	19	17	-0.9	-4.5
94 Oman	..	8.6	9.0	7.1	..	..	..	4.8	93	88	-15.3	-9.9
95 Peru	25.1	0.2	0.8	-2.0	233.7	386.0	-2.9	-6.2	18	10	-0.9	-5.0
96 Iraq	..	..	0.6	..	..	..	..	..	..	..	..	..
97 Dominican Rep.	5.8	1.9	3.8	-0.4	21.8	53.5	-0.7	-1.2	22	23	..	(.)
98 Samoa	0.1	2.0	..	1.2	..	..	..	..	..	..	..	..
99 Jordan	3.9	-0.4	5.8	-3.9	..	6.6	1.0	..	15	14	..	-6.0
100 Mongolia	..	..	0.6	..	-1.3	..	..	..	..	..	..	..
101 China	415.9	9.5	4.1	7.9	5.8	3.5	7.5	..	..	..	..	..
102 Lebanon	..	..	0.6	..	..	..	..	..	..	..	..	..
103 Iran, Islamic Rep. of	139.1	2.7	2.9	-0.8	13.8	14.3	..	-5.1	22	28	-4.6	-4.0
104 Botswana	2.6	9.9	9.9	6.3	12.1	..	..	5.5	29	72	-23.8	12.6
105 Guyana	0.3	-2.7	0.7	-3.2	..	55.6	..	..	..	..	..	..
106 Vanuatu	0.2	2.4	..	-0.5	..	..	..	..	..	..	..	..
107 Algeria	51.6	2.7	4.2	-0.3	6.6	50.0	-0.5	..	..	..	..	..
108 Indonesia	101.2	6.3	5.2	4.1	8.4	5.3	-2.1	1.6	51	63	-2.5	-2.1
109 Gabon	3.7	0.8	5.6	-2.6	-1.7	-2.6	..	..	22	..	-11.9	..
110 El Salvador	5.8	0.8	1.5	-0.6	17.2	11.9	-10.4	-1.2	16	19	-0.9	-0.1
111 Nicaragua	..	..	-0.7	..	432.0	..	..	..	10	..	-4.0	..

HDI rank	Total GNP (US$ billions) 1990	Total GNP (% annual growth rate) 1980-90	GNP per capita annual growth rate (%)		Average annual rate of inflation (%)		Exports as % of GDP (% annual growth rate) 1980-90	Tax revenue as % of GNP (% annual growth rate) 1972-90	Direct taxes as % of total taxes		Overall budget surplus/ deficit (as % of GNP)	
			1965-80	1980-90	1980-90	1991			1972	1990	1972	1990
Low human development	580T	4.4	1.8	1.7	14.5	34.0	0.9	2.6	24	22	-3.4	-6.3
Excluding India	280T	3.2	2.0	0.1	21.3	53.2	0.6	2.6	21	26	-3.7	-4.5
112 Maldives	0.1	10.0	1.8	6.6	..	11.4	..	..	..	..	..	..
113 Guatemala	8.3	0.7	3.0	-2.1	14.6	32.8	-2.8	1.1	14	22	-2.2	-1.8
114 Cape Verde	0.3	5.7	..	3.1	..	14.3	..	..	..	..	..	..
115 Viet Nam	..	..	0.6	..	..	83.1	..	..	..	..	..	..
116 Honduras	3.0	2.2	1.1	-1.2	5.4	28.4	-1.7	..	22	..	-2.9	..
117 Swaziland	0.6	4.5	3.7	1.1	..	..	..	..	..	..	..	..
118 Solomon Islands	0.2	7.0	5.0	3.4	..	..	..	..	..	..	..	..
119 Morocco	23.8	4.3	2.7	1.6	7.2	5.7	2.9	..	19	..	-3.9	..
120 Lesotho	0.8	1.8	6.8	-0.9	13.0	12.9	..	3.3	16	14	-0.9	-2.8
121 Zimbabwe	6.3	2.6	1.7	-0.8	10.8	25.4	..	..	..	50	..	-7.9
122 Bolivia	4.5	(.)	1.7	-2.6	318.4	20.2	1.9	..	..	9	..	-1.9
123 Myanmar	..	..	1.6	..	..	..	..	..	38	17	..	..
124 Egypt	31.4	4.7	2.8	2.1	11.9	22.3	-3.3	..	..	25	..	-6.9
125 São Tomé and Principe	(.)	-1.5	3.3	-4.2	..	25.0	..	..	..	..	..	..
126 Congo	2.3	3.2	2.7	-0.2	0.7	-5.0	8.0	..	21	..	..	..
127 Kenya	9.0	4.2	3.1	0.3	9.2	8.9	-6.1	0.9	44	31	-3.9	-6.8
128 Madagascar	2.7	0.5	-0.4	-2.3	17.1	12.7	-1.7	..	15	..	-2.0	..
129 Papua New Guinea	3.4	1.9	0.6	-0.5	5.3	5.9	-2.0	..	..	54	..	-0.9
130 Zambia	3.4	0.7	-1.2	-2.9	42.3	155.0	..	-4.3	59	40	-13.8	-5.0
131 Ghana	5.8	2.8	-0.8	-0.6	42.7	18.1	7.4	-0.7	21	31	-5.8	0.4
132 Pakistan	42.6	6.3	1.8	2.9	6.7	10.7	0.8	3.2	16	14	-6.9	-7.2
133 Cameroon	11.2	2.9	2.4	-0.3	5.6	0.7	-7.4	..	..	48	..	-3.2
134 India	294.8	5.4	1.5	3.2	7.9	12.8	2.6	2.5	25	19	-3.2	-7.3
135 Namibia	..	..	0.6	..	13.2	..	..	..	..	48	..	7.0
136 Côte d'Ivoire	8.9	0.2	2.8	-3.7	2.7	1.3	-2.7	..	..	..	..	..
137 Haiti	2.4	-0.4	0.9	-2.3	7.2	-1.4	-18.1	..	..	..	..	..
138 Tanzania, U. Rep. of	2.8	2.3	0.8	-0.7	25.7	18.9	-0.8	..	37	..	-5.0	..
139 Comoros	0.2	2.8	0.6	-0.8	..	2.5	..	..	..	..	..	..
140 Zaire	8.1	1.6	-1.3	-1.5	60.9	65.0	-7.4	1.0	23	30	-2.7	1.9
141 Lao People's Dem. Rep.	0.8	3.7	0.6	0.7	..	27.5	..	..	..	..	..	..
142 Nigeria	31.3	0.2	4.2	-3.0	18.2	17.2	4.4	..	49	..	-0.8	..
143 Yemen	..	..	5.1	..	..	29.0	..	..	..	..	..	..
144 Liberia	..	..	0.5	..	..	..	..	0.2	42	35	1.1	..
145 Togo	1.5	1.8	1.7	-1.7	4.8	3.3	-10.3	..	..	..	..	..
146 Uganda	3.8	4.1	-2.2	-0.8	107.0	23.3	1.3	-5.6	24	6	-8.1	..
147 Bangladesh	22.6	3.7	-0.3	1.0	9.6	5.3	0.8	-0.9	8	11	-1.9	-0.4
148 Cambodia	..	..	0.6	..	..	..	..	..	..	..	..	..
149 Rwanda	2.2	1.0	1.6	-2.2	3.8	14.6	-8.6	..	19	..	-2.7	..
150 Senegal	5.3	3.0	-0.5	(.)	6.6	2.1	-2.7	..	18	..	-0.8	..
151 Ethiopia	6.0	1.9	0.4	-1.2	2.1	7.7	-6.4	..	26	..	-1.4	..
152 Nepal	3.3	4.5	(.)	1.8	9.1	9.1	-0.6	3.9	5	13	-1.2	-8.1
153 Malawi	1.7	3.3	3.2	-0.1	14.7	12.7	1.1	1.5	41	40	-6.2	-1.9
154 Burundi	1.2	4.2	2.4	1.3	4.2	2.2	-2.3	..	19	..	(.)	..
155 Equatorial Guinea	0.1	..	..	..	..	-0.3	..	..	..	..	..	..
156 Central African Rep.	1.2	1.4	0.8	-1.3	5.5	39.1	-0.6	..	..	26	..	..
157 Mozambique	1.2	-1.5	0.6	-4.1	36.5	39.1	..	..	..	..	..	..
158 Sudan	..	..	0.8	..	..	55.0	..	..	14	..	-0.8	..
159 Bhutan	0.3	9.7	0.6	7.4	8.4	8.6	..	..	..	30	..	-7.2
160 Angola	..	8.8	0.6	6.1	..	92.2	..	..	..	..	..	..
161 Mauritania	1.0	0.6	-0.1	-1.8	8.8	9.8	1.8	..	..	36	..	-4.2
162 Benin	1.7	2.2	-0.3	-1.0	1.9	0.9	-0.5	..	..	..	..	..
163 Djibouti	..	..	..	..	..	3.2	..	..	..	..	..	..
164 Guinea-Bissau	0.2	3.7	-2.7	1.7	..	84.9	..	..	..	..	..	..
165 Chad	1.1	5.8	-1.9	3.3	1.2	2.2	3.6	..	18	..	-2.7	..
166 Somalia	0.9	1.1	-0.1	-1.8	49.7	..	0.9	..	12	..	0.6	..
167 Gambia	0.2	3.0	2.3	-0.3	..	11.4	..	..	..	..	..	..
168 Mali	2.3	3.8	2.1	1.2	3.0	1.3	0.6	..	..	12	..	-4.6
169 Niger	2.4	-1.3	-2.5	-4.5	3.3	-6.6	1.8	..	..	..	..	..
170 Burkina Faso	3.0	4.1	1.7	1.4	4.6	5.1	1.6	..	19	..	0.3	..
171 Afghanistan	..	..	0.6	..	..	..	..	..	..	..	..	..
172 Sierra Leone	1.0	0.9	0.7	-1.5	56.2	80.8	-5.9	-4.7	36	27	-4.4	-1.4
173 Guinea	2.8	..	1.3	..	..	22.7	..	..	..	..	..	-4.2
All developing countries	2,950T	4.7	2.9	2.5	27.9	39.9	0.1	2.5	35	36	-2.6	-4.9
Least developed countries	84T	2.8	0.6	-0.2	21.6	21.7	1.2	..	21	28	-3.9	-0.8
Sub-Saharan Africa	230T	1.8	1.5	-1.1	22.3	22.6	1.4	..	57	49	-4.0	-2.5
Industrial countries	16,820T	..	2.5	2.2	..	..	-0.2	1.3	..	..	-1.7	-2.3
World	19,770T	..	2.4	2.3	..	..	(.)	1.5	..	..	-1.8	-2.6

Note: Data for industrial countries for this subject area are in table 50.

HDI rank		Life expectancy at birth (years) 1990	Maternal mortality rate (per 100,000 live births) 1988	Population per doctor 1984-89	Scientists and technicians (per 1,000 people) 1986-90	Tertiary full-time equivalent gross enrolment ratio		Daily newspaper circulation (per 1,000 people) 1988-90	Tele-visions (per 1,000 people) 1990	GNP per capita (US$) 1990	Real GDP per capita (PPP$) 1990
						Total (%) 1988	Female (%) 1988				
1	Japan	78.6	16	663	110	39	45	587	620	25,840	17,616
2	Canada	77.0	7	455	177	76	81	228	641	20,380	19,232
3	Norway	77.1	4	503	231	29	31	614	425	22,830	16,028
4	Switzerland	77.4	6	696	202	21	14	463	407	32,250	20,874
5	Sweden	77.4	7	387	262	38	43	533	474	23,780	17,014
6	USA	75.9	13	419	55	70	75	250	815	21,810	21,449
7	Australia	76.5	5	436	50	49	53	249	486	16,560	16,051
8	France	76.4	13	320	83	37	40	210	406	19,590	17,405
9	Netherlands	77.2	14	450	65	27	25	311	495	17,570	15,695
10	United Kingdom	75.7	11	700	..	19	18	395	435	16,080	15,804
11	Iceland	77.8	2	350	..	..	..	..	320	22,090	16,496
12	Germany	75.2	8	380	84	26	24	390	570	22,360	18,213
13	Denmark	75.8	4	399	85	30	33	352	535	22,440	16,781
14	Finland	75.5	15	443	104	38	42	559	497	24,540	16,446
15	Austria	74.8	11	388	21	29	27	357	481	19,000	16,504
16	Belgium	75.2	4	331	..	34	37	305	452	17,580	16,381
17	New Zealand	75.2	18	575	49	30	30	324	442	12,570	13,481
18	Luxembourg	74.9	2	554	..	4	..	389	255	29,010	19,244
19	Israel	75.9	6	350	76	..	..	261	266	11,160	10,840
21	Ireland	74.6	3	681	..	26	24	159	276	10,370	10,589
22	Italy	76.0	6	234	82	19	19	107	424	16,880	15,890
23	Spain	77.0	7	360	36	23	23	82	396	11,010	11,723
25	Greece	76.1	7	351	48	..	..	140	196	6,010	7,366
26	Czechoslovakia	71.8	14	389	..	..	..	507	412	3,190	..
28	Hungary	70.9	21	307	46	..	..	233	410	2,780	6,116
39	Malta	73.4	5	890	..	..	..	153	742	6,690	8,732
40	Bulgaria	72.6	40	340	..	..	..	451	250	2,320	..
41	Portugal	74.0	14	412	..	..	..	38	177	4,950	8,770
48	Poland	71.8	15	487	..	..	..	127	293	1,690	4,237
77	Romania	70.8	..	567	..	..	..	..	194	1,620	..
78	Albania	72.2	100	..	..	..	..	42	86	..	..
	Aggregates										
	Industrial	74.5	26	380	81	..	..	545	348	14,580	14,440
	Developing	62.8	420	5,080	9	..	..	55	50	810	2,170
	World	64.7	370	4,090	22	..	..	148	118	4,010	4,890
	OECD	76.4	11	440	83	44	47	596	310	20,360	18,000
	Eastern Europe incl. former USSR	70.3	48	290	..	..	..	..	428	2,670	6,100
	European Community	75.9	9	330	74	25	25	444	253	17,220	15,710
	Nordic	76.6	7	420	182	35	38	482	513	23,450	16,650
	Southern Europe	75.4	12	320	58	21	21	367	94	12,950	13,140
	Non-Europe	76.8	13	500	79	60	65	725	347	22,480	19,800
	North America	76.0	12	420	67	70	75	798	248	21,670	21,240

Other countries

HDI rank		Life expectancy	Maternal mortality	Population per doctor				Daily newspaper	Tele-visions	GNP per capita	Real GDP per capita
29	Lithuania	71.5	23	218	..	..	..	..	..	3,110	4,913
34	Estonia	70.0	31	220	..	..	..	..	..	4,170	6,438
35	Latvia	69.6	24	204	..	..	..	..	..	3,590	6,457
37	Russian Federation	69.3	47	213	..	..	..	..	..	3,430	7,968
38	Belarus	71.3	22	248	..	..	..	286	268	3,110	5,727
45	Ukraine	70.5	32	228	..	..	..	251	327	2,500	5,433
47	Armenia	71.8	40	227	..	..	..	..	..	2,380	4,741
49	Georgia	72.8	21	170	..	..	..	..	..	2,120	4,572
54	Kazakhstan	68.8	55	242	..	..	..	..	..	2,600	4,716
62	Azerbaijan	71.0	..	255	..	..	..	..	..	1,640	3,977
64	Moldova, Rep. of	68.7	44	251	..	..	..	..	..	2,390	3,896
66	Turkmenistan	66.4	42	274	..	..	..	..	..	1,690	4,230
80	Uzbekistan	69.5	34	276	..	..	..	..	..	1,340	3,115
83	Kyrgyzstan	68.8	63	271	..	..	..	..	..	1,570	3,114
88	Tajikistan	69.6	42	362	..	..	..	..	..	1,130	2,558

Note: Data for developing countries for this subject area are in table 2.

HDI rank		Unemployment rate (%) Total 1990-91	Youth (age 15-24) 1990-91	Adults with less than upper secondary education (%) 1988	Ratio of income of highest 20% of households to lowest 20% 1986-89	Female wages (as % of male wages) 1990-91	Average annual rate of inflation (%) 1980-90	Hazardous and special waste generation (metric tons per km²) 1980-87	Deaths from road accidents (per 100,000 people) 1987-90	Drug crimes (per 100,000 people) 1980-86	Suicides (per 100,000 people) 1987-90
1	Japan	2.1	4.5	33	4.3	51	1.5	1.8	8	31	17
2	Canada	10.2	16.2	34	7.1	63	4.4	0.4	16	225	14
3	Norway	5.5	12.8	48	5.9	85	5.5	0.4	9	116	16
4	Switzerland	1.3	..	22	8.6	68	3.7	3.0	14	129	22
5	Sweden	2.7	6.1	41	4.6	89	7.4	1.2	8	..	19
6	USA	6.6	12.9	23	8.9	59	3.7	28.9	19	234	13
7	Australia	9.5	17.2	41	9.6	..	7.4	(.)	17	403	13
8	France	9.4	19.5	..	6.5	88	6.1	3.6	19	..	21
9	Netherlands	7.0	10.5	48	5.6	78	1.9	44.2	9	38	10
10	United Kingdom	8.9	12.9	48	6.8	67	5.8	16.1	9	..	8
11	Iceland	1.5	..	..	..	80	..	..	11	..	16
12	Germany	4.3	6.4	19	5.7	74	2.7	20.5	..	..	17
13	Denmark	10.6	..	..	7.1	82	5.6	3.0	14	176	24
14	Finland	7.5	13.5	..	6.0	77	6.8	0.4	13	..	29
15	Austria	3.5	..	27	..	78	3.6	2.4	19	77	25
16	Belgium	7.7	..	64	4.6	64	4.4	27.9	20	40	..
17	New Zealand	10.3	18.8	..	8.8	81	10.5	0.2	23	..	14
18	Luxembourg	1.3	..	..	..	65	..	1.5	23	..	20
19	Israel	10.6	..	..	6.6	..	101.4	1.5	..	25	7
21	Ireland	15.8	19.5	..	..	62	6.5	0.3	13	..	8
22	Italy	9.9	30.8	72	6.0	80	9.9	6.8	12	6	8
23	Spain	16.0	31.1	67	5.8	..	9.2	3.4	16	15	7
25	Greece	7.3	..	..	..	68	18.0	..	18	..	4
26	Czechoslovakia	6.6	..	..	..	71	1.9	..	9	..	18
28	Hungary	8.5	..	..	3.2	..	9.0	76.7	15	..	41
39	Malta	3.7	..	..	..	..	..	..	..	..	2
40	Bulgaria	12.0	..	..	..	..	2.3	..	13	..	15
41	Portugal	4.1	8.7	87	..	76	18.2	11.4	23	13	9
48	Poland	..	..	..	3.6	..	54.3	..	13	..	13
77	Romania	..	..	..	..	..	1.8	..	..	..	..
78	Albania	9.1	..	..	..	..	..	..	..	..	..
	Aggregates										
	Industrial	..	..	..	..	..	..	..	..	..	16
	Developing	..	..	..	..	..	..	..	..	..	..
	World	..	..	..	..	..	..	..	..	..	..
	OECD	6.9	13.7	36	6.9	66	4.8	9.7	15	..	14
	Eastern Europe incl. former USSR	..	..	..	..	..	..	..	..	..	21
	European Community	8.7	17.7	..	6.1	75	6.7	8.7	14	..	13
	Nordic	6.0	9.8	..	5.7	84	6.5	0.8	11	..	22
	Southern Europe	11.1	28.9	..	..	78	11.1	..	15	..	7
	Non-Europe	5.7	10.9	27	7.5	..	4.4	10.1	15	..	14
	North America	6.9	13.2	24	8.7	59	3.8	14.6	18	..	13

Other countries

HDI rank											Suicides
29	Lithuania	..	..	..	..	..	..	..	..	..	26
34	Estonia	..	..	..	..	..	..	..	..	..	27
35	Latvia	..	..	..	..	..	..	..	..	..	26
37	Russian Federation	..	..	..	..	..	..	..	..	..	26
38	Belarus	..	..	..	..	..	..	..	..	..	20
45	Ukraine	..	..	..	..	..	..	..	..	..	21
47	Armenia	..	..	..	..	..	..	..	..	..	3
49	Georgia	..	..	..	..	..	..	..	..	..	4
54	Kazakhstan	..	..	..	..	..	..	..	..	..	19
62	Azerbaijan	..	..	..	..	..	..	..	..	..	2
64	Moldova, Rep. of	..	..	..	..	..	..	..	..	..	15
66	Turkmenistan	..	..	..	..	..	..	..	..	..	8
80	Uzbekistan	..	..	..	..	..	..	..	..	..	7
83	Kyrgyzstan	..	..	..	..	..	..	..	..	..	12
88	Tajikistan	..	..	..	..	..	..	..	..	..	5

HDI rank		Intentional homicides (per 100,000 people) 1987-89	Reported rapes (per 100,000 women age 15-59) 1987-89	Drug crimes (per 100,000 people) 1980-86	Prisoners (per 100,000 people) 1980-86	Juveniles (as % of total prisoners) 1980-86	Live births outside marriage (%) 1985-89	Single-parent homes (%) 1980	Divorces (as % of marriages contracted) 1987-90	Suicides (per 100,000 people) 1987-90
1	Japan	1.5	5	31	..	..	1	5	22	17
2	Canada	2.6	23	225	94	..	23	..	43	14
3	Norway	0.9	20	116	..	..	26	4[a]	40	16
4	Switzerland	2.5	18	129	54	..	6	4	33	22
5	Sweden	1.5	43	..	..	..	52	6	44	19
6	USA	8.0	118	234	426	..	27	8	48	13
7	Australia	2.0	44	403	60	6	16	..	34	13
8	France	4.6	17	..	40	1	26	5	31	21
9	Netherlands	..	26	38	27	3	10	5	28	10
10	United Kingdom	1.6	..	..	77	5	25	4[a]	41	8
11	Iceland	..	..	..	..	..	..	..	..	16
12	Germany	3.8	26	..	77	12	10	7	30	17
13	Denmark	5.7	35	176	47	..	45	6	44	24
14	Finland	2.4	19	..	75	8	..	10	38	29
15	Austria	2.3	27	77	87	..	22	7[a]	33	25
16	Belgium	..	..	40	27	14	8	5	31	..
17	New Zealand	2.0	..	..	60	..	25	8	37	14
18	Luxembourg	..	..	..	..	..	12	7	37	20
19	Israel	0.5	4	25	..	32	1	..	18	7
21	Ireland	..	..	..	..	3	12	9[a]	..	8
22	Italy	4.3	4	6	60	13	6	..	8	8
23	Spain	2.0	12	15	49	20	8	..	..	7
25	Greece	1.5	..	..	24	12	2	..	13	4
26	Czechoslovakia	1.1	12	..	..	..	..	..	32	18
28	Hungary	3.6	31	..	142	7	9	..	31	41
39	Malta	0.8	2	..	..	..	1	..	..	2
40	Bulgaria	3.8	21	..	160	2	12	..	12	15
41	Portugal	4.2	5	13	58	12	14	..	13	9
48	Poland	1.9	19	..	204	11	5	..	11	13
77	Romania	..	..	..	..	..	..	..	20	..
78	Albania	..	..	..	..	..	..	..	9	..
	Aggregates									
	Industrial	4.9	48	..	..	..	15	..	33	16
	Developing	..	..	..	..	..	..	..	..	..
	World	..	..	..	..	..	..	..	..	..
	OECD	4.4	52	..	201	..	17	..	35	14
	Eastern Europe incl. former USSR	..	..	..	..	..	11	..	31	21
	European Community	3.4	17	..	58	..	15	..	27	13
	Nordic	2.5	32	..	61	..	44	..	42	22
	Southern Europe	3.3	7	..	..	..	7	..	11	7
	Non-Europe	5.4	75	179	371	..	19	..	39	14
	North America	7.4	110	233	394	..	27	..	48	13

Other countries

HDI rank		Intentional homicides	Reported rapes	Drug crimes	Prisoners	Juveniles	Live births outside marriage	Single-parent homes	Divorces	Suicides
29	Lithuania	..	..	..	..	..	7	..	36	26
34	Estonia	..	..	..	..	..	25	..	47	27
35	Latvia	..	..	..	..	..	16	..	46	26
37	Russian Federation	..	..	..	..	..	14	..	42	26
38	Belarus	..	..	..	..	..	8	..	35	20
45	Ukraine	..	..	..	..	..	11	..	40	21
47	Armenia	..	..	..	..	..	8	..	15	3
49	Georgia	..	..	..	..	..	18	..	19	4
54	Kazakhstan	..	..	..	..	..	12	..	28	19
62	Azerbaijan	..	..	..	..	..	3	..	16	2
64	Moldova, Rep. of	..	..	..	..	..	10	..	31	15
66	Turkmenistan	..	..	..	..	..	4	..	14	8
80	Uzbekistan	..	..	..	..	..	4	..	15	7
83	Kyrgyzstan	..	..	..	..	..	13	..	20	12
88	Tajikistan	..	..	..	..	..	7	..	16	5

a. Around 1970.

HDI rank	Life expectancy at birth (years)		Tertiary enrolment ratio (%)		GNP per capita (US$)		Real GDP per capita (PPP$)		Total education expenditure (as % of GDP)		Total health expenditure (as % of GDP)	
	1960	1990	1965	1987-90	1976	1990	1960	1990	1960	1988	1960	1990
1 Japan	67.9	78.6	13	31	4,990	25,840	2,701	17,616	4.9	5.0	2.9	6.7
2 Canada	71.0	77.0	26	70	8,300	20,380	7,758	19,232	4.6	7.2	5.5	9.3
3 Norway	73.4	77.1	11	43	7,630	22,830	5,443	16,028	4.6	6.6[a]	3.3	8.0
4 Switzerland	71.2	77.4	8	28	8,910	32,250	9,313	20,874	3.3[a]	5.1[a]	3.3	7.8
5 Sweden	73.1	77.4	13	33	9,180	23,780	6,483	17,014	5.9[a]	5.7	4.7	8.6
6 USA	69.9	75.9	40	70	8,190	21,810	9,983	21,449	5.3	5.7	5.2	12.2
7 Australia	70.7	76.5	16	35	7,770	16,560	7,204	16,051	..	..	4.6	8.2
8 France	70.3	76.4	18	37	6,680	19,590	5,344	17,405	3.6	5.7	4.2	8.8
9 Netherlands	73.2	77.2	17	34	6,850	17,570	5,587	15,695	4.9	6.6	3.9	8.6
10 United Kingdom	70.6	75.7	12	25	4,220	16,080	6,370	15,804	3.4[a]	4.7[a]	3.9	6.1
11 Iceland	73.2	77.8	10	25	7,100	22,090	5,352	16,496	..	..	3.5	8.7
12 Germany	69.7	75.2	11	33	7,460	22,360	6,038	18,213	2.4	6.2	4.7	8.6
13 Denmark	72.1	75.8	14	32	8,030	22,440	5,900	16,781	4.0[a]	6.9	3.6	6.6
14 Finland	68.4	75.5	11	47	6,150	24,540	4,718	16,446	4.9	6.8	3.9	7.8
15 Austria	68.6	74.8	9	33	5,360	19,000	4,476	16,504	2.9[a]	5.6[a]	4.6	8.5
16 Belgium	70.2	75.2	15	37	6,830	17,580	5,207	16,381	4.8[a]	6.1[a]	3.4	7.7
17 New Zealand	70.9	75.2	15	41	4,590	12,570	7,222	13,481	2.2[a]	4.9[a]	4.4	7.3
18 Luxembourg	68.2	74.9	..	..	8,430	29,010	6,970	19,244	..	..	..	..
19 Israel	68.6	75.9	20	33	4,080	11,160	3,958	10,840	..	..	1.0[a]	2.1[a]
21 Ireland	69.6	74.6	12	26	2,670	10,370	3,214	10,589	3.0[a]	6.2	4.0	7.7
22 Italy	69.2	76.0	11	31	4,030	16,880	4,375	15,890	4.2[a]	4.8[a]	3.3	7.7
23 Spain	69.0	77.0	6	34	3,090	11,010	2,701	11,723	1.1[a]	5.0	2.3	6.4
25 Greece	68.7	76.1	10	29	2,650	6,010	1,889	7,366	2.0	3.1	3.2	4.8
26 Czechoslovakia	69.9	71.8	14	18	..	..	..	..	..	..	2.9[a]	4.2[a]
28 Hungary	68.1	70.9	13	15	..	..	..	..	..	..	2.6[a]	3.2[a]
39 Malta	68.5	73.4	5	11	1,700	6,690	1,516	8,732	..	..	..	..
40 Bulgaria	68.4	72.6	17	31	..	..	..	..	..	..	2.0[a]	3.2[a]
41 Portugal	63.3	74.0	5	14	1,700	4,950	1,618	8,770	1.8[a]	4.9	0.8[a]	6.1
48 Poland	67.0	71.8	18	22	..	..	..	..	..	..	3.5[a]	4.0[a]
77 Romania	65.5	70.8	10	9	..	..	..	..	..	..	2.0[a]	1.9[a]
78 Albania	62.1	72.2	8	7	..	..	..	..	..	..	..	..
Aggregates												
Industrial	69.0	74.5	22	45	..	..	..	..	..	..	..	..
Developing	46.2	62.8	..	7	..	..	950	2,170	..	..	..	..
World	53.4	64.7	..	16	..	..	..	..	..	..	..	..
OECD	69.6	76.4	19	45	6,330	20,360	6,280	13,000	4.6	5.5	4.6	9.1
Eastern Europe incl. former USSR	67.7	70.3	26	..	..	..	..	..	..	..	..	..
European Community	69.7	75.9	12	32	5,360	17,220	5,050	15,710	3.3	5.5	4.0	7.7
Nordic	71.9	76.6	12	37	7,960	23,450	5,770	16,650	5.4	6.2	4.1	7.9
Southern Europe	67.6	75.5	10	29	3,400	12,950	3,390	13,140	3.3	4.8	3.0	7.2
Non-Europe	69.3	76.8	28	57	7,150	22,480	7,470	19,800	5.2	5.5	5.0	10.1
North America	70.0	76.1	39	70	8,200	21,470	9,780	21,240	5.3	5.8	5.3	11.9

Other countries

HDI rank	1960	1990	1965	1987-90	1976	1990	1960	1990	1960	1988	1960	1990
29 Lithuania	69.1	71.5	..	..	..	..	..	..	..	..	..	..
34 Estonia	68.8	70.0	..	..	..	..	..	..	..	..	..	..
35 Latvia	69.6	69.6	..	..	..	..	..	..	..	..	..	..
37 Russian Federation	..	..	..	..	..	..	..	..	..	..	..	..
38 Belarus	..	..	..	..	..	..	..	..	..	..	..	..
45 Ukraine	..	..	..	..	..	..	..	..	..	..	..	..
47 Armenia	..	..	..	..	..	..	..	..	..	..	..	..
49 Georgia	..	..	..	..	..	..	..	..	..	..	..	..
54 Kazakhstan	..	..	..	..	..	..	..	..	..	..	..	..
62 Azerbaijan	..	..	..	..	..	..	..	..	..	..	..	..
64 Moldova, Rep. of	..	..	..	..	..	..	..	..	..	..	..	..
66 Turkmenistan	..	..	..	..	..	..	..	..	..	..	..	..
80 Uzbekistan	..	..	..	..	..	..	..	..	..	..	..	..
83 Kyrgyzstan	..	..	..	..	..	..	..	..	..	..	..	..
88 Tajikistan	..	..	..	..	..	..	..	..	..	..	..	..

a. Public expenditure only.

Note: Data for developing countries for this subject area are in table 4.

HDI rank	Mean years of schooling (25+)			Scientists and technicians (per 1,000 people) 1986-90	R & D scientists and technicians (per 10,000 people) 1986-89	Expenditure on research and development (as % of GNP) 1989-91	Tertiary graduate ratio (as % of corresponding age group) 1987-90	Science graduates (as % of total graduates)		
	Total 1990	Male 1990	Female 1990					Total 1988-90	Male 1988-90	Female 1988-90
1 Japan	10.7	10.8	10.6	110	60	2.8	12.4	25	40	8
2 Canada	12.1	12.3	11.9	177	34	1.4	14.3	27	34	21
3 Norway	11.6	11.7	11.5	231	49	2.0	23.5	24	30	18
4 Switzerland	11.1	11.5	10.7	202	28	1.8	2.6	40	46	30
5 Sweden	11.1	11.1	11.1	262	62	2.8	10.0	58	67	50
6 USA	12.3	12.2	12.4	55	..	2.9	15.5	24	26	23
7 Australia	11.5	11.6	11.4	50	33	1.3	11.4	30	36	25
8 France	11.6	11.5	11.7	83	51	2.3	12.1	27	..	..
9 Netherlands	10.6	10.4	10.8	65	44	2.2	9.4	32	39	23
10 United Kingdom	11.5	11.4	11.6	..	..	2.3	11.0	42	46	38
11 Iceland	8.9	8.8	9.0	..	47	..	..	..	..	..
12 Germany	11.1	11.7	10.6	84	47	2.9	7.6	43	40	46
13 Denmark	10.4	10.5	10.3	85	50	1.6	7.7	44	48	40
14 Finland	10.6	10.7	10.5	104	43	1.8	10.7	56	65	48
15 Austria	11.1	11.7	10.5	21	19	1.3	3.7	34	45	25
16 Belgium	10.7	10.7	10.7	..	37	1.7	10.2	28	31	25
17 New Zealand	10.4	10.2	10.6	49	..	..	7.0	23	36	11
18 Luxembourg	10.0	10.3	9.8	..	..	..	..	..	..	..
19 Israel	10.0	10.9	9.0	76	59	3.1	5.1	32	35	29
21 Ireland	8.7	8.6	8.8	..	22	1.1	9.2	42	48	27
22 Italy	7.3	7.4	7.3	82	20	1.1	3.7	42	55	26
23 Spain	6.8	7.0	6.5	36	11	0.7	5.6	27	33	21
25 Greece	6.9	7.3	6.5	48	1	0.3	5.3	40	48	32
26 Czechoslovakia	9.0	9.5	8.4	..	69	3.3	4.2	48	60	32
28 Hungary	9.6	9.5	9.7	46	33	2.0	5.4	17	24	12
39 Malta	6.1	6.4	5.9	..	1	(.)	2.1	32	38	21
40 Bulgaria	7.0	7.6	6.4	..	69	2.7	6.4	38	39	37
41 Portugal	6.0	6.8	5.2	..	8	0.5	2.2	30	43	20
48 Poland	8.0	8.3	7.7	..	..	1.2	6.6	32	36	29
77 Romania	7.0	7.4	6.6	..	4	2.6	2.2	68	..	..
78 Albania	6.0	7.0	5.0	..	..	..	1.7	30	39	22
Aggregates										
Industrial	10.0	10.4	9.6	81	41	..	9.4	35	40	26
Developing	3.7	4.6	2.7	9	3	..	1.2	29	..	..
World	5.0	5.8	4.3	22	12	..	3.7	30	..	..
OECD	10.9	10.9	10.9	74	41	2.4	11.3	30	37	25
Eastern Europe incl. fomer USSR	6.7	..	..	..	..	..	5.6	45	48	30
European Community	9.8	10.0	9.6	..	84	2.0	8.0	37	44	33
Nordic	10.9	10.9	10.9	182	52	2.2	12.2	48	56	41
Southern Europe	6.9	7.2	6.5	58	14	0.9	4.3	36	46	24
Non-Europe	11.7	11.7	11.8	79	54	2.7	14.2	25	31	19
North America	12.3	12.1	12.4	67	34	2.8	15.4	24	27	23

Other countries

HDI rank	Mean years of schooling (25+)			Scientists and technicians	R & D scientists and technicians	Expenditure on research and development	Tertiary graduate ratio	Science graduates		
29 Lithuania	9.0	..	..	..	..	..	..	..	..	..
34 Estonia	9.0	..	..	..	..	..	..	..	..	..
35 Latvia	9.0	..	..	..	..	..	..	..	..	..
37 Russian Federation	9.0	..	..	..	..	..	..	..	..	..
38 Belarus	7.0	..	..	..	..	..	..	37	..	..
45 Ukraine	6.0	..	..	..	..	..	..	44	..	..
47 Armenia	5.0	..	..	..	..	..	..	..	..	..
49 Georgia	5.0	..	..	..	..	..	..	..	..	..
54 Kazakhstan	5.0	..	..	..	..	..	..	..	..	..
62 Azerbaijan	5.0	..	..	..	..	..	..	..	..	..
64 Moldova, Rep. of	6.0	..	..	..	..	..	..	..	..	..
66 Turkmenistan	5.0	..	..	..	..	..	..	..	..	..
80 Uzbekistan	5.0	..	..	..	..	..	..	..	..	..
83 Kyrgyzstan	5.0	..	..	..	..	..	..	..	..	..
88 Tajikistan	5.0	..	..	..	..	..	..	..	..	..

Note: Data for developing countries for this subject area are in table 5.

HDI rank		Life expectancy at birth (years) 1990	Maternal mortality rate (per 100,000 live births) 1988	Average age at first marriage (years) 1980-85	Upper secondary gross enrolment ratio 1988	Upper secondary graduates (as % of population of normal completion age) 1988	Tertiary full-time equivalent gross enrolment ratio 1988	Percentage of women in science and engineering fields (third level) 1988	Employed women (as % of total employed) 1990	Administrative and managerial work (% females) 1980-89	Parliament (% of seats occupied by women) 1991
1	Japan	81.4	16	25.1	96	93	45	7	40	7	2
2	Canada	80.5	7	23.1	99	70	81	..	40	35	13
3	Norway	80.5	4	24.0	97	62	31	30	43	22	36
4	Switzerland	80.7	6	25.0	75	83	14	13	37	6	14
5	Sweden	80.4	7	27.6	87	82	43	25	47	..	38
6	USA	79.5	13	23.3	93	78	75	..	42	38	6
7	Australia	79.9	5	23.5	76	..	53	27	38	30	7
8	France	80.4	13	24.3	87	88	40	..	37	9	6
9	Netherlands	80.5	14	23.2	83	59	25	16	35	12	21
10	United Kingdom	78.5	11	23.1	79	67	18	21	40	22	6
11	Iceland	80.7	2	..	..	..	..	..	..	..	24
12	Germany	78.2	8	23.6	..	..	24	28	38	..	20
13	Denmark	78.7	4	26.1	..	..	33	23	40	14	33
14	Finland	79.2	15	24.6	..	..	42	24	44	19	39
15	Austria	78.2	11	23.5	72	57	27	25	39	12	22
16	Belgium	78.5	4	22.4	..	..	37	24	37	13	9
17	New Zealand	78.3	18	22.7	69	..	30	26	39	17	17
18	Luxembourg	78.1	2	23.1	71	57	..	..	34	6	13
19	Israel	77.7	6	23.5	..	..	..	27	35	..	7
21	Ireland	77.4	3	23.4	..	87	24	30	27	16	8
22	Italy	79.3	6	23.2	61	46	19	32	31	38	13
23	Spain	80.0	7	23.1	..	60	23	27	27	6	15
25	Greece	78.3	7	22.5	..	..	..	28	31	15	5
26	Czechoslovakia	75.5	14	21.6	..	..	..	26	43	..	9
28	Hungary	74.6	21	21.0	..	..	..	19	42	..	7
39	Malta	75.2	5	..	..	..	..	10	25	..	3
40	Bulgaria	75.6	40	20.8	..	..	..	44	..	29	9
41	Portugal	77.3	14	22.1	55	..	..	35	41	15	8
48	Poland	75.8	15	22.5	..	..	..	29	..	..	14
77	Romania	73.6	210	21.1	..	..	..	..	..	..	4
78	Albania	74.8	100	..	..	..	..	42	..	..	4
	Aggregates										
	Industrial	77.9	26	23.5	..	..	..	..	42	24	9
	Developing	64.2	420	20.7	..	..	..	..	33	8	12
	World	67.3	370	21.2	..	..	..	..	34	12	11
	OECD	79.7	11	23.7	87	76	47	21	41	24	10
	Eastern Europe incl. former USSR	74.5	48	21.7	..	..	..	40	..	..	..
	European Community	79.1	9	23.4	75	65	25	27	37	19	13
	Nordic	79.8	7	25.9	91	75	38	25	44	18	36
	Southern Europe	78.4	12	23.0	60	51	21	30	31	23	11
	Non-Europe	80.1	13	23.8	93	82	65	..	41	29	6
	North America	79.6	12	23.3	93	78	75	..	42	38	7

Other countries

29	Lithuania	76.4	29	..	..	..	..	..	..	..	..
34	Estonia	74.9	41	..	..	..	..	..	..	..	..
35	Latvia	74.6	57	..	..	..	..	..	..	..	..
37	Russian Federation	74.4	49	..	..	..	..	..	..	..	..
38	Belarus	75.9	25	..	..	..	..	..	..	..	..
45	Ukraine	75.0	33	..	..	..	..	..	..	..	..
47	Armenia	75.2	35	..	..	..	..	..	..	..	..
49	Georgia	76.3	55	..	..	..	..	..	..	..	..
54	Kazakhstan	73.2	53	..	..	..	..	..	..	..	..
62	Azerbaijan	74.8	29	..	..	..	..	..	..	..	..
64	Moldova, Rep. of	72.0	34	..	..	..	..	..	..	..	..
66	Turkmenistan	69.7	55	..	..	..	..	..	..	..	..
80	Uzbekistan	72.6	43	..	..	..	..	..	..	..	..
83	Kyrgyzstan	72.8	43	..	..	..	..	..	..	..	..
88	Tajikistan	72.1	39	..	..	..	..	..	..	..	3

Note: Data for developing countries for this subject area are in table 8.

				Upper secondary education		Tertiary education		Labour force			
HDI rank	Life expectancy 1990	Popu-lation 1990	Mean years of schooling 1990	Enrolment 1988	Graduates 1988	Full-time equivalent enrolment ratio 1988	Engineering and related science enrolment 1988	1970	1985-91	Unemploy-ment 1990-91	Wages 1990-91

Females as a percentage of males (see note)

HDI rank	Life exp. 1990	Pop. 1990	Mean yrs schooling 1990	Enrolment 1988	Graduates 1988	FTE enrolment ratio 1988	Eng. & science enrolment 1988	Labour force 1970	Labour force 1985-91	Unemploy-ment 1990-91	Wages 1990-91
1 Japan	108	103	98	104	108	..	16	64	68	110	51
2 Canada	109	102	97	102	105	114	29	..	..	90	63
3 Norway	109	102	98	112	113	118	27	38	81	85	85
4 Switzerland	109	105	93	85	90	48	42	52	60	125	68
5 Sweden	108	103	100	109	102	130	25	61	92	77	89
6 USA	110	105	102	105	113	116	29	59	83	91	59
7 Australia	109	100	99	71	..	115	40	42	71	93	..
8 France	111	105	102	105	109	119	..	54	75	168	88
9 Netherlands	109	102	104	84	106	81	25	..	..	179	78
10 United Kingdom	108	105	102	106	105	93	..	55	74	..	67
11 Iceland	108	99	103	..	..	..	..	..	..	131	80
12 Germany	109	108	90	91	96	86	24	..	..	120	74
13 Denmark	108	103	98	100	115	120	24	58	85	130	82
14 Finland	111	106	98	130	139	119	35	73	89	62	77
15 Austria	110	109	90	85	110	89	25	..	..	112	78
16 Belgium	109	105	100	..	..	120	34	42	70	201	64
17 New Zealand	108	102	104	106	..	103	48	38	77	87	81
18 Luxembourg	109	105	95	96	117	..	..	35	53	236	65
19 Israel	105	100	82	..	..	..	..	..	..	156	..
21 Ireland	108	99	102	125	112	84	48	36	44	64	62
22 Italy	109	106	99	104	113	95	53	..	..	234	80
23 Spain	108	103	92	115	113	105	28	24	54	194	..
25 Greece	106	103	89	..	..	..	..	..	..	255	68
26 Czechoslovakia	111	105	88	..	..	..	..	80	87	124	71
28 Hungary	111	107	102	..	..	..	..	70	85	83	..
39 Malta	105	103	92	..	..	..	..	27	34	56	..
40 Bulgaria	108	102	84	..	..	..	..	79	86	..	..
41 Portugal	110	107	76	129	..	..	37	34	76	206	76
48 Poland	112	105	92	..	..	..	..	85	83	..	..
77 Romania	108	103	89	..	..	..	..	83	86	..	..
78 Albania	107	94	93	..	..	..	..	..	..	..	..
Aggregates											
Industrial	110	106	99	..	..	..	..	59	77	..	..
Developing	104	96	58	..	..	..	..	..	52	..	..
World	106	99	72	..	..	..	..	..	56	..	..
OECD	109	105	99	103	109	106	29	55	75	128	66
Eastern Europe incl. former USSR	112	109	..	..	..	..	..	..	..	..	..
European Community	109	105	96	103	106	98	34	46	70	168	75
Nordic	109	103	99	112	115	123	27	59	88	89	84
Southern Europe	108	104	90	110	113	99	43	26	58	220	80
Non-Europe	109	104	101	103	110	115	26	60	76	98	59
North America	110	105	101	105	112	116	29	59	83	91	59

Other countries

HDI rank	Life exp. 1990	Pop. 1990									
29 Lithuania	115	111	..	..	..	..	..	..	..	..	..
34 Estonia	115	114	..	..	..	..	..	..	..	..	..
35 Latvia	116	115	..	..	..	..	..	..	..	..	..
37 Russian Federation	116	114	..	..	..	..	..	..	..	..	..
38 Belarus	114	114	..	..	..	..	..	..	..	..	..
45 Ukraine	114	117	..	..	..	..	..	..	..	..	..
47 Armenia	110	104	..	..	..	..	..	..	..	..	..
49 Georgia	111	111	..	..	..	..	..	..	..	..	..
54 Kazakhstan	114	106	..	..	..	..	..	..	..	..	..
62 Azerbaijan	112	105	..	..	..	..	..	..	..	..	..
64 Moldova, Rep. of	110	110	..	..	..	..	..	..	..	..	..
66 Turkmenistan	111	103	..	..	..	..	..	..	..	..	..
80 Uzbekistan	110	102	..	..	..	..	..	..	..	..	..
83 Kyrgyzstan	113	105	..	..	..	..	..	..	..	..	..
88 Tajikistan	108	101	..	..	..	..	..	..	..	..	..

Note: All figures are expressed in relation to the male average, which is indexed to equal 100. The smaller the figure the bigger the gap, the closer the figure to 100 the smaller the gap, and a figure above 100 indicates that the female average is higher than the male. Data for developing countries in this subject area are in table 9.

HDI rank		Population per doctor 1984-89	Maternal mortality rate (per 100,000 live births) 1988	Deaths from diseases of the circulatory system (as % of all causes) 1987-90	Number of new AIDS cases (per 100,000 people) 1990	Occupancy rates in in-patient care institutions (%) 1989-90	Population eligible for public health insurance (%) 1987	Proportion of health bills paid by public insurance (%) 1987	Medical care expenditure price index (1985=100) 1990	Total health expenditure (as % of GDP) 1960	Total health expenditure (as % of GDP) 1990	Private expenditure on health (as % of total health expenditure) 1990
1	Japan	663	16	37	0.2	84	..	..	109	2.9	6.7	28.1
2	Canada	455	7	41	3.4	..	..	..	129	5.5	9.3	25.9
3	Norway	503	4	47	1.3	85	100	100	135	3.3	8.0	4.3
4	Switzerland	696	6	44	6.6	86	98	93	119	3.3	7.8	31.9
5	Sweden	387	7	52	1.4	84	100	95	138	4.7	8.6	10.5
6	USA	419	13	45	15.6	70	25	55	134	5.2	12.2	57.6
7	Australia	436	5	46	3.6	82	..	..	138	4.6	8.2	30.5
8	France	320	13	34	6.6	80	98	77	114	4.2	8.8	25.8
9	Netherlands	450	14	40	2.7	89	72	79	111	3.9	8.6	27.4
10	United Kingdom	..	11	46	1.9	..	100	94	144	3.9	6.1	15.5
11	Iceland	..	2	44	1.2	86	100	..	..	3.5	8.7	13.1
12	Germany	..	8	49	2.1	86	92	91	110	4.7	8.6	26.8
13	Denmark	399	4	45	3.8	82	100	88	124	3.6	6.6	17.2
14	Finland	443	15	50	0.3	84	100	80	140	3.9	7.8	21.2
15	Austria	388	11	51	2.0	82	99	85	122	4.6	8.5	33.5
16	Belgium	331	4	..	1.8	87	93	59	118	3.4	7.7	17.5
17	New Zealand	575	18	46	1.8	..	..	..	172	4.4	7.3	18.3
18	Luxembourg	554	2	47	2.5	..	100	96	125	..	7.2	8.6
19	Israel	..	6	42	0.7	..	..	..	..	1.0a	2.1a	..
21	Ireland	681	3	47	1.5	..	37	71	132	4.0	7.7	26.2
22	Italy	234	6	44	5.2	68	100	82	146	3.3	7.7	24.1
23	Spain	360	7	43	6.6	79	97	84	132	2.3	6.4	21.6
25	Greece	351	7	52	1.3	66	100	88	..	3.2	4.8	24.0
26	Czechoslovakia	389	14	55	..	..	..	..	..	2.9a	4.2a	..
28	Hungary	307	21	52	0.2	..	..	..	..	2.6a	3.2a	..
39	Malta	..	5	50	0.3	..	..	..	..	..	3.2a	..
40	Bulgaria	340	40	62	..	..	..	..	..	2.0a	6.1	38.3
41	Portugal	412	14	44	2.0	69	100	100	172	0.8a	6.1	..
48	Poland	487	15	52	0.1	..	..	..	..	3.5a	4.0a	..
77	Romania	567	..	59	4.1	..	..	..	..	2.0a	1.9a	..
78	Albania	..	100	..	..	..	..	..	..	..	..	..
	Aggregates											
	Industrial	380	26	46	..	..	..	..	..	4.2	8.3	..
	Developing	5,080	420	..	..	..	..	..	..	1.0	..	..
	World	4,090	370	..	..	..	..	..	..	..	..	..
	OECD	440	12	43	6.9	77	67	73	128	4.6	9.1	35.1
	Eastern Europe incl. former USSR	290	49	54	..	..	..	..	..	..	..	..
	European Community	330	9	44	3.8	79	95	85	128	4.0	7.7	23.5
	Nordic	420	7	49	1.7	84	100	91	135	4.1	7.9	13.2
	Southern Europe	320	12	44	5.0	..	99	85	143	3.0	7.2	24.5
	Non-Europe	500	13	42	9.6	75	..	..	127	5.0	10.1	45.5
	North America	420	12	45	14.4	70	25	55	134	5.3	11.9	54.5

Other countries

HDI rank		Population per doctor 1984-89	Maternal mortality rate 1988	Deaths circulatory system 1987-90	AIDS cases 1990							
29	Lithuania	218	23	..	..	..	..	..	..	..	..	..
34	Estonia	220	31	..	..	..	..	..	..	..	..	..
35	Latvia	204	24	..	..	..	..	..	..	..	..	..
37	Russian Federation	213	47	..	..	..	..	..	..	..	..	..
38	Belarus	248	22	51	..	..	..	..	..	..	..	..
45	Ukraine	228	32	53	..	..	..	..	..	..	..	..
47	Armenia	227	40	36	..	..	..	..	..	..	..	..
49	Georgia	170	21	..	..	..	..	..	..	..	..	..
54	Kazakhstan	242	55	49	..	..	..	..	..	..	..	..
62	Azerbaijan	255	..	66	..	..	..	..	..	..	..	..
64	Moldova, Rep. of	251	44	75	..	..	..	..	..	..	..	..
66	Turkmenistan	274	42	53	..	..	..	..	..	..	..	..
80	Uzbekistan	276	34	55	..	..	..	..	..	..	..	..
83	Kyrgyzstan	271	63	49	..	..	..	..	..	..	..	..
88	Tajikistan	362	42	47	..	..	..	..	..	..	..	..

a. Public expenditure only.

Note: Data for developing countries for this subject area are in table 12.

36 Education profile

HDI rank	Years of free full-time compulsory education 1989	Upper secondary gross enrolment ratio 1988	Upper secondary graduates (as % of population of normal completion age) 1988	Secondary technical enrolment (as % of total secondary) 1987-88	Tertiary full-time equivalent gross enrolment ratio 1988	Tertiary engineering and related science enrolment (as % of total tertiary) 1988	Public expenditure on tertiary education (as % of all levels) 1985-90	Public expenditure per tertiary student (PPP$) 1988	Total education expenditure (as % of GDP) 1960	Total education expenditure (as % of GDP) 1988
1 Japan	9	94	90	28	39	26	23	2,504	4.9	5.0
2 Canada	9	98	68	..	76	13	29	7,785	4.6	7.2
3 Norway	9	92	58	56	29	14	15	7,439	4.6	6.6[a]
4 Switzerland	9	82	88	36	21	22	19	10,187	3.3[a]	5.1[a]
5 Sweden	9	84	81	78	38	20	13	6,334	5.9[a]	5.7
6 USA	11	90	74	..	70	14	24	6,386	5.3	5.7
7 Australia	9	92	..	..	49	22	31			4.8[a]
8 France	10	85	85	57	37	32	14	3,780	3.6	5.7
9 Netherlands	11	91	57	55	27	23	30	9,542	4.9	6.6
10 United Kingdom	11	77	65	16	19	..	19	7,960	3.4[a]	4.7[a]
11 Iceland	..	..	..		..	..	..	..	..	..
12 Germany	10	..	..	46	26	27	22	5,085	2.4	6.2
13 Denmark	9	..	..	69	30	25	16	10,847	4.0[a]	6.9
14 Finland	10	..	..	59	38	27	22	5,293	4.9	6.8
15 Austria	9	79	55	64	29	13	19	5,029	2.9[a]	5.6[a]
16 Belgium	10	..	..	45	34	31	17	4,987	4.8[a]	6.1[a]
17 New Zealand	9	67	..	..	30	16	35		2.2[a]	4.9[a]
18 Luxembourg	9	72	52	69	..	..	..	12,238	..	6.0[a]
19 Israel	..	..	..	..	..	..	19		..	..
21 Ireland	9	99	82	18	26	26	19	4,740	3.0[a]	6.2
22 Italy	8	60	43	..	19	13	10	4,250	4.2[a]	4.8[a]
23 Spain	8	94	56	45	23	12	13	1,934	1.1[a]	5.0
25 Greece	9	..	..	28	..	..	20		2.0	3.1
26 Czechoslovakia	..	..	..	..	..	..	16		..	..
28 Hungary	..	..	..	..	..	..	15		..	..
39 Malta	..	..	..	..	..	..	12		..	..
40 Bulgaria	..	..	..	..	..	..	14		..	..
41 Portugal	8	48	..	..	..	23	16	4,451	1.8[a]	4.9
48 Poland	..	..	..	..	..	..	22		3.8[a]	..
77 Romania	..	..	..	..	..	..	10		2.9[a]	..
78 Albania	..	..	..	..	..	..	..		..	..
Aggregates										
Industrial	..	..	..	..	..	..	..	..	..	..
Developing	..	..	..	..	..	..	..	..	..	..
World	..	..	..	..	..	..	..	..	..	..
OECD	9	87	38	72	44	20	21	5,280	4.6	5.5
Eastern Europe incl. former USSR	..	..	..	..	..	..	..	..	..	..
European Community	9	78	42	63	25	22	17	5,120	3.3	5.5
Nordic	9	87	68	73	35	21	16	7,320	5.4	6.2
Southern Europe	8	71	..	48	21	13	12	3,420	3.3	4.8
Non-Europe	9	92	..	78	60	18	24	5,290	5.2	5.5
North America	10	91	..	73	70	14	25	6,520	5.3	5.8

Other countries

HDI rank	Years of free full-time compulsory education 1989	Upper secondary gross enrolment ratio 1988	Upper secondary graduates 1988	Secondary technical enrolment 1987-88	Tertiary full-time equivalent gross enrolment ratio 1988	Tertiary engineering and related science enrolment 1988	Public expenditure on tertiary education 1985-90	Public expenditure per tertiary student (PPP$) 1988	Total education expenditure 1960	Total education expenditure 1988
29 Lithuania	..	..	..	..	..	..	..	..	..	..
34 Estonia	..	..	..	..	..	..	..	..	..	..
35 Latvia	..	..	..	..	..	..	..	..	..	..
37 Russian Federation	..	..	..	..	..	..	..	..	..	..
38 Belarus	..	..	..	..	..	..	14	..	..	..
45 Ukraine	..	..	..	..	..	..	15	..	..	..
47 Armenia	..	..	..	..	..	..	..	..	..	..
49 Georgia	..	..	..	..	..	..	..	..	..	..
54 Kazakhstan	..	..	..	..	..	..	..	..	..	..
62 Azerbaijan	..	..	..	..	..	..	..	..	..	..
64 Moldova, Rep. of	..	..	..	..	..	..	..	..	..	..
66 Turkmenistan	..	..	..	..	..	..	..	..	..	..
80 Uzbekistan	..	..	..	..	..	..	..	..	..	..
83 Kyrgyzstan	..	..	..	..	..	..	..	..	..	..
88 Tajikistan	..	..	..	..	..	..	..	..	..	..

a. Public expenditure only.

Note: Data for developing countries for this subject area are in table 15.

HDI rank		Radios (per 1,000 people) 1990	Tele-visions (per 1,000 people) 1990	Daily newspaper circulation (per 1,000 people) 1988-90	Telephones (per 1,000 people) 1986-88	Passenger cars (per 1,000 people) 1985-89	Book titles published (per 100,000 people) 1988-90	Library books (per person) 1988-90	Annual museum attendances (per person) 1987-90	Annual cinema attendances (per person) 1987-90	Average number of people served by one post office 1986-88
1	Japan	907	620	587	555	263	..	6.1	0.8	1.2	5,100
2	Canada	1,026	641	228	780	455	..	5.6	0.9	3.0	2,000
3	Norway	798	425	614	460	385	88	9.4	1.2	3.0	1,500
4	Switzerland	855	407	463	882	435	206	3.7	1.4	1.9	1,700
5	Sweden	888	474	533	796	417	141	12.9	1.4	2.0	..
6	USA	2,123	815	250	789	588	..	5.8	1.4	4.6	5,800
7	Australia	1,280	486	249	550	435	..	1.5	0.3	2.4	3,400
8	France	896	406	210	608	417	74	1.7	0.2	2.1	3,200
9	Netherlands	906	495	311	659	357	92	5.4	1.1	1.1	5,100
10	United Kingdom	1,146	435	395	477	333	..	3.1	..	1.7	2,700
11	Iceland	787	320	..	477	500	..	11.2	..	4.7	1,800
12	Germany	899	570	390	585	385	..	4.1	1.3	2.2	3,400
13	Denmark	1,030	535	352	882	313	216	9.1	1.7	2.0	4,000
14	Finland	998	497	559	617	385	204	10.7	0.6	1.5	..
15	Austria	624	481	357	543	385	134	7.6	1.6	1.4	..
16	Belgium	778	452	305	499	370	69	5.0	..	1.6	..
17	New Zealand	929	442	324	717	455	..	3.1	0.1	..	2,600
18	Luxembourg	630	255	389	..	455	138	2.1	0.2	1.4	3,500
19	Israel	471	266	261	469	145	..	..	1.5	..	3,100
21	Ireland	583	276	159	265	222	..	4.2	0.2	3.3	..
22	Italy	797	424	107	509	417	43	0.6	0.1	1.7	4,000
23	Spain	306	396	82	396	294	93	1.3	0.4	2.2	3,000
25	Greece	423	196	140	362	143	32	1.3	0.3	..	..
26	Czechoslovakia	587	412	507	255	200	55	6.0	1.3	4.5	2,300
28	Hungary	595	410	233	158	169	79	8.7	1.5	4.3	3,300
39	Malta	527	742	153	471	256	130	3.3	..	0.9	..
40	Bulgaria	438	250	451	140	137	38	10.8	1.7	7.6	..
41	Portugal	218	177	38	219	189	62	2.1	0.3	1.7	1,300
48	Poland	429	293	127	128	128	27	9.1	0.5	1.8	4,500
77	Romania	198	194	..	..	53	9	8.0	0.8	8.8	..
78	Albania	176	86	42	..	..	..	3.8	..	2.2	..
	Aggregates										
	Industrial	1,130	545	348	590	390	61	4.9	0.8	2.9	4,200
	Developing	180	55	50	28	13	6	..	..	..	16,330
	World	360	148	118	130	87	12	..	..	..	14,170
	OECD	1,260	595	310	628	424	83	4.5	0.9	2.7	4,360
	Eastern Europe incl. former USSR	592	308	428	108	65	30	8.9	0.7	4.1	..
	European Community	817	444	253	522	360	71	2.6	0.6	1.9	3,310
	Nordic	925	482	513	711	382	161	10.9	1.3	2.1	2,840
	Southern Europe	541	367	94	434	315	61	1.1	0.3	1.9	3,360
	Non-Europe	1,640	725	347	707	474	..	5.7	1.1	3.4	5,200
	North America	2,017	798	248	788	575	..	5.8	1.4	4.4	5,400

Other countries

HDI rank		Radios	Tele-visions	Daily newspaper circulation	Telephones	Passenger cars	Book titles published	Library books	Annual museum attendances	Annual cinema attendances	Average number of people served by one post office
29	Lithuania	..	..	..	..	..	..	..	..	..	..
34	Estonia	..	..	..	..	..	..	..	..	..	..
35	Latvia	..	..	..	..	..	..	..	..	..	..
37	Russian Federation	..	..	..	..	..	..	..	..	..	..
38	Belarus	306	268	286	..	..	28	..	..	..	..
45	Ukraine	794	327	251	..	..	16	..	..	..	..
47	Armenia	..	..	..	..	..	..	..	..	..	..
49	Georgia	..	..	..	..	..	..	..	..	..	..
54	Kazakhstan	..	..	..	..	..	..	..	..	..	..
62	Azerbaijan	..	..	..	..	..	..	..	..	..	..
64	Moldova, Rep. of	..	..	..	..	..	..	..	..	..	..
66	Turkmenistan	..	..	..	..	..	..	..	..	..	..
80	Uzbekistan	..	..	..	..	..	..	..	..	..	..
83	Kyrgyzstan	..	..	..	..	..	..	..	..	..	..
88	Tajikistan	..	..	..	..	..	..	..	..	..	..

Note: Data for developing countries for this subject area are in table 16.

HDI rank		Labour force (as % of total population) 1989-91	Women in labour force (as % of total labour force) 1990	Percentage of labour force in			Earnings per employee annual growth rate (%)		Percentage of labour force unionized 1989-90	Annual leave days and holidays (days per person in manufacturing) 1990	Weekly hours of work (per person in manufacturing) 1989-91	Expenditure on labour market programmes (as % of GDP) 1990-91
				Agriculture 1989-91	Industry 1989-91	Services 1989-91	1970-80	1980-89				
1	Japan	53	41	7	34	59	3.1	2.0	27	22	45	0.4
2	Canada	50	44	5	25	70	1.8	0.1	35	..	31	2.4
3	Norway	50	45	5	25	70	2.6	1.6	55	31	35	2.2
4	Switzerland	52	37	6	30	64	..	..	26	32	42	0.4
5	Sweden	52	48	3	28	69	0.4	0.9	85	36	37	2.6
6	USA	50	45	3	26	71	0.1	0.9	17	23	34	0.7
7	Australia	64	41	15	23	62	2.9	(.)	42	30	34	1.4
8	France	43	43	7	20	73	..	2.0	12	36	39	2.7
9	Netherlands	41	39	5	22	73	2.5	0.8	25	39	40	3.3
10	United Kingdom	50	43	2	20	78	1.7	2.8	42	33	43	1.6
11	Iceland	..	..	..	..	..	..	..	78	..	47	..
12	Germany	50	40	4	30	66	3.5	1.8	34	43	39	2.2
13	Denmark	57	46	4	27	69	2.5	0.6	73	33	..	5.7
14	Finland	51	47	..	..	..	2.6	2.7	71	47	..	2.1
15	Austria	46	41	8	35	57	3.4	1.9	46	40	..	1.3
16	Belgium	42	41	3	20	77	4.6	-0.1	53	31	34	3.8
17	New Zealand	47	43	9	24	67	1.2	-0.5	51	26	39	2.7
18	Luxembourg	43	35	4	33	63	..	..	50	35	..	1.1
19	Israel	39	41	3	24	73	8.8	-3.4	..	..	36	..
21	Ireland	37	31	13	23	64	4.1	1.8	52	29	..	4.3
22	Italy	42	37	9	20	71	4.1	1.1	40	39	..	1.5
23	Spain	39	35	10	35	55	4.4	0.8	16	36	37	3.5
25	Greece	40	36	22	28	50	4.9	-0.5	25	31	..	0.9
26	Czechoslovakia	50	47	13	50	37	..	..	..	18	..	0.6
28	Hungary	45	46	6	51	43	3.7	2.6	..	..	..	1.6
39	Malta	37	25	3	28	69	..	..	..	..	..	..
40	Bulgaria	50	46	17	38	45	..	..	..	..	..	0.8
41	Portugal	48	43	17	32	51	2.5	0.3	30	36	..	0.8
48	Poland	49	45	24	41	35	..	..	..	..	..	1.4
77	Romania	47	46	31	43	26	..	..	..	20	..	..
78	Albania	48	41	56	26	18	..	..	..	..	..	..
	Aggregates											
	Industrial	49.1	42.4	7.6	25.7	66.7	2.2	1.4	..	..	..	..
	Developing	43.7	32.6	60.5	14.4	25.1	1.3	4.0	..	..	..	..
	World	44.9	34.3	48.2	17.0	34.8	1.6	3.5	..	..	..	..
	OECD	48.7	42.0	5.4	27.1	67.5	2.1	1.4	27	..	..	1.4
	Eastern Europe incl. former USSR	50.3	..	12.6	22.2	65.2	..	..	..	..	..	..
	European Community	45.2	39.8	6.3	25.0	68.7	3.3	1.7	31	..	..	2.3
	Nordic	52.6	46.8	4.9	26.7	68.4	1.7	1.4	74	..	..	3.4
	Southern Europe	41.5	37.0	12.7	26.9	60.4	3.7	0.9	30	..	..	2.1
	Non-Europe	51.3	43.6	4.8	28.5	66.7	1.3	1.2	22	..	..	0.8
	North America	50.3	45.1	3.2	26.3	70.5	0.3	0.8	19	..	..	0.9

Other countries

HDI rank		Labour force	Women in labour force	Agriculture	Industry	Services	1970-80	1980-89	unionized	leave	hours	Expenditure
29	Lithuania	52	..	10	33	57	..	..	..	..	..	..
34	Estonia	51	..	9	33	58	..	..	..	..	..	..
35	Latvia	55	..	9	33	58	..	..	..	..	..	..
37	Russian Federation	53	..	..	..	..	..	..	..	..	..	..
38	Belarus	53	..	..	..	..	..	..	..	..	..	..
45	Ukraine	51	..	..	..	..	..	..	..	..	..	..
47	Armenia	..	..	11	32	57	..	..	..	..	..	..
49	Georgia	37	..	14	30	56	..	..	..	..	..	..
54	Kazakhstan	..	..	20	22	58	..	..	..	..	..	..
62	Azerbaijan	..	..	15	21	64	..	..	..	..	..	..
64	Moldova, Rep. of	..	..	21	26	53	..	..	..	..	..	..
66	Turkmenistan	32	..	..	..	..	..	..	..	..	..	..
80	Uzbekistan	..	..	17	20	63	..	..	..	..	..	..
83	Kyrgyzstan	42	..	16	24	60	..	..	..	..	..	..
88	Tajikistan	..	..	14	19	67	..	..	..	..	..	..

Note: Data for developing countries for this subject area are in table 17.

HDI rank	Unemployment rate (%)			Incidence of long-term unemployment (as % of total unemployment)			Regional unemployment disparity (25% worst regions versus 25% best) 1989	Ratio of unemployment rate of those not completing secondary school to those graduating from third level		Future labour force replacement ratio[a] 1990
	Total 1990-91	Female 1990-91	Youth (15-24) 1990-91	More than 6 months 1990-91	More than 12 months 1990-91	More than 24 months 1986-87		Males 1989-90	Females 1989-90	
1 Japan	2.1	2.2	4.5	38	18	17	1.9	..	..	86
2 Canada	10.2	9.6	16.2	24	7	..	2.0	3.6	2.4	99
3 Norway	5.5	5.0	12.8	39	20	..	1.6	5.5	2.0	94
4 Switzerland	1.3	1.5	..	..	..	..	..	1.0	0.9	78
5 Sweden	2.7	2.3	6.1	16	5	..	2.4	2.6	2.8	83
6 USA	6.6	6.3	12.9	..	6	..	2.0	5.9	4.6	105
7 Australia	9.5	9.1	17.2	50	25	..	1.5	3.7	1.4	106
8 France	9.4	12.2	19.5	58	37	27	1.5	..	..	99
9 Netherlands	7.0	9.5	10.5	63	48	36	1.1	2.5	1.5	83
10 United Kingdom	8.9	5.1	12.9	52	36	25	1.8	4.0	2.4	94
11 Iceland	1.5	1.7	..	..	..	..	..	..	..	124
12 Germany	4.3	4.8	6.4	65	46	30	2.2	4.8	1.9	75
13 Denmark	10.6	12.1	..	60	34	13	1.4	..	..	81
14 Finland	7.5	5.7	13.5	24	7	..	3.3	7.5	8.0	92
15 Austria	3.5	3.7	..	..	..	..	1.3	6.9	2.0	85
16 Belgium	7.7	11.0	..	82	70	53	1.5	2.8	2.9	88
17 New Zealand	10.3	9.5	18.8	39	21	..	1.3	..	..	108
18 Luxembourg	1.3	2.6	..	57	..	10	..	..	..	80
19 Israel	10.6	13.4	..	..	..	..	..	..	..	163
21 Ireland	15.8	11.4	19.5	82	67	43	1.1	..	..	142
22 Italy	9.9	15.4	30.8	87	71	36	2.9	1.9	1.7	82
23 Spain	16.0	23.2	31.1	68	51	38	1.9	1.2	1.7	100
25 Greece	7.3	12.5	..	74	52	19	1.4	0.9	0.5	97
26 Czechoslovakia	6.6	7.3	..	..	..	..	..	..	..	116
28 Hungary	8.5	7.6	..	..	..	..	..	..	..	97
39 Malta	3.7	2.3	..	..	..	..	..	..	..	111
40 Bulgaria	12.0	..	..	..	..	..	..	..	..	99
41 Portugal	4.1	5.8	8.7	65	48	34	2.2	..	..	105
48 Poland	..	..	..	..	..	..	..	..	..	126
77 Romania	..	..	..	..	..	..	..	..	..	115
78 Albania	9.1	..	..	..	..	..	..	..	..	165
Aggregates										
Industrial	..	..	..	..	..	..	..	..	..	105
Developing	..	..	..	..	..	..	..	..	..	..
World	..	..	..	..	..	..	..	..	..	..
OECD	6.9	7.6	13.7	56	28	27	2.0	3.8	2.5	94
Eastern Europe incl. former USSR	..	..	..	..	..	..	..	..	..	..
European Community	8.7	10.8	17.7	66	49	31	2.0	..	..	89
Nordic	6.0	5.7	9.8	32	15	12	2.2	5.5	4.3	87
Southern Europe	11.1	16.9	28.9	78	61	35	2.4	..	..	96
Non-Europe	5.7	5.5	10.9	..	10	..	2.0	..	..	100
North America	6.9	6.6	13.2	..	6	..	2.0	5.6	4.3	104

Other countries

HDI rank	Total	Female	Youth	More than 6 months	More than 12 months	More than 24 months	Regional	Males	Females	Future labour
29 Lithuania	..	..	..	..	..	..	..	..	..	..
34 Estonia	..	..	..	..	..	..	..	..	..	..
35 Latvia	..	..	..	..	..	..	..	..	..	..
37 Russian Federation	..	..	..	..	..	..	..	..	..	..
38 Belarus	..	..	..	..	..	..	..	..	..	..
45 Ukraine	..	..	..	..	..	..	..	..	..	..
47 Armenia	..	..	..	..	..	..	..	..	..	..
49 Georgia	..	..	..	..	..	..	..	..	..	..
54 Kazakhstan	..	..	..	..	..	..	..	..	..	..
62 Azerbaijan	..	..	..	..	..	..	..	..	..	..
64 Moldova, Rep. of	..	..	..	..	..	..	..	..	..	..
66 Turkmenistan	..	..	..	..	..	..	..	..	..	..
80 Uzbekistan	..	..	..	..	..	..	..	..	..	..
83 Kyrgyzstan	..	..	..	..	..	..	..	..	..	..
88 Tajikistan	..	..	..	..	..	..	..	..	..	..

a. Population under 15 divided by one-third of the population aged 15-59.

HDI rank	Real GDP per capita (PPP$) 1990	Country share of industrial market economy (%) 1990	GNP per capita (US$) 1990	Income share Lowest 40% of households (%) 1985-89	Income share Ratio of highest 20% to lowest 20% 1985-89	Total education expenditure (as % of GDP) 1988	Total health expenditure (as % of GDP) 1990	Social security benefits expenditure (as % of GDP) 1985-89
1 Japan	17,616	19.8	25,840	21.9	4.3	5.0	6.7	6.0
2 Canada	19,232	3.4	20,380	17.5	7.1	7.2	9.3	17.3
3 Norway	16,028	0.6	22,830	19.0	5.9	6.6[a]	8.0	17.6
4 Switzerland	20,874	1.4	32,250	16.9	8.6	5.1[a]	7.8	13.3
5 Sweden	17,014	1.3	23,780	21.2	4.6	5.7	8.6	33.7
6 USA	21,449	34.4	21,810	15.7	8.9	5.7	12.2	12.6
7 Australia	16,051	1.9	16,560	15.5	9.6	4.8[a]	8.2	8.0
8 France	17,405	7.0	19,590	18.4	..	5.7	8.8	18.6
9 Netherlands	15,695	1.6	17,570	20.1	5.6	6.6	8.6	27.7
10 United Kingdom	15,804	5.9	16,080	17.3	6.8	4.7[a]	6.1	17.0
11 Iceland	16,496	(.)	22,090	..	..	..	8.7	..
12 Germany	18,213	8.9	22,360	19.5	5.7	6.2	8.6	23.0
13 Denmark	16,781	0.7	22,440	17.4	7.1	6.9	6.6	27.8
14 Finland	16,446	0.8	24,540	18.4	6.0	6.8	7.8	20.6
15 Austria	16,504	0.9	19,000	..	..	5.6[a]	8.5	21.5
16 Belgium	16,381	1.0	17,580	21.6	4.6	6.1[a]	7.7	19.8
17 New Zealand	13,481	0.3	12,570	15.9	8.8	4.9[a]	7.3	12.0
18 Luxembourg	19,244	0.1	29,010	..	..	6.0[a]	7.2	18.8
19 Israel	10,840	0.3	11,160	18.1	6.6	..	2.1[a]	4.0
21 Ireland	10,589	0.2	10,370	..	..	6.2	7.7	19.9
22 Italy	15,890	6.1	16,880	18.8	6.0	4.8[a]	7.7	13.1
23 Spain	11,723	2.7	11,010	19.4	5.8	5.0	6.4	13.4
25 Greece	7,366	0.4	6,010	..	..	3.1	4.8	11.9
26 Czechoslovakia	..	..	3,190	..	..	..	4.2[a]	18.4
28 Hungary	6,116	..	2,780	25.7	3.2	..	3.2[a]	18.2
39 Malta	8,732	(.)	6,690	..	..	..	..	..
40 Bulgaria	..	..	2,320	..	..	..	3.2[a]	14.9
41 Portugal	8,770	0.3	4,950	..	..	4.9	6.1	10.4
48 Poland	4,237	..	1,690	23.9	3.6	..	4.0[a]	11.5
77 Romania	..	..	1,620	..	..	..	1.9[a]	..
78 Albania	..	..	..	..	..	..	..	..
Aggregates								
Industrial	14,440	100.0	14,580	..	..	..	..	14.1
Developing	2,170	..	810	..	..	..	..	..
World	4,890	..	4,010	..	..	..	..	..
OECD	18,000	99.7	20,360	18.1	6.9	5.5	9.1	14.1
Eastern Europe incl. former USSR	6,140	..	2,670	..	..	..	..	..
European Community	15,710	35.0	17,220	18.8	6.1	5.5	7.7	18.5
Nordic	16,650	3.4	23,450	19.3	5.7	6.2	7.9	28.4
Southern Europe	13,140	9.5	12,950	19.0	5.9	4.8	7.2	13.1
Non-Europe	19,800	60.1	22,480	17.6	7.5	5.5	10.1	10.6
North America	21,240	37.8	21,670	15.9	8.7	5.8	11.9	13.0

Other countries

HDI rank	Real GDP per capita (PPP$) 1990	Country share of industrial market economy (%) 1990	GNP per capita (US$) 1990	Lowest 40% of households (%) 1985-89	Ratio of highest 20% to lowest 20% 1985-89	Total education expenditure 1988	Total health expenditure 1990	Social security benefits 1985-89
29 Lithuania	4,913	..	3,110	..	..	..	..	..
34 Estonia	6,438	..	4,170	..	..	..	..	..
35 Latvia	6,457	..	3,590	..	..	..	..	..
37 Russian Federation	7,968	..	3,430	..	..	..	..	..
38 Belarus	5,727	..	3,110	..	..	..	..	..
45 Ukraine	5,433	..	2,500	..	..	..	..	..
47 Armenia	4,741	..	2,380	..	..	..	..	..
49 Georgia	4,572	..	2,120	..	..	..	..	..
54 Kazakhstan	4,716	..	2,600	..	..	..	..	..
62 Azerbaijan	3,977	..	1,640	..	..	..	..	..
64 Moldova, Rep. of	3,896	..	2,390	..	..	..	..	..
66 Turkmenistan	4,230	..	1,690	..	..	..	..	..
80 Uzbekistan	3,115	..	1,340	..	..	..	..	..
83 Kyrgyzstan	3,114	..	1,570	..	..	..	..	..
88 Tajikistan	2,558	..	1,130	..	..	..	..	..

a. Public expenditure only.

Note: Data for developing countries for this subject area are in table 18.

		Total official development assistance (ODA) given							Aid social allocation ratio (%) 1988/90	Aid social priority ratio (%) 1988/90	Aid human expenditure ratio (%) 1988/91	Social priority aid (as % of total aid) 1988/90	Aid to least developed countries (as % of total) 1991
		US$ millions 1991	As % of GNP			As % of central government budget 1990-91	As % of military exports 1991	Per capita (US$) 1991					
HDI rank			1970	1990	1991								
1	Japan	10,945	0.23	0.31	0.32	1.3	100+	77	11.5	32.0	0.012	3.7	15
2	Canada	2,604	0.41	0.44	0.45	2.0	94	92	19.7	46.5	0.041	9.2	27
3	Norway	1,178	0.33	1.17	1.14	2.0	100+	282	24.9	71.9	0.204	17.9	47
4	Switzerland	863	0.13	0.32	0.36	3.2	22	118	34.8	48.3	0.061	16.8	30
5	Sweden	2,116	0.41	0.91	0.92	2.8	14	234	12.3	47.7	0.054	5.9	39
6	USA	9,402	0.31	0.19	0.17	0.8	2	44	15.9	52.4	0.014	8.3	15
7	Australia	1,050	0.59	0.34	0.38	1.3	30	58	14.6	15.7	0.009	2.3	23
8	France	6,530	0.46	0.52	0.54	2.0	4	115	12.0	30.4	0.020	3.6	26
9	Netherlands	2,517	0.60	0.92	0.88	2.7	9	168	21.1	49.1	0.091	10.4	26
10	United Kingdom	3,231	0.42	0.27	0.32	1.2	2	99	11.9	55.2	0.021	6.6	30
11	Iceland	..	..	..	..	..	..	..	..	..	..	..	..
12	Germany	6,890	0.33	0.42	0.41	2.4	21	92	7.8	26.3	0.008	2.1	24
13	Denmark	1,200	0.40	0.94	0.96	3.2	25	231	30.5	71.9	0.210	21.9	37
14	Finland	930	0.09	0.63	0.76	2.0	..	180	34.3	39.7	0.103	13.6	33
15	Austria	548	0.07	0.25	0.34	0.6	81	60	27.0	32.9	0.030	8.9	17
16	Belgium	831	0.48	0.46	0.42	1.2	100+	86	..	..	..	..	30
17	New Zealand	100	0.23	0.23	0.25	0.5	29	..	..	..	..	17.0	..
18	Luxembourg	..	..	..	..	..	..	..	..	..	..	..	..
19	Israel	-1,365	..	-2.90	-3.10	..	..	-28	..	..	..	..	..
21	Ireland	72	0.16	0.16	0.19	0.6	..	..	..	..	..	..	29
22	Italy	3,352	0.17	0.31	0.30	0.7	13	58	21.3	36.5	0.023	7.8	20
23	Spain	1,177	0.01	0.20	0.23	0.6	8	27	..	..	..	..	15
25	Greece	..	..	..	..	..	..	..	..	..	..	..	..
26	Czechoslovakia	..	..	..	..	..	..	..	..	..	..	..	..
28	Hungary	..	..	..	..	..	..	..	..	..	..	..	..
39	Malta	..	..	..	..	..	..	..	..	..	..	..	..
40	Bulgaria	..	..	..	..	..	..	..	..	..	..	..	..
41	Portugal	213	1.05	0.25	0.31	(.)	46	16	..	..	..	..	72
48	Poland	..	..	..	..	..	..	..	..	..	..	..	..
77	Romania	..	..	..	..	..	..	..	..	..	..	..	..
78	Albania	..	..	..	..	..	..	..	..	..	..	..	..
Aggregates													
Industrial		..	..	..	..	..	..	..	..	..	..	..	..
Developing		..	..	..	..	..	..	..	..	..	..	..	..
World		..	..	..	..	..	..	..	..	..	..	..	..
OECD		56,700T	0.33	0.33	0.33	1.3	..	75	15.1	43.2	0.021	6.5	23
Eastern Europe incl. former USSR		..	..	..	..	..	..	..	..	..	..	..	..
European Community		26,970T	0.36	0.41	0.42	1.7	..	89	14.0	41.5	0.024	5.8	26
Nordic		5,420T	0.34	0.90	0.93	2.5	..	228	22.8	58.5	0.124	13.4	39
Southern Europe		4,740T	..	0.28	0.28	0.7	..	43	21.3	36.5	0.022	7.8	..
Non-Europe		24,100T	0.31	0.25	0.24	1.0	..	57	14.3	42.4	0.015	6.0	17
North America		12,000T	0.32	0.20	0.21	0.9	..	49	16.7	50.9	0.017	8.5	18

Other countries

29	Lithuania	..	..	..	..	..	..	..	..	..	..	..	..
34	Estonia	..	..	..	..	..	..	..	..	..	..	..	..
35	Latvia	..	..	..	..	..	..	..	..	..	..	..	..
37	Russian Federation	..	..	..	..	..	..	..	..	..	..	..	..
38	Belarus	..	..	..	..	..	..	..	..	..	..	..	..
45	Ukraine	..	..	..	..	..	..	..	..	..	..	..	..
47	Armenia	..	..	..	..	..	..	..	..	..	..	..	..
49	Georgia	..	..	..	..	..	..	..	..	..	..	..	..
54	Kazakhstan	..	..	..	..	..	..	..	..	..	..	..	..
62	Azerbaijan	..	..	..	..	..	..	..	..	..	..	..	..
64	Moldova, Rep. of	..	..	..	..	..	..	..	..	..	..	..	..
66	Turkmenistan	..	..	..	..	..	..	..	..	..	..	..	..
80	Uzbekistan	..	..	..	..	..	..	..	..	..	..	..	..
83	Kyrgyzstan	..	..	..	..	..	..	..	..	..	..	..	..
88	Tajikistan	..	..	..	..	..	..	..	..	..	..	..	..

Note: Data for developing countries for this subject area are in table 19.

42 Resource flow imbalances

HDI rank	Export-import ratio 1990	Ratio of export to import growth rate 1980-90	Trade dependency (exports plus imports as % of GDP) 1990	Terms of trade (1987=100) 1990	Net workers' remittances from abroad (US$ millions) 1990	Gross international reserves (in months of import coverage) 1990	Current account balance (US$ millions) 1990
1 Japan	124	75	18	91	..	2.6	40,380
2 Canada	108	70	42	109	..	1.6	-17,955
3 Norway	127	288	58	91	-66	4.2	4,991
4 Switzerland	92	92	59	100	-1,980	6.4	7,111
5 Sweden	105	126	49	101	18	2.9	-4,188
6 USA	72	43	16	100	-1,100	2.9	-71,710
7 Australia	91	83	26	115	..	3.3	-14,725
8 France	90	106	37	102	-1,983	2.4	-3,648
9 Netherlands	104	126	92	102	-298	2.5	12,374
10 United Kingdom	83	55	42	105	..	1.3	-16,314
11 Iceland	..	..	..	..	..	..	..
12 Germany	117	108	50	97	-4,556	2.8	62,774
13 Denmark	110	121	51	104	..	2.5	1,551
14 Finland	99	64	..	98	..	3.1	-5,947
15 Austria	84	119	58	92	307	2.9	1,067
16 Belgium	99	152	..	96	-386	..	5,967
17 New Zealand	96	94	43	99	259	3.4	-1,555
18 Luxembourg	..	..	..	..	..	..	..
19 Israel	79	160	51	103	..	3.4	-3,105
21 Ireland	115	203	105	95	..	2.1	-1,249
22 Italy	96	83	32	97	1,181	4.5	-9,487
23 Spain	64	82	29	106	1,747	6.3	-18,023
25 Greece	41	88	48	105	1,775	2.6	-6,438
26 Czechoslovakia	..	..	..	..	..	1.5	-1,175
28 Hungary	..	423	..	87	..	1.2	230
39 Malta	..	..	..	..	..	..	..
40 Bulgaria	..	..	..	..	..	..	-1,710
41 Portugal	65	143	73	105	4,271	8.7	-1,119
48 Poland	..	250	..	103	..	2.9	2,762
77 Romania	..	..	..	..	..	1.7	-3,254
78 Albania	..	..	..	..	..	..	-154
Aggregates							
Industrial	94	..	..	100	..	..	-42,500T
Developing	111	..	42	101	..	3.7	-20,900T
World	97	..	..	101	..	..	-63,400T
OECD	96	90	30	99	-830T	3.0	-36,140T
Eastern Europe incl. former USSR	..	..	..	..	..	..	-3,300T
European Community	97	103	43	101	1,750T	3.0	26,390T
Nordic	109	147	51	100	-50T	3.1	-3,590T
Southern Europe	82	88	33	100	8,970T	5.2	-35,220T
Non-Europe	93	60	19	98	..	2.7	-68,670T
North America	80	49	19	101	-1,100T	2.7	89,670T

Other countries

HDI rank	Export-import ratio 1990	Ratio of export to import growth rate 1980-90	Trade dependency 1990	Terms of trade 1990	Net workers' remittances 1990	Gross international reserves 1990	Current account balance 1990
29 Lithuania	56	..	..	..	..	..	..
34 Estonia	60	..	..	..	..	..	..
35 Latvia	71	..	..	..	..	..	..
37 Russian Federation	129	..	..	..	..	..	..
38 Belarus	89	..	..	..	..	..	..
45 Ukraine	85	..	..	..	..	..	..
47 Armenia	56	..	..	..	..	..	..
49 Georgia	59	..	..	..	..	..	..
54 Kazakhstan	58	..	..	..	..	..	..
62 Azerbaijan	97	..	..	..	..	..	..
64 Moldova, Rep. of	51	..	..	..	..	..	..
66 Turkmenistan	105	..	..	..	..	..	..
80 Uzbekistan	63	..	..	..	..	..	..
83 Kyrgyzstan	55	..	..	..	..	..	..
88 Tajikistan	58	..	..	..	..	..	..

Note: Data for developing countries for this subject area are in table 20.

HDI rank		Military expenditure (as % of GDP) 1960	1990	Military expenditure (as % of combined education and health expenditure) 1977	1990	ODA given (as % of military expenditure) 1991	Armed forces — As % of total population 1987	Per teacher 1987	Per doctor 1987	Annual average exports of major conventional arms to developing countries — US$ millions 1987-91	As % of global arms exports 1987-91
1	Japan	1.0	1.0	10	8	35	0.20	0.2	1.29	3	0.01
2	Canada	4.3	2.0	15	13	27	0.33	0.3	1.54	28	0.13
3	Norway	3.2	3.2	25	23	38	0.89	0.7	3.89	1	(.)
4	Switzerland	2.4	1.6	24	12	28	0.31	0.7	2.02	40	0.19
5	Sweden	2.8	2.4	23	15	50	0.80	0.9	2.98	152	0.71
6	USA	8.8	5.6	54	32	4	0.89	0.9	3.79	4,701	21.97
7	Australia	2.4	2.3	25	15	17	0.43	0.4	2.11	35	0.16
8	France	6.3	3.6	35	24	21	0.98	1.0	3.94	1,728	8.07
9	Netherlands	3.9	2.7	24	19	40	0.74	0.8	3.12	282	1.32
10	United Kingdom	6.4	3.9	43	36	10	0.56	0.6	4.08	1,519	7.10
11	Iceland	(.)	(.)	..	..	..	..	..	..	..	..
12	Germany	4.0	2.8	34	22	20	0.80	1.0	2.85	335	1.57
13	Denmark	2.7	2.0	18	16	53	0.57	0.4	2.21	47	0.22
14	Finland	1.7	1.8	11	14	44	0.69	0.7	3.09	..	..
15	Austria	1.2	1.0	11	8	41	0.73	0.6	3.79	7	0.03
16	Belgium	3.4	2.4	30	20	21	0.92	0.8	2.87	1	0.01
17	New Zealand	1.4	2.0	16	16	13	0.39	0.4	2.20	..	..
18	Luxembourg	1.0	1.1	14	10	..	0.27	0.3	1.43	..	..
19	Israel	2.9	8.4	257	192	..	3.23	2.1	14.39	164	0.77
21	Ireland	1.4	1.3	15	10	14	0.39	0.4	2.80	..	..
22	Italy	2.7	2.1	27	22	18	0.68	0.6	6.07	249	1.17
23	Spain	2.9	1.8	32	23	18	0.84	1.1	2.48	155	0.73
25	Greece	4.8	5.9	124	81	..	2.09	2.6	6.28	5	0.02
26	Czechoslovakia	3.8	3.1	48	..	..	1.29	1.8	4.22	180	0.84
28	Hungary	1.8	2.1	36	..	..	1.00	1.1	2.99	..	..
39	Malta	..	..	..	..	..	0.29	0.3	2.00	..	..
40	Bulgaria	3.2	3.5	41	..	..	1.70	2.1	5.65	..	..
41	Portugal	4.2	3.1	50	37	15	0.65	0.5	2.50	5	0.02
48	Poland	3.0	2.9	47	24	..	1.04	1.1	5.10	4	0.02
77	Romania	2.3	1.4	38	41	..	0.78	1.2	3.73	37	0.17
78	Albania	9.0	..	126	..	..	1.36	1.4	9.33	..	..
	Aggregates										
	Industrial	6.3	..	..	..	..	..	1.0	3.4	..	..
	Developing	4.2	3.4	91	169	..	0.40	0.6	18.0	..	..
	World	6.0	..	..	..	..	..	0.7	14.7	..	..
	OECD	6.4	3.4	43	28	12.0	0.70	0.8	3.3	9,290T	..
	Eastern Europe incl. former USSR	..	..	..	..	..	..	1.4	3.6	..	..
	European Community	4.7	2.9	36	27	18.6	0.80	0.9	3.8	4,330T	..
	Nordic	2.7	2.5	20	17	46.3	0.74	0.7	3.0	200T	..
	Southern Europe	3.3	2.2	39	29	17.6	0.86	1.0	4.7	410T	..
	Non-Europe	7.5	3.8	50	29	7.7	0.66	0.7	3.0	4,930T	..
	North America	8.5	5.3	53	32	4.4	0.83	0.9	3.6	4,730T	..

Other countries

HDI rank											
29	Lithuania	..	..	..	..	..	..	..	..	..	..
34	Estonia	..	..	..	..	..	..	..	..	..	..
35	Latvia	..	..	..	..	..	..	..	..	..	..
37	Russian Federation	..	..	..	..	..	..	..	..	..	..
38	Belarus	..	..	..	..	..	..	..	..	..	..
45	Ukraine	..	..	..	..	..	..	..	..	..	..
47	Armenia	..	..	..	..	..	..	..	..	..	..
49	Georgia	..	..	..	..	..	..	..	..	..	..
54	Kazakhstan	..	..	..	..	..	..	..	..	..	..
62	Azerbaijan	..	..	..	..	..	..	..	..	..	..
64	Moldova, Rep. of	..	..	..	..	..	..	..	..	..	..
66	Turkmenistan	..	..	..	..	..	..	..	..	..	..
80	Uzbekistan	..	..	..	..	..	..	..	..	..	..
83	Kyrgyzstan	..	..	..	..	..	..	..	..	..	..
88	Tajikistan	..	..	..	..	..	..	..	..	..	..

Note: Data for developing countries for this subject area are in table 21.

HDI rank		Urban population (as % of total)			Urban population annual growth rate (%)		Population in cities of more than 1 million (as % of urban population)	Major city with highest population density		Population exposed to 65+ decibels of road traffic noise (%)	Daily travel time to and from work (minutes)
								City	Population per km²		
		1960	1991	2000	1960-91	1991-2000	1990		1980-88	1980	1975-80
1	Japan	63	77	78	1.6	0.5	36	Tokyo	13,973	31	..
2	Canada	69	77	79	1.7	1.0	39	Montreal	6,357	..	49
3	Norway	50	75	79	1.9	0.8	..	..	..	5	46
4	Switzerland	51	60	64	1.2	0.9	..	Lausanne	5,512	11	52
5	Sweden	73	84	86	0.9	0.3	23	Stockholm	3,051	11	..
6	USA	70	75	77	1.3	0.9	48	New York	8,722	7	62
7	Australia	81	85	86	1.9	1.2	59	Sydney	3,318	..	63
8	France	62	74	77	1.3	0.7	26	Paris	20,647	13	54
9	Netherlands	85	89	89	1.0	0.6	16	The Hague	6,386	5	74
10	United Kingdom	86	89	90	0.4	0.3	26	Birmingham	4,444	..	..
11	Iceland	80	91	92	1.6	1.0	..	..	..	..	..
12	Germany	76	85	87	0.6	0.2	15	Munich	4,192	8	52
13	Denmark	74	87	89	0.9	0.3	31	Copenhagen	5,735	12	..
14	Finland	38	60	62	1.9	0.5	34	Helsinki	2,616	..	42
15	Austria	50	58	63	0.8	0.8	47	Vienna	3,689	16	52
16	Belgium	92	97	98	0.4	0.1	..	Brussels	4,160	12	60
17	New Zealand	76	84	85	1.5	0.9	..	..	..	..	37
18	Luxembourg	62	84	87	1.6	0.5	..	..	..	..	..
19	Israel	77	92	93	3.2	1.7	45	..	..	..	..
21	Ireland	46	57	60	1.7	1.5	..	Dublin	4,485	..	..
22	Italy	59	69	72	0.9	0.5	37	Naples	10,342	..	53
23	Spain	57	78	83	1.9	0.9	28	Barcelona	17,433	23	..
25	Greece	43	62	68	1.9	0.9	55	..	..	20	..
26	Czechoslovakia	47	77	83	2.1	1.1	11	Prague	2,821	..	..
28	Hungary	40	61	68	1.6	1.0	33	Budapest	3,954	..	..
39	Malta	70	87	90	1.0	0.6	..	..	..	..	..
40	Bulgaria	39	68	73	2.4	0.9	19	..	..	..	..
41	Portugal	22	34	40	1.9	1.9	46	Lisbon	9,893	..	..
48	Poland	48	62	66	1.7	1.2	28	Warsaw	3,419	..	..
77	Romania	34	53	58	2.2	1.4	18	Bucharest	3,271	..	..
78	Albania	31	35	39	2.8	2.6	..	..	..	..	..
	Aggregates										
	Industrial	61	73	75	1.4	0.8	34	..	..	..	..
	Developing	22	37	45	4.0	4.0	36	..	..	..	..
	World	34	45	60	2.9	2.8	35	..	..	..	..
	OECD	68	77	79	1.2	0.7	36	..	..	..	..
	Eastern Europe incl. former USSR	46	64	67	2.0	1.0	20	..	..	..	..
	European Community	70	79	81	0.9	0.5	26	..	..	..	..
	Nordic	61	78	80	1.2	0.4	28	..	..	..	..
	Southern Europe	49	66	70	1.5	0.9	32	..	..	..	..
	Non-Europe	68	76	78	1.5	0.8	44	..	..	..	..
	North America	70	75	77	1.3	0.9	47	..	..	..	..

Other countries

HDI rank		Urban population (as % of total)			Urban population annual growth rate (%)						
29	Lithuania	39	69	..	..	..	..	..	..	..	..
34	Estonia	57	71	..	..	..	..	..	..	..	..
35	Latvia	56	71	..	..	..	..	..	..	..	..
37	Russian Federation	53	74	..	..	..	..	..	..	..	..
38	Belarus	31	67	..	1.0	..	..	..	..	..	..
45	Ukraine	46	68	..	0.7	..	..	..	..	..	..
47	Armenia	50	68	..	0.6	..	..	..	..	..	..
49	Georgia	42	56	..	..	..	..	..	..	..	..
54	Kazakhstan	44	58	..	..	..	..	..	..	..	..
62	Azerbaijan	48	53	..	0.4	..	..	..	..	..	..
64	Moldova, Rep. of	22	48	..	..	..	..	..	..	..	..
66	Turkmenistan	45	45	..	(.)	..	..	..	..	..	..
80	Uzbekistan	34	40	..	0.3	..	..	..	..	..	..
83	Kyrgyzstan	34	38	..	..	..	..	..	..	..	..
88	Tajikistan	33	31	..	..	..	..	..	..	..	..

Note: Data for developing countries for this subject area are in table 22.

HDI rank	Estimated population (millions)			Annual population growth rate (%)		Total fertility rate 1991	Ratio of 1991 fertility rate to 1960	Contraceptive prevalence rate (%) 1985-90	Dependency ratio (%) 1991	Life expectancy at age 60 (years)	
	1960	1991	2000	1960-91	1991-2000					Male 1989-90	Female 1989-90
1 Japan	94.1	124.0	128.1	0.9	0.4	1.7	81	56	43	20.0	24.4
2 Canada	17.9	27.0	30.4	1.3	1.3	1.8	47	73	48	..	..
3 Norway	3.6	4.3	4.5	0.6	0.6	1.9	68	71	55	18.3	22.9
4 Switzerland	5.4	6.8	7.2	0.7	0.6	1.6	67	71	46	19.1	23.9
5 Sweden	7.5	8.6	9.0	0.5	0.5	2.0	89	78	56	19.1	23.3
6 USA	180.7	252.5	275.3	1.1	1.0	2.0	58	74	52	18.6	22.7
7 Australia	10.3	17.3	19.6	1.7	1.4	1.9	57	76	49	18.8	23.1
8 France	45.7	57.0	58.8	0.7	0.4	1.8	65	81	52	18.8	24.0
9 Netherlands	11.5	15.0	16.1	0.9	0.7	1.7	53	76	45	18.3	23.4
10 United Kingdom	52.4	57.6	58.8	0.3	0.2	1.9	70	81	53	17.4	21.7
11 Iceland	0.2	0.3	0.3	1.2	1.1	2.2	55	..	55	19.5	22.9
12 Germany	72.7	79.9	82.6	0.3	0.4	1.5	62	78	46	17.8	22.2
13 Denmark	4.6	5.1	5.2	0.4	0.2	1.7	64	63	49	17.5	21.7
14 Finland	4.4	5.0	5.1	0.4	0.3	1.8	66	80	49	17.1	21.9
15 Austria	7.0	7.7	8.0	0.3	0.3	1.5	56	71	48	18.1	22.3
16 Belgium	9.2	10.0	10.1	0.3	0.1	1.6	63	81	50	17.6	22.5
17 New Zealand	2.4	3.4	3.7	1.2	0.9	2.1	55	70	51	17.8	21.9
18 Luxembourg	0.3	0.4	0.4	0.6	0.7	1.6	68	..	45	..	..
19 Israel	2.1	4.9	6.3	2.7	2.9	2.9	75	..	67	..	..
21 Ireland	2.8	3.5	3.4	0.7	-0.2	2.2	56	60	62	16.0	20.0
22 Italy	50.2	57.7	58.1	0.5	0.1	1.3	54	78	46	18.3	22.9
23 Spain	30.5	39.0	39.6	0.8	0.2	1.4	50	59	49	..	..
25 Greece	8.3	10.2	10.3	0.6	0.2	1.5	67	..	49	..	..
26 Czechoslovakia	13.7	15.7	16.3	0.4	0.4	2.0	80	95	52	..	..
28 Hungary	10.0	10.5	10.5	0.2	-0.0	1.8	91	73	50	..	..
39 Malta	0.3	0.4	0.4	0.4	0.7	2.1	60	..	51	..	..
40 Bulgaria	7.9	9.0	8.9	0.4	-0.1	1.9	83	76	50	..	..
41 Portugal	8.8	9.9	9.9	0.4	0.1	1.5	49	66	51	18.0	22.0
48 Poland	29.6	38.3	39.5	0.8	0.3	2.1	70	75	54	..	..
77 Romania	18.4	23.3	24.0	0.8	0.4	2.2	93	58	51	..	..
78 Albania	1.6	3.3	3.6	2.3	1.0	2.8	48	..	61	..	..
Aggregates											
Industrial	940T	1,220T	1,290T	0.8	0.6	2.0	65	59	50	16.7	20.9
Developing	2,070T	4,160T	4,930T	2.3	1.9	3.8	60	49	70	..	..
World	3,010T	5,380T	6,220T	1.9	1.6	3.4	61	52	65	..	..
OECD	630T	802T	840T	0.7	0.6	1.8	63	72	49	18.6	23.0
Eastern Europe incl. former USSR	310T	420T	440T	0.9	0.6	2.2	81	33	53	12.6	16.1
European Community	290T	345T	350T	0.5	0.3	1.6	61	76	48	18.0	22.6
Nordic	20T	23T	24T	0.4	0.4	1.9	74	74	52	18.2	22.6
Southern Europe	120T	145T	150T	0.6	0.2	1.5	53	70	48	17.1	21.1
Non-Europe	310T	430T	460T	1.1	0.8	1.9	64	69	49	19.0	23.2
North America	200T	280T	310T	1.1	1.0	2.0	57	74	51	18.6	22.7

Other countries

HDI rank	1960	1991	2000	1960-91	1991-2000	1991	to 1960	1985-90	1991	Male 1989-90	Female 1989-90
29 Lithuania	2.8	3.7	4.0	1.0	0.7	2.0	78	12	52	13.3	17.0
34 Estonia	1.2	1.6	1.7	0.9	0.8	2.2	113	26	49	12.1	15.8
35 Latvia	2.1	2.7	2.8	0.8	0.5	2.0	108	19	49	12.1	15.8
37 Russian Federation	118.8	148.7	155.2	0.7	0.5	2.0	..	22	49	12.0	15.8
38 Belarus	8.1	10.3	10.8	0.8	0.5	2.0	..	13	49	12.9	16.4
45 Ukraine	42.4	52.1	53.8	0.7	0.4	1.9	..	15	52	12.5	15.8
47 Armenia	1.8	3.4	3.6	2.0	0.6	2.6	..	12	54	13.5	16.5
49 Georgia	4.1	5.5	5.8	0.9	0.7	2.1	..	8	52	14.1	17.1
54 Kazakhstan	9.6	16.9	18.3	1.8	0.9	2.8	..	22	61	12.5	16.4
62 Azerbaijan	3.8	7.2	8.0	2.0	1.1	2.8	..	7	61	14.2	18.2
64 Moldova, Rep. of	3.0	4.4	4.6	1.3	0.6	2.5	..	15	56	12.5	14.7
66 Turkmenistan	1.6	3.8	4.5	2.8	2.0	4.3	..	12	82	12.8	15.8
80 Uzbekistan	8.6	21.0	25.2	2.9	2.0	4.0	..	19	69	14.1	17.1
83 Kyrgyzstan	2.2	4.5	5.2	2.4	1.7	3.8	..	25	72	13.0	16.7
88 Tajikistan	2.1	5.5	6.9	3.1	2.6	5.1	..	15	89	15.1	18.0

Note: Data for developing countries for this subject area are in table 23.

HDI rank		Land area (million hectares)	Population density (per 1,000 hectares) 1991	Arable land (as % of land area) 1989	Irrigated land (as % of arable land area) 1989	Forest area (as % of land area) 1989	Internal renewable water resources per capita (1,000 m³ per year) 1990	Annual fresh water withdrawals	
								As % of water resources 1980-87	Per capita (m³) 1980-87
1	Japan	37.7	3,294	11.0	62	66.7	4.4	20	923
2	Canada	922.1	29	5.0	2	38.8	109.4	1	1,752
3	Norway	30.7	139	2.9	11	27.1	96.2	(.)	489
4	Switzerland	4.0	1,701	9.8	6	26.5	6.5	6	502
5	Sweden	41.2	209	6.9	4	68.1	21.1	2	479
6	USA	916.7	275	20.5	10	32.1	9.9	19	2,162
7	Australia	761.8	23	6.4	4	13.9	20.4	5	1,306
8	France	55.0	1,036	32.5	7	26.9	3.0	22	728
9	Netherlands	3.4	4,437	26.7	59	8.8	0.7	16	1,023
10	United Kingdom	24.2	2,382	27.7	2	9.8	2.1	24	507
11	Iceland	10.0	26	0.1	..	1.2	671.9	(.)	349
12	Germany	34.9	2,286	34.2	4	29.7	1.3	26	668
13	Denmark	4.2	1,215	60.2	17	11.6	2.2	11	289
14	Finland	30.5	164	8.1	3	76.2	22.1	3	774
15	Austria	8.3	936	17.6	..	38.7	7.5	3	417
16	Belgium	3.0	3,281	..	..	23.0	0.9	72	917
17	New Zealand	26.8	128	1.8	54	27.3	117.4	(.)	379
18	Luxembourg	0.3	1,465	..	..	..	2.7	1	119
19	Israel	2.0	2,396	16.9	50	5.4	0.4	88	447
21	Ireland	6.9	507	13.8	..	4.9	13.4	2	267
22	Italy	29.4	1,963	30.8	25	22.9	3.1	30	983
23	Spain	49.9	781	31.2	16	31.3	2.8	41	1,174
25	Greece	13.1	776	22.0	30	20.0	4.4	12	721
26	Czechoslovakia	12.5	1,252	39.7	6	36.8	1.8	6	379
28	Hungary	9.2	1,141	54.7	3	18.3	0.6	5	502
39	Malta	0.0	11,125	37.5	8	(.)	(.)	92	68
40	Bulgaria	11.1	812	34.8	30	35.0	2.0	7	1,600
41	Portugal	9.2	1,073	31.6	17	32.3	3.3	16	1,062
48	Poland	30.4	1,258	47.3	1	28.7	1.3	30	472
77	Romania	23.0	1,010	43.0	32	27.7	1.6	12	1,144
78	Albania	2.7	1,200	21.2	..	38.2	3.1	1	94
Aggregates									
Industrial		5,360T	225	13.0	7.0	30.1	7.6	21	1,204
Developing		7,550T	541	16.0	20.0	28.7	6.8	16	523
World		12,910T	409	11.0	16.0	29.1	7.0	17	645
OECD		3,020T	266	12.1	9.2	30.2	10.6	21	1,221
Eastern Europe incl. former USSR		2,340T	177	..	..	..	..	..	..
European Community		230T	1,500	31.0	12.7	24.6	2.4	27	786
Nordic		120T	191	7.5	8.2	51.6	38.1	5	501
Southern Europe		130T	1,108	29.7	20.1	27.8	3.1	30	1,062
Non-Europe		2,670T	161	10.8	8.6	29.6	15.8	18	1,710
North America		1,840T	152	12.7	8.4	35.4	19.1	17	2,122

Other countries

HDI rank		Land area	Population density	Arable land	Irrigated land	Forest area	Water resources	As %	Per capita
29	Lithuania	6.5	574	..	..	..	..	..	..
34	Estonia	4.5	351	..	..	..	..	..	..
35	Latvia	6.4	416	..	..	..	..	..	..
37	Russian Federation	1,707.5	87	..	..	..	..	..	..
38	Belarus	20.8	495	..	..	..	..	..	..
45	Ukraine	60.4	862	..	..	..	..	..	..
47	Armenia	3.0	1,145	..	..	..	..	..	..
49	Georgia	7.0	785	..	..	..	..	..	..
54	Kazakhstan	271.7	62	..	..	..	..	..	..
62	Azerbaijan	8.7	837	..	..	..	..	..	..
64	Moldova, Rep. of	3.7	1,188	..	..	..	..	..	..
66	Turkmenistan	48.8	77	..	..	..	..	..	..
80	Uzbekistan	44.7	469	..	..	..	..	..	..
83	Kyrgyzstan	19.8	225	..	..	..	..	..	..
88	Tajikistan	14.3	383	..	..	..	..	..	..

Note: Data for developing countries for this subject area are in table 24.

HDI rank	Commercial energy consumption per capita (kg of oil equivalent)		Total commercial energy consumption (billion kg of oil equivalent)		Percentage share in world consumption	Annual rate of change in commercial energy consumption (%)		Commercial energy consumption in kg of oil equivalent per $100 GDP	
	1965	1990	1965	1990	1990	1960-74	1980-90	1990	Indexed (1965=100)
1 Japan	1,474	3,563	146	440	5.3	10.7	2.1	15	9
2 Canada	6,007	10,009	118	267	3.2	6.0	2.1	47	18
3 Norway	4,650	9,083	17	39	0.5	5.9	1.9	36	15
4 Switzerland	2,501	3,902	15	26	0.3	5.9	1.5	12	11
5 Sweden	4,162	6,347	32	54	0.7	4.9	1.7	24	14
6 USA	6,535	7,822	1,270	1,955	23.6	4.1	1.5	36	20
7 Australia	3,287	5,041	37	86	1.0	5.6	2.2	29	18
8 France	2,468	3,845	120	218	2.6	5.8	1.1	18	15
9 Netherlands	3,134	5,123	39	77	0.9	8.7	1.3	27	14
10 United Kingdom	3,483	3,646	189	209	2.5	1.7	0.8	21	10
11 Iceland	..	..	..	..	..	..	..	..	..
12 Germany	2,478	3,491	188	277	3.4	4.5	0.3	19	10
13 Denmark	2,911	3,618	14	19	0.2	5.5	-0.1	14	9
14 Finland	2,233	5,650	10	28	0.3	9.1	3.0	..	..
15 Austria	2,060	3,503	15	27	0.3	5.1	1.5	17	11
16 Belgium	..	2,807	..	28	0.3	..	..	15	8
17 New Zealand	2,622	4,971	7	17	0.2	5.7	5.4	39	32
18 Luxembourg	..	..	..	..	..	..	..	..	..
19 Israel	1,574	2,050	4	10	0.1	9.6	2.3	18	16
21 Ireland	1,504	2,653	4	9	0.1	4.7	0.5	22	12
22 Italy	1,564	2,754	82	159	1.9	8.3	0.9	15	12
23 Spain	901	2,201	29	86	1.0	8.5	1.5	17	14
25 Greece	615	2,092	5	21	0.3	13.2	2.7	37	37
26 Czechoslovakia	3,374	5,081	48	80	1.0	3.1	0.8	..	..
28 Hungary	1,825	3,211	19	34	0.4	3.9	1.4	..	..
39 Malta	..	..	..	..	..	..	..	..	..
40 Bulgaria	1,788	4,945	15	44	0.5	9.8	1.7	..	..
41 Portugal	506	1,507	5	15	0.2	8.3	2.8	26	22
48 Poland	2,027	3,416	64	130	1.6	4.1	1.2	..	..
77 Romania	1,536	3,623	29	84	1.0	8.0	1.3	..	..
78 Albania	420	1,152	1	4	(.)	12.5	3.1	..	..
Aggregates									
Industrial	3,387	4,937	2,521T	4,443T	53.7	6.0	1.4	..	..
Developing	204	517	709T	2,084T	..	6.2	5.1	68	50
World	936	1,316	3,230T	6,527T	..	6.2	4.5	..	..
OECD	3,565	5,101	2,390T	4,057T	49.0	6.1	1.4	25	15
Eastern Europe incl. former USSR	..	..	..	..	..	5.6	1.3	..	..
European Community	2,243	3,253	730T	1,118T	13.5	5.9	1.0	19	12
Nordic	3,539	6,092	74T	140T	1.7	6.1	1.6	24	13
Southern Europe	1,167	2,372	140T	284T	3.4	8.9	1.5	17	14
Non-Europe	4,802	6,528	1,570T	2,774T	33.5	6.3	1.8	30	16
North America	6,486	8,033	1,380T	2,222T	26.8	4.3	1.6	37	20

Other countries

HDI rank									
29 Lithuania	..	..	..	..	..	..	..	..	..
34 Estonia	..	..	..	..	..	..	..	..	..
35 Latvia	..	..	..	..	..	..	..	..	..
37 Russian Federation	..	..	..	..	..	..	..	..	..
38 Belarus	..	..	..	..	..	..	..	..	..
45 Ukraine	..	..	..	..	..	..	..	..	..
47 Armenia	..	..	..	..	..	..	..	..	..
49 Georgia	..	..	..	..	..	..	..	..	..
54 Kazakhstan	..	..	..	..	..	..	..	..	..
62 Azerbaijan	..	..	..	..	..	..	..	..	..
64 Moldova, Rep. of	..	..	..	..	..	..	..	..	..
66 Turkmenistan	..	..	..	..	..	..	..	..	..
80 Uzbekistan	..	..	..	..	..	..	..	..	..
83 Kyrgyzstan	..	..	..	..	..	..	..	..	..
88 Tajikistan	..	..	..	..	..	..	..	..	..

Note: Data for developing countries for this subject area are in table 25.

HDI rank		Major city with most days of high sulfur emissions City	Days with over 150 UG/m³ 1980-87	Emissions of traditional air pollutants (kgs per 1,000 people) 1980	Municipal waste per capita Kilograms 1985-89	Municipal waste per capita Change since 1975 (%) 1985-89	Industrial waste per unit of GDP (tons per million US$) 1985-89	Waste paper recycled (as % of paper consumption) 1965	Waste paper recycled 1988	Spent nuclear fuel inventories (kg of heavy metal per 1,000 ha) 1988	Population served by waste water treatment plants (%) 1980-87	Hazardous and special waste generation (metric tons per km²) 1980-87
1	Japan	Tokyo	0	..	394	15.3	235	37	48	149	39	1.8
2	Canada	Montreal	10	78	632	20.6	155	15	21	12	62	0.4
3	Norway	..	..	26	475	11.9	35	20	..	(.)	43	0.4
4	Switzerland	..	..	17	427	44.0	..	33	61	176	85	3.0
5	Sweden	..	..	33	317	..	37	21	48	46	100	1.2
6	USA	New York	8	64	864	33.3	186	..	30	19	74	28.9
7	Australia	Sydney	2	40	681	..	146	16	30	(.)	..	(.)
8	France	..	..	20	304	33.6	89	27	33	231	50	3.6
9	Netherlands	Amsterdam	1	19	467	0.7	50	34	54	59	90	44.2
10	United Kingdom	Glasgow	14	37	353	8.9	97	29	30	1,279	84	16.1
11	Iceland	..	..	..	..	..	..	..	..	..	..	..
12	Germany	Frankfurt	20	28	331	0.1	95	27	41	135	87	20.5
13	Denmark	Copenhagen	0	28	469	..	41	13	31	(.)	98	3.0
14	Finland	Helsinki	2	34	608	..	221	..	34	13	74	0.4
15	Austria	..	..	21	228	..	211	25	49	(.)	67	2.4
16	Belgium	Brussels	12	21	313	..	104	..	36	85	23	27.9
17	New Zealand	Christchurch	0	24	662	..	15	..	18	..	88	0.2
18	Luxembourg	..	..	..	..	..	..	..	..	..	83	1.5
19	Israel	Tel Aviv	3	..	..	..	..	..	21	(.)	..	1.5
21	Ireland	Dublin	1	..	311	..	87	..	..	..	11	0.3
22	Italy	Milan	29	15	301	17.0	94	17	27	48	30	6.8
23	Spain	Madrid	35	27	322	49.8	27	28	37	56	29	3.4
25	Greece	Athens	9	17	314	21.3	123	..	..	(.)	1	..
26	Czechoslovakia	..	..	..	..	..	..	..	49	..	..	..
28	Hungary	..	..	..	..	..	..	..	29	..	..	76.7
39	Malta	..	..	..	..	..	..	..	..	..	..	..
40	Bulgaria	..	..	..	..	..	..	..	..	756	..	..
41	Portugal	..	..	12	231	..	292	..	41	(.)	13	11.4
48	Poland	Warsaw	10	..	..	..	..	..	..	(.)	..	..
77	Romania	..	..	..	..	..	..	..	..	(.)	..	..
78	Albania	..	..	..	..	..	..	..	..	..	..	..
Aggregates												
	Industrial	..	..	..	..	..	..	..	..	..	..	..
	Developing	..	..	..	..	..	..	..	..	..	..	..
	World	..	..	..	..	..	..	..	..	..	..	..
	OECD	..	..	42	529	..	152	27	35	30	60	9.7
	Eastern Europe incl. former USSR	..	..	..	..	..	..	..	..	..	..	..
	European Community	..	..	25	328	..	87	26	35	254	57	8.7
	Nordic	..	..	31	443	..	38	18	40	22	83	0.8
	Southern Europe	..	..	19	303	..	82	21	32	34	26	..
	Non-Europe	..	..	63	703	..	197	32	34	13	63	10.1
	North America	..	..	65	841	..	183	15	29	16	73	14.6

Other countries

HDI rank												
29	Lithuania	..	..	..	..	..	..	..	..	..	..	..
34	Estonia	..	..	..	..	..	..	..	..	..	..	..
35	Latvia	..	..	..	..	..	..	..	..	..	..	..
37	Russian Federation	..	..	..	..	..	..	..	..	..	..	..
38	Belarus	..	..	..	..	..	..	..	..	..	..	..
45	Ukraine	..	..	..	..	..	..	..	..	..	..	..
47	Armenia	..	..	..	..	..	..	..	..	..	..	..
49	Georgia	..	..	..	..	..	..	..	..	..	..	..
54	Kazakhstan	..	..	..	..	..	..	..	..	..	..	..
62	Azerbaijan	..	..	..	..	..	..	..	..	..	..	..
64	Moldova, Rep. of	..	..	..	..	..	..	..	..	..	..	..
66	Turkmenistan	..	..	..	..	..	..	..	..	..	..	..
80	Uzbekistan	..	..	..	..	..	..	..	..	..	..	..
83	Kyrgyzstan	..	..	..	..	..	..	..	..	..	..	..
88	Tajikistan	..	..	..	..	..	..	..	..	..	..	..

49 National income accounts

HDI rank	Total GDP (US$ billions) 1990	Agricultural production (as % of GDP) 1990	Industrial production (as % of GDP) 1990	Services (as % of GDP) 1990	Consumption Private (as % of GDP) 1990	Consumption Government (as % of GDP) 1990	Gross domestic investment (as % of GDP) 1990	Gross domestic savings (as % of GDP) 1990	Tax revenue (as % of GNP) 1990	Central government expenditure (as % of GNP) 1990	Exports (as % of GDP) 1990	Imports (as % of GDP) 1990
1 Japan	2,943	3	42	55	57	9	33	34	13	17	9	7
2 Canada	570	..	..	..	59	20	21	21	19	23	23	21
3 Norway	106	..	..	..	50	21	21	29	36	46	35	27
4 Switzerland	225	..	..	..	57	13	29	30	..	..	29	32
5 Sweden	228	3	35	62	52	27	21	21	39	42	28	27
6 USA	5,392	..	..	..	67	18	16	15	18	24	7	9
7 Australia	296	4	31	65	61	18	21	21	25	26	12	14
8 France	1,191	4	29	67	60	18	22	22	38	43	19	21
9 Netherlands	279	4	31	65	59	15	21	26	43	53	51	49
10 United Kingdom	975	..	..	..	63	20	19	17	32	35	20	24
11 Iceland	..	..	..	..	..	..	..	..	..	..	..	..
12 Germany	1,488	2	39	59	54	18	22	28	27	29	28	24
13 Denmark	131	5	28	67	52	25	17	23	34	41	31	28
14 Finland	137	6	36	58	21	27	26	28	31	21	21	20
15 Austria	157	3	37	60	55	18	25	27	32	39	28	34
16 Belgium	192	2	31	67	62	14	21	24	42	49	76	77
17 New Zealand	43	9	27	64	63	17	22	21	39	47	21	22
18 Luxembourg	..	..	..	..	..	..	..	..	..	..	..	..
19 Israel	53	..	..	..	59	29	18	12	34	51	24	30
21 Ireland	43	..	..	..	55	16	21	29	44	55	71	62
22 Italy	1,091	4	33	63	62	17	21	21	38	49	17	18
23 Spain	491	..	..	..	62	15	26	22	28	34	13	20
25 Greece	58	17	27	56	71	21	19	8	..	..	13	33
26 Czechoslovakia	44	8	56	36	51	21	30	28	45	61	..	..
28 Hungary	33	12	32	56	62	11	23	27	47	55	..	..
39 Malta	..	..	..	..	..	..	..	..	..	..	..	..
40 Bulgaria	20	18	51	31	54	18	29	28	56	77	..	..
41 Portugal	57	..	..	..	66	13	32	21	34	43	32	50
48 Poland	64	14	36	50	54	7	31	39	37	40	..	..
77 Romania	35	18	48	34	68	5	34	27	31	34	..	..
78 Albania	..	..	..	..	..	..	..	..	..	..	..	..
Aggregates												
Industrial	16,200T	4	37	59	..	..	..	..	24	..	..	..
Developing	3,000T	17	36	47	63	12	26	26	15	..	19	21
World	19,200T	7	37	56	..	..	..	..	23	..	..	..
OECD	16,00T	3	37	60	61	17	22	22	23	28	16	16
Eastern Europe incl. former USSR	..	13	44	43	57	12	30	31	..	..	..	..
European Community	6,000T	3	34	63	59	18	22	23	34	39	25	26
Nordic	460T	4	32	64	52	25	20	23	35	40	30	26
Southern Europe	1,700T	5	33	62	62	16	23	21	35	44	17	20
Non-Europe	9,300T	3	41	56	63	15	22	22	17	22	9	10
North America	5,960T	..	..	..	66	18	16	16	18	24	8	11

Other countries

HDI rank	Total GDP (US$ billions) 1990	Agricultural production (as % of GDP) 1990	Industrial production (as % of GDP) 1990	Services (as % of GDP) 1990	Consumption Private (as % of GDP) 1990	Consumption Government (as % of GDP) 1990	Gross domestic investment (as % of GDP) 1990	Gross domestic savings (as % of GDP) 1990	Tax revenue (as % of GNP) 1990	Central government expenditure (as % of GNP) 1990	Exports (as % of GDP) 1990	Imports (as % of GDP) 1990
29 Lithuania	..	28	32	42	63	20	30	18	..	48	..	..
34 Estonia	..	16	40	44	65	13	30	22	..	33	..	..
35 Latvia	..	18	43	39	57	11	33	33	..	43	..	..
37 Russian Federation	..	16	36	48	47	22	33	31	..	47	..	..
38 Belarus	..	..	..	..	..	..	34	..	..	34	..	..
45 Ukraine	..	..	..	..	..	..	..	..	..	38	..	..
47 Armenia	..	..	..	..	..	..	..	..	..	36	..	..
49 Georgia	..	..	..	..	..	..	..	..	..	32	..	..
54 Kazakhstan	..	..	..	..	54	9	26	..	..	37	..	..
62 Azerbaijan	..	..	..	..	..	..	15	..	..	32	..	..
64 Moldova, Rep. of	..	..	..	..	..	..	..	..	..	35	..	..
66 Turkmenistan	..	..	..	..	..	..	..	..	..	42	..	..
80 Uzbekistan	..	..	..	..	..	..	..	..	..	46	..	..
83 Kyrgyzstan	..	34	28	38	67	17	34	..	..	38	..	..
88 Tajikistan	..	..	..	..	..	..	..	..	..	..	..	..

Note: Data for developing countries for this subject area are in table 26.

HDI rank	Total GNP (US$ billions) 1990	Total GNP (% annual real growth rate) 1980-90	GNP per capita annual growth rate (%) 1965-80	GNP per capita annual growth rate (%) 1980-90	Average annual rate of inflation (%) 1980-90	Average annual rate of inflation (%) 1991	Exports as % of GDP (% annual growth rate) 1980-90	Tax revenue as % of GNP (% annual growth rate) 1972-90	Direct taxes as % of total taxes 1972	Direct taxes as % of total taxes 1990	Overall budget surplus/deficit (as % of GNP) 1972	Overall budget surplus/deficit (as % of GNP) 1990
1 Japan	3,141	4.1	5.1	3.5	1.5	1.9	-3.1	1.4	66	75	-1.9	-2.9
2 Canada	543	3.3	3.3	2.4	4.4	2.7	-1.0	-0.3	61	59	-1.3	-2.9
3 Norway	98	3.1	3.6	2.7	5.5	1.9	0.7	2.5	24	22	-1.5	0.7
4 Switzerland	219	2.3	1.5	1.7	3.7	5.2	-0.1	..	15	..	0.9	..
5 Sweden	202	2.1	2.0	1.8	7.4	7.0	1.2	2.0	30	21	-1.2	3.2
6 USA	5,446	3.2	1.8	2.2	3.7	3.6	-2.1	0.8	63	56	-1.5	-4.0
7 Australia	291	3.2	2.2	1.7	7.4	2.1	-1.8	1.4	67	72	-0.2	1.9
8 France	1,100	2.2	3.7	1.7	6.1	3.0	1.1	1.3	18	19	0.7	-2.2
9 Netherlands	259	1.9	2.7	1.4	1.9	2.7	1.4	0.7	34	34	(.)	-4.9
10 United Kingdom	924	2.7	2.0	2.5	5.8	6.9	-0.9	0.4	44	45	-2.7	0.8
11 Iceland	5	2.4	..	1.2	..	8.0	..	..	..	..	..	..
12 Germany	1,411	2.2	3.0	2.2	2.7	4.4	1.8	0.8	21	17	0.7	-1.3
13 Denmark	114	2.1	2.2	2.1	5.6	2.1	2.1	1.1	43	44	2.7	-0.4
14 Finland	130	3.6	3.6	3.1	6.8	5.2	-3.1	1.1	32	33	1.2	0.1
15 Austria	147	2.1	4.0	2.0	3.6	3.8	2.3	1.1	22	21	..	-4.4
16 Belgium	155	1.4	3.6	1.2	4.4	3.0	3.3	1.1	32	36	-4.4	-6.4
17 New Zealand	43	1.4	1.7	0.6	10.5	4.4	-1.1	3.0	68	62	-3.9	4.3
18 Luxembourg	11	4.3	..	3.9	..	2.1	..	..	..	..	..	..
19 Israel	51	3.2	3.7	1.5	101.4	..	-3.6	1.8	44	43	-15.7	-4.3
21 Ireland	33	1.4	2.8	1.1	6.5	-1.3	4.1	2.2	32	41	-5.5	-5.3
22 Italy	971	2.4	3.2	2.2	9.9	7.1	-1.2	2.2	18	38	-8.7	-10.4
23 Spain	429	3.1	4.1	2.7	9.2	6.9	2.1	2.2	18	30	-0.5	-3.6
25 Greece	60	1.2	4.8	0.8	18.0	19.3	-0.7	..	13	..	-1.7	..
26 Czechoslovakia	49	1.5	..	1.3	1.9	41.3	..	..	..	26	..	-7.1
28 Hungary	30	1.4	5.1	1.5	9.0	28.1	..	..	..	21	..	0.8
39 Malta	2	3.1	..	3.6	..	..	..	..	..	..	..	..
40 Bulgaria	20	2.5	..	2.3	2.3	295.6	..	..	..	51	..	-1.5
41 Portugal	51	3.0	4.6	2.4	18.2	14.0	..	..	..	26	..	-5.0
48 Poland	64	1.8	..	1.2	54.3	64.9	..	..	..	32	..	-2.4
77 Romania	38	1.5	..	1.1	1.8	180.6	..	..	..	21	..	0.9
78 Albania	..	..	..	..	..	35.5	4.4	..	..	..	..	..
Aggregates												
Industrial	16,820T	..	2.5	2.2	..	..	-0.2	1.3	..	..	-1.7	-2.3
Developing	2,950T	..	2.9	2.5	..	39.9	0.1	2.5	35	36	-2.6	-4.9
World	19,770T	..	2.4	2.3	..	..	(.)	1.5	..	..	-1.8	-2.6
OECD	15,780T	3.0	2.9	2.4	4.8	4.3	-0.9	1.1	42	47	-1.7	-3.2
Eastern Europe incl. former USSR	..	..	..	..	..	99.1	..	..	..	..	..	9.3
European Community	5,520T	2.3	3.1	2.1	6.7	5.8	0.7	1.3	25	30	-2.1	-3.4
Nordic	550T	2.6	2.7	2.3	6.5	4.6	0.4	1.7	32	29	0.2	1.3
Southern Europe	1,550T	2.6	4.0	2.3	11.1	9.4	0.9	2.2	18	34	..	..
Non-Europe	9,510T	3.5	2.9	2.6	4.4	3.0	-2.3	1.0	64	62	-1.6	-3.3
North America	5,990T	3.2	1.9	2.2	3.8	3.5	-2.0	0.7	63	56	-1.5	-3.9

Other countries

HDI rank	Total GNP (US$ billions) 1990	Total GNP 1980-90	1965-80	1980-90	1980-90	1991	Exports	Tax revenue	1972	1990	1972	1990
29 Lithuania	10	..	..	..	..	175.9	..	..	..	..	..	-2.8
34 Estonia	6	..	..	..	..	118.9	..	..	..	..	..	2.9
35 Latvia	9	..	..	..	..	103.0	..	..	..	..	..	1.6
37 Russian Federation	480	..	..	..	..	104.7	..	..	..	..	..	..
38 Belarus	32	..	..	..	..	92.5	..	..	..	..	..	3.5
45 Ukraine	121	..	..	..	..	79.3	..	..	..	..	..	-0.6
47 Armenia	7	..	..	..	..	100.3	..	..	..	..	..	7.1
49 Georgia	9	..	..	..	..	116.1	..	..	..	..	..	1.3
54 Kazakhstan	42	..	..	..	..	83.3	..	..	..	..	..	2.8
62 Azerbaijan	12	..	..	..	..	50.0	..	..	..	..	..	1.2
64 Moldova, Rep. of	10	..	..	..	..	..	..	..	..	..	..	0.5
66 Turkmenistan	6	..	..	..	..	..	..	..	..	..	..	1.7
80 Uzbekistan	28	..	..	..	..	..	..	..	..	..	..	-0.9
83 Kyrgyzstan	7	..	..	..	..	93.6	..	..	..	..	..	0.4
88 Tajikistan	6	..	..	..	..	..	..	..	..	..	..	..

Note: Data for developing countries for this subject area are in table 27.

	Sub-Saharan Africa	Arab States	South Asia	South Asia excl. India	East Asia	East Asia excl. China	South-East Asia	Latin America and the Caribbean	Latin America and the Caribbean excl. Mexico and Brazil	Least developed countries	All developing countries	Industrial countries	World
Table 2: Profile of human development													
Life expectancy	51.8	62.1	58.4	56.7	70.2	70.5	62.6	67.4	67.7	51.0	62.8	74.5	64.7
Access to health services	60	89	..	78	..	100	59	86	83	62	72	..	..
Access to safe water	41	82	71	64	72	86	53	81	70	47	68	..	..
Access to sanitation	26	55	17	28	97	99	52	72	67	22	55	..	..
Calorie supply (% of req.)	93	122	100	99	112	120	113	114	107	90	107	..	..
Adult literacy rate	47	51	42	40	74	..	84	85	87	45	65	..	..
Prim. and sec. enrolment	46	71	62	46	88	..	76	86	84	42	73	..	..
Newspaper circulation	11	41	..	14	..	..	38	94	110	6	50	304	130
Televisions	23	107	29	22	38	151	60	164	139	9	55	545	148
GNP per capita	490	1,730	450	700	610	6,180	900	2,130	1,540	240	810	14,580	4,010
Real GDP per capita	1,200	3,380	1,250	1,690	2,220	..	2,590	4,490	3,630	740	2,170	14,440	4,890
Table 3: Profile of human deprivation (in millions unless otherwise stated)													
No health services	..	..	..	..	..	..	..	..	..	200T	1,200T	..	..
No safe water	..	..	..	..	..	..	..	..	..	250T	1,300T	..	..
No sanitation	..	..	..	..	..	..	..	..	..	350T	2,000T	..	..
Dying before five (thousands)	3,600T	900T	5,300T	..	950T	..	1,100T	750T	..	420T	12,600T	300T	12,900T
Malnourished children	..	..	..	..	..	..	..	..	..	40T	200T	..	..
Out-of-school children	..	..	..	..	..	..	..	..	..	100T	330T	..	..
Illiterate adults	140T	60T	400T	120T	..	..	..	40T	..	170T	920T	..	..
Illiterate females	..	..	..	..	..	..	..	..	..	150T	600T	..	..
Total poor	..	..	..	..	..	..	..	..	..	300T	1,300T	..	..
Rural poor	..	..	..	..	..	..	..	..	..	250T	1,000T	..	..
Table 4: Trends in human development													
Life expectancy													
1960	40.0	46.7	43.8	43.1	47.5	54.7	45.3	56.0	56.6	39.0	46.2	69.0	53.4
1990	51.8	62.1	58.4	56.7	70.2	70.5	62.6	67.4	67.7	51.0	62.8	74.5	64.7
Infant mortality													
1960	165	165	164	161	146	83	126	105	103	170	149	35	128
1991	103	67	93	97	28	25	58	49	48	114	71	14	64
Access to safe water													
1975-80	25	71	30	27	70	70	15	60	57	21	36	..	..
1988-90	41	82	71	64	72	86	53	81	70	47	68	..	..
Calorie supply (% of req.)													
1965	92	88	88	86	87	97	87	102	100	88	90	..	..
1988-90	93	122	100	99	112	120	113	114	107	90	107	..	..
Adult literacy													
1970	28	30	33	26	..	..	67	76	81	29	46	..	..
1990	47	51	42	40	74	..	84	85	87	45	65	..	..
Prim. and sec. enrolment													
1970	26	46	45	35	66	76	59	69	73	29	55	..	..
1987-90	46	71	62	46	88	..	76	86	84	42	73	..	..
Real GDP per capita													
1960	..	1,310	700	940	730	..	1,000	2,140	2,410	580	950	..	..
1990	..	3,380	1,250	1,690	2,220	..	2,590	4,490	3,630	740	2,170	..	..
Table 5: Human capital formation													
Adult literacy rate													
total	47	51	42	40	74	..	84	85	87	45	65	..	..
male	58	63	55	52	85	..	89	87	89	56	75	..	..
female	36	39	29	27	63	..	79	83	85	33	55	..	..
Literacy at age 15-19	..	72	63	55	93	100	95	94	95	59	82	..	..
Mean years of schooling													
total	1.6	2.8	2.4	2.4	5.0	7.8	4.4	5.2	6.4	1.6	3.7	10.0	5.0
male	2.2	3.9	3.5	3.4	6.2	9.6	5.2	5.3	6.5	2.3	4.6	10.4	5.8
female	1.0	1.7	1.3	1.5	3.7	6.0	3.6	5.1	6.2	0.9	2.7	9.6	4.3
Scientists and technicians	..	13.7	3.6	3.3	10.0	44.6	..	29.6	29.7	..	8.9	81.0	22.2
R & D scientists	..	..	2.3	1.4	..	..	..	5.3	4.8	..	3.2	40.5	12.2
Tertiary graduates	0.2	2.3	0.7	..	..	..	2.6	2.5	2.4	0.3	1.2	9.4	3.7
Science graduates	23	24	37	..	..	..	24	25	28	18	29	35	30
Table 6: Narrowing South-North gaps (expressed as % of average North)													
Life expectancy													
1960	58	68	63	62	69	79	66	81	82	57	67	100	..
1990	70	83	78	76	94	95	84	90	91	68	84	100	..
Under-five mortality													
1960	75	76	76	77	89	93	78	88	88	75	80	100	..
1990	84	92	87	86	98	98	94	95	95	83	90	100	..
Calorie supply													
1965	74	71	71	69	70	78	70	82	81	71	72	100	..
1988-90	70	91	75	74	84	89	84	85	80	67	80	100	..
Adult literacy													
1970	28	30	33	26	..	..	67	76	81	29	41	100	..
1990	47	52	42	40	75	..	85	86	88	45	66	100	..
Access to safe water													
1975	25	71	30	27	70	70	15	60	57	21	36	100	..
1988-90	41	82	71	64	72	86	53	81	70	47	68	100	..

	Sub-Saharan Africa	Arab States	South Asia	South Asia excl. India	East Asia	East Asia excl. China	South-East Asia	Latin America and the Caribbean	Latin America and the Caribbean excl. Mexico and Brazil	Least developed countries	All developing countries	Industrial countries	World
Table 7: Widening South-North human gaps (expressed as % of average North)													
Real GDP per capita													
1960	14	21	12	16	15	17	13	37	46	9	17	100	..
1990	8	23	9	12	15	..	18	31	25	5	15	100	..
Mean years of schooling													
1980	17	21	25	25	54	70	39	48	57	17	38	100	..
1990	16	28	24	24	50	78	44	52	64	16	37	100	..
Overall enrolment													
1980	6	37	27	15	7	57	21	52	57	8	20	100	..
1987-90	5	33	16	9	9	91	25	46	60	7	18	100	..
Fertility													
1965	46	43	48	45	48	62	51	55	60	47	50	100	..
1991	29	36	43	34	86	95	54	59	56	31	49	100	..
Telephones													
1980	10	21	7	13	5	34	11	32	47	7	12	100	..
1986-88	3	7	1	3	4	54	5	14	12	1	5	100	..
Table 8: Status of women													
Life expectancy	53.6	63.6	58.6	56.7	71.9	73.5	64.5	70.2	70.4	52.0	64.2	77.9	67.3
Maternal mortality rate	690	320	570	600	130	110	340	210	210	740	420	26	370
Age at first marriage	19.1	21.2	18.7	18.8	22.5	24.2	21.3	21.9	21.9	18.9	20.7	23.5	21.2
Literacy at age 15-24	37	49	37	31	82	..	87	89	91	36	65	99	69
Primary enrolment	42	72	..	63	100	100	96	..	..	45	86		
Secondary enrolment	14	44	29	21	43	85	43	57	59	12	36	..	..
Tertiary enrolment	1.5	9.7	3.6	1.9	2.1	25.6	5.8	16.3	23.1	1.2	4.9	..	..
Tertiary sciences	12	26	21	..		15	..	..	..	14	20	22	21
Admin. and managerial staff	..	..	2	..	10	4	13	18	18	..	8	24	12
Labour force	34	13	22	13	43	38	41	32	30	29	33	42	34
Parliament	..	4	6	5	21	8	11	9	9	9	12	9	11
Table 9: Female-male gaps (female expressed as % of male)													
Life expectancy	107	105	100	100	105	109	106	109	108	104	104	110	106
Population	102	97	93	94	94	100	101	100	100	100	96	106	99
Literacy													
1970	42	36	41	36	85	..	72	91	91	38	54	..	..
1990	64	59	54	53	74	..	89	96	96	58	72	..	..
Mean years of schooling	46	57	36	44	60	62	69	96	96	43	58	99	72
Primary enrolment													
1960	52	57	46	36	90	..	77	95	94	44	61	..	..
1988-90	85	81	90	74	100	100	96	99	100	81	94	..	..
Secondary enrolment	64	71	59	54	79	99	91	99	100	58	74	..	..
Tertiary enrolment	32	60	36	36	50	54	43	89	85	28	51	..	..
Labour force	55	16	29	17	75	63	70	48	44	48	52	77	56
Table 10: Rural-urban gaps													
Rural population (% total)	69	47	73	72	64	30	70	28	31	80	63	27	55
Urban access to health services	87	100	..	..	..	..	..	..	..	85	90	..	..
Rural access to health services	..	82	..	54	..	..	..	..	..	..	..	..	..
Urban access to safe water	79	97	79	79	88	93	73	91	85	61	85	..	..
Rural access to safe water	28	67	69	60	68	69	45	56	41	45	60	..	..
Urban access to sanitation	47	90	47	67	100	99	57	90	86	45	76	..	..
Rural access to sanitation	18	28	6	11	82	..	55	34	33	15	40	..	..
Rural-urban disparity													
health	..	82	..	..	..	..	..	..	..	..	..	..	..
water	35	69	87	76	77	70	62	62	48	74	71	..	..
sanitation	38	29	13	16	82	..	96	38	38	33	77	..	..
child nutrition	67	..	..	..	..	..	..	..	..	80	82	..	..
Table 11: Child survival and development													
Women with prenatal care	66	51	61	46	..	98	62	66	63	51	63	..	..
Births attended	38	52	63	43	94	97	65	63	64	31	66	..	..
Low-birth-weight babies	13	11	29	27	6	4	12	10	8	18	16	..	..
Infant mortality rate	103	67	93	97	28	25	58	49	48	114	71	14	64
Breast-feeding at one year	84	66	..	74	..	..	70	34	40	82	68	..	..
One-year-olds immunized	61	84	86	75	97	87	85	79	78	60	83	..	..
Underweight children	31	..	58	48	..	..	37	12	14	42	36	..	..
Wasted children	13	..	23	..	..	..	..	4	4	15	14	..	..
Stunted children	44	..	63	60	..	..	43	23	30	50	48	..	..
Under-five mortality rate	165	95	136	..	38	..	86	63	..	..	104	16	93

	Sub-Saharan Africa	Arab States	South Asia	South Asia excl. India	East Asia	East Asia excl. China	South-East Asia	Latin America and the Caribbean	Latin America and the Caribbean excl. Mexico and Brazil	Least developed countries	All developing countries	Industrial countries	World
Table 12: Health profile													
Access to health services	60	89	..	78	..	100	..	86	83	62	72	..	..
Access to safe water	41	82	71	64	72	86	53	81	70	47	68	..	..
Access to sanitation	26	55	17	28	97	99	52	72	67	22	55	..	..
People per doctor	24,380	2,850	3,570	6,120	1,010	900	6,340	1,220	1,300	22,590	5,080	380	4,090
People per nurse	2,400	900	2,900	5,830	1,370	530	1,230	990	860	4,620	1,870	150	1,510
Nurses per doctor	9.9	3.5	1.5	1.5	0.8	..	5.4	1.4	1.9	6.9	2.7	3.1	2.8
Maternal mortality rate	690	320	570	600	130	110	340	210	210	740	420	26	370
Health expenditure													
1960	0.7	0.9	0.5	..	..	..	..	1.4	1.5	0.7	1.0	4.2	..
1988-90	3.1	5.6	3.2	3.1	4.2	6.4	3.7	3.5	3.1	2.4	3.7	..	..
Table 13: Food security													
Food production per capita	95	109	113	99	132	..	114	105	98	93	115	..	..
Agricultural production	22	11	28	25	20	9	19	10	12	37	17	..	..
Calorie supply per capita	2,250	2,970	2,220	2,170	2,650	2,820	2,500	2,690	2,510	2,130	2,490	..	..
Calorie supply as % of req.	93	122	100	99	112	120	113	114	107	90	107	..	..
Food import dependency													
1969/71	6.5	29.9	4.3	7.9	3.2	..	10.0	..	..	..	6.7	..	..
1988/90	10.2	49.5	6.1	16.7	7.0	..	9.9	18.7	11.3	11.3	10.5	..	..
Cereal imports	7,850T	35,050T	11,820T	11,370T	23,620T	9,900T	8,580T	18,900T	7,870T	8,770T	109,480T	..	..
Food aid	500T	140T	250T	200T	22T	..	34T	110T	90T	600T	1,100T	..	..
Table 14: Education flows													
Primary intake, total	67	81	..	85	..	..	98	100	100	65	91	..	..
Primary intake, female	59	74	..	80	..	..	..	..	100	54	76	..	..
Primary enrolment	46	78	..	69	100	99	..	86	78	49	83	..	..
Primary repeaters	18	10	5	8	..	..	..	12	8	15	8	..	..
Primary completers	62	81	..	61	81	91	72	50	61	53	69	..	..
Transition to second level	44	68	..	..	..	..	..	78	..	47	63	..	..
Primary entrants to secondary	21	53	..	68	51	..	..	..	52	21	48	..	..
Secondary enrolment	17	51	38	27	49	87	45	48	52	16	40	..	..
Secondary repeaters	17	18	..	11	..	..	..	5	6	15	7	..	..
Tertiary enrolment	2	12	6	4	3	36	12	17	22	2	7	45	16
Table 15: Education imbalances													
Prim. pupil-teacher ratio	41	26	45	44	22	30	27	28	29	45	34	..	..
Sec. technical enrolment	7.5	15.0	..	..	8.5	15.3	..	16.5	19.2	4.7	9.8	..	..
Tertiary science enrolment	29	36	33	36	25	32	..	34	31	31	32	39	36
Tertiary students abroad	14.2	6.2	2.1	7.9	3.2	3.2	2.3	1.0	1.2	7.9	2.9	..	..
Education expenditure													
1960, % of GNP	2.4	3.5	2.1	..	..	..	..	2.1	2.5	1.3	2.2	..	..
1988-90, % of GNP	3.4	6.1	3.4	3.7	2.8	3.5	2.9	3.6	2.9	2.8	3.4	..	..
% total public exp.	13.9	17.1	9.0	10.2	12.8	21.6	9.1	16.4	15.5	11.5	11.9	..	..
Prim./sec. educ. expenditure	67.6	67.5	72.0	73.6	70.3	76.5	65.8	56.5	52.5	73.2	65.4	..	..
Higher educ. expenditure	19.6	21.0	15.8	14.2	15.9	12.2	19.0	20.6	28.0	18.2	18.4	..	..
Table 16: Communication profile													
Radios	150	260	90	100	210	690	150	340	350	100	180	1,130	360
Televisions	23	107	29	22	38	151	60	164	139	9	55	545	148
Newspaper circulation	11	41	14	14	..	..	38	94	110	6	50	304	130
Telephones	18	43	8	18	22	..	29	84	69	4	28	590	130
Passenger cars	15	22	2	3	1	27	12	73	51	2	13	390	87
Book titles	3.1	5.3	2.6	6.1	9.6	..	4.1	6.4	8.2	2.3	5.9	61.0	12.0
Cinema attendances	0.3	1.1	6.1	1.1	4.3	4.3	6.2	2.2	0.7	..	..	3.0	..
People per post office	40,620	17,290	6,310	10,600	20,660	..	13,640	12,090	12,880	39,390	16,330	4,200	14,170
Table 17: Employment													
Labour force	38.6	28.2	36.7	30.1	58.4	43.8	44.1	38.5	38.7	38.2	43.7	49.1	44.9
Women in labour force	33.9	13.3	22.0	13.3	42.9	38.0	40.8	31.8	29.6	29.4	32.6	42.4	34.3
Labour force in agriculture													
1965	79.0	63.0	72.3	..	..	..	..	44.0	41.6	83.2	72.0	22.2	56.5
1989-91	66.4	36.0	59.7	50.2	71.5	23.6	57.8	24.1	21.8	72.4	60.5	7.6	48.2
Labour force in industry													
1965	8.1	13.9	12.1	..	..	..	..	20.9	21.2	5.8	11.3	36.4	19.0
1989-91	9.4	18.3	12.3	17.0	14.4	32.6	11.3	26.2	25.5	7.7	14.4	25.7	17.0
Labour force in services													
1965	12.9	23.1	15.6	..	..	..	..	35.1	37.2	11.0	16.7	41.4	24.5
1989-91	24.2	45.7	28.0	32.8	14.1	43.8	30.9	49.7	52.7	19.9	25.1	66.7	34.8
Earnings growth rate													
1970-80	-1.5	..	..	..	..	..	..	2.0	0.6	..	1.3	2.2	1.6
1980-89	..	..	3.1	..	4.3	..	5.9	..	..	..	4.0	1.4	3.5

	Sub-Saharan Africa	Arab States	South Asia	South Asia excl. India	East Asia	East Asia excl. China	South-East Asia	Latin America and the Caribbean	Latin America and the Caribbean excl. Mexico and Brazil	Least developed countries	All developing countries	Industrial countries	World
Table 18: Wealth, poverty and social investment													
Real GDP per capita	1,200	3,380	1,250	1,690	2,220	..	2,590	4,490	3,630	740	2,170	14,440	4,890
GNP per capita	490	1,730	450	700	610	6,180	900	2,130	1,540	240	810	14,580	4,010
Income share: lowest 40%	..	..	..	..	..	..	..	..	..	..	..	..	..
Highest 20%/lowest 20%	..	..	..	..	..	..	..	..	..	..	..	..	..
Gini coefficient	..	..	..	..	..	..	..	..	..	..	..	..	..
People below poverty line													
total	..	..	..	..	..	..	..	..	..	70	32	..	..
urban	..	..	..	..	..	..	..	..	..	62	25	..	..
rural	..	..	..	..	..	..	..	..	..	72	36	..	..
Education expenditure	3.4	6.1	3.4	3.7	2.8	3.5	2.9	3.6	2.9	2.8	3.4	..	..
Health expenditure	3.1	5.6	3.2	3.1	4.2	6.4	3.7	3.5	3.1	2.4	3.7	..	..
Social security benefits	..	..	..	..	..	..	..	..	..	..	..	..	..
Table 19: Aid flows													
ODA received	15,100T	9,100T	6,720T	5,060T	2,290T	120T	5,340T	4,860T	4,480T	14,810T	45,100T	..	..
ODA as % of GNP	10.0	4.3	1.2	2.1	0.3	0.3	1.8	0.4	1.3	15.1	1.5	..	..
ODA per capita	31	42	6	14	2	2	12	11	22	29	11	..	..
ODA per poor person	..	..	..	..	..	..	..	..	..	..	..	..	..
Social allocation ratio	18.0	16.9	17.6	19.9	16.3	46.2	17.5	17.1	16.5	18.9	16.9	..	..
Social priority ratio	43.3	61.8	49.4	50.2	18.6	12.0	35.6	38.1	40.1	47.8	44.9	..	..
Human expenditure ratio	0.779	0.449	0.104	0.210	0.009	0.017	0.112	0.026	0.086	1.364	0.114	..	..
Social priority aid	7.8	10.4	8.7	10.0	3.0	5.5	6.2	6.5	6.6	9.0	7.6	..	..
Table 20: Resource flow imbalances													
Total debt	107	90	25	24	14	14	54	42	65	96	39	..	..
Debt service ratio													
1970	4.7	..	..	..	..	..	..	14.4	11.9	4.5	13.3	..	..
1990	21.3	..	18.2	10.4	10.5	10.7	20.0	25.3	26.5	20.5	20.4	..	..
Workers' remittances	-0.4	..	1.4	4.2	..	..	..	0.8	0.5	2.3	1.1	..	..
Export-import ratio	127	96	85	97	101	80	91	144	186	58	111	94	97
Trade dependency	46	58	21	28	55	83	96	22	33	29	42	..	..
Terms of trade	100	95	90	89	103	102	96	111	110	101	101	100	101
Gross international reserves	1.9	3.5	1.8	1.6	4.5	2.2	4.0	3.9	5.5	2.1	3.7	..	..
Current account balance	-4,100T	9,900T	-14,900T	-5,100T	11,900T	-2,800T	-13,200T	-3,800T	5,700T	-11,500T	-20,900T	..	..
Table 21: Military expenditure and resource use imbalances													
Military exp. as % of GDP													
1960	0.7	4.9	2.8	..	..	..	..	1.8	2.1	2.1	4.2	6.3	6.0
1990	3.8	..	3.6	4.5	3.3	3.3	2.7	1.7	2.7	2.8	3.4	..	..
as % of health/educ. exp.													
1977	86	154	104	146	144	201	94	36	52	89	91	..	..
1990	108	275	115	211	..	..	..	64	95	146	169	..	..
Armed forces													
as % of population	0.2	1.4	0.2	0.4	0.4	2.3	0.6	0.3	0.5	0.3	0.4	0.8	0.5
per teacher	0.9	1.7	5.0	1.0	0.5	2.5	0.8	0.4	0.6	1.1	0.6	1.0	0.7
per doctor	76	26	7	15	6	18	25	4	6	77	18.0	3.4	14.7
Arms imports													
total	1,180T	7,750T	6,400T	2,890T	1,800T	1,640T	1,420T	1,390T	1,080T	2,260T	21,330T	..	..
as % of nat'l imports	2.6	9.0	9.2	4.4	0.7	1.0	0.8	1.4	2.5	3.3	3.1	..	..
Table 22: Growing urbanization													
Urban population, %													
1960	15	30	17	16	20	36	18	49	52	8	22	61	34
1991	31	53	27	28	36	70	30	72	69	20	37	73	45
2000	38	60	33	34	49	76	37	76	73	26	45	75	60
Urban pop. growth rate													
1960-91	5.2	4.6	3.9	1.9	2.0	2.2	1.7	3.7	3.3	5.3	4.0	1.4	2.9
1991-2000	5.3	3.9	4.1	2.0	3.1	0.8	2.1	2.5	2.5	5.8	4.0	0.8	2.8
Pop. in cities over 1 million	29	38	..	..	31	74	..	45	42	35	36	34	35
Pop. in largest city	28	28	12	25	10	50	..	27	36	34	18	..	..
Highest population density	..	..	..	..	..	..	..	..	..	..	..	..	..
Table 23: Demographic profile													
Population													
1960	210T	90T	600T	150T	700T	40T	230T	210T	100T	240T	2,070T	940T	3,010T
1991	520T	220T	1,220T	350T	1,250T	70T	460T	450T	210T	520T	4,160T	1,220T	5,380T
2000	680T	270T	1,470T	450T	1,390T	80T	540T	520T	240T	680T	4,930T	1,290T	6,220T
Population growth rate													
1960-91	2.9	2.9	2.3	2.7	1.8	1.8	2.2	2.5	2.4	2.5	2.3	0.8	1.9
1991-2000	2.8	2.3	2.1	2.8	1.3	1.5	1.8	1.6	1.5	3.0	1.9	0.6	1.6
Ratio of pop. growth rates	129	119	97	119	94	44	92	71	75	126	98	..	..
Population doubling date	2015	2025	2025	2025	2050	2040	2030	2025	2025	2015	2025	..	..
Total fertility rate	6.5	5.3	4.4	5.6	2.2	2.0	3.5	3.2	3.4	6.1	3.8	2.0	3.4
Ratio of fertility growth rates	97	72	71	83	39	35	59	54	62	92	60	65	61
Contraceptive prevalence	15	32	38	23	71	78	47	58	53	16	49	59	52
Population density	245	211	1,876	1,032	1,120	414	941	224	217	285	541	225	409

	Sub-Saharan Africa	Arab States	South Asia	South Asia excl. India	East Asia	East Asia excl. China	South-East Asia	Latin America and the Caribbean	Latin America and the Caribbean excl. Mexico and Brazil	Least developed countries	All developing countries	Industrial countries	World
Table 24: Natural resources balance sheet													
Land area	2,040T	1,260T	670T	340T	1,150T	180T	490T	2,010T	970T	1,540T	7,550T	5,360T	12,910T
Arable land	6	4	34	16	9	3	12	7	6	6	16	13	11
Irrigated land	6	26	35	45	40	10	23	10	14	10	20	7	16
Forest area	29.5	6.0	15.4	9.4	14.0	16.4	55.3	47.3	36.3	28.5	28.7	30.1	29.1
Renewable water resources	7.4	1.0	3.3	6.1	2.5	2.2	13.7	24.1	24.8	11.4	6.8	7.6	7.0
Deforestation	0.5	..	2.1	1.4	..	..	..	1.5	0.9	0.6	1.1	..	..
Production of fuelwood	3.6	3.1	2.5	2.8	1.7	-1.7	2.3	2.4	2.3	3.0	2.3	6.5	3.0
Fresh water withdrawals													
% of water resources	5.0	68.3	19.1	21.8	16.1	17.8	4.9	6.4	7.0	6.4	16.4	21.0	17.3
per capita	120	1,058	756	1,110	477	737	266	510	565	259	523	1,204	645
Table 25: Energy consumption													
Consump. per capita (kg oil equiv.)													
1965	204	348	117	192	182	282	115	537	701	42	204	3,387	936
1990	282	1,202	247	287	651	1,851	284	1,035	1,013	63	517	4,937	1,316
billion kgs.													
1965	49T	39T	318T	268T	139T	9T	126T	76T	9T	9T	709T	2,521T	7,230T
1990	140T	252T	294T	99T	785T	95T	127T	439T	193T	32T	2,084T	4,443T	6,527T
Annual rate of change													
1960-74	9.1	8.6	5.8	9.2	4.1	11.3	7.3	7.6	6.7	9.0	6.2	6.0	6.2
1980-90	2.7	7.2	6.2	6.8	5.7	7.4	4.2	3.1	2.5	4.7	5.1	1.4	4.5
Consump./$100 GDP													
1990	58	80	67	53	118	31	37	45	60	27	68	..	..
(1965=100)	61	53	61	35	63	17	33	36	47	89	50	..	..
Table 26: National income accounts													
Total GDP	240T	280T	440T	180T	660T	300T	310T	970T	320T	86T	3,000T	16,200T	19,200T
Agricultural production	22	11	28	25	20	9	19	10	12	36	17	4	7
Industrial production	35	43	26	21	41	41	37	36	38	22	36	37	37
Services	43	46	46	54	39	50	44	54	50	42	47	59	56
Private consumption	63	64	70	73	55	62	57	66	71	82	63	..	..
Government consumption	16	15	12	22	8	8	10	12	9	13	12	..	..
Gross domestic investment	17	26	22	20	37	35	34	19	15	15	26	..	..
Gross domestic savings	21	21	18	16	40	36	33	21	21	5	26	..	..
Tax revenue	24	15	10	8	..	14	18	14	14	12	15	24	23
Central gov't expenditure	..	..	18	19	..	16	21	26	18	..	..	28	..
Exports	25	23	8	11	22	32	46	13	22	10	19	..	..
Imports	21	28	10	13	29	51	53	10	15	18	21	..	..
Table 27: Trends in economic performance													
Total GNP	230T	170T	510T	220T	710T	300T	310T	910T	300T	84T	2,950T	16,820T	19,770T
Total GNP growth rate	1.8	1.7	4.6	3.6	9.5	9.5	5.7	1.8	0.9	2.8	4.7	..	..
GNP p.c. annual growth rate													
1965-80	1.5	3.0	1.4	1.2	4.2	5.2	3.6	3.8	2.0	0.6	2.9	2.5	2.4
1980-90	-1.1	-1.4	2.0	0.3	3.0	8.1	3.6	-0.3	-1.0	-0.2	2.5	2.2	2.3
Annual rate of inflation													
1980-90	22.3	7.7	8.3	9.3	5.8	5.1	8.3	171.6	128.3	21.6	27.9	..	..
1991	22.6	28.8	11.8	9.4	3.8	10.9	20.4	432.1	194.2	21.7	39.9	..	..
Exports/GDP growth rate	1.4	-0.5	1.0	0.3	-3.0	-8.7	0.6	3.4	4.3	1.2	0.1	-0.2	(.)
Tax revenue/GNP growth rate	..	4.5	2.1	2.0	..	0.9	2.1	..	1.5	..	2.5	1.3	1.5
Direct taxes													
1972	57.3	16.7	22.3	18.0	..	33.2	31.4	38.6	37.1	21.1	34.7	..	..
1990	48.8	25.2	19.4	19.6	..	38.4	42.9	35.1	31.7	27.9	36.4	..	..
Budget surplus/deficit													
1972	-4	-1.7	-3.9	-4.7	..	..	-3.4	-1.5	-2.1	-3.9	-2.6	-1.7	-1.8
1990	-2.5	-3.5	-6.1	-4.5	..	-0.7	0.8	-7.9	-1.9	-0.8	-4.9	-2.3	-2.6

	High human development		Medium human development		Low human development		High-income	Middle-income	Low-income	
	All countries	Developing countries	All countries	Excl. China	All countries	Excl. India			All countries	Excl. China and India
Table 2: Profile of human development										
Life expectancy	74.0	70.6	68.0	65.4	56.5	54.4	76.4	67.2	61.9	54.7
Access to health services	..	94	..	68	..	65	..	79	..	66
Access to safe water	..	79	73	75	62	50	..	82	65	49
Access to sanitation	..	85	84	65	20	27	..	71	50	28
Calorie supply (% of req.)	..	123	114	116	98	96	..	118	103	93
Adult literacy rate	..	91	76	79	49	50	..	79	59	52
Prim. and sec. enrolment	..	88	86	84	58	49	..	83	71	53
Newspaper circulation	285	197	..	55	..	13	319	104	..	17
Televisions	486	184	67	114	28	25	600	161	31	29
GNP per capita	13,480	3,470	940	1,690	360	360	20,570	2,350	360	350
Real GDP per capita	13,500	6,290	2,710	3,660	1,110	1,140	18,170	4,830	1,510	1,320
Table 3: Profile of human deprivation (in millions unless otherwise stated)										
No health services	..	..	..	..	..	..	..	..	..	..
No safe water	..	..	..	..	..	..	..	..	..	..
No sanitation	..	..	..	..	..	..	..	..	..	..
Dying before five (thousands)	..	..	..	..	..	..	..	..	..	..
Malnourished children	..	..	..	..	..	..	..	..	..	..
Out-of-school children	..	..	..	..	..	..	..	..	..	..
Illiterate adults	..	..	..	..	..	..	..	..	..	..
Illiterate females	..	..	..	..	..	..	..	..	..	..
Total poor	..	..	..	..	..	..	..	..	..	..
Rural poor	..	..	..	..	..	..	..	..	..	..
Table 4: Trends in human development										
Life expectancy										
1960	67.3	58.5	48.5	50.4	42.6	41.4	69.6	54.1	44.2	41.0
1990	74.0	70.6	68.0	65.4	56.5	54.4	76.4	67.2	61.9	54.7
Infant mortality										
1960	42	83	139	124	165	166	30	111	158	162
1991	17	31	42	53	96	99	8	46	77	98
Access to safe water										
1975-80	..	68	42	42	30	28	..	48	28	22
1988-90	..	79	73	75	62	50	..	82	65	49
Calorie supply (% of req.)										
1965	..	107	88	92	89	89	..	95	88	89
1988-90	..	123	114	116	98	96	..	118	103	93
Adult literacy										
1970	..	83	60	60	31	28	..	61	31	28
1990	..	91	76	79	49	50	..	79	59	52
Prim. and sec. enrolment										
1970	..	73	64	61	41	34	..	64	51	34
1987-90	..	88	86	84	58	49	..	83	71	53
Real GDP per capita										
1960	5,910	3,140	1,010	1,680	670	740	6,310	1,840	700	740
1990	13,500	6,290	2,710	3,660	1,110	1,140	18,170	4,830	1,510	1,320
Table 5: Human capital formation										
Adult literacy rate										
total	..	91	76	79	49	50	..	77	60	55
male	..	93	84	85	63	64	..	84	71	66
female	..	91	67	74	39	43	..	75	47	44
Literacy at age 15-19	..	97	93	93	66	66	..	91	78	66
Mean years of schooling										
total	9.3	6.6	4.8	4.8	2.3	2.2	10.8	5.5	3.3	2.3
male	9.5	7.1	5.8	5.4	3.3	3.1	10.9	6.1	4.3	3.1
female	9.1	6.1	3.8	4.2	1.3	1.4	10.7	5.0	2.2	1.5
Scientists and technicians	76.3	49.8	10.8	15.2	2.9	1.7	80.6	25.1	5.9	4.1
R & D scientists	33.0	9.4	..	..	2.4	2.1	42.3	..	..	..
Tertiary graduates	9.8	2.9	1.2	2.4	0.6	..	11.4	3.0	0.6	0.6
Science graduates	29	32	31	26	..	20	28	29	31	17
Table 6: Narrowing South-North gaps (expressed as % of average North)										
Life expectancy										
1960	..	85	70	73	62	60	..	78	64	59
1990	..	95	91	88	76	73	..	90	83	73
Under-five mortality										
1960	..	92	84	86	76	77	..	89	79	77
1990	..	98	96	95	86	86	..	94	89	85
Calorie supply										
1965	..	86	71	74	72	72	..	76	71	72
1988	..	92	85	87	73	72	..	88	77	89
Adult literacy										
1970	..	87	63	63	32	29	..	64	33	30
1988-90	..	92	77	80	49	51	..	80	60	53
Access to safe water										
1975	..	68	42	42	30	28	..	48	28	22
1988-90	..	79	73	75	62	50	..	82	65	49

| | High human development | | Medium human development | | Low human development | | | | Low-income | |
	All countries	Developing countries	All countries	Excl. China	All countries	Excl. India	High-income	Middle-income	All countries	Excl. China and India
Table 7: Widening South-North human gaps (expressed as % of average North)										
Real GDP per capita										
1960	..	50	19	24	11	11	..	34	13	10
1990	..	44	18	25	8	8	..	33	10	9
Mean years of schooling										
1980	..	59	49	42	23	22	..	42	36	24
1990	..	66	48	48	22	21	..	55	33	23
Overall enrolment										
1980	..	62	15	33	23	13	..	41	14	8
1987-90	..	66	13	31	15	11	..	40	10	7
Fertility										
1965	..	63	48	54	47	45	..	52	47	46
1991	..	68	66	53	38	33	..	58	50	35
Telephones										
1980	..	48	10	21	8	14	..	27	5	11
1986-88	..	27	5	9	2	3	..	15	2	2
Table 8: Status of women										
Life expectancy	77.6	73.8	69.8	67.5	57.3	55.6	79.7	70.1	63.0	55.9
Maternal mortality rate	45	120	170	220	590	610	23	220	480	630
Age at first marriage	23	22	22	21	19	19	24	22	20	19
Literacy at age 15-24	98	93	82	81	41	42	99	84	60	47
Primary enrolment	..	..	98	..	..	..	..	89	85	62
Secondary enrolment	..	65	44	50	26	20	..	57	33	23
Tertiary enrolment	..	22.7	3.7	10.4	3.6	2.7	..	13.8	2.2	1.5
Tertiary sciences	..	..	..	23	20	16	21	..	20	17
Admin. and managerial staff	22	13	11	13	3	..	24	..	7	..
Labour force	40	29	39	33	26	27	42	32	33	28
Parliament	9	8	16	8	7	7	10	6	13	8
Table 9: Female-male gaps (female expressed as % of male)										
Life expectancy	110	110	105	105	103	105	109	109	103	105
Population	105	100	96	99	97	100	104	102	96	100
Literacy										
1970	..	90	59	..	44	45	..	74	44	46
1990	..	98	80	87	59	65	..	89	66	66
Mean years of schooling	97	86	65	75	39	43	99	81	51	47
Primary enrolment										
1960	..	95	83	..	50	50	..	82	50	50
1988-90	..	100	99	95	99	81	..	94	90	86
Secondary enrolment	..	99	82	88	62	63	..	88	68	64
Tertiary enrolment	..	80	57	75	41	35	102	72	45	34
Labour force	68	42	66	54	39	42	75	50	54	44
Table 10: Rural-urban gaps										
Rural population (% total)	27	25	58	42	72	71	22	40	71	74
Urban access to health services	..	100	..	..	98	94	..	..	..	94
Rural access to health services	..	..	81	..	..	59	..	74	89	62
Urban access to safe water	..	88	90	92	78	77	..	94	81	76
Rural access to safe water	..	48	59	56	56	40	..	68	61	41
Urban access to sanitation	..	..	90	81	47	54	..	90	69	50
Rural access to sanitation	..	..	72	52	11	18	..	..	38	20
Rural-urban disparity										
health	..	..	..	..	..	63	..	..	..	..
water	..	55	66	61	72	52	..	72	75	66
sanitation	..	..	80	73	23	33	..	..	55	54
child nutrition	..	..	..	..	75	..	..	89	80	40
Table 11: Child survival and development										
Women with prenatal care	..	72	..	60	64	59	..	64	63	58
Births attended	..	70	80	66	55	42	..	69	65	39
Low-birth-weight babies	..	6	8	11	23	19	..	10	18	17
Infant mortality rate	..	31	42	53	96	99	..	46	77	98
Breast-feeding at one year	..	27	..	57	..	80	..	46	82	..
One-year-olds immunized	..	80	91	86	76	66	..	82	84	70
Underweight children	..	11	24	26	47	36	..	19	41	38
Wasted children	..	..	8	9	..	..	..	8	16	12
Stunted children	..	..	38	31	..	..	..	30	52	50
Under-five mortality rate	..	..	..	..	..	..	..	..	..	..

	High human development		Medium human development		Low human development		Low-income			
	All countries	Developing countries	All countries	Excl. China	All countries	Excl. India	High-income	Middle-income	All countries	Excl. China and India
Table 12: Health profile										
Access to health services	..	94	..	68	..	65	..	79	..	66
Access to safe water	..	79	73	75	62	50	..	82	65	49
Access to sanitation	..	85	84	65	20	27	..	71	50	28
People per doctor	500	1,010	2,210	3,760	8,490	13,600	450	1,740	5,980	15,000
People per nurse	240	740	1,270	1,090	2,550	3,270	140	770	2,100	3,280
Nurses per doctor	3.0	1.7	2.0	3.7	3.6	5.5	4.2	2.4	2.7	6.3
Maternal mortality rate	45	120	170	220	590	610	23	220	480	630
Health expenditure										
1960	..	1.2	0.8	0.7	0.6	0.7	..	..	0.8	0.5
1988-90	..	4.6	3.7	3.9	3.2	3.3	..	4.2	3.1	3.6
Table 13: Food security										
Food production per capita	..	99	122	108	108	100	..	104	119	102
Agricultural production	..	9	16	13	30	29	..	12	29	28
Calorie supply per capita	..	2,900	2,660	2,680	2,250	2,270	..	2,800	2,420	2,310
Calorie supply as % of req.	..	123	114	116	98	96	..	118	103	93
Food import dependency										
1969/71	..	19.2	6.1	12.2	5.9	8.5	..	12.7	3.7	7.0
1988/90	..	36.4	10.4	18.0	7.8	12.9	..	21.2	6.3	12.9
Cereal imports	..	21,680T	62,590T	48,870T	25,540T	25,090T	..	67,970T	37,120T	22,960T
Food aid	..	..	210T	190T	900T	850T	..	310T	810T	740T
Table 14: Education flows										
Primary intake, total	..	..	99	97	..	69	..	94	91	79
Primary intake, female	..	..	..	96	..	59	..	92	67	61
Primary enrolment	..	92	96	92	67	..	..	88	82	61
Primary repeaters	..	..	8	10	9	14	..	10	8	13
Primary completers	..	78	75	69	..	61	..	69	70	64
Transition to second level	..	..	65	72	..	47	..	69	59	50
Primary entrants to secondary	..	..	52	57	..	23	..	55	44	24
Secondary enrolment	..	61	50	52	31	23	..	52	37	25
Secondary repeaters	..	..	..	..	..	15	..	10	5	11
Tertiary enrolment	39	24	7	13	5	4	48	16	4	4
Table 15: Education imbalances										
Prim. pupil-teacher ratio	..	29	24	25	43	41	..	28	36	39
Sec. technical enrolment	..	12.8	9.4	12.4	..	6.0	..	12.7	7.7	7.1
Tertiary science enrolment	35	33	25	36	32	31	34	39	27	32
Tertiary students abroad	..	2.7	3.7	4.3	6.6	11.7	..	5.3	4.7	10.1
Education exp. as % of GNP										
1960	..	2.2	2.2	2.5	2.3	2.3	..	2.4	2.0	1.9
1988-90	..	3.5	3.3	3.6	3.5	3.9	..	4.0	2.7	2.6
% total public exp.	..	11.9	12.9	13.6	10.3	12.2	..	14.7	10.8	11.0
Prim./sec. educ. expenditure	66.2	62.9	64.5	64.0	71.1	71.5	66.5	63.5	66.8	64.0
Higher educ. expenditure	21.2	20.1	17.5	17.1	18.0	19.2	21.4	17.4	18.4	19.8
Table 16: Communication profile										
Radios	1,040	510	210	240	110	130	1,270	350	140	130
Televisions	490	180	71	120	31	25	600	160	30	29
Newspaper circulation	280	200	..	62	..	15	320	100	..	20
Telephones	500	160	29	59	10	15	630	90	7	6
Passenger cars	340	71	15	39	5	10	420	60	2	5
Book titles	55.0	32.3	6.0	6.9	1.9	2.2	86.0	11.0	4.1	2.5
Cinema attendances	3.0	2.1	1.7	1.7	5.1	1.6	3.0	1.5	5.4	1.9
People per post office	6,150	13,310	17,190	11,790	15,680	28,080	4,720	12,490	16,980	23,840
Table 17: Employment										
Labour force	47.1	35.9	50.6	39.5	37.0	36.2	48.8	40.9	45.7	36.5
Women in labour force	39.7	29.4	38.9	33.2	26.2	26.7	41.9	31.9	33.1	27.7
Labour force in agriculture										
1965	29.0	27.7	73.3	53.6	74.4	75.4	13.0	52.9	78.1	76.5
1989-91	8.1	16.2	61.5	38.3	63.2	63.8	5.1	26.1	67.8	61.3
Labour force in industry										
1965	31.6	32.0	11.0	17.7	10.1	8.6	45.9	18.9	8.9	8.1
1989-91	26.2	32.5	15.6	19.3	11.1	11.3	27.2	23.0	12.1	10.4
Labour force in services										
1965	39.4	40.3	15.7	28.7	15.5	16.0	41.1	28.2	13.0	15.4
1989-91	65.7	51.3	22.9	42.4	25.7	24.9	67.7	50.9	20.1	28.3
Earnings growth rate										
1970-80	..	..	..	..	..	..	..	..	..	..
1980-89	..	..	..	..	..	..	..	..	..	..

	High human development		Medium human development		Low human development				Low-income	
	All countries	Developing countries	All countries	Excl. China	All countries	Excl. India	High-income	Middle-income	All countries	Excl. China and India
Table 18: Wealth, poverty and social investment										
Real GDP per capita	13,500	6,290	2,710	3,660	1,110	1,140	18,170	4,830	1,510	1,320
GNP per capita	13,480	3,470	940	1,690	360	360	20,570	2,350	360	350
Income share: lowest 40%	..	..	..	..	..	..	..	..	..	..
Highest 20%/lowest 20%	..	..	..	..	..	..	..	..	..	..
Gini coefficient	..	..	..	..	..	..	..	..	..	..
People below poverty line										
total	..	..	..	..	..	..	..	..	..	..
urban	..	..	..	..	..	..	..	..	..	..
rural	..	..	..	..	..	..	..	..	..	..
Education expenditure	..	3.5	3.3	3.6	3.5	3.9	..	4.0	2.7	2.6
Health expenditure	..	4.6	3.7	3.9	3.2	3.3	..	4.2	3.1	3.6
Social security benefits	..	..	..	..	..	..	..	..	..	..
Table 19: Aid flows										
ODA received	..	1,050T	14,120T	11,950T	29,900T	28,230T	..	22,000T	23,000T	19,180T
ODA as % of GNP	..	0.2	0.8	0.9	4.7	9.1	..	0.8	2.6	7.3
ODA per capita	..	5	7	14	16	28	..	17	9	25
ODA per poor person	..	..	..	..	..	..	..	..	..	..
Social allocation ratio	..	22.7	14.7	14.6	17.6	18.0	..	15.1	17.0	17.7
Social priority ratio	..	20.5	34.7	37.6	49.7	49.9	..	39.2	49.9	52.4
Human expenditure ratio	..	0.009	0.041	0.049	0.411	0.817	..	0.047	0.221	0.677
Social priority aid	..	4.7	5.1	5.5	8.7	9.0	..	5.9	8.5	9.3
Table 20: Resource flow imbalances										
Total debt	..	38	32	39	58	94	..	40	38	84
Debt service ratio										
1970	..	..	11.0	..	11.3	9.0	..	13.7	11.5	8.0
1990	..	19.1	20.0	23.0	25.2	23.7	..	21.0	19.2	25.5
Workers' remittances	..	..	..	..	2.0	3.6	..	1.9	1.0	2.7
Export-import ratio	96	125	114	113	81	86	93	115	99	96
Trade dependency	31	63	37	38	28	40	31	41	30	41
Terms of trade	103	107	101	101	97	97	100	103	99	99
Gross international reserves	3.0	3.8	4.0	3.2	2.2	2.3	3.0	3.4	4.3	2.7
Current account balance	-27,700	11,400	-9,100	-21,100	-27,200	-17,400	29,400	-30,700	-12,600	-14,700
Table 21: Military expenditure and resource use imbalances										
Miltary exp. as % of GDP										
1960	6.2	1.9	6.9	2.6	2.2	2.5	5.4	7.5	6.5	3.5
1990	3.4	2.5	3.7	3.7	3.6	3.9	3.4	3.4	3.0	2.8
as % of health/educ. exp.										
1977	38	96	86	80	100	124	36	80	105	127
1990	..	..	230	..	105	123	..	193	120	174
Armed forces										
as % of population	0.7	0.6	0.5	0.7	0.3	0.4	0.7	0.6	0.3	0.3
per teacher	0.9	0.8	0.6	0.9	0.7	1.0	0.8	1.0	0.6	0.9
per doctor	4	6	9	15	27	44	3	12	19	46
Arms imports										
total	..	1,930T	11,280T	11,120T	8,490T	4,980T	..	11,790T	6,280T	2,610T
as % of nat'l imports	..	1.0	3.1	3.7	7.9	5.2	..	2.6	5.0	2.3
Table 22: Growing urbanization										
Urban population, %										
1960	60	52	25	36	16	15	69	41	17	13
1991	73	75	42	58	28	29	78	60	29	26
2000	76	80	54	65	34	36	79	66	38	33
Urban pop. growth rate										
1960-91	1.7	3.6	4.0	4.2	4.2	4.7	1.3	3.3	4.0	4.9
1990-2000	1.0	2.2	4.0	3.1	4.5	4.9	0.7	2.4	4.7	5.1
Pop. in cities over 1 million	38	51	33	40	34	36	36	41	30	33
Pop. in largest city	..	..	13	23	17	27	..	28	11	25
Highest population density	..	..	..	..	..	..	..	..	..	..
Table 23: Demographic profile										
Population										
1960	990T	110T	1,110T	450T	910T	470T	620T	720T	1,550T	450T
1991	1,340T	220T	2,120T	950T	1,920T	1,050T	800T	1,320T	3,030T	1,000T
2000	1,430T	250T	2,440T	1,130T	2,360T	1,340T	840T	1,520T	3,580T	1,250T
Population growth rate										
1960-91	1.0	2.2	2.1	2.4	2.4	2.6	0.8	2.0	2.2	2.6
1991-2000	0.7	1.4	1.6	1.9	2.3	2.7	0.5	1.6	1.9	2.5
Ratio of pop. growth rates	..	62	92	85	107	122	..	76	101	117
Population doubling date	..	..	..	..	..	..	..	..	..	..
Total fertility rate	2.0	2.8	2.9	3.6	5.0	5.8	1.8	3.3	3.8	5.5
Ratio of fertility growth rates	63	53	47	57	77	87	63	61	60	82
Contraceptive prevalence	61	62	64	53	31	19	72	47	48	24
Population density	230	330	530	260	590	380	250	240	860	450

	High human development		Medium human development		Low human development				Low-income	
	All countries	Developing countries	All countries	Excl. China	All countries	Excl. India	High-income	Middle-income	All countries	Excl. China and India
Table 24: Natural resources balance sheet										
Land area	6,040T	700T	3,390T	2,440T	3,480T	3,190T	3,230T	6,140T	3,540T	2,310T
Arable land	12	9	8	7	12	7	12	9	12	7
Irrigated land	8	14	23	16	17	15	7	13	28	19
Forest area	..	..	29.9	35.1	28.6	29.1	30.1	35.4	24.3	29.0
Renewable water resource	10.4	12.6	7.2	13.2	5.8	8.9	10.7	13.2	4.3	8.2
Deforestation	..	..	..	..	0.8	0.7	..	1.3	0.9	0.7
Production of fuelwood	5.5	0.6	1.9	1.9	2.9	3.4	6.9	2.0	2.5	3.3
Fresh water withdrawals										
% of water resources	20.1	14.0	16.2	16.4	16.8	15.7	22.8	15.6	15.7	13
per capita	1,124	762	493	532	536	472	1,270	540	504	462
Table 25: Energy consumption										
Consump. per capita (kg oil equiv.)										
1965	3,065	810	229	316	96	91	3,618	622	128	67
1990	4,347	1,718	703	848	182	140	5,155	1,339	340	102
billion kgs.										
1965	2,600T	102T	547T	417T	90T	41T	2,350T	649T	218T	39T
1990	4,700T	363T	1,480T	786T	335T	140T	4,100T	1,350T	1,040T	157T
Annual rate of change										
1960-74	6.4	8.4	5.8	8.9	6.4	7.9	6.0	9.0	5.0	7.2
1980-90	1.8	3.4	5.4	4.9	5.0	4.3	1.5	4.2	5.3	4.6
Consump./$100 GDP										
1990	26	46	81	51	59	44	25	48	111	49
(1965=100)	16	31	50	33	74	70	15	33	80	58
Table 26: National income accounts										
Total GDP	16,950T	780T	1,710T	1,350T	540T	290T	16,020T	2,220T	940T	320T
Agricultural production	4	9	16	13	30	29	3	12	28	28
Industrial production	37	38	39	38	28	27	37	38	34	31
Services	59	53	45	49	42	44	60	50	38	41
Private consumption	61	66	59	62	71	73	61	64	60	68
Government consumption	16	10	12	13	13	13	16	15	10	11
Gross domestic investment	22	25	28	25	20	18	22	24	29	24
Gross domestic savings	23	27	29	25	16	13	22	24	29	21
Tax revenue	23.4	14.0	..	16.0	13.1	15.0	23.4	19.2	13.7	15.8
Central gov't expenditure	28	18	..	27	21	25	28	25	..	24
Exports	16	30	17	18	11	17	16	19	14	19
Imports	17	36	17	18	15	22	17	20	14	21
Table 27: Trends in economic performance										
Total GNP	17,550T	730T	1,750T	1,330T	580T	280T	15,870T	2,880T	1,020T	310T
Total GNP real growth rate	3.1	4.5	4.7	3.2	4.4	3.2	3.1	3.3	6.8	4.4
GNP p.c. annual growth rate										
1965-80	2.7	3.9	4.0	3.8	1.8	2.0	3.0	3.1	2.7	1.9
1980-90	2.4	2.9	2.5	0.8	1.7	0.1	2.4	1.3	4.6	1.6
Annual rate of inflation										
1980-90	20.9	94.4	32.4	68.7	14.5	21.3	5.1	65.4	10.1	17.5
1991	30.8	35.1	62.0	149.6	34.0	53.2	4.0	104.5	19.7	45
Exports/GDP growth rate	-2.1	-5.7	3.9	2.6	0.9	0.6	-1.1	-0.3	2.0	-0.1
Tax revenue/GNP growth rate	1.4	1.4	..	2.9	2.6	2.6	1.4	2.7	2.0	1.8
Direct taxes										
1972	..	37.7	..	37.2	23.6	21.0	..	36.2	30.6	37.4
1990	..	43.1	..	40.8	22.2	26.1	43.6	35.3	29.6	38.9
Budget surplus/deficit										
1972	-1.7	-2.3	-2.4	-2.4	-3.4	-3.7	-1.7	-2.5	-3.3	-3.4
1990	-2.2	0.1	..	-6.6	-6.3	-4.5	-3.2	1.1	-5.7	-3.8

Selected definitions

Aid human expenditure ratio The percentage of a donor's GNP going to human priority areas in recipient countries or the amount of official development assistance received for human priority areas expressed as a percentage of the recipient country's GNP.

Aid social allocation ratio The percentage of official development assistance that goes to the social sector.

Aid social priority ratio The percentage of social sector official development assistance that goes to human priority areas.

Births attended The percentage of births attended by physicians, nurses, midwives, trained primary health care workers or trained traditional birth attendants.

Budget surplus/deficit Current and capital revenue and grants received, less total expenditure and lending, minus repayments.

Calorie supply See *Daily calorie supply*.

Child malnutrition See *Underweight, Wasting* and *Stunting*.

Child mortality See *Under-five mortality*.

Contraceptive prevalence rate The percentage of married women of childbearing age who are using, or whose husbands are using, any form of contraception: that is, modern or traditional methods.

Current account balance The difference between (a) exports of goods and services (factor and non-factor) as well as inflows of unrequited private transfers but before official transfers and (b) imports of goods and services as well as all unrequited transfers to the rest of the world.

Daily calorie requirement per capita The average number of calories needed to sustain a person at normal levels of activity and health, taking into account the distribution by age, sex, body weight and environmental temperature.

Daily calorie supply per capita The calorie equivalent of the net food supplies in a country, divided by the population, per day.

Debt service The sum of repayments of principal (amortization) and payments of interest made in foreign currencies, goods or services on external public, publicly guaranteed and private non-guaranteed debt.

Dependency ratio The ratio of the population defined as dependent, under 15 and over 64 years, to the working-age population, aged 15 to 64.

Direct tax Taxes levied on the actual or presumptive net income of individuals, on the profits of enterprises and on capital gains, whether realized on land sales, securities or other assets.

Domestic investment (gross) Outlays in addition to the fixed assets of the economy plus net changes in the level of inventories.

Domestic savings (gross) The gross domestic product less government and private consumption.

Earnings per employee Earnings in constant prices derived by deflating nominal earnings per employee by the country's consumer price index.

Education expenditures Expenditures on the provision, management, inspection and support of pre-primary, primary and secondary schools; universities and colleges; vocational, technical and other training institutions; and general administration and subsidiary services.

Employees Regular employees, working proprietors, active business partners and unpaid family workers, but excluding homeworkers.

Enrolment ratio (gross and net) The gross enrolment ratio is the number enrolled in a level of education, whether or not they belong in the relevant age group for that level, expressed as a percentage of the population in the relevant age group for that level. The net enrolment ratio is the number enrolled in a level of education who belong in the relevant age group, expressed as a percentage of the population in that age group.

Exports of goods and services The value of all goods and non-factor services provided to the rest of the world, including merchandise, freight, insurance, travel and other non-factor services.

Female-male gap A set of national, regional and other estimates in which all the figures for females are expressed in relation to the corresponding figures for males, which are indexed to equal 100.

Fertility rate (total) The average number of children that would be born alive to a woman during her lifetime, if she were to bear children at each age in accord with prevailing age-specific fertility rates.

Food aid in cereals Cereals provided by donor countries and international organizations, including the World Food Programme and the International Wheat Council, as reported for that particular crop year. Cereals include wheat, flour, bulgur, rice, coarse grain and the cereal components of blended foods.

Food import dependency ratio The ratio of food imports to the food available for internal distribution: that is, the sum of food production, plus food imports, minus food exports.

Food production per capita index The average annual quantity of food produced per capita in relation to that produced in the indexed year. Food is defined as comprising nuts, pulses, fruit, cereals, vegetables, sugar cane, sugar beets, starchy roots, edible oils, livestock and livestock products.

Future labour force replacement ratio Population under 15 divided by one-third of the population aged 15 to 59.

Gini coefficient A measure that shows how close a given distribution of income is to absolute equality or inequality. Named for Corrado Gini, the Gini coefficient is a ratio of the area between the 45° line and the Lorenz curve and the area of the entire triangle. As the coefficient approaches zero, the distribution of income approaches absolute equality. Conversely, as the coefficient approaches one, the distribution of income approaches absolute inequality.

Government expenditures Expenditures by all central government offices, departments, establishments and other bodies that are agencies or instruments of the central authority of a country. It includes both current and capital or developmental expenditures but excludes provincial, local and private expenditures.

Gross domestic product (GDP) The total for final use of output of goods and services produced by an economy, by both residents and non-residents, regardless of the allocation to domestic and foreign claims.

Gross enrolment ratio See *Enrolment ratio*.

Gross national product (GNP) The total domestic and foreign value added claimed by residents, calculated without making deductions for depreciation. It comprises GDP plus net factor income from abroad, which is the income residents receive from abroad for factor services (labour and capital), less similar payments made to non-residents who contribute to the domestic economy.

GNP per capita and growth rates The gross national product divided by the population. Annual GNPs per capita are expressed in current US dollars. GNP per capita growth rates are annual average growth rates that have been computed by fitting trend lines to the logarithmic values of GNP per capita at constant market prices for each year of the time period.

Health expenditures Expenditures on hospitals, health centres and clinics, health insurance schemes and family planning.

Health services access The percentage of the population that can reach appropriate local health services on foot or by the local means of transport in no more than one hour.

Immunized The average of the vaccination coverages of children under one year of age for the four antigens used in the Universal Child Immunization Programme (UCI).

Income share The income in both cash and kind accruing to percentile groups of households ranked by total household income.

Infant mortality rate The annual number of deaths of infants under one year of age per 1,000 live births. More specifically, the probability of dying between birth and exactly one year of age times 1,000.

Inflation rate The average annual rate of inflation measured by the growth of the GDP implicit deflator for each of the periods shown.

International reserves (gross) Holdings of monetary gold, special drawing rights (SDRs), the reserve positions of members in the IMF, and holdings of foreign exchange under the control of monetary authorities expressed in terms of the number of months of imports of goods and services these could pay for at the current level of imports.

Labour force The economically active population, including the armed forces and the unemployed, but excluding homemakers and other unpaid caregivers.

Least developed countries A group of developing countries established by the United Nations General Assembly. Most of these countries suffer from one or more of the following constraints: a GNP per capita of around $300 or less, land-locked, remote insularity, desertification and exposure to natural disasters.

Life expectancy at birth The number of years a newborn infant would live if prevailing patterns of mortality at the time of its birth were to stay the same throughout its life.

Literacy rate (adult) The percentage of persons aged 15 and over who can, with understanding, both read and write a short simple statement on their everyday life.

Low birth-weight The percentage of babies born weighing less than 2,500 grammes.

Malnutrition See *Underweight, Wasting and Stunting*.

Maternal mortality rate The annual number of deaths of women from pregnancy-related causes per 100,000 live births.

Mean years of schooling Average number of years of schooling received per person age 25 and over.

Military expenditures Expenditures, whether by defence or other departments, on the maintenance of military forces, including the purchase of military supplies and equipment, construction, recruiting, training and military aid programmes.

Net enrolment ratio See *Enrolment ratio*.

North See *South-North gap*.

Official development assistance (ODA) The net disbursements of loans and grants made on concessional financial terms by official agencies of the members of the Development Assistance Committee (DAC), the Organisation for Economic Co-operation and Development (OECD), the Organization of Petroleum Exporting Countries (OPEC) and so on, to promote economic development and welfare, including technical cooperation and assistance.

ODA for social investment Official development assistance for the combined areas of health, education, social services, rural and urban development and water and sanitation.

Population density The total number of inhabitants divided by the surface area.

Poverty line That income level below which a minimum nutritionally adequate diet plus essential non-food requirements are not affordable.

Primary education Education at the first level (International Standard Classification of Education [ISCED] level 1), the main function of which is to provide the basic elements of education, such as elementary schools and primary schools.

Primary intake rate Number of new entrants into first grade, regardless of age, expressed as a percentage of the population of official admission age to the first level of education.

Primary school completion rate The proportion of the children entering the first grade of primary school who successfully complete that level in due course.

Purchasing power parities (PPP) See *Real GDP per capita*.

Real GDP per capita (purchasing power parities [PPP]) The use of official exchange rates to convert the national currency figures to US dollars does not attempt to measure the relative domestic purchasing powers of currencies. The United Nations International Comparison Project (ICP) has developed measures of real GDP on an internationally comparable scale using purchasing power parities (PPP) instead of exchange rates as conversion factors, and expressed in international dollars.

Rural-urban disparity   A set of national, regional and other estimates in which all the rural figures are expressed in relation to the corresponding urban figures, which are indexed to equal 100.

Safe water access   The percentage of the population with reasonable access to safe water supply, including treated surface waters, or untreated but uncontaminated water such as that from springs, sanitary wells and protected boreholes.

Sanitation access   The percentage of the population with access to sanitary means of excreta and waste disposal, including outdoor latrines and composting.

Science graduates   Tertiary education graduates in the natural and applied sciences.

Scientists   Persons with scientific or technological training—usually completion of third-level education in any field of science—who are engaged in professional work on research and development activities, including administrators and directors of such activities.

Secondary education   Education at the second level (ISCED levels 2 and 3), based on at least four years' previous instruction at the first level, and providing general or specialized instruction or both, such as middle schools, secondary schools, high schools, teacher-training schools at this level and schools of a vocational or technical nature.

Secondary technical education   Education provided in those second-level schools that aim at preparing the pupils directly for a trade or occupation other than teaching.

Social security benefits   Compensation for loss of income for the sick and temporarily disabled; payments to the elderly, the permanently disabled and the unemployed; family, maternity and child allowances and the cost of welfare services.

South-North gap   A set of national, regional and other estimates in which all the figures are expressed in relation to the corresponding average figures for all the industrial countries, which are indexed to equal 100.

Stunting   The percentage of children, between 24 and 59 months, below minus two standard deviations from the median height-for-age of the reference population.

Technicians   Persons engaged in scientific research and development activities who have received vocational or technical training for at least three years after the first stage of second-level education.

Terms of trade   The ratio of a country's index of average export prices to its average import price index.

Tertiary education   Education at the third level (ISCED levels 5, 6 and 7), such as universities, teachers' colleges and higher professional schools—requiring as a minimum condition of admission the successful completion of education at the second level or evidence of the attainment of an equivalent level of knowledge.

Trade dependency   Exports plus imports as a percentage of GDP.

Transition from first- to second-level education   Number of new entrants into secondary general education, expressed as a percentage of the total number of pupils in the last grade of primary education in the previous year.

Under-five mortality rate   The annual number of deaths of children under five years of age per 1,000 live births averaged over the previous five years. More specifically, the probability of dying between birth and exactly five years of age times 1,000.

Underweight (moderate and severe child malnutrition)   The percentage of children, under the age of five, below minus two standard deviations from the median weight-for-age of the reference population.

Unemployment   The unemployed comprise all persons, above a specified age, who are not in paid employment or self-employed, are available for paid employment or self-employment and have taken specific steps to seek paid employment or self-employment.

Wasting   The percentage of children, between 12 and 23 months, below minus two standard deviations from the median weight-for-height of the reference population.

Water sources, internal renewable   The average annual flow of rivers and aquifers generated from endogenous precipitation.

Classification of countries

Countries in the human development aggregates

High human development
(HDI 0.800 and above)

Argentina
Armenia
Australia
Austria
Bahamas
Barbados
Belarus
Belgium
Brunei Darussalam
Bulgaria
Canada
Chile
Costa Rica
Cyprus
Czechoslovakia
Denmark
Dominica
Estonia
Finland
France
Georgia
Germany
Greece
Hong Kong
Hungary
Iceland
Ireland
Israel
Italy
Japan
Kazakhstan
Korea, Rep. of
Kuwait
Latvia
Lithuania
Luxembourg
Malta
Mexico
Netherlands
New Zealand
Norway
Poland
Portugal
Qatar
Russian Federation
Singapore
Spain
Sweden
Switzerland
Trinidad and Tobago
Ukraine
United Kingdom
Uruguay
USA
Venezuela

Medium human development
(HDI 0.500 to 0.799)

Albania
Algeria
Antigua and
  Barbuda
Azerbaijan
Bahrain
Belize
Botswana
Brazil
China
Colombia
Cuba
Dominican Rep.
Ecuador
El Salvador
Fiji
Gabon
Grenada
Guyana
Indonesia
Iran, Islamic Rep. of
Iraq
Jamaica
Jordan
Korea, Dem. Rep. of
Kyrgyzstan
Lebanon
Libyan Arab Jamahiriya
Malaysia
Mauritius
Moldova, Rep. of
Mongolia
Nicaragua
Oman
Panama
Paraguay
Peru
Philippines
Romania
Saint Kitts and Nevis
Saint Lucia
Saint Vincent
Samoa
Saudi Arabia
Seychelles
South Africa
Sri Lanka
Suriname
Syrian Arab Rep.
Tajikistan
Thailand
Tunisia
Turkey
Turkmenistan
United Arab
  Emirates
Uzbekistan
Vanuatu

Low human development
(HDI below 0.500)

Afghanistan
Angola
Bangladesh
Benin
Bhutan
Bolivia
Burkina Faso
Burundi
Cambodia
Cameroon
Cape Verde
Central African
  Rep.
Chad
Comoros
Congo
Côte d'Ivoire
Djibouti
Egypt
Equatorial Guinea
Ethiopia
Gambia
Ghana
Guatemala
Guinea
Guinea-Bissau
Haiti
Honduras
India
Kenya
Lao People's Dem. Rep.
Lesotho
Liberia
Madagascar
Malawi
Maldives
Mali
Mauritania
Morocco
Mozambique
Myanmar
Namibia
Nepal
Niger
Nigeria
Pakistan
Papua New Guinea
Rwanda
São Tomé and Principe
Senegal
Sierra Leone
Solomon Islands
Somalia
Sudan
Swaziland
Tanzania,
  U. Rep. of
Togo
Uganda
Viet Nam
Yemen
Zaire
Zambia
Zimbabwe

Countries in the income aggregates

High-income (GNP per capita above $6,000)	Middle-income (GNP per capita $501 to $6,000)		Low-income (GNP per capita $500 and below)
Australia	Albania	Malaysia	Afghanistan
Austria	Algeria	Mauritius	Bangladesh
Bahamas	Angola	Mexico	Benin
Bahrain	Antigua and Barbuda	Moldova, Rep. of	Bhutan
Barbados	Argentina	Mongolia	Burkina Faso
Belgium	Armenia	Morocco	Burundi
Brunei Darussalam	Azerbaijan	Namibia	Cambodia
Canada	Belarus	Nicaragua	Central African Rep.
Cyprus	Belize	Oman	Chad
Denmark	Bolivia	Panama	China
Finland	Botswana	Papua New Guinea	Comoros
France	Brazil	Paraguay	Equatorial Guinea
Germany	Bulgaria	Peru	Ethiopia
Greece	Cameroon	Philippines	Gambia
Hong Kong	Cape Verde	Poland	Ghana
Iceland	Chile	Portugal	Guinea
Ireland	Colombia	Romania	Guinea-Bissau
Israel	Congo	Russian Federation	Guyana
Italy	Costa Rica	Saint Kitts and Nevis	Haiti
Japan	Côte d'Ivoire	Saint Lucia	India
Kuwait	Cuba	Saint Vincent	Kenya
Luxembourg	Czechoslovakia	Samoa	Lao People's Dem. Rep.
Malta	Djibouti	Senegal	Liberia
Netherlands	Dominica	Seychelles	Madagascar
New Zealand	Dominican Rep.	Solomon Islands	Malawi
Norway	Ecuador	South Africa	Maldives
Qatar	Egypt	Suriname	Mali
Saudi Arabia	El Salvador	Swaziland	Mauritania
Singapore	Estonia	Syrian Arab Rep.	Mozambique
Spain	Fiji	Tajikistan	Myanmar
Sweden	Gabon	Thailand	Nepal
Switzerland	Georgia	Trinidad and Tobago	Niger
United Arab Emirates	Grenada	Tunisia	Nigeria
United Kingdom	Guatemala	Turkey	Pakistan
USA	Honduras	Turkmenistan	Rwanda
	Hungary	Ukraine	São Tomé and Principe
	Indonesia	Uruguay	Sierra Leone
	Iran, Islamic Rep. of	Uzbekistan	Somalia
	Iraq	Vanuatu	Sri Lanka
	Jamaica	Venezuela	Sudan
	Jordan	Yemen	Tanzania, U. Rep. of
	Kazakhstan	Zimbabwe	Togo
	Korea, Dem. Rep. of		Uganda
	Korea, Rep. of		Viet Nam
	Kyrgyzstan		Zaire
	Latvia		Zambia
	Lebanon		
	Lesotho		
	Libyan Arab Jamahiriya		
	Lithuania		

Countries in the major world aggregates

Least developed countries

Afghanistan
Bangladesh
Benin
Bhutan
Botswana
Burkina Faso
Burundi
Cambodia
Cape Verde
Central African Rep.
Chad
Comoros
Djibouti
Equatorial Guinea
Ethiopia
Gambia
Guinea
Guinea-Bissau
Haiti
Lao People's
Dem. Rep.
Lesotho
Liberia
Malawi
Maldives
Mali
Mauritania
Mozambique
Myanmar
Nepal
Niger
Rwanda
Samoa
São Tomé and
Principe
Sierra Leone
Solomon Islands
Somalia
Sudan
Tanzania
Togo
Uganda
Vanuatu
Yemen
Zaire
Zambia

All developing countries

Afghanistan
Algeria
Angola
Antigua and
Barbuda
Argentina
Bahamas
Bahrain
Bangladesh
Barbados
Belize
Benin
Bhutan
Bolivia
Botswana
Brazil
Brunei Darussalam
Burkina Faso
Burundi
Cambodia
Cameroon
Cape Verde
Central African
Rep.
Chad
Chile
China
Colombia
Comoros
Congo
Costa Rica
Côte d'Ivoire
Cuba
Cyprus
Djibouti
Dominica
Dominican Rep.
Ecuador
Egypt
El Salvador
Equatorial Guinea
Ethiopia
Fiji
Gabon
Gambia
Ghana

Grenada
Guatemala
Guinea
Guinea-Bissau
Guyana
Haiti
Honduras
Hong Kong
India
Indonesia
Iran, Islamic Rep. of
Iraq
Jamaica
Jordan
Kenya
Korea, Dem.
Rep. of
Korea, Rep. of
Kuwait
Lao People's
Dem. Rep.
Lebanon
Lesotho
Liberia
Libyan Arab
Jamahiriya
Madagascar
Malawi
Malaysia
Maldives
Mali
Mauritania
Mauritius
Mexico
Mongolia
Morocco
Mozambique
Myanmar
Namibia
Nepal
Nicaragua
Niger
Nigeria
Oman
Pakistan
Panama

Papua New Guinea
Paraguay
Peru
Philippines
Qatar
Rwanda
Saint Kitts and
Nevis
Saint Lucia
Saint Vincent
Samoa
São Tomé and
Principe
Saudi Arabia
Senegal
Seychelles
Sierra Leone
Singapore
Solomon Islands
Somalia
South Africa
Sri Lanka
Sudan
Suriname
Swaziland
Syrian Arab Rep.
Tanzania, U.
Rep. of
Thailand
Togo
Trinidad and
Tobago
Tunisia
Turkey
Uganda
United Arab
Emirates
Uruguay
Vanuatu
Venezuela
Viet Nam
Yemen
Zaire
Zambia
Zimbabwe

Industrial countries

Albania
Armenia
Australia
Austria
Azerbaijan
Belarus
Belgium
Bulgaria
Canada
Czechoslovakia
Denmark
Estonia
Finland
France
Georgia
Germany
Greece
Hungary
Iceland
Ireland
Israel
Italy
Japan
Kazakhstan
Kyrgyzstan
Latvia
Lithuania
Luxembourg
Malta
Moldova, Rep. of
Netherlands
New Zealand
Norway
Poland
Portugal
Romania
Russian Federation
Spain
Sweden
Switzerland
Tajikistan
Turkmenistan
Ukraine
United Kingdom
USA
Uzbekistan

Countries in the developing and industrial aggregates

Sub-Saharan Africa

Angola
Benin
Botswana
Burkina Faso
Burundi
Cameroon
Cape Verde
Central African Rep.
Chad
Comoros
Congo
Côte d'Ivoire
Djibouti
Equatorial Guinea
Ethiopia
Gabon
Gambia
Ghana
Guinea
Guinea-Bissau
Kenya
Lesotho
Liberia
Madagascar
Malawi
Mali
Mauritania
Mauritius
Mozambique
Namibia
Niger
Nigeria
Rwanda
São Tomé and Principe
Senegal
Seychelles
Sierra Leone
Somalia
South Africa
Swaziland
Tanzania, U. Rep. of
Togo
Uganda
Zaire
Zambia
Zimbabwe

Arab States

Algeria
Bahrain
Egypt
Iraq
Jordan
Kuwait
Lebanon
Libyan Arab Jamahiriya
Morocco
Oman
Qatar
Saudi Arabia
Sudan
Syrian Arab Rep.
Tunisia
United Arab Emirates
Yemen

Latin America and the Caribbean

Antigua and Barbuda
Argentina
Bahamas
Barbados
Belize
Bolivia
Brazil
Chile
Colombia
Costa Rica
Cuba
Dominica
Dominican Rep.
Ecuador
El Salvador
Grenada
Guatemala
Guyana
Haiti
Honduras
Jamaica
Mexico
Nicaragua
Panama
Paraguay
Peru
Saint Kitts and Nevis
Saint Lucia
Saint Vincent
Suriname
Trinidad and Tobago
Uruguay
Venezuela

East Asia

China
Hong Kong
Korea, Dem. Rep. of
Korea, Rep. of
Mongolia

South-East Asia and Oceania

Brunei Darussalam
Cambodia
Fiji
Indonesia
Lao People's Dem. Rep.
Malaysia
Myanmar
Papua New Guinea
Philippines
Samoa
Singapore
Solomon Islands
Thailand
Vanuatu
Viet Nam

South Asia

Afghanistan
Bangladesh
Bhutan
India
Iran, Islamic Rep. of
Maldives
Nepal
Pakistan
Sri Lanka

OECD

Australia
Austria
Belgium
Canada
Denmark
Finland
France
Germany
Greece
Iceland
Ireland
Italy
Japan
Luxembourg
Netherlands
New Zealand
Norway
Portugal
Spain
Sweden
Switzerland
United Kingdom
USA

Eastern Europe and former USSR

Albania
Armenia
Azerbaijan
Belarus
Bulgaria
Czechoslovakia
Estonia
Georgia
Hungary
Kazakhstan
Kyrgyzstan
Latvia
Lithuania
Moldova, Rep. of
Poland
Romania
Russian Federation
Tajikistan
Turkmenistan
Ukraine
Uzbekistan

Nordic countries

Denmark
Finland
Iceland
Norway
Sweden

Southern Europe

Albania
Greece
Italy
Malta
Portugal
Spain

European Community

Belgium
Denmark
France
Germany
Greece
Ireland
Italy
Luxembourg
Netherlands
Portugal
Spain
United Kingdom

Non-European countries

Australia
Canada
Israel
Japan
New Zealand
USA

North America

Canada
USA